Understanding Christian Mission

Understanding Christian Mission

Participation in Suffering and Glory

Scott W. Sunquist

a division of Baker Publishing Group
Grand Rapids, Michigan

Published by Baker Academic
a division of Baker Publishing Group
P.O. Box 6287, Grand Rapids, MI 49516-6287
www.bakeracademic.com

Printed in the United States of America

Library of Congress Cataloging-in-Publication Data

Sunquist, Scott, 1953–
Understanding Christian mission : participation in suffering and glory / Scott W. Sunquist.
pages cm
Includes bibliographical references and index.
ISBN 978-0-8010-3615-6 (cloth)
1. Missions. 2. Trinity. I. Title.
BV2061.3.S86 2013
266—dc23 2013012148

13 14 15 16 17 18 19 7 6 5 4 3 2 1

In keeping with biblical principles of creation stewardship, Baker Publishing Group advocates the responsible use of our natural resources. As a member of the Green Press Initiative, our company uses recycled paper when possible. The text paper of this book is composed in part of post-consumer waste.

This book is dedicated
with great respect
to my strong and gentle
pilgrim companion
on this missionary journey,
without whom this book
would not have been produced:
Nancy.

οὐχὶ ταῦτα ἔδει παθεῖν τὸν χριστὸν
καὶ εἰσελθεῖν εἰς τὴν δόξαν αὐτοῦ;
Was it not necessary that the Messiah should *suffer* these things and then enter into his *glory*?

Luke 24:26

Contents

Acknowledgments

Most important in the production of this book has been contributions from friendships, conversations, papers, worship, and conferences with Asian and African seminary and Bible college students in the past twenty-five years. As I wrote each page I sensed my former students reading over my shoulder checking for accuracy and authenticity. Some of these former students are now bishops and seminary professors leading the church in their respective contexts. They have become my teachers. The penultimate chapter in this book (on partnership) describes my experience in mission through these former students—now colleagues in mission.

Second, I must acknowledge the good response and patience of my missiology students in Pittsburgh, Cairo, Sabah, and Pasadena who read through parts of this manuscript and usually ended up asking, "Dr., where is chapter four?" Well, I can say to them all now, here are the chapters that were promised. Thank you all for your comments, advice, and patience.

Third, I must acknowledge three institutions that have given me some space to work out these ideas and to write unhindered. The Evangelical Theological Seminary in Cairo gave me an opportunity to lecture on the main theme of this book, and then get feedback from thoughtful faculty and students. Sabah Theological Seminary gave me a wonderful flat with a view of the sunrise over Mt. Kinabalu and the sun setting over the South China Sea. Teaching through much of this material and talking with Lundayeh, Rungus, Kadazan-Dusun, Dyaks, Chinese, Iban, and many other ethnic groups helped me to frame missiological issues in the midst of "the nations." Special thanks must go to the principal of Sabah Theological Seminary, Dr. Thu En Yu; to his wife, Brenda; to Dean Chung Song Mee; and to Dean Wilfred John and his wife, Mery. Special appreciation must be expressed to Pittsburgh Theological Seminary, especially to the board, Dean Barry Jackson, and President Bill Carl for awarding me a sabbatical to finish the volume, and for support to travel and teach these materials on different continents. The World Mission Initiative at the seminary became a place of missional practice and reflection. Thanks to my long-term partner in mission, Dr. Don Dawson, for his support through the years. The material is much richer and contains echoes of the nations thanks to this support.

Fourth, I want, once again, to thank the wonderful faculty administrator at Pittsburgh Theological Seminary, Holly McKelvey. Her faithfulness and diligence in keeping manuscripts organized, arranging travel schedules, and ordering books from libraries and book distributors have made this labor much easier. My student assistants, Mike McKee and Shae Cole, have been a great help in research and editing. Since this is designed primarily as a textbook, I asked for and had feedback from students on many chapters. I would like to thank Charles Cotherman for reading through most of the chapters in their earlier incarnations. Also, I have much appreciation for comments from Rev. Anthony Rivera, Rev. Eugene Blackwell, Cindy Rancurello, and Rev. Paul Roberts. My sons Elisha and Jesse also read chapters and made helpful comments. Daughter and son-in-law Bethany and Joshua Lomelino suggested the cover image and provided the photograph. Son-in-law and scholar of ancient Christian literature Timothy Becker challenged me (gently) on two of my theology chapters. I made many of the corrections he suggested. My daughter Caroline Becker helped greatly with editorial work at the last minute. It is wonderful to collaborate with my daughter again on a book on mission. My wife of thirty-seven years, Nancy, has been a dialogue partner for me, and we have been involved in mission practice all our married life. I am involved in mission today because of her encouragement before we were married. I thank her for reading over most of the book and making the volume much clearer and cleaner.

This book never would have been written if Brian Bolger of Baker Academic had not suggested I do it. Thanks to you, Brian, and special thanks goes to the editor who suffered with me through the final stages of the project: James Ernest. A good editor is hard to find, and I have found one of the best. Thank you, James.

As the book was going to press, I moved from Pittsburgh to Pasadena and had the opportunity for my PhD students to read through the manuscript and make more observations and helpful comments. Fuller Theological Seminary has been a great support to my academic work already, and for this, Nancy and I are very grateful.

Thanks to all of you for helping this become a better book. I apologize for not taking your good advice when I should have, and I pray that God would overrule my decisions, and that this work will be of some encouragement to the people of God as we participate in the mission of God in each context, throughout the world.

Preface

Christian mission is as personal as a missionary's daughter dying of malaria, and it is as cosmic as the restoration of all things. In between the two—expressed in the two—is suffering and glory. God's plan is incomprehensible unless we enter into discussion of both God's glory and the way of suffering. The great saints of the past knew this, Scripture reveals this, and the life of our Savior illustrates this basic truth of the *missio Dei*, the mission of God.

I have come to this conclusion through academic study, but also through personal experience and the testimony of some great missionaries and lesser-known saints of the past. There was a time when an introductory book of theology, social science, or history had to claim objectivity and neutrality. Today we know better. Objectivity is elusive, and we have learned something about the personal nature of knowledge. This volume makes no claim to be objective, but it does seek to give a clear understanding of Christian mission from a participant-observer position. My particular influences have come from my missionary work with my family (in East Asia), travels (mostly in Asia and Africa), scholarship, and teaching. I have been very fortunate to have worked the past twenty-five years in ecumenical contexts writing global (intercultural and ecumenical) history. This life of mission and scholarship has led me to produce a book that may seem to the reader more a description of missional Christian existence than an introduction to missiology.

The reader will find that this volume is held together by a cord of three strands: history, theology, and ecclesiology. It has become my conviction that the history and globalization of Christianity since the sixteenth-century reformations must be understood before pursuing the study of missiology. The work of the Jesuits in Asia and Latin America in the sixteenth and seventeenth centuries, and the work of the Moravians and German Lutherans in the eighteenth century are foundational for contemporary missiology. Their work in identifying with people in mission, in studying local contexts, and in taking risks of personal identity are still germane to mission work today. Thus, I spend a great deal of time on Christian history (not just "mission history")—mostly on the period from the sixteenth century on.

A historical study of Christian mission, however, must not stand alone. After looking at the historical contexts, it is necessary to think theologically and biblically about missiology. Missiology must be firmly rooted in a trinitarian understanding of God from which emerge various structures (means of accomplishing mission) and practices. However, even though I look at the theology of mission in a classical fashion (Father, Son, and Holy Spirit), I am quite aware that our knowledge of God and of God's mission is revealed contextually in Jesus Christ. Jesus Christ reveals God and God's desire for the nations to us.

Finally, missiology must become the work of the church in each age, to each place. This volume, then, is not an inductive piece where we simply look over the evidence of Scripture and then say, "See, that is what Christian mission is and that is what it does." All such "inductive" works are slightly deceived, because we bring questions and experiences to our reading of history and of Scripture. Through both my life and my study, I have come to the following conclusion, which shall serve as the thesis of this book: *Mission is from the heart of God, to each context, and it is carried out in suffering in this world for God's eternal glory.*

This may seem a little unconventional or eccentric for an introductory volume on mission, and yet there are basic concepts here that I believe are of central importance in the understanding of and integral participation in Christian mission. Firstly, we note that mission is from God's heart—grounded in God's love. Secondly, mission is to particular contexts—it is contextual or incarnational. Thirdly, mission has a temporal reality—it participates in the suffering of God. And, finally, it has an eternal dimension—reflecting God's character, God's glory.

In a rather remarkable piece of writing, one of the earliest Protestant mission theorists, Jonathan Edwards,[1] made the following comments about God's mission in his *Dissertation Concerning the End for Which God Created the World.*

> The emanation or communication of the divine fullness, consisting in the knowledge of God, love to God, and joy in God, has relation indeed both to God and the creature: but it has relation to God as its fountain, as it is an emanation from God; and as the communication itself, or thing communicated, is something divine, something of God, something of his internal fullness; as the water in the stream is something of the fountain; and as the beams are of the sun. And again, they have relation to God as they have respect to him as their object: for

1. See, for example, Ronald E. Davies, *Jonathan Edwards and His Influence on the Development of the Missionary Movement from Britain* (Cambridge: Currents in World Christianity Project, 1996).

> the knowledge communicated is the knowledge of God; and so God is the object of the knowledge: and the love communicated, is the love of God; so God is the object of that love: and the happiness communicated, is joy in God; and so he is the object of the joy communicated. In the creature's knowing, esteeming, loving, rejoicing in, and praising God, the glory of God is both exhibited and acknowledged; his fullness is received and returned. Here is both an *emanation* and *remanation*. The refulgence shines upon and into the creature, and is reflected back to the luminary. The beams of glory come from God and are something of God, and are refunded back again to their original. So that the whole is *of* God, and *in* God, and *to* God; and God is the beginning, middle and end in this affair.[2]

Missiology, then, is viewed through the twin lenses of the human and the divine, the temporal and the infinite. There is an incarnational trajectory to this volume that will be revealed from chapter to chapter. We are participating with the Triune God who is always sending out to reconcile and redeem. If any consensus has developed about mission during the past century, it is that Christian mission is rooted in the mission of God (*missio Dei*) rather than in a particular task (planting churches) or a particular goal (making converts). Unfortunately, the concept of *missio Dei* has been a plastic one for many missiologists, taking the shape of almost any confessional family and being molded around most any theological system or contextual need. In this volume, we will assume that God's mission is the basic concern in studying Christian mission, but we will define the concept of *missio Dei* based on historical, biblical, and theological material. *Missio Dei* must be understood as a foundational concept that launches the church from the place of worship and fellowship into the frontiers of God's reign. Living such a life, participating with God in such a movement, is costly and painful, and yet, in the end, it is glorious.

A word needs to be said about suffering. Writing in an age described as postcolonial, but from the United States—a country recognized by many scholars today as an empire more than a nation-state—it may seem strange to raise the issue of suffering. The West has worked hard in the past centuries to avoid or placate all suffering. Modern science and technology is based on the commonly accepted goal of relieving suffering and making life, from cradle to grave, easier. Science is even in the secular business of being the healer and conqueror of death. A truly contextual missiology, one might suggest, should emphasize victory and conquest, not suffering. In contrast to our culture, however, we believe that *God* is the one who heals and conquers death. We also see, however, that God does not heal all illnesses, and we believe that God enters into our suffering and endures our death and alienation. Suffering is inescapable as a central element in God's redemption. It is one of the central concepts in this volume for two reasons.

2. Jonathan Edwards, *Ethical Writings: The Works of Jonathan Edwards* (New Haven: Yale University Press, 1989), 8:435.

Firstly, having started out in life fairly well-protected from suffering, I was exposed to human suffering during our sojourn in Asia. The masses of people sleeping alongside the road in the metropolis of Madras (Chennai), the pictures of thousands suffering from disease and unhealthy water during the annual monsoon floods in Bangladesh, and the millions of people living in squalor—drinking from the same river they bathe in—in Jakarta began to open my eyes to the reality of suffering. Then there came news reports from Christian leaders in Indonesia, Vietnam, Laos, India, and other countries of persecution from Muslim mobs, Communist governments, or Hindu fundamentalists. And then I began to work through the research for writing volume 2 of *History of the World Christian Movement*. The overwhelming and sustaining image that I came away with is of the massive suffering of Christians as Christianity has developed in each new region. Suffering is very much a part of Christian existence, as well as human existence in general. On top of all of this "observation" of human suffering came my own experience of suffering. I suppose we will all suffer the loss of friends, family, and/or fortune at some point, but sudden, tragic loss leaves scars and redirects thoughts and life decisions. Thus suffering has become a part of my thought and my life as I study and participate in God's mission.

Secondly, I have learned of suffering in my biblical study. A few years ago, I spent a year in 1 Peter. I read through the text many times in English and then worked through it verse by verse in Greek; my Greek only slightly improved, but my understanding of the book got much better. I can still remember the impact the first chapter had on me. We are chosen pilgrims, wandering around with something of far greater value than gold: "an inheritance that can never perish, spoil or fade . . . kept in heaven for you. . . . In all this you greatly rejoice, though now for a little while you may have had to suffer grief in all kinds of trials" (1 Pet. 1:4, 6). What struck me then, and what has stayed with me, is the permanence of the inheritance (also called salvation) and the fading memory of suffering. The argument is clinched in 1:10–11:

> Concerning this salvation, the prophets, who spoke of the grace that was to come to you, searched intently and with the greatest care, trying to find out the time and circumstances to which the Spirit of Christ in them was pointing when he predicted the sufferings of Christ and the glories that would follow.

The sufferings of Jesus Christ and the glory that would follow—this was the key that the prophets looked for, and this is the identity of the Messiah that stays with us today. As people who participate in Christ's salvation, we also are called through suffering (which is temporary) to that which is glorious (and eternal).

What follows has been shaped by others, both saints in our age and saints in the history of the church, but I have put it together in the form you now see. I trust that you will suffer through it . . . to the glory of God.

Introduction

What you are about to read is an introductory book on missiology: the study of Christian mission. Unlike biology (the study of living things) or even Christology (the study of the person and work of Christ), the study of missiology as an academic discipline has developed fairly recently. Many students of theology, and even more church members, know more about the meaning of psychology or necrology, than of missiology. There is some confusion as to whether missiology is basically a practical science that helps missionaries prepare for their work, whether it is a historical science that reveals a different dimension of church history, or whether it is a theological discipline that broadens or realigns theological studies.[1] Mission, like liturgy, pastoral care, or preaching, is rooted in right thinking about the task, but it must also involve a practice. Although there are practical outcomes and specific practices that will be encouraged or discouraged, what the individual, church, or society actually does is rooted in what they think about God, humanity, the church, and the world. Therefore, as an introduction, this book is primarily concerned with right thinking about Christian mission, right thinking about the church, and pointing toward faithful practices.

This is a theological inquiry rooted in an understanding of God that is informed by most other areas of theological studies: biblical studies, hermeneutics,

1. See Francis Anekwe Oborji, *Concepts of Mission: The Evolution of Contemporary Missiology* (Maryknoll, NY: Orbis Books, 2006), especially chap. 2, "Mission and the Growth of Missiology in Theological Education" (41–56). Also see the bibliography for a range of approaches to the study of Christian mission. Stanley H. Skreslet provides a helpful overview of the issues involved in the study of missiology in "Who Studies Christian Mission and Why?" in *Comprehending Mission: The Questions, Methods, Themes, Problems, and Prospects of Missiology* (Maryknoll, NY: Orbis Books, 2012), 1–20. In general, evangelical missiology books focus more on motivation, biblical foundations, and practice, whereas ecumenical studies focus more on theory, theology, and history.

history, practical theology, ecclesiology, and ethics. Other supportive areas such as cultural anthropology, sociology of religion, history of religions, and psychology feed into the study, but part of the argument of this book is that missiology must resist being taken captive by the social sciences.[2] Missiology is first concerned with thinking correctly about the Triune God—the God who by his very nature is a sending God—rather than with particular practices or programs. In fact, until fairly recently in Christian history, the word "mission" (sending) was used in theological discourse of the Trinity, not of missionary practices. The Father sending the Son and the Father and Son sending the Holy Spirit was a "mission" discussion. It was not until late in the sixteenth century that the early Jesuits first used the word *missio* to speak of Christian people being sent to non-Christian people.[3] It has been commonly accepted since the late eighteenth century that "mission" primarily refers to the church's task to carry out the will of the Father in the world. Again, my point is that such work must be grounded in right thinking. Good practice flows out of good thinking in context. Although this is not a book on the history of missiology, it is important to look briefly at the discipline's history in order to understand the approach this book will take.

History of the Concept and the Study of Christian Mission

Many disciplines that we commonly accept as standard fare today are actually very new to the social sciences and to tertiary education. The academic disciplines of sociology, economics, and anthropology are less than 150 years old. In fact, it took about half a century for those three disciplines to become distinct. In the wake (or we might say the exhaust) of the industrial revolution, scholars began to study the worsening conditions of cities and realized that they were using new approaches involving the study of human activity *in communities*. One of the great proponents of these rising studies was a scholar who became something of a patron saint for sociology: Charles Darwin. These new social scientists (in the mid- to late nineteenth century) were working under the evolutionary and progressive assumptions that all societies would move forward to a higher level of existence (eugenics), and it was therefore the ethical imperative of scholars to help each society to move "up" (social Darwinism). At best, this was expressed as the social gospel; at worst it was

2. The captivity of missiology to the social sciences is not determined by one's theology. Conservative, fundamentalist, Pentecostal, and liberal theologians are equally prone to such captivity. When missiology turns into sociological studies of what "works," then we have turned away from proper missiological centeredness on the knowledge of God and the *missio Dei* as revealed in the life of Jesus Christ.

3. From David Bosch, *Transforming Mission: Paradigm Shifts in the Theology of Mission* (Maryknoll, NY: Orbis Books, 1991), 1.

"the white man's burden" to help lesser peoples. Only in the early twentieth century did the social sciences begin to take on clearer definition. Today they are firmly entrenched in our liberal arts curriculum. It is hard to imagine an "educated" college graduate in the twenty-first century who has not spent at least some time in the well-established disciplines of sociology and economics.

Missiology also began to develop as a field of study in the nineteenth century; however, mission studies had little institutional support until the latter part of the twentieth century.[4] Both disciplines were initiated by the movement of people: the social sciences by urbanization (the movement of people to cities), and mission studies by the movement of missionaries around the world. Careful critical reflection upon mission did not really develop until *after* the modern missionary movement began (nineteenth century).[5]

There had, however, been some earlier attempts to promote missional reflection—in the shadow of the Crusades and of ongoing Muslim presence in southern and eastern Europe.[6] In the thirteenth and fourteenth centuries, there were three important theological figures who began to engage in missiological thinking: St. Raymond of Pennyfort, St. Thomas Aquinas, and Raymond Lull.[7] Raymond of Pennyfort (1175–1275) had a special concern to confront the "infidels," not through war, but through preaching (he was true to his Dominican order: the order of preachers). Concerned that a way should be found for Muslims and Jews to convert and be baptized, he requested the greatest scholar of the age, Thomas Aquinas (1225–74), to write a handbook to encourage their conversion. Thomas's smaller summa, the *Summa Contra Gentiles*, is a type of systematic theology with the Jewish or Muslim neighbor in mind. In fact, it provides us with a rather complex summary of mid-thirteenth-century knowledge. Still, in the back of his mind was the need to explain Christian thought to non-Christians. It was a scholastic,

4. For a comprehensive history of the study of mission, missions, or missiology, see Johannes Verkuyl, *Contemporary Missiology: An Introduction* (Grand Rapids: Eerdmans, 1978), 18–88; David Bosch speaks about paradigm shifts in the understanding and practice of mission rather than in the academic study of mission (*Transforming Mission*, chaps. 5–10); see also Olav Myklebust, *The Study of Missions in Theological Education*, 2 vols. (Oslo: Hovedkommisjon Forlaget Land og Kirke, 1955–57). Roman Catholic perspectives on this history are given by Karl Müller, *Mission Theology: An Introduction* (Nettetal: Steyer Verlag-Wort und Werk, 1987), 30–50; and Oborji, *Concepts of Mission*, 41–50.

5. There is one major earlier exception to this. According to Jan A. B. Jongeneel (*Philosophy, Science, and the Theology of Mission in the 19th and 20th Centuries* [Frankfurt am Main: Peter Lang, 1997], 2:19), it was Gisbertus Voetius (1589–1676), founder of Utrecht University, who first did systematic Protestant reflection on Christian mission.

6. In chap. 1 we will look at the earlier missiological reflection and strategies. Here we look at the earliest reflections and then the development of the discipline of missiology.

7. We could easily add Dominic de Guzman (St. Dominic) and Francis Bernidone (St. Francis), since both were motivated to preach and serve in ways that would extend the church across boundaries. However, neither developed a "missiology" that was different from other religious orders in the middle ages.

Christendom apologetic with a missiological heart and mind behind it: the earliest missiology undertaken.

Raymond Lull (Raimundo Lulio, 1232–1315), one of the first missiologists, was a practitioner, a theoretician, and a strategist. Lull, like his namesake from Pennyfort, was a Spaniard who had an interest in reaching out to Muslims. His concern was to "conquer" the "Mohammedans"—through prayer rather than violence. To this end, he argued for missionaries to be trained not only in Scripture and theology, but also in languages such as Arabic, Hebrew, and "Chaldean." Lull made three trips to North Africa, and on the third trip he was stoned by an angry Muslim mob in Tunisia. He eventually died from his wounds on his home island of Majorca.[8] Lull had developed a whole strategy of evangelism, apologetics, and language study for the sake of a more proper engagement of the Roman Catholic Church with Islam. As is often the case with mission in the church, Lull's ideas and concerns were marginalized by the church in his time; militant models overwhelmed his missional model. Until the time of the Jesuits in the late sixteenth century, there was no one else who took such a missional approach to the church and to theology.

The modern practice and reflection upon mission begins with the Jesuits[9] in the late sixteenth century, and continues with discussions among the orders and then the arrival of the first Protestants in India, the Caribbean, and Africa in the eighteenth century. The contemporary academic study of missiology, as we know it now in seminaries and Christian colleges, is mostly the result of reflection upon the work of this modern mission movement.[10]

The first series of mission lectures that we know of were those given by Johann Friedrich Flatt (1759–1821) in 1800 at the University in Tübingen. As with most early lectures on mission subjects, these intersected the fields of practical theology, ethics, and biblical study. It seems there was no follow-up. In 1832 we read of J. T. L. Danz of Jena, a church historian, writing about the "study of missions" as if it were becoming a discipline, but in fact the "study" was slow in coming. It was another thirty-two years (1864) before a clear plea for the study of missiology was made, this time by Karl Graul (1814–64), the director of the Leipzig Mission. By this time, mission study was slowly becoming a concern of both mission societies and universities. In words that could almost be used today, Graul said, "This discipline must gradually come to the point where she holds her head up high; she has a right to ask for a place in the house of the most royal of all science, namely,

8. Majorca (Mallorca) is an island off the east coast of Spain that was ruled by various Muslim rulers until 1229, when it was annexed to Aragon.

9. This is not exactly true, for the earliest Augustinians, Franciscans, and Dominicans in the Americas and in Africa were thinking about their task and translating Scriptures, prayers, and catechisms in the early sixteenth century. See chap. 2 for more discussion of their work.

10. For further study of history of mission studies, see Jongeneel's *Philosophy, Science, and the Theology of Mission.*

theology."[11] Unfortunately, whether because of the rising secularization of Western education, or the embarrassment of symbiotic empire and missionary enterprises, the discipline never reached a point where "she [could] hold her head up high." Even today, when those of us who are teachers of missiology introduce ourselves as such, we cringe, hoping that we don't have to explain exactly what this means.

The first major move forward for mission education in Europe was the establishment of a chair in "Evangelistic Theology" at New College, Edinburgh, in 1867. The first occupant was the person who proposed establishing the chair, the famous Scottish missionary to India Alexander Duff. This chair is often cited as the first professorship in missions in all of Christendom,[12] so the title of the chair teaches us something about the understanding of the discipline at that time. Evangelism was seen as the core of Christian mission and missionary work, and mission was studied as a theological discipline. (At other times, however, mission has been studied as a practical discipline, or as a historical discipline.) By the time this first chair was abolished, mission study was much more accepted in Western Europe. Ironically, this chair in mission, or evangelistic theology, was abolished the year before an epoch-making missionary conference was held in the very same buildings: the 1910 Edinburgh Missionary Conference.

While in Europe mission studies were becoming more established late in the nineteenth century, in North America another Presbyterian seminary was pioneering in the area of mission studies. Princeton Theological Seminary established a chair in "Pastoral Theology and Missionary Instruction" in 1836, at about the time the first Presbyterian Mission Board was being established (Synod of Pittsburgh, PA, 1837). Again, the title of the chair is telling: the Princeton Presbyterians identified mission studies with pastoral theology, and considered it a practical rather than theological discipline. Unfortunately, the establishment of this chair reflected a temporary commitment to mission studies rather than a change in theological awareness (the chair ceased to exist in 1839).

More significant for the discipline than the establishment of these academic chairs were individuals and their scholarship. Gustav Warneck (1834–1910) is universally recognized as the pioneer missiologist. A professor and a prodigious writer from Halle University, Warneck founded the *Allgemeine Missions Zeitschrift*, the first missionary periodical for the "scientific study of mission," in 1874 and published the first survey of Protestant missions in 1901 (*Abriss einer Geschichte der protestantischen Missionen von der Reformation bis auf die Gegenwart: ein Beitrag zur neueren Kirchengeschichte*). These publications

11. As quoted from Oborji, *Concepts of Mission*, 44.

12. Olav G. Myklebust, *The Study of Missions in Theological Education* (Oslo: Egede Institute, 1955), 187.

began the study of mission history and, at the same time, began the division in theological discipline between mission history and church history. This was an advantage for the study of mission in some ways, but the artificial dichotomy it created also did much to isolate missiology from the rest of the theological curriculum. Comprehensive global Christian histories, histories that did not divide mission from the rest of the church, were not undertaken until the beginning of the twenty-first century.[13] In most educational institutions there are still two types of history being taught (or, in many cases, one type being neglected). Warneck also published the first textbook on the study of missiology (*Evangelische Missionslehre*, in 5 volumes, 1892–1905). Following his lead, Josef Schmidlin (1876–1944), also a German, pioneered Roman Catholic missiology. Schmidlin died in one of Hitler's concentration camps in 1944, and Warneck died almost at the very time of the Edinburgh Missionary Conference in 1910.

With these two major figures, missiological studies expanded in North America and Europe. A chair in mission studies was established at the Roman Catholic faculty in Münster in 1910, at Rome's Gregorian University in 1923, and at Urban University in 1933. Other Roman Catholic schools followed, but in both Roman Catholic and Protestant schools missiology did not become a standard part of the theological curriculum, as other new practical disciplines (homiletics, pastoral counseling, pastoral care, etc.) or theological disciplines (ecclesiology, contextual theology). "Mission was something completely on the periphery (and this was most noticeable in Protestantism) and did not evoke any theological interest worth mentioning."[14] Even without a clear place within the wider theological discipline, mission studies prospered during the twentieth century due to the growth of missions and missionary engagement, and also because of the developing ecumenical movement. As we will see in the next chapter, the International Missionary Council produced or provoked much of the richest missiological reflection of the first six decades of the twentieth century. Some of the greatest theologians of the age (Barth, Brunner, Bonhoeffer, Visser't Hooft, Blauw, Hoekendijk, and Newbigin) were involved in its discussions and publications. Mission societies for the academic study of mission were also developed: the Fellowship of Professors of Mission of the Atlantic Seaboard (1917), the International Association of Mission Studies (1966/1972), the Association of Professors of Missions (1952),[15] the Association of Evangelical Professors of Missions (1965), the Association of Evangelical Professors of Missions (1968, later renamed the Evangelical Missiological Society in 1990), the American Society of Missiology (1972), and the International Association

13. One of the first would be Dale Irvin and Scott Sunquist, *History of the World Christian Movement*, 2 vols. (Maryknoll, NY: Orbis Books, 2001–12).

14. Oborji, *Concepts of Mission*, 46.

15. Prior to the 1960s, "missions" (with an "s") was the term used to describe God's mission. The change to contemporary parlance took place in the 1960s and 1970s.

of Catholic Missiologists (2000). Many other societies were organized to promote, organize, or strategize for world mission, but those mentioned above were primarily established for the study of Christian mission.

Mission, Missions, Missionary, Missiology, Missional: What Is in a Word?

Most companies in the twentieth century have a mission, a purpose, a method, and a goal for making products and providing services. McDonald's mission, for example, is "to be our customers' favorite place and way to eat." Contemporary culture has co-opted the word "mission," which was originally used of the Trinity and then of God's mission to the world. I want to be clear about word usage from the beginning, so I offer a few brief definitions. "Mission" is the overarching term describing God's mission in the world (the *missio Dei*), or Christian mission in general. Thus, when I use "mission" (in the singular), I am talking about the *missio Dei*, the mission of God to bring about redemption of the world, or human participation in this mission. In the plural—"missions"—I am generally talking about particular mission societies or organizations. Consistency is lacking in this distinction, for there are many lay people and some mission authors who talk about teaching or studying "missions," when what they are really studying is the larger topic of the mission of God. I will be consistent in this volume, speaking of missions only when I am talking about organizations or institutions that carry out God's mission.

The third term may seem obvious, but it has engendered some controversy in the last four decades. A "missionary" is, quite simply, one who is sent. Theologically speaking, the missionary is sent by God (John 20:21), but practically and ecclesiologically, a missionary is sent by a church or an ecclesiastical body. When a missionary is sent by one of thousands of missions, there is still the need for a local church to be the primary sending body, since mission is the work of the church—the church universal, through a local, particular church. The controversy over the term "missionary" in past decades comes from the assumed imperialistic or paternalistic baggage that is associated with it. In an effort to achieve distance from older missionary models, other terms have been suggested and tried, but none of the alternatives caught on, since to change a biblical term[16] requires the ecumenical church to harmoniously affirm the new vocabulary. "Fraternal workers" was tried for a while but, as concern for women's rights grew, this gender-exclusive term was dropped. Next the term "mission co-workers" was tried, but it was rather clumsy, and

16. "Missionary" is a biblical term because it is simply the Latin word *missio* (to "send") used to translate the Greek word for "apostle" (*apostello*), meaning "sent one." The apostles were sent ones, and so the clear connection of disciples of Jesus Christ being sent ones is lost if we drop the usage of "missionary."

most non-Western church leaders simplified it to missionary anyway. Thus "missionary" is still the universally accepted term, even for those who are engaged missionally as tent-makers. A missionary is an apostle, one who is sent from the heart of God to proclaim the present and coming Kingdom of God to all the nations of the earth.

The fourth term, "missiology," is simply the study of God's mission. This study (which is the subject of this book) involves using the following academic disciplines: the social sciences (especially sociology and cultural anthropology), theology, biblical interpretation, Christian history, study of religions, and practical theology. Depending upon the institution and the missiologist, the study of missiology may be more of a practical science, a historical science, or a theological and philosophical study. I will call upon all of these disciplines in this volume, but my predisposition is to comprehend missiology as more of a theological concern, rooted in careful biblical and historical work. Practical applications are so varied that to focus on approaches, methods, or specific practices is much too limiting (too culturally specific). Thus, we begin with what is commonly accepted by theologians and missiologists today throughout the world: we study missiology as the *missio Dei*, or the mission of God.[17] This expression became a major theme in missiological discussions after World War II and put missiological study in a whole new theological universe. Missiological discussion now begins not with what the church should do, or what a missionary must believe (or do), but with what God has done and what God is doing. Our role, as we participate with God in his mission to his creation, is to respond in obedience, gratitude, and joy. This is obviously a much broader and inclusive definition of mission; it is also a much deeper, even mysterious, missiological understanding. We begin with the deep work of God in confronting the powers and conquering death and evil, and we follow through with his work of reconciliation, peace, and even glorification. Mission is not only about planting churches; it is a much more profound and, we might say, more foundational work. Missiology is, then, a major dimension of theological study. It is a study that moves toward an understanding of God; it is a study of God's nature and activity in sending to his creation prophets, priests, kings, and even his own Son to bring about and then announce the redemption of his world.

The fifth and final term is the newest of our terms. In fact, the adjectival form of mission, "missional," was coined in the 1990s in an effort to recover the missionary nature of every local church. The recovery of the local church's missionary vocation came as a result of theological discussions in

17. An excellent survey of the use of the term *missio Dei* is found in the PhD dissertation of John Flett, "God Is a Missionary God: *Missio Dei*, Karl Barth, and the Doctrine of the Trinity" (PhD diss., Princeton Theological Seminary, 2007). It was revised and published as *The Witness of God: The Trinity,* Missio Dei, *Karl Barth, and the Nature of Christian Community* (Grand Rapids: Eerdmans, 2010).

the ecumenical movement beginning with the 1938 Tambaram (Madras) International Missionary Council (IMC) meeting. This opened up a discussion that continued through the rest of the century on what it means, theologically and practically, for the church—for any and every local church—to participate in God's mission.

Missiology Applied to the West

It was J. E. Lesslie Newbigin, English Presbyterian missionary to India, who developed missional thought for the Western church. His writings, especially in the 1980s and 1990s, influenced the thinking of Western missiologists and church leaders who were no longer thinking theoretically about churches in the West having a missional responsibility. Newbigin identified that the West had become a mission field.

The decline of Christianity in the West and the advent of Asian religions in the cities of the West revealed the need for local churches to assume their missional nature once again. When most of the surrounding culture was Christian, or at least tolerant of Christian values and holidays, it was easy for Western churches to forget the missional nature of the church. It was George Hunsberger and the "Gospel in Our Context" movement who, through publications, workshops, and conferences, raised the issue and gave meaning to the new adjectival use of mission. Today, there is much confusion over what it means to be a "missional church," but I use it here to mean the responsibility of each and every church to participate in God's mission in all its fullness.

Theology Starts with Mission

Missiological reflection is both the context of all theology and the first movement in theological reflection. This understanding of theology as coming out of the reflection of the faith on the frontiers of faith is commonly accepted today. The earliest Christian theological reflections are found in the New Testament. Luke's two-part volume was written while on a missionary journey. Paul's letter to the Romans was written to prepare the way for his missionary visit to Rome, as he passed through on his way to Spain. He wrote theology as a church planter, "on a mission." In fact, each of the New Testament writings comes out of the missionary engagement of the church with the world. Therefore, it is necessary to have a missional hermeneutic for reading the Bible—but especially for reading the New Testament.[18] The New Testament writings were reflections on missiological praxis.

18. C. J. H. Wright, *The Mission of God: Unlocking the Bible's Grand Narrative* (Leicester: Inter-Varsity, 2006). Part 1, "The Bible and Mission," provides a missional hermeneutic for reading the Bible. See also the pioneering article by James V. Brownson, "Speaking the Truth

The Martyrdom of Bishop Polycarp of Smyrna

This work of the apostolic fathers was written from one church (Smyrna) to another church (Philomelium) as an encouragement—describing how their bishop gave a faithful "testimony" (witness, or *martyria*) in his life and his death. He himself was the missionary encounter between faith and non-faith, and his story then became a testimony to others. When we read both of his martyrdom and then his letter to the Christians at Philippi, we realize that Polycarp was a type of missionary bishop, concerned with the spread of the faith and the integrity of the church.

As we move out of the earliest period of Christian writings and into the second and third centuries, we discover that these writings also come out of the context of a missionary engagement. Most of the major Christian writings of this period are apologetic in nature, either addressed to people in authority defending the Christian belief and cause or written to strengthen the Christian community in its witness to the broader culture. Origen's famous response to Celsus's attacks on Christianity (*Contra Celsum*) is quite typical of the period; theological awareness, reflection, and writing are based in the missionary encounter. This has always been the case, and it is still the case today.[19] "Mission is the mother of theology," as well as the mother of the New Testament texts.[20] Neither the second- and third-century writers, nor the New Testament writers, were systematic theologians sitting in ivy-covered citadels contemplating the character and will of God. They were persecuted, hurried, and harried apostles (read "missionaries") challenging the religious, political, and social structures of their time—proclaiming a Kingdom that was above all kingdoms and authorities of this world. It was this mission that birthed biblical and theological reflection.

Some Definitions of Mission

How do we define mission? As David Bosch once said during an informal discussion in Princeton, "Christian mission is the church crossing frontiers. There must be some crossing of barriers—whether they be linguistic, economic, cultural, or religious—and there must be some communication of the message

in Love: Elements of a Missional Hermeneutic," *International Review of Missions* 83 (July 1994): 479–504.

19. For further discussion of the missiological dimension of theology, see Andrew Kirk's chapter "What Is Theology? And Theology of Mission?" in his book *What Is Mission? Theological Explorations* (Minneapolis: Fortress, 2000), chap. 1. See also Bosch, *Transforming Mission*, 489–98, for a discussion of "mission as theology."

20. Martin Kähler, *Schriften zur Christologie und Mission* (Munich: Chr. Kaiser Verlag, 1908), 190, translation from Bosch, *Transforming Mission*, 16.

of Christ."[21] Like Bosch, we have already noted that mission involves both sending and the crossing of boundaries of faith or belief, but can we be more specific? Missiologists in recent years have given greater definition to mission, drawing on theological reflection, biblical studies, and the church's engagement in mission. Before offering my own definition, then, it will be helpful to lay out some of the definitions that are currently being used by major missiologists.

David Bosch begins his magnum opus, *Transforming Mission*, with a three-page interim definition. He begins this section by saying that Christian faith is intrinsically missionary, and if it is not, "it denies its very *raison d'être*."[22] He explains further that mission will always remain indefinable and that the most we can hope for is to formulate some *approximations* of what mission is all about.

Bosch puts forward his own series of approximations on mission before his in-depth biblical, historical, and theological study of the *missio Dei*. At the end of his book, he says much more directly:

> In our mission, we proclaim the incarnate, crucified, resurrected, and ascended Christ, present among us in the Spirit and taking us into his future as "captives in triumphal procession." . . . Mission is quite simply, the participation of Christians in the liberating mission of Jesus, wagering on a future that verifiable experience seems to belie. It is the good news of God's love, incarnated in the witness of a community, for the sake of the world.[23]

Andrew Kirk, in his book *What Is Mission?*, begins with a definition not of mission but of a related concept, theology of mission:

> The theology of mission is a disciplined study which deals with questions that arise when people of faith seek to understand and fulfill God's purposes in the world, as these are demonstrated in the ministry of Jesus Christ. It is a critical reflection on attitudes and actions adopted by Christians in pursuit of the missionary mandate. Its task is to validate, correct, and establish on better foundations the entire practice of mission.[24]

What is important in both of these definitions is the understanding that there is a content or a theological understanding that is communicated in Christian mission. In later chapters, Kirk unfolds the meaning of Christian mission as announcing the good news; transforming cultures; providing justice for the poor; promoting encounter, dialogue, and witness among the religions of the world; building peace in a world of violence; and caring for the environment. Moreover, all this is to be done in partnership. Regarding mission to

21. In a discussion with faculty and PhD students in the history department at Princeton Theological Seminary in 1986.

22. Bosch, *Transforming Mission*, 8–11.

23. Ibid., 518.

24. Kirk, *What Is Mission?*, 21.

Bosch Defines Mission

Missiologist David Bosch draws up a list of eleven approximations for understanding mission:[a]

1. Mission involves the dynamic relationship between God and the world.
2. Mission cannot be directed by biblically immutable and objective laws of mission.
3. The entire Christian existence is missionary.
4. The church is missionary by its very nature.
5. There is no dichotomy between foreign and national missions.
6. Mission is grounded in the gospel itself.
7. The missionary task is "as coherent, broad, and deep as the need and exigencies of human life."
8. Mission involves the whole church bringing the whole gospel to the whole world.
9. Mission is both God's "yes" to the world and at the same time it is God's "no."
10. Mission includes the essential dimension of evangelism, but it is not synonymous with evangelism.
11. The church is a sign and sacrament for the world, pointing (as the first fruits) to the coming Kingdom.

a. Bosch, *Transforming Mission*, 8–11.

political life, the church's mission is three-fold: prophetic task, servant task, and evangelistic task.

In a similar fashion, Francis Anekwe Oborji, a Nigerian Roman Catholic, includes numerous dimensions in his definition of worship. He writes of mission as conversion, church planting, inculturation, dialogue, service of God's reign, ecumenical dialogue, and contextual theologies. In his conclusion, he focuses upon three themes that are central to a definition of Christian mission: proclamation, evangelization, and contextual theologies. He sees these three elements as working together with the clear goal of Christian mission being "evangelization and church formation."[25]

Bevans and Schroeder, in their book *Constants in Context*, also recognize the nexus of concerns that crop up when we try to define mission. As with the above books, much of their volume is written to try to give definition to the concept. However, in the first part of the book they follow the Conciliar and Roman Catholic trajectories from the World Council of Churches ("Conciliar") and

25. Oborji, *Concepts of Mission*, 210.

from the Second Vatican Council (Roman Catholic), commenting that "mission takes the church beyond itself into history, into culture, into people's lives, beckoning it constantly to 'cross frontiers.'"[26] They remind the reader that "Christians are themselves called to witness and proclaim the good news to the world: 'It is unthinkable that a person should accept the Word and give himself to the Kingdom without becoming a person who bears witness to it and proclaims it in his turn.'"[27] Regarding the goal of mission, they note that the goal is not the expansion of the church for its own sake, but that people are invited into the church so that they can join a community dedicated to preaching, serving, and witnessing to God's reign. At the end of their volume, they conclude: "There is one mission: the mission of God that is shared, by God's grace, by the church. It has two directions, to the church itself (*ad intra*) and to the world (*ad extra*). . . . Mission has a basic three-fold office of word (*kerygma* or proclamation), action (*diakonia* or service), and being (*koinōnia* or *martyria*—community or witness/martyr)."[28]

Six Constants in Missiology

Bevans and Schroeder put forward six constants in Christian mission that transcend particular cultures, times, and places, so as to anchor the theology and practice of mission. They give these constants as questions:

1. Who is Jesus Christ and what is his meaning?
2. What is the nature of the Christian church?
3. How does the church regard its eschatological future?
4. What is the nature of the salvation it preaches?
5. How does the church value the human?
6. What is the value of human culture as the context in which the gospel is preached?[a]

a. Bevans and Schroeder, *Constants in Context*, 34.

Bevans and Schroeder's constants of Christian mission are questions that anchor theology and practice. There are many other definitions of mission that I could point to, but these four missiologists raise the important themes that we will be tracing in the coming pages.[29]

What Type of Missiology Is This?

This textbook is a missiology in three parts: a descriptive section (history); a prescriptive or constructive section (theology); and an issues section (contemporary themes). There is an internal logic to this outline. Before discussing

26. Stephen Bevans and Roger Schroeder, *Constants in Context: A Theology of Mission for Today* (Maryknoll, NY: Orbis Books, 2004), 8.
27. Ibid., quoting from the Vatican II document *Evangelii Nuntiandi* 24.
28. Definitions in this passage are my own.
29. You will find my working definition of mission at the beginning of part 2.

missiology for today, we have to understand the historic context that has brought us to the place we are today. History reveals some of the divisions we have in missiological thinking, the way ideas have developed over time, and some of the successes and failures we have witnessed in carrying out God's mission. History will help us evaluate the critique of missions and empire, of missionaries creating "rice Christians," and of missionaries "making one more Christian and thus one less Chinese." We will also learn about some of the remarkable work missionaries have accomplished—work that will challenge our thinking about God's mission and our responsibility today.

Modern missiology really began with the Jesuits (Roman Catholic) in the sixteenth century and then with the Moravians (Protestant) in the eighteenth century. In both cases, modern missionary practice and thinking began at the fringes, not at the center, of Christendom. Questions that these pioneers raised are still relevant today. Does this mean that we denigrate the sacrificial work of earlier missionary encounters? Not at all. In fact, we will see the value of these earlier encounters in the constructive section in part 2 of this book.

Chapter 1 covers the earliest monastic missionary movement, as a foundation for the modern period. Chapters 2 and 3 examine the early modern mission (Roman Catholic, Protestant, and Orthodox) from the time of Xavier (1506–52) up to the middle of the nineteenth century. In the early nineteenth century, Protestant missions was just catching up to Roman Catholic missions; Protestants were still in a formative stage. After the middle of the nineteenth century, Roman Catholic missions were redeveloping after a near collapse in the shadow of the French Revolution, and Protestant missions were moving from the fringes to the center. I use the end of the Second Opium War in China (1842) as a cutoff point between early modern missiology and the period of history in which the missionary movement peaked.

Chapter 4 covers the zenith of the modern missionary movement, from 1842 to 1948. During this period, mission budgets were major financial outlays for churches in Europe and North America, mission was a dominant global concern, and the missionary force continued to grow, even through two world wars. The final history section, chapter 5, covers a turbulent period of Christian history that I refer to as the waning and reconception of Christian mission. The Western missionary force began to decline and missionary thought dissipated beginning in the 1960s. The year 1961 is an important marker, because it was the year of the integration of the International Missionary Council into the World Council of Churches, it was the year that the first Pentecostal churches joined the WCC, and it was also the year before the Second Vatican Council opened (1962–65)—in which Roman Catholic understanding of ecclesiology developed in new ways that greatly influenced both ecumenical relations and missionary work. This was also the beginning of the decline of Western mainline missions. Missionary work in the 1850s has more in common with missionary work in the 1950s than missionary work in the 1950s does with that of the 1970s.

I have called the period from the 1960s to the end of the twentieth century the "worldwide reversal" of Christianity. Chapter 5 also explores the postcolonial missiologies that developed in the last half of the twentieth century. This is the first chapter where the major players are global and ecumenical. Of the four streams of Christianity—Orthodox, Roman Catholic, Protestant, and Spiritual—it is the last that begins to assert itself above all others. The Spiritual churches include Pentecostal churches, but are mostly made up of churches that spring up through inspiration of the Holy Spirit: indigenous churches, unregistered churches, Muslim background churches, unbaptized believers, and culture Christians. Spiritual churches are defined by their authority coming from the Holy Spirit more than from a particular tradition. This final historical chapter (chap. 5) sets the stage for part 2 of this volume.

Part 2 is the constructive section, in which I develop a trinitarian model of missiology. Taking into account the last half of a millennium of missiological practice and thinking, and working with biblical texts, patristic texts, and contemporary trinitarian theology, I develop a missiology that is trinitarian, catholic, and evangelical. This is a tall order, but it is based upon some primary biblical concerns. First is the concern for unity. I take very seriously Jesus's high priestly prayer in John 17 and that his major concerns are twofold regarding the glory of God: that God's glory be revealed to all the world, and that the followers of Jesus be united in this mission of glory-revealing. This being the case, I will develop a theology of mission that is the following: trinitarian, meaning that it is rooted in the original meaning of *missio* in theological discussion (the sending nature of God); catholic, meaning that it includes all of the church; and evangelical, meaning that it is centered in the good news revealed in the life of Jesus Christ. This discussion takes up the heart of this volume, chapters 6 (the sending Father), 7 (the suffering and sacrificing Son), and 8 (presence, participation, and power of the Holy Spirit).

Finally, part 3 of this volume covers contemporary themes, or issues that are central to living out such a trinitarian theology of mission today. In chapter 9, I discuss the nature of the church and the practice of Christian life in the local church. There is much discussion and confusion about what the church is today, which is caused in part by confrontations with postmodern culture, as well as the growth of Christianity in persecuted regions. These two issues, plus the rapid decline of Christianity in the "Christian West," have caused a rethinking of what the local church should be. I look at the local church as a place of community, worship, and mission. These are the constituent parts that make up the church, and they must be seen together as the expression of the Kingdom of God. In chapter 10, I look at the nature of the church as a witnessing community. "Witness" is a good word to sum up the missional presence of any Christian community, but what does it mean? In this chapter, I try to recover a holistic sense of witness and give examples of holistic witness as a catalyst to further thinking.

Chapter 11 focuses on a major concern of mission for the twenty-first century: mission and the city. Humankind has always formed communities that have expanded into towns and cities. We read of cities—both good (Jerusalem and the New Jerusalem) and evil (Babylon)—in the Bible. There are even books in the Bible named for cities: Corinthians, Philippians, Colossians, and of course Romans. However, in the twenty-first century, cities have grown to such enormous size and complexity that missionary thinking must specifically look at what it means to be a missionary presence in these new megacities.

Chapter 12 discusses another major theme in missiological thinking today: global partnership. Here I respond to the global occurrence of Christian communities in most regions of the world. Partnerships of all types are developing between churches, missions, leaders, and governing bodies throughout the world. How is this faithful participation in God's mission, and what are the concerns that need to be addressed? Finally, in chapter 13, I look at mission and spirituality, remembering the earliest missionary work that grew out of spiritual vitality and spiritual discipline (monastic). This is a chapter that is, I believe, unique among books on mission. Many of the earliest missionary writings came out of deep spiritual experiences, and many of these writings became spiritual "best sellers." Christian mission is a matter of the heart as well as the head, a matter of devotion as well as decision. Ignatius of Loyola, the founder of both the Jesuit missions and the Spiritual Exercises is a reminder that the warp of spirituality and the woof of mission make up one fabric.

The three parts of this book are approached with nine guiding contextual concerns. Twenty years from now, these concerns may be different, meaning that this theology of mission would look different as well. It is the very nature of theology—especially of missiology—that it both comes out of specific contexts and speaks to specific contexts. Thus, there is a place for an ecumenical missiology, but there is also a place for local missiologies that speak to specific contexts and situations. A missiology for China today would raise different issues than a missiology for Iceland or Peru. Still, an ecumenical missiology such as this one is needed to see the overall *missio Dei* as being one: "There is one body and one Spirit—just as you were called to one hope when you were called; one Lord, one faith, one baptism; one God and Father of all, who is over all and through all and in all" (Eph. 4:4–6). In the following section I identify the major contextual concerns that have guided this volume.

Nine Contextual Concerns

1. Theology must be *ecumenically informed* (globally and from many church confessional families). As I mentioned above, it is just not acceptable for churches, denominations, missions, or individuals to move forward in mission

as if they are the only ones faithful in mission. It takes great humility to work with others, but theologically it is absolutely necessary that we work to express our missiology as one. To this end, this volume is part of a growing body of missiological literature dedicated to listening to others and to Scripture, and to speaking words that will bring Christians together in this great global, and even cosmic, work of the church.

2. This study is based upon the assumption that *all Christian mission is inadequate*, but that all Christian mission has its own significance. Therefore, a theology of mission must be big enough to include various strands of Christianity that express the *missio Dei*. However, a missiology must also be focused enough to be distinguished from the Rotary or local Garden Club. I try to say some things very clearly and boldly, but also to give proper latitude to the breadth of God's work in the world. In our world of both Christian divisions and Christian persecution, it is necessary to embrace clarity and charity.

3. My work is built with the conscious realization of *three twenty-first-century characteristics of Christianity*. Firstly, Christianity is mostly non-Western. Any mission text or mission conference that was held before the 1980s was dealing with a different context, in which most of the church, and most of the missionaries, came from the North Atlantic. This is not true today. With each day, the percentage of Western Christians and Western Christian missionaries is declining. Secondly, Christianity is growing outside the older boundaries of Protestant, Catholic, and Orthodox churches. The shift to spiritual and indigenous forms of Christianity occurred throughout the twentieth century, but shifted most dramatically after World War II, with the rise of decolonialization. This makes discussion about missions and churches much more difficult. Newer associations have developed, newer churches and groupings of churches have emerged, redrawing the ecclesial and missions maps. In the 1950s we could talk about the documents of the World Council of Churches and know that they represented much of the Protestant mission thinking in the world. This is no longer the case.

Thirdly, global Christianity in the twenty-first century is much less "modern"—meaning organized, rational, and pyramid-like in organization. Spiritual churches are, by their very nature, led by the Spirit, and the Spirit, like the wind (John 3), is neither predictable nor organized (as we would understand order). The Protestant church in China is a good example of what we are talking about. The very organized church in China (China Christian Council) is becoming increasingly marginalized, and the mass movement of Christianity toward unregistered churches is the main story. However, it is very hard to get statistics on unregistered churches, and it is even more difficult to discover their "order" or organization. Christianity is much more of a movement than an institution in the twenty-first century, although it is always both. In short, Christianity today is more pneumatic than in recent centuries. Some of this will come out in chapter 5, on the contemporary context of mission, but it needs to be stated upfront that the postmodern world, a world that is "flatter"[30] and more globalized than ever before, is our context for missionary engagement.

4. I write with an awareness that the major issues of missiology today have to do with *religious encounters, political presence, and ongoing human-induced tragedies* (starvation, disease, violence, etc.). These are the practical and real concerns that will always be at our prayer altar as we study the subject matter. In some ways, these issues have always been the context of missionary activity, but with the rise of contemporary communications and global connectedness, we must deal with these issues more directly than ever before. It is very important to hold these issues before us, because the global media does not share the same compassion for the world. Popular media, by its very nature, can only focus upon a few "sensational" and "attractive" areas of suffering. Christian missionary involvement must not be bound to what is popular, popularly known, or even what seems like "viable" mission. All of the suffering world is the concern of the *missio Dei*, and therefore of our missiology.

5. It is important to be clear *who the dialogue partners are* in such a task. There are numerous writers, mission leaders, and theologians with whom I could interact. I have limited myself, however, to a few of the major figures. These include the following: David Bosch, Andrew Kirk, Lesslie Newbigin, Stephen Bevans and Roger Schroeder, Francis A. Oborji, Timothy Tennent, Vinoth Ramachandra, Paul Knitter, Matteo Ricci, Ludwig von Zinzendorf, the Cappadocians, and others from the ancient church (Simeon the New Theologian, Ephrem, Narsai, Ignatius of Antioch, Irenaeus, and the "solitaries" of *The Philokalia*). It is a mixed group, but it is a good representation of the contemporary, the early modern, and the ancient—of East and West. The mixture of conversation partners is intentional, and is intended to guide us through contemporary discussions while keeping us rooted in the Great Tradition of the church. Loss of the grounding or ballast of tradition may cause us to misrepresent God's mission and God's people. While modern contextual theologies are being developed—and are serving the church well—there is at the same time the need to look back and remember the lifeline that we are all part of. There is, at root, one Christianity and one church—as diverse and conflicted as it often appears.

6. I believe that mission is really a *dimension of our spirituality*, not a contrast to it. Bosch's *Spirituality of the Road*[31] is a reminder that missional engagement must be understood as a matter of identification with Christ. Whether a church or a person engages in mission and how that mission is done is more a matter of spirituality than anything else. Thus, from the be-

30. See Thomas Friedman's *The World Is Flat: A Brief History of the 21st Century* (New York: Farrar, Straus & Giroux, 2005).

31. This book is a compilation of lectures Bosch gave to the Mennonite Missionary Study Fellowship in 1978. It was published by Herald in 1979 and reissued in 2001.

ginning, I do not think of mission primarily as a practical science, but more as a spiritual theology. It brings together theological study and personal and corporate piety.

7. In writing this volume, I have some contemporary encounters before me that remind me of *Christianity's uniqueness*. In the West today we are conflicted about uniqueness. We want to affirm each community's right to define its own terms, its own reality. At its best, this is radical communal integrity, but at worst, this is radical communalism. At the same time, we are not comfortable with a community that interprets reality in a way that is not in the "flow" of the increasing hedonism and secularism of the twenty-first century. The West today looks more like Rome in the first centuries of the Common Era than the Christendom of the past thousand years. Our Western world is decaying from within, and its empire is now only a fading glory. It no longer has the order or the goodness to impose its will on the world. In the midst of this conflicted Western context, we affirm the uniqueness of God's redemption. Grace still transforms and conquers evil. This grace, seen in humility and humiliation, is not a power the world recognizes, but it is a powerful grace that transforms the world. At the same time, this uniqueness also reveals that it is God's justice, not ours, that must be proclaimed. We see this uniqueness also in the simple teaching of Christ that one's life is fulfilled when that life is laid down. Other religions and ideologies offer paths, works, exercises, or approaches to god (or paths to "release"). Jesus offers something more powerful—grace—and asks only for surrender.

8. Following Andrew Walls,[32] I am guided, especially in the history section (part 1), by the understanding that Christianity is both *incarnational* (Jesus tabernacles among us, and so is at home in all cultures) and a *pilgrim faith* (Christians are not at home; we are pilgrims and refugees). Of all of Walls's many contributions to mission theory and history, this may be his greatest. He sees clearly that two principles are at work in Christianity throughout its history, and from its beginning. The incarnational is an ongoing and purposeful move to be part of a culture; Christianity must be translated into a culture, and the gospel must speak Foochow as well as Spanish, Arabic, and modern Greek. It is this diversity—of the gospel in its many cultural expressions—that Christians must celebrate and that God embraces. At the same time, the pilgrim principle is at work in Christianity. The gospel is (and is only) the gospel of Jesus Christ. It has specific content and meaning, and it comes not to affirm all that is in a local culture, but enters into the culture to lift it up and clean it off. Cultures, societies, and governments always have a love-hate relationship with the gospel of Jesus Christ, since it both affirms and challenges. Affirmation

32. See Andrew Walls's two volumes *The Missionary Movement in Christian History: Studies in the Transmission of Faith* (Maryknoll, NY: Orbis Books, 1996) and *The Cross-Cultural Process in Christian History* (Maryknoll, NY: Orbis Books, 2002).

and rejection, incarnation and pilgrimage, are always at work in Christianity and are always a stress and a hope within Christian mission.

9. Finally, I affirm, almost as an extension of Walls's two principles, that throughout history *Christianity is centered and intercultural* (two essential elements). As we mentioned before, there is a strong core or deep foundation to Christian mission. And yet, almost paradoxically, there is great flexibility and contextual variety within missiology. The title of Bevans and Schroeder's book, *Constants in Context*, expresses it well. We have a center—the cross—that unites all Christians throughout time and space. And yet, we also have a great variety of cultural expressions and translations. I am aware that these two—centeredness and cultural diversity—must always be before us and must also be both affirmed and critiqued according to trinitarian theology.

The "Dogmatic Constitution on the Church"

Here are the opening words of the "Dogmatic Constitution on the Church" (*Lumen Gentium*) from the Second Vatican Council:

> Christ is the Light of nations. Because this is so, this Sacred Synod gathered together in the Holy Spirit eagerly desires, by proclaiming the Gospel to every creature, (1) to bring the light of Christ to all men, a light brightly visible on the countenance of the Church. Since the Church is in Christ like a sacrament or as a sign and instrument both of a very closely knit union with God and of the unity of the whole human race, it desires now to unfold more fully to the faithful of the Church and to the whole world its own inner nature and universal mission. This it intends to do following faithfully the teaching of previous councils. The present-day conditions of the world add greater urgency to this work of the Church so that all men, joined more closely today by various social, technical and cultural ties, might also attain fuller unity in Christ.

History, Theology, and Practice

To bring this introduction to a conclusion, I would like to remind the reader that such a work as this, a work that starts from historical awareness, builds a constructive theology that is trinitarian in essence and biblical in awareness, and that ends with practical applications—such a work is at heart an ecclesiology. From start to finish, missiologists have come to the conclusion that missiology is about the church; it is from the church and it must build the church. It was to a young church of frightened Jews in Jerusalem that Jesus first gave the commission that we are now studying. Twenty centuries later, Christians of all backgrounds and confessions continue to push into this reality. The recent use of the term "missional" to modify the noun "church," is only one indication of this. The missional and emerging church movements are closely linked, through their missional predispositions, to engage the world and specific local cultures with the gospel. Vatican II documents such as *Gaudium et Spes* ("Pastoral Constitution on the Church in the Modern World"), *Lumen Gentium* ("Dogmatic Constitution on the Church"), and *Ad Gentes* ("Decree on the Church's Missionary Activity"), as well as Pope Paul VI's Apostolic Letter *Evangelii Nuntiandi* (1975), are all indications that the Roman Catholic Church sees the church as missionary in its very essence.

The church is a sacrament for the world: a sign of our unity with Christ and of the church's universal mission. Vatican II is clear that the church is not a static institution simply maintaining order and dispensing grace to all who attend. The church has become a tabernacle; God with the nations. Protestants have come to agree. Although it was the towering Protestant theologian Karl Barth who provided much of the missiological reflection and fodder for future theologians, it was Emil Brunner in 1931 who said it most memorably and clearly: "The church exists by mission, just as a fire exists by burning."[33] Much later, but equally emphatically, Adrian Hastings stated it this way: "The church does not so much *have* a mission—as if the church somehow existed *prior* to its task—rather it *is* mission as such; indeed, as the phrase goes, the church of Christ does not so much have a mission as the mission of Christ has a church."[34]

33. Emil Brunner, *The Word in the World* (New York: Charles Scribner's Sons, 1931), 11.
34. Quoted in Bevans and Schroeder, *Constants in Context*, 8.

Part I

Suffering and Glory in History

The Mission Movement

We begin our study of missiology with history. We do this for three reasons. First, Christianity is one of the few historical or "secular"[1] religions that exists. God created, and with that creation time began. Beginning with God's revelation to Abraham (a call to a specific family and a specific geographical location), Christian heritage is a clear break with local hierophanic[2] and cyclical faiths (which I describe below). God, in Christ, entered into this mundane world of sin and grace, of pain and joy, lifting up physical existence and redeeming time-bound life.[3] The physical world that moves from moment to moment, the place where time will

1. "Secular" is used for this world (Latin, *saeculum*), or for worldly existence. Christianity has a "this-worldly" concern, as seen most clearly in the incarnation.

2. Scholars of religion use this term to designate nature religions marked by sacred places, times, and seasons. Most of the religions of the ancient Near East were built around such imminence of the sacred. "Hierophanic" is from Greek roots indicating a local appearance or manifestation of the holy or the sacred; it should not be confused with "hierophantic," which refers to priestly religion.

3. See Scott Sunquist, *Time, Cross, and Glory: Understanding Christian History* (Downers Grove, IL: InterVarsity, forthcoming), chap. 1, "Time, Creation, Redemption."

"sweep [us] all away"[4]—this is the place of God's redemption and therefore of Christian mission. Mission is through all of time and into all of creation.

In contrast to this view of time and history, most religions of the world, responding to human problems (pain, suffering, aging, death, injustice) find the answer in escape from the physical world. For example, in ancient Greek thought, the spiritual is superior to the physical. The realm of "idea" is superior to the realm of physical human life. Early Gnostic influences in Christianity were rejected again and again because they denigrated time and the physical world. The goal in most religions is to escape the physical world and to exist, even if in a semi-animated state, in the spiritual realm. Hinduism and Buddhism also denigrate the physical world, having as their goal escape from the endless cycle of suffering in this world.[5] If we can talk about holiness in Buddhism it would be to be "unattached" from this world and its desires. Thus, in most religions, this physical world, with its brokenness, suffering, decay, and death, is nothing but an endless cycle. There is no progress, no moving forward: only escape. Christianity radically critiques this cyclical view of reality. In the incarnation, God has entered time—and he therefore sanctifies historic events. Through the resurrection, he redeems time—by conquering evil in a specific place in a particular time. The incarnation itself is a divine shout of joy regarding this world of time and matter. History is meaningful and carries sacredness within it. The biblical texts tell a story—the story of God in his created world—the story of redemption, in time, moving toward a glorious goal, for all of the nations. As Newbigin expresses it, mission is to the end of time and to the end of the earth.[6]

My second reason for starting with history is that Christian mission, as an expression of the mission of God, is a process that takes place in history and therefore has historical dimensions and implications. Christian mission must respond to historical contexts as it speaks to historical contexts. Christianity roots the individual in a community in a particular context, and it does this by grafting the person into the vine of life. The elevation of the Christian from strictly secular and historical realities, so that the heart and mind are in Christ Jesus (Col. 3), makes it possible for the Christian to have a missional presence that has the power to transform this earthly existence. Complete identification with the secular (this world) means one has no critical distance and therefore no leverage with which to transform this world. Christian mission takes place in the world, it is for the world, but it is from God. Thus, Christian mission is both influenced by the historical and exists for the sake of influencing what is historical. Christian mission is not an otherworldly activity, in the sense that it provides a spiritual dimension that takes us out of, or raises us above, the

4. Psalm 90 reminds us of God's time and eternity.

5. In Hinduism the goal is *moksha*, or "release," and in Buddhism it is *nirvana* (*nibbana*), a state of enlightenment where a person is fully liberated and at perfect peace.

6. Lesslie Newbigin, *The Open Secret* (Grand Rapids: Eerdmans, 1978), 1.

daily grind. This would be more akin to Buddhist meditation or New Age spirituality as personal therapy. Christian mission is *for* the world that we believe God created, God loves, and God continues to redeem. Christians are invited to participate in this historical work of God in his creation.

Third, I begin with history because, quite obviously, we are not originating mission in the twenty-first century. We are participating with a long line of saints and sinners who have been more or less faithful to God in time and space. On one hand, we must recognize the great work of those in the past and find ways to build on this. On the other hand, we must make careful judgments about where our past participation in mission has not been faithful to God's mission. We should always be searching for what has been done and what has been left undone as we step into the path of mission faithfulness. History is our context. Martyrs, apostles, and saints are our instructors. Mission is not merely an abstract theory that we discuss, that academics play with during scholarly conferences. Mission is also not something that we read from the Bible, as if the Bible were a modern set of missionary instructions. This is the mistake of much missionary literature today: the Bible is treated as a twenty-first-century handbook on mission and the Great Tradition of the saints, and the complex issues of the present are ignored.

I want to affirm that mission does not exist apart from the historical reality of Christ's body speaking and acting in the world. What has gone on in the past centuries helps to explain where we are today. My focus in the first part of this book will be with recent history (the past five hundred years!), but I will also give an overview of themes from the first fifteen hundred years. The reason for my greater concern with recent centuries is self-evident: this history most directly influences our present reality. Earlier historical periods are no less important, of course, but many others have written that history at length.[7] I will move quickly through the earlier periods and then focus on the new mission theology and practice that began with the Jesuits in the sixteenth century. This more recent history reveals the issues, the struggles, and the themes that give context to our contemporary discussions on Christian mission. Two major themes begin in the sixteenth century that reveal why I begin my historical analysis there: globalization of Christianity and the Reformation (beginning in 1482).[8] European church divisions and globalization

7. For example, Kenneth Scott Latourette, *A History of Christian Expansion*, 7 vols. (London: Eyre & Spottiswoode, 1939–45); Stephen Neill, *A History of Christian Missions* (New York: Penguin, 1986); Dale Irvin and Scott Sunquist, *History of the World Christian Movement*, 2 vols. (Maryknoll, NY: Orbis Books, 2001/2012); Adrian Hastings, *A World History of Christianity* (Grand Rapids: Eerdmans, 1999); Justo González, *The Story of Christianity*, 2 vols. (San Francisco: Harper & Row, 1984).

8. This is the date the Portuguese established their first tropical fort at Elmina on the Gold Coast, marking the beginning of their encounter with Africa. A year later, Martin Luther was born.

occurred almost concurrently. Therefore, I begin with the major trends in missionary activity during this period of great creativity in Christian theology, trends that were stimulated by early encounters with modernity and with other religions and cultures. This was a period when cultural and religious intolerance was finding its way toward greater tolerance. It was a period of empire building, rapidly growing technology, and cross-cultural encounters. It was also the period of early secularization and pluralism.[9] What could be more appropriate for today?

9. David Bosch notes that secularization and pluralism are two of the major issues opposing modern missiology today. See *Transforming Mission: Paradigm Shifts in the Theology of Mission* (Maryknoll, NY: Orbis Books, 1991), 1–4.

1

Ancient and Medieval Mission

Earliest Christianity developed without the privileges of political tolerance, cultural understanding, or translation into the common languages of the age. From the start, the followers of Jesus had a sense of mission and identity with Jesus, but they were a marginal group of Jewish outsiders speaking only Aramaic or Greek. Slowly the heartbeat of Jesus's mission for all nations and languages pulsated in the body of Christ, crossing cultural and imperial barriers in Africa, Asia, and Europe. By the high Middle Ages, the missional impulse had developed communities of Jesus followers from China to Spain and from Scotland to Ethiopia.

Earliest Christianity: Suffering Missional Presence

Christian mission from the earliest centuries after the death, resurrection, and ascension of Jesus Christ was mission from a position of weakness. No kingdoms or princes supported the fledgling religious movement, which was often misunderstood as a sect of Judaism. Christians were ridiculed by the Jews for their insistence that Jesus was the Messiah, and they were criticized by the pagan Romans for being "atheists" (not worshiping the pagan gods or the "genius" of the emperor). We know now that Christianity grew in all levels of society (not just among the poor and disenfranchised), but more among women than among men.[1] Persecution both scattered the believers, sending

1. Rodney Stark has two convincing arguments. First, he argues that there were a large number of women who were attracted to Christianity because of the elevated status that Jesus's

them to establish new communities of Jesus followers, and strengthened the resolve of the believers. Suffering has a way of focusing one's life and thoughts. It must not be forgotten that Christianity was born in suffering and oppression, inspired by a prophet who was identified with suffering (*passio*: to suffer). Small communities spread along trade routes, in port cities, and along the Old Silk Route that stretched from the Mediterranean all the way to old Cathay (China). Very soon followers of Jesus were in Gaul, Spain, Ethiopia, India, and present day Central Asia. There was no one center, no single strategy, but there was a united understanding that the message was about the meaning of Jesus for all people,[2] and the life of Jesus within his followers. In less than two hundred years the message was being spread in Syriac, Latin, Greek, and Aramaic.[3]

What kept the early Christians together when there was so little in the way of central structure or dominant authority? Earliest Christianity was *movement* with little *institution*. It was united by a common belief that Jesus Christ was raised from the dead and that his teaching and life was to be spread to all people. All people were to be united in worship of Jesus as Lord. Thus, both the call to mission and the call to worship kept Christians united across languages and empires.[4] Worship was a shared experience that involved common liturgical phrases and structures. The liturgy pointed to the life and work of Jesus and gave structure to basic beliefs about the person of Jesus and the triune nature of God. The early Jesus movement was persecuted and fragmented, but it retained great zeal for mission. Later, when Scriptures were becoming standardized, it was the liturgy that provided the standard for what was authentic Jesus material and what was not. The Bible was a much later standard.

The first major shift took place when these struggling missional and worshiping communities began to garner royal support. When kings and other rulers began to convert, mission theology was turned upside down. Abgar IX (who ruled 179–86), the Christian king of the Roman client kingdom of Osrhoene (the capital of which was Edessa); Tiridates the Great, the Armenian king (who converted to Christianity in 301); and Constantine the Great (who ruled 306–37) were three of the earliest Christian rulers. All were in western

---

teachings gave women (chap. 5 in *The Rise of Christianity: How the Obscure, Marginal Jesus Movement Became the Dominant Religious Force in the Western World in a Few Centuries* [Princeton: Princeton University Press, 1996]). Second, he argues that many people of status were in the early movement because cults and new religious movements always attract more from the elite than from the poor. See also Michael Green, *Evangelism in the Early Church* (London: Hodder & Stoughton, 1970).

2. Often called the "Paschal mystery" (for the suffering, death, resurrection, and glorification of Jesus Christ) remembered in the celebration of the Eucharist.

3. Two hundred years later, Christians in Arabia were developing the Arabic language through Christian writings.

4. It is to be noted that the earliest Christians lived in two empires and many other "enemy" nations. The Roman and Parthian (Persian) empires had a heated border in Syria, where Christianity was growing.

Asia and all ushered in a new age of missionary understanding. Since both Armenia and Osrhoene were client kingdoms, or bargaining properties for Rome and Persia, it is the later semi-converted Roman emperor Constantine who really set in motion a new understanding of Christian identity, and thus of Christian mission.[5] Suddenly, under the rule of one emperor, Christianity was transformed from persecuted minority cult to favored faith. This imperial support continued in the West (Europe) even when non-Christian tribes invaded from the north and the east. The story was very different in Asia, where imperial support waned and large intercultural faiths (Zoroastrianism, Hinduism, and later Islam) persecuted Christian communities. Christian mission looks very different when Christianity is a royally favored faith.

In Asia, the revival of the Zoroastrian religion with imperial support in Persia, followed by the rapid spread of Islam in western Asia, meant that Christian liturgical development, theology, and practice occurred in a contentious missional context. While Asian Christians struggled to survive in a hostile anti-Christian context, European Christians, with the support of the empire, developed their understanding of the church for about one thousand years without that type of pressure—without their earlier missional context. With Europe cut off from most of Africa and Asia, the missional story became the long process of converting Western culture, not sending missionaries to other regions of the world. As post-Constantinian Western society became more a part of the church (not necessarily more Christian), its connections to the outside world were cut by the expansion of Arab-Islamic culture. And when Christianity is not able to express itself missionally, to outsiders, it turns in upon itself. As Bosch says so clearly, "The Christian faith . . . is intrinsically missionary. . . . Christianity is missionary by its very nature, or it denies its very *raison d'être*."[6]

Not only was this long period of ecclesial development in Europe almost devoid of missional context, it was also in a "Christendom" context that involved political and religious cooperation.[7] Thus mission turned inward, with the support and power of the state, as a movement to keep the church unified and pure. In the big picture of European history, Christian mission—which reaches out with the love of God in Jesus Christ to outsiders—was co-opted. To the east, in Zoroastrian and later Muslim Persia, Christians were further and further marginalized, and they lost the opportunity to witness outside of

5. "Christendom" is the term given to the political and religious cooperation that began with Constantine's conversion and rule. Arguments for and against Constantine's conversion as genuine and good are found in Peter J. Leithart's *Defending Constantine: The Twilight of an Empire and the Dawn of Christendom* (Downers Grove, IL: InterVarsity, 2010).

6. David Bosch, *Transforming Mission: Paradigm Shifts in the Theology of Mission* (Maryknoll, NY: Orbis Books, 1991), 8.

7. There was a missional context in that pagan tribes continued to flood into Europe from Asia. Slowly they were converted, mostly by monastic endeavors.

their community. European Christianity became Christendom; Asian Christianity was a melet community.[8] Both lost their purpose and promise for the larger society—entrapped by royal intervention in Europe and enclosed by melet structures in Asia.

Monasticism: Spirituality in Mission

In the Eurasian context of Christianity, roughly from the fourth through the fifteenth centuries, Christian mission was kept alive not from the ecclesial center but from the margins.[9] It was monastic movements of outreach, study, and renewal that continued the church's mission. The rise of monasticism in the fourth century was in part a missional renewal movement: to tear the church away from its early captivity to worldly power and riches. Christians sought to find an appropriate way to continue the basic understanding of the spiritual life. And what was the basic way of understanding the spiritual life in the early church? The life *in Christ* is the life that *imitates Christ*. Both of these elements were foundational from long before the development of monasticism in the fourth through sixth centuries. Christians are, in an ontological sense, "in" Christ Jesus, living the life of Jesus Christ (in community) for the world. But Christians, on a secular level, are also persons who endeavor to imitate Christ: both working out their salvation and knowing that God is at work within them. The earliest noncanonical Christian writings were very clear that the Christian was to imitate Christ in humility, in preaching, and in care for the poor. Representative of this understanding is Ignatius's exhortation to the Ephesians regarding their life as a witness:

> Pray continually for the rest of humankind as well, that they may find God, for there is in them hope for repentance. Therefore allow them to be instructed by you, at least by your deeds. In response to their anger, be gentle; in response to their boasts, be humble; in response to their slander, offer prayers; in response to their errors, be steadfast in the faith; in response to their cruelty, be meek; do not be eager to imitate them. Let us show by our forbearance that we are their brothers and sisters, and let us be eager to be imitators of the Lord, to see who can be the more wronged, who the more cheated, who the more rejected, in order that no weed of the devil may be found among you, but that with complete purity and self-control you may abide in Christ Jesus physically and spiritually.[10]

8. A melet (or millet) community is a ghetto community allowed to exist among a majority faith (Zoroastrianism and later Islam) but prevented from engaging the larger culture in any form of witness.

9. There were few popes like Gregory the Great, who sent out missionaries to unevangelized tribes in Europe and beyond. See Bede's *Ecclesiastical History of the English People*, ed. Betram Colgrave and R. A. B. Mynors (Oxford: Oxford University Press, 1969).

10. Ignatius, *To the Ephesians* 10. Ignatius died, at the latest, in 117.

Ignatius, greatly concerned in this letter for church order and unity, does not neglect the foundational concern of Christian witness through humility, gentleness, suffering, and identification with Jesus Christ. A slightly later writing, the apologetic work *The Epistle to Diognetus*,[11] expands on the purpose or genetic makeup of the church. Apologetic writings of the ancient church comprise some of the earliest theological literature: theology in defense of the faith or theology for outsiders, that they might come to faith. Theology develops on the missional edge of the church. *The Epistle to Diognetus* is a memorable and recognizable writing that identifies the missional presence and developing theology of the earliest Christians.

The incarnational principle of Christianity is evident in that Christians eat local food and dress like local people. However, although enculturated, Christians are not captive to any local culture.[12] Christians are a missional presence, pointing to the Kingdom. When this missional presence became normative and popular, many fled to deserts and caves to maintain their sacredness and Christlike detachment from the world ("suffer as strangers"). Continuing the passion of Christ was hard to imagine when society honored Christian bishops and priests.

When the emperor became tolerant and then supportive of the church, to the point of inviting the leaders to his palace in Nicaea, Christian humility and humiliation seemed to slip away. It was difficult to follow the lowly suffering Christ in an age of affluence and comfort. Therefore the taproot of monasticism—asceticism—started as a spiritual recovery. St. Antony in the desert was an Elijah figure in the wilderness, fighting demons and the temptations of demons. Many people cannot see an explicit missionary intent or vision in this. However, even this spirituality was an inspiration to mission, as we will see.

Asceticism Turns Monastic and Missional

The monks of the deserts in Egypt and Syria were an inspiration and catalyst to Christians living in cities. Their theology was a practical theology that inspired many to live as Christ lived, by the grace that Christ made available.[13] One of those who was greatly inspired by the desert monks was the traveling

11. The earliest known apologetic work, dated late second century (before 200). I discuss the epistle further in chap. 9.

12. A very similar idea is taught by the semi-converted but very important early Asian apologist Bardaisan of Edessa in his *Book of the Laws of Countries*, trans. H. J. W. Drijvers (Assen: Van Gorcum, 1965), 61: "But in whatever place they are and wherever they may find themselves, the local laws cannot force them to give up the law of their Messiah, nor does the Fate of the Guiding Signs force them to do things that are unclean for them."

13. The early desert writings found in places like the *Philokalia* were theological treatises that we might call practical theology today, for the language about God was directed to the behavior and life of the individual.

Epistle to Diognetus on Christians in Society

For Christians are not distinguished from the rest of humanity by country, language, or custom. For nowhere do they live in cities of their own, nor do they speak some unusual dialect, nor do they practice an eccentric way of life. This teaching of theirs has not been discovered by the thought and reflection of ingenious people, nor do they promote any human doctrine, as some do. But while they lived in both Greek and barbarian cities, as each one's lot was cast, and follow the local customs in dress and food and other aspects of life, at the same time they demonstrate the remarkable and admittedly unusual character of their own citizenship. They live in their own countries, but only as nonresidents; they participate in everything as citizens, and endure everything as foreigners. Every foreign country is their fatherland, and every fatherland is foreign. . . . In a word, what the soul is to the body, Christians are to the world.[a]

a. *The Epistle to Diognetus*, in Michael W. Holmes, *The Apostolic Fathers in English* (Grand Rapids: Baker Academic, 2006), 295–96.

priest Basil, who later became Bishop of Caesarea. Basil was inspired by their discipline and devotion, but he was troubled by their absolute solitude: "A life passed in solitude is concerned only with the private service of individual needs. This is openly opposed to the law of love which the Apostle fulfilled, who sought not what was profitable to himself, but to many that they might be saved."[14] Basil knew that the privatized spiritual life was fraught with dangers. "The first [danger] and greatest is that of self-satisfaction. Since the solitary has no one to appraise his conduct, he will think he has achieved the perfection of the precept. Secondly, because he never tests his state of soul by exercise he will not recognize his own deficiencies." But even greater than these was the concern that, alone, one could not show mercy, charity, or compassion. "Wherein will he give evidence of his compassion, if he has cut himself off from association with other persons. . . . Whom, therefore will you wash? To whom will you minister?"[15]

And so, under the guidance of Basil, monasticism began to be transformed from spiritual renewal and a school of personal holiness with limited missional concern to a missional community designed for holiness and service to the other. Monasticism was no longer only about separation from the world. Slowly it began to develop as "separation from" in concert with "involvement in." Basil moved monastic houses nearer to cities, so the monks and nuns could go outside of their walls and serve the poor and needy. "This kind of life has as

14. From Basil's "Longer Rule, Question 7," quoted from John W. Coakley and Andrea Sterk, eds., *Readings in World Christian History*, vol. 1, *Earliest Christianity to 1453* (Maryknoll, NY: Orbis Books, 2004), 145.

15. Ibid., 146.

its aim the glory of God according to the command of our Lord Jesus Christ, who said: "So let your light shine before men that they may see your good works and glorify your Father who is in heaven" (Matt. 5:16).[16]

The monastic structure, as a structure alongside the local church, became normative in Persia ("Sons and Daughters of the Covenant"), Ethiopia, Egypt, North Africa (St. Augustine lived in a type of monastic house), Italy, Germany, France, Britain, and even China. Some of these houses had more formal and strict rules than others, but all were dedicated to the holy life, for the sake of the church and its mission. As the monastic communities spread, they brought with them education and care for the poor in each new community. In Europe, it was the monastic structure, more than the local church structure, that catechized the invading tribes and illiterate European masses.

Therefore, monasticism was slowly renewed or transformed into a missiological structure as new houses were started in frontier regions. Monasteries preserved the writings of the early church (especially the Scriptures) and they later became the foundational institutions for the rise of modern universities. Monasteries, and the monks and nuns who inhabited them, became a spiritual guidebook for the laity: role models. We see this from the very beginning in Athanasius's "Life of Anthony" (ca. 360), as well as in the later calendar of saints, most of whom were monks. Although there were different patterns to the spread of monasticism—from the peripatetic monks who wandered around planting churches and monasteries, to the eremitic monks in the wilderness—its missiological purpose, which all branches held in common, became one of the strongest pillars of monastic life.

The monastic movement was the leading partner in the conversion of cultures within Christendom.[17] Every monastery was a missional presence of Christian practice in a largely unconverted countryside (*paganus*, or pagan, means country-dweller, or rustic). The polytheistic mind and life of tribal Europe was slowly evangelized, and the broader culture converted, through the growing monastic presence. Christian practice, as well as architecture, art, and literature developed a European Christian culture. This story has been told often. One of the best-known leaders in the monastic conversion of cultures is St. Patrick (d. 493), the English slave and then missionary to Ireland. Upon his conversion, Patrick returned to his land of enslavement and began a Christian movement that brought about literacy, rule by law, monastic schools, and better treatment for slaves and women. Celtic culture was developed by the conversion and discipleship of large numbers of the Irish in a short period of time. This began a movement out from Ireland whereby monastic houses

16. Anna M. Silvas, ed. and trans., *The Asketikon of St. Basil the Great* (New York: Oxford University Press, 2005).

17. Or what has more recently been called the church's mandate for "culture making." See Andy Crouch, *Culture Making: Recovering Our Creative Calling* (Downers Grove, IL: InterVarsity, 2008).

Extreme Monasticism

The often misunderstood Symeon the Stylite lived thirty-seven years on top of a pillar. Feeling his private prayer and fasting time increasingly interrupted by people who visited him seeking prayer and advice, he decided to remove himself from the ground and stay atop a pillar where he would not be so easily bothered. But his increased height off the ground seemed to attract both advice-seeking pilgrims and curious onlookers. And so Symeon purportedly took time each afternoon to speak with and even provide instruction to people who came to visit. He was quite literally a signpost of the Kingdom.

were built, texts were copied, and the pagan Celts began to read about Jesus and then bring him to new regions as they wandered. The Celtic missionary movement this initiated spread throughout Ireland, Scotland, parts of England, and to the Low Countries of the Continent. This Celtic monastic movement is one of the clearest examples of how monasticism developed as the main missionary structure even into the age of exploration.

Missionary Monks in Asia

To the east, outside of Europe, the monastic lifestyle flourished even when the empire (Persian) did not become Christian. At times the monastic ideal seemed a little too austere, but, for the most part, these Sons of the Covenant were the pioneers and the models of godliness.

Similar to the Celtic bands who built small monasteries, translated Scriptures, and moved on, the Persian monks were also a restless lot, moving farther and farther to the east. By the end of the fifth century, in spite of severe persecution under the Sassanid Dynasty, monastic vocation and seminary education thrived. The famous School of the Persians at Nisibis was reported to have over a thousand students living in monastic cells, which were former horse stables. Trained in Bible and exegesis (and virtually nothing else), they wandered along the Silk Road across the rooftop of Asia. In 635, the first Christian monks we know of arrived in China. Alopen and other Persians were granted a place to live near the Chinese emperor and translated their Scriptures into Chinese. Thus the missionary dimensions of monastic faith came to the fore as Persians, speaking and worshiping in Syriac, were translating, with the help of Buddhist monks, the Christian texts for Chinese royalty. As in Europe, the basic method of evangelization was to reach the ruler, with the understanding that the people would follow. This is not the time to go into the long and fascinating story of early mission to China,[18] but for our purposes it is important to know that it was monks who first brought Christian teaching to the Pacific. In fact, the monastery was so important that it is not clear if the

18. See Samuel Hugh Moffett, *History of Christianity in Asia*, vol. 1 (San Francisco: HarperSanFrancisco, 1992); and Kenneth Scott Latourette, *A History of Christian Missions in China* (New York: Macmillan, 1992).

Persian monks were planting monasteries or churches in China.

The monastic structure for mission was evident even in streams of monasticism that are often thought of as schools for holiness, rather than missionary outposts. The most important writings of the Orthodox tradition are collected in *The Philokalia* ("love of the beautiful").[19] These writings, many of them by solitaries (Mark the Ascetic and Evagrios the Solitary, among others), constitute a core of Orthodox writings accepted across the world and through the centuries.

The Philokalia

This is a four-volume collection of texts written between the fourth and fifteenth centuries by spiritual masters of the Orthodox Christian tradition. The full title in English might be rendered, "The Love of the Beautiful of the Watchful (Attentive) Fathers." It was first published in 1782 in Greek, then translated into Slavonic, Russian, and finally English. The writings come out of years of contemplation and reflection on the name of Jesus, the passions, and the inner life of the soul. After the Bible, it is regarded as the second most influential book in the recent history of the Orthodox Church and the root of many modern Orthodox spiritual revivals.

Many of the ascetic sites from which these saints were writing were not missionary sites, but the impact of their writings, often focusing on the holy life, have been foundational for missionary existence. One of the great teachers of the Orthodox Church, whose writings are found in *The Philokalia*, is the later saint Symeon the New Theologian (942–1022). He was considered new because he was accepted as a theologian for the Orthodox Church much later than the first two great theologians: the apostle John and Gregory of Nazianzus. Symeon expressed a missional theology that emphasized Christian devotion and discipline as including preaching to the nonbeliever and care for the poor. Such theology could not be lived in isolation from the world. Symeon brought together the "two main lines of authentic Byzantine spirituality: the intellectualism of the school of the Alexandrians [Origen, Clement, Evagrios, Basil, etc.] . . . and the 'affective' school of the heart, represented by the writings of Pseudo-Macarius, Diadochos of Photike, John Climacus, Hesychius and Philotheus."[20]

For Symeon, the missionary life of the monk is one of ascetic sacrifice, in an attitude of broken and contrite love, for the sake of casting the net of salvation to the whole world. Although monastic theology is not a missionary theology, the structure of the monastery and the life in the monastery became the form and life for the church's missionary outreach and conversion of tribes and nations.

19. *The Philokalia*, 4 vols., trans. G. E. H. Palmer, Philip Sherrard, and Kalistos Ware (New York: Faber & Faber, 1979). This work should not be confused with the *Philokalia* of Origen, an anthology of his writings created by Basil of Caesarea and Gregory of Nazianzus.

20. From the introduction by George Maloney to *Symeon the New Theologian: The Discourses* (New York: Paulist Press, 1980).

Symeon's Missionary Monasticism

We see here, in the following discourse delivered to his monks, how it is that the life of Jesus and the example of the apostles were central to the Eastern monastic tradition.

> However great your zeal and many the efforts of your asceticism, they are all in vain and without useful result unless they attain to love in a broken spirit (Ps. 51:9). . . . He [Jesus] willingly endured His life-giving sufferings, in order that He might deliver man, His own creature, from the bonds of hell, and restore him and lead him up to heaven. Moved by love the apostles ran that unceasing race and cast on the whole world the fishhook and net of the word to drag it up from the deep of idolatry and bring it safe into the port of the kingdom of heaven. Moved by love the martyrs shed their blood that they might not lose Christ. Moved by it our God-bearing Fathers and teachers of the world eagerly laid down their own lives for the Catholic and apostolic Church.[a]

a. George Maloney, *Symeon the New Theologian: The Discourses* (Mahwah, NJ: Paulist Press, 1980), 45.

Mission and Monks in the Middle Ages

In this cursory survey we have seen a variety of missiological approaches to and through monastic structures, mostly working from a position of weakness rather than power. However, while we acknowledge that the mission of God was carried out through monastic structures, we must also recognize that the monastic structures themselves were not the mission of God. Monastic structures worked with church structures—seeking the full conversion of cultures. As the church became wealthy, monasteries also benefited from wealthy patrons. One of the basic vices (later called cardinal sins) that was of grave concern to the earliest monastic movement—avarice—became the strange bedfellow of large monastic houses. Monastic life often became comfortable and convenient, and so reforming movements (Cluny in the tenth and eleventh centuries, the Cistercians in the twelfth century, and St. Francis in the thirteenth century) sprang up, calling monastic life back to simplicity, purity, and mission. But corrupting forces were strong. In the very century in which Cluniac reforms were taking place, and in the early stages of the Franciscans, monastic corruption took a new turn with the rise of militant monks. The Knights Templar[21] began soon after the first Crusade (1096–99) as a religious order called to protect pilgrims traveling to the holy sites. Supported by wealthy Europeans, mostly French, these militant monks became quite influential in the church and in European society. They were among the most important warriors in the Crusades, but they also built bridges and

21. First called the "Poor Knights of the Temple of King Solomon," since their first house was located in Jerusalem at the site of King Solomon's temple.

roads and were even involved in banking. The Knights Templar were only one of many such militant monastic orders.[22] Piety and patronage, mission and militancy, had come together in the twelfth century, corrupting the original purpose of monastic life.

The story is a complex one: Princes worked with bishops and monks to consolidate power and wealth. The hard work and discipline of the monks often brought about prosperity and larger and larger holdings of real estate. With the increasing wealth and power of medieval Christendom, monastic houses and religious orders sometimes became oppressive, and later became tools of secular oppression. The monastic structure, which began as a structure of renewal calling individuals to faithful life in Christ, took on a more missional purpose to serve both the unloved and the unreached. Later, this same structure lent itself to power and, at times, domination. How did this happen? In part it happened as a natural consequence of monastic discipline, and in part it happened through the unholy marriage of prince and prior. Both secular and religious rulers benefited from the alliance. Finally, with the rise of Islam and the consequent insulation of Christian Europe from the rest of the world, missional presence became more and more difficult. With the rise of the Muslim Seljuk Turks in the eleventh century and then the Ottoman Turks in the thirteenth century, Christian missionary expression was limited to worship in Christendom Europe or through the Crusades in west Asia. It became more and more difficult for monastic life to move out into frontier areas. Christian life, even monastic Christian life, turned in upon itself. The religious life in Persia was greatly limited by the Islamic caliphs of the eighth through the fifteenth centuries. In a sense, Persian Christianity lost its vitality—which it derived from missional contact. In contrast, monasteries in Europe often became wealthy establishments and, at other times, became instruments of oppressive political structures. Monks began to support Crusades and accepted bribes for positions of authority. It is a history of power, money, and isolation that should be remembered by the church today. This position of power and privilege continued even as Europe became less isolated in the fifteenth and sixteenth centuries.

One interesting example of this paradox in Christian theology is Bernard of Clairvaux (1090–1153), one of the most winsome and influential leaders of the High Middle Ages. Bernard is known as a great monastic leader (helping to found over 160 monasteries), a honey-mouthed preacher, a great moral leader, a promoter of devotion to Mary, an author of devotional classics such as his work on the Song of Songs, and is remembered as "the spiritual master of the

22. Other militant orders that were founded between the eleventh and fifteenth centuries include Teutonic Knights, Livonian Brothers of the Sword (aka "Christ Knights"), Knights of Saint Mary, etc.

path of love."[23] Yet, as a church leader in Christendom Europe, he was also a powerful political leader. One of his most famous works, *On Consideration*, was written to Pope Eugenius III, one of his former monks. In this work, Bernard counsels his former student as to how to carry out his duties as pope and how to balance the delicate relationship of church and state. When asked to help with the promotion of the second Crusade to protect the "Christian lands," Bernard preached and wrote to encourage French nobles, priests, monks, and "the faithful people of Eastern France and Bavaria" to support the Crusade.

> The enemies of the Cross have raised blaspheming heads, ravaging with the edge of the sword the land of promise. For they are almost on the point . . . of bursting into the very city of the living God, of the holy places of the spotless Lamb with purple blood. Alas! they rage against the very shrine of the Christian faith with blasphemous mouths, and would enter and trample down the very couch on which, for us, our Life lay down to sleep in death. What are you going to do then, O brave men? What are you doing, O servants of the Cross? Will you give what is holy to the dogs, and cast your pearls before swine?

After exhorting the French to stop fighting against each other, he has a strong rhetorical section imploring the French to do for God what he could do with his angels, but looks for humans to do.

> But now, O brave knight, now, O warlike hero, here is a battle you may fight without danger, where it is glory to conquer and gain to die. If you are a prudent merchant, if you are a desirer of this world, behold I show you some great bargains; see that you lose them not. Take the sign of the cross and you shall gain pardon for every sin that you confess with a contrite heart.

The mission of the monks had turned into the military engagement of crusaders. Carrying the cross, the symbol of the suffering, gentle, and compliant Savior, had become an oppressive sign of military conquest: from passion to power and from humility to hubris.

Bernard is not the only spiritual leader of the age to support the Crusades, but he is one of the clearest and most visible. This devout and influential monk supported the Knights Templar and even outlined their Rule. Powerful symbolism is evident in the fact that the first Knights Templar house was built out of the Al Aqsa Mosque, which in turn had been built on the Temple Mount, where it was assumed the Temple of Solomon had been built. Thus, a militant monastic house was on top of a Jewish temple and Muslim mosque. Christian monastic structures and purposes were being remade into the image of the Muslim Turks they resisted.

23. Jean LeClercq in the introduction to *Bernard of Clairvaux: Selected Works*, trans. G. R. Evans (Mahwah, NJ: Paulist Press, 1987), 7.

Reform in Monastic Missional Identity

As noted in the introduction, the newer religious orders of the Franciscans and Dominicans did not develop a new missiological understanding or theory, even though they were committed to ministries that crossed boundaries of faith. Dominic founded his Order of Friars Preachers as a way of preparing missionary friars to preach orthodoxy in regions where heterodox doctrines threatened the church. One of his main concerns was the Cathars, a growing Gnostic sect of Christianity that was spreading rapidly in southern France.[24] The pope's two approaches to the Cathars (send Crusades to attempt to kill them, and issue a show of pomp and power to attempt to win them) were failures. In contrast, Dominic advocated preaching: "It is not by the display of power and pomp, cavalcades of retainers, and richly-houseled palfreys, or by gorgeous apparel, that the heretics win proselytes; it is by zealous preaching, by apostolic humility, by austerity, by seeming, it is true, but by seeming holiness. Zeal must be met by zeal, humility by humility, false sanctity by real sanctity, preaching falsehood by preaching truth."[25] The Dominicans (approved in 1216) became an order of preachers to help the church resist heresy through good preaching. At about the same time, St. Francis founded his Order of Friars Minors (founded 1210). The Franciscans embraced the virtues of evangelical poverty while preaching repentance and caring for the most needy. Francis sought to preach to all, possibly even to the Sultan of Egypt during the Crusades. His was a recovery of early monastic missionary identity: humility and suffering. According to tradition, his identification with the passion of Christ was so complete that he developed the stigmata (nail marks) on his own hands.

Out of this same medieval world, another movement was started that remained outside of the official church, but that was driven by many of the same concerns for renewal. Peter Waldo, a wealthy merchant from Lyon, had a sudden conversion to evangelical poverty (not unlike St. Francis) in or around 1175. As a result, he sold most of his goods, found a copy of the Scriptures in French, and began to preach for conversion and against wealth. His movement was not approved by the papacy, so these preachers (both men and women) traveled throughout Europe as "heretics." The significance of this movement is that it was a semi-monastic movement that preached in the vernacular and focused on the Christian life as a life of poverty. They were called the "Poor of Lyon."

These three movements recovered some of the missional intent of Christianity, in that they were speaking to newer contexts, but they did so very much

24. See Mark Gregory Pegg, *A Most Holy War: The Albigensian Crusade and the Battle for Christendom* (New York: Oxford University Press, 2008).

25. Quoted from Alexander Clarence Flick, *The Rise of the Medieval Church* (New York: Putnam's Sons, 1909), 522.

within older patterns of monastic life and practice. Mission out of weakness was not the normal pattern of the period, but these three movements pointed back to earlier monastic humility and forward to contemporary mission movements in the non-Western world. Unfortunately, in later years, the Franciscans and Dominicans were domesticated and used by political powers, so their ministry, too, became ministry from a platform of power, rather than weakness.[26]

One of the few pioneers who pushed out of Europe during this period—a prophet figure who pointed ahead to future missiology—is Raymundo Lullus (1232–1315). Lullus was ahead of his time, not only in thinking about *how* to reach Muslims with the Christian message, but also, as I noted in the introduction, in his missionary work from a position of weakness and vulnerability. Although his work was from powerlessness, being a medieval man, he still had access to patrons for his academic work. He wrote in four languages, especially Arabic, at a time when Muslims were still ruling large portions of Spain. Lullus tried to interest popes, kings, and princes in establishing colleges for training missionaries to evangelize the Muslims. As a result of his advocacy, before he died, chairs in Hebrew, Arabic, and Chaldean were established at the universities of Bologna, Oxford, Paris, and Salamanca. Lullus worked with the greatest academic of the time, Thomas Aquinas, convincing him to write a theology for missionary apologetics toward Muslims: *Summa Contra Gentiles* (1259–64). "The [*Summa Contra Gentiles*] is a classic manual for Christian doctrine intended for the use of Christian missionaries in Spain."[27] However, this was not "modern" missions, for it contained two medieval characteristics: dependency upon kings and rulers to support the missionary work and a primary focus toward Jews and Muslims. In a sense, missionary work was still envisioned as extending European cultural forms of Christendom.

Lull, along with the Dominicans and the Franciscans, straddled the medieval and the modern in his work. However, no modern missionary movement came from the noble leadership of lay Franciscans like Lull or Dominican scholars like Thomas Aquinas. The Muslims and Jews in Spain were not converted through a scholastic defense of the truth (Thomas's approach to apologetics), nor through prayer alone. It was through secular power that the Moors and Jews were expelled and then compelled to sign a treaty in 1492. The Capitulation of 1491,[28] or the Treaty of Granada, granted Muslims freedom to live, worship, and carry on business under Christian rulers. The freedom and peace this treaty brought, however, was illusive. As late as 1507, the Cardinal of Granada (the famous Franciscan, Francisco Ximenez de Cisneros,

26. The Dominicans, for example, became very influential through education and were called upon to support the often corrupt and violent work of the Inquisition.

27. From Anton C. Pegis's notes in the translated volume of *Summa Contra Gentiles* (Notre Dame, IN: University of Notre Dame Press, 1955), 17.

28. There were actually two treaties: one of surrender (November 25, 1491) and one of 1492 that gave the Muslims protection and a degree of respect while living under Christian rulers.

1436–1517) was leading troops against Muslim forces, and as late as 1517 he was gathering up and burning copies of the Qur'an. It is out of this context, and with this mind-set, that Roman Catholics began (after the *Reconquista* of Spain) to move out of the Iberian Peninsula, exploring, conquering, and evangelizing far beyond the Crusader states of the Near East. Mission and conquest were intertwined as Europeans moved out from Western Europe in search of spices and Christians.

2

Colonial Missions, Part 1

Globalization of Roman Catholicism

The 350 years from 1492 to 1842 are the period in which Christianity became a global faith. Much of the development of Christianity was in completely new lands: North America, South America, the Caribbean, West Africa, South Africa, Japan, and regions of Southeast Asia. However, some of the development was in lands where Christianity was an ancient faith that had been severely restricted or persecuted for centuries: Egypt, Ethiopia, India, Persia, Lebanon, Turkey, and China. Christianity had never encountered such a diversity of cultures, languages, and religions in one century as it did from the time of Christopher Columbus's mission in the Caribbean (1492) to the beginning of the Jesuit mission to China (1582). In this chapter I will describe these encounters by looking at the various regions where Christian missions were initiated. This was a period in which missionary ideas, strategies, and theologies were developed. The new contexts encountered by Christians, as much as European ideas or theories of the missionaries, directed missionary practice at this time, so I have organized our study by regions. This chapter begins with Africa, where Portuguese exploration and evangelization first spilled out of Europe. Then we will move to Latin America, where both Spanish and Portuguese royalty laid claims of patronage. Next we will look at Asia, where Europeans met their biggest challenge: large, ancient, and intercultural religions. At the end of the chapter we look at how Christian missions transformed cultures, but also how cultures were constantly transforming the meaning and practice of these missions.

Mission and Early European Overseas Movements

Modern world religious history, not only modern Christian history, was determined in the hundred-year period from the middle of the fifteenth century to the middle of the sixteenth century. Two major shifts took place during that time that transformed Christianity and shaped the modern global religious landscape. Chronologically, the first major transformation was the spread of Christianity to Africa, the Americas, and Asia. Christianity was already in parts of Asia and Africa, but its presence was limited, and Christian communities were in the minority, hemmed in by major rulers and religions. The Portuguese, however, began to explore down the west coast of Africa in the 1450s, which opened up new areas of Christian presence. It was a pivotal time for all of global history, because the Chinese had already explored the east coast of Africa thirty years earlier and were in a position to dominate all of Asia and Africa.

The Chinese began their explorations in 1405 under the Yongle Emperor, eighteen years before Portuguese explorations began under Henry the Navigator. While the Portuguese saw Africa, and later the Americas and Asia, as great economic and missional opportunities, the Chinese saw nothing but inferior cultures. The Chinese had no need for exploring further; they brought back giraffes for the emperor, and decided that they had no need to leave China. After all, they were the Middle Kingdom between heaven and earth. The massive Chinese ships (three times larger than the Portuguese ships) were put up in dry dock and eventually rotted. With China out of the picture, global colonization—from about 1492 to 1948—became a matter of Europeans imposing their will and designs on the non-Western world. And part of that "European will" was Christianity. After nearly sixteen centuries of Christianity, newer regions were finally hearing for the first time about the life of Jesus Christ. This was the first major global shift that took place from approximately 1450 to 1550; Christianity broke out of its European and West-Asian captivity.

The second major shift that took place during this period was the division of Christianity from two major families (Roman Catholic and Orthodox) into four major families. The Reformation added two additional Christendom families: those of the magisterial reformers (Anglicans, Reformed, Lutherans), and the radical reform movement, which we will call the Spiritual family. The magisterial Protestant churches seemed at the time a completely different form of Christianity—but from a distance of a half a millennium, we now see that they were mostly hotly contested debates over interpretations of ritual and words. I don't want to minimize the significance of many of these disagreements, but compared with the fourth family of Christianity (radical or Spiritual), the Protestant division should be understood to be more of a slight mutation. Starting in the Reformation period, the Spiritual churches broke away from the reigning assumption that Christianity was interwoven with secular authorities and structures. The Spiritual churches viewed Christians as "called out" communities whose witness was, in part, to have communities separated from culture that responded to the spiritual call of God rather than the mandates of magistrates. Groups like the Mennonites, and later Pentecostal and independent churches, were radical departures from the less dramatic reforms of the magisterial reformers.

These two major shifts (global Christianity initiated by the Portuguese and four major divisions that we still live with today) set in motion a new direction for Christianity and Christian mission. Christian mission became far more complex and diverse because of these social transformations.

The earliest missionaries who worked outside of the Mediterranean Judeo-Muslim-Christian world were the monks, friars, and priests who sailed with the Spanish to the Americas and with the Portuguese to Africa and Brazil. They sailed not as ambassadors for the pope and Christendom, but as employees of the Spanish and Portuguese kings. Under the royal patronage granted by the pope (*Patronato Real* in Spanish, or *Padroado* in Portuguese), Christianization of newly discovered and occupied lands was to be carried out by the kings of Spain and Portugal. No other Christian countries could travel the world at that time, and it was common knowledge that kings were responsible for the Christian faith in their lands. Thus, the earliest evangelization of the Americas, of the coastlands of Africa, and almost all of the coastlands (and some inland areas) of Asia were initiated by the bidding, and enabled through the financial support, of Iberian rulers.

Until the arrival of St. Francis Xavier and two other Jesuits in Goa, India, in 1542 (assigned to this task in 1540, the year of the Order's Foundation), missionary work was carried out by three orders constituted in the thirteenth century: Augustinians, Dominicans, and Franciscans.[1] Thus, the initial contact outsiders had with Christianity was with friars—all committed to lives of poverty. Friars are mendicants, meaning they have no possessions and beg for their daily provisions. In the case of the Americas, these orders were provided for by the patronage of the king of Spain. In time, however, their provision would come from newly formed Christian communities and from the lands that they were given by the crown. Christian mission would become a political affair once again.

Where Were the Protestants?

Before looking at what I call the first modern mission movement, we need to answer an obvious question: If the sixteenth century was the century of

1. The Carmelites, the fourth mendicant order founded in the fourteenth century, were excluded by the king of Spain from working in Spanish territories in the Americas. The Carmelites did begin a smaller work in Brazil under the Portuguese crown in 1580.

St. Francis Xavier, missionary pioneer in strategy and spirituality, is depicted here looking at the suffering Christ in glory while his own heart flames with passion while pierced with a cross.

both European migrations and the diversification of the Western church, why do we not find Protestant and Spiritual churches involved in the modern overseas missionary enterprise? The first answer is the clearest and most direct: Protestant churches did not have ships. Swiss Reformed Churches, Mennonites, and German Lutherans were all from countries that would come late to trade by sea.[2] The first overseas movement came from newer technologies in ship development originating in Portugal and Spain, and these were Roman Catholic countries. Secondly, and related, Roman Catholic countries were already in contact with other religions and other cultures: Spain's rulers were Muslim from the eighth century up to 1492; and Roman Catholic countries bordered Muslim regions in Iberia as well as Eastern Europe. Protestants were mostly landlocked, with Roman Catholic neighbors (or adversaries). Thirdly, Christian mission for Protestant and Spiritual churches was primarily directed toward renewal or evangelism (it was described as both) of Roman Catholics. Mission, from the Protestant and Spiritual perspective, was at their doorstep. Fourthly, Protestant and Spiritual churches rejected monasticism, which had been the basic missionary structure since the fourth century. They may have had good reason to reject monastic abuses, but in rejecting monasticism completely they lost an institutional dimension that was largely dedicated to missionary activity. Finally, Reformation theology developed a belief that the apostles had evangelized the world in the first centuries, so the commands found in Matthew 28, Mark 16, and Acts 1 were no longer valid.[3] An exception to this general rule was the Anabaptist churches of the Spiritual stream who believed that they

2. The earliest British explorer, John Cabot, was an Italian (Giovanni Caboto). The Protestant Brits certainly had access to the sea, but until they defeated the Spanish in 1588 (initiating a nineteen-year undeclared war) they did not have freedom to sail, explore, and evangelize.

3. Norman Thomas has arranged basic texts from the Reformation that show the dispensational nature of the theology of Calvin and Luther and how it prevented the promotion of mission. See chap. 3, "The Protestant Reformation," in *Classic Texts in Mission and World Christianity* (Maryknoll, NY: Orbis Books, 1995).

should evangelize throughout Europe. The Anabaptist tenant of believer's baptism retained the close association between preaching, conversion, and faith. Commenting on Mark 16:15–20, Balthasar Hubmaier remarked, "Well, it is stated very clearly: 1. go, 2. preach, 3. he who believes, 4. and is baptized, 5. will be saved. Here you see a well-structured speech of which no single letter will fall. It must be kept as it is."[4] His was not, however, the majority view of non-Catholics in the sixteenth and seventeenth centuries.

Protestants missed out on nearly two centuries of modern mission as they fought to survive and as they developed their own institutions. When Protestant missions finally began, it was indebted to Roman Catholic royal missions, as we will soon see.

Jesuits as the First Modern Missionaries

I have noted the political and even military nature of much of the Roman Catholic missionary work beginning in the early modern period of European expansion. In the midst of this global movement of Christianity, most missionary work being done followed the Christendom pattern of the previous five hundred years. The major exception was the missionary order founded in 1540 by a former Spanish soldier whose leg had been shattered by a cannon ball. The new order was the Society of Jesus, and the founder was the Basque Spaniard Íñigo López de Loyola (Ignatius of Loyola, 1491–1556). The "Jesuits" as they were called, were based on a new spirituality and held a new understanding of mission. In fact, the modern usage of the word "mission" has been attributed to the Jesuits, who extended its use from the Trinity (the Father sending the Son, and the Son sending the Spirit) to the church's participation in God's sending.[5] The Jesuits, in their work outside of Europe, developed a missionary strategy that took local cultural contexts seriously. What was different about the Jesuits, and why are they considered the first "modern" missionaries?

First, Jesuit spirituality was centered on the carefully worked out Spiritual Exercises of Loyola. Every Jesuit, from Spain to Brazil and from France to Japan, was committed to this new monastic spirituality. Ignatius's *Exercises*, unlike most monastic rules, was for the purpose of *personal* discernment. Thus, it was not dependent upon a community, or upon fixed hours, and could be individualized (and even made available to laity) in month-long retreats of silence. It was, and continues to be, a method of spiritual formation and personal discernment for mission in the world. Jesuits were formed by the basic structure of self-examination according to the life (especially the sufferings) of Christ. The four weeks of meditations embedded in the Exercises focus on

4. Ibid.

5. David Bosch, *Transforming Mission: Paradigm Shifts in Theology of Mission* (Maryknoll, NY: Orbis Books, 1991), 1.

sin, the life of Jesus, the sufferings and death of Jesus on the cross, and the resurrection and glorification of Christ. Jesuit spirituality is built around the life of Jesus Christ. It is, after all, the Society of *Jesus*.

Second, Jesuits were activists, not contemplatives. Their spirituality was directed toward active mission and educational work in the world. Following their leader, who attempted missionary work in Jerusalem, the Jesuits engaged in global mission and educational work at a rapidly growing rate. By the time Ignatius died, in 1556, there were over one thousand Jesuits, and they had founded seventy-four colleges on three continents. Education would soon become a major method of mission toward Muslims and "pagans."

Third, Jesuits, more than any other religious order, imbibed the best of European Renaissance education and brought this to the farthest corners of the world. Jesuits brought modern mathematics, astronomy, painting, architecture, and map making to Japan, China, and Latin America. They became linguists, translating some of the first dictionaries, grammars, and then catechisms into local languages. Their commitment to education and learning had its taproot in their appreciation of other cultures. Jesuits studied non-European cultures as part of God's creation, while many other Europeans of the period tended to denigrate indigenous cultures as evil, inferior, or insignificant.

Fourth, stemming from their focus on education, the Jesuits developed an approach to mission that has been described as the "Catholic inculturation paradigm."[6] I believe that it was their culturally rich Renaissance education, coupled with their Jesus-centered spirituality, that shaped this part of their approach to mission. Jesuits studied local cultures. They appreciated more than denigrated, and entered into more than rejected, non-Western cultures. In the introduction I referred to the church as living within the tension of the incarnational and the pilgrim principle. The Jesuits lived out this tension more clearly than most, and in ways that became the model for the early Protestant missionaries. (For example, when the first Protestant missionary to China, Robert Morrison, was preparing to go to China, he studied Chinese from Jesuit texts that were available in England.) The Jesuits pioneered in intentional incarnational awareness. In the following few pages, we will look at some examples of how the Jesuits lived out these principles and therefore how they laid the foundation for modern Christian mission, be it Catholic, Protestant, or Spiritual.

Some Jesuit Pioneers

The Jesuit pioneer who pointed the way for future Jesuit enculturation in mission is also the best known of all Jesuit missionaries: Francis Xavier (1506–52).

6. William Burrows, "A Seventh Paradigm? Catholics and Radical Inculturation," in William Saayman and Liippies Kritzinger, eds., *Mission in Bold Humility: David Bosch's Work Considered* (Maryknoll, NY: Orbis Books, 1996).

Xavier was part of the original followers of Ignatius in Paris, and he was the first to be sent to Asia, arriving in 1542 in the Portuguese colony of Goa, India. During his first five hectic years in Asia, Xavier worked with children in Goa and in Tamil Nadu; he founded the important Jesuit Moluccan Mission in the East Indies; and he helped to develop the Jesuit college in Goa. Then, in 1547, he happened to meet one of the most colorful figures in mission history, and the real catalyst to Xavier's new approach to mission: the Japanese fugitive Yajiro.[7] Yajiro, after murdering a man in Japan, escaped on a Portuguese ship and learned about Christianity from Europeans. By the time he met Xavier, he was eager to be baptized. He wrote his own testimony, translated the Gospel of Matthew into Japanese, and memorized most of it. He had a very strong desire to teach his newfound faith to his own family and to his countrymen. Xavier, always looking toward the next mission frontier, was eager to help Yajiro reach the Japanese. Yajiro guided Xavier as to how this must be done. The Japanese will have to see the teachings of Jesus lived out, he told the Jesuit; they will not be convinced by the "Christian" witness of Portuguese sailors, nor will they be convinced by "voluntary poverty." They will need to see that Christianity has dignity fitting of an emperor, and they will need to examine the moral life of its founder. Xavier followed Yajiro's lead and became a student of Japanese culture. As a student of Japanese culture, he learned that the strategic goal must not be to reach the emperor, but the local rulers, or *daimyos*. In addition, he learned that the Japanese imitate the Chinese, and so it was important to reach the Chinese first, then the Japanese would follow. Xavier, through the guidance of Yajiro, developed a missionary approach that involved careful study of local cultures (especially languages and religions) and then addressed European adaptation to those cultures. Xavier's commitment to reaching the Japanese led him to sail to China. It seems odd today, but Xavier was convinced that it was culturally appropriate and necessary to convert the Chinese first. No simple task, we might add.

Following in Xavier's train were a host of Jesuits who found ways to adapt the gospel to enhance its reception in China and Japan. In five hundred years of missionary work in Japan, Xavier and his colleagues had the greatest success, and their work was only rebuffed by a sudden change in imperial rule.[8] However, the approach of Xavier was developed further (and standardized, to a degree) by the Jesuit visitor, Alesandro Valignano. His positive assessment of East Asian cultures led to a remarkable cultural exchange, and a similar evaluation of East Asian cultures and pattern of missions was later followed by Protestants.

Another important Jesuit who illustrates the Catholic inculturation paradigm and who opened the doors for Christian witness in China for the first time

7. Also "Yajir," and in some of the earliest Jesuit writings, "Anjiro."

8. The rise of the Tokugawa Empire brought on severe and persistent persecution, all but annihilating the Christian movement that was growing so fast in the southern islands. The first major anti-Christian edict was in 1614.

since the eighth century was Matteo Ricci (1552–1610). Ricci began his work with another Jesuit, Michael Ruggieri, by (illegally) finding a tutor to help them learn the Chinese language in Macao, China. They then received permission to move onto the mainland in Zhaoqing, where they continued to study both language and Confucian thought. They were led to believe that they would be received better if they adapted the religious form (dress, living conditions, and diet) of the local Buddhist bonzes. Shaving their heads and changing their dress, they assumed, would help distance them from the Portuguese sailors, and help local people understand them to be religious leaders—which they were. However, in late Ming China, Buddhist monks were not held in high regard, and so the duo readapted themselves to Chinese culture—this time as members of the Confucian literati: scholars. Ruggieri returned to Europe, but Ricci pursued his study of Confucius, while maintaining his Ignatian spiritual disciplines. Eventually, Ricci accomplished his goal of moving to the capital, Beijing, and earning the respect of the Confucian literati by memorizing and discussing the Confucian classics.

Ricci's contributions to the spread of Christian faith were easily matched by his contributions to Chinese society. Christian mission, for Ricci, was a much larger cultural project. Through literature, map making, clock making, mathematics, astronomy, and calendar making, Ricci, and the Jesuits who followed, both made the gospel understandable in a Chinese context and became agents of change in Chinese society.[9] Aware of the need to be respected as a scholar, and the need to contribute to society, the Jesuits won a hearing and began a Roman Catholic movement in late Ming and early Qing China, which continues today. However, an open question concerning this approach is still being asked: When Christianity is presented as a royal religion, is the religion of the humble Suffering Servant really being proclaimed? It is a fair question, and yet recent research reveals that the Jesuits did not just reach the rulers and well-educated in the cities. Many, and maybe even most, of the Jesuits were struggling in smaller towns, presenting the Christian faith in much more humble settings and with much more humble methods.[10] Theirs was a mission that engaged cultures from the top to the bottom.

There are many other examples of Jesuit missiology that we could examine. For further study, and to deepen our understanding of this modern approach, I will later look at the approach that Roberto de Nobili (1577–1656) took to reach upper-caste individuals in South India. For further understanding, we could also look at the work of Alexandre de Rhodes with the indigenous leaders of the people of modern-day Vietnam, or we could look at the reductions (*reducciones de indios*) of the Jesuits in South America, where indigenous

9. As a matter of full disclosure, it must be admitted that Jesuits also helped with manufacturing cannons that helped the first emperor of the new Qing Dynasty, Nurachai, defeat the Ming Lords.

10. See Liam Matthew Brockey's *Journey to the East: The Jesuit Mission in China, 1579–1724* (Cambridge, MA: Harvard University Press, 2007).

people were gathered, catechized, and trained in basic skills. In each case, a studied awareness of local language, culture, religions, and society was foundational to their missionary work. From this knowledge, and with the daily spiritual exercises designed by their founder, the Jesuits sought ways to bring the nations to faith in Jesus Christ. We turn now to look more closely at how Roman Catholicism truly became a world religion, region by region.

Roman Catholic Mission in Africa

As the Portuguese sailors cautiously moved out of Iberia, they followed the winds and coastlines south, along the northwest coast of Africa. In their movement, they established patterns of setting up secured port cities (rather than large empires), trading in captured slaves, and carrying out the pope's orders to establish the church along with the Portuguese presence. Prince Henry the Navigator was a devout Roman Catholic and the third son of King João, who had a fascination with sailing. He developed a school for sailors and used enhanced sailing technology to spread the Catholic faith. His first movement out from Portugal was actually called a Crusade against the Moors (1415), the Muslims of North Africa. Thus, mission and Christianization began in Africa as Crusade and *reconquista*, or as a reconquest of Christian lands long ago taken by Muslim Arabs. The Portuguese chronicler de Zurara wrote that Henry's purpose was "to extend the Holy Faith of Jesus Christ and bring it to all souls who wish to find salvation [seeking for] . . . a Christian Kingdom that, for love of our Lord Jesus Christ would help in that war."[11] In other words, not unlike Christopher Columbus, who would arrive on the scene half a century later, Christian mission and conquest was linked with the search for a mythical Christian king, "Prester John," who was to have ruled a Christian kingdom on the other side of the Muslims. India was the goal, and spices were the reward. The motives of early modern missions seem mixed and confused to us today, but at the time this all made perfect sense; the idea was to conquer the world for Christ the King, and his vicar on earth, the pope. Making money through trade in the process was another pleasant catalyst.

Quickly, Henry and the Portuguese learned both of the lucrative trans-African trade and of the extensive lands to the south. They pressed on and by 1450 had established ports in Ceuta (off the coast of Morocco), the Cape Verde Island, and São Tome. These new ports, the beginning of Portugal's global shoestring empire, were populated with Portuguese sailors and African slaves. Very soon, they were peopled with mixed race, semi-Catholic children from African wives and girlfriends. The Portuguese established forts and churches for the sailors, and later, in their African forts, they built holding centers

11. Desmond Seward, *The Monks of War* (New York: Penguin, 1972), 183.

for captured slaves. For over 350 years, Christianization and the slave trade would reside uneasily together in West Africa. Unlike the later Dutch and British, however, for the Portuguese, intentional expansion included intentional missionary activity. Kings financed Christian mission, but kings—African kings—also opened and closed doors for European activity in West Africa.

African Themes in Early Modern Mission

A number of themes dominated the unique West African missionary work of the fifteenth through the eighteenth centuries. First, the approach, much like the work in medieval Europe, involved reaching rulers: *cuius regio, euius religio* ("whoever is the ruler, that is the religion"). The Portuguese first sent an envoy to the Manikongo (king of the Kongo) Nzingu Kuwu (1484), who in turn sent his son Mvemba Nzinga to Portugal to be educated. The prince returned, baptized as Alfonso, and even though his father returned to the faith of his fathers, the young Christian prince remained within the Catholic faith. Alfonso made Christianity the religion of his empire, tearing down the traditional temple, building a church, and then renaming the capital São Salvador (Our Savior). It was an assumed pattern that had only limited success. The same pattern was repeated elsewhere in western Africa, as well as in southern and eastern Africa. Most Christians, not just those involved in African missions, assumed this practice (missions must work to convert the rulers of a culture) because hardly any premodern societies were pluralistic. A people or a nation had one religion. Mission, it was understood, required converting the ruler first and subsequently the people.

A second dominating theme at the time was that Roman Catholic missions were constantly plagued by their association with the slave trade. From the beginning, there were mixed signals about Portuguese intentions and confusion about the meaning of the Christian religion. European priests got off the same boats that were then loaded with Kongolese slaves. Granted, the slaves were not captured by the Europeans (they were purchased from local African rulers), but the meaning was the same: "Do you want to save us or enslave us?" Several of the priests were directly engaged in the slave trade. King Afonso complained to King Manuel, "Today our Lord is crucified anew by the very ministers of his body and blood." The conversion of some of the African leaders, historically considered, seems to be more genuine than that of the European Catholics. The later Dutch and British Protestants would face the same problem, as they inherited this dehumanizing trade.

One quick example will suffice. In 1624, when the people of Ndongo (east of Luanda) were being evangelized, a treaty was struck with the local queen, Nzingha a Mbande (1582–1663). Luanda was a city built on slavery and the slave trade, and the Portuguese only added to this immorality by exporting some of their own convicts to the city. Queen Nzingha was sent as an ambassador on behalf of her brother, the king, to negotiate peace with the Portuguese. She was impressed with the power of the Portuguese and their beautiful buildings, and so, after consultation about their religion, she converted and was baptized. She took the Christian name Queen Dona Ana de Souza; it was a political and religious alliance. However, the Portuguese quickly betrayed the newly baptized Dona Ana; she escaped with her life and returned to her indigenous faith. Allying herself with the Yaka (Jaga) people, she developed her kingdom as a haven for freed or returned slaves and as a military force against the Portuguese. A thirty-year war ensued. It is easy to see from this one story how remarkable it is that any church at all was planted in Western Africa under the Portuguese.

Third, one of the early Roman Catholic strategies, later picked up by Protestants, was to bring promising African leaders (usually young princes) to Europe to help shape them into European Christians. The assumption was that Christianity would develop in Africa to look very much like European Christianity. Rather than try to mold these African leaders into European Christians while in Africa, it was thought the process would be easier and less costly if African Christian leaders were brought to Europe to be formed properly. They needed to see, hear, smell, and experience the best of Christendom to know what they were supposed to reproduce in Africa. Alfonso's son, Henrique, was sent to Lisbon to study for the priesthood. He was ordained a bishop by order of Pope Leo X before returning to serve the Kongolese church as the first African bishop to serve in São Salvador. Henrique himself seemed to have returned to serve as a political leader more than anything else. Nonetheless, the first African bishop served in São Salvador, West Africa, before Calvin wrote his *Institutes of the Christian Religion* and before Loyola formed his "Society" in Paris. Unfortunately, even this very imperialistic approach to mission did not have long-term Christian influence. It would not be until the twentieth century that many African bishops, Catholic, Anglican, or Lutheran, would be ordained to lead the African church.

The Roman Catholic Church engaged in a similar practice in East Africa, sending African princes and potential church leaders to study in India. Some of these did return, and so some of the evangelization of East Africa was done from India.

Jacobus Elisa Johannes Capitein (b. ca. 1717; d. 1747) was an African scholar who adapted much of his theology and life to that of the Dutch imperialists.

Protestants also carried out the practice of evangelizing and catechizing Africans in England, Denmark, and the Netherlands. A Fante youth, later named Jacobus Elisa Johannes Capitein, was taken to the Netherlands at the age of eleven and given a complete Dutch classic Christian education. A painting of him at the age of twenty-five indicates that his Christian calling came in Dutch apparel. He was ordained and sent to work with his own people as a "chaplain" of the Dutch West India Company. He had some success through translation and a school that he established for local youth. However, the Dutch experiment was an isolated one; this was not a long-term strategy. The training of Africans in Europe had a greater impact on ending the slave trade than on evangelizing Africa.[12]

Fourth, and quite unexpectedly, early West African Christianity showed many of the later elements of African indigenous Christianity. This was not at all part of the European missionary strategy or vision. In fact, one could say that this development happened despite Western strategies and beliefs. How could these early Christendom missionaries ever guess that something as African as dreams from departed ancestors and female prophets would become elements of Christianity in Africa?

Fifth, the approach of most of the missionary religious orders in Africa was to confront and destroy indigenous fetishes and architecture. This was not only a European understanding of the conversion of life and culture; the very first conversion, of the Manikongo himself, involved the burning of religious items and the destruction of the indigenous temple.[13] The new religion must displace the old; new temples are built on the ruins of the old. This is the approach that the Capuchins working in West Africa took. Because Capuchins were seldom Portuguese, and they came later under the direction of the *Propaganda Fide* (papal missions rather than being sent by the Portuguese crown), their work was less confused with political ends. These friars cared first and foremost about building up an African church. They were far more effective in the first few decades of their work in Kogo and Soya (from 1645) than the previous century of Portuguese work had been. Their method was to confront and destroy religious fetishes or buildings and baptize and catechize new converts. Although baptisms multiplied, long-term Christian catechetical training did not. Thus, during the seventeenth and eighteenth centuries, growth was sporadic in large part because of the poor long-term catechetical work. Later it was described

12. Cf. Lamin Sanneh, *Abolitionists Abroad: American Blacks and the Making of Modern West Africa* (Cambridge, MA: Harvard University Press, 2001), 24–31; Jehu Hanciles, "Back to Africa: White Abolitionists and Black Missionaries," in Ogbu U. Kalu, ed., *African Christianity: An African Story* (Pretoria: University of Pretoria Press, 2005), 191–216; Ron Milland, "Editing Race: The Mediation of Equiano's 'Interesting Narrative' and the Correlating Black Aesthetic," in Chima J. Korieh, ed., *Olaudah Equiano and the Igbo World: History, Society, and Atlantic Diaspora Connections* (Trenton, NJ: Africa World Press, 2009), 369–80.

13. This was more like Saint Boniface (Wynfryth) chopping down the sacred Oak of Donar as a challenge to the gods. Having escaped the judgment of the gods, he cut up the great oak and built a chapel dedicated to St. Peter (732).

West African Female Prophets

Three important women prophets of West African Christianity from the sixteenth through the early eighteenth centuries were Queen Nzingha (Dona Ana de Souza); a Kongolese woman named Apollonia Mafutta; and another Kongolese, Dona Beatriz Kimpa Vita (d. 1706). In each case, elements of West African indigenous religious belief and practice are mixed with biblical elements and political concerns of the time period.

Apollonia lived during a time when the famous Christian capital of São Salvador was in ruins and the Kongolese Christian King Pedro IV was residing in a new capital on Mt. Kibangu. Apollonia had visions from Mary, the mother of Jesus, who told her to communicate to the Kongolese people that her Son was grieved that the Christian capital was in ruins. Apollonia was a prophet to her people, calling them back to faithfulness through rebuilding the capital. She proved her visions through various miracles, one of which was finding a rock in a river with the face of Jesus upon it.

Kimpa Vita's story is far more complex, involving her being possessed by the spirit of Saint Anthony of Padua, dying each Friday, being raised from the dead each Monday, and receiving revelations directly from God during these times of death. But again there was a call back to faithfulness, portrayed as an African Christian kingdom. These prophetic women function for us as a foretaste of elements of twentieth-century African Christianity. They also reveal something of African resistance both to European rule and to European missionaries who were often allied to that foreign rule.

that the people were "without leader, light, or cross" (*sine duce, sine luce, sine cruce*). Royal baptisms with no teaching about the Christian life reduced Christianity to a veneer and finally to a fading memory in most of West Africa.

Thus, the early modern mission work in Africa had signs of ongoing cultural or imperial domination, like the Crusades only with more emphasis upon commerce—and especially slaves. The innovation of bringing the best and the brightest to Europe to make them European Christians was an assumed strategy, but one that had little long-term impact. The confusion of European motives and ministries greatly hampered the work. In addition, the lack of long-term, sustained leadership training (catechetical as well as priestly formation) ensured that any Christian presence that might develop would be forever dependent upon foreign priests. This was a weakness not only in Africa but also in Central and South America in both Spanish and Portuguese missionary work.

Latin America: Mission, Conquest, and Resistance

Some of what we have observed about the Roman Catholic approach in Africa was also true in Latin America and the Caribbean. For our purposes here we only need to highlight features that were unique to this part of the western hemisphere. In Latin America, we need to distinguish between Christian mission under the Spanish and under the Portuguese. The Spanish, in general, were soldiers wherever they went. The Portuguese tended to be sailors. Soldiers conquer large areas of land, and sailors establish ports. In the history of Spanish America, we hear of conquerors like Pizarro in the Andes and Cortez in New Spain (Mexico). In less than a century, the Spanish had conquered from Texas to the Straits of Magellan. If the First Nations people of present-day Florida and Texas had not been so strong and confident, the Spanish would have conquered most of the southern United States from Florida to the Pacific as well.

The Portuguese, on the other hand, were happy to set up trading ports and only later (and only in Brazil) did they establish a colonial territory. Both Iberian conquerors were racist, looking down on all non-Europeans, and especially darker-skinned people. The Spanish had a well-defined class system that was imposed both in Latin American society and in church. The Iberians were rulers; mixed-race people (mulattos and mestizos) were given limited authority and honor; indigenous people and dark-skinned Africans were least respected. Priests and monks in South America and the Caribbean, for most of colonial history, were fully of European descent. Iberian culture was imposed upon the continent and local cultures and peoples were oppressed. However, conquistadors were not priests, and sailors were not monks. The missionary work of the church was, by necessity, linked to Iberian expansion—but it was not identical to it.

Important questions arise: Did the monks and friars fully embrace the same assumptions as the soldiers and sailors? Did missionaries work as agents of the colonial powers, or did their contact with indigenous people (and later with African slaves) influence their missionary work? As with most historical questions, the answers are not simple. The Franciscans, Dominicans, and Augustinians who came to the "New World" came to Christianize, not to enslave, oppress, or get rich. Still, they were sixteenth- and seventeenth-century Europeans, and so they shared most of the basic assumptions about cultures, religion, and politics. What we see is that long-term involvement in missions tended to clarify the missiology of many and pollute the motives of others. The Spanish established ranches or villages of indigenous people called *encomiendas*, and the rulers of these plantations were called *encomienderos*.[14] Friars often functioned as *encomienderos*—entrusted with the lives of indigenous people—and as such they often became wealthy. Other friars, monks, and some secular priests became more and more conscious of the injustices inflicted upon the indigenous people and responded through their missionary work, through their writings, and through protest.

14. From the Spanish *encomendar* meaning "to entrust."

Missionary Resistance to Empire

One of the best-known examples of missionary resistance is Bartolomé de Las Casas (1484–1566). De Las Casas first came to the Caribbean as part of a Spanish expedition, arriving in Hispaniola in 1502, and for his work he was awarded his own *encomiendero*. In this position, he was able to use local people, abusing them as necessary, to provide free labor under the guise of civilizing and evangelizing them. His participation in the mistreatment of people was an experience that changed his mind and broke his heart. He became the first priest to be ordained in the Indies, and then he headed back to Spain to protest the treatment of indigenous people in the Americas. He argued for reforms. He argued his case before the Archbishop of Toledo, returned to America for another two years, and then, back in Spain in 1517, he argued his case with the son of the German emperor, the young Carlos I. Carlos was the ruler of parts of Italy and the Low Countries as well as Spain and the new lands being conquered in America. Carlos, who had just been elected Holy Roman Emperor (Charles V) listened to de Las Casas describe the cruel treatment of the gentle and humble people of the Americas. The priest defended their humanity, their capacity to receive the faith, to practice self-government, and to exercise reason.[15] Charles V condemned the cruel practices—without completely outlawing the system. The leadership of missionaries like de Las Casas did eventually bring about de jure reform, if not de facto reform. In 1542 the king of Spain issued what were called the New Laws (*Leyes Nuevas*) to provide protection for the indigenous people. Although generally ignored in the Americas, the laws forbade enslavement of indigenous peoples and dissolved the *encomiendas*. It is interesting to note that Charles V, in 1518, not only had problems with a Dominican priest in *Hispanolia*, he also had problems with an Augustinian monk in Wittenberg, Germany: Martin Luther.

De Las Casas may be one of the better-known reformers in the Americas, but he was not alone. Many Dominicans, Franciscans, and later Jesuits pushed against the normal European treatment of indigenous people, and some opposed the treatment of slaves, and even the institution of slavery itself. Here I give a sampling of the friars and monks who resisted the cultural norms of the time and helped to reveal something of the church and its missionary understanding.

1. Antonio de Montesinos (Dominican, ca. 1486–1530) was one of the first missionaries to speak out against the atrocities regarding the treatment of the indigenous peoples. He arrived in the Caribbean in 1510; by Advent of 1511 this preacher spoke strongly against the terrible conditions created by the cruel enslavement of the *encomienderos*. His sermon of December 21 directly attacked the Spanish rulers in the New World, even suggesting

15. From Dale Irvin and Scott Sunquist, *History of the World Christian Movement*, vol. 2 (Maryknoll, NY: Orbis Books, 2012), chap. 1, "The Conquest and Christianization of America."

that the barbaric treatment of local people put the salvation of the Spanish in jeopardy—that the Spanish were no better than the Moors. Opposing the common understanding that certain people were inferior and not worthy of the spiritual and worldly blessings that others receive, de Montesinos named the indigenous people as worthy not only of just treatment but even of the precious gospel of God.

2. Juan de Zumárraga was the first bishop of New Spain (Franciscan, 1527), and he assumed from the beginning that it was his responsibility to defend the "Indians." The remaining Aztecs he regarded as under his charge. It is actually quite amazing that he simply assumed that his parish included all souls in the geographic region of New Spain, even non-Christians. He traveled to Spain and brought back people to help "convert the culture and society" of New Spain: teachers for schools, people to run hospitals and to establish a college. In addition, he brought back artisans and the first printing press in the Americas. His mission was a broad-based cultural mission that involved all areas of society and all people in his parish.

3. Antonio de Valdevieso (d. 1550) has earned, for his reforming efforts, the epitaph "First Christian Martyr in the Americas."[16] Valdevieso was the third bishop of Nicaragua and Costa Rica and, soon after being appointed, he advocated and promoted reforms for the human treatment of the indigenous peoples. When he attempted to implement the *Leyes Nuevas* (New Laws), mentioned above, the local *encomienderos* rose up against the good bishop and killed him. Simple advocacy of Spanish law was a dangerous position to take as a missionary.

4. Alonso de Sandoval[17] (Jesuit, 1576–1652) was a Spaniard who was educated with the best of American Jesuit schooling, and he chose to use his education—theological and practical—in advocacy of the plight of the Africans in the Americas. Almost his entire ministry was spent in caring for, educating, catechizing, and baptizing slaves. Located in the important port city of Cartegena (on the Caribbean coast in Colombia), Sandoval was there when the newly arrived Africans stepped off the boat. He was also there to bury those who died before their time, due to mistreatment. De Sandoval published the first major treatise on the beliefs, practices, and suggested approaches to evangelism of Africans: *De Instauranda Aethiopum Salute* (*On Procuring the Salvation of the Ethiopians*). Although not opposed to all slavery, he spoke out unequivocally against the African slave trade as an institution and argued for the full inclusion of Africans in the Catholic faith. It is interesting that this

16. He may be the first martyr in South America. In fact in 1542, eight years earlier, Franciscan friars were killed in present-day Kansas in North America while establishing a mission among the Wichita nation. De Padilla, Juan de la Cruz, and Luis de Escalona are likely the first Christian martyrs in the Americas.

17. See Alonso de Sandoval, *Treatise on Slavery*, ed. and trans. Nicole von Germeten (Indianapolis: Hackett, 2008).

Jesuit scholar and reformer begins his study of mission to the African slaves with a study of Africa. Sandoval took indigenous cultures very seriously. Other missionaries followed in his train, advocating for ministry to, and at times liberation of, African slaves: Pedro Claver, from Spain (Jesuit, 1580–1654); Epiphane de Moirans, from France (Capuchin, 1644–89); and Francisco José de Jaca, from Spain (Capuchin, ca. 1645–88).

5. Gerónimo de Loayza, first archbishop of Lima (Dominican, 1498–1575), defended the need for Christian work to be done in local languages. As archbishop, he called the first two Church Councils for the Americas, both held in Lima (1551 and 1567). These councils, especially the second council, made it clear that all those to be baptized were to be catechized in their own languages. However, the second Lima council also established the racist pattern of separate churches for local converts and for Iberians, and it prohibited indigenous men from being trained for the priesthood. We should remember that the councils were not missionary meetings, and the bishop was salaried by the king of Spain. There are many other stories that are worth telling and worth hearing regarding missionary resistance to colonial policies and practices, but these few give us an idea of the issues that were important for Roman Catholic missions in Latin America.

The Liminal World of Missions in Latin America

Roman Catholic missions to the Americas were often overwhelmed by the colonial structures and attitudes toward non-Iberians and non-Catholics. However, careful examination shows ongoing resistance to Spanish and Portuguese rule, to its violent and oppressive racism, its disregard for human rights, and its worship of mammon. Mission was all men's work, for missionary work was done by religious orders—single women would not have fared well in the frontiers of the Americas. With the advent of female missionary work in the nineteenth century, Roman Catholic mission diversified and greater efforts were made to educate women as part of the mission work. Catholic mission was very much indebted to the Council of Trent, which was occurring during the earlier missions in Latin America (1545–63). Theological and sacramental developments that had come through the High Middle Ages and were institutionalized by Trent were affirmed in the Americas. Ceremonies, festivals, the church calendar, church architecture, celebration of the sacraments, honoring of the saints, pilgrimage sites, and confraternities were all brought over from Iberia—providing a nearly seamless blanketing of the church across the Atlantic. However, the context in the Americas was different—so, as missional work was carried out, issues were raised that reveal the tensions involved in bringing Iberian Christianity across the Atlantic.

First, we see in the reformers and bishops listed above a central concern for the evangelization of the indigenous peoples. Priests, monks, friars, and bishops were in the Americas to evangelize local people, and later to evangelize slaves. Second, in contrast to the accepted practices and beliefs of this late Renaissance and early Enlightenment period, many monks and friars believed that the indigenous people were fully human, and therefore should be treated justly and expected to learn a catechism. The cultural racism of missionaries was dulled by church duty and pastoral practice; friars, working closely with indigenous people, learned to love their congregations. Third, the missionary task was understood broadly as including all people and all of culture. I have not expounded upon the Jesuit villages or *encomiendas*, but they developed new crops and diets for indigenous people, and working with indigenous people, the Jesuits also learned languages, printed books, and developed art and music. Much of the "culture" that was developed was transplanted (and only minimally adapted) European culture, but there was at least some attempt to mitigate this broad cultural approach to mission. Finally, we see a common difficulty for missionaries: they were often caught between empires and nations, laws and customs, colonial authorities and the authority of their faith. At their best, and when pointing most clearly to the Roman Catholic understanding of mission, they rested uneasily as European invaders with a message of grace. Too often, and certainly after the first two hundred years, the church (including its missionaries) had become far too comfortable supporting the colonial status quo, a status quo that was hierarchical, racist, and oppressive to the masses of Latin American and Caribbean Christians.

Asia and Mission to Religious Nations

In Asia, Christian mission met its greatest difficulty and reaped its most meager results. The greatest difficulty was bringing Christian teaching and life to centers of ancient, multicultural faiths. Latin America and Africa were both filled with traditional societies that each followed their own particular religion. In Asia, there were transcultural or multicultural religions, like Buddhism, that were practiced by people from many different nations speaking many different languages. Some of these religions predated Christianity (Buddhism and Hinduism) and others were newer, but also transcultural (Islam and Sikhism). In addition, Christian missionaries in Asia also encountered much larger populations and large literate civilizations. It is hard to downplay the tremendous difference of context between most of the Americas—largely migrant and nomadic people with only a few settled nations—and the ancient Indian, Korean, Japanese, Chinese, Thai, and Vietnamese civilizations. The Chinese (to use just one example) had forgotten more regarding the arts, math, and technology than most nations ever knew. Missionaries who traveled to Asia during the sixteenth through eighteenth centuries had similar attitudes and understandings as the missionaries in Africa or Latin America, but the unique Asian context drew out issues and concerns that were not evident elsewhere. We look here at some of the basic issues of Christian mission that are revealed through the missionary encounters with these transcultural faiths and ancient civilizations.

When Pope Alexander VI issued his important bulls of donation, *Inter caetera* and *Eximiae devotionis*, in the fifteenth century, in effect he gave the kings of Portugal and Spain spiritual authority in what the bulls considered newly "discovered" lands.[18] Portugal was given the authority and responsibility to evangelize all lands discovered to the east of their own Cape Verde Islands,[19] and Spain was responsible to evangelize all lands to the west. Thus, moving out from Iberia, Portugal was responsible for most of Africa and Asia. Portugal was to provide for all of the priests and missionaries and to pay to erect churches in all of the lands they claimed. No appeal was to be made to Rome. The first encounter that the Portuguese had with Asians was in South India; they were helped in getting there by Arab Muslim sailors from East Africa. It is significant that throughout the Indian Ocean, across to the South China Sea and the central Philippines, the Portuguese, and later the Spanish, encountered Persian, Arab, and Indian Muslim traders. Islam had completed its spread, through trade, all the way to the gates of Manila by 1500. Everywhere Catholic missionaries landed, Muslim traders preceded them—until they reached Japan and China.

South Asia: Caste and Christ

When the Portuguese arrived in India, they encountered ancient Christians (Prester John), and they encountered the early Muslim Mughal Empire (founded in 1526 by Babur, grandson of Tamerlane). Meeting the St. Thomas Christians was a hopeful occurrence; encountering the Muslim rulers was troubling. Christians had little to no success in their Christian witness to the Ottoman, Seljuk, and Mamluk empires in West Asia and Egypt. Their success in South and Southeast Asia would be similar. Even though the Indian Muslim empire was much more pluralistic than other Muslim empires, Christian missionary work had virtually no impact there. In fact, Christian witness has never had a great impact upon Muslim populations. Missionary work in Asia moves around and among, but not *in*, Muslim communities. Of all populations, Europeans most wanted to convert Muslims, but desire and will alone (even with careful planning) brought meager results.

18. These are commonly called the "Bulls of Donation" of 1493. Since all of the lands of the world are under the care of the Vicar of Christ (the pope) it was his responsibility (as it was understood at the time) to make sure that all "new lands" were given the gospel of Christ. Kings, as servants of the church, were to carry out this Christian duty.

19. Actually, 370 leagues west of the Cape Verde Islands.

In India and Ceylon (Sri Lanka), the Portuguese, and later the French and other missionaries, worked mostly among Buddhists (both Mahayana and Theravada) and Hindus. Encounters with Hinduism raised two new issues for Europeans: pluralism and caste. In Latin America and Africa, the Europeans had been the racists, with a clear understanding of who was on the top (Portuguese, with light skin) and who was on the bottom (African slaves with dark skin). In India, the social context was more complex—and more detrimental to missionary work. Whereas missionaries could talk to and evangelize and worship with indigenous people in the Americas, in India the caste system prevented people in lower castes (artisans) from worshiping with, or even eating with, people who were from the royal caste (Brahmin caste). When missionaries first reached India, they sought to gather people into communities regardless of caste or vocation. However, Europeans were viewed (because they smelled, they ate meat, and they wore leather) as being lower caste—so they had little success in reaching people who were higher on the social rung. The global strategy of reaching the rulers (and then the people will follow) was virtually impossible in India.

One person (among many) who fought against the European identity and endeavored to reach upper-caste Hindus by entering the upper caste was the Jesuit Roberto de Nobili. The Jesuits sent de Nobili inland to work in Madurai in 1606, when most of the Europeans were working among fisherfolk on the coast (very low caste), among the St. Thomas Christians, or attempting to reach the rulers in the Mughul royal court. The statement that de Nobili began to make with his new missionary work in this Tamil region was that it is not necessary to become a foreigner to become a Christian. You can become a Christian as an upper-caste Indian. This is significant, because most Catholic missions in the seventeenth century assumed that to become Christian, one must culturally become a European Christian. The Jesuits, as we have seen with Xavier and Matteo Ricci, sought to adapt the Christian message and life to local cultural contexts. For Ricci, it meant becoming a Confucian literati. For de Nobili, it meant becoming an upper-caste sannyasi ("renouncer"), or holy man. He refused to wear leather, he ate only vegetables and rice, he studied Sanskrit texts, and he became fluent in Tamil and Tamil literature. De Nobili attracted other upper-caste Hindus through his Tamil poetry and songs and his knowledge of the ancient Indian texts.

The results were not dramatic (less than one hundred converts in the first three years), but it was the first time a community of upper-caste Indians had formed a church. This small success was, however, attached to a large controversy: whether or not it was appropriate to allow caste to divide the church and to allow such extreme adaptation to a particular Indian context. Two other results accompanied this Jesuit approach. First, a number of Indian gurus began to come to faith, and, when they did, their students followed. In some regions of Tamil Nadu this brought persecution against the Hindu converts;

many new Indian Christians had to meet in secret. A second result, totally unpredicted, is that this Indian form of Christianity actually worked to open the door to larger numbers of lower-caste Indians. In part, these lower-caste people saw Christianity as a way out of the bondage of caste: as Christians they were no longer bound by caste and so the gospel brought liberation, the possibility of learning to read and of pursuing less demeaning forms of labor. It is important to note these unintended results, because they continue to be a major part of Christianity in India today.

Earlier contacts with Hinduism by Catholics created conversions and conflict. Some understood the Christian faith in Indian dress, others rejected the Christian faith as a challenge to the basic order of Indian society. This is another theme, not only in India and not only in Christian missionary work among Hindus, but in all of Asia: the Asian concern for social order. Since Asian nations are mostly built around intercultural religions living in mutuality with national rulers, the possibility of conversion is seen as destabilizing the nation. A good Thai is a good Buddhist. A good Malay is a good Muslim. A good Japanese is a good Shintoist (and Buddhist). Conversion to Christianity was often seen as the act of a traitor, and the close identity of many missionaries with European powers (and their guns and cannons) only reinforced this perception. This helps to explain the limited success the Jesuits often had in places like Japan, China, India, and Vietnam (at the time Anam and Cochin China). The Roman Catholics were the first to encounter this enormous issue in Asian missionary work. When large numbers of people began to convert, even in very "Asian ways," in areas like East China, Vietnam, and Japan, persecution soon followed. It is one of the major themes in Asian Christianity.[20] For Japanese Christians, obeying a Japanese Christian *daimyo*, even going to battle for Japan against the Koreans (as the earliest Japanese Christians did), was not enough to prove loyalty. In Japan—as was the case in China, Vietnam, and Korea—a change in dynasty meant a change in Christian fortunes.

East Asia and Mission Conflicts

Christianity was growing in Japan at a very rapid rate in the late sixteenth and early seventeenth centuries, thanks to the Jesuit approach promoted and devised by Alesandro Valignano (1539–1606), the Jesuit Visitor for East Asia.[21] Local rulers (*daimyos*) were coming to faith, and their subjects were following. Some of the first Asian artwork and first translations of Scriptures, prayers,

20. For a further discussion of persecution and martyrdom as a mark of Asian Christianity, see chap. 7, "Asia," in Mark Hutchinson, Donald Lewis, and Richard Pierard, *A Guide to Global Evangelicalism* (Downers Grove, IL: InterVarsity, 2012).

21. See Andrew C. Ross, *A Vision Betrayed: The Jesuits in Japan and China, 1542–1742* (Maryknoll, NY: Orbis Books, 1994), and J. F. Moran, *The Japanese and the Jesuits: Alesandro Valignano in 16th Century Japan* (New York: Routledge, 1993).

and liturgies were done under Valignano's guidance. But at the end of the sixteenth century, a new dynasty came to power under the leadership of Tokugawa Ieyasu (ruled 1598–1614). In the early years of his reign, he ignored the rapid growth of Christianity in the south (in and around present-day Nagasaki) as he consolidated his rule. But after consolidation in the north, Ieyasu turned to the south where most of the Christian *daimyos* fought to prevent him from coming to power. In 1614, Ieyasu issued a very harsh anti-Christian edict whereby all churches in Japan were to be closed, all missionaries were to leave the country, and all practice of Christianity, public and private, was banned. The religions of Japan were Shintoism, Buddhism, and Confucianism, the edict declared. Christianity was the religion of foreigners who wished to take over the country. All Japanese were to be enrolled in one of the Buddhist sects, initiating a Buddhist revival and leading to Christian martyrdoms and defections from the faith. Sixty missionaries who refused to leave were decapitated or hung upside down on crosses to die.[22] Only two or three thousand Japanese were killed, but many more defected, and some fled to the hills and mountains to survive. Such reversals of fortune are unique to Asia. There are similar stories of changed fortunes out of concern for social order in Vietnam, Cambodia, Thailand, Myanmar, China, Sri Lanka, and India.

Missions Transforming Cultures Transforming Mission

Another important theme that developed in the seventeenth and eighteenth centuries in Asia was the conflict that developed between Europeans as they worked in different Asian contexts. Part of the conflict was over approach and strategy, such as the Jesuit adaptation approach, which focused on reaching the leaders of a nation first, a strategy that often (and especially in Asia) involved giving expensive gifts. In opposition to the Jesuit approach was the Franciscan approach of working with the poor. Closely related to this conflict (which became magnified in Japan and China) was the conflict between Europeans from different countries. In some regions, most of the missionaries were Italian; later came the Spanish, and then came French or Portuguese missionaries. When the Spanish friars (Franciscan) arrived in Japan in 1593, an approach had already been established by the Jesuits (which involved keeping their distance from the Portuguese sailors). The Jesuits built relationships with local rulers, earning their respect through giving gifts, dressing appropriately, and learning the language well. The Franciscans came to work with the poor and sick and, frankly speaking, were suspicious of the ostentatious lifestyle of the Jesuits, nestled so close to Japanese rulers. Franciscans did not understand the need to keep their social distance from the Spanish sailors who were now

22. The Japanese punished Korean Christians in the same way in the early decades of the twentieth century in Korea.

arriving from "New Spain." The Japanese were suspicious that these Europeans wanted to rule Japan. It appeared to be true, as revealed by a tragic incident in 1597. The Spanish galleon, *San Felipe*, ran aground loaded with weaponry and missionaries in 1597. The captain was questioned by the Japanese, and word was carried back to Emperor Hideyoshi himself that the Spanish were in fact spreading their conquest from Mexico and the Philippines to Japan. Six Franciscans who had been on the ship and three Japanese Jesuits who may not have been on it were seized, along with another fifteen Japanese Franciscans from a hospital. Two others voluntarily turned themselves in to the Japanese. These twenty-six Christians each had an ear sliced off and were paraded through the streets in humiliating fashion before being executed by crucifixion. The emperor ordered that the bodies of these Nagasaki martyrs be left on the crosses for nine months as a warning to those who would further befriend the Christians.

Christ, Confucius, and Christianity

Other conflicts between missionary approaches and nationalities did not create such sudden and tragic results, but were divisive, nonetheless. In China, the nearly two-hundred-year struggle over how Christians should view the Chinese Confucian rites and ceremonies was much more intricate and delicate, but equally divisive. The Jesuits, beginning with Matteo Ricci, worked to understand how the Christian faith could be presented in ways that would be understandable, without requiring the converts to become in any sense European. They were asking the right questions, even if their answers were sometimes unpopular. "What does it mean to become a Chinese Christian? Can a Chinese become a Christian and not have to deny her or his 'Chineseness'? Do some of the habits and rituals of the Chinese reflect Christian values and morals, but in different forms?" These questions were being answered in China (and in Chinese), but Vatican authorities, including the pope himself, were evaluating the answers and practices in Italy (in Italian and Latin). Such questions divided the Roman Catholic Church as it attempted to fulfill its missionary calling, a calling originally carried out by political leaders, not missionaries.

Mission to the Top or from the Bottom?

One dimension of this missionary division had to do with the long-term mission strategy that said political leaders must be reached before the nation or tribe will receive the faith. This had been the practice in European history, and in most premodern cultures it continued to be true. To put it bluntly, if the ruler is not favorable, there will be no Christian mission. In Europe, in 1555, a similar principle was articulated in a Diet called by Emperor Charles V, who earlier had listened to de Las Casas argue concerning the just treatment of

Americans. This meeting established a tentative religious peace in Germany by articulating that the faith of the ruler in the realm was to be the faith of the people.[23] But was the principle an indelible Christian principle or just a matter of pragmatic interest? It had proven to be effective and necessary in Africa, but in Asia it was proving very expensive and nearly impossible to carry out. The Jesuit approach was based on the premise that the best and brightest—the rulers and scholars—needed to be reached, and then the people would follow. Franciscans, Austin Friars, and others did not agree. The friars reasoned that Jesus's words "Blessed are the poor" clearly indicated that the lower classes, peasants, and farmers should be reached first. Jesuits were criticized for the large budgets that were necessary to purchase "gifts fit for a king." Occasionally ships went down in the Indian Ocean or the South China Sea with Jesuit treasures to be presented to *daimyos*, or Chinese provincial rulers. When the contents of the loss were revealed, it was clear that Jesuit mission looked a lot like international diplomacy, and was proving just as costly. Should missionaries seek to save the lost and the poor (a bottom-up approach) or reach the rulers and leaders (a top-down approach)? This question of strategy is also a question of theology, and it persists even up to the present.

New Religious Orders

Another aspect of mission during this period (not *only* in Asia but *particularly* in Asia) was the development of new structures for mission, new religious orders. Structures are the means of accomplishing mission, and they are just as necessary to Christian mission as a robust theology.[24] Almost all Christian missions from the Roman Catholic Church were carried out by monastic and mendicant orders—some meeting particular needs within Europe, and some meeting missionary needs overseas. New orders or congregations were being founded to meet these needs, many with specific charisms: education, medical care, work with the poor, women's orders, and so on. For example, the Augustinian Recollects (1609) were a Spanish reform movement within the Augustinian order dedicated mostly to the contemplative life but, out of necessity, their major work in the Philippines was evangelization and church development. Here we see that the missionary context often helped to reshape the original charism of the order. Other religious orders were founded specifically to evangelize the poor, such as the Vincentians, founded by a former captured galley slave, St. Vincent de Paul (1581–1660). De Paul had a special interest in ministering to slaves working on galleys along the coast of North Africa (he ransomed some twelve hundred slaves) and caring for the incurable dying. Soon, he himself was sent as a missionary to Madagascar. Many

23. This Diet is not to be confused with the Lutheran Diet of Augsburg in 1530, which produced the Augsburg Confession.

24. See the discussion of William Carey below.

other religious orders were founded, focusing on apostolic work of some type, but the greatest number of new orders would not be founded until the Roman Catholic missions were revived (after the French Revolution) in the nineteenth century.

The first women's religious order founded in Asia was the Lovers of the Holy Cross, founded in 1670 as both a contemplative and apostolic mission. In the Philippines, the Religious of the Virgin Mary was founded by a Filipina woman, Ignacia del Espiritu Santo, in 1684. Influenced by her Jesuit confessor, the order set apart women to aid in the education of young women and in the personal sanctification of all women. The Holy Ghost Fathers (Congregation of the Holy Spirit, or Spiritans) was founded in the early eighteenth century with a specific concern to care for the most desperate and needy of people both in France and overseas. Quickly, the Spiritans began to focus on work among African slaves in French Guyana and later in East Africa.

From Royal Missions to Church Missions

Another major issue of this period for the Roman Catholic Church was the transition from royal or imperial missions to papal or church missions. As was noted above, all of the early Roman Catholic work overseas was, per the pope's instruction, to be directed and financed by the rulers of Spain and Portugal. Such an arrangement made sense when there was no other option, when the Iberian rulers controlled all travel and global finances, but by the seventeenth century things had changed. Both Spain and Portugal were losing their global influence, missions were perennially underfunded and understaffed, and Spanish and Portuguese ships were meeting on the "other side" of the world. The Curia (the central governing body of the Catholic Church) was coming to the realization that kings were not meant to be directing missions. By the beginning of the seventeenth century, there were churches planted in areas that were being cared for under a mission structure (*padroado*) with no episcopal oversight. Thus, in 1622, Pope Gregory XV issued the bull *Inscrutabili Divinae*, which formed a papal mission society called the Sacred Congregation for the Propagation of the Faith (SCPF). The Congregation was established as a means to organize and regulate Catholic affairs outside of Catholic lands—and to spread the faith to new lands and peoples. Overriding the patronage structures of Portugal and Spain, the pope, under the prefect (president) of the SCPF, appointed apostolic vicars for different regions. These apostolic vicars would organize the missionary work in a region and coordinate outreach and ministry among various congregations and/or religious orders. What is of particular interest for us is to hear how this Congregation, working through the Vatican, understood mission work. In an instruction sent out in the thirty-seventh year of the SCPF (1659), after two generations of learning and working with cultures around the world, we read the following:

> Do not regard it as your task, and do not bring any pressure to bear on peoples, to change their manner, customs, and uses, unless they are evidently contrary to religion and sound morals. What could be more absurd than to transport France, Spain, Italy, or some other European country to China? Do not introduce all that to them, but only the faith, which does not despise or destroy the manners and customs of any people, always supposing that they are not evil, but rather wishes to see them preserved unharmed. . . . Do not draw invidious contrasts between the customs of the peoples and those of Europe; do your utmost to adapt yourselves to them.[25]

The transference from royal (patronage) missions to papal missions (and then a global Roman Catholic Church) took a long time. One of the major losses in the transfer was the zeal that some of the early missionaries had to equip local priests and bishops early on. The vision of people like Alexandre de Rhodes to have local Christians do the catechizing, and the vision of the Jesuits to train Japanese priests in Japan, did not become the standard position or concern of Catholic missions.

Unintended Results: Renewing Asian Religions

One of the unintended results of Christian engagement with Asian Hindus, Muslims, Sikhs, and Buddhists, from this period up to the middle of the nineteenth century, has been the stimulation of reform and renewal (as well as division) in these faiths. The Sikh religion, founded in the first decades of the sixteenth century, was regularized in part *because* of contact with Western missionaries. Guru Gobund Singh (d. 1708) established the sacred texts as well as other ritual practices, bringing order to a previously diverse religion. It is well-known that when European missionaries first arrived in India, Hinduism was a diverse network of religious practices (albeit with similar rituals, a common social structure, and a shared understanding of karma and reincarnation). "Hinduism" became a single religion as missionaries and other outsiders began to make observations and write about their Indian encounters. One of the first Baptist missionaries in India, William Ward, helped to give Hinduism its own self-definition with the publication of his work *Account of the Writings, Religion and Manners of the Hindoos including Translations from Their Major Works, in 4 volumes*, published in 1811. Some Hindus engaged Christian missionaries, or studied at Christian schools, and brought Christian teachings (often ethical and moral teachings) to bear upon Hindu practices. Rammohan Roy (1772–1833) encouraged Scottish missionary Alexander Duff to set up schools in India and to include teaching of the Bible; he was especially

25. Quoted from Stephen Bevans and Roger Schroeder, *Constants in Context: A Theology of Mission for Today* (Maryknoll, NY: Orbis Books, 2004), 192, but taken from *Sacra congregatio de propaganda fide, Collectanea* 10/300 (Rome, 1907), 103. This quotation can be found in many places, which reveals how important it is to an understanding of Christian mission.

attracted to the New Testament. Influenced by Christian teaching, Roy was led to reject the idolatry of Hinduism and to promote monotheism behind all its avatars. Having worked in the British service for a number of years, he became acquainted with Christianity and then, upon returning to Calcutta, began study of the Bible in Greek and Hebrew. In 1820, Roy published his work *The Precepts of Jesus: The Road to Peace and Happiness*, a work that, like Mahatma Gandhi years later, promoted following the teachings of Jesus as superior moral precepts. Roy, with much criticism and some friction, brought a new challenge to Hinduism that helped to bring about renewal. At the same time, his openness to Christianity, without seeing a need to convert, brought a new challenge to missionaries. When challenged by other Hindus about reading the Bible in Duff's academy, it was the enlightened Roy who defended Duff's approach. "Read and judge for yourself. Not compulsion, but enlightened persuasion, which you may resist if you choose."[26] In 1828, the ideas of Rammohan Roy were institutionalized in the founding of the *Brahmo Samaj* ("Community of the One God"), a social and religious movement within Hinduism. *Brahmo Samaj* became the conduit of many new movements within Hinduism, and helped Hinduism to communicate itself to the Western world. The encounter with transcultural religions became more and more complex in Asia, renewing, strengthening, and diversifying the very communities the missionaries were trying to reach. It is in Asia, beginning in the sixteenth century, that cultural anthropology, interreligious dialogue, and religious pluralism originate.

Persecution: The Christian Birthmark

As an epilogue, it should be noted that in Asia, more than in other regions, this early modern period marks the return of Christian persecution. In Latin America, large populations were decimated by disease, and smaller royal centers (Aztecs and Incas) were dominated by Spanish conquistadors; persecution was related to military conquest, not religious belief. Violence against Christians in Africa was primarily against slave traders and sailors; the greatest suffering came from disease (the life span of missionaries in the tropics of Africa and Asia up until the twentieth century was less than ten years).[27] In Asia, there were two factors that were unique: most of the countries were not completely colonized, and missionaries encountered transcultural faiths supported by rulers. As a minority and a foreign presence, missionaries had to negotiate their presence and package their message carefully. Persecution

26. Quoted from Stephen Neill, *History of Christianity in India* (Cambridge: Cambridge University Press, 1985), 309.

27. Life spans varied greatly, but a commonly quoted figure for nineteenth-century missionaries in Africa is that they lived, on the average, eight years after their arrival. In Thailand, before the last decade of the nineteenth century, the life span was under five years.

of the missionaries and of young Asian Christians was common. The Jesuit Alexandre de Rhodes was only able to spend ten years in Vietnam out of his twenty years in the region. He was repeatedly expelled and even imprisoned. Many of his young disciples were imprisoned, and some were killed. However, despite this violent context, the Vietnamese Catholic Church became one of the strongest in Asia. Only in the Philippines, where the Spanish established themselves throughout as colonial lords, did the Catholic Church have greater success.

Japan is called the Land of Asian Martyrs because of the severe persecution of Christians after the rise of the Tokugawa Empire. A final gasp of Christian presence was crushed in 1637 when Christians in the Arima prefecture, persecuted with an 80 percent tax, finally revolted against their anti-Christian *daimyo*, Matsukura Shigeharu. This Christian revolt was led by a fifteen-year-old prophetic leader, Amakusa Shiro; the Christian farmers went to battle with crosses and angels on streaming banners. After an initial victory, the oppressed farmers were crushed; some thirty-seven thousand of them starved to death after seeking refuge in Hara Castle in Shimabara. The Shimabara Rebellion marks the end of a tumultuous, though at times promising, "Christian Century" in Japan.

In other countries, there was not the strong Christian movement—but persecution was still a near neighbor of both missionaries and new indigenous Christians. The first real advance of Christianity in Korea was not prompted by missionaries, but by Confucian Korean priests who brought back Christian texts from China. There were many conversions, and the Korean converts requested the help of foreign Christian priests. Then came the persecution. Christian teaching was not considered *chonghak* ("correct teaching"), or the true teaching of Confucianism. The Korean officials labeled it *sahak* ("deviant teaching"). By 1802, over five hundred Korean Christians had been killed, many of them well-educated Confucianists, but also a large number of wealthy women.

At about the same time, in India, a period of intense persecution of Christians was taking place. Mughul ruler Fateh Ali Tipu (ruled 1782–99) came to power from the region of Bangalore and eventually exerted his rule as Sultan across much of Southern India. Southern India contained the few significant Christian communities that existed in India at that time. The greatest impediment to Tipu's efforts of expansion was the British, whose interests in the south were growing. Tipu sought alliances with the Persians, Afghans, and even the French in his efforts to extend his rule. When the British openly opposed him, Tipu lashed out against the Christians in his territories, including those of indigenous Indian identity. Priests were arrested and church buildings destroyed. Some twenty-five thousand Christians in South Kanara were put in chains and marched into exile in Srirangapatnam—with as many as ten thousand dying of disease and hunger on the way. Christian men were forced to undergo circumcision and take Muslim names. Women were given to Muslim men in marriage. Over the next decade, Tipu's religious policy softened considerably, but by then the Christian population had been dramatically reduced.

These are a few of the more dramatic instances of Christian persecution in Asia, but throughout Asia persecution remained a shadowy reality for every new church and the neighbor of every new convert. Christian mission was shaped by this experience and through its response, as it sought protection from colonial powers and as it sought to avoid conflict and rejection. But instead of European colonial powers serving to protect Christian missionaries, what happened is that into the nineteenth century these powers mostly acted as aids to Asian religions, often protecting indigenous people from being exposed to Christian missionaries. The results of these colonial policies continue to have an impact on Christian communities today.

3

Colonial Missions, Part 2

Orthodoxy, the Americas, and Modernity

Having surveyed colonial-era missions in Africa, Latin America, and Asia, we now turn west to look at the often-neglected early missionary work in the Middle East, among ancient cultures and Muslim overlords. Then, after looking at the diverse work in North America, we will look at the earliest Protestant missionary work and draw some conclusions about the early modern missionary period.

Middle East: Re-Centering the Orthodox

A new issue was raised with the rise of early modern Roman Catholic missions to regions contiguous with Europe: what does Christian mission look like in Muslim areas that have ancient Christian communities? For the Roman Catholic Church the goal was twofold. First, missionary work meant working to bring the Coptic, Maronite, St. Thomas, or Orthodox Church under the oversight of the papacy. The pope, as the Vicar of Christ, was the ruler of all Christians—those not acknowledging his authority must do so. The second goal was to properly catechize these "Oriental Christians," and work together to bring Muslims and other non-Christians to the faith. Roman Catholic ecclesiology prevented missionaries from recognizing Christians from these ancient churches and so, in the presence of an expanding Ottoman Empire, envoys from Rome wooed all four of the sixteenth-century's Coptic popes (Egypt). At one point the Coptic Church nearly took the offer, hoping for protection from the Ottoman Turks in exchange for submission to the Roman pope. Gregory XIII of Rome sent a delegation to Egypt to try to convince John XIV of Cairo to accept the offer. A special council was called, and bishops and monks met in Egypt in February of 1583. The council was divided. Those who refused to submit reminded the council that their ancestors had resisted other churches and other religions, and that there was now a long line of martyrs praying that the church would remain faithful. On the other side were more practical and political arguments. The church was suffering under the Turks, and they needed protection. No decision was made at that time, as the Coptic Pope John XIV died suddenly, leaving the Copts without a leader. Rome continued to try to bring other African and Asian Orthodox churches under its authority in subsequent centuries. It eventually had limited success in parts of West and South Asia, but not in Africa. For its part, the Coptic Church continued to suffer under the heavy hand of Turkish rule for another two hundred years.

The question of Orthodox independence, in Egypt, Ethiopia, and throughout the Middle East, was closely related to the political and social issues of living under or around Muslim rulers. The Italians were sailing in the Mediterranean Sea, while the Portuguese were sailing around the whole continent of Africa to India. A religious alliance at such a time was seen by some as a Christian duty, but for others it was seen as selling out. Sometimes the military preceded the religious delegation. In 1541 the Portuguese arrived with four hundred soldiers and canons, led by Vasco da Gama's son, Cristóvo da Gama, to aid the Christian emperor in Ethiopia. In retaliation, the Muslims turned to the Ottoman Turks, who sent some eight hundred troops. This proved to be decisive in turning the tide against the Portuguese and Ethiopian forces. De Gama and 160 other Portuguese were beheaded, the Turks were released to return home, and the war seemed to be over. However, international conflict continued as European Catholics pushed both to convert Ethiopians and to impose European military aid. Colonial expansion at times looked more like a continuation of the Crusades, or, from the other side, like a new Islamic jihad.[1] In between battles, Catholics (mostly Jesuits) worked to bring the Ethiopian church under the authority of Rome. With all of the respect that the Jesuits had for other cultures, including the similarities they recognized between Orthodox and Catholic liturgies, the Jesuit mission must be seen as misguided and ultimately detrimental to African Christianity.

It should be noted that Christian mission in the Orthodox world, mostly in the Middle East, was being carried out in the midst of four large Muslim empires, all in conflict with each other. The Ottomans were pressing in on

1. In fact, most of these "struggles" against Christian kingdoms were called jihads by Muslim rulers. The Ottomans carried out jihad against the Byzantine Empire and, until the late eighteenth century, were again at the gates of Vienna.

Europe in the fifteenth century. They had finally taken Constantinople, the last toehold for the Byzantine Empire, and in 1480 their ships had landed on Italian soil in an effort to conquer Rome. To the east of the Ottomans was the Safavid Dynasty (1500–1736) in Persia, Shi'a Muslims who prevented the spread of the Sunni Ottomans to the east. Farther east, Muslims were extending their Mughal Empire in India, and in Egypt the Mamluk Dynasty ruled and dominated most of Arabia and the Gulf states. Christians encountered Muslim rulers from Morocco to Mindanao; from Turkey to Ethiopia and from the Balkans to India, they encountered ancient Christian churches whose members were living under Muslim rulers.

Catholic and, beginning in the nineteenth century, Protestant missionaries sought to make contact with these ancient churches. To the credit of both Catholics and Protestants, there was a concerted effort made to understand, reach out to, and support the Coptic Church, Maronite Church, St. Thomas Church, and others. Roman Catholics would listen to and observe the Mass to look for orthodoxy as a prerequisite of future fellowship. The evaluation was generally positive, and so some churches were brought into fellowship with the Vatican as "Eastern Rite Catholic Churches." Those churches that were brought into the Roman Catholic fold had the benefit of being part of a much larger ecumenical church without having to change their theology, liturgy, or language. Unfortunately, such decisions weakened the Orthodox churches by taking away members, priests, and buildings. The situation in India is a good example of this.

Christianity in India has ancient, if not apostolic, origins.[2] By the fifteenth century, Christianity had remained or become concentrated along the southwest Malabar Coast, and the Indian Christians had adapted to caste society by becoming upper-caste traders and business people. The liturgy was carefully followed in the Syriac language, a language many of the priests no longer understood. These Christians, however, were very devout. Some among the Portuguese described the Indian Christians as lovers of fasts and long sermons. They were also devoted to the cross (depicted in East Syrian tradition without a body) and to their prayers. Churches contained no images such as those found in Roman Catholic churches or Hindu temples. Before the arrival of the Portuguese, Indian churches were built in the local style, resembling a Hindu *pagoda* (or temple) with a cross on the top and floors "painted" with cow dung. Churches had lamps and umbrellas in the local style. Rather than a statue (or collection of statues) in the front of the sanctuary, there was a copy of the Syriac Bible, often in gold leafing, on an elaborately carved stand. Men and women sat on opposite sides of the church and everyone bowed in

2. For a discussion of its origins, see Father Mundadan's excellent discussion in *History of Christianity in India*, vol. 1 (Bangalore: Church History Association of India, 1989); or Samuel Hugh Moffett, *A History of Christianity in Asia*, vol. 1 (Maryknoll, NY: Orbis Books, 1992).

three directions upon entering: forward to honor the cross; to the right, in the direction of the baptismal font; and to the left, where the Eucharistic bread was located. Portuguese sailors and early missionaries initially reached out to these Christians (more than to their Muslim neighbors) in an effort to include them in the Roman Catholic communion.

In the early years, after an initial fiasco whereby Vasco da Gama hurled bombs at the Indians (killing Muslims, Hindus, and even three of his own Franciscan missionaries), the Portuguese developed cordial relations with St. Thomas Christians. Soon, however, the Thomas Christians realized that Portuguese sailors could not always be trusted and at times seemed as difficult as the "Ishmaelites" (Muslims). A key Indian figure who negotiated the relationship between his own Indian Christians and the Europeans was Mar Jacob, the Metropolitan of Cranganore from 1504 to 1551. Mar Jacob helped to negotiate trade treaties for the Europeans, and he was well respected by both the Franciscans and the later Jesuit missionaries. For example, early in his relationship with the Europeans he translated a Latin prayer into Syriac for use in the St. Thomas churches. The Thomas Christians, as a community, were of two minds about these Europeans; the Europeans were quickly becoming a dominant force in the Indian Ocean, but their religion seemed to be part of the dominating cultural force. As with many peoples of Africa, Asia, and Latin America, it was difficult for the Thomas Christians to separate Christian good will from colonial oppression. When Mar Jacob died, in 1551, there was no leader of his stature and wisdom to navigate the troubled waters of international Christian diplomacy. For over a century, Thomas Christians were taken to Rome to attempt to influence them to "convert." Some churches began to use the Roman Catholic liturgy, while others resisted. The issues that divided the two sides were as much cultural and linguistic as they were theological.

A major Synod, held in 1599, marks a turning point in Roman/Thomas Church relations. At the Synod of Diamper, Roman culture and religion was imposed upon the St. Thomas Church. The goal was to bring unity between the church in India and the church in the West—but the effect was the division and weakening of the Indian Christian community and the neutralization of much of the witness to the surrounding Muslim and Hindu communities. European priests gave sermons ridiculing the Chaldean Patriarch, to whom the Indian church had been accountable for about thirteen hundred years. Although mostly religious concerns were expressed, the overall impression—and one of the main reasons for resistance—was that the Synod was part of an overall plan to Westernize the ancient Indian church.

Christian mission to the ancient Christian churches was unique and generally involved cultural and structural concerns rather than missionary work. In general, Roman Catholic mission was more gracious among those furthest from the faith, and more militant and culturally rigid among Christian communities. If the Crusades and *Reconquista* seemed to spill over into what often looked like Christian conquest in Latin America, then the Reformation battles seemed to be spilling over where there were existing Christian churches in Asia and Africa.

North America: First Nations People and the People of Many Nations

There is no single pattern for the evangelization of North America. The mission history is mostly a history of migrations of various Europeans, along with small attempts at mission and large demographic decline due to European diseases. In North America, Christianity was spread mostly by migration, not missionaries. Most of the early migrants from northern Europe had little to no concern for indigenous people. Except where Roman Catholic ships or soldiers landed (French in Quebec, Spanish in the Southwest), Europeans brought devastation rather than salvation to First Nations peoples. Like Australia, New Zealand, most of Latin America, and the Caribbean, the indigenous people were overwhelmed or even exterminated by European emigration.[3] In the early period of modern missionary work—roughly from 1600 to the 1820s—First Nations people were seldom a priority. The Spanish missions in California and in Texas came later but, as a result of the loss of Spanish lands to the United States, they struggled to maintain their witness. These Spanish missions followed the pattern of settling transient communities of Navajo or Apache on missions and teaching basic farming and other skills alongside the Catholic faith.

Some of the earliest Protestant missionary work that occurred in North America is often forgotten. Protestant mission does not begin with the great pioneer William Carey in 1793 in India, nor does it begin with Bartholomew Ziegenbalg and the German Pietists in 1709 (also in India). The earliest Protestant interest in mission to unreached people arose because of the opportunities that presented themselves in North America. Proximity can change one's mind-set. The vague interest was expressed by King Charles I of England in granting the charter to the Massachusetts colony with one of the express purposes to "win and invite the natives of the country to the knowledge of the only true God and Saviour of mankind and the Christian faith." The original Seal of Massachusetts expresses this concern: a lone "Indian" is pictured; the ribbon of text extending from his mouth is a plea taken from Acts 16:9, "Come over and help."

Virtually no Anglicans initiated mission work to indigenous peoples in North America—but other Protestants did. Puritan pastor John Eliot, working in Roxbury, Massachusetts, began by learning the Algonquin language, and

3. For example, virtually no indigenous peoples were left in the Caribbean Islands.

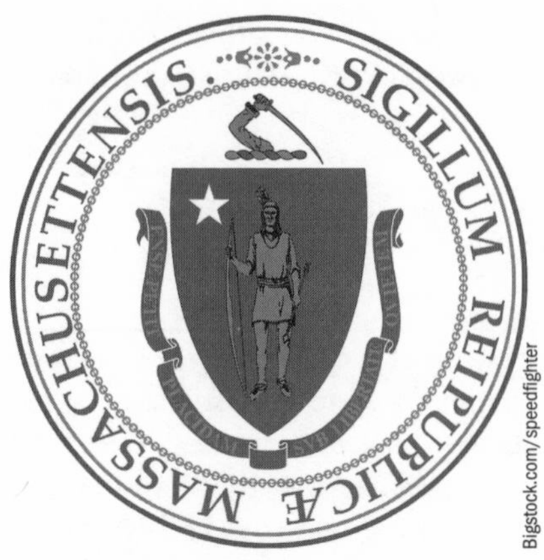

Seal of the State of Massachusetts retains the First Nation person, but without the "call."

soon he knew it well enough to begin to preach (1646). Following a Roman Catholic pattern, he gathered the faithful into Christian towns ("praying towns" similar to *encomiendas*) for training, as well as for safety. But, unlike the Roman Catholics, Eliot, as a Protestant, translated the Bible and focused on Bible teaching. By 1661 he had published a New Testament in "Moheecan"—the Old Testament was done in 1663. The work was of great historic import, even though it did not become a pattern for other settlers. By 1671 there were over thirty-six hundred Indian Christians in fourteen "praying towns," and by the time of Eliot's death in 1690 there were twenty-four preachers trained to carry on the ministry. The story ends tragically, however, for increasing migration of Europeans pushed the First Nations peoples off of their lands, and Christian villages were abandoned in the midst of regional wars. Except for a few isolated pioneers and Puritans, other early settlers did not travel across the Atlantic for missionary purposes.[4] What is of note, however, is the early pattern that developed of enculturation and conversion of indigenous people while allowing them to live in their own communities, speak their own language, and follow their own trained leaders. It was certainly an interesting pioneering vision: indigenous people walking around in European clothes, attending Puritan worship, but reading Bibles in their own language and listening to the Word proclaimed by their own people.

Most of the early intentional mission in North America was Roman Catholic, and, since it followed similar patterns and was based on similar concerns and issues as elsewhere in the world, we need not take much time with it here. Jesuit work in Quebec followed a slightly different pattern than in South America, in that many of the Jesuits traveled with the seminomadic Micmacs, Montagnais, Huron, and Algonquins, rather than settling them in towns or villages. The Jesuits sought to create a form of Roman Catholicism that would communicate Christianity and at the same time win acceptance by these various First Nations peoples. As in other missionary settings, translation work was done and Christian cultural development (writing hymns, prayers, etc.) was part of the missionary work. Similar to the missionary

4. Other isolated cases would be the Mayhew family and their ministry on Martha's Vineyard, and later David Brainerd. See Henry Warner Bowden, *American Indians and Christian Missions* (Chicago: University of Chicago Press, 1981).

work in the Pacific, Latin America, and the Caribbean, diseases struck within a few decades—decimating the indigenous populations.[5] Thus, with rapid migration to North America, a largely underpopulated continent, the percentage of indigenous people rapidly decreased through the years. Most of the "missionary" work was actually chaplaincy to various immigrant groups: German Lutherans, French Catholics, Scotch Presbyterians, Dutch Reformed, Irish Catholics, and others.

Before moving on, however, we need to address one major mission theme that is unique in the Americas: missionary work to another "migrant" group, African slaves. It is one of the great historical ironies and tragedies that the people who were evangelizing Africans were also the very people who were enslaving them. Of course, they weren't exactly the same people—but to an African, as to a St. Thomas Christian in India, these Europeans were all of the same mold. We have noted above that there were some Catholic orders that focused on work among the slaves (we should include the work of the Holy Spirit Fathers)—the same became true of Protestants. Those who worked among slaves—for their evangelization and welfare, as well as for their liberation—tended to be evangelicals. Wesley, one of the main leaders in the evangelical revivals of the eighteenth century, spoke and wrote against slavery, and the earliest work among slaves in the Caribbean was done by German Pietists and Baptists. As a result of the work of these churches among slave communities, most of the early African American church leaders were in only a few denominations: Baptist, African Methodist Episcopal, and African Methodist Episcopal Zion. Two of the first African American pioneers, George Liele (first ordained) and David George, were both Baptist.

In addition, evangelical churches tended to be less hierarchical and therefore more democratic. Evangelical worship was easier for newcomers, like slaves or the illiterate, to enter into. Evangelicals also had the spiritual and theological foundation for work among slaves and freed slaves. Other churches that were more hierarchical, like the Anglicans, Roman Catholics, and Lutherans—churches that were more identified with European ethnic groups or nations—developed ministries to African Americans in the middle of the nineteenth century. The impact of this ministry—to the most oppressed and estranged—was tremendous. Slaves and freed slaves, through their own suffering and alienation from their own culture, became more Christian than the European immigrants.[6]

5. Contact with Europeans did not bring diseases and massive death to the people of South Asia, Africa, or East Asia. It is likely that the intermittent contact with Europeans over centuries had created some antibodies in Africans and Asians that had never developed in island peoples and people of the western hemisphere. See Jared Diamond's *Guns, Germs, and Steel: The Fates of Human Societies* (New York: Norton, 2005).

6. For a fuller description of why and how slave religion developed, see Albert J. Raboteau, *Canaan Land: A Religious History* (New York: Oxford University Press, 2001).

Protestant Paradox: Killing Catholics and Imitating Catholics

Protestant missions developed in the wake of Roman Catholic missions; they developed similarly in some ways and differently in others. Protestants were not Catholics, but they were living in the same period of European expansion and Enlightenment. Here we will note some of the new dimensions of mission that came out of Protestant missions (before the great age of Protestant missions in the middle of the nineteenth century). Most of these differences are the fruit of a different theology, different political contexts, and a different period of time. Protestant missions were not supported by their kings (with the notable exception of King Frederick IV of Denmark), they came after hundreds of years of Roman Catholic mission experience, and they emphasized knowledge of the Scriptures. However, like their Roman Catholic predecessors, Protestant missionaries studied local cultures and wrote important books on local religions, beliefs, and customs. Also like Roman Catholic monks and friars, Protestants tended to move inland—beyond colonial borders. Missionaries were not bound by colonial military or political power, but they did rely on colonial support when it was needed or helpful. Protestants also imitated Catholics in much of their architecture and worship, bringing patterns that were familiar and common in Europe. They, like their Roman Catholic counterparts, were very diverse in their approaches to different regions, but developed more academic approaches to literate societies in places like China and India, and were more attracted to serve within these ancient civilizations.

Before there were Protestant missions, there were private trading companies from Protestant countries. The Dutch and British each had both an East India Company and a West India Company. These were private companies that acted almost as shadow empires, with the power of military and ability to coin money. By today's description, they would be like hyper-multinational companies. They had enormous power and the protection of governments. They imposed European will upon Asians and Africans, but did not impose or force their religion. In fact, the Dutch and British companies resisted mission as interfering with good business. They also despised and attacked Roman Catholic colonial forts with impunity, showing far greater violence against European Christians than against Asian or African Muslims. In the seventeenth and eighteenth centuries, these multinational companies were led by Protestant businessmen with post-Reformation (anti-Catholic) zeal. In West Africa, Ceylon, Malacca (Malaya), and the East Indies, the Portuguese were soundly routed by the Dutch, who razed Catholic churches or turned them into Protestant churches. The Portuguese presence, and therefore the Catholic witness, suffered dramatically, losing control of important trading centers and losing pastoral care of many non-European Catholics.[7]

7. One of the great heroes of the Sri Lankan church, Joseph Vaz, was inspired to reach out to and support the oppressed Catholics in Ceylon.

Protestant missions began with chaplains working with Dutch and British citizens living and traveling overseas. A very few of these chaplains took interest in the local or indigenous people, but it was very difficult for them to find the time to learn a local language and begin to translate Scriptures (in a chaplain's spare time). One of the great exceptions to the rule, but coming relatively late, was a number of Anglican chaplains who were inspired by the pastoral and missional vision of Charles Simeon (1759–1836) who served as a type of university pastor at Holy Trinity Parish in Cambridge. He inspired and helped to recruit a number of the early chaplains who served with the East India Company in Asia. Probably his best-known disciple from Cambridge was the pioneer in Persia, Henry Martyn (1781–1812), who transferred from law to theology in preparation for missionary work under the influence of Simeon. Martyn "burned out for God" after only seven years in Calcutta, translating the New Testament into Urdu and then into Persian. He was able to personally present a copy of his Persian New Testament to the Shah. His work was of such high quality that his translations were still being used after two hundred years. Mission extending out of chaplains to European traders and then to indigenous people was rare—and it would not be the way forward for Protestant missions.

Protestant Pioneers in India

Another exception to the basic Protestant pattern is the Danish missionary work started by an enlightened (and competitive) king. King Frederick IV of Denmark realized that the Portuguese were spreading their religion to their lands in India and, being a king, he reasoned that he should do the same. Deferring to his very wise chaplain, Franz Julius Lütkens, contact was made with Pietists in Germany (specifically Lütkens's friend August Hermann Francke) and missionaries were selected. Although there were many Danish (Lutheran) priests, Lütkens intuitively knew that missionary work required a certain type of Christian leader—and the renewal movement going on in Germany would be ideal training ground for missionaries. He was perceptive. From the Pietist renewal movement in Halle, Germany, not only did Asian Protestant missions begin, but also some of the earliest Protestant missionary work in the Caribbean, Greenland, North America, and South Africa. Initiative came from the Danish king, resistance came from the colonial administrator in Tranquebar, and financial support came (in large part) from England. It was a unique pattern, for almost no other Protestant nations were supporting missionary work at the time. However, excluding the "home missions" work of the English dissenters in New England, the work of Bartholomew Ziegenbalg and Henry Plütschau in India marks the beginning of the modern Protestant missionary movement in 1706. Protestant missions began as an ecumenical and international partnership.

The earliest Protestants working in Asia soon developed priorities and strategies that became almost a template for Protestant missions.[8] First, the Pietists believed that the Indians were fully able to receive knowledge of God—so it was important for the missionaries to understand Indian religion and culture in order to communicate that knowledge well. Thus, one of the first concerns of Ziegenbalg was to understand local religions. His first publication was a book entitled *Genealogy of the Malabar Gods*. Missionaries realized the value of such a study, but Europeans did not, so this important book was not published until 1867 (154 years after it was written). Secondly, these German pioneers made language study a priority, and especially translation of the Scriptures. Ziegenbalg had a New Testament in Tamil completed by 1714, just eight years after his arrival. Language study and Bible translation would be central in all Protestant work. Thirdly, education—including schools for boys and girls—was also important in Protestant missions. Ziegenbalg learned the importance of education and schools from his mentor, Franke, in Germany. Fourthly, most Protestant missions would bring with them the best of secular education—not just literacy and study of the Bible. Like the Jesuits in China and Japan, for Protestants the modern study of science and math was a key component of Christian missionary work. Fifthly, the early German missionaries were clear that their goal was not schools or literature, but churches led by Indians. Protestants in later years were not so clear, but in the earlier Protestant work the ultimate goal was local churches, led by local Christians; education, literacy, and (later) medical work were penultimate.

Protestant Characteristics in Mission

When the pioneer English-speaking missionary William Carey (1761–1834) went to India in 1793, eighty-seven years after the Germans, he followed similar patterns of missionary work. (One cannot overemphasize the priority these German Protestants gave to language work, culture learning, and Bible translation.) In sending his son Jabez off with Jabez's wife to Amboina (the East Indies) in 1814, William gave the following instructions:

> Labour incessantly to become a perfect master of the Malay language. In order to do this, associate with the natives, walk out with them, ask the name of everything you see, and note it down; visit their houses, especially when any of them are sick. Every night arrange the words you get in alphabetical order. Try to talk as soon as you get a few words, and be as much as possible one of them. A course of kind and attentive conduct will gain their esteem and confidence and give you an opportunity of doing much good.[9]

8. It should be noted that some of the principles express Roman Catholic approaches from the Jesuit tradition of cultural adaptation.

9. From George Smith, *The Life of William Carey, DD: Shoemaker and Missionary, Professor of Sanskrit, Bengali, and Marathi in the College of Fort William, Calcutta* (London: John Murray, 1887), 76.

Language learning was both a missionary means and a ministry pattern.

William Carey is more important for another Protestant characteristic in missions: the mission society. During a time in which most Protestants had no interest in missions, believing that the apostolic call was fulfilled by the apostles, Carey's call to missionary work was a call to establish the "means" to carry out the missions work. The short title of his famous book tells it all: "An Enquiry into the Obligation of Christians to Use Means for the Conversion of Heathens."[10] Roman Catholics were ready for missionary work with their many religious orders dedicated to lives of self-denial. They had means to carry out the work that the pope commissioned. Protestants, however, had cut out of their faith the monastic structure for mission that had helped to evangelize the West. The concept of voluntary societies, as a parallel structure for mission, was not a theological conviction—it was a practical necessity. These societies were often built around a denomination or ecclesial tradition, but their founders and their foundations were much more ecumenical and focused on the work of mission—not the structure of European Christendom. As Andrew Walls has noted, "There never was a *theology* of the voluntary society. The voluntary society is one of God's theological jokes, whereby he makes tender mockery of his people when they take themselves too seriously."[11] Imitating monastic structures, voluntary mission societies leaned toward (in the age of Enlightenment) pragmatism and tended to take a businesslike approach. It was, as it were, an incarnational missionary structure that made sense and worked for Protestants in the West. Later, we will see that Asians, Latin Americans, and Africans are not wedded to this structure or means.

Another characteristic of Protestant missions has to do with its foundation or catalyst. What, we might ask, has motivated Protestant missions? This is less of a question for Roman Catholics, since in this early period the mandate and means came with the responsibility of exploring and colonizing secular societies. Secular rulers and church rulers worked together to spread the influence of the Iberian king and the Kingdom of Christ. This dual mission, as we have seen, could take violent forms (see the sidebar).

Protestants, on the other hand, had virtually no motivation for missionary work for centuries—but then something happened. It was not just that they developed means of transportation and so decided to get involved in mission; British and Dutch ships had been traveling around the world for centuries before Protestant missionary work began. No, the modern Protestant mission movement began as a product of, or response to, European movements

10. The full title ends with "in which the religious state of the different nations of the World, the success of former undertakings, and the practicability of further undertakings is considered."

11. "Missionary Societies and the Fortunate Subversion of the Church," in Andrew Walls, *The Missionary Movement in Christian History: Studies in the Transmission of Faith* (Maryknoll, NY: Orbis Books, 1996), 246.

Secular and Sacred Mission "Collaboration"

Perhaps one of the worst and most violent examples of "mission" involving the collaboration of secular rulers and church rulers was in the reading of the *Requerimento* or "demand" to people in the Americas before the *conquistadores* attacked. The *Requerimento* (read in Spanish) explained that the local people were to submit to the authority of the Spanish since God, who rules over all, has, through his vicar (the pope), given to the Spanish king the responsibility to bring all people under subjection to Christ. They were warned that they should immediately submit: "But, if you do not do this, and maliciously make delay in it, I certify to you that, with the help of God, we shall powerfully enter into your country, and shall make war against you in all ways and manners that we can, and shall subject you to the yoke and obedience of the Church and of their Highnesses."[a] Spanish conquest was often wedded to religious domination.

a. See Luis Rivera Pagan, *A Violent Evangelism: The Political and Religious Conquest of the Americas* (Louisville: Westminster John Knox, 1992).

of renewal.[12] In fact, almost all Protestant missions have been marked by renewals and revivals. The Pietist movement in Germany fueled the earliest mission movement, both through Danish missions and the cross-cultural German ministries that spread to the Low Countries, to England, and through groups like the Moravian Brethren. Directly related to the Pietist movement was the Great Awakening; its leaders (the Wesley brothers, George Whitefield, Jonathan Edwards, and others) all promoted and inspired missionary work. Edwards's biography of David Brainerd, a young missionary to First Nations peoples in New Jersey and Pennsylvania, was widely read on both sides of the Atlantic, and it became a major inspiration to other overseas missionary work. Catholic missions came from the center; Protestant missions came from the edges. Renewals, by definition, are a challenge to the status quo and the existing center—they come up from the grassroots, not down from the authorities. Until Protestant missions became mainstream in the middle or toward the end of the nineteenth century, it was fired by the zeal and creativity of the edges of Western Protestantism.

The Enlightenment and Mission

Although I have mentioned it in passing, we need at least a brief discussion on something that David Bosch discusses in an eighty-three-page chapter: the

12. What Andrew Walls and Ogbu Kalu have written about Africa is also true for Asia, the Pacific, and (to a lesser extent) North America. See Walls, "The Evangelical Revival, the Missionary Movement and Africa," in Walls, *Missionary Movement in Christian History*.

Enlightenment.[13] Protestant missions evolved in the milieu of the Enlightenment, colonialism, and awakenings. All three make up the context of the rise of Protestant missions, and all three have shaped the modern understanding of mission, Roman Catholic and Protestant. The Enlightenment was the product of Christian thought and culture but soon became its nemesis. In short, the opening of human investigation and inquiry brought about the modern study of science, based upon the empiricism of Bacon and the rationalism of Descartes. Modern science laid the foundation for enormous advances in technology, travel, communications, medicine, and production. These advances have enabled much of modern mission to take place, as science and technology have been used as bridges for Protestant missions. However, modern rationalism also flattened the created world as described in Scripture to a world of phenomena. What was once a benediction of "world without end" (*saecula saeculorum*) now simply becomes the secular: what we can sense and therefore manipulate. Modern science has also created two major issues that we might call theological compromises, and which still trouble us today.

First, the Enlightenment—with its subject-object scheme and scientific approach to the world—has dichotomized most of mission into what is observable and what is not observable (and therefore of less importance). As a result, mission is often understood as particular works of mercy and justice that can be measured (laws against widow burning, new schools, declining illiteracy rates) and the spiritual ministry of evangelism and catechetical training, which is less concrete. In an effort to be more scientific, some missions have counted converted noses—but most people realize that this is denigrating to the work of the Kingdom. Modernity, the product of the Enlightenment, has left us with a choice: to prioritize evangelism or to prioritize social justice. This is a sharp departure from ministry and mission as expressed either in Scripture or in the early church. God's creation and God's redemption has been bisected by Enlightenment thought, and the body has not been put back together. Where modernity has not been critiqued, churches and missions fall into thinking in terms of this and other dichotomies. Once you dichotomize, you are forced to prioritize, and this is the problem.

Secondly, modernity tends to be optimistic and progressive. Enlightenment thought brought about many modern inventions and perspectives that opened up the world to being grasped—but also to being abused. "There is nothing we can't solve if we put our mind to it," is the modern mind-set. Protestant missions developed such an optimism by the end of the nineteenth century. However, there is also a progressive mind-set related to this optimism that suggests what we did in the past was inferior and where we are going is better.

13. For an excellent discussion of, and even a wonderful introduction to, the basic elements of the Enlightenment, see chap. 9, "Mission in the Wake of the Enlightenment," of David Bosch, *Transforming Mission: Paradigm Shifts in the Theology of Mission* (Maryknoll, NY: Orbis Books, 1991).

Voltaire, Anti-Religion, and Early Secularization of Europe

While Voltaire was vocally opposed to the church in France, he was equally opposed to religious oppression and violence in Islam. Writing to Frederick II of Prussia in December 1740, he said the following about Mohammed: "But that a camel-merchant should stir up insurrection in his village; that in league with some miserable followers he persuades them that he talks with the angel Gabriel; that he boasts of having been carried to heaven, where he received in part this unintelligible book, each page of which makes common sense shudder; . . . he delivers his country to iron and flame; that he cuts the throats of fathers and kidnaps daughters; that he gives to the defeated the choice of his religion or death . . ."[a] All religion was repugnant to Voltaire, and France would slowly follow a similar disregard for religion in the following centuries.

a. Georges Avenel, ed., *Oeuvres complètes de Voltaire* (Oxford: Voltaire Foundation, 1869), 7:105.

Thus Christian mission was generally measured in terms of secular progress and advancement. Often, as has been expressed by many missionaries, the *results* of Christianity were proclaimed rather than *Christianity itself*. Making progress, measuring results, and advancing civilization are progressive and optimistic goals. Christian mission has always been concerned about progress (conversion is a movement forward). However, with the Enlightenment, progress took on new meaning, becoming a Christian ideology.

One of the results of the Enlightenment was new political theorizing, which laid the foundation for modern democracies. Most new democracies had a foundation of Christian, or at least deistic, teaching behind them. In France, the new movement against the oppression of the monarchy was at the same time a movement against the church. The church was closely wedded to royal oppression (the church owned about 15 percent of all of the land in France). The new intellectuals were not theologians in France, but *Philosophes*, men (and a few women) who decried enslavement to superstition, saints, and sovereigns. Jean Jacques Rousseau (1712–78), as much as any of the French writers, encapsulates the movement in a word: *liberté* (freedom). His most famous work, *The Social Contract* (1762), opens with the following sentence: "Man is born free, but everywhere is in chains." What was of central importance for Rousseau became a defining characteristic for all Western societies: freedom is valued as the supreme, most treasured social value. However, this was freedom without bounds and without duty. Voltaire took the basic concepts and put them in a more dramatic and confrontational form. For example, he loathed the French Roman Catholic Church and attacked it with the cry, "*Écrasez l'infâme!*" (Crush the loathesome thing!).

And so the Roman Catholic Church, if not crushed, did face a major setback for decades. The French Revolution caused a major decline in Catholic missionary activity, perhaps the greatest loss being the closing down of the Society of Jesus. At the very time Protestant missions were expanding, buoyed by early Enlightenment ideas, Roman Catholic missions were in a sudden and rapid decline, caused by many of these same ideas.

The last part of the nineteenth century and most of the twentieth century would be a time of remarkable growth in Western missions, both Catholic and Protestant, and would lay the foundations of modern worldwide Christianity. We turn now to that story.

4

Western Missions

Christianization, Civilization, and Commerce (1842 to 1948)

The modern missionary movement began in the early decades of the nineteenth century, but it wasn't until the middle of the century that it was in high gear. With numerous agencies being founded, hundreds of missionaries going overseas, and millions of pounds, dollars, francs, and deutschmark supporting the cause, modern missions quickly came to the fore of Western Christianity. What had started on the fringes had arrived at center stage. An observer at the end of the First Opium War in China in 1842[1] would have a hard time believing just how important the missionary movement had become to Western Christianity, especially in light of the struggles that William Carey had endured just fifty years earlier. Once foreign missionary work became an abiding concern of Protestant and Catholic churches in the West, missiological reflection also began to move toward center stage. During the late nineteenth century, classic mission reflection developed, focusing upon establishing indigenous churches that had their own internal integrity. By

1. First Opium War, 1839–42; Second Opium War, 1856–60. The result of the wars was that the foreign nations had extended their freedom to travel, settle, evangelize, and even (for the British) sell opium once again. China had been humbled into submission physically (the emperor's summer palace was burned down), morally (opium was again forced upon the Chinese), and spiritually (missionaries were free to study Chinese and settle throughout the empire). It is in this context that Christian missionaries began arriving in large numbers.

the beginning of the twentieth century, theological reflection was combined with issues of social progress, ecumenical unity, and world religions. With the rise of global Communism, the collapse of the largest Christian nation (Russia), followed by the First World War and the Great Flu Epidemic, missiology took on a myriad of new challenges. Christian "advance" was not a foregone conclusion; progressivism had received a mortal wound. Previously, Christian missions were focused on reaching other religious people. Now, a new secular context was arising out of the ashes of Western Christendom, and the new ideologies that were produced challenged the very possibility of "faith" in Western societies. Then, after the Second World War, came a period of decolonialization and nationalism. New challenges to the mission of the church came in the form of the removal of missionaries from many countries in Asia, Africa, and newly constituted Muslim, Buddhist, and Hindu nations. The missionary movement (along with much of Western Christendom) entered a period of dual crises of survival and of unity. This long century from the "opening of China" to the beginning of the decline of Christianity in the West raised many of the missiological issues that have persisted into the twenty-first century.

In this chapter we will trace this very influential global mission movement; a movement that, ironically, was also the mother to both the modern movement of decolonialization and revivals in Asian religions. First, we will look at the growth of the movement itself from its "home base" in North America and Europe. Second, we will look at one of the major controversial themes of the period: the relationship of Christian missions with colonialism and colonial powers. Third, we will discuss some of the major mission ideas and theories that developed during the "Great Century" of Christian mission, both Roman Catholic and Protestant.[2] Fourth, we will look at another major theme of the period: the relationship between Christian mission and Christian unity. We will follow this major theme through the earliest ecumenical conferences of the period that inspired churches both toward mission involvement and toward developing a theology and practice of cooperation. Fifth, we will take a closer look at one of the most important church conferences of the modern period, the Edinburgh 1910 Ecumenical Missionary Conference, and examine some of the ideas that were generated from that conference. We will briefly look at some of the early conferences related to Life and Work (LW) and Faith and Order (FO), as well as the missionary conferences of the International Missionary Council (IMC). It was these three movements, rooted in mission discussions, that led to the formation of the World Council of Churches in 1948. Finally, we will take a look at the rise of Pentecostalism and independency: global movements that began in the first years of the twentieth century,

2. This is the title Kenneth Scott Latourette gave the long century from 1800 to 1914 in his volumes on the *History of the Expansion of Christianity*.

and which provided a strong new vitality to global missionary work. These are movements that quickly brought the Spiritual churches to center stage in global Christianity. Through this panorama-like view over the mission and mission theology terrain, we will see the ongoing contextual dimensions of Christian mission, as both missionaries and mission theorists struggled to remain faithful to the commission of Christ on a rapidly changing global stage. More importantly for today, we will see how quickly the missionary movement adjusted according to the global changes taking place in the world, and this will help us better understand issues of theological reflection on mission in changing contexts.

Growth of the Modern Mission Movement

Structures follow mission or, more accurately for the Protestant missionary movement, institutions follow renewal. When William Carey and Adoniram Judson sensed God's call to carry the gospel of God across the seas, they precipitated the formation of societies that would take on the responsibility of raising funds, organizing churches, providing support, and eventually deciding who would be sent and where.[3] As we have seen, the earliest Protestant missionary work was often accomplished not through mission societies but through chaplains who traveled with colonial governments to serve the British, Dutch, or Danish traders and soldiers. In their "spare time" some of these chaplains developed important missions. For the most part, chaplains learned a local language and began nominal work—but chaplains were hired by companies (not governments) to carry out ministry for the international business community and the local support: sailors, soldiers, wives, and their children. Mission for them was an avocation, not a vocation.

With the growth of interest in this new missionary movement came new structures. The English Baptist Society (1792) was one of the first, but others quickly followed. Some societies began as ecumenical and cooperative societies (e.g., the London Missionary Society, 1795; the New York Missionary Society, 1800; the Boston Female Society for Missionary Purposes, 1800; the British and Foreign Bible Society, 1804; the American Board of Commissioners for Foreign Missions, 1810; etc.). However, most of these quickly became the channel of one, or only a few, denominations. Others were founded from the start as denominational societies, seeking to replicate their polity and theology around the globe (e.g., the [Anglican] Church Mission Society, 1799; the Wesleyan Missionary Society, 1813; the [Presbyterian] Western Foreign

3. Carey was the first British Baptist missionary to India (1793). He is considered the father of English-speaking Protestant missions. Judson was the first Congregational-turned-Baptist missionary to Asia (Burma) sent by the American Board of Commissioners for Foreign Missions (1812).

Mission Society, 1831; etc.). In fact, Protestant missionary societies multiplied extremely fast after the first decades of the nineteenth century, while Roman Catholic religious orders (the basic mission structure of Catholicism) grew most rapidly in the middle and late nineteenth century. It took the Roman Catholic Church a long time to recover from the multiple blows of the French Revolution, the suppression of the Jesuits, and the aftermath of the rule of Napoleon Bonaparte. For much of the early nineteenth century, Roman Catholic orders were playing catch-up to the rapidly expanding Protestant mission enterprise. As we have noted, Roman Catholic mission has mostly been carried out by religious orders, and therefore by celibate monks, friars, and (later) nuns. Many of the most influential religious orders were founded in the nineteenth century (e.g., the Congregation of the Holy Cross, 1837; the Religious of the Sacred Heart of Mary, 1849; the Mill Hill Fathers, 1866; the Society of Divine Word, 1875; etc.). These orders were generally founded to respond to a particular vocation or to express a specific charism, such as education for children, care for the sick, the training of young men, or care for dying. After the middle of the nineteenth century, many of the newer orders were female. Roman Catholic women in mission were celibate; Protestant women were mostly wives and mothers. The growth of structures for mission, both Protestant and Catholic, men and women, followed the revivals of religion. Mission practice and strategy was being developed, and societies multiplied in response to human needs.

Newer orders and societies for missionary work were inspired by renewals and awakenings at "home." In North America, there were awakenings both in the cities of the East Coast and on the frontier, beginning with the 1800 frontier revival in Kentucky and running on and off throughout the century. These awakenings inspired both missionary outreach to the settlers (who were generally a rough lot) as well as to indigenous peoples. Awakenings awakened people both to the grace of God in their own lives and to their responsibility to share this grace and love with others.[4] Mission theology and practice was developing out of the experience of these awakenings.

As a result, the nineteenth century became the century of voluntarism in the United States, with thousands of benevolent societies being formed to care for the poor, the widows, and the lost, as well as to bring the gospel to the nations. The YMCA and YWCA are emblematic of the response of the laity through voluntarism.[5] The responsibility to preach and to heal was seen as one responsibility. It was the same awakening spirit that inspired the long struggle against slavery in England, and which also inspired foreign missionary activity focused on church planting. In fact, if we follow the trail carefully, we can see

4. Technically, the term "awakening" was used in the eighteenth century to mean "awakened to one's sin," and therefore the search for God's mercy and grace.

5. The YMCA was founded in 1844 and the YWCA in 1855, both in London, England.

that missionary outreach led freed slaves to Christ, provided for their education, and then supported their call for an end to slavery. It was the missionary movement that gave voice to the slave, and it was—incidentally—a strong, clear, and theologically articulate voice for the equal treatment of all people. Olaudah Equiano was one of the freed slaves who spoke to the conscience of the Western white Christian. His 1789 book, *The Interesting Narrative of the Life of Olaudah Equiano*, was one of the major weights that tipped the scales of justice in favor of ending slavery.[6] Awakenings inspired mission, which was the catalyst to people moving out and bringing the good news even to the slave. Freed slaves founded some of the first missionary societies in North America with a primary concern for reaching slaves in the Caribbean and for bringing the gospel back to Africa.[7]

Above we saw how slavery, colonization, and mission became a Western cultural web in West Africa with the early Roman Catholic missions. This matrix of economic and religious motivations continued later as the Protestant countries became the dominant players. Western Christian nations were driven more by business and profits than Christian witness. However, beginning late in the eighteenth century and continuing through the early nineteenth century, Christian awakenings and the attendant missionary outpouring was a game-changer for mission, Africa, and slavery. Missionaries and awakened Western leaders began to respond to the blight of slavery on Western civilization. One way this awakened conscience of the West was expressed was in the formation of new nations in Africa. Missionary sensitivities and awakened zeal overflowed the banks of mission societies.

One of the most interesting examples of this is the founding of the nation of Sierra Leone in 1787. Britain's awakened conscience was indebted to the preaching of people like John Wesley, who consistently resisted slavery. As evangelical societies and gatherings increased, so did the sense of moral responsibility in an age of urbanization and industry. A group of benevolent politicians and other philanthropists formed the "Committee for Relieving the Black Poor," which sought a solution for the many poor, homeless (often recently freed) black people in Britain. Their answer was to give them a new chance in life by providing land in West Africa where they could return, develop some industry and agriculture, and then pay back the British government for

6. Oddly enough, Equiano's book, which promoted freedom and was inspired by the Bible and Christian duty, was published in the same year as the very secular French Revolution, which also called for freedom (*Liberte!*).

7. David George, escaped slave, became a great preacher and evangelist in Savannah, then in Nova Scotia, and finally in Sierra Leone. Others like Lott Carey (1780–1828) started missionary movements. Roman Catholic black missions started later. Established societies took up the vocation of releasing slaves, and later societies were founded specifically for ministry to freed slaves. One example is Saint Joseph's Society for Colored Missions in 1871 (an offshoot of the Mill Hill Missionary Society).

the "costs of repatriation." One of the leaders of this group was the famous evangelical leader, abolitionist, and scholar Granville Sharp. Sharp's conscience was pricked after he witnessed a young African, Jonathan Strong, being beaten nearly to death. After this experience, Sharp studied law and began to work for the anti-slave movement. The "Committee" had struck on something (repatriation) that they reasoned killed at least two birds with one missionary stone. In sending Africans back to Africa, they reasoned, the Africans would be happy to return "home," and the Brits would be happy to be rid of the public inconvenience. The problem was that the new "province of freedom" in West Africa was not really home for many of those who were put on the ships. African slaves came from all over West Africa—some from as far away as East Africa. These people spoke many different languages, and some only spoke English. Only in a theoretical sense was a particular part of African soil "home" for these freed slaves.

The first effort was a disaster: on April 8, 1787 (on the third attempt), 411 passengers—a menagerie of African Americans, African Caribbeans, and African English, along with ex-soldiers, adventurers, a few craftsmen, officials, and seventy London prostitutes—left for "Granville Town" (named for Granville Sharp). Within three months, a third of the group had died from disease, and within a year only 133 (only one third) had survived.

The Committee regrouped and, now with the support of abolitionist William Wilberforce and with a newly organized company (Sierra Leone or Lion Mountain Company, 1791), a whole new endeavor was launched. Having learned important lessons from the first failed attempt, this time (January 1792) 1,190 baptized Christian Africans from Nova Scotia set sail for "Freetown," with a missionary purpose. This was Christian mission, liberation, justice, and national politics all working together. Five ships arrived with fully formed Christian communities seeking to bring back the gospel that they had received in the West. They marched on shore singing the hymns of Isaac Watts and settled on land purchased by evangelicals of the Clapham group in England. The largest number of "missionaries" and the greatest success in missions in Africa until the middle of the nineteenth century were freed slaves establishing evangelizing Christian communities in West Africa.[8] They had their own preachers and sense of calling and didn't even receive a Western "missionary" for twenty years.

The year of Sierra Leone's successful repatriation was the same year (1792) that the Baptist William Carey set sail for India (although his arrival in India was significantly delayed because of the British resistance to Christian missions at the time). It was also the same year the Moravian Brethren began their work

8. See Lamin Sanneh, *Abolitionists Abroad: American Blacks and the Making of Modern West Africa* (Cambridge, MA: Harvard University Press, 1999), and Andrew Walls, *The Cross-Cultural Process in Christian History* (Maryknoll, NY: Orbis Books, 2002), 94–96.

in southern Africa. The Moravian Brethren were not Christendom Africans, establishing a Christian state in Africa. They were dissenters and revivalist evangelicals who required personal conversion of all their community and then expected to see the signs of that grace and conversion in transformed lives. By personal history, they were founded upon abolitionist and biblical ideals, as were the pioneers of the Sierra Leone colony. "Their conversion to Christianity in vast numbers represents one of the most spectacular achievements in modern mission history and 'the first mass movement to Christianity in modern Africa.'"[9]

Another Christian-influenced repatriation mission program was initiated by Americans: the American Colonization Society (ACS). Such colonies as Sierra Leone and what would soon become Liberia ("land of the free") were a direct threat to the ongoing slave trade. Slaving colonies were still very active in the early nineteenth century, even as the British were moving toward abolition. In the midst of this environment, the ACS negotiated the use of land to establish a free colony for freed slaves and their families. Resistance came not only from European slave traders, but also from local African rulers who were more interested in getting money for their land (or from selling slaves) than hearing moral or religious teachings from Americans. The colony suffered greatly from the resistance of African slave traders, from disease, and from lack of organization. Although one quarter of the original settlers died in the first year, missionaries continued to arrive and did what they could to stem the onslaught of disease.[10]

Christian mission was not limited to mission societies; awakened Christians found many ways to fulfill a calling to missionary faithfulness in the midst of social injustices. By the middle of the nineteenth century there were awakenings among businessmen that produced noontime prayer meetings and outreach to the poor in the cities. The YMCA movement (1844) was started by evangelicals in Britain for the purpose of reaching out to young men in the cities, trapped in the worst of the Industrial Revolution. Later, their witness was taken to university campuses, and then to cities and universities overseas. One of the great leaders of revival, a derivative of awakenings,[11] was Dwight

9. From Jehu Hanciles, "White Abolitionists and Black Missionaries," in Ogbu Kalu, ed., *African Christianity: An African Story* (Pretoria: University of Pretoria Press, 2005), 205.

10. Tropical diseases, especially malaria, devastated missionary personnel in tropical Africa and Asia. The experience of the Basel Mission in the early nineteenth century was typical. The three-year survival rate for missionaries on the Gold Coast from 1828 to 1843 was 20 percent. After the 1850s the survival rate increased dramatically. In the first twenty-five years (1828–53), two-thirds of the missionaries had either died, left the mission, or were removed. From Jon Miller's *Missionary Zeal and Institutional Control: Organizational Contradictions in the Base Mission on the Gold Coast, 1828–1917* (Grand Rapids: Eerdmans, 2003), 21.

11. There is no clear consensus on the terminology, but most historians appreciate a marked difference between the "awakenings," or renewals, of the eighteenth and early nineteenth centuries and the revivalism of the later nineteenth century. One of the main differences was a

L. Moody (1837–99). Moody worked in the streets of Chicago for the YMCA, but later became a great revival preacher, both in the United States and in Great Britain. By the 1880s he was also speaking to university students every summer at Northfield in Massachusetts, although Moody himself never attended college. From these gatherings, another movement was birthed: the Student Volunteer Movement for Foreign Missions (SVM). Traveling secretaries would help to organize university students into mission fellowships, and these students were challenged to make a commitment to serve as a foreign missionary. The international network of student fellowships became the Student Christian Federation in 1895, which became the incubator for mission and later ecumenical leaders. This was an international mission movement among students, and therefore mission led by laity, not clerics or even denominational leaders.

Societies multiplied and diversified as movements outgrew their structures, and as more and more Western Christians accepted the claims of mission advocates that the Great Commission was still a valid call for modern disciples. Other motives had priority in earlier centuries, but in the nineteenth and early twentieth centuries, Matthew 28:16–20 became the primary motivation. Mission became mainstream and mainline, finding expression in every way imaginable. Children's missionary organizations were formed to help raise the awareness of the needs for Sunday school classes in Africa and Asia. Women's missionary societies were formed to reach women who could not be reached by men because they lived in harems or zenanas in Asia and Africa. It is estimated that approximately 60 percent of the missionaries sent out by the end of the century were women. Many single women went out with the women's societies, while almost all male missionaries were married (their wives also considered full-time missionaries).[12] What makes this statistic even more surprising is that, until 1822, we do not have record of a single woman ever serving as a Protestant missionary.[13] Roman Catholic female religious orders were the parallel to the Protestant women's societies. Before the 1850s, almost all foreign missionary work, both Catholic and Protestant, was considered the primary responsibility of men. Societies were also formed to reach China (the China Inland Mission), the Sudan (Sudan Interior Mission), Africa (Africa

---

theology that determined a practice. Whereas Jonathan Edwards was "surprised" by the work of God, Charles Finney, in his *Lectures on Revival*, tells how a revival can be inspired (not quite "produced"). Revivals often work toward a particular response and effect.

12. Dana Robert, *American Women in Mission: A Social History of Their Thought and Practice* (Macon, GA: Mercer University Press, 1996). See also Dana Robert, "Missionaries Sent and Received Worldwide, 1910–2010," in David Barrett and Kenneth Ross, eds., *Atlas of Global Christianity* (Edinburgh: Edinburgh University Press, 2010), 258. In 1910, 55 percent of Protestant and 62 percent of Roman Catholic missionaries were female.

13. Betsy Stockton, educated and then released from her slavery by President Ashabel Green of the College of Princeton, was the first single missionary as well as the first black and former-slave missionary. She served as an educational missionary first in the Sandwich Islands (Hawaii), then in Canada (with indigenous children), and finally in Philadelphia.

Inland Mission), South America (Andes Evangelical Mission), and some societies focused just on two or three areas but in different continents.[14]

All of this activity meant that more and more areas of the world were being exposed to missionary outreach, and at the same time being exposed to Western culture and imperialism. There was a constant increase in activity, funding, organization, and zeal in the Western churches throughout the nineteenth and early twentieth centuries. Missionary outreach became big business—well organized with plans, consultations, and greater centralization of activities. In some ways, it was reflecting the culture of the late Industrial Age and the newly arising Gilded Age. The church was becoming (or at least looking more like) a powerful multinational corporation—spreading the glad tidings in the form of churches, mission stations, hospitals, and schools. The impact was seen in a multitude of ways, both intended and unintended. Churches were connecting with each other in cooperative ventures. Women became Christian leaders and pioneers in reform and even church planting—initially through revivals and later through mission societies. The missionary momentum was set by revivals and awakenings, but by the middle of the nineteenth century it was given a further push by secular powers of global economics and colonialism. Colonial powers had a checkered relationship with missionaries, but in the high Victorian Era missionaries began to look to empires as their advocates.

The Sticky Problem of Mission, Colonialism, and Power

One of the key themes of this period, the period of high imperialism, is the relationship between missions (and missionaries) and Western colonialism. Nineteenth- and twentieth-century missionary work was prompted by renewals or awakenings at home, but this was not the only factor in its growth, for there were awakenings in the early eighteenth century that did not express themselves in foreign missionary activity. The second element that made the missionary movement possible was global trading and colonialism. To put it plainly, colonialism made travel to the "mission field" possible. Increased contact with China, the Ivory Coast, India, and later with Japan and Korea awakened the conscience of Western Christians both to need and to possibility. Missionary literature included many drawings, etchings, and then photos of the "unreached natives" in faraway places. Thus, there was a push (awakenings) and a pull (images) to the missionary movement.

This chapter begins with the ominous date of 1842 for a reason. This was the end of the First Opium War. With the end of the war, treaty ports were opened to foreign trade, to foreign residence, and to foreign missionaries. In fact, China was forced open for trade and for missionaries by foreign gunships. Coming

14. For example, the United Presbyterian Church in North America had only three mission fields: India, Ethiopia, and Sudan.

off of those ships were opium traders with their kegs of Indian-produced opium, and missionaries with their Hong Kong–printed tracts and Scriptures. In the eyes of the Chinese, there was little difference between the two drugs. Most of the Protestant missionaries saw this opportunity as a divine work of God; China had been resistant to the gospel for centuries, and now it was "opened." Roman Catholics viewed it a little differently. Although missionary work had been difficult after the "Rites Controversy," Roman Catholic missionaries had continued to work secretly, and at times more openly, with their many congregations along the coastal regions. Now, however, a massive influx of missionaries began. India may have been the "jewel in the crown" for the British Empire, but China was certainly the jewel for Western missionaries. More than any other country, China captured the imagination of Westerners as the ultimate mission field. David Livingstone became a famous explorer and missionary in Africa, but he, like many European missionaries, wanted to go to China. Before 1842, LMS, Presbyterian, or Anglican missionaries would settle for working with the Chinese in Malaya or Indonesia, building a "wall of light" around China—but once China "opened," missionaries flooded into the country. Malaya and Indonesia decreased as China increased. Of course, it was colonial guns that had made this benevolent work possible.

It is tempting, therefore, to see missionary work as riding on the coattails of Western colonialism. While missionaries are not imperialists, they are often pragmatists. When it seemed difficult to move out farther, to go to new regions, or to reach new peoples, missionaries would find a way. Missionaries had been attempting to reach the Chinese long before the Opium Wars, and so the "Unequal Treaties" were seen as answers to missionary prayers. Catholic missionaries, however, even during the "closed" century, continued to find ways to minister to their flocks—and so the Roman Catholic Church continued to grow during the last half of the eighteenth century in China. The first Protestant missionary, Robert Morrison, arrived (illegally, we might add) in 1807 to study Chinese and to begin translating the Bible into Chinese. British vessels would not take him to China, so he sailed to New York, where it took him a month to get the support and security of an American vessel to take him to China. At that time, any Chinese person teaching their language to a foreigner could be killed for sedition; both colonial powers and Chinese officials resisted missionary incursions. Ironically, in the coming decades it would be the missionary knowledge of the Chinese language that made secular (colonial) treaties possible. These early missionaries were devout linguists and spiritual pragmatists. One of the first medical missionaries, American Methodist Peter Parker, helped to translate the second of the "Unequal Treaties," the 1844 Treaty of Wanghia (Wangxia), which prevented Americans from being involved in the opium trade, but also allowed missionaries to take up residence in China. In general, missionaries were the earliest presence in inland regions, they knew the culture and language better than most colonialists, and they had very different goals from the traders. Their commitments to reach the Chinese at times compromised the integrity of their message, but, in general, multinational companies and colonial governments resisted missionary initiative—unless they could use them. Colonialists were also pragmatists but with different goals in mind.

Again, we must not confuse missionaries with traders, or evangelists with soldiers. Missionaries used trading companies and governments when it was convenient or necessary, but they were often excluded by those same people. In fact, their motives for traveling to Asia or Africa often brought the missionaries into direct conflict with colonial governments and trading companies. In contrast to common assumptions of the past half of a century, it is clear today that colonialists and colonial companies harmed as much as aided the work of missionaries. Without going into this long history, a few examples will make the point. It is common knowledge that the Portuguese sailors and soldiers were a great embarrassment to the Jesuits, Augustinians, and others working in Asia, Africa, and Brazil. Even when the kings of Portugal and Spain were patrons of Catholic mission, their support was less than adequate and their representation as Christian colonialists less than pristine. Many missionaries sought to distance themselves from their fellow Europeans. Roberto de Nobili finally came to the conclusion that missionaries must cut themselves off from identification with the *parangi* (foreigners) if the gospel was to have any impact upon India. Portuguese sailors were poor models of Christian virtues.

After about a century of Portuguese domination in the coastlines of Africa and Asia, the Dutch were in the ascendancy, displacing Portuguese Catholics at every port and town they could. Dutch Protestants, with little concern for missionary outreach, set back Roman Catholic missions more than any African or Asian government. Catholics were slaughtered and churches closed across two continents. The Dutch had no funding or structure for missionary outreach, and so their immediate impact upon mission was to cause decline. In the East Indies, the Dutch were careful to protect Muslim rulers and their religion. In a similar fashion, the British East India Company would not support missions at all in the early decades. And so William Carey had to begin his missionary work on Danish (Lutheran) lands in India—even though there was a great expanse of British soil in India by the time he arrived in 1793. As late as 1874, the British (no longer a private trading company) continued to protect Muslims from Christian missionaries. The 1874 Treaty of Pangkor (Malaya), between the British and the Sultan of Perak, confirmed the local ruler and promised him both British advisers and British protection. The treaty also promised that the local customs and religion would be respected. Thus, missionary work was proscribed in the Malay states, except among the Chinese and the Indians. The British colonial government established a precedent—protecting Muslims from evangelism—which continues to this day. Colonialists and missionaries were all people of their age, seeking to influence the world of "lower civilizations." Missionaries sought to influence for the sake of Christ and his church, planting churches and developing leaders for these churches. Colonialists built empires for earthly kings and secular kingdoms and, in doing so, used local people to serve the profits and power of the Dutch, or British, or French. At times these contrasting motives were fortuitously aligned, but more often they were in conflict with each other.

Africa, outside of a few coastal areas, is a special case because colonial empires came so late to Africa. Whereas Christians were actively planting churches, schools, and monasteries in the Americas, China, India, and Southeast Asia in the Roman Catholic period and the early Protestant period, the interior of Africa was not brought under imperial control until the last decades of the nineteenth century. For most of Africa, the European colonial period was less than a century long. Coming as late as it did, missionary attitudes in most of Africa were shaped by the newer ideas of social Darwinism and the racist attitudes of its cultural superiority. Once again, missionaries preceded the colonial advance, and we see this most clearly in the life of David Livingstone (1813–73). Livingstone was appointed by the LMS to work in South Africa, but his resistance to slavery—both Arab and Dutch Afrikaner—resulted in the destruction of his mission station in South Africa in 1851. He was convinced that the ongoing Arab (Omani Muslim) slave trade was an evil that must be resisted. As a missionary, he concluded that only Western colonial trade could put an end to Muslim slave trading. Thus, his explorations were driven by more than a personal goal to map the interior of Africa; he sought to open up intercontinental trade in Africa to bring the benefits of trade and Western science and knowledge to Africans. Thus, his call for Christianity, civilization, and commerce was a Christian call to elevate the life of Africans and at the same time resist their enslavement by Arab traders. Seen in this light, his mission was holistic and complex—even if Victorian.

The work and zeal of missionaries opened up Africa to Western European nations. Coastal areas were already set up as colonies by the Portuguese, Spanish, British, and Dutch, but through a series of meetings in Berlin, home of a new rising power (Germany), Africa was systematically carved up by the Europeans to harvest minerals and profit European markets. In 1884, German Chancellor Otto von Bismarck called a conference in Berlin to coordinate the European colonization of Africa. At the time, 80 percent of Africa was not yet under European control. By 1914 the European countries of Belgium, Great Britain, France, Portugal, Italy, Germany, and Spain had carved Africa into fifty nations—with very little regard for the over one thousand ethnic nations and languages already in existence. The Berlin Conference mandated that countries could not lay claim to a region unless it was actually occupied—so suddenly European immigrants began arriving in inland regions to "claim" their territories. In general, this occupation and subjugation of Africa drained the land of minerals, impoverished local people, disrupted local nations, allowed both missionaries and traders to penetrate deeper into the continent, and helped to create the contemporary political and economic problems that plague Africa today. European colonialism in Africa, especially in Rhodesia (Zimbabwe, a private kingdom of a single British entrepreneur), South Africa, and the Belgium Congo, was a violent, oppressive, and unjust period of colonial history. During this shameful period of history, missionary work often stands out as a civilizing and salting influence in the midst of the oppression and subjugation of local peoples and cultures. And yet, Christian missionaries too often shared the same superior attitudes as the colonialists—looking down on local cultural expressions, importing the forms as well as the content of the Christian religion to Africa. Appreciation of African cultural life came late to missionaries working under colonial governments in Africa. Ogbu Kalu has expressed some of this missionary dilemma well: "As Christianity was locked into the civilization project, the white image of black people darkened, creating the turbulent responses that characterized the century and embedded the contemporary issues of gospel, cultural authenticity and race in African Christianity."[15]

Mission Theories and Practice: 1840s to 1910

After the first decades of the nineteenth century, missionary work began to come under scrutiny and study. Formal study of mission theory and practice came later,[16] but early theological reflection came from two sources: the missionaries on "the field" and the mission secretaries back in the West. Most of the earliest missionaries were like William Carey—committed Christians with little formal education but uncommon and innate ability. Driven mostly by biblical responsibility, they developed a theology of their work within their practice. They were also remarkably astute observers of local cultures, and so we have a continuous line of early anthropological and religious observations from the sixteenth- and seventeenth-century Roman Catholic writers through the nineteenth-century Catholic and Protestant missionaries.[17] The modern study of missiology owes its origins to missionary reflection and scholarship, and yet this study came very late, resting uneasily in the divinity schools of the West.[18] Mission theology was developing *in medias missio* (in the midst of mission). Here we will focus on seven major themes of that reflection.

15. Ogbu Kalu, "Christianity in Africa in the 19th Century," in *Clio in a Sacred Garb: Essays on Christian Presence and African Responses* (Trenton, NJ: Africa World Press, 2008), 112.

16. See the introduction to this book for a discussion of the earliest faculty positions in mission studies.

17. See "The Nineteenth-Century Missionary as Scholar," in Andrew Walls, *The Missionary Movement in Christian History* (Maryknoll, NY: Orbis Books, 1996), 187–98.

18. The classic study of the early period of mission study in theological education is still O. G. Myklebust's *The Study of Missions in Theological Education* (Oslo: Egede Instituttet, 1955).

1. *Views of Non-Western Peoples: From Sympathetic to Racist*

Most of the earliest Protestant missionaries came to the field with an ecclesially and biblically informed view of the other, rather than a view informed by university education. There was a basic understanding that every person and every race should hear the gospel, and that meant that different people groups needed to understand it in their own language. Thus, from the outset there was an innate value attached to newly encountered cultures and people (God's Word can inhabit their language), even if the smells, habits, or religious practices of these cultures at times seemed abhorrent to missionaries. In early missionary records we see very little of the extreme racist and supremacist language that we see by the end of the nineteenth century and into the twentieth century.[19] Greater wealth, working with expanding empires and the academic discipline of social science (linked with social Darwinism), changed missionary perspective. The first two of these factors are common knowledge, but the third may have been the most important. By the end of the nineteenth century, and with the impact of the university-centered Student Volunteer Movement, missionaries were arriving in Africa and Asia with much better education—and part of that better education included having studied the social sciences. The rising study of social sciences was dominated at that time by a view of progress and development applied to nations, civilizations, and races. The same confident view of social progress described by James Dennis,[20] missionary to the Middle East, in his *Christian Mission and Social Progress*, led others to talk about the "white man's burden," and still others to conclude that some races were superior to others. Western "civilization" was seen as Christian civilization and Western mission was understood as extending the full benefits of that Christian civilization to other cultures. Missionaries, compared to colonialists, took their civilizing mission with a grain of salt. The worst of the scientific view of racial or cultural superiority led colonizers and imperialists like King Leopold II to actions such as the genocidal practices in the Kongo, and led Cecil Rhodes to express the hubris of world domination this way: "I contend that we are the first race in the world, and that the more of the world we inhabit the better it is for the human race."[21] Rhodes's policies in Rhodesia opened the door for large migrations of British to the best lands in south and southeast Africa. Rhodes was resisted by many indigenous leaders, and by many missionaries.

19. David Bosch discusses the different attitudes of missionaries toward race, and more specifically nationalism and colonialism, that developed in the period of high imperialism between 1880 and 1920 (*Transforming Mission: Paradigm Shifts in the Theology of Mission* [Maryknoll, NY: Orbis Books, 1991], 302–13).

20. James Dennis, *Christian Mission and Social Progress: A Sociological Study of Foreign Missions*, 3 vols. (New York: Fleming H. Revell, 1897–1906).

21. Klaus Koschorke, Frieder Ludwig, Mariano Delgado, and Roland Spliesgart, *A History of Christianity in Asia, Africa, and Latin America, 1450–1990* (Grand Rapids: Eerdmans, 2007), 208.

Missionaries resisted such theology and practice, even as they breathed the same air of racial and cultural superiority.[22]

By the time of the critical Edinburgh World Missionary Conference, racist views, attached to a sympathetic awareness of the "white man's burden," had penetrated the missionary conscience. Julius Richter, pastor, missiologist, and future professor in Berlin, spoke at the Student Volunteer Convention in Rochester, New York, before attending the Edinburgh Conference as a delegate. Just six months before Edinburgh 1910, he called students in America to engage in "the evangelization of primitive races, all those dark, dull peoples, low in civilization, even lower in religious and moral standards. . . . What a disadvantage it is for modern missions that their spheres of work among the primitive races are so widely scattered and diversified."[23] Richter was one of the key continental delegates at Edinburgh. Such language was not the dominant view, but it was, nonetheless, quite a common assumption, not only among Germans.

2. *Confrontation with Other Religions*

A second major theme in the development of mission thinking in the nineteenth and early twentieth centuries is the issue of religions: particularly Islam and Hinduism.[24] The late eighteenth and early nineteenth centuries were a period of Islamic resurgence in Africa. In East Africa, as we have noted, Omani Muslim traders and other Arab Muslims were extending their trade and influence. In West Africa, there was a revival of Islam among the Fulani, including jihads against indigenous religious practices that had become part of African Islam. One "renewer of the faith" (*mujaddid*), al-Hajj Umar ibn Sa'id Tal (Umar Tall: 1797–1864), was driven by his sense of calling as a *mujaddid*, to spread and revive the faith. His conquests of other African regions were despised by some, but his resistance to French colonialism earned him the respect of the Senegalese and the Gambians. Umar Tall was a religious warrior, both with the sword and with the pen. His famous written work *Rimah* had the full title, *The Book of the Lances of the League of the Compassionate (Allah) at the Throats of the Satanic Party.* The satanic party was the partially converted and worldly Muslims of the region. Christian missionaries and

22. As an example of the tension, we see this story: In 1895 the African Christian King Khama of the Bamangwato traveled with LMS missionaries to speak against Cecil Rhodes's control over their land, as he had extended his control over Matabeleland. Khama (1835–1923) ruled his people as a Christian king, paving the way for both the modernization and Christianization that laid a foundation for the modern nation of Botswana. We might add that Rhodesia, now Zimbabwe, has had a much more contentious history.

23. Julius Richter, "The Decisive Hour in the History of Protestant Missions," in *Students and the Present Missionary Crisis* (New York: SVMFM, 1910), 119.

24. In chap. 8 I will talk about theology of religions in general, and in chap. 9 I discuss religions and community.

mission leaders in Europe, aware of the resurgence of Islam in Africa and the defense of Muslim Turkey against Russia in the Crimean War, held out little hope that Muslims could be reached by missionaries. In the 1860s there were already figures such as the explorer Richard Burton who went so far as to anticipate an Islamic conquest of Africa. The editor of the proceedings of the 1888 London missionary conference virtually took this "discouraging fact" for granted.[25] This was the context for the development of missionary thinking about missionary work in Islamic contexts: an uncharacteristic pessimism in the age of progress.

Turning to the Middle East, early missionary work was almost exclusively with the ancient churches, rather than with the majority Muslim population. This was in part a missionary model: to work with existing churches, bringing about renewal, which would (following the Western pattern) bring about a renewed interest in missionary outreach. The Muslims would be reached by revived Orthodox churches, or so many thought. By the last decades of the nineteenth century this idea was abandoned, as Orthodox churches strongly resisted both the attempted Protestantization (especially the introduction of newly printed Bibles) and the Romanization of their congregations. Some missions developed specific strategies that would address Muslim trade and resist Muslim subjugation of African peoples. David Livingstone's call for commerce in Africa, we have noted, was his holistic missionary approach to slavery and Islam. If there were no other economic alternatives, the Muslim-dominated slave trade would continue. It was a matter of Christian duty to resist this trade, with more noble, viable, and moral trade. We might question the results, but the sentiment showed his Christian concern for Africans, as well as for Africa. Many Christian missionaries called for European nations to rise up and resist the spread of Islam. In contrast, most colonialist powers did not want to insult or disturb local communities (especially Muslim) in their effort to promote business profits. The British and French were notorious for protecting Muslim communities from evangelism.[26]

In 1868, in North Africa, we see another response to Islam in the founding of the Missionaries of our Lady of Africa, better known as the White Fathers by the French Archbishop of Algiers, Father Charles Lavigerie (1825–92). Lavigerie's vision was to resist the French colonial government's policy of quiet tolerance of Islam. His vision was to use his base in Algiers to evangelize all of Africa. He founded a society for men in 1868, and in the next year a missionary society for women, to promote this vision. Lavigerie received inspiration from Daniel Comboni's plan for the "Rebirth of Africa" or, as

25. Andrew Porter, "Evangelicalism, Islam, and Millennial Expectation in the Nineteenth Century," in Dana Robert, ed., *Converting Colonialism: Visions and Realities in Mission History, 1706–1914* (Grand Rapids: Eerdmans, 2008), 67.

26. Generally speaking, the British would not allow missionary work among local Muslim populations in Africa and Asia. The Treaty of Pangkor (1874) is just one example.

Camboni expressed it, to "Save Africa through Africa." Lavigerie's missionaries wore white, like the Algerian Arabs, and wore Rosary beads around their necks that looked like the Muslim *mesbaha* beads—only with a cross at the end. They spread to equatorial Africa, campaigning against slavery. Committed to the evangelization of Africa by Africans, he founded one of the first seminaries in Africa, and he founded other schools for the education of the poor. Understandably, the first three African Catholic bishops were all trained by the White Fathers. Lavigerie's strategy of centering the mission in Carthage and Algiers rather than in France, his adaptation to local cultural forms, and his focus on African agency have earned him the honor of being the most innovative Roman Catholic mission strategist of the nineteenth century. Here was a strategy that resisted cultural domination, colonial domination, and Islamic domination of Africa.

Protestant missionary ideas about Islam were shaped through their experiences in Egypt and the Middle East. Missionary work among Muslims was creative and strong, even if its results were meager at best. From the inception of its missionary work in Egypt from 1854 until 1880, the American Presbyterian mission had only seventy-five converts, mostly from very poor families. By 1900 the total had only grown to 140.[27] One of the most important strategies was the use of literature, and so missionaries printed tracts and booklets in Arabic, and the Van Dyke translation of the Bible was considered the most important event for reaching Muslims.[28] Schools were also used to attract Muslim children and their families. Thousands of students did enroll, but like the distribution of literature (even through Egyptian Christian hands) the response to the gospel was minimal, though the schools were greatly appreciated.

If tracts and elementary education were an approach to Muslims at a grassroots level, then the work of scholars was an attempt to reach the leaders of Muslim cultures. Egypt, with the largest and best-educated Arab Muslim population, was a center for Christian academic missionary work among Muslims. Part of the strategy of the educational work was to reach Muslim scholars, such as graduates of Al-Azhar University in Cairo, and then train them to be evangelists among Muslims in the Middle East. This seemed a good strategy on paper, but there were, in fact, few who became well-known evangelists. The brothers Mikha'il (formerly Mohammad) and Kamiel had

27. From Andrew Watson, *The American Mission in Egypt, 1854–1896* (Pittsburgh: United Presbyterian Board of Publication, 1904), 360, as quoted in Tharwat Wahba's PhD thesis, "The Practice of Mission in Egypt: A Historical Study of the Integration Between the American Mission and the Evangelical Church of Egypt, 1854–1970" (London School of Theology, 2008), 86. Some of the information below comes from Dr. Wahba's careful analysis.

28. The Van Dyke Arabic New Testament was completed in 1860 and the Old Testament in 1865. Funded by the American Bible Society and the American Syrian Mission, it was begun by Eli Smith and completed by Nasif al Yaziji, Boutros al Bustani, and Yusuf al-Asir under the direction of Cornelius Van Allen Van Dyke. Literature that was produced to reach Muslims bore titles such as "The Witness of the Qu'ran," "The Guidance," and "The Balance of Truth."

been students in Al-Azhar, converted, and then became effective evangelists of the American Mission in Egypt. Another convert, Ahmad Fahmy, had to leave the country so his family would not kill him. He became a medical doctor after studying in Scotland and then served, safely, as an LMS missionary in China—a prophetic witness for future missionary work from the non-Western world. For the Anglican Church in Egypt, it took a Turkish Muslim convert, John Ahmed Tewfik, to help guide the way for the Anglican witness to Muslims.

Among the scholars of Islam working in the Middle East, two of the best known were Temple Gairdner (1873–1928) and Samuel Zwemer (1867–1952). The first an Anglican scholar, the second a Reformed (and later Presbyterian) missionary practitioner and scholar, they represent the gentle and the direct approaches to Christian witness among Muslims. One of the most accomplished scholars of Arabic of his time, Gairdner's approach was to make the gospel beautiful and poetic rather than have it come down on Muslims like a club or hammer. "We need a song note in our message to the Muslims, not the dry cracked note of disputation, but the song note of joyous witness, tender invitation."[29] He followed his own advice, creating music, drama, and poetry, and used all these plus pictures to present Christian teachings to Muslims. Gairdner also brought the Episcopal Publishing House to Cairo and produced *Orient and Occident*, a periodical that became his mouthpiece and the world's window into his singularly creative approach to mission in an Islamic context. Zwemer's approach was more direct and confrontational. He was very knowledgeable about Islamic history and texts and used them to point out weaknesses and inconsistencies. He was critical of the lack of interest and effort that the American Mission showed in evangelistic work among Muslims. Even though their approaches were different, Gairdner was involved in getting Zwemer to Egypt from Arabia, and the two helped found a Cairo Study Center, in which missionaries could study Islam and Arabic (later it became the School of Oriental Studies). Much of the later academic approach to Islam turned into religion departments in schools like the American University of Cairo.

Hinduism had always been resistant to Christian missionary activity for two reasons: caste required a racist or classist approach to mission, and pluralism made a mockery of "proclamation." The concept of caste separated all of human existence, while Christian work sought to bring people together in community. Recognizing caste meant accepting what the gospel sought to break down (Eph. 2:11–22). Some of the early Jesuits, however, as we have noted, tried to reach the upper castes directly—but the acceptance of caste distinctions had limited impact. Those who recognized the value and power of

29. Quoted from the *Biographical Dictionary of Christian Missions*, ed. Gerald Anderson (New York: Macmillan, 1998), s.v. "Gairdner, Temple."

Christian teaching were those who had the most to gain from conversion: the *dalits*, or those who were not even part of the scheduled castes ("outcastes"). Missionary reflection on caste and approaches in the Hindu context were redirected when mass movements to Christianity began late in the nineteenth century, mostly among the *dalits* and tribals. Missionary activity bifurcated, some working among the most needy, encouraging mass movements to Christianity, while others focused on academic discussion and dialogue with educated Brahmins. We noted in the last chapter that early Christian missionaries in India unwittingly inspired a Hindu Renaissance through their literary and educational work. This movement continued through the end of the nineteenth and into the twentieth century. The missionary scholar J. N. Farquhar (1861–1929) expressed explicitly a theology that most missionaries probably supported implicitly. He called Christianity *The Crown of Hinduism* (1917). Hinduism, especially after a century of absorbing many of the challenges and concepts of Christianity, could no longer be easily dismissed as demonic—or as something to be displaced. Values and insights in Hinduism, possibly like the law of Israel, found its crown in Jesus Christ—the fulfillment of the law and ritual. It was not until the later part of the twentieth century that a more thoroughgoing Christian theology of religions and dialogue would appear.

3. Indigenous Leadership: The Three-Self Principle

Although limited in number, the work of local Muslim converts in evangelism proved to be effective in the Middle East. This raises one of the major theological issues of the late nineteenth and early twentieth centuries in missionary thought: the role of foreign and local support in building up an indigenous church. There are four Protestant mission theorists—two administrators, one missionary, and one missionary-pastor theorist—who are generally given credit for developing the concept of "three-self" (self-government, self-support, and self-propagation) in missionary work: Henry Venn (1796–1873), of the Anglican Church Missionary Society in Britain; Rufus Anderson (1796–1880), a Congregationalist of the American Board of Commissioners for Foreign Mission; Roland Allen (1868–1947), an Anglo-Catholic with Pentecostal sensitivities; and John L. Nevius (1829–93), missionary to Shandong, China, from the American Presbyterian Church. There is no need to go into detail regarding the nuances of their approaches, but it is necessary to see how important this discussion and debate was to missionary work. The majority of problems in missionary work were brought on by the differing contexts in which missionaries worked. In most places, the Western missionary had much more money, was considered of much greater value, and had much more education than local people. Thus, missionary societies could build large mission stations that were self-contained communities. With such large and expensive infrastructures, it became hard to "turn over" the control (and the assets) to local people who had less education and less experience as administrators and church leaders. Thus, control of the church remained, for long periods of time, in missionary hands—with little understanding as to how the local people would ever be able to lead their own local churches.

The Congregational mission "tyrant"[30] (as he was called) Rufus Anderson pioneered a robust theology to correct this problem. His theology of mission was birthed during his famous 1854–55 deputation trip to visit mission stations (as they were called) in Syria, India, and Constantinople. On this trip, he convinced the missionaries of the logic of his "recommendations to break up the large stations, found village churches, ordain native pastors for them, and give up English language secondary schools in favor of vernacular-language schools."[31] Anderson had a clear vision of what the missionary task should be, later expressed as the mission's policy: "Missions are instituted for the spread of a scriptural, self-propagating Christianity. This is their only aim." By 1869, Anderson was uncompromising in his belief that the Pauline model needed to be imitated today, even among poorer people, for the early church was also made up mainly of poor people. Anderson wrote:

> The means employed were spiritual; namely the gospel for Christ. The power relied upon for giving efficacy to these means was divine; namely the promised aid of the Holy Spirit. The main success was among the members of the middle and lower classes of society; and the responsibilities for self-government, self-support, and self-propagation were thrown at once upon the several churches.[32]

The concern for "three-self" churches and the focus on the lower classes would be resisted by many missionaries, but it became a standard phrase in mission thinking. Related to self-support was the concern that education not be elitist; that is, it must not be done in English, but in local languages and local dialects. Again, this would be a major point of conflict in the larger missions as education competition developed and higher education was promoted—using English. The language or terms of "three-self" used by Anderson were used in the same way in 1949 and 1950—eighty years later—by the founders of the Three-Self Patriotic Movement (TSPM):[33] Wu Yaozong, Han Wenzao, and others in the People's Republic of China.

30. Anderson ended up serving for forty-four years as an ABCFM mission administrator and became one of the best-known mission strategists in the world. Church leaders recognized that he would make a greater contribution to the newly started ABCFM, and so he became the "tyrant who ruled the American Board, the Prudential Committee, and the missionaries with an iron hand." See R. Pierce Beaver, "The Legacy of Rufus Anderson," in *Occasional Bulletin of Missionary Research*, July 1977, 94.

31. Ibid.

32. Rufus Anderson, *Foreign Missions: Their Relations and Claims* (New York: Scribner, 1869), 61.

33. The partner arm of the China Christian Council.

Other theorists had different emphases, but the same overall concern. Venn talked about the intentional "euthanasia" of the mission from the very start; all missionary work should be designed from the beginning to be turned over to the young Christians of that culture, so that the missionaries can leave. Nevius, from his early work, established a church and leadership training program and moved away in less than three years, handing the ministry over to fresh converts. He wrote about his plan in a letter to his board in 1861, and in a series of articles in the *Chinese Recorder* in 1886,[34] that were later reprinted as a book entitled *Methods of Mission Work* (1895). The articles, written for missionaries working in China, are very carefully nuanced in their understanding of work and relationships. In them, Nevius makes a direct attack on the old way of doing missions: paying foreign agents, paying for buildings, relying on foreign missionaries to do most of the evangelism, building big institutions, and so on. He was especially vehement about training church leaders in their local villages rather than sending them away for three or four years of education in a big city. Thus, the three-self principles were rooted in indigenous localized education. Nevius's ideas were not often applied in China, except in the province in which he and his wife worked (Shandong), but they were applied by Presbyterians working in Korea, especially by the Underwoods and Moffetts in northern Korea.[35]

4. Modernity and Mission: Planting Churches and Developing Institutions

As we move from the middle of the nineteenth century through the early twentieth century, one of the major shifts that begins to take place is the development of more "scientific" approaches to mission. With the advent of medical research, the discovery of harmful bacteria, and the rise of the social sciences came new approaches and, therefore, new understandings of missionary work. Medicine and education, which had previously been important tools for missionaries, began to become the goal of many missionaries and missions. Hospitals and schools were the main purpose of many of the missions of this time period—something easily measured by looking at the budgets of mission societies. Schools were expensive to run, and they required a constant flow of money to keep them open. Educational work started out with basic primary education for literacy and Bible knowledge. These primary

34. This was the year of the founding of the Student Volunteer Movement in America, which would send thousands of well-educated missionaries to China in the next decades. It was just two years after Horace Allen left Shanghai to become the first medical missionary, and first Presbyterian, to work in Korea.

35. For a fuller discussion of the Nevius Method in Korea, see Samuel Hugh Moffett, *History of Christianity in Asia* (San Francisco: HarperSanFrancisco, 1992), 2:536, as well as Allen D. Clark's *History of the Korean Church* (Seoul: Christian Literature Society of Korea, 1961), 112–16.

schools developed into a network of high schools, and eventually colleges were founded for the training of local doctors, teachers, nurses, accountants, and pastors. These colleges became universities in the second decade of the twentieth century, imitating the research universities of the West. Conflicts arose within mission societies because the largest voting bloc on the mission stations would often be the university faculty. Most of these faculty members came to Japan, China, India, or Kenya to teach a subject—not to carry out missionary activity. Purposes and goals began to diverge.

It was in this environment, in the late nineteenth and early twentieth centuries, that both Protestant and Catholic missions and religious orders began to see divisive issues coming to the fore. Some of the issues that brought about division included the requirement of attending chapel services or Bible classes, the way that the Bible was taught at the colleges and seminaries, and the amount of money that missions should spend for campus buildings versus church planting.

Colonial powers made matters more complex when they began to standardize education in their overseas lands, often limiting or forbidding religious education in mission schools that received government support. Colonial governments did not want to anger local Hindus or Muslims. Educationalists reflected much of the social Darwinism of John Dewey's educational theory.[36] Most missionaries, on the other hand, reflected more of John R. Mott's evangelistic zeal: "The Evangelization of the World in this Generation."[37] Both were modern, progressive, and optimistic. The flowering of modernity in Western culture was a slow and steady growth that produced the healing power of antibiotics (for much of modernity serves humanity well), but also the blight of two world wars and a Gulag.

Modernity was magnified in missionary contexts. The Western Enlightenment confidence in human ability brought with it skepticism of religious belief and the habits and values that it engendered. Missionaries after the beginning of the twentieth century carried both confidence and doubt, both secular abilities and religious critiques. The first two decades of the twentieth century, the decades of "the Fundamentals" and of the Presbyterian controversy,[38] were also the decades of mission controversy. The situation was global, and there are examples from every continent. The observation of a Christian university

36. In 1919 John Dewey was invited by his Chinese and Japanese graduates to lecture on education in China and Japan. See Scott W. Sunquist, "American Christian Mission and Education: Henry W. Luce, William R. Harper, and the Secularization of Christian Higher Education," in *Christian Mission and Education in Modern China, Japan, and Korea: Historical Studies*, ed. Jan A. B. Jongeneel et al. (Hamburg: Peter Lang, 2008), 1–14.

37. This was the watchword of the Student Volunteer Movement. See Dana L. Robert, "The Origin of the Student Volunteer Watchword, 'The Evangelization of the World in Our Generation,'" *International Bulletin of Missionary Research* 10 (1986): 146–47.

38. Bradley J. Longfield, *The Presbyterian Controversy, 1922–1936: Fundamentalists, Modernists, and Moderates* (New York: Oxford University Press, 1991).

professor in Uruguay in 1916 provides us with one. Professor Monteverde was showing the future missionary John Mackay some of the intricacies of student ministry in Latin America.

> Monteverde described and discussed the student problem in South America, as it had never been opened up to Mackay before, and Mackay was greatly impressed by his ideas. Although the cultural, intellectual, and scientific standards in Latin America were high, the spiritual and moral aspects of education were not. Religion and science were opposed to each other, agnosticism prevailed in the universities, authentic Christianity is not understood because the Gospels are not studied. Monteverde realized the importance of reaching the student class through special lectures in a secular hall, through the establishment of secondary schools that would prepare students for achieving secular educational standards and also provide sound religious instruction, the YMCA program could reach university students, the basis of pure religion could be presented at Student Camps, and Christian literature could be distributed.[39]

The relationship between modern science and theology posed one of the biggest missionary challenges to date. In other contexts, however, modern science was seen as a divine "method" for mission—so science lectures, using chemistry to create surprising results, were used to attract Chinese people in villages. It is this dependence upon science and the new social sciences that provides the context for the writings of many of the mission theorists mentioned earlier. People like Roland Allen, John Nevius, and Rufus Anderson asserted that it is not our human ability or knowledge but the Holy Spirit in the local Christian that is the power and presence of Christian mission. These voices, and other similar voices, were hardly heard, however, until later. Was Christian mission about producing social and educational results, or was it still something more complex and mysterious, something more spiritual, which brought about a variety of results? For most Western missionaries before World War I, the optimism of modern knowledge was almost inebriating. But soon it was hard to separate modern approaches from the perceived goals of Christian civilization; the product was becoming the process.

Some of the newer missions, especially faith missions, focused solely on church planting and leadership training. They were expressing a side of a Western theological split that would later be called fundamentalism. The larger and wealthier missions, which were promoting higher education, had personnel on both sides of the Western debate: both modernists and fundamentalists. Many of the theological battles raging at this time (especially regarding the interpretation of Scripture and views of Jesus Christ and the atonement) were

39. Mackay, *Diary*, August 22, 1915, in Eduardo Monteverde, "Latin-American Students and Religion," *Student World* 9, no. 4 (1916): 121–32. Quoted from John Metzger, *The Hand and the Road* (Louisville: Westminster John Knox, 2010), 73–74.

also fought out within mission societies. Modernists tended to be more elitist, supporting better education (in the English language) and focused on larger urban areas. The newer faith missions—China Inland Mission, Sudan Interior Mission, South America Mission—focused on inland and less populated areas, working to establish churches and basic education only.

5. *Role of Women in Mission*

In recent decades, it has become clear that the role of women in mission, especially during the nineteenth and twentieth centuries, had been greatly undervalued. In fact, the *majority* of the missionary work was done by women during this time period. It was not feasible for women to accompany *conquistadores* to the Americas or to go with slave traders to Africa in the sixteenth and seventeenth centuries. Roman Catholic women became much more involved in missions once life was safer for single women in overseas empires. After the revival of Roman Catholic missions in the wake of Napoleon, women's religious orders became very involved in both educational work and social care for the needy. One of the great contributions of Roman Catholic women was the development of schools, and therefore literacy, for women in countries where women were excluded from education and thus prevented from having control over their own lives.

Protestant women, in most of the nineteenth century, were necessary partners in mission, and therefore Mount Holyoke College was founded in order to educate women for the mission field.[40] Fedelia Fisk (1816–64), niece of the ABCFM missionary to the Middle East Pliny Fisk, was called to missionary work while she was a teacher at Mount Holyoke. Recruited to work among "Nestorian girls" in 1843, she opened a boarding school at Urmia, applying the "Mount Holyoke Principles." Her training at Mount Holyoke prepared her to be a teacher and an evangelist. During her time working with these East Syrian Orthodox girls, she said her goal was to "make Nestorian girls better wives and mothers and to revive their Christian faith." Apparently she did so, for a number of revivals occurred during her time of tenure.

Other women began to work in the medical field, but one of the largest contributions of women was reaching out to women who could not be reached by men because of social and religious restrictions. Women formed their own mission societies and the term "women's work for women" became a common expression for the work of the newer women's societies. By the end of the nineteenth century, a Presbyterian woman in the United States could be sent by one of ten Presbyterian women's mission societies. In fact, the largest entry in Edwin Munsell Bliss's 1891 *Encyclopedia of Missions: Descriptive, Historical, Biographical, Statistical* is on "Women's Work for Women."

40. Founded by Mary Lyon in 1837 as the Mount Holyoke Female Seminary in South Hadley, Massachusetts.

There were over forty women's missionary societies in all. The involvement of women in mission, especially at such a high level, was unprecedented in Christian missions at that time.

"Women's work for women" had a global impact that would be hard to overestimate. Young girls were learning to read, and soon some of the first college-educated women in Asia and Africa were coming through programs run by Christian women. On the mission field, women converts modeled their lives on those of missionary women and soon became teachers. They were empowered to preach and teach the Bible and to plant churches. As it was in the early church, the liberation through the gospel from various social and cultural oppressions women experienced became a great attraction. Women in many mission fields began to lead the way in the growing global Christian movement. For example, one of the first female converts in Burma (Myanmar) was Ma Min Lay who, upon her conversion, imitated Ann Judson and started a school for girls. One of the first schools for girls in Asia was started by a young Christian woman who continued the missionary liberation of women, a movement rooted in missionary cultures in the West. Christianity began to challenge Asian, African, Pacific Island, and Latin American assumptions about the value and place of women in society.

6. *Missionary Motivation and Purpose*

I have already hinted at the changing or broadening of missionary motives that occurred through the nineteenth and early twentieth centuries. For most of the nineteenth century, the motivation for Christian missions was primarily the command of Scripture and, more specifically, the commission of Jesus Christ. As an act of obedience, or as an expression of the love of God, Christians were to move out in mission to those who had not heard the gospel. Modernity brought more secular, or social, motives to the fore (such as better health and education). But there were other movements of education, religious revival, and theological conflict that began to diversify motives and goals.

First, the impact of various revivals was pervasive, not only in motivating people to missionary involvement, but also in developing new motivations for mission. Revivalism in the mid-nineteenth century contained a critique of the contemporary church and a longing for the fulfillment of the Kingdom. Many "primitivist" groups arose, some orthodox and others highly syncretistic. A longing for the return of Christ, in light of present corruptions in church and society, was the foundation for Adventist groups and many holiness groups. One of the new groups, which emerged in England but had a global impact, was the Plymouth Brethren, led by John Nelson Darby (1800–82). Darby, originally Anglican (the Church of Ireland), came to realize in the late 1820s that the Kingdom of God as described in the Bible was only barely visible in the expression known as the church. He reasoned that the Bible does not describe "churches" as they exist in the modern world, but the Bible describes local house fellowships attending to the Word, breaking bread, and evangelizing their communities. He began such meetings in Dublin, simply calling them "Brethren," and ended up founding a new theological movement known as dispensationalism. Without full-time paid clergy, but with much missionary zeal, the informal gatherings spread to North America, then aboard ships, and then overseas. Brethrenism was spread mostly by laypeople, not by ordained clergy or even full-time missionaries. Besides the more informal gatherings led by lay people, the Brethren were also marked by a premillennial eschatology based on the conclusion that the church was irretrievably corrupt and that Jesus would soon come and directly establish his thousand-year reign. Pessimistic regarding the world's condition, the movement was zealous and optimistic regarding missionary work. These views were widely spread through an annotated Bible that was published with specific dispensationalist and premillennialist ideas: the Scofield Reference Bible (1909), by the American Cyrus I. Scofield. This annotated Bible not only promoted premillennialism, it was also cessasionist regarding spiritual gifts (tongues, healings, casting out demons), taught a "young earth" (4,004 years old), and outlined a clear seven ages or "dispensations" of God's work on earth. This theology was foundational for many missionaries, and soon it was an important foundation for rising fundamentalism. If the church and society were not going to be reformed in this age—that is, not until Jesus returns and does it himself—there is little reason for social engagement. Instead, the focus of mission should be on saving souls. At about the same time that this theology was developing, the great American evangelist D. L. Moody was turning from a classic form of evangelicalism to a more narrow fundamentalism. He said that he used to give families bread and a Bible on Sunday and that the next week they still needed more bread, but the Bible would last. Moody moved from the more holistic mission of the YMCA to a reductionistic form of proclamation. As he described it, "God has given me a lifeboat and said to me, 'Moody, save all you can.'" By the end of World War I, there were missionaries going overseas who were trained in newer Bible colleges and sent by newer missionary societies—all of which were dispensationalist and premillennialist.[41] Many Bible schools were founded from the 1880s through the Second World War—most with clear teachings about eschatology: Nyack College (CMA, 1882), Moody Bible Institute (1886), Boston Missionary Training School (now Gordon College, 1889), Bible Institute of Los Angeles (now Biola, 1908), Toronto Bible College (1894), and Fort Wayne Bible Institute (Mennonite, 1905).[42] This theology, motivation, and expectation was an entirely new perspective in Christian mission.

41. Moody Bible Institute, for example, still requires faculty to hold to a premillennial eschatology. Some of the newer missions were the Sudan Interior Mission, Africa Inland Mission, and South American Mission.

42. There were fewer Bible schools for mission founded in Europe. Those that were founded were founded later and seldom with the strong millennial overtones. One of the first founded for

Related to this new emphasis upon a specific eschatology, many dispensationalists, and later many Pentecostals (discussed below), looked for a special place for Israel in God's fulfillment of Scripture. According to dispensationalists, the present age (or dispensation) is the age of the church, but the church age does not negate the continuing role that God has for Israel. Israel's promises from God—including the promised land and the Messiah coming to Jerusalem (Jesus's return)—are still valid. Thus, dispensational missionaries have a special concern for Israel, and they feel that God has a special will, separate from the church, for the Jews. When the British, with the help of Zionist forces, captured Palestine in 1917 and Lord Balfour issued his declaration that there should be a "national home for the Jewish people," dispensationalists quickly became supporters of Jewish political identity. Protestant fundamentalist, Pentecostal, and dispensationalist support of Israel—as part of God's unfolding mission—continues to be a particular theme for some Christians in mission to this day.[43]

In opposition to the fundamentalist concern for saving souls and an ongoing salvific role for Israel was the social gospel movement. More elitist, and with a greater emphasis upon secular learning, the social gospel movement was led by people like Charles Sheldon (*In His Steps*, 1897), Washington Gladden, and Walter Rauschenbusch (*Christianity and the Social Crisis*, 1907).[44] Social gospel preachers were committed to a view of history that might be described as more postmillennial (although they would not identify themselves this way). According to this view, things will gradually get better—through missionary work transforming societies one step at a time. This theology called people to social transformation as both the process and the final product of missionary activity. Some missionaries held together the fundamentalist concern for "saving souls" with larger concerns for the poor and suffering in the world, but it became harder to navigate the very divisive theological terrain after the Great War. By 1932, Pearl S. Buck, recently having been awarded the Pulitzer Prize for Literature (*The Good Earth*), asked the question, "Is there a case for Foreign Missions?" Her answer was neither clear nor convincing.[45]

---

missionary purposes was H. Grattan Guinness's East London Institute for Home and Foreign Missions.

43. This special place for the Jews, and especially for Jerusalem, was a nineteenth-century preoccupation. Levi Parsons (1792–1822) said that such an eschatology inspired some Native Americans. He said some American Indians who gave $5.87 left a note that said, "To our forefathers in Jerusalem." The Jews, they believed, must be first converted before Jesus will return. From Daniel O. Morton, *Memoir of Rev. Levi Parsons, Late Missionary to Palestine* (1824; facsimile, New York: Arno, 1977), 217–18.

44. There are many books written between 1900 and 1925 on the social gospel, but a good overview is given by Shailer Matthews in *The Social Gospel* (Boston: Pilgrim Press, 1910).

45. See Grant Wacker, "Pearl S. Buck and the Waning of the Missionary Impulse," in *Church History* 72 (2003): 852–74.

Fourthly, the most thoroughgoing historical and biblical theology of mission of the period was articulated from Germany. The pioneer in this Herculean task was the German "Father of Modern Mission Study," Gustav Warneck (1834–1910). Warneck taught at the University of Halle, the home of German Pietism and the spiritual home of modern Protestant missions. David Bosch notes that he had three "large traditions" in him, all strong and thoroughly braided together: confessional Lutheran, the pietistic, and the German cultural Protestant.[46] His magnum opus, *Evangelische Missionslehre* (*Protestant Missions*, 1903),[47] contained the first thorough evaluation of missionary work, biblically, ethically, theologically, and historically considered. Bosch is correct: the work is thoroughly Lutheran, concerned with planting churches as the central task of mission; but there is also a strong Pietist flavor, a concern for culture and nation (even blood). The first part of the book gives six elements as the foundation for mission. The first and primary foundation for Christian mission is that Christianity (and even Christendom) contains the "complete and final revelation from God." Mission is a natural necessity, since Christ is the completion of all of humanity and of each person. "Redemption is God's gracious gift providing points of contact to a man fallen in sin until such a time as a stubborn rejection of this gift becomes apparent." The second foundation is ethical: the need for humans to abide by God's design for creation. Third, Warneck argues that mission is a central biblical theme—from Genesis to Revelation (Warneck is the first individual to read the Bible in this way).[48] His biblical-theological basis, mostly Pauline (especially from Ephesians) describes the church as "a new social structure transcending all natural human ties and possessing a universal character." Closely related is his fourth basis: the ecclesiastical foundation. This is a very important basis for mission, because it reminds us that missionary theology of the nineteenth and early twentieth centuries was focused upon planting churches: both the means and the end of missionary work. Warneck says, the church is "the institute of healing (*Heilsanstalt*) for all humanity. . . . She must engage in mission for her own sake [as well]. From it she exists; if she were to give it up, she would be cutting off her very own lifeline."

The fifth foundation we might call "ethnologic." Missionaries must build bridges to the religious and cultural life of others. Here Warneck describes how cultures are fallen and how missions have the responsibility "to hear the faint strains of Our Father," and raise this up, in a sense redeeming each and every culture. His final basis is the historic foundation. Warneck reflects a paternalistic age in which the missionary had a responsibility to lift people

46. David Bosch, *Witness to the World: The Christian Mission in Theological Perspective* (Atlanta: John Knox, 1980), 137.

47. The following quotations are taken from chap. 3 of Johannes Verkuyl's *Contemporary Missiology: An Introduction* (Grand Rapids: Eerdmans, 1978).

48. See the introduction to part 2 below for a discussion of the biblical story and the *missio Dei*.

and their cultures to a higher level. More than any Protestant before his age, however, he thoroughly described the missionary task and purpose.

Teaching at Halle at the same time was theologian Martin Kähler (1835–1912). Kähler gives a different perspective on missional understanding, writing as a theologian (one of the first theologians to include mission in his writings). In his *Schriften zu Christologie und Mission*, Kähler grounded mission in the atonement. In Kähler's view, from the atonement followed the Christian's debt of gratitude to bring this message to all people. Mission is an essential aspect of Christian faith, and the courage Christians have to carry out this witness comes from the knowledge that Christ has conquered death and the Kingdom is coming now. Mission, for Kähler, comes first; both the church and theology come after mission. This is true chronologically in the Bible (Paul reflects on mission, and this becomes the beginning of theology) as well as theologically (mission precedes ecclesiology). As David Bosch puts it, "Theology did not originate as a luxury in a world-dominating church; it was, rather, the result of an emergency when the church, engaged in mission, was by circumstances forced to theologize."[49] Later, Emil Brunner would express it more dramatically and memorably when he wrote, "The Church exists by mission as fire exists by burning."[50] Mission theology, purposes, and goals were undergoing great transition from the 1850s to the 1930s, and one of the biggest concerns was how to hold all of this together. Is it possible for the church to be one in mission with such a diversity of goals and such an assortment of understandings of the enterprise?

7. *Mission and Unity*

A final theological theme of this period is the relationship of Christian unity and Christian missionary activity. Although it was one of the major themes of Christianity in the twentieth century, this was a uniquely Protestant theme until the 1960s. Prior to the modern missionary movement, Protestantism had continued to divide since the days of the Protestant Reformation in the early sixteenth century. Missionary cooperation and shared concerns brought many churches and movements together as never before.

Christian Unity and Christian Mission

From the founding of the first Protestant missionary societies in 1792 (English Baptist Missionary), 1795 (the Missionary Society, later the "London Missionary Society"), and 1797 (the Netherlands Missionary Society, *Nederlandsche Zendelinggenootschap*), Protestant missionary ideas were grounded in cooperation and unity. Before the end of the first decade of the nineteenth century, English missionary William Carey was calling for a meeting of all

49. Bosch, *Witness to the World*, 138.
50. Emil Brunner, *The Word and the World* (New York: Charles Scribner's Sons, 1931), 108.

missionaries in South Africa between 1810 and 1812. The meeting did not take place, but the impulse has not been forgotten.[51] Up until the mid-1830s, missionary and mission society cooperation was taken for granted, but then denominational identity began to be a major occupational hazard to unity in mission. In about 1835 denominational mission societies began to multiply and the cooperation that was previously evident in the London Missionary Society, the Danish-Halle Mission, and the American Board of Commissioners for Foreign Missions began to disappear.

With the rise of denominationalism and the attendant divisions of mission came the need for new forms of cooperation and unity. Thus, in 1888, at the London Centenary Conference on the Protestant Missions of the World, the concept of "comity," or denominational cooperation, developed.[52] At the Centenary Conference (June 9–19, 1888), twelve hundred mission advocates attended with forty US mission societies, six Canadian societies, fifty-four British societies, and fifteen Continental societies represented. Two of the main topics taken up were the problem of the liquor trade in Africa and the ongoing opium trade "inflicted upon" China by the English. From this important conference the "World Missionary Committee" was formed, which helped to coordinate missionary work globally. This new coordination regarding world evangelization required ongoing communication. Comity arrangements were not exactly new, for informal agreements had been made as early as the 1830s in Protestant missionary work in the Pacific and India.[53] Now, however, a pattern of sharing major urban areas, but dividing up the work in more rural areas, was becoming a standard way of operating.

Two other major ecumenical conferences for mission were held at the beginning of the twentieth century: the Ecumenical Missionary Conference (New York, 1900) and the World Missionary Conference (Edinburgh, 1910). The 1900 conference, with 162 mission board members in attendance, highlighted views on cooperation by twenty-five missionary leaders. This was the "institutional era" of missionary work, in which major effort, time, and money were applied to the development of schools, hospitals, and other institutions. At the 1900 conference a major issue that was discussed was the degree that these (often large and expensive) institutions should be started and run cooperatively. Although there was no absolute consensus at that time, there was

51. Norman E. Thomas begins his survey *Missions and Unity: Lessons from History, 1792–2010* (Eugene, OR: Cascade, 2010) with "William Carey's Pleasing Dream and Its Antecedents" (3–11).

52. Earlier mission conferences were held on both sides of the Atlantic, more as inspirational congresses than working meetings with official delegates. In 1846 the London Missionary Conference had eight hundred mission leaders from fifty-two mission societies and began the cooperative work known as the Evangelical Alliance. This was followed by the 1854 Union Missionary Conference in New York, the 1860 Liverpool Missionary Conference, and the 1878 Mildmay, London Missionary Conference.

53. See Thomas, *Missions and Unity*, 32.

much greater cooperation subsequent to the conference. This, in turn, became the foundation for church unions, first in Asia and later in the West. Another type of cooperation came through the newly founded faith missions, which accepted people of many different denominations.

Unity was promoted most at the beginning of the twentieth century up to the beginning of the Second World War through women's missionary societies, the Student Volunteer Movement (SVM), and its related World Student Christian Federation (WSCF). Nondenominational women's cooperations began early, but with the founding of the Woman's Union Missionary Society in 1861, a new level of female participation, leadership, and unity began. At the 1900 New York Conference, women's work programs were coordinated, and as a follow up, a Central Committee for the United Study of Foreign Missions was established, which ended up producing millions of copies of textbooks and other materials for the study of missions.[54]

Of all of these movements, the greatest impact on the modern ecumenical movement was the SVM and WSCF. These related movements had their foundation in a summer conference for students held at D. L. Moody's campus in Northfield, Massachusetts, in 1886. Recruiting university students from some of the best American universities, a new type of missionary began to go overseas, and these new missionaries had a new sense of community. Leaders of the twentieth-century ecumenical movement came up through the ranks of the nineteenth- and early-twentieth-century Student Volunteer Movement. People like Robert E. Speer, Robert Wilder, and John R. Mott created a unity of purpose and a common identity among college students that carried over into their missionary work. This sense of identity and common experience made the coordination of international ecumenical meetings natural and easy. The earliest missionary movement in North America was instigated by students (the Haystack Movement, 1806),[55] and in a similar way students were the catalyst both for twentieth-century missions and for mission unity.

Edinburgh World Missionary Conference and the Ecumenical Movement[56]

When we think of major church conferences that have defined Christianity for a period, or for an age, we think immediately of major early ecumenical

54. See Robert, *American Women in Mission*, 260–69.

55. See Ryan Shaw, "A Haystack That Changed the World," in *Evangelical Missions Quarterly* 42 (2006): 480–85; David M. Howard, *Student Power in World Missions* (Downers Grove, IL: InterVarsity, 1979).

56. For further reading, see Frampton F. Fox, ed., *Edinburgh 1910 Revisited: Give Us Friends; An Indian Perspective on 100 years of Mission* (Bangalore, India: CMS, 2010); and Brian Stanley, *The World Missionary Conference, Edinburgh 1910* (Grand Rapids: Eerdmans, 2009). For a contemporary response, see W. H. T. Gairdner, *Echoes from Edinburgh, 1910* (New York: Fleming H. Revell, 1910).

councils like Nicaea and Constantinople; we think of the Council of Trent, which clarified Roman Catholic doctrine for half a millennium; and we should also think of the World Missionary Conference held at Edinburgh in 1910. This conference is not comparable to other ecumenical gatherings, the results of which continue to pervade the church, and yet this was a unique Protestant mission conference. It is a conference that both modern-day ecumenical leaders and modern-day evangelical leaders claim as their heritage. It is significant that not one but four major events were held to celebrate the centennial of the Edinburgh Conference.[57] It is not my place to rehearse the planning, events, and results of the conference; however, one of the major trajectories of missionary thinking came out of this conference, and so I want to trace some of the major themes of mission thinking that are still with us today. Here we will look briefly at what happened, and then identify some of the major themes of the conference, and how these themes continued through the middle of the twentieth century.

The conference was headed up by American Methodist layman John R. Mott (1865–1955)—YMCA, SVM, and WSCF leader. Mott was a master motivator, connector, and planner. Under his leadership, Edinburgh 1910 was a massive, professional, and carefully planned nine-day meeting that, judging by its organization and global scope, could easily have been confused for a meeting of Parliament or an annual stockholders' meeting of a multinational corporation. The delegates were official, representing their churches or missions, and two years of planning and surveying had laid the foundation for the nine-day conference. The meetings were marked by optimism, zeal, and industry; its watchword was taken from the World Student Christian Federation: "The evangelization of the world in this generation." Eight commissions were established with about twenty-eight members in each, the representation being determined by the amount of money spent on missionary work. Thus there were ninty-two British members, fifty-one from the United States, and only twenty-two from France, Germany, Holland, Switzerland, and Scandinavia. Lord Balfour, who seven years later would call for a Jewish homeland, brought the greetings to the delegates, noting that,

> By common consent there is just now a great opportunity. Nations in the East are awakening. They are looking for two things: they are looking for enlightenment and for liberty. Christianity alone of all religions meets these demands in the highest degree.[58]

Of the British representatives, about one-half were Anglicans, and they were only included because it was decided that Latin America would not

57. The conferences were held in Edinburgh, Seoul, Cape Town, and Boston.

58. World Missionary Conference, *The History and Records of the Conference* (New York: Fleming H. Revell, 1910), 9:145.

be treated as a mission field. (Many Anglicans were Anglo-Catholics who would not support a conference that would discuss evangelizing Catholic Latin America.) This disagreement over what defines a mission field marks a significant issue that continues to divide Protestant missions up to the present. Nine volumes of records were produced, and an ongoing organization, or "Continuation Committee," was established—both ensuring the ongoing impact of this conference. What follows are a few of the major themes and then a discussion of later issues leading up to 1961, when the missionary and church unity streams came together.

First, the conference marks the height of Western progressivism, optimism, and even of colonial arrogance in mission. Few Christian leaders questioned the assumption that the West was going to do something for the world. It was hard to imagine any other option at the time, and yet, theologically, we can critique such hubris—even as it was nurtured in Protestant piety and devout worship. The following decades would prove the shallowness of these assumptions.

Second, the conference marks the beginning of what might be called big business meets big church. From this conference, a business model for church organization, especially for missions and planning, began to take over. Careful planning, short-term and long-range plans, representation according to annual budgets—all were business models appropriated by the church. Alliances with governments and new business tycoons also became normative.

Third, it is seldom noted that this was a mission conference, not a clergy conference. People did not have to be bishops, moderators, or even pastors to participate. Mott was never ordained. The Protestant missionary movement was always a place in which lay leadership, including women, flourished. If we trace this back to its roots we find that nineteenth-century revivals opened the door for lay leadership as never before. The Reformation treasured the priesthood of all believers, but it was the revivals and the missionary movement of the nineteenth century where the priesthood of all believers really took on flesh.

Fourth, here at the end of the "Great Century for Protestant Missions," there was still a common evangelistic zeal and purpose. Even though much of the evangelistic zeal was mixed with a cultural agenda (as with Lord Balfour's declaration above), there was still a Christian consensus about evangelization. By common consent there was now a great opportunity, there was a great need, and the Christian gospel was the answer. Groups as diverse as James Hudson Taylor's China Inland Mission, American and British Baptists, and the Anglican Church could come together for this evangelistic purpose. It is unfortunate that this was the end of such a broad coalition in the West.

Fifth, this was still the age of white male leadership in the church. Few women were involved in leadership, there were only seventeen Asian delegates, and no African, Latin American, or Pacific Island delegates were invited.[59] Even with a half a century of discussion and work at three-self principles of missionary work, in 1910 the missionary task was still firmly in the hands of Europeans and North Americans. A few of the Asians who were present spoke, and their names should be remembered. The President of Meiji Gakuin College, Reverend Kajinosuke Ibuka, as well as the ex-minister of education for Korea, Yan Chi Ho, made brief addresses. The most telling and prophetic address was made by a future bishop of the Anglican Church in Dornakal, South India, Vendanayagam Samuel Azariah (1874–1945). Azariah was a great example of three-self church leadership, having founded the completely indigenous and self-supporting Indian Missionary Society in 1903. However, at Edinburgh, Azariah swam against the tide of optimism and the happy feelings of cooperation and said very directly that, as much as he respected missionaries, they did not treat Indians as friends or as equals. "The problem of race relations is one of the most serious problems confronting the church today. . . . The relationship between the European missionaries and the India workers is far from what it ought to be, and . . . a certain aloofness, a lack of mutual understanding and openness, a great lack of frank intercourse and friendliness exists throughout the country." His concluding comments to his speech were winsome, uncompromising, and memorable:

> Through all the ages to come the Indian Church will rise up in gratitude to attest the heroism and self-denying labors of the missionary body. You have given your goods to feed the poor. You have given your bodies to be burned. We also ask for *love*. Give us FRIENDS.[60]

Finally, Edinburgh marks the end of missional consensus and optimism—but it marks the beginning of the modern ecumenical movement, which includes Orthodox churches. The Edinburgh conference affirmed that there should be an ecumenical gathering specifically to extend the cooperation from mission to church issues of faith and order. Four months later, the General Convention of the American Episcopal Church made such a call: "We believe that the time has now arrived when representatives of the whole family of Christ, led by the Holy Spirit may be willing to come together for the consideration of questions of Faith and Order. We believe further, that all Christian Communions are in accord with us in our desire to lay aside self-will, and to put on the mind which is in Christ Jesus our Lord." The call was made, in light of Jesus's high priestly prayer (John 17) that "they may be one . . . that the world may

59. Edinburgh 1910 was dominated by men, but women were strongly encouraged by John R. Mott, the moderator, to speak. A separate section to discuss women's missions was set up at the conference. See Stanley, *World Missionary Conference*, 87.

60. V. S. Azariah, "The Problem of Cooperation between Foreign and Native Workers," in *History and the Records*, 9:306–15 (emphasis is in the original records).

believe." It was the missionary bishop from the American Episcopal Church, Bishop Brent, who initiated the call and who led the conference, which was finally held at Lausanne in 1927. It is also quite significant that the Orthodox were included. Relationships that developed through the World Student Christian Federation (SVM International) made this conference possible. John R. Mott, Nathan Söderblom, and Strenopoulos Germanos all met at a WSCF conference in Constantinople in 1911. Strenopoulos was later Archbishop Germanos of Thyatira and, in that position, in 1920 was instrumental in the Ecumenical Patriarch's "Encyclical unto all the Churches of Christ"—a call to Christian unity. The Lausanne meeting was remarkable in bringing together 127 Orthodox leaders among the over four hundred participants. Thus began the second of the three major streams of the modern ecumenical movement: Faith (confession) and Order (ordination, sacraments, etc.).

Between the first major ecumenical conference for mission in 1910 and the second meeting for faith and order in 1928 (the Jerusalem Conference), the world had changed. Three major changes altered the tone and the focus of the second ecumenical meeting. First was the arrival of the Pentecostal movement, which we will look at below. It is difficult to overemphasize the impact of this movement, both for the sake of mission and for the sake of interchurch relationships. Second was the rise of atheistic communism. The "collapse" of Orthodox Russia immediately following the Edinburgh Conference was a shock to all of Christendom. Just as the "Christian Century" was beginning, the largest Christian country became anti-Christian. Again, at the risk of appearing overly dramatic, it is hard to overestimate the impact this had on the Christian church, and especially upon Christian leaders. The third major event that took place was the First World War. Europe had not had such devastation—Christians killing other Christians—since the religious wars following the Reformation. Thus, as Christians gathered to talk about mission again in 1928, this time in Jerusalem, it was a humbled and even humiliated group of leaders who gathered. They had originally planned to meet much earlier, but the Great War had prevented them from meeting. Now they were meeting eighteen years after the Edinburgh Conference—and after their countries had been at war. With the rise of Communism in Russia, the hope of global cooperation was greatly reduced. Whereas the 1910 Conference shouted the watchword of the Student Volunteer Movement, "the evangelization of the world in this generation," the Jerusalem Conference seemed to whisper, "Religions must unite against secularization."[61]

Without going into great detail, we can identify some of the major themes in this early ecumenical movement up to the founding of the World Council

61. Just a year after the 1928 meeting there were riots between Muslims and Jews over the use of the Wailing Wall, making it clear to the world that uniting religions against secularization would not come easy.

of Churches (1948). First was the call for missionary activity to be recovered as an essential activity of the whole church. A theological misperception had developed in the nineteenth century, as missionary societies were developing as structures separate from the church; mission was therefore seen as an extracurricular or even extraecclesial activity. Edinburgh stated, and later conferences tried to reaffirm, that evangelism "is incumbent on every member of the Church. . . . The missionary task demands from every Christian, and from every congregation, a change in the existing scale of missionary zeal and service."[62] The ecumenical movement would not move away from this conviction, even if the message often fell on deaf ecclesial ears. Not only did the ecumenical movement affirm the universal call of the whole church to mission, but, beginning in 1910 and becoming much more pronounced after World War II, it was affirmed that every church was *in* a mission field—therefore the church is always in a missionary context. Volume two of the Edinburgh report (*The Church in the Mission Field*) made this clear: "The whole world is the mission field and there is no church that is not a church in the mission field."[63] Both of these statements—the universal call of all Christians to mission, and the universal presence of the church in mission—were radical then and still seek fulfillment in our time.

A second theme that continued from Edinburgh 1910 was the division of ecclesial functions into three parts. This was unintentional (and there may not have been any way around it at the time), but the ecumenical movement moved in three functional areas: Edinburgh 1910 and the 1928 meeting in Jerusalem representing the church in mission, a movement that became the International Missionary Council; the second stream, from the seed planted in 1910, was the work for unity in issues of "Faith and Order"; and the third stream that held special concern for "Life and Work," or cooperation in social responsibility. The first conference for life and work was held in the shadow of World War I, and it was called the Universal Christian Conference on Life and Work (Stockholm, 1925). The experience of the Great War moved many Christians to take more direct responsibility for social and political issues. This first conference sought "to unite the different churches in common practical work . . . applied to the solution of contemporary social and international problems."[64] This was an age when Western churches were still powerful, with strong political voices, and so they reasoned that it was necessary to provide social leadership to prevent ongoing injustices and violence.

A third theme that would persist for most of the century was the issue of Western control of missions and "younger churches," as they were called in non-Western lands. Soon after the 1910 Conference, John R. Mott headed

62. World Missionary Conference, *History and the Records*, 9:109.

63. Ibid., 2:4.

64. Quoted from Thomas, *Missions and Unity*, 57.

Three Streams of Ecumenism

For our understanding of missiology, it is noteworthy that the three vital streams mentioned here were somewhat related, but for nearly forty years ecclesial unity related to the mission of the church was being discussed in three (until 1948) and then two (until 1961) separate movements. In 1948 the Faith and Order, and Life and Work movements merged to form the World Council of Churches, but not until 1961 was the International Missionary Council fully integrated into the larger ecumenical movement of the WCC. This fragmented approach was not a healthy way to envision and enact the mission of unity in the church, for it was too easy to assume that church order or sacraments had nothing to do with mission, or that mission had nothing to do with the work of the laity in society.

out to Asia to help organize national councils—that is, councils of local churches, in which their leaders could confer together. This is one of the great practical results of the Edinburgh meeting. Various churches planted by schismatic Western churches came together in national councils in Asia, the Middle East, Latin America, and Africa. These were not conferences that brought people together for a single meeting or single purpose—these were *councils* that began to represent Protestant Christianity in each country or region, and this at the same time (and often before) there were functioning councils in Western nations. By the time of the Jerusalem meeting of the International Missionary Conference in 1928, there were twenty-six national councils. But even with the formation of these national councils, releasing control of missions and national churches was a long and slow process for many Western missions. Many non-Western Christian leaders recognized the need for their churches to be independent from Western control. As a result, in 1971 there was a major call for a moratorium on Western missions from Kenyan Presbyterian John Gatu. The debate continued in Africa and Asia for years.[65]

One of the immediate results of the national councils is that they soon brought about unions of national churches—far ahead of such unions in the West. The Church of Christ in China brought together many churches in 1927 (excluding Lutherans and Anglicans) around the simple confession of faith in Jesus Christ as revealed in the Scriptures. The Church of Christ in Japan (Nippon Kirisuto Kyodan) was formed in 1940, and the Church of Christ in Thailand was formed in 1934 (mostly from Presbyterian churches, but with the understanding that it would eventually be the Protestant Church in Thailand).

A final theme, which we will look at in greater depth in the next chapter, is the evolving view of mission and other religions. The 1910 World Missionary Conference backed away from a blanket condemnation of all world religions,

65. See Rodger C. Bassham, *Mission Theology* (Pasadena, CA: William Carey Library, 1979), 160n85, for a discussion of the primary literature.

but instead spoke about respect for religions ("sympathy" was used) and understanding for what they tell us about other people. Still, there was a clear commitment to proclaim "the truth" of the gospel to people of all faiths. A number of factors challenged this common assumption, chief among these were the rise of atheistic Communism in Europe and Asia, the empathic study of world religions in universities, and religious violence in the early decades of the century (Muslims killing Armenians and Christians killing Christians in Europe). Jerusalem gave a strongly christological statement in the end, but there was tension concerning how to talk about secularization and other religions. The overwhelming shadow of secular states and the decline of Christianity tempted many to see other religions as the allies of Christianity and Christian mission. The debate surfaced more clearly in the 1930s, and it stretched ecumenical unity to the breaking point in the 1960s and 1970s.

Mission Theology Traversing Global Angst: 1928 to 1948

Global social and political events are both the context for missionary activity and the focus of that activity. The global context of the 1930s and 1940s was a tumultuous period for Christian mission. The crash of global markets in 1929 caused a rapid decline in financial support for overseas missionary work. At that very time it was becoming clear that persecution of the Orthodox Church in Russia was on the rise, an anti-Christian movement in China had set back much missionary work, and the ongoing expansion of the Japanese empire in the Pacific, along with internal strife in China, challenged ongoing missionary involvement. And yet, as we look back more than eighty years later, we now see that the biggest challenge to Christian mission came from within the church—from its own theological trends in the West. Japanese imperialism ended, Russian Communism ended, and the civil strife in China (after passing through a violent period) ended up creating a paradoxically healthy and contentious environment for Christian growth. It was Western, not overseas, mission contexts that were the problem.

In the 1930s, however, none of this could be seen. Following the 1928 Jerusalem meeting, an extensive study was done on world mission, supported by seven North American mission boards and financed by John D. Rockefeller. *Rethinking Missions: A Laymen's Inquiry after One Hundred Years*, edited by Harvard philosophy professor William Ernst Hocking (1932), focused on missionary work in India, Burma, China, and Japan, and the conclusions guided by professor Hocking prescribed a new approach to mission which must "be willing to give largely without any preaching, to cooperate wholeheartedly with non-Christian agencies for social improvement."[66] American optimism and pragmatism drove the theology of the report, and it created

66. William Ernest Hocking, *Rethinking Missions: A Laymen's Inquiry after One Hundred Years* (New York: Harper & Brothers, 1932), 326.

a major upheaval in mission circles. The common search for truth among people of all religions, and the primacy of social improvement, dislodged mission theology from christological and trinitarian foundations. As a result, the Dutch theologian Hendrik Kraemer, missionary to the East Indies, was commissioned to prepare a biblical and theological study for the 1938 meeting of the IMC to be held in Tambaram (Madras). His study, *The Christian Message in a Non-Christian World*,[67] was a missiological fortress, a 450-page study built largely on "biblical realism." "The realism of the Bible . . . simply takes seriously, on account of a robust and sane intuition, the fact that God is God and that if He is God, his Will is the Ground of all that is." The two positions—that there is continuity between Christian faith and other faiths (as in the Hocking report), and the view that there is absolutely no continuity between God's revelation and human beliefs (Kraemer)—were outlined in these two works. Protestant Christianity was greatly polarized regarding its mission and view of non-Christian religions before the Second World War.

The Madras meeting was a significant meeting for mission theology, being held on the eve of another world war, and being held in India. It made a strong affirmation that the church, *every local church*, is the locus of mission. "It is the Church and the Church alone which can carry the responsibility of transmitting the Gospel from one generation to another, of preserving its purity, and of proclaiming it to all creatures. . . . The place where this task is centered is the local church or congregation."[68] Again this conference affirmed that every church is located in a mission field, and that mission involves personal transformation as well as social engagement. The conference was small, but its reports and theological reflection were significant. Its significance was underscored immediately, as its delegates' nations were soon at war with one another in Africa, Asia, and Europe. Not only was every place a place of mission, but every place was a place of conflict.

When the IMC was able to piece together another meeting in the ruins of World War II, it was a humbled group of church leaders who met in Whitby, Ontario, in 1947. The war had left many missions orphaned from their sending churches, and many hundreds of hospitals, schools, and church buildings in Europe, Africa, and East Asia were destroyed. There was no time for mission thinking; it was a time for rebuilding, for picking up the pieces, and also for picking up "where we left off." From the missionary and mission society correspondence of the period, it is clear that there was little thought of anything but rebuilding. Few people recognized, until the cries for independence in the 1950s and 1960s, that Christian mission had turned a corner. It would no longer be the sole prerogative of the West.

67. Hendrik Kraemer, *The Christian Message in a Non-Christian World* (London: Edinburgh House, 1938).

68. International Missionary Council, *The Madras Series, 1938: Findings* (New York: IMC, 1939), 24, 26.

The title of the conference at Whitby in 1947 was "Partners in Obedience," and only 112 delegates from forty nations were present to affirm the need for all Christians to partner together in evangelistic and social outreach. Partnership had been a concept earlier, but now it took center stage.[69] It would become a major concept in mission for over six decades, and it continues to be a driving force today. Both J. H. Oldham and John R. Mott had retired, so a new group of leaders were stepping forward, and many of the younger leaders did not have the history of the 1910, 1928, and even 1938 conferences. Of note, this conference dropped the language of "Christian and non-Christian nations," since it was recognized that true partnership, and a genuine recognition that mission was in every location, would mean that such labels were no longer appropriate. Very forward looking, the conference called for "absolute spiritual equality" in Christian witness to the whole world.[70] It was an ideal, but it was one of the cases where an honest ecumenical theology looked beyond the present reality to the church's hope for the future.

A year later (1948), the World Council of Churches held its first meeting in Amsterdam, after being formally constituted ten years earlier. A Dutch theologian, W. A. Visser't Hooft, was the general secretary (1938–66), and the title of the first assembly was quite appropriate: "Man's Disorder, God's Design." While studying God's order or plan for the world, the assembly was also soon made aware of a huge new problem, along with promoting the renovation of missions: more than 350,000 Arab refugees had been moved from their homes in order to found the state of Israel. Like a small cloud on the horizon, the Balfour Declaration of decades earlier was now beginning to be a major global issue for countries and for Christians. One hundred and forty-seven churches officially joined at this first assembly, making it the largest representative council of Christians outside of the Roman Catholic Church. In Section 2 of its Report the first assembly affirmed that the purpose of God is to reconcile all persons to himself through Jesus Christ, and therefore they reported, "we have been burdened by a sense of urgency. We have recaptured something of the spirit of the apostolic age, when the believers went everywhere preaching the word."

The assembly had much discussion about peace, great hope for the formation of the United Nations, and soon new worries because of the rise of Communism in China and the war in Korea. In looking at this history of mission in the nineteenth and twentieth centuries, one cannot avoid the conclusion that mission is always carried on in imperfect, and often contentious and violent, contexts. While interviewing a missionary couple who worked in the Middle East beginning right after World War II, I will never forget the husband's first

69. See chap. 12 for a fuller discussion of partnership.

70. International Missionary Council, *The Witness of a Revolutionary Church: Statements Issued by the Committee of the International Missionary Council, Whitby, Ontario, Canada, July 5–24, 1947* (New York: International Missionary Council, 1947), 173–84.

sentence. "We lived through four regional wars."[71] "Man's Disorder, God's Design" was definitely an appropriate name for this first assembly. Three months later, the United Nations, with much help from the WCC and Christian leaders like Roman Catholic Jacques Maritain and Orthodox Charles Malik, would pass the Universal Declaration for Human Rights.

Mission, Pentecostalism, and Independency

Of the three major themes of Christianity in the twentieth century, Pentecostalism and related "Spiritual" forms of Christianity is possibly the most important—along with the ecumenical movement and the sudden reversal of Christianity to non-Western forms. I will call Pentecostalism and independent forms of Christianity "Spirit churches": churches that identify themselves as led by the Spirit rather than schisms from the sixteenth century (Protestant churches), centered in Rome (Roman Catholic Church), or following a theology from the early church councils (Orthodox). These Spirit churches changed the way mission was expressed and carried out. In some ways, the indigenous movements were a sign of the success of Western missionary work and their nineteenth-century principles. On the other hand, indigenous churches that began in places as distant as China and the Ivory Coast were often founded in opposition to the "mission churches." They had indigenous elements (drums, dancing, indigenous languages, etc.) that missionaries had too frequently rejected as inappropriate at best and pagan at worst.

At the very time of the Edinburgh meeting, a meeting in which no African Christian leaders were invited to participate, there was a major African movement beginning in Liberia. The former Anglican (now independent) African prophet William Wade Harris (a Liberian) began preaching along the coast of West Africa beginning in 1913. Earlier, he had served time in prison for fighting for greater British control of Liberia. But, while incarcerated, he had a vision from the angel Gabriel who told him to remove all of his Western clothes (including his new American shoes) and walk barefoot, to carry a large staff topped with a cross, and to preach to Africans, as an African. And so he did—accompanied by three wives. They would sing and dance, and he would preach. They used dried gourds for instruments. Soon thousands were destroying their fetishes and seeking baptism in any existing church (Protestant or Roman Catholic). Harris's movement was only one of many indigenous movements that were founded by prophets (male and female) who resisted white colonial control, and who preached a clear but simple message of conversion.[72]

71. From interviews that were conducted for Scott W. Sunquist and Caroline Becker, *A History of Presbyterian Missions, 1944–2007* (Louisville: Geneva, 2008).

72. Others include David Brown Vincent or Mojola Agbebi (1860–1917); Simon Kimbangu (1887–1951), who founded Église de Jésus Christ sur la terre par son envoyé spécial (or The Church

Types of African Independent Churches

Indigenous forms of Christianity began to develop on a large and diverse scale in Africa beginning in the 1880s. These African-initiated movements can be classified as four general types:

1. *Ethiopian*: Looking back to Ethiopia in the Old Testament as its inspiration and model in resistance to Euro-American leadership and oppression.
2. *Zionist*: Originally inspired by missionaries from the West (New Jerusalem or Zion, Illinois) who focused on faith healing, equipping local leaders, and speaking in tongues.
3. *Prophet or Spirit Churches*: Based on sacred spaces, and led by a prophet with a dream or vision.
4. *Revival Type*: These churches start as revivals of existing European mission churches. They were found mostly in East Africa in the 1920s and 1930s and then in Nigeria in the 1970s. Some new churches were started (Aladura Churches in Nigeria), but mostly the people stayed in their churches.

There are a number of identifiable causes of these independent or indigenous movements but, for our purposes, only a few of them are important, in that they help us understand Roman Catholic and Protestant missionary work in Africa in the nineteenth and first half of the twentieth century. First, missionary authoritarianism has been identified as a major contributing factor. There were many well-educated and strong Christian leaders among Africans by the twentieth century, yet missionaries continued to exercise control over Africans at almost every level. A second contributing factor is that many of the missionary churches were "low church" regarding worship, with only limited or understated practice of rituals. The African independent (or indigenous) churches retained or recovered the central importance of ritual from indigenous African practices. Thirdly, there was a desire among Africans to retain more of their traditions. Many missionary church services looked and sounded like European (or North American) worship services that had been transported to African soil. African Christians felt they had lost much of their personal identity, and wanted to express that identity within their worship. A fourth factor giving rise to the indigenous churches and revival movements was the longing for a greater emphasis on the Old Testament.

of Christ on Earth by His Special Envoy Simon Kimbangu); Samuel Bilehou Joseph Oschoffa (1909–85) and his Christianisme Céleste (or Celestial Church of Christ), Benin; Moses Orimolade (1879–1933) and the Church of the Cherubim and Seraphim; Isaiah Shembe (1870–1935) and the iBandla lamaNazaretha (Nazareth Baptist Church); Mangena Maake Mokone (1851–1931), founder of the Ethiopian Church; and Elliot Kenan Kamwana (1872–1956) and his Watchtower.

Ritual, family, tribal identity, and other themes that are very strong in the Old Testament resonated strongly with most Africans. This was their world, and it was a world with no division between secular and sacred. Finally, most Protestant and Catholic missionaries, before the rise of Pentecostalism, were working within an Enlightenment (closed-universe) framework. They believed that God was present and that he would work to bring people to faith, but they didn't really expect the Holy Spirit (or his adversaries) to "show up." Africans were expectant—they lived in a world in which mediums manipulated the spirits and ancestors were present. Thus, African indigenous movements mark a recovery of spiritual power to confront evil. The world of the Bible was easier for the African to understand and accept than it was for the Western missionary. When African Christianity emerged, it reshaped Christianity not only by starting new churches but also by reshaping the Western mission churches. Anglican bishop and revival leader from Uganda Festo Kivengere commented, "When principle, doctrine, or structure becomes the center instead of Jesus, before we know it we are left with our dos and don'ts and have lost the Lord Jesus. Are you willing to have the Spirit smash the structure or your principle, so that Jesus may have the preeminent place?"[73] Thus, we can see the influence African Christianity began to have on the global missionary movement.

The other major Spirit movement that influenced missions was Pentecostalism, also taking off around the time of the 1910 Edinburgh meeting. Once again, the Pentecostal movement can be understood both as resistance and response: resistance to what is perceived as a Spiritless, or lifeless, Christianity, and response to the call of Christ in mission. Pentecostalism exploded across the globe in missionary outreach. Two major streams of nineteenth-century revivalism fed into twentieth-century Pentecostalism: Wesleyan perfectionism and Keswick holiness. Wesleyan perfectionism taught that a person should seek and could attain perfect intention of love in all that they do. The doctrine was often taught as a second enduement of power from the Holy Spirit that would enable perfect love. The Keswick Conventions in England, beginning in 1875, promoted "practical holiness" and developed a theology that emphasized that the normal Christian should experience "fullness of the Holy Spirit." Their emphasis upon filling and fullness of the Holy Spirit allowed for many "fillings" for power—not only for one's own sanctification but for ministry and mission. Keswick spirituality had a direct impact upon German Pentecostalism, A. B. Simpson (founder of the Christian and Missionary Alliance Church), and the Great Welsh Revival of 1904–5. The Welsh Revival spread its wings around the world to places as far as Korea, China, Africa, Australia, and India. All of these movements, with their recovery of

73. Quoted from Richard K. MacMaster, *A Gentle Wind of God: The Influence of the East Africa Revival* (Scottsdale, PA: Herald, 2006), 242.

the central role of the Holy Spirit in the church,[74] began to link dreams, visions, healings, tongues, and casting out demons with the work of mission and evangelism. The Welsh Revival preacher Evan Roberts (1878–1951) was only twenty-six when, he says, "I was taken up into the divine fellowship for about four hours. What it was I cannot tell you, except that it was divine." These revivals opened up a new type of mission, not planned like a large business or corporation (the IMC model), but dependent upon the direct leading of the Holy Spirit. While still in the midst of the global transformation of Christianity, and especially Christian mission, Roland Allen (famous Anglican author of *Missionary Methods: St. Paul's or Ours?*) penned a book that contributed a greater understanding of the seemingly chaotic new missionary work being done: *Pentecost and the World*.[75] It was a helpful way of viewing world mission in a Pentecostal vein: as continuing the story of the Acts of the Holy Spirit.

Whereas in the late nineteenth century we could not even begin to talk about Spirit churches, by the end of the twentieth century it had become common knowledge that the Pentecostal and indigenous churches were among the largest and fastest growing in the world. For example, in the twentieth century, African indigenous churches grew from about forty thousand converts to an estimated fifty-four million at the beginning of the twenty-first century. Their influence has been even greater than the remarkable 15 percent growth in Christian population on the African continent. These and other Spirit churches have challenged modern views of mission by their reliance on the Holy Spirit and his gifts and by focusing less on the practical means of carrying out the mission of God. We will look at this more carefully in chapter 8. While this deeply spiritual movement was taking off in the 1950s and 1960s, another movement in the West was, figuratively speaking, pulling the church back to earth: secularization. The 1960s is called the secular decade, but it was also the decade of the charismatic movement and the rise of evangelicalism. We now turn to the turbulent period from the 1950s to the present.

Ecumenical Conferences and Themes from 1910 to 1961

Mission, Church Union, and Life and Work

1910 Edinburgh Missionary Conference (8 sections)
"The Evangelization of the World in this Generation"

74. I say "recovery" because Protestant Reformers focused a great deal upon Scripture, grace, and Jesus Christ but very little on the Holy Spirit. See Craig Van Gelder, *The Ministry of the Missional Church: A Community Led by the Spirit* (Grand Rapids: Baker Books, 2007), 24.

75. Roland Allen, *Pentecost and the World: The Revelation of the Holy Spirit in the "Acts of the Apostles"* (Oxford: Oxford University Press, 1917).

1925 Stockholm Sweden: Universal Christian Conference on Life and Work
"Doctrine Divides, Service Unites"

1927 Lausanne: World Conference on Faith and Order
"Both agreements and disagreements were noted . . . "

1928 Jerusalem: International Missionary Council
"Religions Against Secularization"

1937 Oxford Life and Work Conference
"Church, Community and State . . . The primary duty of the church to the state is to be the Church"

1937 Edinburgh: Faith and Order
"We are one in faith in our Lord Jesus Christ, the incarnate Word of God"

1938 Madras, Tambaram: International Missionary Conference
"The younger churches became the majority" (guided by Kraemer's book *The Christian Message in a Non-Christian World*)

1939 Amsterdam: First World Conference of Christian Youth

1947 Oslo: Second World Conference of Christian Youth
"Jesus Christ is Lord"

1947 Whitby, Ontario: International Missionary Conference
"Partnership in Obedience"

1948 First Meeting of the World Council of Churches, Amsterdam
"Man's Disorder, God's Design"

1951 Rolle, Switzerland; pivotal meeting of the Central Committee of the WCC
"Ecumenical . . . is properly used to describe everything that relates to the whole task of the whole Church to bring the Gospel to the whole world."

1952 Willingen, Germany: International Missionary Conference
"Missionary Obligation of the Church . . . There is no participation in Christ without participation in His mission to the world."

1952 Lund, Sweden: Faith and Order
"The Lund Principle" states that churches should act together in all matters except where deep differences of conviction prevent them.

1952 Kottayam, South India: Third World Conference of Christian Youth
"Jesus Christ the answer—God in Christ, reconciling the world unto himself"

1954 Evanston: World Council of Churches (Second Assembly)
"Jesus Christ: The Hope of the World"

1958 Accra, Ghana: International Missionary Council
"The Christian Mission at this Hour" ("It is Christ's Mission, not Ours")

1960 Lausanne: Fourth World Conference of Christian Youth

1961 New Delhi: World Council of Churches (Third Assembly)
"Jesus Christ, the Light of the World" [Integration of the IMC with WCC]

5

The Waning and Reconception of Christian Mission

Postcolonial Missiologies (1948 to Present)

The 1950s was the lull before the storm; the 1960s was the storm.[1] The 1950s was a conservative period of rebuilding, restarting, and remaking what had been lost. Many countries in Asia and Africa were gaining their independence, and national churches were also beginning to raise up local leaders as never before. For many mission societies it was a period of hopeful rebuilding after the devastation of the Second World War. Countries like Japan and China saw a brief but large influx of missionaries seeking to rebuild Asian nations on Christian foundations. Missionary and mission society correspondence from this time indicates that little had changed in Western missionary thinking. Ecumenical discussion was far ahead of the practical missionary work being carried on, but this discussion did not always trickle down to the missionaries and their societies. Most missionaries and mission boards still understood mission as the responsibility of the West: to build churches, hospitals, and schools for Africa, Latin America, and Asia. Money was being raised to rebuild what had been lost in the war and to repair what

1. The 1960s was the decade of the Beatles; the assassinations of John F. Kennedy, Malcom X, and Martin Luther King Jr.; the Vietnam War, the Cold War, and the Cuban missile crisis; miniskirts; landing on the moon; Rachel Carson's *Silent Spring* warning of the environmental crisis; the Six Days' War; hippies; and the independence of thirty-two African nations. The 1960s, socially speaking, was a turbulent period for most regions of the world.

had been neglected. Most Western missionaries still considered it their responsibility to evangelize non-Western nations. Rebuilding institutions, building and rebuilding churches, and evangelizing non-Christian people groups were consistent themes in the early post–World War II era.

The Not-So-Conservative 1950s

However, there were changes in the world and changes in the Western church that were beginning to emerge in the "conservative" 1950s. First, the '50s marked the largest and most sudden remapping of the world in human history. Ralph Winter calls the period from 1945 to 1969 the "25 unbelievable years."[2] According to Winter, 99 percent of the non-Western world that was under colonial control gained independence in this quarter of a century. Independence created a very different context for Christian mission. Many "new countries" that had been under the rule of a Christian European country gained independence and took on a different religious identity: Hindu Nepal, Muslim Pakistan, Muslim Morocco, Buddhist Cambodia, and so on. Other countries took on a Marxist ideology that also challenged Christian missionary assumptions: the People's Republic of China, North Korea, the USSR, Vietnam, and Laos. Christian missions had, in a very short period of time, come up against fascism, Marxism, and the revival of Asian religions. Missionaries had seen in Germany and Japan that fascism could become an ideology that used religion. Now they were learning that communism is an ideology that acts like religion.

Very soon these countries began to assert their independence in religious matters, removing missionaries and using government funds to support the building of temples, mosques, or wats. Thousands of missionaries had to change their status or location. China had been the largest mission field, but with the "liberation" under the Maoists, missionaries were quickly removed and the Three-Self Patriotic Movement (TSPM) was subsumed under the new communist government. No one dreamed that this jewel in the missions crown would be "lost" so quickly. In subsequent decades the news was even worse than the original prognosis. Churches were taken over and turned into political party offices. Clinics were now closed or run by government agencies. All but one seminary was closed. In other countries, like India, where missionaries had great freedom under British rule, suddenly the rules of missionary engagement changed. Christian churches in India could no longer rely on missionary leadership. The ideology of Warneck and others assumed that the great European empires were God's way of evangelizing the world. What would happen now that "God's way" was destroyed?

2. Ralph D. Winter, *The 25 Unbelievable Years, 1945–1969* (South Pasadena, CA: William Carey Library, 1970).

Missions and Their Struggle to Adapt

The world was changing and, in subtle ways, so was the church and theological reflection about the church. Subtle and then dramatic changes in Christian approach, attitude, and placement were beginning to emerge in the 1950s. In 1944 most of the six hundred Presbyterian missionaries from the United States working in East Asia were working in China—but the Pacific War, followed by the communist liberation,[3] changed all of that. In 1954, there were only 333 Presbyterian missionaries working in East Asia, and none of them were in China.[4] Many missionaries to China, and most missions that had been working in China, were now working in Taiwan, Indonesia, Malaysia, Singapore, and Thailand. It was a foretaste of the future of Christian mission. The self-determination of peoples in each country would redraw the mission map, as well as the religious map, of the world. Out of necessity, most mainline missions now gave credence to the leadership of national church bodies as never before. Methodists, Anglicans, and Presbyterians from numerous nations deferred to the General Assembly of the China Christian Council. Local churches, as early as 1948, were to request missionaries—a pattern that would become dominant after the 1960s—rather than the mission boards making the decision from London, Basel, or New York. Requests were to be made from local churches to their synod, these requests were to be passed on to the General Assembly, and the General Assembly would pass on the request to various mission boards in the West. It was neater, clearer, and more businesslike in design than it was in practice. But even with this new sense of order and focus, missionary presence did not fully recover. Missionary presence (almost all Western) in the world was highest right before the Great Depression (about 1927–29); the numbers did not begin to recover until the 1950s. The new high mark of missionary activity (1958–60) was lower than the high mark in the 1920s. Global missionary presence did not fully recover until the sudden rise of evangelical missions in the 1960s and 1970s—and when it did, it was less and less Western. Mainline missions continued their decline from about 1960 to the present. Faith missions, evangelical missions, and non-Western missions more than replaced this loss. While missionary work was slowly being transformed by world events, some things were already beginning to change.

Ecumenical Movement in the 1950s

During the period of "lull before the global storm," the ecumenical movement continued to move forward with new programs, studies, and assemblies.

3. Perspective is important. For many Chinese, the Communist revolution was liberation. For others the rise of Communism meant loss, imprisonment, and/or death.

4. Scott W. Sunquist, "East Asia: Destructions, Divisions, and Abundance," in Scott W. Sunquist and Caroline N. Becker, *A History of Presbyterian Missions: 1944–2007* (Louisville: Geneva, 2008), 194–96.

The chairman for the IMC from 1947 to 1958 was John Mackay, president of Princeton Theological Seminary. A Scotsman who learned Castilian Spanish to work among university students in Latin America and who then worked with the Presbyterian mission agency in New York before taking on his role at Princeton, Mackay was well-suited for his role in global mission. Mackay moved mission thinking forward in his teaching, in his work in South America, and in his leadership in the IMC. He developed and taught a required course for all students: a course on how to think about the global church in unity and mission. By 1965 his lectures were collected and put into book form: *Ecumenics: Science of the Church Universal* (1965).[5] For Mackay, and many mission leaders at the time, the broader category of "ecumenics" framed the missionary work of the global church. Unity, cooperation, partnership, and equality were leading concerns in the ecumenical movement in the 1950s. In 1958, Mackay reported that the age had now come when full partnership of Western and "newly independent churches" was transforming "the Protestant Christian mission from a unilateral Western sending operation into a missionary enterprise with a world-wide base and a world-wide field of operation."[6] Looking back half a century later, this and other pronouncements appear both prophetic and overly optimistic. For all of the rhetoric of "fully independent" churches and "full partnership" among them, the global church was still far from being (fully) equal in partnership according to any measure of equality: education, experience, finances, or organization. Vitally important was the fact that real partnership was now affirmed, and this language prepared the global church for independence, which is the prerequisite for partnership.

The Triune God, the Church, and the World

The next major IMC meeting (1952), held in Willingen, Germany, was important in that it began a new direction in mission thinking: placing mission within the larger secular story. Once again a Dutch theologian would challenge cherished assumptions. Johannes Christiaan Hoekendijk (1912–75) made a strong attack on the "church based" mission thinking that went back a century to the writings of Rufus Anderson and other promoters of the three-self mission theology. For Hoekendijk, this theology made the church the center of mission thinking and this was an "illegitimate center."[7] God's concern is to bring his *shalom* to the

5. We know that this was Mackay's approach from the early 1950s. He argued in 1951 at the Central Committee of the WCC that the study commissioned at Whitby, "The Missionary Obligation of the Church," should instead be called "The Calling of the Church to Mission and to Unity." For Mackay you can't talk about mission without talking about unity, and the term for this is "ecumenics." It is a good term to reclaim.

6. Mackay's 1957 speech to the General Assembly of the Presbyterian Church in the USA, quoted by R. Pierce Beaver in *From Missions to Mission* (New York: Association Press, 1964), 39.

7. See Hoekendijk's article "The Church in Missionary Thinking," *International Review of Missions* 41 (1952): 324–36.

world—and the church is only the means by which his much greater work would be accomplished. The church is instrument, not center, nor goal. In retrospect, we can see that these ideas would move the ecumenical movement from ecclesiology to eschatology as the primary framework for missiological discussions. This eschatological approach (*shalom* in final reconciliation) and the focus on the world rather than the church would bear their full fruit in the 1960s.

A second major theme that came out of 1952 was what might be called a recovery of fully trinitarian engagement in mission theology. A radical christological orientation, in large part influenced by neo-orthodoxy, had dominated most mission discussions until this point. From 1952 on, a more trinitarian foundation for mission was established. This should be understood as a recovery of the theology of the ancient church as it first struggled to make sense of and explain the person of Christ, the work of the Holy Spirit, and their relationship to the Father. Now mission was understood as a part of the nature of the Triune God—God in community fully reconciled and bringing about the reconciliation of all of creation. "The missionary movement of which we are a part has its source in the Triune God Himself."[8]

Out of this conference, only seven years from the end of the Second World War, and possibly with the reconstruction and rebuilding of societies in mind, came a strong statement on the identification of the church with the world and the need of the church to "listen" to the world. "The Lord of the Church identified Himself wholly with mankind, so must the Church also do. . . . [The Church must] discern in it the sure signs of God's sovereign rule."[9] Mission was moving from being a church activity to being God's activity; from paying attention to the church to paying attention to the world; from a theology of present activity, to God's final act to bring about *shalom*. Most of the 190 delegates and advisers at the conference may not have been clear about these changes at the time, but this was the new direction for ecumenical missiology. This new direction began in 1952 and fully blossomed in the mid- to late 1960s. In a sense, mission was seen as much larger and more inclusive; mission was becoming more secular. How mission would be carried out now hinged on how one understood "sure signs of God's sovereign rule." This was a critical variable that exposed this theology to a logical fallacy; there are many interpreters of the times, but most people see their own reflection in their prophetic vision. This weakness aside, Willingen promoted the *missio Dei* rather than the *missio ecclesia* or the *missio Christi*. To this day, starting with the missionary nature of God rather than the missionary calling of the church or even Jesus as the Missionary of God has proven to be an enduring theological gift for missiology and for Christian theology.

8. Norman Goodall, ed., *Missions under the Cross: Addresses Delivered at the Enlarged Meeting of the Committee of the International Missionary Council at Willingen, 1952* (London: IMC, 1953), 189.

9. Ibid., 190.

The theological movement or call for the churches to listen to the world, to the longings and needs of the people, developed into a heightened concern for social issues in the IMC and the WCC. Issues of social justice and racism were discussed much more openly as church leaders looked for ways to express mission from a position of strength.[10] The WCC, headed up by Western Christians who still had remarkable resources and political standing in the West, saw it as their Christian duty, in light of the eschatological future, to work toward "the Responsible Society," marked by social reconciliation. The combined voices of church leaders could still have an impact on political policy, international relations, and social discourse.[11] Continuing to advocate mission as involving church planting and evangelism, the broader concerns of God's rule in all of life began to be interpreted in new ways with strong voices.

These themes continued at the Second Assembly of the WCC held in Evanston, Illinois, in 1954.The WCC now represented 132 member churches from forty-two countries. The eschatological approach, combined with an expanded view of evangelism (to include all that will come about), tended to collapse the goal of mission into the process of the mission. In other words, the goals of reconciliation or justice were defined as proclaiming the good news, which meant that racial reconciliation became evangelism. We begin, here, to see the broadening of the term "evangelism," as it became an expression for all (or any part of) that which had traditionally been called "mission." Evangelism still meant bringing persons to faith in Christ, but it now also meant helping to bring about social transformation and incorporating people into the life of the church.[12] Also of note at this assembly, and something that would also come to light in the Roman Catholic Church at the Second Vatican Council, is that the understanding of the laity in God's mission was affirmed with great clarity. The church is not just clergy in mission, it is the whole body called to witness to Jesus Christ. As always, contexts (local and global) set the stage for missional theology. At this assembly, the world was becoming more and more caught up in the Cold War; the statement on "Responsible Society" was a way of providing a Christian critique of all governments and political systems—East and West. A second major issue of the time was segregation and racial injustices in places like the United States and South Africa. Again,

10. See, for example, W. A. Visser 't Hooft, *The Ecumenical Movement and the Racial Problem* (Paris: UNESCO, 1954), and, much earlier, J. H. Oldham, *Christianity and the Race Problem* (New York: George H. Doran, 1924).

11. For example, Reinhold Niebuhr appeared before senate committees in the 1940s, and churches set up offices in Washington, DC, and near the United Nations as part of a broader mission of the church. Christendom—the cooperative arrangement between church and government—was still alive through the 1950s.

12. Here I am following the excellent summary by Rodger C. Bassham, *Mission Theology, 1948–1975: Years of Worldwide Creative Tension—Ecumenical, Evangelical, and Roman Catholic* (Pasadena, CA: William Carey Library, 1979), 37–40.

in light of an eschatology of hope, the assembly made it clear that any segregation is contrary to the gospel. The type of unity that the WCC represented was explained (we are not a "super church"), and the authority of the WCC was also explained (only by the weight of its own wisdom with the constituent churches).

Mission as Integral to the Church

In 1958 the IMC met again (in Accra, Ghana), and this would be the last meeting in which the missionary arm of the ecumenical movement met separately. This meeting prepared the way for the integration of the IMC into the WCC in 1961. A major part of the assembly was taken up with discussions about whether or not it was a good idea that the WCC (which is not a church) should take in the IMC (which is not a mission). Some felt that the missionary dimension would be diluted or completely lost in discussions of order and unity;[13] others felt that, if mission is the heart of the church, then the church (represented by the WCC) should not be without its heart; still others felt that the WCC was not universally accepted and acceptable by all IMC members, so union would force some to either opt out or compromise. In the end, the vote was strongly in favor of integration (fifty-eight to seven national councils), but, without unanimity, tensions continued and some divisions would later occur.

Of great importance for missionary thinking was the decision at this assembly to take on further study of the "Theology of Mission" and a joint study with the WCC on "The Word of God and the Living Faiths of Men." The latter of these two would become a major theme in ecumenical theology in the following three decades. In the pattern of Edinburgh 1910, the preparation for integration into the WCC called for careful study. Out of this careful study, involving regional meetings with pastors, scholars, and mission leaders, came a number of publications. Most important, and still helpful reading regarding ecclesiology and mission, is the study on *The Missionary Nature of the Church* by Johannes Blauw,[14] as well as the IMC-commissioned book written by D. T. Niles of Ceylon (Sri Lanka), *Upon the Earth*.[15] At each regional meeting the delegates were presented with ten questions to discuss, and Niles

13. Two Anglicans spoke strongly against it: Max Warren and Stephen Neill (who said the WCC had little interest in mission and so the IMC would just become one of ten or twelve departments of the WCC). See Paul E. Pierson's article "Lessons in Mission from the 20th Century: Conciliar Missions," in Jonathan Bonk, ed., *Between Past and Future: Evangelical Mission Entering the 21st Century* (Pasadena, CA: William Carey Library, 2003), 76.

14. This volume summarized and provided a critique of biblical theology of mission and the church. Johannes Blauw, *The Missionary Nature of the Church: A Survey of Biblical Theology of Mission* (New York: McGraw-Hill, 1962).

15. This was published in 1962, reflecting material from the twelve regional meetings held on six continents. D. T. Niles, *Upon the Earth* (New York: McGraw-Hill, 1962).

summarized seven common factors that came out of those global discussions. They are worth noting here:

1. Criticism concerning missionary foreignness
2. Questions about missionary justification
3. Issues relating to missionary unity
4. Problems of missionary frustration
5. The spread of the sectarian spirit
6. The voice of the African revolutions
7. The challenge of resurgent religions

These seven issues came not from theologians or mission administrators but from missionaries and local Christian leaders who were on the frontiers of mission. Niles gives an example of how broader church issues illumined missiological issues. A Sinhalese Baptist minister in Ceylon expressed the Buddhist attitude toward Christianity.

> There has been a psychological aversion to Christianity on the part of the Buddhist public on the ground that it is a foreign religion, couched in an alien paraphernalia, introduced to this country by foreign missionaries. It is also regarded as a powerful ally of Western Culture and of Western Imperialism. . . . Another motive behind the resurgence of Buddhism is concerned with the supposed danger which the impact of Christianity has on our national culture. This impact, according to our critics, is so strong and harmful, that if the Christian Church is allowed to continue its way any longer, there might be a sort of cultural disintegration in our land.[16]

Contextualization and national identity were not theoretical constructs, but were matters of life and communication; are missionaries communicating the gospel or their cultural values?

Closely related to these studies was a far more critical event for the future direction of mission theology—the 1960 World Student Christian Federation (WSCF) conference held at Strasbourg. Although the movement of students into missionary careers had dropped beginning in the 1920s, the movement of Christian students continued to have vitality both within the ecumenical movement and in newer evangelical movements. Nothing reveals more about the different concerns and approaches to missions than the 1960 WSCF conference contrasted with the meetings of groups like Inter-Varsity Fellowship (in the UK, IVF), InterVarsity Christian Fellowship (in North America, IVCF), and Campus Crusade for Christ (in the United States, CCC). (We will look at this comparison in more detail later.) WSCF in the 1950s was led by future

16. Ibid., 27.

leaders of the WCC and IMC, and so what happened in one had a direct bearing upon the other.[17] Students pioneered the new theology of mission, as they had pioneered the modern mission movement in the nineteenth century. In 1956 a long-term (five-year) study on the life and mission of the church was planned, looking at what might be responsible participation of the church in the world. Before the five-year study was over, a major teaching conference for students was held (1960) with major theologians presenting: Karl Barth, Lesslie Newbigin, D. T. Niles, and W. A. Visser 't Hooft. The most impressive speaker according to the students, however, was the forty-eight-year-old Dutchman, Johannes C. Hoekendijk. Hoekendijk's language of mission had developed further as he emphasized more strongly the full identity of the church with the world. Earlier, in a 1950 article for the *Ecumenical Review of Mission*,[18] Hoekendijk gave a "call to evangelism" that both broadened and deepened the understanding of evangelism. Hoekendijk may very well have been the first writer to define evangelism as the preaching of the *shalom* of God. "The aim of evangelism can be nothing less than what Israel expected the Messiah to do, i.e., He will establish *shalom*. And *shalom* is much more than personal salvation." In fact, the goal of salvation is much more comprehensive than what had been envisioned in the past. Hoekendijk identified salvation (and the evangelism that brings it to the individual) with the complete, eschatological fulfillment of salvation: "realization of hope . . . the redemption of the whole of creation." Hoekendijk then rejected two contemporary ideas of evangelism: propaganda (reproducing ourselves) and *plantatio ecclesiae* (planting churches). Anticipating later "missional church" language, Hoekendijk stated that the church is not the product of evangelism, but the church itself is apostolic:

> I believe in the Church which is a function of the Apostolate, that is, an instrument of God's redemptive action in this world. . . . The Church is nothing more (but also nothing less!) than a means in God's hands to establish *shalom* in this world.[19]

Then he comes to his classic presentation of the threefold proclamation of God's *shalom*:

- proclaimed *(kerygma)*
- lived *(koinōnia)*
- demonstrated *(diakonia)*

17. WSCF leaders included Philippe Maury of France, Robert Mackie, D. T. Niles, and Philip Potter. Lesslie Newbigin also came up through the WSCF movement.

18. Johannes C. Hoekendijk, "Call to Evangelism," *Ecumenical Review of Mission* 39 (1950): 167–75.

19. Ibid.

The following decades indicate that people heard Hoekendijk's words in different ways. Some heard a call to speak less and live more; mission became for these people a call to serve the world and, in this sense, Hoekendijk anticipated the secular decade of the 1960s. God's call would be discovered as we searched for the places where God was already at work, and we would then participate with God in these movements of liberation on the way to *shalom*. Others heard here a call to more consistent and holistic mission. For these people, mission was not just a call to "make converts" or plant churches; mission was a call for us to participate in God's larger work of redemption in the world. We follow Jesus into the world and, as the body of Christ, we serve, proclaim, and build community in his pattern.

The church was not simply removed from the center of mission—the church was almost viewed as a hindrance to mission. Hoekendijk expressed, with great accuracy and zeal, the students' frustration with ecclesial structures, or what was later expressed as "the rigidity of organizations and institutions [as] one of the major obstacles, if not the greatest to the missionary enterprise of the Church."[20] One of those who participated at the conference was WSCF committee member Frank Engel. He commented on the 1960 Strasbourg "teaching conference," the brainchild of D. T. Niles, in the following manner:

> D.T. [Niles] delivered the first address at Strasbourg and experienced what he had been warned of. The student audience reacted against his "teaching" concept. This was a rare occasion when this extraordinarily able communicator "missed the bus". He had to alter his approach.
>
> Much has been written about "Strasbourg" for it had a disturbing impact. It became a moment of great change and it ushered in that decade of change. It had been planned in the light of the steadily developing theological thought of the previous 35 years, and beyond that, of the lessons of more than a century of Protestant missionary experience. (One issue of *The Student World* had been devoted to the lessons of history, in preparation for Strasbourg.) But by July 1960, unnoticed, almost subterranean, elements broke through the surface, rather like molten lava bursting through new fissures or orifices in a volcano. There was Hans Huykoendyk [*sic*] of the Netherlands calling for the "de-sacrilizing" of the Church in the light of the emergence of the secular age.[21]

Hoekendijk's language (of "dereligionizing Christianity" or "desacralizing the church") would become the language of the 1960s, a language that broke open discussions, but it never became the standard language of mission. Pioneering in new and extreme language about the church in mission, the

20. From D. T. Niles (*Upon the Earth*, 29), quoting a follow-up document from the Strasbourg conference.

21. Frank Engel, *Living in a World Community* (Hong Kong: WSCF, 1994), 45.

WSCF moved into a period of internal struggles and rapid decline.[22] The language and the debate of the Strasbourg meeting became the language of the WCC in the 1960s. The more traditional language of other theologians would slowly find its way back during the 1970s, but by then its meaning had changed.

Thus, by 1960 there was clarity about the church being formed in mission and unity. There was commitment to the ideas that the mission of God is bigger than the church, and that it is the church that participates in the mission of the Triune God. There was also agreement that mission must have an eschatological perspective—looking toward the fulfillment of all things or the expression of the full *shalom* of God in this world. However, the means of carrying out that mission, the structure of the church in mission, and the meaning of the evangelistic calling of the church were all unsettled and unsettling issues. This was the situation in which the mission structure (IMC) became integrated into the WCC in 1961 at the New Delhi General Assembly.

Mission in a World Turned Upside Down: 1960–2000

A number of developments in Christianity exploded upon the world stage with little forewarning. No one predicted the collapse of the Berlin Wall in 1989. Few people imagined that the violent apartheid social system in South Africa would end without great violence or even civil war. No one imagined that China would become the most competitive free market in the world, while remaining a communist country. No one (at least no one in the ecumenical movement) dreamed that Christianity and other religions would remain so vital into the twenty-first century. No one dreamed that the twentieth century would be the century of both ecumenism and Pentecostalism. Finally, no one predicted that Christianity would recenter outside of the West within one generation: between 1965 and 1990. These global developments (and many more) came about suddenly, quietly, and with little warning. Christianity, in the midst of these global transformations, was showing a new strength, resiliency, and adaptability. Christian mission and mission theology took off in different directions in light of these changes, and that is what I would like to look at in the remaining sections of this chapter.

The years 1960 and 1961 provide an excellent point of departure. I have noted above the impact of the WSCF theological development at Strasbourg; in the next year the pivotal Third Assembly of the World Council of Churches was held in New Delhi. At this assembly the missionary (IMC) and church unity (FO and LW) streams of the ecumenical movement joined. It was expressed as the integration of the International Missionary Council with the

22. Robin Boyd, *The Witness of the Student Christian Movement: "Church ahead of the Church"* (Geneva: WCC, 2007).

World Council of Churches. For some, this was the obvious direction of the ecumenical movement, but for others it was considered a great mistake. Max Warren prophesied, for example, that such an integration would mean that mission concerns would be lost or overwhelmed. Most, however, felt that this would bring missionary concerns into their proper context—into the church. Ecclesiology is the natural home for missiology. This is how the Assembly itself explained the integration.

> For the churches which constitute the World Council this means the acknowledgment that the missionary task is no less central to the life of the church than the pursuit of renewal and unity.[23]

Not only did "renewal and unity" join with mission, but a new and more explicit "basis" for the World Council of Churches was approved. The previous basis was unambiguous and simple—a way of including as many churches as possible:

> The World Council of Churches is a fellowship of churches which accept our Lord Jesus Christ as God and Savior.

This "basis" had been written and approved at the planning meeting for the World Council held in Utrecht in 1938. The committee of fourteen represented the Life and Work and the Faith and Order conferences on this simple basis. Thus, from 1938 to 1961 the basis of ecumenical cooperation, coming out of the German period of the Barmen Declaration, focused upon the divinity and authority of Jesus Christ. Although the statement did exclude some groups like Unitarians, by 1960 the statement was considered a little too brief. It lacked the theological clarity of early church councils. At New Delhi, the basis was expanded to clarify any ambiguities:

> The World Council of Churches is, "A fellowship of churches which confess the Lord Jesus Christ as God and Savior, according to the scriptures, and therefore seek to fulfill together their common calling to the glory of the one God, Father, Son, and Holy Spirit."

Thus, the basis became christocentric, trinitarian, confessional, and scriptural. Adding these simple elements ("confess"; "to the glory"; "Father, Son and Holy Spirit"; and "according to Scripture") made it clear that unity would be built around traditional and ancient orthodoxy. The year 1961 also marks the joining of a large contingent of Orthodox churches with the WCC, the joining of the first Pentecostal churches (two from Chile), and the first observers from the Roman Catholic Church.

23. From *New Delhi Report* (New York: Association Press, 1962), 4.

The years 1960 and 1961 were pivotal years for mission, theological clarity in mission, and Christian unity. Covering this period we will look at six major themes in Christian mission in the half century from 1960 to 2010. First, we will look at how 1960s theology (the secular decade) both opened up Christian mission to a careful analysis of missional contexts and lost much of the spiritual language, worship, and power of earlier Christian mission. Closely related to the development of secular mission was a propensity to collapse all mission into social justice. A type of missional reductionism occurred in the 1960s and 1970s that drove many away from the WCC; the search for "movements of liberation" became ideological for many theologians. Secondly, we will look at the complex development of mission and religions. Since the 1910 Edinburgh Conference, mission theology had become more and more nuanced and careful in its language about "living faiths" and Christian mission in the context of those faiths. In the 1960s this became a central concern, using the newer language of "dialogue." Great diversity developed among Christians from around the world as to what dialogue meant, what the goal was, and how it related to witness and conversion. Thirdly, we will look at the remarkable changes that took place in global Catholicism as a result of the Second Vatican Council. Vatican II opened the Roman Catholic Church to more direct contact and dialogue with Protestants and Orthodox regarding Christian mission. Fourthly, we will look briefly at the nationalizing of missions and the decline of the church in the West. Nationalizing missions (turning over the authority and property of the mission to national churches) took place while churches in the West were in rapid decline. The decline of Christianity in the West was the result of a long period of germination of Enlightenment ideas. The Enlightenment brought many good gifts to society, but by the twentieth century it also bore the spoiled fruits of spiritual doubt and church decline. Fifthly, we look at the rise of evangelical cooperation as distinct from the WCC and the ecumenical movement. The tensions that developed between secular theologies and theologies of liberation within the ecumenical movement produced fissures in Protestant cooperation. Thus, by the end of the 1960s and up to the present, we can talk about three major streams of mission involvement and reflection: Roman Catholic, conciliar Protestant (aligned with the WCC), and non-conciliar Protestant (evangelical and Spiritual churches). Finally, we will look at the most remarkable shift that occurred in Christianity in 2000 years: the sudden rise of non-Western Christianity and Spiritual forms of Christianity. Almost all of the reflection on mission that has occurred in the past five centuries has been European and North American. Now, however, in the twenty-first century, mission activity and reflection are mostly Asian, African, and Latin American. The Western church has passed the mantel of leadership in mission. Some Western churches are aware of this shift; most have not fully grasped what this means.

Secular Theologies, Christianity, Liberation, and Salvation

The "turn to the world" that occurred in theology and mission in the 1960s had certain ambiguities that led (at times) to some strange conclusions. In 1972, an article was published in the *International Review of Mission* that discussed salvation in purely secular terms—as liberation brought by the savior figure Mao Tse Tung.[24] As the author expressed, if we look at salvation in this world, we can see the work of Mao as bringing salvation to China. The process is not complete, and it is not perfect, but the parallels with Jesus open up new understandings of what "salvation today" really means.[25] What such an article shows us is that, in a search to identify the "movement of God" in the world and then participate in that movement, it is often difficult to discern genuine works of God. Ideologies that *look* like the work of God often creep in. One person's liberator is another person's oppressor. Mao, the liberator, became one of the most tragic rulers in human history.[26] This example demonstrates how difficult and even misleading it is for the church to make large prophetic statements interpreting world events. We usually get it wrong. Nineteenth-century "Adventist" and "millennial" movements are proof that prophetic interpretations of history are best left alone.

Race and Reconciliation

Wherever movements of liberation from oppression were found, there were theologians who would write about the Spirit of God behind those movements. Some liberation movements, however, were more obviously divinely congruent with Scripture than others. The civil rights movement in the United States and the struggle against apartheid in South Africa are two such movements, and both were important in framing mission theology in the 1960s through the 1980s. Although race issues had been discussed throughout the twentieth century in relation to the church and mission, the urgency for change and the culpability of the Western church came to the fore at the 1968 General Assembly of the WCC held at Uppsala, Sweden. At this meeting it was affirmed

24. Raymond Whitehead, "Salvation and the Chinese Revolution," *International Review of Mission* 61, no. 244 (1972): 327–41.

25. "Salvation Today" was the name of the CWME five-year study that culminated in the 1972–73 meeting in Bangkok, Thailand. See *Bangkok Assembly 1973: Minutes and Report of the Assembly* (Geneva: WCC, 1973).

26. Mao developed a morbid fascination with death and saw it as a helpful tool in ruling the Middle Kingdom. There are now many biographies on Mao that have unmasked his personal life and the social results of his policies. It is now estimated that over fifty million people died unnecessarily—both directly and indirectly—under his rule. See Li Zhi Sui, *The Private Life of Chairman Mao* (New York: Random House, 1996); and Julia Chung and Jon Halliday, *Mao, the Unknown Story* (New York: Anchor, 2006). See the excellent evaluation of deaths caused by various wars and by Mao's policies on the following website: http://necrometrics.com/20c5m.htm.

that "the world sets the agenda for mission," and in 1968 that meant American civil rights and apartheid. The assembly was held in the shadow of the assassination of Martin Luther King Jr. (April 4, 1968). This was even more significant, because King was to have been one of the plenary speakers at the assembly. The goal of mission was expressed as the "new humanity," a new humanity formed in the likeness of Christ, exhibiting social engagement as a primary sign.

As a commitment "to be" this new humanity, the WCC established its controversial "Program to Combat Racism" in 1969. Funds were allocated to help the church be in solidarity with those fighting against racism; "combat" and "fighting" were at times ambiguous terms. Funds were allocated to support families and provide medical care for freedom fighters in Southern Africa, but money was also used for the legal defense fund for the radical activist Angela Davis (a communist party member) in the United States (1971). This type of radical solidarity with militant revolutionary figures had a very negative impact upon support for the WCC and national Christian councils. Most of the criticisms of the "Program to Combat Racism" were extreme and unjustified, but one $10,000 grant to help Angela Davis went a long way to discrediting the ecumenical movement as a whole. The WCC and mainline churches supporting the WCC had a major public relations crisis beginning in the 1960s and mission funding dropped dramatically.[27]

Reconciliation to Revolution to Liberation

Shalom led to "reconciliation," which then led to "revolution" as a catchword for mission in the later 1960s and 1970s. Martin Luther King Jr. was a model of reconciliation through peaceful resistance. For many ecumenists, liberation fighters in southern Africa became agents of God's work in the world—more so than the local church. In fact, the local church was developing a poor reputation since the strong call of Hoekendijk in 1960, in which he alluded to the church as a prison: "Are there no revolutionaries here? People who do not want to improve or to modify the structures and institutions of our Christian life but who are ready to break out of these prisons?"[28] Studies on the church ("Missionary Nature of the Church," "The Missionary Structure of the Congregation," and "The Church for Others"), and a developing theology of "presence" over "witness" or "proclamation," dovetailed with this revolutionary theology of mission. The church was no longer the arena of mission; in fact, many viewed the church as a hindrance to mission. Probably the most important study in promoting this new view of church was the 1967

27. Anecdotal evidence is much easier to find than statistical analysis of the funding decline in light of the policies of the Program to Combat Racism.

28. Quoted from Theo Gill in "Historical Context for Mission, 1944 to 2007," in Sunquist and Becker, *History of Presbyterian Missions*, 28.

study "The Church for Others." Containing both a North American and a European group section, this document turns the church outward to find its full identity in movements of liberation. Mission (a particular type of mission) swallows up all worship, preaching, liturgical, and even nurturing elements of the church. The church can be found wherever people struggle to bring about greater justice and reconciliation in their communities.[29]

What we see in retrospect is not that mission was becoming bigger or more complex (as was thought at that time), but rather that mission theology was suffering from an ideological reductionism. Mission was reduced to the quest for social justice. In this reductionism there developed an impatience that was reflected in semantics; from "reconciliation" and *shalom* people quickly moved to talk of revolution. Theologies of revolution or theologies of liberation developed out of genuine situations of oppression coupled with attendant hope. Latin America was one place of long-term oppression by a small number of wealthy landowners paying very small wages to laborers who did not even own their own land. The Roman Catholic Church (and later some Protestant churches) were often complicit, having much to lose in opposing the status quo of the oppressors. Thus, liberation from oppressive situations often involved divisions within faith communities. Matters were made more complex by the strong Marxist critique that often came with Christian theologies of liberation. A number of Marxist movements were calling for justice for laborers at this time; how was their call and their struggle different from the Christian call for justice? Is it possible to use Marxist analysis in a Christian way to help bring the Kingdom of God, or is this improper contextualization?

In fact, liberation theology was a new type of contextualization, and it differed both from older liberal theology and from Marxism—two ideologies to which it has been compared. Unlike earlier liberal theologies, liberation theology was strongly biblical (focusing on the person of Jesus), and it was "from below." Liberal theology of the nineteenth and early twentieth centuries did not speak of Jesus the way liberation theology did, and liberal theology, which was more of an academic movement, tended to be more elitist. Unlike Marxist revolutionaries, however, liberation theologians were theologians; they understood human sin, and they did not sell out to a utopian vision. All utopias end in violence; they make promises they cannot keep and end up forcing their will on both people and structures. Liberation theologians were more realistic and more theological. We might say that liberation theologians

29. I think this is a fair summary. Some people took this very seriously, and in doing so, all but extinguished the local church. I came across a pastor in New Jersey who was trying to rebuild a church that had lived out this Church-for-others mind-set. The previous pastor (who studied with one of the authors of "The Church for Others") convinced the congregation to meet on Sunday mornings to go out and serve in their communities. No worship. No Sunday school. No sacraments. In five years, the church was nearly closed. The church had almost dissolved into the world.

were both worldlier and more divine than either earlier liberal theology or Marxists.[30]

These theologies did not come out of the WCC but were developed by Christians working with the poor, and thus provided a corrective to the church *for* others. Here was a theology that expressed in its formation a "church *with* others." Looking at biblical passages about God's special concern for the poor—what became a "preferential option for the poor"—opened up the global church to its own complicity in oppression, and it challenged Christians in the West to think in terms of "first steps" in theology. Is it valid to theologize about mission from a position of privilege and safety, or should greater identification with the Suffering Servant be a requirement for real theological reflection? Liberation theologies became, more accurately, theologies of suffering with the poor rather than theologies of confrontation and violence. One of the structural changes in missional presence that developed out of or within liberation theology was the *communidades ecclesiais de base* (CEB: base, or grassroots, Christian communities). These local gatherings of Christians were the natural product of a theology *with* the poor developed by Brazilian archbishop of Olinda and Recife, Dom Hélder Pêssoa Camera (1909–99). His life in the squatters' settlements in Rio de Janeiro earned him the title "Bishop of the Favelas." Here was a Roman Catholic ecclesial change that did what WCC was discussing in the 1960s, but accomplished the missional transformation without a loss to the basic church structure.

Mission and Religions, Dialogue and Witness

A second major development in the last half of the twentieth century had to do with the relationship between Christian faith and witness and other religions. Sometimes terminology says a lot. Previous to the twentieth-century ecumenical movement, other religions or religious people were called "pagans," followers of "primitive religions," or "heathens." By the middle of the twentieth century, Hindus or Buddhists were called "people of other religions," then "people of other faiths," and finally "people of other living faiths." This reveals a new respect for the full humanity of the person as well as a respect for the beliefs of others. This new approach—from a direct proclamation of the gospel, to a more passive Christian "presence," to a thoughtful "dialogue"—all occurred in the 1960s. The discussion has been almost exclusively Asian and Middle Eastern until recent years. Asia has been the mother of all world religions, including Christianity, and it was from people like D. T. Niles that the major

30. I am thinking here of Míguez Bonino, Segundo, and Gutiérrez. Much of this analysis follows that of Bosch, *Transforming Mission*, 432–47.

studies were first encouraged.[31] Most all of the major writers on religious issues have been from Asia or have worked in Asia: M. M. Thomas, D. T. Niles, Stanley Samartha, Paul Devenandan, Lesslie Newbigin, and so on. Earlier statements that came out of these consultations focused on respect for people of other religions and love for individuals of other faiths. They rightly focused on people—not on religions as systems of thought and life.

The central concept that came out of these discussions was that of dialogue rather than witness. What was accomplished from these discussions on Christian mission and people of other living faiths? First, as we noted above, an approach developed that begins with the biblical record of God's relationship with all humankind and ensures humility and trust. Dialogue requires listening, and listening makes it possible to communicate with greater clarity and accuracy. It was noted that Jesus questioned, spoke, and listened in a way that established dialogical relationships with others—peasants, those in authority, and even Gentiles. Second, the dialogical approach was defined and given some structure. For example, in the 1967 Kandy Statement, three realities are given for the basis of dialogue: (a) Christians are in human solidarity with all people; (b) all of humanity lives in the same universal history; and (c) all humans are created in the image of God (and Christ died for every person).[32] Third, for the most part the statements on dialogue held together two things: the need to listen and speak on an equal footing with others, and the uniqueness of Christian faith. "[A] Christian's dialogue with another implies neither a denial of the uniqueness of Christ, nor any loss of his own commitment to Christ."[33] Evangelism was not excluded under the new emphasis on dialogue, but the method and understanding of evangelism was changing.

Another dimension of religious understanding was the awareness that people of faith need to work together to struggle against the ills of society. Problems of violence, injustice, and disaster relief require cooperation of all people. The struggle for peace requires that people of faith understand each other so that lasting peace can be established on the basis of mutual respect.[34] In order for greater understanding to develop in social contexts, the WCC encouraged and sponsored dialogue sessions with people of other faiths. One of the first was held in 1970 at Ajaltoun; four Buddhists, three Hindus, three Muslims, and twenty-eight Christians gathered for an official dialogue. Through such sessions, walls of misunderstanding were lowered, genuine relationships were developed, and issues of common concern were discussed. In this way, the

31. Niles first raised the subject at the 1954 Evanston Assembly of the WCC, and then it developed into a major study, "The Word of God and the Living Faiths of Men."

32. From "Christians in Dialogue with Men of Other Faiths," *International Review of Missions* 56, no. 233 (1967): 338–43.

33. *The Uppsala Report* (Geneva: WCC, 1968), 29.

34. *Bangkok Assembly, 1973: Minutes and Report of the Assembly of the CWME of the WCC, December 31, 1972 and January 9–12, 1973* (New York: WCC, 1973).

WCC was defining an area of mission (that had been a part of mission work for centuries) in a more structured way.[35] At the time of the Nairobi Assembly of the WCC (1975), people from other faiths were invited to discuss section 3: "Seeking Community: The Common Search of People of Various Faiths, Cultures and Ideologies."

By 1979 a very helpful document was produced to provide theological structure to the concept of dialogue: *Guidelines on Dialogue with People of Living Faiths and Ideologies*.[36] This document gives helpful advice and also points to the ambiguities and potentially divisive nature of genuine dialogue. The document is helpful in its description of the way Christians should approach theological questions:

> Approaching the theological questions in this spirit, Christians should proceed with repentance . . . with humility . . . with joy . . . with integrity. . . . All these would mean an openness and exposure, the capacity to be wounded which we see in the example of our Lord Jesus Christ and which we sum up in the word vulnerability.

Helpful guidance is also given regarding the theological foundation for dialogue:

> It is Christian faith in the Triune God—Creator of all humankind, Redeemer in Jesus Christ, revealing and renewing Spirit—which calls us Christians to human relationship with our many neighbours. Such relationship includes dialogue; witnessing to our deepest convictions and listening to those of our neighbours.

But then the difficult questions and ambiguities are faced squarely:

> Christians engaged in faithful "dialogue in community" with people of other faiths and ideologies cannot avoid asking themselves penetrating questions about the place of these people in the activity of God in history. They ask these questions not in theory, but in terms of what God may be doing in the lives of hundreds of millions of men and women who live in and seek community together with Christians, but along different ways.

The boundaries of interreligious dialogue are often stretched beyond what the church will permit. This happens when dialogue moves to interfaith worship

35. Wherever missionaries were involved as pioneers or wherever they worked outside of colonial control, interreligious dialogue was part of their daily lives. We have seen this in the work of the early Jesuits in Asia, but it was also evident in the work of missionaries like E. Stanley Jones. See *Christ at the Round Table* (New York: Abingdon, 1928) for a discussion of his dialogue sessions where everyone (the best informed and respected from all faiths) would be invited to share the deepest of their own spiritual experiences in life. No judgments were made, for all came to listen and learn.

36. *Guidelines on Dialogue with People of Living Faiths and Ideologies* (Geneva: WCC, 1979).

and toward a common world or global theology. However, most people in the WCC, as well as the non-conciliar and Roman Catholic traditions, understand the value of dialogue as a way of living in mission rather than as an ideology or a type of theological reductionism.[37]

Revolution in Roman Catholic Missiology

Roman Catholic mission theology before World War II was still very much an expression of the First Vatican Council and Pope Pius IX's *Syllabus Errorum* ("Syllabus of Errors") and his encyclical *Quanta Cura* ("With Great Care," issued on the same day—December 8, 1864). These were documents that were defensive in orientation, telling Catholics about the errors and vices of the modern world.[38]

There was a mission theology behind the "Syllabus of Errors" and the First Vatican Council, and this theology was elaborated further through later encyclicals.[39] Mission was understood to be the responsibility of European churches to preach the light of the gospel and plant viable churches among all peoples. A strong emphasis was placed upon indigenous priests and bishops, but this aspect of Catholic missiology was late to develop in practicality. After over 450 years of mission work there were still only sixty-eight Asian and twenty-five African Roman Catholic bishops.[40] One major issue leading up to the Second Vatican Council was the problem of the nationalities of missionaries. French, Portuguese, and Spanish colonialism often made it difficult for other nationalities to work on their lands. Rome struggled against nationalism in mission, even as colonialism was being dismantled.

The calling of a Second Vatican Council (called January of 1959, held 1962–65) came as a surprise to church leaders, for Pope John XXIII was seventy-seven when he was elected as a "stop-gap" pope. If calling a council was a surprise, the content and decisions of the council were even more surprising. Many of the theologians who had earlier been silenced or disciplined for

37. There is a more thorough discussion of theologies of religion in chap. 8 on the Holy Spirit.

38. Many helpful summaries and analyses of Christian mission in the light of the Second Vatican Council have been written. A simple introduction to the Council, the theology of the RCC leading up to the Council, and the theology following the Council is given in Stephen Bevans and Roger Schroeder, *Constants in Context: A Theology of Mission for Today* (Maryknoll, NY: Orbis Books, 2004), 244–55.

39. Bassham, in his book *Mission Theology, 1948–1975*, 300, lists five encyclicals that were important for mission: *Maximum Illud* (1919, Benedict XV), *Rerum Ecclesiad* (1926, Pius XI), *Evangelii Praecones* (1951, Pius XII), *Fidei Donum* (1957, Pius XII), and *Princeps Pastorum* (1959, John XXIII).

40. Richey Hogg, "Some Background Considerations for *Ad Gentes*," in *International Review of Missions* 56, no. 223 (2011): 287.

"Syllabus of Errors" of the Vatican Council, 1864

Some of the "errors" that were condemned were obvious threats to Christianity: "absolute liberty"; the state having the right over church property; the state having the final say over a child's education; the belief that teachings of the church are harmful to society; and the belief that divine revelation is imperfect. Other articles in the "Syllabus" (there are eighty total) include calls to return to the pre-Reformation era relationship of church and state (e.g., when the pope's worldly power was defended by the state, and the Roman Catholic Church was to be the sole religion in a given country). Some of the errors that were identified were prophetic—outlining the very decline of Christianity in the West that later took place. The elevation of human reason over religion, the spread of secular authority into the church, and the decline of Christian marriage were all identified as problems in this 1864 document. The "Syllabus" and *Quanta Cura* were a great encouragement to the faithful, but a bane to liberal scholars and rulers of Europe.

their *nouvelle théologie* were invited to help provide leadership at the council. It was this *nouvelle théologie* that was the underlying theology of the Second Vatican Council. Some of the scholars of this theological movement of "Ressourcement"[41] included Henri de Lubac, Dominican Yves Congar, Hans Urs von Balthasar, Étienne Gilson, Jean Daniélou, and Joseph Ratzinger (later Pope Benedict XVI). These were theologians who were engaging ancient texts (Daniélou and Lubac began the important volumes of early Christian writings, *Sources Crétiennes*, begun 1942) and at the same time engaging the modern world. This helps to explain some of the major shifts that took place in Roman Catholic ecclesial and missional thinking that began with Vatican II. We look here at six of the shifts that took place and how they played out in later events in the Roman Catholic Church.

New Directions for the Roman Catholic Church

First, the council marks a change in approach from excluding non-Catholics, to finding ways to include and unite all Christians. Clearly some of this concern came out of the modern context of church divisions, but it also came out of the extensive biblical and patristic study that guided the theologians. Rather than affirming that outside of the Roman Catholic Church there is no salvation, the "Decree on Ecumenism" talks about Orthodox, Protestants, and other Christians as "separated brethren." The goal of Christian unity was now approached through the Kingdom of God and the body of Christ rather than through the movement of all Christians into the Mother Church.

41. Returning to the sources of the faith: Scripture and the ancient writings.

Second, the council rooted the identity of the church in the mission of God (*missio Dei*) in Jesus Christ. Remarkably, one of the most important Catholic documents of the twentieth century, the "Dogmatic Constitution on the Church" (*Lumen Gentium*), does not begin with sacraments or preaching or priestly orders, but with the following sentences:

> Christ is the Light of nations. Because this is so, this Sacred Synod gathered together in the Holy Spirit eagerly desires, by proclaiming the Gospel to every creature, to bring the light of Christ to all men, a light brightly visible on the countenance of the Church. Since the Church is in Christ like a sacrament or as a sign and instrument both of a very closely knit union with God and of the unity of the whole human race, it desires now to unfold more fully to the faithful of the Church and to the whole world its own inner nature and universal mission.[42]

The first footnote in *Lumen Gentium* is Mark 16:15: "He said to them, 'Go into all the world and preach the gospel to all creation.'" The language of Vatican II is very similar to that of the scholars working on missional ecclesiology at the same time in Geneva. Years later, in 1976, Lesslie Newbigin would say the following of the local church: it must take seriously "the full secular reality of its place. . . . 'Taking seriously' will mean recognizing the church's calling to be for that place its calling to be a sign, a foretaste and instrument of God's purpose to sum up all things in Christ as that purpose relates to *that* place."[43]

Third, Vatican II's theology of the church shows development in the doctrine of the Holy Spirit (under charisms of work), which strengthens a trinitarian ecclesiology rather than a christological ecclesiology. As other scholars have noted, a trinitarian model both reflects the biblical record more faithfully and avoids a strong hierarchical approach to the church. Trinitarian ecclesiology points to the communal essence of God and allows for a greater focus on the laity.

This emphasis upon the role of the laity in the church and mission is the fourth characteristic of Vatican II. The "Decree on the Apostolate of the Laity," describes the responsibility of all laity in all vocations to share in the vocation of all Christians to the apostolic life, "But the laity likewise share in the priestly, prophetic, and royal office of Christ."

Fifth, the council opened up the church to more genuine encounters with cultures through its foundational document on Revelation, *Dei Verbum* ("Dogmatic Constitution on Divine Revelation"). Paragraph 22 calls for the "Word of

42. All quotations from Vatican II documents come from the Vatican website: http://www.vatican.va/archive/hist_councils/ii_vatican_council/.

43. "A Local Church Truly United," in Choan-Seng Song, ed., *Growing Together in Unity: Texts from the Faith and Order Commission on Conciliar Fellowship* (Geneva: Faith and Order, 1978), 232–33.

Church as Sign, Instrument, and Foretaste of the Kingdom: J. E. Lesslie Newbigin

Bishop Newbigin described the church as sign, instrument, and foretaste of the Kingdom a number of times—including in *The Open Secret* ([Grand Rapids: Eerdmans, 1978], 110), but he was thinking this way much earlier. In the 1958 publication for the IMC entitled *One Body, One Gospel, One World: The Christian Mission Today*, he used the following language, "But in finding ways of escape from the wrong kind of colonialism we must not lose the true foreignness of the Church. The Church can never be wholly at home in the world and the fact that in its life and mission it deliberately and systematically transgresses the boundaries of nation and culture is an indispensible symbol and instrument of its supernatural calling" (31). In that same document he also talks about the church as a foretaste. Speaking of the church, he says, "It is the place where the fruit of Christ's mission is already present in foretaste and as an earnest of that which is to come. It is the place where the forgiveness of sins, peace with God through Jesus Christ, and eternal life in Him, are already enjoyed in foretaste" (19). The influence of Newbigin's eschatological ideas on the church are especially evident in chapter 7 of *Lumen Gentium*.[a]

a. A candid and full discussion of Protestant dialogue and mutual sharing regarding the church and mission around Vatican II can be found in Thomas Stransky, "The Observers at Vatican II: A Unique Experience at Dialogue," *Centro Pro Unione* 63 (Spring 2003): 8.

God to be accessible at all times," and states that "suitable and correct translations are [to be] made into different languages, especially from the original texts." In the same paragraph, Catholics are instructed to do these translations "in cooperation with the separated brethren as well." This one little paragraph opened up the Catholic Church to deeper contextual missionary engagement in cultures, and opened up the sacred Scriptures and Catholic worship to people throughout the world. It caused an enormous transformation in the meaning of worship and in the meaning of the spiritual life for many Catholics; they were encouraged to read the Bible in their own language.

Finally, and related to the above issue, Vatican II opened up the church to a new and positive engagement with the world. Vatican I was defensive and protective; Vatican II was affirming and open to dialogue with the world. This was expressed in a number of ways. Theologically, Vatican II is open to engagement and a subsequent search for unity with Orthodox and Protestant churches. Politically, the council dropped the Roman Catholic nation ideal and was open to Christian presence as a pilgrim people among other peoples. Socially speaking, there was a special decree on technology, *Inter Mirifica* ("Decree on the Media of Social Communications"), which was a very forward-looking document that recognized the need to seek a fuller conversion of cultures. Christian responsibility, and an apostolic relationship with cultures, requires the church to engage cultures with the use of newer technologies and media. Again, this would have great implications for Roman Catholic involvement in apostolic witness.

Roman Catholic Missiology after Vatican II

The aftermath of the council may have brought more *aggiornamento* ("bringing up to date") than the Curia expected. Bevans and Schroeder have commented that "for Roman Catholics, the updating introduced through the Second Vatican Council brought refreshing new life, but also chaos. . . . Thousands of priests, sisters and brothers left rectories and religious communities; and social and political agendas sometimes fueled further tensions within the church."[44] Regarding mission, there were both positive and negative effects. Certain reforms regarding religious orders relaxed some of the guidelines and encouraged greater engagement with the world. However, the call for "adaptation to the changed conditions of our time" ended up with complex, but basically negative, consequences for religious vocations. A rapid decline of nuns, monks, friars, and priests followed Vatican II.[45] This decline (40 percent decline of American men studying for the priesthood from 1965–70) was not a direct result of Vatican II; however, the greater openness to the world that Vatican II encouraged did make possible some extreme responses, or what Benedict XVI has called "excessive secularism." In parallel with the radical call for a secular church in Protestant circles, Roman Catholic Ronan Hoffman, in 1967, called for mission structures to dismantle—for every church member should be a missionary.[46] This was the "Church for Others" in Roman garb. It was the 1960s.

Another result of the council was a more direct church engagement in countries suffering under or perpetrating long-term injustices and oppression. The council called for such an engagement.[47] Theologies of liberation began to be articulated soon after the important Conference of Latin American Bishops (CELAM) in Medellín, Colombia (1968), in which the Latin American bishops were to reflect on implementing the ideas of Vatican II. Three years later, Gustavo Gutiérrez's groundbreaking book *A Theology of Liberation*[48] was published. There were similar movements expressed throughout the Roman Catholic world, and greater attention given to local contexts, to the laity, and to social issues. The shift was coordinated globally through the newly formed

44. Bevans and Shroeder, *Constants in Context*, 251.

45. See Rodney Stark and Roger Fink, "Catholic Religious Vocations: Decline and Revival," in *Review of Religious Research* 42, no. 2 (2000): 135–45.

46. Identified by Bevans and Schroeder, *Constants in Context*, 251. See Ronan Hoffman, "The Changing Nature of Mission," *Washington Service* 19, no. 1 (1968): 5–12.

47. Second Vatican Council, *Gaudium et Spes* (1965).

48. Gustavo Gutiérrez, *A Theology of Liberation: History, Politics, and Salvation* (Maryknoll, NY: Orbis Books, 1973).

Synod of Bishops, established by Paul VI after Vatican II. The Third General Conference of the Synod of Bishops (1974), a gathering of bishops from ninety-five countries, was a key meeting that discussed at length the important document on evangelization in the modern world. Two important conclusions are found in the final document issued by Paul VI, *Evangelii Nuntiandi* ("The Evangelization of the Modern World"): (1) "The task of evangelizing all people constitutes the essential mission of the Church." Thus, ecclesiology derives its meaning and task from its evangelistic calling. However, evangelism was not narrowly defined. (2) "Evangelizing means bringing the Good News into all the strata of humanity, and through its influence transforming humanity from within and making it new." Evangelism does first involve an "interior change," but it must also convert the behaviors and lives of people.[49] By affirming the understanding of the church and mission from Vatican II, *Evangelii Nuntiandi* affirmed that mission is the task of all Christians, that our understanding of evangelization comes from the example of Jesus Christ, and that the church in each location has the responsibility of "assimilating the essence of the gospel message and transposing it." In addition, *Evangelii Nuntiandi* reflected some of the concerns of the Latin American bishops (from the Medellín gathering) affirming that liberation of all people is the extension, or fulfillment, of evangelization.

Since the 1970s, Roman Catholic missiology has developed through the regional gathering of bishops (e.g., Conference of Asian Bishops) and pastoral institutes. As a result, the Roman Catholic Church has developed ways of training the priests and religious that are contextually appropriate. These pastoral institutes provide the vehicle to bring various congregations together to learn by listening to each other's contexts.[50] Many of the same issues the WCC has faced have been guiding issues for the Roman Catholic Church: dialogue and theology of religions; Pentecostalism and the charismatic movement; and openness to the world in a context of poverty, human suffering, and growing technologies. The world, on one level, does set the agenda—and mission thinkers of all communions are reflecting on the same tides of change.

Nationalizing Missions and the Decline of the West

The end of the twentieth century was the time of independence for many nations in Africa and Asia, and a time of nationalizing for many missions. As Christianity was losing its influence (and membership) in the West, in the

49. Quotations taken from *Evangelii Nuntiandi* (December 8, 1975).

50. I have had the good fortune of participating in a Pastoral Institute in South Africa where priests and religious from all over Africa were given the opportunities to talk about local social issues and pastoral issues, and then, in the context of Bible study, worship, and meals, groups were given the opportunity to discuss together the pastoral and missional issues.

non-Western world Christianity was growing. Although the expressed goal of all missions was that all churches and institutions would eventually be under indigenous leadership, the reality of this was much more complex. By the middle of the twentieth century, missions were running large hospitals, schools, colleges, and even universities. All of these large institutions were subsidized by European and North American donations. Simply "turning over" these institutions to local church councils was highly problematic. Three-self, as a goal, had two major flaws: money and control. Many of the institutions had such large budgets that a local Indian or Indonesian or Kenyan church could never begin to support such a hospital or school. At the same time, it was problematic for European churches to simply send money, as if they were shifting from mission to welfare agency. Control was also a big issue. There was a great deal of personal and institutional ownership of these institutions. What if the local church council did not take care of the mission compound or the school? What if the school closed? Some Western leaders felt they should ensure that the institutions survived and thrived into the future—even at the expense of local indigenous leadership.

Discussions of what was called "full integration" of missions into the local churches took decades, and there was no one rule for how it took place. The priority was always to have indigenous leadership at the helm and local financial support of all institutions and churches. Thus, there was a strong push for leadership training after World War II. Numerous Bible schools and seminaries in the non-Western world were begun in the 1950s. Most missions worked out the process of integration in the 1950s and 1960s, but when it finally took place few missionaries were pleased with how it happened, and few mission executives were lauded by the missionaries that worked in their organization. Missionaries were often sent home. Many of these missionaries had been working for decades in a certain area: they had learned a new language (or two), they had families and relationships that gave their lives stability and meaning, and suddenly (or so it seemed) they were told that they had to go "home." I have studied this process fairly carefully in the Presbyterian Church (USA), and I am not sure it could have been done in a way that would have avoided the pain, loss, and long-term grief.[51] Not only missionaries experienced this pain; local church leaders also felt great pain in this process. Often local leaders were told by offices in the West, "You are now an independent church, so we will be calling back half of our missionaries. We would like you to tell us which ones you would like to stay."[52] Of course, this approach was very painful for national leaders who had grown to work well with many of these missionaries. Culturally, in most regions of East Asia, it would be

51. See Sunquist and Becker, *History of Presbyterian Missions* for discussions of this process. See especially Caroline N. Becker, "Missionaries Speak," 132–53.

52. As told to me in Chiang Mai, Thailand, 1990.

impossible to "save face," and tell someone to leave. Many local leaders were not prepared to handle large budgets (huge by local standards), and so the temptation to use church money to take care of family was great, and often not resisted. Corruption was almost encouraged by the lack of accountability and training that preceded most of the integration.

With integration came a new model of missionaries being requested rather than sent. Having given full autonomy to a national church, the Western missions would take requests for missionaries rather than making these decisions from London, Paris, or New York. It was a good idea, but it was difficult to implement. Many countries no longer had a "mission station" presence, and so the Western offices were in contact only with national church leaders. Sometimes this worked well, but, once again, it left many individuals with too much power and too little partnership in their work. Western missionaries were often requested for "projects" or short-term work. Mission was being redefined as "person in the gaps" rather than as an incarnational presence. The incarnational presence comes long term to learn the language, the culture, and to fully participate with the Christian community in mission. In interviewing retired missionaries, comments like the following, about the period of integration, were common.

> They dissolved the missions and left no structure. No longer was language study a priority. Previously you had to pass language study before you would be approved. [For example], Arabic is two years full-time language study, at least. In 1968 you had to come for five years for your first term of work before you would go on furlough. Term appointments were destructive of mission work because missionaries did not fully engage the culture. Nationals used to say—come to live with us and die with us.[53]

The concept and goals of the missions were missiological common sense. As one missionary from Egypt said, "We were always trying to work ourselves out of a job." The application of these concepts, however, was not always done well, or in ways that were contextually appropriate. In the big picture of things, the process of integration did empower, strengthen, and develop local churches. The national churches became stronger, and most of them grew once the transfer had taken place. Nationalism, decolonialism, and mission integration were all expressions of global awakening of cultures and nations.

In some countries, governments pushed the missions out of the country by nationalizing mission schools and/or hospitals. In Pakistan, between September and October of 1972, the "Government of Pakistan nationalized all privately managed colleges and schools, including Christian colleges and schools, thus effectively undermining a key historical component of Presbyterian mission

53. Taken from notes from a group interview of retired missionaries in New Wilmington, Pennsylvania, July 2, 2005.

there."[54] Other countries stipulated the schools could continue only if Christian instruction were an elective course of study. Some governments told mission schools they must require instruction in Buddhism, Hinduism, or Islam—but not Christianity. Local churches were caught in the odd missionary situation of promoting education and promoting Buddhism, or giving up on the whole vocation of educational ministry.

At the same time that integration of missions was taking place, the churches in the West were going through (and continue to go through) a rapid decline. Funding for mission work went down, and this accelerated the decline of Western missionary presence in the world. Through the first decade after World War II, Christian mission was still on the radar screen of most Western Christians. Missionaries were volunteering to "rebuild" and even re-evangelize areas where the war had destroyed lives and institutions. But this changed in the 1960s, when mission became a peripheral work of the church—and by the 1980s, mission "at our doorstep" became more important. Western churches became preoccupied with their own programs, and at times their own survival. Churches were closed and often bought by local businesses or other religious groups. I note this briefly here because it had a great impact upon mission understanding as well as mission support. What was lost in the mainline churches in mission, however, was picked up by newer Pentecostal and evangelical churches.

Evangelical Emergence

Our fifth major theme is the reemergence on the global stage of evangelicalism. We have seen the impact that evangelicalism had in world mission in the eighteenth and nineteenth centuries. The roots of evangelicalism stretch deeply into late seventeenth and early eighteenth century German Pietism, English Puritanism, and later awakenings in the eighteenth and nineteenth centuries. Evangelicals are very conscious of those roots and often reaffirm this heritage when given the opportunity. Evangelicalism as a stream of Protestantism seemed to have been largely seduced into fundamentalism in the early parts of the twentieth century, while those who did not become separatist and postmillennial continued within mainline Christianity. However, the 1960s changed everything. The perceived neglect of evangelism in the WCC and the strong social statements coming out of the 1960s left many evangelicals wondering where they belonged. The shift seemed sudden, but there were early rumblings. Beginning in the last decades of the nineteenth century, mission societies had been founded with a clearly evangelistic priority (or a particular eschatology or view of the atonement), and yet many evangelicals continued to participate in the ecumenical movement. There were signs of evangelical resurgence in

54. John Webster, "South Asia," in Sunquist and Becker, *History of Presbyterian Missions*, 291.

the founding of faith missions and Bible colleges. Those evangelicals who remained in the ecumenical movement struggled to accept the broader social witness of the ecumenical movement from the very beginning. However, it was among students that the first signs of change in mission would be detected. In 1910, a major decline in the Student Christian Movement (SCM) came about through the defection of large segments to the more evangelical Inter-Varsity Fellowship, which traces its roots to the Cambridge Inter-Collegiate Christian Union (CICU).[55] Thus, Inter-Varsity Fellowship spread its movement to Canada and the United States by 1938. Newer evangelical student groups were the furnace of renewal for missions after the Second World War.[56]

The years 1941–42 are an important marker for the rise of evangelicalism. In those years InterVarsity Christian Fellowship (USA) was founded and the National Association of Evangelicals was envisioned. A prophetic statement was made by Harold Ockenga at the gathering of evangelical leaders in St. Louis in 1942. His address, "The Unvoiced Multitudes," became a rallying cry for evangelicals to unite for a common public witness, and to stop withdrawing from social responsibility.[57] It was a call to leave the fundamentalist mentality and return to the roots of evangelism and social engagement. Thus, there was an evangelical movement with separate structures in place before the 1960s. Statements and addresses at ecumenical gatherings in the 1960s made it very difficult for these evangelicals to continue to live in two worlds. After the 1968 meeting of the Uppsala Assembly of the WCC, Donald McGavran from Fuller Theological Seminary devoted a whole issue of his *Church Growth Bulletin* to the "betrayal by the WCC." The title of the issue was "Will Uppsala Betray the 2 Billion?"[58] Other evangelicals, like John Stott and David Hubbard, tried to engage the WCC by attending and participating. Evangelicals were emboldened, but they also sensed that other structures were needed to

55. CICU traces its roots back to the 1848 Cambridge Prayer Union ("to make Jesus known to students in Cambridge") but was founded as a Christian Union in 1877. The Oxford Union was founded two years later. The CICU website explains the growth of the Inter-Varsity movement in the following manner: "Initially CICCU became part of the Student Christian Movement, formed in 1889; however, the CICCU left the SCM in 1910 because the SCM had drifted to the view point that Jesus' death on the cross was not at the centre of their message. Recognizing the seriousness of this issue, OICCU and other CUs followed them in this split, and together they founded the Inter-Varsity Fellowship of Evangelical Unions (now UCCF, the 'Universities and Colleges Christian Fellowship') in 1928." See http://www.ciccu.org.uk/faq.php#howciccubegin.

56. Another group started at UCLA in 1951, Campus Crusade for Christ (now called "Cru"), started by businessman Bill Bright. In 2011 there were about twenty-five thousand full-time missionaries working with CCC globally.

57. The indefatigable, but ever gracious, Ockenga helped to found Fuller Theological Seminary, Gordon-Conwell Theological Seminary, and the periodical *Christianity Today*. These three institutions reflect the recovery or reemergence of evangelicalism. All have a strong element of missional commitment.

58. The estimated two billion were those who had not heard the gospel.

Courtesy of the Billy Graham Center Archives, Wheaton College

Billy Graham conferring with the Emperor Haile Selassie at the Berlin 1966 World Congress on Evangelism. On Billy Graham's left is Professor Otto Debelius, who is speaking to Carl Henry, cofounder of *Christianity Today*.

communicate clearly the evangelical core of mission and to gather younger churches around that message and task.

In 1966 a "World Congress on Evangelism" was organized in Berlin under the sponsorship of the Billy Graham Association and *Christianity Today*. The title of the volume on the congress is "One Race, One Gospel, One Task." The emphasis was on the gospel for all nations (one race) and the responsibility of all Christians to engage in that work (one task). It was the first large-scale international gathering of Christians that was not part of the Roman Catholic Church or the ecumenical movement. The congress was held on the heels of the Second Vatican Council and it included (surprisingly, I might add) about three hundred observers from the Roman Catholic and Jewish faiths. There were twelve hundred participants in all, including the evangelical sympathizer (but Orthodox Christian) Emperor Haile Selassie, who stood on the platform with Billy Graham. Speakers included Bishop Otto Dibelius (Lutheran), John Stott (Anglican), Corrie ten Boom, Francis Schaeffer, and a host of speakers from Asia, Africa, and Latin America. Many participants were evangelicals within ecumenical churches; others were from independent churches or evangelical denominations.[59]

The Lausanne Covenant, 1974

Berlin 1966, the first major evangelical meeting, was a statement and a call to faithfulness to an evangelical witness. In 1974, the same year as the important

59. The full list of speakers and many of the addresses are available at the Billy Graham Center Archives: http://www2.wheaton.edu/bgc/archives/GUIDES/014.htm.

Third Synod of Roman Catholic Bishops, a new ecumenical and evangelical mission movement was started with the gathering of evangelical leaders from around the world in Lausanne, Switzerland. Twenty-seven hundred delegates attended from 150 nations. The purpose of the gathering was to unite evangelicals for mission[60] and the title of the congress was, "Let the Earth Hear His Voice." In the midst of that discussion a number of issues surfaced. First, there was an animated discussion about social responsibility; the issue was pressed by Latin American participants including René Padilla and Samuel Escobar. Lausanne would become more inclusive and thorough in its understanding of mission as a result of its listening process.[61] A second issue that emerged came from one of the great innovators of mission in the twentieth century, Ralph Winter. Winter argued that the biblical concept of nation (*ad gentes*) was not talking about modern political nation states, but about ethnic groups. Therefore, world evangelization should identify "unreached people groups" and develop strategies for reaching them. This concept was used to discuss and plan for world evangelism after 1974 with numerous statistical projects designed to track the planting of churches in every people group in the world.

Like the 1910 Edinburgh meeting, the 1974 Lausanne meeting became institutionalized as a movement. The covenant was signed, and many people from around the world joined in. A "Continuation Committee" was selected, specific issues were discussed, meetings were held around the world, and booklets were produced to provide reflection and guidance on various issues. There have been two follow-up international gatherings, one in Manila in 1989, and one in Cape Town in 2010. The "Cape Town Commitment" is a substantial theological statement that, in many ways, completes the discussions of the previous decades. Other studies have been done under the auspices of the Lausanne Committee on World Evangelization and nearly thirty Lausanne Occasional Papers have been produced, covering a variety of topics related to mission. Lausanne has been the central place, along with the World Evangelical Alliance,[62] in which Protestants of all backgrounds gather around the central concern for evangelism in participating in the *missio Dei*.

Contributions of Evangelical Missiology

Evangelicalism has made a number of contributions in mission thinking since the 1960s, many of which came to the surface in 1974. The concept of

60. "To encourage and stimulate the involvement of churches, denominations, ministries, networks, and individuals in the cause of world evangelization."

61. At the 2010 Lausanne Meeting in Cape Town, Padilla and Escobar expressed their appreciation to John Stott for making a special trip to Latin America after the 1974 Congress to listen to their concerns and then continue to voice these issues in the Lausanne Movement.

62. Founded in 1951 as the World Evangelical Fellowship, it is a fellowship of churches that identify as evangelical from 127 nations. It is not specifically a missionary fellowship.

unreached people groups is one I have already noted. Also, church planting among people of the same cultures as a "natural" means of church growth has been a strategy discussed since the 1950s. This "Homogeneous Unit Principle" is a core concept in the Church Growth Movement of Donald McGavran.[63] Another contribution is the Evangelism in Depth movement, which came out of the work of the Latin America Mission under the leadership of R. Kenneth Strachan. Strachan said that the strength of any movement was based on its ability to mobilize all of its members in propagating its beliefs.[64]

Another contribution evangelicals made during this period was the idea of training pastors and church workers in their own location rather than bringing them out to a large city for residential theological education. Called "Theological Education by Extension," the movement originated from the observation of missionaries working in Guatemala: they noticed that most of the people who went to seminaries did not stay in ministry very long. The pastors were coming from rural areas and small towns and, after living three or four years at a residential seminary, they often did not return to their towns—or they did not fit in. It was decided, in large part under the leadership of Ralph Winter, to take theological education to the people. The experiment began in 1963, and soon it spread throughout the world. In this model, some of the education is done by correspondence, some in seminars run at a central site, and some through traveling teachers. Today, we would call this a blended model of education.

There are many other concepts and strategies that were developed by evangelicals at the end of the twentieth century, but two more recent concepts are worth mentioning. When working among highly resistant societies, such as in Muslim villages, different levels of contextualization were identified: C1 up to C6.[65] A C1 approach would be to transplant the same cultural form of Christianity (language, worship style, liturgy, and architecture) that was the culture of the missionary. This had often been the case in the past. C2 would adapt the local language, but little else would be adapted. C6 is the opposite extreme, in which a person or a family or a village might be Muslim in every way—except that they are followers of the prophet Isa (Jesus) and they read the Injil (Arabic New Testament). This has given language to various discussions

63. McGavran's first book outlining some of these ideas from the Indian context was *The Bridges of God: A Study in the Strategy of Missions* (New York: Friendship Press, 1955). This was later followed by *Church Growth and Christian Mission* (New York: Harper & Row, 1965), among others.

64. See Strachan's description in his article "Call to Witness," *International Review of Missions* 53, no. 210 (1964): 191–200. The application was to the evangelization of a region or a country, but it should be noted that this focus on lay involvement in mission was also expressed in the WCC study on the church and in the Vatican II documents.

65. See John Travis, "The C1 to C6 Spectrum: A Practical Tool for Defining Six Types of Christ-centered Communities (C) Found in the Muslim Context," *Evangelical Missions Quarterly*, 1998: 407.

about the levels and appropriateness of forms of contextualization.[66] Another strategy that has come out of evangelicalism, developed by Campus Crusade for Christ, was a single media tool translated into more languages than any movie in the world: "The Jesus Film." The film is an acted-out version of the Gospel of Luke with a brief call to follow Jesus at the end of the film.

What we see here is that the Lausanne Movement has helped to foster and spread many new approaches and concepts for world mission. It has been a marketplace for evangelical missional ideas, and a catalyst for many new movements. Lausanne still describes itself as a movement, a place where people can get connected and develop new partnership—more as individuals than as representatives or as institutions. Individuals volunteer, or opt in, to participate in Lausanne: it is not a movement of institutions but of individuals.

Evangelical Diversity and Cooperation

Evangelicalism in mission is among the most diverse forms of Christianity in the world today. The Cape Town 2010 gathering of four thousand people represented 198 nations, and among some of those nations, there are many different ethnic groups and languages. There were many Pentecostals at the gathering, but the worship was very Anglican, and one of the official (Christian) languages was Arabic. Because of the emphasis upon unreached people groups, diversity of cultures is given a high priority, and the more "grassroots approach" to delegate selection brings local social and moral issues to the fore.

With the ferment of ideas, studies, and new approaches coming from the Lausanne Movement, and with the recent studies of the WCC, the Synod of Bishops, and Curia of the Roman Catholic Church, there is unprecedented opportunity for genuine engagement and cooperation at all levels of the church. The WCC document *Mission and Evangelism: An Ecumenical Affirmation* (1982),[67] placed alongside the document on evangelism from the Synod of Bishops, *Lineamenta* ("The New Evangelization for the Transmission of the Faith," February 2011), and the Lausanne 2010 "Cape Town Commitment," reveals that they share many of the same commitments. Studied together, these documents reveal greater unity within the global missional task than we have seen since the Reformation.

It must be remembered that many evangelicals pulled out of the WCC, basically in protest that the ecumenical movement was reducing mission to

66. In contrast to this approach, a much more carefully nuanced and broader-range discussion of contextual approaches is given by Stephen Bevans in his classic presentation, *Models of Contextual Theology*, rev. ed. (Maryknoll, NY: Orbis Books, 2002).

67. This document is more thorough than the more recently produced preparatory paper "Mission and Evangelism in Unity Today" (2005). Both are found on the WCC website: www.oikumene.org.

social engagement. When they did so, there was very little conversation with either Roman Catholics or ecumenical Protestants. In the first decades of the twenty-first century we live in a different context. We now have a long history of evangelical and Roman Catholic dialogue on mission (1977–84), and evangelicals have a much greater engagement in issues of social justice as part of the work of evangelization. With these elements in place, there is the opportunity to develop greater trust and partnership across confessional boundaries. The biggest issue preventing greater cooperation and trust in mutual mission today is not the official statements but ongoing prejudices and insecurities in local contexts.[68]

Pentecostal and Indigenous Resurgence

We have noted the resurgence of Spiritual forms of Christianity in the twentieth century, movements which often have no relationship to Protestant or Roman Catholic forms of Christianity, except that they share the same Bible. Some of these movements (indigenous and Spiritual) started as rebellion against Western forms of Christianity. We might say the ongoing C1 types of mission work created a context for indigenous movements, inspired by the Holy Spirit, to emerge. The explosion of Spiritual forms of Christianity may have started in the early twentieth century, but it was the 1960s and 1970s when it penetrated mainline structures in the form of the charismatic movement. This is significant, because the charismatic movement bridged the division between classic Pentecostalism (which came out of fundamentalism and Wesleyan perfectionism) and mainline Protestant and Catholic communions. The difference can be seen in how a mainline church makes a decision and how a charismatic mainline church makes a decision. The former will ask someone to open with prayer, and then they will do a study, set up committees, come back with reports, pray, and then vote on a decision. The latter may call for a three-hour prayer meeting. The Spiritual movements brought back the expectation that God, through the Holy Spirit, will answer, heal, and cast out demons. There is great diversity of leadership styles, worship, liturgy, and even types of missionary activity among Spiritual churches, but what they have in common is an expectancy that the Holy Spirit will act and will speak.

Many of the largest churches and Christian movements in the world today would have to be described as Spiritual churches. Much of the movement to Christianity in China is Spiritual—with long prayer meetings, healings, prophecy, and an expectation for power in mission; the Spirit leads, and functions and

68. Another important point of division is the degree to which certain groups raise up their particular theological doctrines (e.g., the role of Mary, postmillennialism, meaning of the Eucharist) and moral issues.

forms follow. The largest church in Korea (actually, in the world) is Pentecostal, and the largest church in the Ukraine was started by a Spiritual Christian leader from Nigeria. Spiritual forms of Christianity tend to be "boundless." They cross boundaries of race and language with little resistance; they cross social or economic boundaries very easily; and they cross denominational boundaries with little concern. Spiritual churches are marked also by "extreme outreach." These churches are centered on the gospel of Christ for others, and are generally more concerned to reach others than they are to get advanced degrees or build the right churches. Finally, most of these movements have a larger role for women in leadership because they are led by the Spirit, not by a particular tradition or institution. Women also are given dreams and visions, and women also are given the gift of evangelistic preaching. This has been a boon for missionary outreach in areas where women have been liberated by such models and by such a message. As the movement becomes more institutionalized, some of these traits get domesticated, but for over a century the mark of extreme outreach continues to be evident.

Spiritual forms of Christianity are immensely influential in mission today. Classic Pentecostalism (including some African indigenous churches and other indigenous churches) represents over 15 percent of the world's population. This is an enormous change. One of the reasons for this is that, in many areas, the world of Spiritual Christianity is the world of local people. In most of Africa, for example, traditional beliefs accept the presence of the spiritual world, the importance of dreams, and the possibility of healings and demon possession. This is the world of the Bible, and it is the world of most Spiritual churches. Many missionaries will have no ministry if they cannot pray for healing or if they don't know what to do with a demon possessed girl. One exorcism goes a long way in bringing about the conversion of a whole family, even of a whole village.[69] Pentecostals, and Spiritual Christians in general, find ways of living in the modern, secular, and technological world while keeping their soul in the spiritual world, which is pleading through the missionary to "come and follow me."

Mission and Missiology from the New Center

It is tempting to think of the late-twentieth-century explosion of missionary activity from Africa, East Asia, South Asia, and Latin America as being mission from the margins, but by the 1980s the non-Western world was not on the margins of Christianity, but had become the center of Christianity, at

69. See Robert Solomon, *Living in Two Worlds: Pastoral Responses to Possession in Singapore* (Frankfurt am Main: Peter Lang, 1994). This is a study of ministry among former Hindus regarding demon possession and how to handle the pastoral issues related to the exorcism of a family member.

least in terms of numbers and vitality. When we look back at what happened in the five hundred years since the rise of Roman Catholic missions in the age of exploration, it is quite remarkable to see how the religious globe has changed. Christianity has not only broken out of its Western European–isolated existence, but now Christian mission is primarily being initiated from regions that Europeans did not even know existed five hundred years before. Equally significant is how diverse the models of mission have become. Iberian missionaries were supported by royal governments, organized by religious orders in service to the pope. Protestant initiative was much more individualistic and voluntaristic, with more complex relationships to churches and colonial governments. Now mission from Korea, Nigeria, Brazil, India, Malaysia, and China is often from countries where Christians are a struggling minority. Mission is not from "Christian nations" to "non-Christian nations." Thus we have seen in this overview a remarkable transformation in the understanding of the "missionary" and the "missionized."

We have also seen an equally remarkable transformation in how unity in mission is expressed. We have seen that in the post-Reformation period, for over 150 years, Protestants and Catholics were killing each other in Europe as well as in Africa and Asia. Ethnic identity was firmly welded to religious identity, as Dutch Reformed soldiers killed Portuguese Catholics all along the Portuguese Empire. As late as the mid-twentieth century there was much competition and little love among the various Protestant and Catholic groups—but that is less and less the case. Major movements of the 1960s have changed all of that. Teaching in Protestant schools in Asia and North America, I often have Roman Catholics in the class, preparing for some type of missionary outreach. I do not want to overplay the picture, because much distrust still remains, and yet this is a very different world for mission, and it may be that the context of ongoing persecution in the West (from secular ideologies) and from the non-West (from religious governments) minimizes Christian divisions. Persecution is not only the seed of the church—it can be the seed of church unity.

Christian mission is now carried on in a postcolonial, post-Marxist, and postmodern globalized world. No one knows exactly what that means. We do, however, have some hints. It means that the scars of colonial oppression and the deep wounds of communist gulags remain with us. It means that the globalized economies and movements of people that began in the sixteenth century have moved people and altered economies dramatically—moving both the poor and the rich into Christian communities. We also know that some of the same issues of secularism, technology, religions, church unity, and the meaning of church have not changed.

Part 2 of this book presents a way of thinking of the *missio Dei* built upon the movement we have just studied. We will look back at Scripture and tradition and build a theology that is vigorous enough to stand against persecution, both physical and ideological, but that is lithe enough to move among the many winds of change in our contemporary context. It is a theology of mission that honors the goal of revealing God's glory among the nations, through the very simple concept given by Jesus, the Missionary of God: "Unless a seed goes into the earth and dies, it cannot produce more seeds."[70]

70. Translation given in a worship service in Kota Kinabalu, April 2011.

Part 2

The Suffering and Glory of the Triune God

Trinitarian Mission in Scripture

In the history of Christianity we can see, as in a mirror darkly, Christian mission as the public movement of God through broken individuals and institutions. We have seen the church at times almost ignore its charter or commission from Christ, and at other times we have seen moments of humble, suffering service in the pattern of Jesus Christ to bring about the redemption of people and cultures. Part 1 of this book has been descriptive, highlighting movements, cultural shifts, and ideas that help us to understand the missionary nature of the church, especially in the last five hundred years. At times the history of missions is very confusing, and mission itself, the main cord of God's love in human history, seems obscured and hard to follow. Beginning in this way, with history, demonstrates that all Christian theological discourse is contextual: it is rooted both in a time and place. Mission is built around the faithfulness of God encountering the ebb and flow of human history. We have looked at the historical context of mission thinking and activity as a way of examining themes and issues (both good and bad) that are part of our history. We may not like some of what we have discovered—such as the connection between Christian mission and imperialism, or the way in which Christian mission has often been wedded to Western ideas of progress—but this history impacts how mission is often perceived today, so it is necessary to bring it out into the open. What has happened in the past has created perceptions that need to be reviewed and critiqued. Some of the historical models of mission and the ideas and commitments it entailed should not be forgotten. For example, in the twenty-first century, with global travel having become so easy, many local churches sponsor mission trips, and people travel around the world with very little awareness of historical concepts such as the "three-self" principle, contextual appropriateness, or the need to learn the local language. We want to remember some of these important concepts that have been learned, as well as avoid some of the subtle errors of the past. History is a hard schoolmaster.

The history section has highlighted many forgotten lessons and movements, and yet I have left out much more history than I have included—in order to tell a story. If you want to know a person, sit and listen to their family history. We need to continue to sit and listen to our family history, even as we reframe that history. Therefore, the brief history in the previous section is just that; it is not all there is to say. In preparing for mission work in any region of the world, one should do more detailed study of the history of mission in that region in order to be sensitive to the specific issues that are present within that context. What is offered in the previous section should simply point in the right direction for further and more specific study. Now, in part 2, we come to the constructive section, which seeks to recover, re-center, or renew the *missio Dei* for the church today. We have looked at the historic context and, with that history in mind, we now ask: how should we understand God's mission today? We are moving from history to theology and then to proclamation. The task of theology and good preaching is to give guidance to the church, and that is what we seek to do now.

The constructive section includes both part 2 and part 3. In part 2, we will look briefly at how to develop a theology of mission that is true to Scripture and Tradition, and that is relevant to the church in the twenty-first century: a three-legged stool of sacred Scripture, the Great Tradition, and local context. For most missiologists, as well as contextual theologians, the first and third of these "legs" on our missiological stool are obvious; theology must be done with the Bible and our contemporary world in view. However, I wish to also, even if only in a cursory manner, bring in a third element, and that is the Great Tradition of the church. By the Great Tradition, I mean all in the Christian tradition that points back to the apostolic teaching.[1] The Great Tradition is a

1. The Great Tradition has been defined as "what has been taught in all places, at all times by the whole Church." This may sound good theoretically, but once we try to explore what it means, we quickly discover it is an impossible guide.

needed ballast for the moving, shifting, and turning contexts that missiology must navigate. When missiology is done using the three legs of Scripture, Tradition, and context, we have the great saints who have gone before us as counselors and guides. We have some accountability to the early councils and the great apologists and the early church fathers. We are not alone. We are accountable to God and to the body of Christ, the church, through the ages. Our sudden new insights and revelations of what must be done today are often flights of fancy or forays into frontiers without a map. Including the Great Tradition in our missiology is like having all the saints of the past looking over our shoulder praying for our faithfulness in mission.

A quick example of how important this is today may help. It is possible to study the Bible, find some inspiring passages, and build a whole theology around, say, John 3:16. One could certainly do much worse. Then, however, a person might go off and preach and teach with the goal that their audience would "believe" (praying a one sentence prayer of salvation). This might be seen as a sufficient and complete missionary work. My wife and I have visited many churches in the past few years in Singapore, Malaysia, Egypt, South Africa, and the United States. We are surprised to see the loss of two important elements of the missionary nature of the church: contextualization and the confession of sin. Many of these churches look, sound, and sing exactly alike—with no apparent awareness of the context around them. The sermons are often made up of encouraging comments and supportive stories—"God loves you; God loves the whole world." Most of these churches have no place for confession of sin in their worship. The worship moves from praise (almost always meaning standing and singing songs for twenty to forty-five minutes), to offering, to preaching.

The Great Tradition is a reminder that the core of the faith, what makes faith possible, is the work of God (grace) and our response of faith (confession of sin) and obedience. Faith has meaning, and in the classic Anglican prayer it is expressed as "the prayer of humble access": "We do not presume to come to this thy Table, O merciful Lord, trusting in our own righteousness, but in thy manifold and great mercies. We are not worthy so much as to gather up the crumbs under thy Table. But thou art the same Lord, whose property is always to have mercy."[2] This is just one example of how the Great Tradition (for, until recently, all church communions had elements of confession in worship) provides guidance and mooring for the church in mission. After attending a worship service where there is no confession of sin, I have often wondered what "gospel" message is being proclaimed if the congregation does not see that confession is essential to being in God's presence. And so I will bring some ancient Christians into the constructive sections that follow.

2. From the 1662 edition, which is a revision of the 1559 Book of Common Prayer.

Three Characteristics of This Trinitarian Theology of Mission

Many others have preceded me in this important task, so we might ask: "What is unique about this particular description of mission? What is offered here that is more important, complete, or accurate than other attempts?" Three elements, I believe, are unique and make this next section important for the church today.

First, as was mentioned in the introduction, this missiology is developed biblically; it is rooted in the life, teaching, and ministry of Jesus Christ that the mission of God, the *missio Dei*, is a matter of *our participating with Jesus Christ in his suffering love for the greater glory of God to be revealed.* This gives a critical edge and a particular point of view to this description of mission that will exclude other views. The summary above comes out of historical and theological study, along with experience in the global church over the past decades. It is unusual, as a statement of mission, in that it focuses upon "suffering love." Quite frankly, I think that Tradition and Scripture critique any and all gospels of health and wealth; God is not primarily interested in our happiness in this life. I hope to defend what follows as a better way to understand the mission of God—rather than starting with cultural assumptions about happiness and fulfillment, or with an ahistorical biblical basis of mission, or even with a contemporary paradigm based upon previous paradigm shifts. Christian theology—especially the theology of mission—must begin with the Trinity as revealed in Scripture and in Tradition; this approach will reveal the importance of the suffering love of the Trinity.

Second, and closely related to the first, these two constructive sections envision *mission as a fundamental dimension of Christian existence*, and therefore the approach is more integrated and inclusive than other mission approaches. Mission is clearly a matter of ecclesiology. This is one of the major contributions of the ecumenical movement to the study of mission.[3] Mission has come out of the eighteenth and nineteenth centuries, in which it was a special task that some Christians elected to participate in by forming special missional structures. The missional church movement of the twentieth century came out of discussions of the ecumenical movement and was energized by Newbigin's challenge in his 1984 Warfield Lectures at Princeton Theological Seminary, which asked the question, "Can the West be Converted?"[4] This lecture pointed to the missionary nature of the church universal as applied to the West. The West had become a mission field in the minds of many missiologists as never

3. See the excellent study of mission in the theology of Karl Barth by John Flett: *The Witness of God: The Trinity, Missio Dei, Karl Barth, and the Nature of Christian Community* (Grand Rapids: Eerdmans, 2010).

4. In the opening paragraph, Newbigin admitted that he had stolen the title of the lecture from General Simatoupong of Indonesia when he muttered the question under his breath at a meeting in Bangkok. See *Princeton Seminary Bulletin* 6, no. 1 (1985): 25–36.

before. But mission is also a matter of basic discipleship. The rough spiritual waters of the 1960s revealed the importance of mission as the responsibility of all people of God. The apostolic nature of Christian discipleship is assumed here. Thus, I push against earlier assumptions that when we talk about Christian mission we are basically talking about a special calling—a second or higher calling. There may indeed be a special calling, but mission is first a general call of and for all Christians. Those who are called to Christ are sent by Christ; thus, mission is fundamental to Christian existence.

Coming out of this second characteristic of the approach presented here is my assumption that, third, *mission is primarily a matter of spirituality*; it is a way of participating in the life of Jesus Christ within a world at enmity with the One who created us. The spirituality of Christian mission is a major theme in Roman Catholic and Orthodox mission—less so among Protestants. You will find on the following pages a strong emphasis upon mission as an expression of spiritual life in God, as I try to recover some assumptions of the spiritual life that come from the ancient church. My study of history has led me to believe that many of the errors and tragedies of Christian mission come from a lack of spiritual awareness or from misplaced spirituality. Those who have stood fast with Christ in the midst of great persecutions and temptations have much to teach us about our identity with Christ. Persecutions will not decrease in the future, and so Christian spirituality should be a major concern. We are invited to share in the sufferings of Christ as a part of our participation in his mission: this is the spiritual life.

A Definition of Christian Mission

As promised earlier, part 2 begins with a definition of Christian mission. The introduction to this book presented four representative definitions or areas of concern in mission. Now that we have looked at the modern history of the missionary movement and evaluated some of the shifting ideas and patterns of missionary engagement, it is time to offer a definition of Christian mission that will guide our trinitarian understanding of the missionary God.

> Christian mission is the church's participation in the Triune God through the suffering of Christ, who was sent by the Father for the redemption and liberation of the world, by means of the conversion of individuals and cultures, in the power of the Holy Spirit, to the end that God be glorified in the nations and in all of his creation.

This definition recognizes the nature of mission (it is God's work), the extent of mission (all of creation), and the means of mission (Jesus Christ). It recognizes that mission is not a private affair: it is both personal (not private) and corporate. And it recognizes that mission involves a cultural mandate through nations or cultures. The Great Commission (Matt. 28:19) is focused upon cultures, and so is the heavenly vision (showing the completion of mission) in Revelation 7:9. This definition also reveals the way of suffering and the ultimate goal of mission: God's glory. The phrase "redemption and liberation" is used to describe the penultimate goal of mission. There are many words we could use to describe the salvation that God brings (salvation, reconciliation, eternal life, forgiveness, resurrection, etc.). It is clear that no one word can capture all that God has done, so I have chosen two words that are broadly inclusive of all that God has done. These two words are deeply embedded in the biblical text, especially the Old Testament, so I use them in tandem. This definition is not the final word, but it will help guide us in the following chapters.[5]

The Bible and Theology

Many missiological works begin with Scripture, as if what is recorded in the Bible can be directly applied to a local church or mission agency today. The tendency is to pull out favorite verses to support a particular view, neglecting the more inclusive biblical meaning of mission. Most "biblical-basis" mission approaches utilize direct commands and specific "going" texts. Mission, however, is much bigger and more pervasive than a few important texts; the entire Bible is a missiological text—and we need to view specific sending texts within the whole text of Scripture.[6]

In the next three chapters we will look at mission biblically and theologically through the Great Tradition's lens of the Triune God. In this, I am following much of the theological work of missiology in the twentieth century. Mission is not centered on the individual, on the mission society, on social movements, on the local church, or even on the church universal. These have all been seen as the center of missiology in the past. Instead, mission flows out of the divine nature of the Holy Trinity as revealed in Scripture. In chapter 6 we look at the nature of God the Father as the creating and sending Father. Chapter 7 looks at Jesus as the sent, suffering, and sacrificial Son. Jesus's identity cannot be separated from his work as the missionary sacrifice of God. Chapter

5. It may be helpful to compare this definition with the earlier definitions we mentioned in the introduction.

6. Much can be said about the Bible and mission. One of the best works in recent years (correcting Bosch's neglect of the Old Testament) is Christopher Wright's *The Mission of God: Unlocking the Bible's Grand Narrative* (Downers Grove, IL: InterVarsity, 2006), but many other authors in recent years have helped us to read the Bible with missional eyes: Andreas J. Köstenberger, Peter T. O'Brien, James Brownson, David Bosch, John R. W. Stott, William Larkin, Martin Hengle, Chuck Van Engen, Walter Kaiser, F. Hahn, Roger Hedlund, Joel Green, Beverly Gaventa, and Richard Bauckham, among others. I have benefited from many of these and other commentators.

8 discusses the Holy Spirit as the presence, participation, and power of God in enacting the *missio Dei* in each context and in each life.

"David Ford, at the end of his comprehensive survey of contemporary theology, concludes that any adequate theology has to be 'self-involving,' 'world-involving,' and 'God-involving.' God ultimately is the author of theology, the whole nature and culture forms the horizon[,] and the subject matter 'has a specific concern with the radical transformation of selves.'"[7] It is my hope that the following chapters on the theology of mission will be both involving and transforming.

7. Andrew Kirk, *What Is Mission? Theological Explorations* (Minneapolis: Fortress, 2000), 9.

6

The Creator God as the Sending Father

Missional Scripture, Missional God

World religions have sacred books. These books are sacred in that they speak of what is holy, and most are considered to have a holy origin. Sacred books contain proverbs, poetry, and narrative, and they prescribe holy or virtuous behaviors. All this is true for the Christian Bible, but in addition, the Bible tells a story of God and God's creation that reveals that God is a loving Father. The loving Father, as in the story of the prodigal son, goes out to extend his love. He moves toward his creation, and he sends to his creation. Furthermore, the New Testament contains writings that come from a mission or missionary context. Thus both God the Father and the sacred texts reveal a missional story.

Bible as Missionary Document

We begin with the simple statement that the Bible is a missionary (or missional) text.[1] Andrew Kirk takes the next step, saying: "There can be no

1. Bosch drives home the point in *Transforming Mission: Paradigm Shifts in the Theology of Mission* (Maryknoll, NY: Orbis Books, 1991): "The history and theology of early (NT) Christianity are first of all 'mission history' and 'mission theology.' The beginnings of missionary theology are therefore also the beginnings of Christian theology as such" (16). Martin Kähler (1908): "Mission is the mother of theology. . . . Theology began as an accompanying manifestation of the Christian mission and not as a luxury of the world dominating church." There is

theology without mission—or to put it another way, no theology which is not missionary."[2] From beginning to end the Bible is a history of God's activity: God's sending of his will,[3] his Word, his prophets, his own Son, and his apostles to humanity for the sake of redeeming his creation. Fundamentally, it is the story of God sending out from his own self to create, redeem, and glorify.

Before looking at Scripture in more detail, one vignette will illustrate the difficulty of understanding this point. I asked a friend about his recent writing project, and he said that he was writing a commentary on Romans. As this has already been done a number of times, I asked the obvious question: "What is your angle, or the issue you will use as a lens for looking at this important book?" He said that he will look at it using postcolonial theory. I responded, "Well, don't forget that Paul was a missionary, so you want to honor something of that authorial intent, I am sure." Silence. In his mind, mission had nothing to do with Paul or with Romans. I had given him a whole new perspective.

Contrary to the approach of many scholars, Paul was not a modern-day theologian sitting in his air-conditioned office reflecting on word usage, how he was really helping Jews and Gentiles resist empire, or how he was going to convince everyone that love is the answer. Paul was commissioned to deliver a message from Jesus Christ and was struggling with languages, finances, rejection, and lack of places to stay. He was especially struggling and praying to establish new Christian communities along the highways of the late Roman Empire. He was persecuted for his stubborn refusal to deny his commission. His intent was to proclaim the Kingdom, and his writings were all in service of that commitment (or commission). His writings were, in fact, missionary letters, and they should be read *at least* from this perspective. They also shed light on matters of ethics, moral behavior, and relations to civil authorities—but incidentally, not essentially.

When we say that the Bible is essentially a missionary document, we are beginning to reveal a normal and reasonable hermeneutic. The Bible has been read, and continues to be read, in many ways—some more defensible than others. Interpretation in the twenty-first century is as confusing as ever. Enlightenment assumptions have detached the reader from the text in a type of sterile analytical approach. Students in seminary still struggle with letting the text touch them, change them—and they are especially resistant to having the text get under their skin. The scientific approach the Enlightenment promotes

---

also a growing bibliography on missional hermeneutics, or reading the Bible with an awareness of its missional character. One of the best early statements was given by James V. Brownson, "Speaking the Truth in Love: Elements of a Missional Hermeneutic," in *International Review of Mission* 83, no. 330 (2011): 479–504. See also Christopher J. H. Wright, *The Mission of God: Unlocking the Bible's Grand Narrative* (Downers Grove, IL: InterVarsity, 2006), 29–69; and J. Andrew Kirk, *What Is Mission? Theological Explorations* (Minneapolis: Fortress, 2000), 7–22.

2. Kirk, *What Is Mission?*, 11.

3. In Syriac his *ith*, which is a sign or nod.

has taught generations of scholars to stand above the text and critique it according to approved historical methods. The higher critical method that developed in the nineteenth century subjected the Scriptures to the scientific lab, whereby the text was examined, dissected, and parts were removed.[4] For most students struggling to apply this approach, there is little life left in the body of Scripture. Lifeless and dismantled, Scripture has no internal coherence, no narrative meaning, no integrity, and therefore no power. From this approach, many adjectival theologies developed. Once the Scripture had been dismantled, it then became available for personal or communal ends. Again, some uses are more legitimate than others. For example, liberation theologies found a particular and necessary theme for contexts in Latin America and made it primary. The theologies and contextual concerns that drove liberation theology are a central theme of the biblical narrative. However, I have probably heard more seminary sermons on Micah 6:8, Exodus 3, and Luke 4 than all other texts in the Bible. These are important themes and texts, and I will examine some of these passages in the following pages; however, from liberation theologies came communal theologies (and even personal theologies) that were based upon a hermeneutic that was both modern and postmodern. The text decreased as personal and/or communal concerns increased. Scriptures have been conveniently useful rather than communally vital.

The postmodern element of these adjectival theologies is in the assumption that communities of discourse (my community) can and must create the meaning of the text. This comes from a completely understandable and even defensible proposition: people have been crushed by others imposing on them the control of discourse. It can be the discourse of slavery ("they are not capable of the same type of moral behavior") or the discourse of sexism ("God made women to submit to men"), but whatever the oppressive language used, the total loss of shared meaning cannot be the answer. Words have to have some shared meaning, something for everyone, or there can be no social intercourse or even any real communication.

A Missional Hermeneutic

A Christian missional hermeneutic requires two elements that may be countercultural. A Christian missional reading of the Bible requires that we read

4. Early church and medieval exegetes were quite aware of biblical inconsistencies and anomalies, but it was in the nineteenth century that the Bible became subject of intense critique. Under the leadership of scholars like F. C. Baur (1792–1860), David Friedrich Strauss (1808–74), and the Tübingen School, New Testament study shifted from knowledge of the text (and synthesizing the teachings of the text) to critique of the text and a search to understand the historical development of texts. The real historical Jesus was obscured, by the texts written by subjective "believers," and so the search for the real, historical Jesus, dominated much of New Testament studies for 150 years.

Scripture (in some way) as it has always been read. If we find that we are discovering absolutely unique readings of the Bible, we are on thin ice. Christians honor the Bible as their sacred text, and therefore we trust that Origen, Anselm, Matteo Ricci, and Mother Teresa are getting the same basic message. In addition, a Christian missional reading must major on what the Scripture majors on. This means that (contra Marcion) *all* of Scripture should contribute to our understanding of God's mission. Thus, there must be some basic, shared understanding of Scripture for all, and there must be meaning that flows through all of Scripture—from Genesis through Revelation.

One quick example may help. There is much talk today about the importance of tolerance and diversity. This is our twenty-first-century context for mission. Generally speaking, the entire world sees the need to tolerate difference and to celebrate diversity. This, I believe, is an expression of the postmodern celebration of individual communities of discourse. But on what basis and to what extent should Christians support diversity? This is a missiological question regarding the engagement of the gospel with a contemporary social issue. How do we proceed? Christopher Wright is very helpful in talking about the Bible and diversity:

> The Bible got there [contextual, diverse cultures, narrative] before postmodernity was dreamed of—the Bible which glories in *diversity* and celebrates multiple human *cultures*, the Bible which builds its most elevated theological claims on utterly *particular* and sometimes very *local* events, the Bible which sees everything in *relational*, not abstract, terms, and the Bible which does the bulk of its work through the medium of *stories*.[5]

We can see that the whole story of Scripture glories in particular cultural life. But Scripture also critiques diversity as an ideology; Scripture does not honor diversity as an abstract and absolute concept. Scripture indicates that there are types of diversity that God glories in: age, gender, and cultures. God speaks about honoring people of age and of loving and caring for children. In fact, both children and the elderly are signs of God's blessings. God also embedded in his very good creation male and female, and both are given the very Spirit of God. Finally, God glories in the diversity of cultures: this is seen in the affirmation of a specific culture in the incarnation, in the Scriptures being recorded in different languages, and in salvation being proclaimed to all ethnic groups (*panta ta ethnē*, Matt. 28:19). Here is an example of Scriptural meaning making sense across cultures, having a "normative" function that speaks into contemporary culture.

We must also look at all of Scripture to understand community, justice, God's love, the poor, diversity, and holiness. From a global biblical awareness

5. Christopher Wright, *The Mission of God: Unlocking the Bible's Grand Narrative* (Downers Grove, IL: InterVarsity, 2006), 47, italics original.

will come the specific teaching for a particular context. The same is also true for the concept of mission; except when it comes to mission, "the whole canon of Scripture is a missional phenomenon in the sense that it witnesses to the self-giving movement of this God toward his creation and us, human beings in God's own image."[6] Mission is not just one of the themes in Scripture; I believe it is one of the major two threads that holds all of Scripture together.[7] In addition, as I noted above concerning the apostle (missionary) Paul, mission has to do with the very formation of Scripture and is the context for most of the books of the Bible.

Interpreting Scripture itself has a missiological dimension. We should remember that interpreting Scripture along with the Great Tradition of the church means that we are always interpreting through different cultural lenses. The cultures of twelfth-century France, or fifth-century Persia, or eighteenth-century North America are very different. They spoke different languages, which carried different concerns, and they had different resources available to them for interpreting the Bible. This does not mean that their communities of discourse were *absolutely* different, however. Ephrem the Syrian wrote most of his theology as hymns or as poetic homilies. He spoke Syriac and wrote theology as a psalmist. We can still understand his theology, but it takes some time to "enter his world," to translate the Syriac, and then to understand what he was doing with images and wordplay. Yes, as one of the interpreters of Scripture, he adds to our understanding of the whole of Scripture as a narrative. Writing on the near side of medieval Scholasticism and of the later Enlightenment, he, and other ancients like him, became a witness to the overall story of Scripture.

The Bible: God's Story

The whole message of the Bible is the story of God's love for and relationship with his creation. It is important—both for understanding mission theology and for the message of our own missionary work—to know the story of Scripture and to be able to tell it. The Bible is God's story told through different authors, speaking different languages, in different times, using a variety of literary forms. But it is the single story of God: a public story or "open secret"; that is, the story of God for all of his creation. It does not purport to be a private or ethnic story, even though it speaks about God's "holy nation" and about "God's own people." The story reveals that God is the only God, the only One who creates, and that he creates all things good. The first chapter of Genesis reveals that he created and ordered all things to be under his sub-lord, the one to whom he has given his very image: humanity. Creation is

6. Ibid., 48.
7. The other related theme is God's glory.

ordered with three creation kingdoms in the first three days and three creature kings the second three days.[8] Humans, as image bearers ("very good"), are the creature kings over the plants and animals. The Covenant God, Creator King, rules over all of his creation in Sabbath rest.

Creation Elements	Creation Lords
Day One: Day and Night	Day Four: Sun and Moon/Stars
Day Two: Heavens and Seas	Day Five: Birds and Fish
Day Three: Earth/Plants	Day Six: Animals and Humans (*imago Dei*)
Day Seven: Creator King Ceases Creating and Rests	

Covenant love is sent to God's creation with blessings for fidelity and curses for neglect. Humanity refuses to be faithful, refuses to honor God as God, and so it suffers the loss of relationship, purity, and place. Cast out of God's immediate presence, humanity is reminded of God's love through the law, and yet the ongoing story is of humanity's rejection of God and search for other gods, including the god of self. Most of the scriptural story is about humanity's disobedience, God's call to return, God's sending of messengers (judges, kings, prophets), and finally God's sending of his own Son to fulfill covenant love.[9] Fulfilling God's covenant love meant that Jesus fulfilled the promises and requirements of the Law and the Prophets. He showed us how to live, and he conquered death, through death, for us. From the beginning of the story, God has invited his image bearers to be in relationship with God and to share his purpose for creation. The climax of the story is in three parts:

- Jesus lives a holy life, suffers, and dies fulfilling the law.
- Jesus rises from the dead, conquering sin and death.
- Jesus sends his Spirit, anointing his body (the church) to continue his work.

Running through the whole story is God's relationship to "his people" through a covenant of love.[10] He extends, confirms, and calls people to his covenant through specific individuals: Abraham, Joseph, Moses, Joshua, Elijah,

8. Borrowed from Meridith Kline's "Genesis" in *The New Bible Commentary*, ed. D. Guthrie, 3rd rev. ed. (Downers Grove, IL: InterVarsity, 1970), 79–114.

9. This is the interpretation of Scripture given by Jesus in Matthew 21:33–46.

10. One does not have to be a specifically Reformed Covenant theologian to recognize the basic relationship of God with his people as a covenantal relationship. Stuart J. Foster unpacks the fuller meaning of covenant for mission in the article "The Missiology of the Old Testament," *International Bulletin of Missionary Research* (October 2010): 205–8. "The missiological purpose of covenant concepts in the Old Testament can be put in the following terms: The covenant structure highlighted relationship with Yahweh and, within that relationship, elevated exclusivity, security, accountability, and purpose."

Isaiah, and others. The covenant is renewed and opened to others through specially anointed ones: through the specific to the general, finally through his Son to the nations.

The Bible is a love story, the story of a loving God who will not let go and watch his people reap their own destruction. He is constantly sending (*missio*), reminding, calling, forgiving, and judging. His concern is for all of creation, because, unlike the gods of the nations, he is the creator of all peoples and all places. All of the inhabited earth and every nation is his.

Themes in God's Story

Reading the whole story over and over again, there are some remarkable themes that develop. One is the *depth of human sin* and the terrible forgetfulness of God's chosen people. God's life-giving law is forgotten as soon as it is proclaimed. The nation of Israel is depicted as God's chosen vessel, but seldom have the heroes in a story been portrayed so poorly. Reading through the Bible with my teenage son one year, he said to me, after reading a few chapters in Judges, "Dad, did you read the passages in the Bible this morning? How could the Bible have such terrible stuff?" We went out and got the morning paper and read the headlines. I remarked something about how little had changed and how honest God is in Scripture.

A second issue that rises when reading through the Bible in the twenty-first century is how much *God judges*, kills, and warns people. Many today have simply misconstrued the hard texts of Scripture as being ancient people projecting their own violence upon God, and yet if that were true then we would have to similarly explain the more endearing qualities of God in the Old Testament: forgiveness, longsuffering, and deep and abiding love (*hesed*) that is also part of God's character. Both are strong themes in the complex love story of Scripture. A third theme that is woven through all of Scripture is the way that God chooses individuals to bear his message to all people. What is often called *the particular for the universal* is undeniably the way God chooses to act in Scripture. This underscores the personal or relational nature of God. God's law is an expression of his personality, and he continues to point to his sweet law ("sweeter than the honey," Pss. 119:103 and 19:10) through individual people. There are many other remarkable themes that we could focus on, but one more is unique to Christianity: *grace*. One cannot talk honestly about Christianity if the word grace, or the concept of unmerited favor from God, is not mentioned. All religions (at some basic level) establish a way to deal with suffering and death. These ways are prescriptions for behavior to release or win a god's or the gods' favor. The Bible alone has this amazing (even troubling, when it comes to some of the Old Testament texts) story of God's grace preceding our work, and even enabling our virtues. Even in forms of Christianity that seem works-oriented, grace is the foundation. "Of myself, there is absolutely nothing I can do. For without Thee I would not have come into existence from non-existence; without Thee I cannot live or be saved . . . for 'though the horse be made ready for battle, salvation comes from the Lord.'"[11]

So there we have a general description of the biblical story. We can argue about what could be left out and what should be added, but every Christian in the world should recognize this basic story as the story of God recorded in Scripture. Some might ask, "Does this mean that you are imposing a metanarrative upon the text and thus upon other people? Are you saying that this one narrative that you have described should control all people?" Yes. There is a basic story that is communicated to all communities of discourse, to all nations or cultures.[12] There is a common assessment of the problem of humanity (as all religions have a common assessment), and there is also a solution that is grand and glorious enough to include all of humanity. There is one God over all, and so the story of God is absolutely inclusive. However, we also have to be honest and say, "No, this is not a common, cookie-cutter type of story." This is a story that is quite mysterious in the way it adapts to each culture and to each person. Like the personal God who is the subject of the story, this narrative speaks to each and every heart uniquely and intimately. And it also speaks to each and every culture specifically and redemptively. Some will enter the story through a healing. Some will enter through the message of forgiveness. Some will enter the story through judgment and the fear of death. This story is unabridged, complete, and exhaustive in how it comes and then becomes shaped around the needs, longings, pain, and loss of each person and every culture. It is a grand narrative that is also a glorious and mysterious particular narrative. Let's look more closely at the author of this narrative, God the creator.

God the Creator

The first word in a mission theology is not "savior" or "salvation," but "creator" and "creation." One cannot talk about how creation is redeemed until we know who created it to begin with.[13] Only the One who created the world has the right and the ability to redeem it. We often forget that creation is a major theme in salvation. In the first centuries of Christianity, one of the

11. St. Peter of Damaskos, "How to Acquire True Faith," in *Philokalia* 3:165. The text quoted is Prov. 21:31.

12. Evidence of the universal nature of this story comes from missionaries who have met people who read the Bible, without teacher or commentary, and understand the call to discipleship, to follow Jesus.

13. This is true thinking apologetically or evangelistically. God as creator makes it possible to see God as the redeemer of his creation. Theologically speaking, I would reverse the order: we only know God the creator through Jesus Christ who has revealed the Father's love to us.

major movements that tried to decenter Christianity was Gnosticism, which was based on a faulty view of creation.[14] Gnosticism is based upon a "secret knowledge" that has to do with creation, a type of knowing about what is behind God. Gnostics were working with much of the same material as the Christians (Judaism, Greek philosophies, and canonical material), but added to this material were other religious materials, secret teachings, and noncanonical writings about Jesus. Since Gnostic teachings were focused on Jesus, it is often hard to tell the difference between Christian writings and Gnostic writings. But there is, in fact, a world (pardon the pun) of difference. Gnostics taught that creation was an aborted error coming from the arrogance of the Mother figure, Sophia. Creation was not good; it was not intended. Consequently, they taught that Christ was an Aeon (or emanation) who only appeared to be "material" and who came to release people from bondage to the material world. Gnosticism has a pessimistic view of the material world, and a salvation that is partial (only the spiritual is redeemed). Creation (i.e., the material world) for all Gnostics was seen to be a prison of the spirit and thus fundamentally evil.[15] Therefore, the mission of Jesus and the identity of Jesus were far different from the Jesus depicted in the Christian story.

Early apologists understood this, and so, when talking about salvation or the incarnation (the heart of salvation in the Orthodox tradition), they would inevitably talk about creation—and so shall we.[16] One of the most important early theological works on the incarnation is called "On the Incarnation" (*De Incarnatione Verbi Dei*) by St. Athanasius of Alexandria (300–373).[17] In this work defending the meaning of the incarnation of God in Jesus Christ, Athanasius begins in the first chapter by saying that we have to start with creation if we are going to talk about redemption.

> But to treat this subject it is necessary to recall what has been previously said; in order that you may neither fail to know the cause of the bodily appearing of the Word of the Father, so high and so great, nor think it a consequence of His own nature that the Saviour has worn a body; but that being incorporeal by nature,

14. Much has been written on Gnosticism in the early church, and there are various interpretations concerning the time of earliest development and the path of development of Gnostic concepts. For an introduction to some of the issues, see the survey article by Michael Allen Williams in Daniel Patte, ed., *The Cambridge Dictionary of Christianity* (Cambridge: Cambridge University Press, 2010), 461. See also Bentley Layton, *The Gnostic Scriptures: A New Translation with Annotations and Introductions* (Garden City, NY: Doubleday, 1987); and Kurt Rudolph, *Gnosis: The Nature and History of Gnosticism* (San Francisco: Harper & Row, 1983).

15. See Dale Irvin and Scott Sunquist, *History of the World Christian Movement* (Maryknoll, NY: Orbis Books, 2001), 1:115–28, for a discussion of Gnosticism and the Catholic opponents.

16. Of note, the largest number of commentaries in the early church were on the Hexameron, or the first six days of creation. This underscores how important a clear understanding of creation was to understanding the salvation of Jesus Christ.

17. Athanasius's book is on the incarnation, but the focus is on the economy of salvation. How does the incarnation, as God's salvific work, make sense?

> and Word from the beginning, He has yet of the loving-kindness and goodness of His own Father been manifested to us in a human body for our salvation. It is, then, proper for us to begin the treatment of this subject by speaking of the creation of the universe, and of God its Artificer, that so it may be duly perceived that the renewal of creation has been the work of the self-same Word that made it at the beginning. For it will appear not inconsonant for the Father to have wrought its salvation in Him by Whose means He made it.[18]

It is a little circuitous, but still a reasonable and convincing argument. The same Word who created all things (Gen. 1 and Col. 1) is the Word who became incarnate in Jesus Christ (John 1, Col. 1, and Phil. 2). So the renewal of creation is accomplished by the same Word who created it "in the beginning." Salvation points back to creation, and in doing so points to the creator. Athanasius goes on to discuss different views of creation, saying that some believe creation comes to be "of itself" (like the Epicureans) and therefore they believe there is no "Providence." Others, like Plato, say that God made the world from what already existed. But, says Athanasius, this is not a creator God, just a God who fashions from what there is: he is less than God. Jewish and Christian teaching was unique: God created absolutely ex nihilo (out of nothing).[19] There is absolutely no continuity between God and his creation, meaning nothing flows out of God or is birthed from God. Creation is creation, absolutely. Athanasius then spends over a chapter on the Old Testament and creation, explaining how God created humanity for relationship with himself, out of his loving kindness:

> You are wondering, perhaps, for what possible reason, having proposed to speak of the Incarnation of the Word, we are at present treating of the origin of humanity. But this, too, properly belongs to the aim of our treatise. For in speaking of the appearance of the Saviour among us, we must speak also of the origin of humanity, that you may know that the reason of His coming down was because of us, and that our transgression called forth the loving-kindness of the Word, that the Lord should both make haste to help us and appear among humanity.

Salvation and the mission of God must be understood first from creation.[20] This is not just an academic exercise, however, for it means that all of creation is connected to mission, just as all of creation is connected to the incarnation.

18. This and the following quotation are taken from *On the Incarnation* 3–4. Gender specific language has been changed to inclusive language. See http://www.ccel.org/ccel/athanasius/incarnation.ii.html.

19. To be exact, the doctrine was not fully developed until the early third century. See Gerhard May, *Creatio ex Nihilo: The Doctrine of "Creation out of Nothing" in Early Christian Thought*, trans. A. S. Worrall (London: T&T Clark, 1994).

20. See also Anselm's *Cur Deus Homo* for a similar but much later theological argument of the incarnation from creation.

The early Greek Christians understood this connection because of how they understood humanity in creation. Humanity, as we noted above, is special within creation—but what does this specialness mean? Looking at the place of humanity in creation in Genesis 1 and 2, the fall of humanity in Genesis 3, and the renovation of creation through the incarnation in Romans 5, 6, and 8, humanity is seen as a microcosm of the universe. Humanity, by bearing the image and glory of God in creation, keeps all in harmony. Only humanity is made of the dust (sharing physical components with the rest of creation) and yet has God's breath within (thus sharing the spiritual realm). The human being is a microcosm of the world:

> "He is an entire world which contains—not just symbolically, but actually—all the physical, chemical and spiritual components of the world." "Man stands as a mirror and also a summation of the World." There is an interchangeability whereby man is the world and the world is a man. "Man and the world coexist in an indissoluble relationship and unity."[21]

Thus, when humans sin and are cast out from the garden, it is not just humanity who suffers. "The whole creation has been groaning" (Rom. 8:22), waiting for "the children of God to be revealed" (v. 19). When "all things are made new," humanity will again be restored to the role of priest of creation: a microcosm that holds together the cosmos, albeit on a small scale. There is a direct connection between human sin and the fall of creation. There is also a direct connection between human restoration and the restoration of the universe.[22] Humanity bears the very image of God; humanity is made from the dust but contains the animating Spirit of God. When the image bearer is broken, creation is broken. Later, we will look at what this should say to us about mission and ecology, evangelism and global warming.

To understand how radical Yahweh worship was in the ancient Near Eastern world, it is helpful to look at Yahweh in historic context. This will help us to understand the meaning of God, the only God, as creator of all. Monotheism is

21. Anastes G. Keselopoulos, *Man and the Environment: A Study of St. Symeon the New Theologian*, trans. Elizabeth Theokritoff (Crestwood, NY: St. Vladimir's Seminary Press, 2001), 41. Maximos the Confessor maintained clearly that the whole world is a man: "Man composed of soul and body is a world" (*Mystagogy* 7). Even John Calvin recognized and appreciated this understanding of anthropology. See *Institutes of the Christian Religion* 1.3.1.

22. A contemporary presentation of this comes from the WCC Inter-Orthodox discussion on creation (Consultation in Sofia, Bulgaria, October 1987). In discussing the creation of humanity, the document says, "The reference to the 'image of God' is to be understood in terms of Jesus Christ, since he is explicitly identified with it (2 Cor. 4:4; Col. 1:15; Heb. 1:3). . . . In the created world only the human being combines material and spiritual elements. Human existence is thus differentiated from non-human creation in a qualitative way. In light of this fact, the Church Fathers often speak of the human being as a 'little world,' a 'microcosm' of the whole of creation. . . . Humankind then stands on the boundary (*methorion*) between the material and the spiritual world as a connecting link" (pars. 8–10).

critical to all we have spoken of. The religions of the Middle East, from which God called Abraham and the patriarchs, were religions built around the sprits and cycles of nature. Deities were called upon for specific concerns or needs. In the past, these religions were called *hierophanic* religions (from the Greek for sacred, or priestly). Specific places and times and events held a sacredness that mediated between the earthly and the sacred realms. There would be divine manifestations at specific places in which humans could communicate with their gods. These religions were not only *heirophanic*, but they were also cyclical, following the seasonal cycles of an agrarian culture.[23] Bavinck points out some basic traits of these religions:

- The nations were virtually identical with their gods.
- These nations were incarnations of their deities, therefore nations were divided by worship.
- The gods were tutelary powers protecting "their" people.
- These nations worshiped the forces of nature in their gods.
- The god-worlds of these nature religions were divine counterparts of the earth.
- Those conquered must worship the conquering nation's god. Thus, conversion was by coercion only.

We can quickly see some of the differences and similarities of these early religions to the worship of Yahweh, the creator God, over all, who does not share his throne, or his worship, and who is not limited to place or time.

- Israel's religion was based upon history and the historic acts of God. God is revealed in the Exodus from Egypt.
- Yahweh is a universal God, who created everything and who is due all honor.
- Yahweh is a God of revelation and promise (future). Nature gods are cyclical, not grounded in hope for a future.
- Yahweh elected a people to serve the nations, the poor, and the stranger. God is revealed as having love and grace, as well as justice.
- Yahweh's compassion and future involves the nations (see below).
- In this "history" of God is revealed a covenant of compassion and judgment—compassion for those who submit to the covenant and accept God's offer (even pagans such as Ninevites), and judgment for those who reject God's offer.

23. See the classic Reformed missiology by Johan Herman Bavinck, *An Introduction to the Science of Missions* (Philadelphia: P&R, 1960), 13.

Here we see the break between ancient Near Eastern cultures and the revelation of Yahweh for the nations: one God over all of creation, who works through history, and whose revelation and grace are inclusive.[24] Monotheism is the taproot of all of these differences. There is continuity with local cultures and practices, especially with the concept of harvest and planting festivals, and yet in Yahweh these celebrations mark historic events (e.g., Passover) and God's character as he acts in history. God is not called Ba'al or any other national or cultural name. God is not controlled by the manufacturing of idols; in fact, God is absolutely clear that no "thing" can represent him. God "is" God, and he is called . . . Yahweh.

Fatherhood of God

Does it matter what God is called? Yes—for a name, biblically speaking, reflects the character or being of the one named. Here is a story to illustrate how a Chinese couple expressed this concept. At a local church in Malaysia, where the Chinese are a strong ethnic minority in a sea of Islam, a Chinese woman came across the street to a church to ask for help. Her husband was dying of cancer, and she didn't know what to do. She needed physical help, taking care of him, and she needed emotional help; she had avoided all thoughts of death until this point in life. The church responded: they cared for her husband, fixed meals, and prayed with the woman. And then, the woman began praying on her own. As a Chinese religionist she knew what to call her idols (Guan Yin, the Goddess of Mercy, Buddha, etc.), but now she was in a fix. She asked the church worker, "When I pray, what do I call God? Does God have a name, or do I just say, 'God?'" The church worker told her that Jesus tells us that we should call God "Father." "Our Father in heaven, hallowed be your name" (Matt. 6:9).

Was the church worker right? Yes, Jesus teaches us how to pray, and Jesus is identified as the Son of God—so the relationship of God the Father to the Son is preserved in this language. This is also the language of the rest of the Bible: Jesus calls God Father, Peter calls God Father (Acts 2:33; 1 Pet. 1:2, 3), Paul calls God Father (Rom. 1:7; 15:6; etc.), the author of Hebrews calls God Father (Heb. 1:5; 5:5), James calls God Father (James 1:17), John calls God Father (1 John 3:1), and Jude calls God Father (Jude 1:1). In a sense, Father is the proper name for God—not indicating gender, but rather his relationship to the Son and to us. We might ask, "Why not Mother?" The simple answer is that we are not given "Mother" as a name for God. The deeper reason may

24. The Psalms were read daily by the ancients, and they were all considered Messianic, meaning Jesus is revealed in every psalm. However, many psalms are also focused on history and on creation. Thus, the Psalms underscore our argument here about the sui generis nature of God and his unique creation. The creation psalms include Pss. 8, 19, 29, 33, 65, and 104.

be that "mother" or "mother earth" was a common designation for a goddess who brought forth creation from her own being. She "birthed" creation from her womb. God the Father creates *ex nihilo*. A mother god points to a creation that shares her essence. This is not the biblical story. The biblical account, as we have seen, protects the *sui generis* nature of creation and the absolute separateness or holiness of God. Many adjectives can describe God (a lion, a strong tower, shepherd, king, fortress, and even a bird), but only one name is appropriate: Father.

Father language also protects the trinitarian nature of God: Father, Son, and Holy Spirit. The Father begets the Son. This is the language given for the one God, and it is language that has been defended—even in the shadow of over thirteen hundred years of misunderstandings from Islamic communities. Muslims criticize Christians for teaching that God had a Son, or that Mary could have given birth to God, or that Mary had intercourse with God. Even with the challenge and persecution from Muslim cultures over the centuries, Father language for God has persisted.[25] Classic dialogues between Muslims and Christians through the ages have focused on the unity versus the tri-unity of God.

Trinitarian language for God has always been expressed as Father, Son, and Holy Spirit: the Father sending the Son to the world, and the Son sending the Holy Spirit. Mission, or the sending nature of God, is tied up with trinitarian language and meaning. It is important to preserve this language in mission because it is the language that has been given to us, because it is the language which has been the church's language, and because of our commitment to ecumenical unity. God as Father, Son, and Holy Spirit unites Christians in all of time and throughout the world.[26] A missiology that divides Christians on such a basic level as language about God has abdicated one of the fundamental concerns: the unity of God and of God's people. Trinitarian language has always revealed God as in community, as sharing attributes and a common love and relationship. Trinitarian language expresses that the Word of the Father moves out from God, in relationship, to proclaim the Kingdom of God, and to invite others into the community and the communion of the Triune God.

25. In the eighth-century Apology (or Dialogue) of Patriarch Timothy of Baghdad before Caliph Mahdi, we read the following exchange: "And our King [Mahdi] said to me: 'Do you not say that He was born of the Virgin Mary?'—And I said to his Majesty: 'We say it and confess it. The very same Christ is the Word born of the Father, and a man born of Mary. From the fact that He is Word-God, He is born of the Father before the times, as light from the sun and word from the soul; and from the fact that He is man He is born of the Virgin Mary, in time; from the Father He is, therefore, born eternally, and from the Mother He is born in time, without a Father, without any marital contact, and without any break in the seals of the virginity of His Mother.'" From A. Mingana, ed. and trans., *Woodbrooke Studies*, vol. 2 (Cambridge: Heffer, 1928).

26. Oneness Pentecostals and Unitarians would be the exception. But they are exceptions.

Eighth-Century Christian-Muslim Dialogue

The Persian Patriarch Timothy I recorded a two-day dialogue in 781 with the Caliph Mahdi in Baghdad. Much of the discussion concerned the nature of God as absolute and singular (Mahdi) or as the Trinity of Father, Son, and Holy Spirit (Timothy). Mutual respect was evident in the dialogue, but the Caliph ("King") had questions: "He said to me: 'O Catholicos, a man like you who possesses all this knowledge and utters such sublime words concerning God, is not justified in saying about God that He married a woman from whom He begat a son.'" Father language for God and Son language for Jesus was a stumbling block. The two days of discussion revolved around the nature of God as Trinity. "And our King said to me: 'Did not Jesus Christ say, I am going to My God and to your God?'—And I said: 'It is true that this sentence has been said by our Savior, but there is another sentence which precedes it and which is worthy of mention.'—And the King asked: 'Which is it?'—And I said: 'Our Lord said to His Disciples "'I am going to My Father and to your Father, and to My God and your God.'"—And our King said: 'How can this be? If He says that He is His Father, He is not His God, and if He is His God, He is not His Father; what is this contradiction?'—And I replied to him: "'There is no contradiction here, O God-loving King. The fact that He is His Father by nature does not carry with it that He is also His God by nature, and the fact that He is His God by nature does not imply that He is His Father by nature.'" God as Father and the triune nature of God are not compromised in Christian encounters with other cultures and religions.

One final note concerning God as Father is necessary before we move on. Father, as the name for God, does point to the concept of Father as the One who guides and disciplines (Deut. 4:36; 11:2; Job 5:17; Ps. 94:12; Heb. 12:5–12). The Old Testament is very clear that God's character is both loving and just; it is forgiving, but also disciplining. God's justice can be a frightening prospect, but his grace is ever surprising. Scriptures teach that the beginning of wisdom is the fear of the Lord. In a world of family violence and child abuse, we have to be careful not to misunderstand this biblical concept, but neither should we reject it just because it is difficult. Scripture is uncompromising, and the ancients knew well that the fear of the Lord is foundational for spiritual life. However, fear and discipline are abstract nouns that need to be filled with the right content. "Fear of God" in the Bible refers to being filled with awe and respect.[27] God as Father is feared not for his anger or for his unpredictable punishment, but for the exact opposite: for his predictable and trustworthy righteousness. In fact, he is to be feared for his love, the ancients tell us.

27. The basic Hebrew word for fear (*yare'*) often is translated "awe" for overwhelming respect as in, "It took my breath away." There are other Hebrew words for fear that have more to do with terror, dread, or trembling.

Fear of God is the standard description of a holy and virtuous person in the Bible.[28] The one who does not fear God is called a fool. Therefore, we are called to honor God the Father in all that we do, and this is summarized as "the fear of God." "Fear is the son of faith and the shepherd of the commandments. He who is without faith will not be found worthy to be a sheep of the Lord's pasture."[29] God our Father is to be feared, loved, and worshiped by all the nations.

Mission, God's People, and the Nations

We have noted before the scriptural concept of God's calling a people to himself to reach all people: the particular for the universal. In this regard, one of the key passages in Scripture is Genesis 12:1–3:

> The Lord had said to Abram, "Go from your country, your people and your father's household to the land I will show you. I will make you into a great nation, and I will bless you; I will make your name great, and you will be a blessing. I will bless those who bless you, and whoever curses you I will curse; and all peoples on earth will be blessed through you."

It is a promise reaffirmed (Gen. 17:4–7, below) and central to the whole biblical story, and it includes a family, many nations, and land.

> As for me, this is my covenant with you: You will be the father of many nations. No longer will you be called Abram; your name will be Abraham, for I have made you a father of many nations. I will make you very fruitful; I will make nations of you, and kings will come from you. I will establish my covenant as an everlasting covenant between me and you and your descendants after you for the generations to come, to be your God and the God of your descendants after you.

Later this calling of a specific man and his family to become a blessing to the nations is continued in the responsibility of God's chosen people to care for the nations and to be God's people for the nations. Other nations were to look at Israel, God's chosen, and know about God's justice and holiness. God's people were to be signposts of God. Unfortunately, much of the Old Testament record is of God's missionary nation being missionized by the idolatrous nations. The Israelites too often convert to the worship and ethics of the nations around them. The influence is to be from God, through the priests and prophets, to the people, and then out to the nations, but that just does not happen. In order to remain pure in devotion to Yahweh, Israel is not to take on

28. Genesis 20:11; 22:12; 42:18; Exodus 9:30; 18:21; 20:20; and many others.
29. Ilias the Presbyter, in "Gnomic Anthology IV" 137. This is found in *Philokalia* 3:65.

covenantal relationships that will bind them to the lifestyle or the worship of the nations. However, they continue to be attracted to local fertility worship (Asherah, Ba'al, etc.), reverting back to the older hierophanic practices. All too often, the Israelites proved to be bad missionaries. It was because of the "wickedness of [the] nations" (Deut. 9:5) that Israel was to drive them out, but the nations remained, and Israel became entangled in their wickedness and in their false practices. And yet, the hope and the promise of God—that all the nations would be blessed through Abraham, a man of faith—remained. Isaiah 40:5 says that "the glory of the Lord will be revealed, and all people will see it together," not just Israel. Isaiah 2:2–4 is even more specific about the future hope for the nations.

> In the last days the mountain of the LORD's temple will be established as the highest of mountains; it will be exalted above the hills, and all nations will stream to it. Many peoples will come and say, "Come, let us go up to the mountain of the LORD, to the temple of the God of Jacob. He will teach us his ways, so that we may walk in his paths." The law will go out from Zion, the word of the LORD from Jerusalem. He will judge between the nations and will settle disputes for many peoples. They will beat their swords into plowshares and their spears into pruning hooks. Nation will not take up sword against nation, nor will they train for war anymore.

All of the nations are involved in God's future. The Lord's temple was built by his people, but it will be a house of prayer for the nations (Isa. 56:7 and Mark 11:17). Abraham's promise will blossom into a commission and eventually into a blessing for the nations. The chosen people, even in their own worship, are reminded of their duty to tell of God's glory to all the nations, to tell them that idols are nothing (God is King!), and to warn them of the coming judgment (Ps. 96). Israel's worship is to flow into testimony ("Declare . . . his marvelous deeds," Ps. 96:3), teaching ("All the gods of the people are idols, but the LORD made the heavens," v. 5), and warning ("He comes to judge the earth," v. 13). All the nations are included in God's mission, not because Israel is sent out (they are not commanded to "go"), but because the nations come to Jerusalem. This is attractive or centripetal mission. In contrast, the New Testament portrays centrifugal mission: God sending people out to the nations. Eventually the message will get out to all the nations; eventually there will be peace and reconciliation (*shalom*) upon earth as the many will be blessed through the chosen. This describes a method of communicating the message (or warning) from God. But what is the content of that message? What is it that Israel is to communicate and what is it that they are to live? In brief, Israel has had revealed to them their need for redemption and the means of that redemption. God has embedded this message of redemption in their culture in two ways: in his law and in their periodic and seasonal festivals.

Redemption in the Old Testament

There are many words, analogies, and stories of God's salvation work in the Old Testament, but the one strongest word that is reinforced again and again in Israel's storytelling, festivals, and rituals is "redemption."[30] Redemption was embedded in the spiritual DNA of Israel because the sacrificial system was based upon the requirement of a blood sacrifice to redeem Israel from their sins, property law was indebted to the concept of redemption (see Lev. 25 and 27), and kinship responsibilities also involved redemption.[31] Redemption, in the law, in history, and in future hope is God's work on behalf of his creation. He is the redeemer of humanity—of all of creation. This is expressed in many ways in the Bible, it is fulfilled in Jesus Christ, and it is proclaimed by his church. How does the Old Testament express redemption?

There are many images of redemption in the Old Testament. The first and dominant image is of Israel being redeemed from the Egyptians.[32] God portrays the Israelite enslavement as a situation that required a redeemer. God "hears the cries of his people" and redeems them. It is a costly redemption: many animals and all the Egyptians' firstborn sons died before redemption was accomplished. Redemption is costly. This act of redemption is a prototype and image of salvation for all of Jewish and Christian history. The Psalms (see 78, 80, and 81) refer to the history of God's redemption of the Israelites from Egypt. Negro spirituals focus on the exodus as a primary theme of redemption: "Go down Moses, way down to Egypt; and tell old Pharaoh, 'Let my people go.'" The people (or Israel) are the slaves, and "Egypt" is the slaveholder. The Israelites are redeemed to worship Yahweh, so there is a *purpose* for redemption. Liberation is not simply for liberation's sake. An earlier image of redemption, oddly enough, is that the Israelites are redeemed *into* Egypt. Joseph was sold into slavery and, through that enslavement, God released him to be the savior

30. In Hebrew, *ga'al*, having the basic meaning of to buy back, or specifically the duty of a kinsman to buy back from slavery, or of begetting children on behalf of a dead brother. It has another meaning of to avenge by blood or to require blood. An argument could be made for liberation as the best way to summarize God's salvific work since the exodus from Egypt is a major image for all of Israel's history, but even there, the word redemption is used: Exodus 6:6–7 reads, "Therefore, say to the Israelites: 'I am the LORD, and I will bring you out from under the yoke of the Egyptians. I will free you from being slaves to them, and I will *redeem* you with an outstretched arm and with mighty acts of judgment. I will take you as my own people, and I will be your God. Then you will know that I am the LORD your God, who brought you out from under the yoke of the Egyptians.'" Liberation comes with a cost, and redemption has within its meaning a cost for the freedom that will follow.

31. We might argue that atonement is a better word (or another word) for God's salvation. I think it best to think of redemption as the whole process of God's reclamation project of humanity. Atonement is, in a sense, the price paid, or the process that leads to redemption. The atoning sacrifice redeems. The atonement is the price, redemption the result.

32. Redemption is liberation, especially in the Exodus account. However, the term "redeem" includes the means, cost, and goal of salvation. The term "liberation" is broader and less specific.

of Israel. It may seem paradoxical, but this image of redemption emphasizes kinship duty in redeeming family.

Samson—blinded and humiliated, standing in the temple of Dagon and then bringing the whole temple down upon the idol, himself, and all the worshipers—is a type of redemption of the name of Israel's God. Jonah's death-to-life experience can be seen as a type of redemption: he "dies," is resurrected, and then returns with the message of life. The Ninevites are saved in spite of, or because of, Jonah's disobedience and redemption. Moses, holding up a bronze serpent in the wilderness so that all who lift up their eyes and look on the serpent will be saved, is also an image of redemption. The Israelites are being judged (again) for their grumbling, and God's redemption comes when the serpent is lifted up. One of the most obvious images of redemption in the Old Testament is the story of Ruth. Ruth's husband passed away, and Ruth, a Moabite, returned to her husband's family and sought redemption from her husband's next of kin, Boaz. It is a remarkable story of devotion to a mother-in-law, patience, wooing, righteous obedience to the law, and faithful duty to a foreign woman. Ruth, a Moabite woman, is four generations away from King David.

The liberation from Egypt is one of the major redemption images. The other dominant redemption image is the system of sacrifices culminating with the annual Day of Atonement (Yom Kippur). There were daily, weekly, monthly, and then five annual sacrifices or offerings instituted by God (see Num. 28). The Passover and Yom Kippur were strong reminders of the cost of redemption. Again and again we read that an animal, without blemish or defect, is to be offered as a sacrifice, or "to redeem." Redemption, in images and the sacrificial system, is the biblical pattern. Looking forward to the eventual redemption of humanity, not only for healing and freedom in this life, but to conquer death, is imaged in Psalm 49 (vv. 7–9, 15, emphasis mine).

> No one can *redeem* the life of another or give to God a ransom for them—the ransom for a life is costly, no payment is ever enough—so that they should live on forever and not see decay. . . . But God will redeem me from the realm of the dead; he will surely take me to himself.

The One who created is the One who can and must redeem. Redemption is costly, it is a family responsibility, and it is central to the overall narrative of Israel. Redemption is not complete in the Old Testament, for there are many passages that talk about its completion involving all of the nations, and all of creation (e.g., Isa. 55:6–13).

Conclusion

Christian mission is not an extracurricular activity of the church, nor is it an imposed or secondary theme in Scripture. I have shown that Scripture itself

Jesus Creates, Redeems, and Graces: Mark the Ascetic

One of the most influential of Eastern theologians, though largely unknown to Protestants, is Mark the Ascetic or Mark the Monk. His writings, as well as other ancient ascetical writings, have had a major influence upon renewal movements in Orthodoxy, not to mention in the revivals of the eighteenth century. Included in the *Philokalia*, Mark's writings are pithy and deep theological statements that describe the theological life of the believer. When speaking about Jesus Christ, Mark expresses the complete work of Christ from creation, through redemption, and to sustaining grace:

> Christ is Master by virtue of His own essence and Master by virtue of His incarnate life. For He creates man from nothing, and through His own blood redeems him when dead in sin; and to those who believe in Him He has given His grace.[a]

a. Mark the Ascetic, "On Those Who Think That They Are Made Righteous by Works: Two-Hundred and Twenty-Six Texts," in *The Philokalia* 1:127.

is a missional form of literature, with significant portions of it written by missionaries. If we don't read with that understanding, we are ignoring one of the main cords of Scripture. We have seen that Scripture tells the story of God, a public story that is the story not just of Jews and Christians, but is the universal story of human history. In short, Scripture is the description of God, the creator of the universe, whose covenantal love is initiated by the Father, and entrusted to his people, who are to be a light for the nations. His redemptive love is revealed in various historical acts and images of the Old Testament that point toward a future fulfillment. What I hope has become clear in this brief survey is the extent and depth of God's redemptive work. All of creation is involved, but it is primarily through humanity, the microcosm of the universe, that God lavishes his love and responsibility upon the world. The image of God (that is us) must be restored to its proper function as God's sub-lords in creation.

This theology of mission is trinitarian. However, we must remember that when we talk about the Trinity we are talking about one God whose three persons have one divine will, one love, and one work. We have spoken here about God the Father as the creator, but God's work is not as functional or mechanical as that. It may be misleading to speak too much of God the Father as the creator when in fact Scripture is clear that all of creation comes through and is for Jesus Christ (John 1, Col. 1).[33] The redemption of creation is the work of God and it is accomplished primarily through the cross, and yet that

33. This is a reason it is not acceptable to pray to a functional Trinity: "In the name of the Creator, Redeemer, and Sustainer." The Holy Spirit is involved in creation and applies redemption. Jesus is also part of creating the universe and he also sustains all things; all things hold together in him.

redemption is applied through the work of the Holy Spirit. The Triune God is involved from beginning to end. Thus, redemption—buying back or winning back to original ownership and purpose—leads us to Christology. Beginning with the early church writings, the connection between creation and redemption has been a major theme in Christian theology.

Jesus Christ has full ownership or mastery over humans because: (1) his divine essence demands it, and (2) he has both created humanity and redeemed humanity through the cross. We turn now to Jesus Christ, the Suffering Son, as the Missionary of God.

7

Jesus, Sent as the Suffering and Sacrificing Son

The Centerpiece of Christian Mission

A missionary working among Muslim villages in Southeast Asia tells of a typical conversation with a thoughtful Muslim. In the pattern of E. Stanley Jones,[1] this missionary engages local people in religious discussions about their personal experience of Allah.[2]

> "Tell me, what is the biggest issue or problem that your religion deals with?"
> "How to be forgiven of our sins," is usually the response.
> "And how does that happen according to your religion? How are you forgiven?"
> "We pray five times a day, we give alms, we fast, we recite the creed and we make a pilgrimage to Mecca."
> "That's wonderful, and so you are then sure that your sins are forgiven?"
> "No, we are never sure."

1. Jones, the prolific and creative Methodist missionary to India, would set up round tables representing some of the most respected of various religions. Each person would share the deepest longings and experiences of faith. Jones believed that when the best of each religion (in terms of spiritual experience) was expressed, Jesus would rise up as the most significant among the religions. See E. Stanley Jones, *Christ at the Round Table* (New York: Abingdon, 1928).

2. In Bahasa Malaysia or Indonesia, Allah is the term for God used by both Christians and Muslims.

"That is so sad. I actually know that I cannot please God and that I cannot be forgiven by means of my good deeds, and yet I know that my sins are forgiven because of what God has done for me . . ."

So the conversation goes, according to this missionary. I do not put this forward as a model for missionary conversations, but simply to lift up this simple truth: Christian faith, and the message of the missionary, is focused on the work God has done through Jesus Christ rather than on the works we must do. It may seem simplistic and blatantly obvious, but it is often forgotten that all of the work and all of the words of Christian mission flow out of the work God has done in Jesus Christ. We are invited to participate in and give witness to that message, and Jesus is both the message and the messenger.

In the last chapter, we discussed the trinitarian foundation of redemption that involves the fulfillment of redemptive images and acts in the coming Messiah of God. God's salvific plan, as seen through Christian lenses, always pointed to its fulfillment in the Son of God, who is the Son of Man. Jesus Christ is the mission of God. It is his life, his words, his coming, his going, and his promised return that embodies the salvation promised and now sealed. When we look into the face of Jesus Christ we see God's suffering love, but we also see his glory. The same Jesus who wept over Lazarus and bled on the cross also fed the five thousand, raised Lazarus from the dead, and was revealed in glory on the mountain. The same Jesus did not open his mouth to protest his punishment, and yet opened the mouth of the grave. The same Jesus who endured the whips of the Romans sent a man who denied him to proclaim his message to the Romans. Jesus is the suffering love of God for the world. Jesus Christ is the salvation of God. In fact, Jesus Christ is the sacrifice of God (revealing the means of salvation), he is the Missionary of God (revealing the method), and his life exegetes the message (revealing the meaning).

Jesus, however, is known almost exclusively through the writings of the New Testament, writings that are already a step away from Jesus, since they are in a foreign language (translated from Aramaic to Greek). Translation of the divine presence took place in the incarnation, and translation of Jesus's life occurs in the New Testament record. This reveals something of the missionary nature of the New Testament: it is meant to be translated—to fully embody—into every language and culture. More than that, I affirm, alongside many others, that the New Testament is a missionary document. "The decisive difference between the Old and New Testaments is mission. The New Testament is essentially a book about mission."[3] Christopher Wright correctly points out that "the text in itself is a product of mission in action."[4] The authors of the

3. David Bosch emphasizing that in the Old Testament there is no Christian mission. Here he is quoting H. Rzepkowski's "The Theology of Mission," *Verbum SVD* 15 (1973): 79–91.

4. Christopher Wright, *The Mission of God: Unlocking the Bible's Grand Narrative* (Downers Grove, IL: InterVarsity, 2006), 49.

New Testament were apostles (sent ones) and martyrs (witnesses), reflecting on the meaning of the missionary of God (Jesus) even as they were sharing in his sufferings. It is not imposing mission upon the text to do a missiological reading of the New Testament—it is a matter of being honest with the text. By means of analogy, I do not read my grandmother's letters to her fiancé fighting in France in 1915 as if she were reflecting on just war theory. She was not. These were love letters of hope, and so an honest reading of them places them in the context of the Great War, of family loyalties, of hopes of a future marriage, and of loss. Paul was a missionary reflecting on his vocation and expressing hope for its future expressed in fledgling communities. Peter and John heard Jesus say, "As the Father sent me, I am sending you" (John 20:21), and so they had a sense that they were sent. All three of these apostles accepted that specific call. The New Testament documents must first be read as missionary letters and portraits concerning the Missionary of God.

Furthermore, theology rooted in the New Testament begins as missional reflection. The earliest reflections on Jesus (Christology) come out of the early Christian encounter with Greco-Roman culture. For the Jews, Jesus was the promised Messiah (*Christos*). For the Hellenists and the non-Jews, Jesus was Lord (*Kurios*), the word substituted for Yahweh in the Old Testament. When Paul says that Jesus is "Lord," he is both saying that Jesus (not Caesar) is Lord, and he is saying Jesus is Lord (the designation for Yahweh in the Septuagint). It is both a deeply political and a deeply religious statement. Even political theology begins with Paul's reflections on Rome and John's apocalyptic vision of Babylon and the New Jerusalem (Rom. 13 and Rev. 13). Theological reflection on the person of Christ, on the nature of the church, on the meaning of salvation, begins with the missionary encounter of the gospel in local contexts. The earliest theological reflection and, in a sense, all newer theological reflections, emerge through the missionary encounter with local cultures and societies. And so we can affirm that mission is "the mother of theology." The New Testament texts reveal for us that mission is a primary category for our understanding of theology and, specifically, of Christology. Ecclesiology, as we will see, must flow out of this missional Christology. Theological reflection on the New Testament documents that does not acknowledge the context of missional engagement is disingenuous, and, by extension, a theology without a mission is no true theology, and a church without a mission is no true church.

The New Testament, Jesus Christ, and Christian Mission

The New Testament is the record of the missionary activity of God through his people, but how do we understand its content? In continuity with the Old Testament, we see that the New Testament records God's continued missionary activity of sending the *particular* for the *universal*. Jesus is sent to reconcile the world (creation) to God (creator). The Gospel records are intentionally written as a type of biography or story of the life of Jesus of Nazareth—so that others will become disciples.[5] In the New Testament the advent of Jesus marks the beginning of the end: the promised anointed one (Messiah) has come, salvation has been proclaimed, and sin (and resulting death) has been conquered. Jesus is both the work and the message of God. Jesus is also both the suffering servant and the satisfactory sacrifice. Jesus brings the answer to the human condition; he is the perfect human; and he points to the fullness of humanity to come. Jesus can say, "The Kingdom of God is among you," when he is present, because he is the king of that Kingdom.[6] Christian mission is trinitarian, but it pivots around the divine-human person of Jesus Christ.

"Christ the Pantocrator" by Eileen McGuckin (www.sgtt.org)

An important Orthodox icon is of Christ Pantocrator, or the Almighty. Jesus is depicted as ruling over all, holding the New Testament in his hand. He is the Word of God, and the New Testament speaks primarily of him. In some Western depictions, Jesus actually points to the open Bible as if to say, "This is about me."

Thus, when we talk about Christian mission in and through the New Testament, we must be clear about how we read the New Testament. We are not just reading about private religious myths, we are reading about public truth that was revealed to many and intended for all. One of the main arguments against heretics such as the Gnostics in the early church, an argument most clearly expressed by Irenaeus, was that their truths were taught in secret and are only later revealed. The true teachings of and about Jesus are public in nature. Therefore, the common understanding of their origin and accuracy gives a certain validation to the Gospels, to the apostolic writers, and to the Great Tradition that develops from these writings. For the church through the ages, this public identity of Jesus Christ with the Scriptures has been a cornerstone of orthodoxy. Reliability is not the only issue. Such identity with Jesus also gives a certain authority and even power to the texts. Another way of looking at this identity of the Messiah with the Scriptures

5. This is not the place to go into great detail about the nature of "story," but many Christian novelists have recognized the essential nature of "story" reflected in the life of Jesus. See Donald Miller's *A Million Miles in a Thousand Years* (Nashville: Thomas Nelson, 2009) for a creative discussion of story built upon the work of Robert McKee in his *Story: Substance, Structure, Style, and the Principles of Screenwriting* (New York: HarperCollins, 1997).

6. Luke 17:21. "Among" is also translated "within" you, which is equally valid and preferred by the Orthodox Church. The Greek word *entos* can mean "within" or "among"; however, since it was a group of Pharisees who asked Jesus the question, it is more likely that he meant "among" them.

is to look at the authority Jesus claimed—again publicly—over the Torah. In Matthew 5, five times Jesus quotes from the Law, or from expositions of the Law in the Old Testament, and then he says, "But I say to you . . ." Jesus is claiming authority over the Torah, over the law of God. He is therefore superior to Moses who merely received the law and, more than this, he is superior to the law itself. He is claiming to *be* Torah, we might say—just as later he claims to be the temple (John 2:19). In a dual way, then, Jesus is the message and the messenger of God. As missionaries we preach Jesus, we point to Jesus and explain his work. But Jesus, as the very Word of God, simply spoke. When he spoke, it happened, and when he acted, his words gave the true interpretation. As Vinoth Ramachandra expresses it, "Jesus was the Word-Act of God."[7] There was no division or disruption between his speech and act. His words were the power of God in the first century, as the words God spoke in creation were the creative Word of God, "in the beginning." Thus, the New Testament is more than just a story about Jesus and guidelines for how we should live.

We do not read the New Testament as God merely giving us an example, a model for how we should live. In some ways, the mission *is* Jesus, embodied in the sacred text.[8]

Jesus did provide a pattern, but he is also the promise. One passage in John, a passage expressed as from the lips of Jesus, puts our missiology and interpretation in proper christological perspective:

> Again Jesus said, "Peace be with you! As the Father has sent me, I am sending you." And with that he breathed on them and said, "Receive the Holy Spirit. If you forgive anyone's sins, their sins are forgiven; if you do not forgive them, they are not forgiven." (John 20:21–23)

Here we see the triple sending motif: Jesus was sent by the Father; Jesus sends, or breathes the Holy Spirit out "on them"; Jesus sends us out "in the same way." If we are to understand Christian mission, it is clear that we must understand the nature of Jesus's "sentness"—his work, message, and essence—and we need to understand how it is that he sends all who follow him. Thus Jesus as missionary, Jesus as message, and Jesus as sending Messiah are all part of a study of Jesus in the mission of God. We learn from him and are sent like him, as derivative missionaries: deriving our purpose and power from the Messiah, the Sent One.

As a composite of missional texts, we should also note the overall structure of the New Testament. The New Testament starts with four biographies of

7. See Vinoth Ramachandra, *The Recovery of Mission: Beyond the Pluralist Paradigm* (Grand Rapids: Eerdmans, 1997), 179–223.

8. This is visually depicted in much Christian art and iconography that has Jesus standing and holding onto a Bible, as if to say, "Here I am."

the same person. As a Muslim friend of mine once noted after reading the New Testament for the first time, "It's kind of repetitive, isn't it?" These four biographies provide much material for New Testament scholars to argue about, but for the Christian who reads with the eyes of faith, the Gospel accounts give four perspectives on the one Messiah. Matthew emphasizes the fulfillment of Jesus Christ as the promised Jewish Messiah; Luke, the historian, records more information about women and the poor; Mark is more direct and straightforward; and John is more philosophical, recording "I am" statements about Jesus of Nazareth. All four biographies are told as stories moving from birth through his teaching and works of power—slowly revealing his identity—and then suddenly coming to betrayal, tragic death, the surprising resurrection (which should not have been a surprise), a dénouement of final instructions, and ascension. As we noted above, it is a great story, and it is told with all the pathos and passion of the "Greatest Story Ever Told."[9]

Next we have a history book (Acts) about the Jesus people carrying out his final instructions amidst great opposition, under the power and direction of the Holy Spirit. What follows next is a series of twenty-one missionary letters, written (so it seems) to explain what is going on and at the same time to encourage faithfulness to the final instructions. Most of the material in the twenty-one missionary letters of the New Testament is about what to believe and how to live. I believe this is important to note: the overwhelming majority of the New Testament is about Jesus's life and teachings and the teachings and life of his followers. Very little in these missionary letters is concerned about how these communities are to order themselves. The final book is a revelation from God. If we step back and look at the overall literary order of the New Testament, it is quite amazing. After all of the biographies, the history, and the letters, we have a vision or apocalyptic writing as directly given to John by God: "A revelation from Jesus Christ, which God gave to him to show his servants" (Rev. 1:1).

The book of Revelation has important meaning for our study of missiology. Although variously interpreted through the years,[10] it is a vision that John had during worship ("on the Lord's Day," 1:10), and it is a revelation of and about Jesus Christ. Thus, it is a christological piece about worship. Much ink has been spilled about the historical and social interpretation of the book of Revelation, but it is fundamentally a book about worship and about Jesus.[11]

9. Title of the 1949 novel by Fulton Oursler and the 1965 movie produced by George Stevens.

10. See Ben Witherington's *Revelation*, The New Cambridge Bible Commentary (Cambridge: Cambridge University Press, 2003), 1–64, for a survey of scholarship and interpretation of Revelation.

11. Robert Mounce, among others, identifies four lines of interpretation: (1) preterist, or contemporary-historical; (2) historicist (speaking about the present time); (3) futurist, or eschatological; and (4) idealist, or timeless symbolic (therefore allegorical). See Robert H. Mounce, *The Book of Revelation*, rev. ed. (Grand Rapids: Eerdmans, 1998), 24–30.

> Revelation is explicitly designated for public reading in a liturgy (1:3) most likely a Eucharistic liturgy. From the heavenly celebration that met John's eyes and ears in chapter 4, there follows, throughout his book, one heavenly liturgy after another.[12]

Worship in Orthodox churches is patterned after Revelation, filled with songs of worship and focused on Jesus, the Lamb of God. Since this is a Revelation of Jesus Christ, through it we come to understand more fully who Jesus is in the heavenly realm. Many titles are used for Jesus (Christ, Son of God, Son of Man, Logos), but the two main titles are Lord (twenty-three times) and Lamb (twenty-eight times).[13] This is significant when we think about Christian mission, because as depicted in Revelation, in worship—the goal of mission—we come to see Jesus as God (Lord) and as the One who conquered all evil in his death (Lamb). Revelation is filled with cosmic battles and conflicts; evil seems relentlessly to return. But Satan, the great dragon that leads people to greed, lust, and power, is defeated by the blood of the Lamb. The Lamb who was slain unites earth and heaven, and so worship is a heavenly experience breaking into the earthly existence. Justice for the hungry, the exposed, and the oppressed comes through the worship of the Lamb by all of God's people. All of Revelation is worship, so we can say that, on one level, worship brings the victory of the Lamb over the evils and injustices of the world.

It is not too much to say that worship has a missional dimension, pushing back the powers of darkness and revealing the victory of the Lamb to the entire earthly and heavenly realms. In worship, we remember the martyrs who have given a faithful witness (*martyria*, 20:4); Babylon and all her oppression and sins are conquered (chaps. 17 and 18); we celebrate the gospel for every language and nation (14:6–7); we celebrate that the sacrifice of Jesus and our testimony conquers the great deceiver, Satan (12:10–12); and we live into the future hope of the victory of Christ revealed, the same hope that we proclaim and live in mission (21:22–27 and chap. 22). Worship is a missional act, and mission has as its goal worship of the Lamb by all the nations of the world (7:9–10).

In the New Testament, from the biographies of Jesus to the Revelation of heavenly worship, the mission of Jesus Christ is revealed, promoted, and celebrated. From beginning to end the story is about Jesus Christ, and main themes are built around right worship and the means of reaching that worship through obedience to God's mission. All nations are invited, and all other lords are to be vanquished. They are vanquished, however, by laying down earthly power and by submitting to the Lord who is the Lamb. Worship and mission reinforce and reflect each other. Worship flows out to testimony (witness), and the witness to others leads to thanksgiving and praise for conquest over sin.

12. Wilfrid J. Harrington, OP, *Revelation*, Sacra Pagina (Collegeville, MN: Liturgical Press, 1993), 30.

13. Witherington, *Revelation*, 28.

The central image of this story is the cross, and the central participation or celebration is the Eucharist. Christian mission must always in some way point to the cross and seek to celebrate this mercy for us in Eucharistic splendor. In summarizing the message he was handing on to others, Paul said to the Corinthians:

> Now, brothers and sisters, I want to remind you of the gospel I preached to you, which you received and on which you have taken your stand. By this gospel you are saved, if you hold firmly to the word I preached to you. Otherwise, you have believed in vain. For what I received I passed on to you as of first importance: that Christ died for our sins according to the Scriptures, that he was buried, that he was raised on the third day according to the Scriptures. (1 Cor. 15:1–4)

From this simple proclamation flows the mission of God that was entrusted to others to bring about the transformation of all of creation. It was for this cosmic mission that Jesus, the Messiah, was sent.

Messiah Is the Missionary of God

Jesus is both Messiah and Missionary of God. The earliest followers of Jesus were Jews who, upon his death and resurrection, understood Jesus fully in messianic terms. In Matthew's genealogy (Matt. 1), in Peter's confession (Matt. 16:16), in Peter's first sermon (Acts 2), and in Stephen's testimony and final sermon (Acts 7), Jesus is identified as the Messiah, or as the specially anointed and promised one of God. All of the early witnesses, as good Jewish citizens, were aware that they were proclaiming that the Messiah had come. Jesus did nothing to dissuade this belief; in fact, he encouraged it in his discussion about the law, his need to go to Jerusalem, and his request to his closest friends not to make the announcement that he is the Messiah too soon (the messianic secret). "Do not think that I have come to abolish the Law or the Prophets; I have come not to abolish them but to fulfill them" (Matt. 5:17). Although Jesus quickly proclaimed himself as the Messiah to non-Jews, for whom this language and expectation was foreign, his messianic identity was, and still is, critical. The Missionary of God, Jesus Christ, has his identity in the prophetic expectation from the Pentateuch, Psalms, and Prophets. Jesus is not an afterthought of God; he is portrayed as the forethought now revealed. He doesn't create a new identity by what he does, he reveals (*apokalyptō*)[14] what he has always been, and what Israel has always hoped for. The importance of this for mission is that we better understand Jesus the Missionary, who is the message, through all of Scripture. Marcion got it wrong, but his tendency

14. Revelation 13:8 describes Jesus as the Lamb who was slain from the creation of the world. Thus, we can see in worship, Jesus is not an afterthought, but a forethought of God.

or weakness is still very much alive.[15] It is tempting to view the church's mission as starting with and being founded on Jesus—from his baptism to his ascension.[16] A brief look at some significant images and teachings about the identity of Jesus the Messiah will help fill out our understanding of Jesus and our mission in Jesus Christ.

Messianic Images in the Old Testament

From the very beginning of the Jesus story (the infancy narratives), the apostolic witness affirmed that Jesus was the promised Messiah. "Look, the virgin shall conceive and bear a son, and they shall name him Emmanuel," which means, "God is with us" (Matt. 1:23 quoting Isa. 7:14, NRSV). Jesus's birth was a mysterious messianic birth and his identity was a mysterious theophany: God with us. The geographic references also affirmed his identity: Bethlehem (Matt. 2:6 quoting Mic. 5:2) and Egypt (Matt. 2:15 quoting Hosea 11:1). His identity from earliest childhood to his final days was marked by suffering: "A voice was heard in Ramah, wailing and loud lamentation, Rachel weeping for her children; she refused to be consoled, because they are no more" (Matt. 2:18 quoting Jer. 38:15 NRSV). And at the end of his life numerous quotations from the Old Testament are brought forward including one of the most troubling of all, "My God, my God, why have you forsaken me?" (Matt. 27:46 and Mark 15:34 quoting Ps. 22:1). It is interesting that one of the clearest passages from the Psalms that the apostolic witness saw as messianic was Psalm 22. It speaks of betrayal, suffering, mocking, having his clothes divided, suffering, but having no broken bones, and having his hands and feet pierced. Clearly the conquering Messiah was also acknowledged to be a suffering savior in the earliest years of Christian witness.

Sacrifice

We have seen in the Old Testament imagery about redemption the importance of sacrifice in the rhythms of Israel's community life. When Jesus is identified as the Lamb of God by John the Baptist (John 1:29, 36) and when we read in Revelation that Jesus is the Lamb, Jews would immediately think of Abraham's lamb (Gen. 22:8) or the Passover lamb, marking salvation from the angel of death and liberation from Egyptian servitude. The Messiah is

15. Marcion (d. 155) taught that the creator God, the God of the Old Testament, YHWH, was an evil God and so the Old Testament had no relevance. Jesus taught love; in contrast, the evil God of the Old Testament was violent and (since he created) attached to the material world, which is inferior to the spiritual.

16. It is here we augment David Bosch's approach, who, for other reasons, glanced over the Old Testament in his magnum opus, *Transforming Mission: Paradigm Shifts in Theology of Mission* (Maryknoll, NY: Orbis Books, 1991), 16–20.

named Jesus, which means "God saves" (or Yahweh is salvation). He is given this name to identify his mission: Jesus is to save his people from their sins (Matt. 1:21). Thus, as we look at the fullness of God's mission through Jesus and the church, we must hold on to the central concern in this mission, which is found in the very name of the promised Messiah: God saves (from sin).

To Fulfill the Law

The early Jewish followers of Jesus understood that when Jesus said he came to fulfill the law, he was literally fulfilling scriptural images and notions of God's salvation. Thus, the Old Testament is quoted frequently by New Testament writers, and by Jesus himself.[17] From finding fulfillment of the Law in Jesus, Christians soon began to see all of the Old Testament, especially the Psalms, as messianic—or about Jesus. Thus, understanding Jesus and his mission is not just about studying the Gospels; it is also about understanding Jesus as the Word, in the words of Scripture. In the Psalms, Jesus is the righteous one and the Lord. He is the one in whom we take refuge, who defends the cause of the poor, who gives deliverance to the needy, and who crushes the oppressor (Ps. 72:4). Jesus, the Messiah and Missionary of God, is understood as the fulfillment of all that was in Scripture concerning God's will and work. He is the Jewish Messiah who has broken out to become the Lord of the nations. "Declare his glory among the nations, his marvelous works among all the peoples. . . . Say among the nations, 'The Lord is king!'" (Ps. 96:3, 10 NRSV). Acts 2 reveals a paradigm of the universal nature of Christ's salvation when all the nations heard in their own languages followers of Jesus "speaking about God's deeds of power" (Acts 2:11 NRSV). Then there is a transition from Jewish Messiah to universal Lord in the first Christian sermon, when Peter concludes, "Therefore let the entire house of Israel know with certainty that God has made him both Lord and Messiah, this Jesus whom you crucified" (Acts 2:36 NRSV). The universal nature of the Messiah's lordship was again affirmed in Acts 10, when a non-Jewish group of people received a special revelation from God and then received the same Holy Spirit the Jerusalem Jews had received upon hearing the gospel of Jesus Christ proclaimed. Again, the early Christians could see that Jesus was more than a Jewish Messiah. He was "a light for the Gentiles" (Isa. 42:6 and 49:6), and so salvation would be proclaimed to the ends of the earth (49:6).[18]

17. See Leonhard Goppelt, *Typos: The Typological Interpretation of the Old Testament in the New*, trans. Donald M. Madvig (Grand Rapids: Eerdmans, 1982); Steve Moyise, *Evoking Scripture: Seeing the Old Testament in the New* (New York: T&T Clark, 2008); Stanley E. Porter, ed., *Hearing the Old Testament in the New Testament* (Grand Rapids: Eerdmans, 2006); and John M. Court, *New Testament Writers and the Old Testament: An Introduction* (London: SPCK, 2002).

18. Jesus was sent to Israel with a view to the nations. Both must be emphasized, affirming this Jewish heritage and foundation, and the universal extent or purpose (see John 1:11; Matt. 15:21–28; and, of course, John 3:16).

Universal Lord

The universal nature of Jesus's lordship reflects a unique quality of both Jesus and of the witness we bear. Since Jesus is the universal Lord, there are no other lords and no other saviors who can save. Jesus's claims are universal (Mark 2:1–12; John 12:32) and his apostles concurred as seen in their witness (Acts 4:12; Rom. 10:5–17). What is unique is not just the claim of universal salvation through Jesus Christ alone, but also the means of that salvation. As we noted in the opening paragraph of this chapter, in Jesus Christ redemption has come as a free gift. Jesus offers a costly grace: costly for him, full of grace for us (Acts 15:11). There are others who offer paths and methods for salvation, but Jesus Christ offers it as a free gift. Forgiveness precedes empowerment to change, rather than the other way around. There are many common threads and themes in other prophetic and savior figures,[19] but Jesus is presented as the unique Lord of all and his offer (grace) is also like none other.

Sent from God

Another unique characteristic of Jesus is the clear teaching that he is the sent one from God. Other prophets and savior figures come, often with special signs and strange portents, but Jesus is predicted to be sent, has a foretold mission, and then is self-consciously fulfilling the mission for which he was sent. "I was sent only to the lost sheep of Israel" (Matt. 15:24); "I must proclaim the good news of the kingdom of God to other towns also, for that is why I was sent" (Luke 4:43); "As the Father has sent me, I am sending you" (John 20:21). But for what purpose or what mission was Jesus sent?

Here is where missionaries and mission societies must find common understanding. There are Christians who would follow the Jesus of Mahatma Gandhi (Jesus of the Sermon on the Mount),[20] or the reduced Jesus of higher criticism,[21] or the revolutionary Jesus of militant liberationists,[22] or even the pacifist Jesus of the Mennonite tradition. It is not our place here to cover all the Jesus material of the past centuries, but we do need to ask the question and answer as honestly as possible: for what reason was Jesus sent? However, the reader will have to wait for the answer to this question until a later section

19. We could compare Jesus with Zoroaster and Siddhartha Gautama, or, for example, with the contemporary wonderworker and philosopher Apollonius of Tyana. See *Apollonius of Tyana* by Philostratus, ed. and trans. Christopher P. Jones, Loeb Classical Library (Cambridge, MA: Harvard University Press, 2006).

20. See William W. Emilsen, *Gandhi's Bible* (Delhi: ISPCK, 2001).

21. There are many, but one of the most widely known is John Dominic Crossan, *The Historical Jesus: The Life of a Mediterranean Jewish Peasant* (San Francisco: HarperSanFrancisco, 2000).

22. There are many varieties here, each coming out of situations of oppression. For one of the earliest, see James Cone, *Black Theology and Black Power* (New York: Seabury, 1969), which focused upon the social context of African Americans in the 1960s.

("Mission of Jesus"). What we can and must say here is that the mission of Jesus and the life of Jesus must be understood as one piece. We must not reduce Jesus to a moral teacher, or an atoning sacrifice, or a healer, or a liberator, or an empire resister. The life of Jesus, in some sense, is his mission: incarnation and birth, teachings and works of power, passion and death, resurrection and ascension. We cannot choose to focus only on his teaching; this is misuse of the biblical material and disregards his life, including his conflict with evil, and his passion. It is all of one fabric, and together it is the content of our mission.

Jesus the Lord Is the Suffering Savior

We come now near to the heart of the missional identity of Jesus and also of those who follow him and are sent by him. As was mentioned in the preface, we are not being true to the gospel message if we neglect the place of suffering in mission. The central symbol of Jesus is the cross and the central identity of Jesus in worship is the Lamb and the Eucharist.[23] We need to pause for just a moment to consider this: it must be the greatest paradox of all creation, or the greatest irony in the entire world, that the Deceiver is deceived, thinking that he has killed "Life." Or, to look at it another way, the powers of the air are defeated when God is lifted up to die in the air. Hubris is conquered by humility and avarice by poverty. It is so counterintuitive, so unexpected and mysterious, that it is easy to see why the history of the church is filled with people who would avoid suffering and choose to help God be victorious through the use of worldly powers. But, of course, this is to be deceived by the Deceiver. And missionaries have often been deceived in this way, when they have possessed the power to insulate themselves from suffering.

Before launching into texts describing the meaning and place of suffering and death, we must first make a quick foray into text criticism, since the passion of Jesus has been one of the most controversial issues in studies of the historical Jesus. Jesus's prediction and passive acceptance of his death have been questioned. From as early as David Friedrich Strauss (1836) up to the last decade of the twentieth century, with the writing of John Dominic Crossan, Jesus scholars have given the Passion Narratives "a very critical going-over."[24] Jesus's death was not so much denied, but its meaning and his passive

23. As a side note, one of the most famous films about Jesus was called *The Passion of the Christ*.

24. A summary is given by Dale C. Allison in *Constructing Jesus: Memory, Imagination and History* (Grand Rapids: Baker Academic, 2010), 388. David Friedrich Strauss, *The Life of Jesus Critically Examined* (German original, 1836) is the classic in this tradition of skeptical historical analysis (trans. George Eliot, ed. Peter C. Hodgson [Philadelphia: Fortress, 1972]). John Dominic Crossan, *Who Killed Jesus? Exposing the Roots of Anti-Semitism in the Gospel Story of the Death of Jesus* (San Francisco: HarperSanFrancisco, 1996).

Dale Allison on Jesus's Purposed Death

"To entertain the suggestion that Jesus did not go to his death willingly requires positing either a widespread conscious cover-up or a catastrophic memory failure in the early Christian sources. Perhaps some will find one of those options plausible. I consider it much more likely that, in this particular instance, our sources are not bereft of memory. Jesus's decision to die, whenever made and whatever the motivation and whatever this precise interpretation, left a vivid impression. Indeed, next to the fact that Jesus was crucified by order of Pontius Pilate, his acquiescence to his fate is probably the best-attested fact about his last days. At some point, he determined to assent to his miserable end, accepting it as the will of God."[a]

a. Allison, *Constructing Jesus*, 433. In the first seventeen pages of the same book, Allison discusses how recent studies of memory aid in our interpretation of Gospel materials about Jesus.

acceptance were strongly critiqued. Recently, Dale Allison has argued—first from Pauline material, then from comparison of Paul (on Jesus) to Mark (and John), and finally from memory studies—that Jesus's passive acceptance of his death, as a meaningful fate, is nearly undeniable.

A sudden and tragic death has a tremendous effect on one's memory. Anyone who has experienced the sudden death of a loved one can affirm that the Gospel memory of Jesus is realistic. The events around the passion (suffering and death) jump out in stark relief compared to the rest of the person's life. And so Mark's Gospel, according to Martin Kähler,[25] is about 40 percent Passion Narrative. That the last week takes up 40 percent of the narrative of a person's life reflects the truth that "a tragic and cruel death draws attention to itself," so that it "'eclipses the retelling of their living—the way they died takes precedence over the way they lived.'"[26] Jesus's passion should be understood today not only as a historic event, but as the central and defining event of the life of Jesus: a weeklong process of submission to God's will that was later described as Jesus's humility and obedience (Phil. 2:1–8).

This being the case, how does Scripture understand suffering and, I add, its relationship to God's glory?[27] Four major themes about Jesus's suffering and

25. Martin Kähler summarizes that "one could call the Gospels passion narratives with extended introductions." *The So-called Historical Jesus and the Historic, Biblical Christ*, trans. and ed. Carl E. Braaten (German original, 1896; Philadelphia: Fortress, 1964), 80n11.

26. Allison, *Constructing Jesus*, 423. Here Allison is quoting from Edward K. Rynearson, *Retelling Violent Death* (Oxford: Oxford University Press, 2001), ix, x.

27. There has been recent scholarship on the cross and atonement theology that has criticized the whole notion of God the Father sending the Son to be killed as a cruel expression of filicide (killing one's son). Moltmann has answered this charge noting that this is not child abuse, but it is the love of the Triune God: "If Paul speaks emphatically of God's 'own son,' the not-sparing and abandoning also involves the Father himself. In the forsakenness of the Son, the Father also

glory will be mentioned here, because they relate directly to our understanding and practice of mission.

Suffering as a Sign of the Messiah

First, temporary suffering (including death) and eternal glory is a primary sign or designation of Jesus. First Peter 1:10–12 tells how the prophets of old sought (through the Spirit of Christ in them) to find out the time and circumstances that salvation would come to this world. The key to finding salvation was given when the Spirit of Christ in them "predicted the sufferings of the Messiah and the glories that would follow" (v. 11). Peter had just mentioned to this scattered group of disciples that suffering is temporary (1:6), but the rewards, like precious gold (and like the Word of God) last forever (1:9, 24–25). Luke portrays the resurrected Jesus making this connection directly to some early disciples, showing that the suffering and the glory to follow was predicted by the prophets: "'Did not the Messiah have to suffer these things and then enter his glory?' And beginning with Moses and all the Prophets, he explained to them what was said in all the Scriptures concerning himself" (Luke 24:26–27). Immediately after this, the connection is made between four important themes: suffering, glory, mission, and the Holy Spirit's empowerment.

> He said to them, "This is what I told you while I was still with you: Everything must be fulfilled that is written about me in the Law of Moses, the Prophets and the Psalms." Then he opened their minds so they could understand the Scriptures. He told them, "This is what is written: The Messiah will suffer and rise from the dead on the third day, and repentance for the forgiveness of sins will be preached in his name to all nations, beginning at Jerusalem. You are witnesses of these things. I am going to send you what my Father has promised; but stay in the city until you have been clothed with power from on high." (Luke 24:44–49)

The key to recognizing the Savior is to see his suffering and passion, which is followed by his glory, revealed first in the resurrection, and later in the mission carried out by his apostles.[28]

Suffering Conquers Evil

Second, suffering vanquishes evil. Again, this is counterintuitive, for how can suffering and death—defeat—conquer anyone or anything? And yet

---

forsakes himself. In the surrender of the Son, the Father also surrenders himself, though not in the same way." I might even venture to say that the Triune God suffers. Jürgen Moltmann, *The Crucified God: The Cross of Christ as the Foundation and Criticism of Christian Theology*, trans. R. A. Wilson and John Bowden (New York: Harper & Row, 1974), 243.

28. There are many other supporting passages we could look at. See also John 17:1–5 and Romans 8:18.

this is one of the major themes of salvation in Scripture. Jesus's life and the worship we have described in Revelation are pictured as a battle against evil.[29] We may not like warfare imagery, but it is found throughout Scripture. This, however, is a very different type of warfare. It is through gentleness and submission that the evil one is slain. John records Jesus's explanation of such an ironic victory plan in chapter 12. To those who asked to see him, Jesus tells of the coming hour for the glorification of the Son of Man and connects this glorification with a kernel of wheat, which must die in order to bear fruit (vv. 21–24). He goes on to speak with a troubled yet confident heart about his call to glorify his Father's name and be lifted up from the earth so that he might draw all people to himself (vv. 27–33). In these passages we see the relationship between suffering and glory, but we also see the relationship between death and victory (bearing fruit, drawing all people to himself). Thus, the victory he will win will be in drawing all people to himself. The salvation of the nations is the victory he wins over the prince of this world, the evil one who holds humanity captive. The irony of suffering and death hiding ultimate victory is expressed in many hymns and gospel songs.[30] Blood, as well as the cross, are symbols of the passion and death of Jesus Christ, and here is where the cosmic victory is won. His death is the weapon that defeats all earthly and heavenly powers.

Suffering Christ, Suffering Church

Third, the passion of Christ is not unlike the suffering church. In fact, our identity in Jesus Christ includes our call to suffering with him. This does not mean that the church should seek out suffering or become flagellants.[31] Our call to suffering simply reveals the reality that the mission of Jesus Christ, which is now the mission of God carried out by the church, will be resisted. Jesus's response to this resistance, and the church's response, is to speak clearly, act faithfully, and receive the rejection in gentleness and humble submission. "But rejoice inasmuch as you participate in the sufferings of Christ, so that you may be overjoyed when his glory is revealed" (1 Pet. 4:13). Like our Savior, suffering will be followed by the revelation of the glory of God. Writing to a scattered and persecuted church, Peter encourages them further with these remarks: "If you suffer as a Christian, do not be ashamed, but praise God that you bear that name" (v. 16). Mark records Jesus himself preparing the disciples

29. Allison (*Constructing Jesus*, 19) summarizes that what we do know about Jesus (which he concludes makes Jesus an "apocalyptic prophet") is in part that he is combating evil. "According to the sources as a whole, Jesus was an exorcist who thought of himself as successfully combating the devil."

30. The refrain "There is pow'r, pow'r, wonder-working pow'r in the precious blood of the Lamb" is one example. Lewis E. Jones, 1899.

31. Mostly a thirteenth- and fourteenth-century movement of self-mortification through whipping oneself.

Peter's Confession of Christ: A Call to Suffering

"Who do people say I am?" They replied, "Some say John the Baptist; others say Elijah; and still others, one of the prophets." "But what about you?" he asked. "Who do you say I am?" Peter answered, "You are the Messiah." Jesus warned them not to tell anyone about him. He then began to teach them that the Son of Man must suffer many things and be rejected by the elders, chief priests and teachers of the law, and that he must be killed and after three days rise again. He spoke plainly about this, and Peter took him aside and began to rebuke him. But when Jesus turned and looked at his disciples, he rebuked Peter. "Get behind me, Satan!" he said. "You do not have in mind the concerns of God, but merely human concerns." Then he called the crowd to him along with his disciples and said: "Whoever wants to be my disciple must deny themselves and take up their cross and follow me. For whoever wants to save their life will lose it, but whoever loses their life for me and for the gospel will save it" (Mark 8:27–35).

for a future of rejection and suffering at the turning point in the Gospel, the confession of Peter (Mark 8:27–35).

This passage links Jesus's identity with his suffering and glory, and links his followers' calling to cross-bearing. Bearing a cross is an image of self-denial and even death. It is a call to extreme obedience. Paul absorbed this teaching into his own life and expressed his identity with Jesus in mission in the following way: "Now I rejoice in what I am suffering for you, and I fill up in my flesh what is still lacking in regard to Christ's afflictions, for the sake of his body, which is the church" (Col. 1:24). The suffering of the missionary, for the sake of the church, is completing the work of Jesus Christ, or is participating in the work of Jesus Christ in vanquishing the powers of evil.

Suffering and Spiritual Life

Finally, suffering is an expression of missional spirituality closely related to humility, gentleness, and obedience. As depicted in Scripture, Jesus accepted the will of the Father, even though it was a bitter cup ("*Abba*, Father. . . . Take this cup from me," Mark 14:36). Even Jesus, according to Scripture, struggled with the call to obedience. Faithful witness is a spiritual battle, and the victory is for others, not ourselves. Our victory over sin, which involves our path of passion, is part of our witness. We see this in many places, including the *locus classicus* Philippians 2, but we see this most clearly in the martyrdom of Stephen in Acts 7:51–60. Stephen's faith was crowned with martyrdom (witness). In this witness a number of key elements come together: Stephen spoke words of judgment clearly and directly. There was resistance to his message. The Holy Spirit strengthened Stephen and gave him a sustaining vision. His vision linked his witness to his identity in Christ: he saw Christ—the Suffering Servant—in glory. And, finally, in the midst of his suffering—as he gave witness—he prayed. Stephen's prayer is a prayer of humility centered on salvation in Jesus Christ and on forgiveness. Christian spirituality is centered on humble witness through suffering.

An Intermission on Evangelism: What Is the Good News (Euangelion)*?*

When this good news of Jesus Christ as the Messiah was proclaimed, what was actually said? We have looked at the central purpose of Jesus seen through these prophecies and expressed by Jesus and those closest to him. There is a tendency among Christians to want to reduce this message to a handy booklet, to a tract, or to a single verse. And yet the evangelistic message is multifaceted. How can we best understand it in all of its mystery and power? Jesus himself seemed to give very different messages to different people. Think of the following examples:

- Nicodemus, the Pharisee, was told he had to start over or be born again (John 3:3).
- A demon-possessed man in the synagogue was simply told to "Be quiet" (Luke 4:35).
- Levi the tax collector was told to "Follow me" (Luke 5:27).
- The Samaritan woman fetching water at the well was told, "Whoever drinks the water I give them will never thirst. . . . Go call your husband and come back" (John 4:14, 16).
- The paralyzed man at the Sheep Gate in Jerusalem was asked, "Do you want to get well? . . . Get up! Pick up your mat and walk" (John 5:6–8).

As we can see, the message that Jesus spoke to people was quite varied depending upon the context and the person or persons addressed. Some he judged in no uncertain terms: "You brood of vipers!" (Matt. 3:7; 12:34; and 23:33). Others he spoke to with great compassion: "He said to her, 'Daughter, your faith has healed you. Go in peace and be freed from your suffering'" (Mark 5:34). To some he spoke very directly: "'One thing you lack,' he said. 'Go, sell everything you have and give to the poor, and you will have treasure in heaven. Then come, follow me'" (Mark 10:21). But others he left totally confused: "The disciples came to him and asked, 'Why do you speak to the people in parables?' He replied, 'Because the knowledge of the secrets of the kingdom of heaven has been given to you, but not to them'" (Matt. 13:10–11). Context is not everything, but it is a critical component when thinking about the message of Christ and the message of the church.

On the other hand, the message of Jesus Christ is very simple, for it is generally summarized in the New Testament simply as good news (*euangelion*). The core of Christian mission, what David Bosch calls the "heart" of mission, is evangelism: giving witness to the gospel. The noun "gospel" (*euangelion*) is used seventy-five times in the New Testament (fifty-eight times by Paul). As a verb (to evangelize, preach, proclaim: *euangelizomai*) it is used fifty-three times (twenty by Paul). Thus the word "gospel" or "to preach good news"[32] is used a total of 128 times in the New Testament. It is very important that we have a grasp of the central meaning of the gospel, as well as the breadth of the meaning of the gospel.

Ten Statements about the Gospel

The following are ten statements about the gospel that should help us in thinking of how we communicate the message of the Messiah, which is our message to the nations.

1. The gospel is a summary of the life and teachings of Jesus Christ. On one level the gospel is Jesus. The Gospel of Mark begins, "The beginning of the good news about Jesus the Messiah, the Son of God" (Mark 1:1). The good news, the gospel, is the full story of Jesus Christ. Thus, when we say gospel, we are using shorthand for all that Jesus is and all that he did while on earth. This means that both Jesus's concern for the poor and his judgment upon hypocrites are part of the gospel of Jesus Christ.

2. The gospel is what Jesus taught. When we read the Sermon on the Mount and when we think over the parables and stories that Jesus told, we are thinking of strands in the larger fabric of the gospel (Jesus's teachings). Jesus's teachings about how to live and how to trust and follow him ("faith") are the gospel—not just moral teachings. The gospel is about trusting Jesus and his teaching, even becoming part of him (John 15).

3. The gospel is the message from God to all people or, more precisely, to all ethnic groups. In Mark 13:10 we read, "And the gospel must first be preached to all nations." In parallel passages, Scripture states that this gospel is for the entire world to hear (Matt. 24:14; Mark 14:9). The gospel has universal meaning and intent.

4. The gospel is the message preached by the apostles. Thus, there is continuity expressed in the New Testament between what Jesus was teaching and

32. The verbal form meaning to tell the good news is often simply translated "to preach." There are other words used in the New Testament for "to preach" (*kerysső*, *katangellō*, etc.). In most of the instances, the meaning of the word is to preach to those outside of the church, to proclaim the good news of Jesus Christ in order to bring others to faith. Thus, it is safest to think of "preaching" in the New Testament as we commonly understand "evangelizing." When Paul says, "Preach (*keryssōn*) the word; be prepared in season and out of season; correct, rebuke and encourage—with great patience and careful instruction" (2 Tim. 4:2), his concern is obviously missional. He is concerned to bring people to faith and help them resist other cultural lords (desires, myths, etc.).

what his followers were teaching. In Acts 8 we read that John and Peter (v. 25) as well as Philip (v. 40) went about preaching the gospel. Whether it be the centrality of the cross, the concern for sin, or even the nature of the Kingdom of God, it is one gospel.

5. The core message of the gospel is about the grace of God offered for all of humanity. When Peter was called to speak to Cornelius (not knowing why) he summarized to the Jewish believers in Jerusalem what he said in the following way:

> God, who knows the heart, showed that he accepted them by giving the Holy Spirit to them, just as he did to us. He did not discriminate between us and them, for he purified their hearts by faith. Now then, why do you try to test God by putting on the necks of the Gentiles a yoke that neither we nor our ancestors have been able to bear? No! We believe it is through the grace of our Lord Jesus that we are saved, just as they are. (Acts 15:8–11)

This experience, which required special visions of revelation for both Peter and Cornelius, prevented Christianity from becoming a Jewish sect. From first to last it was the grace of God that saved all people: Jews who walked with Jesus, as well as Cornelius and his household. Grace plus nothing is the gospel message.[33]

6. The gospel of grace is centered on the meaning of the cross of Jesus Christ. Paul speaks of the gospel as parallel to the message of the cross. "For Christ did not send me to baptize, but to preach the gospel—not with wisdom and eloquence, lest the cross of Christ be emptied of its power. For the message of the cross is foolishness to those who are perishing, but to us who are being saved it is the power of God" (1 Cor. 1:17–18). Thus our earlier discussion of suffering as a core element of Jesus Christ comes out in Paul's preaching of the gospel. The cross does not express the full extent of the gospel preached, but it does show the intent of God's message and messenger.

7. Because the gospel is a gospel of grace, it is also a gospel of judgment. Grace is available because the evil powers have been vanquished. If there is no judgment of evil, there is no grace for others. The cross is a judgment on sin and death. The outworking of this gospel is seen in the rejection of all vanquished idols. Christian virtues are now possible and vices are hamstrung. Thus, the gospel message includes the call to live into the new life, which recognizes the defeat of the other lords. "Since then you have been raised with Christ, set your heart on things above, where Christ is, seated at the right hand of God" (Col. 3:1). The gospel includes the call to "put on" Christ and to

33. Acts 20:24 also summarizes the core understanding of the gospel. Paul, in summarizing his ministry before the Ephesian elders, said, " . . . if only I may finish the race and complete the task the Lord Jesus has given me—the task of testifying to the gospel of God's grace." It is the gospel about or concerning God's grace.

"put off" the old nature.[34] Thus, the "sin lists" we find in the New Testament (e.g., Mark 7:21; 1 Cor. 5:9–13) are lists of behaviors we now reject, because their lords are defeated.

8. The gospel is to be preached in a manner that reveals its nature: The gospel is truth, and so it must be preached truthfully. The gospel is grace and humility, and so it must be preached with grace and humility. In 2 Corinthians 4:2–5, Paul talks about how the gospel is to be preached, not in secret or deceptive ways, but openly, honestly, with no pretense or prejudice. The gospel has its own power (derived from its truth and glory) and therefore doesn't need us to help it by compromising (using deception, distortion, or shameful methods).[35]

9. The gospel of Jesus Christ has supreme value. In many ways this is communicated through Jesus's life (take no staff or cloak, only the gospel when you are sent out, Luke 9:1–6) and Paul's letters (Phil. 1, Gal. 1 and 2, etc.). Paul was willing to be imprisoned, and even die, as long as Christ was being proclaimed (Phil. 1:15–18). All other virtues and issues of justice and mercy must and will flow from this supreme value—that Christ is proclaimed.

10. The gospel has its own power to transform individuals. "For we know, brothers and sisters loved by God, that he has chosen you, because our gospel came to you not simply with words but also with power, with the Holy Spirit and deep conviction" (1 Thess. 1:4–5; see also 2 Tim. 1:8). The gospel has this power because it is the Word of God. In receiving and then preaching the gospel, people receive the Holy Spirit and are then empowered to participate in the conquest over evil and sin (in their own lives). And so Paul could say, "I am not ashamed of the gospel, because it is the power of God that brings salvation to everyone who believes" (Rom. 1:16).

Gospel of Words and Works

One final note about preaching the gospel of the Kingdom (Matt. 24:14) and doing the works of the Kingdom. For the biblical writers there is power in both. Jesus enacted the Kingdom, but he also preached the Kingdom. His words and his works had power. Jesus responded to situations with a touch of the hand, a word of encouragement, or a word of judgment, and in each case there was power. We, however, tend to be reductionistic: promoting verbal evangelism alone, or promoting works of mercy alone. Jesus does not recognize this dichotomy. I think an analogy from the family is helpful at this point. Any wife will tell you that words are cheap when it comes to proving

34. Both in the New Testament and in much early Christian literature there is the image of clothing for salvation. St. Ephrem the Syrian talks about salvation as putting on "the Robe of Glory," or a "garment of light." See Sebastian Brock's *St. Ephrem the Syrian: Hymns on Paradise* (Crestwood, NY: St. Vladimir's Seminary Press, 1990), 66–72.

35. See also 1 Corinthians 1:17, which explains that when we use our own power or wisdom in preaching the gospel, we are stripping it of its power. The gospel has its own power.

love in a marriage. "You tell me you love me, but you never lift a finger to help out around the house." Love must be expressed in deeds of love, in acts of mercy. On the other hand, no parent should ever try to raise their children without saying powerful and transformative words of support, "We love you so much." "We were so proud of how hard you worked on your project." Buying presents is shallow and misleading when words can and must express love with precision. Words from parents are needed to express why they do certain things (like feeding vegetables when three meals of donuts seems perfectly reasonable). On the other hand, I have seen parents destroy children with words ("Why can't you do well in school like your sister!?"), and then again I have heard parents empower and build up children with words ("You never cease to amaze us!"). The same is true of actions, for actions can destroy a child. Child abuse steals a young person's soul. The gospel must be spoken and lived, preached and practiced. Words must be proven in acts of love, and acts must be interpreted by words. Jesus is our model for both living out and proclaiming the gospel to the nations.

Is Jesus Our Missionary Model?

Is Jesus really our missionary model, or should we be thinking about Jesus as our message? In what way do we "follow" Jesus as our missionary model or example? Do we sell all we have and wander around on foot collecting disciples and living off of others? What leads us to this question is the important and revealing resurrection appearance recorded by John.

> On the evening of that first day of the week, when the disciples were together, with the doors locked for fear of the Jewish leaders, Jesus came and stood among them and said, "Peace be with you!" After he said this, he showed them his hands and side. The disciples were overjoyed when they saw the Lord. Again Jesus said, "Peace be with you! As the Father has sent me, I am sending you." And with that he breathed on them and said, "Receive the Holy Spirit. If you forgive anyone's sins, they are forgiven; if you do not forgive them, they are not forgiven." (John 20:19–23)

This is a key passage for understanding the missionary nature of our calling as disciples and our identity in relationship to Jesus; if we are called *to* Jesus Christ, we are sent *by* Jesus Christ.[36] We note in this passage that, at first, the disciples were frightened—only when Jesus comes into their midst and they recognize the key to his identity (marks of suffering) are they filled with joy.

36. For a full discussion of the concept of coming to Jesus and being sent by Jesus in the Gospel of John, see Andreas J. Köstenberger, *The Missions of Jesus and the Disciples According to the Fourth Gospel, with Implications for the Fourth Gospel's Purpose and the Mission of the Contemporary Church* (Grand Rapids: Eerdmans, 1998), 176–98.

Peace (*shalom*) is declared to them two times, and then he utters the Johannine commission, "As the Father has sent me, I am sending you." It is a simple grammatical construction that is loaded with meaning.[37] The Father sent the Son who sends his disciples, even as he sends the Holy Spirit.

There are many ways we can look at this sending, but let me suggest a few that are important for missionary vocations. Jesus was sent in the power of the Holy Spirit, and he sends his disciples in the same power; related to this (or perhaps the flip side of it), Jesus was not sent with worldly power or influence. In fact, he was relatively poor, from a suspicious birth, he was persecuted, and he was almost killed soon after his birth. Jesus was sent to be among the poor, to walk with them, and to heal and cast out demons from those who were oppressed. He did spend some time with the wealthy, but often it was to call them to let go of their riches and to choose him as Lord instead of their wealth. Jesus was sent in continuity with the Old Testament law, affirming it and even raising the standards (see the Sermon on the Mount, Matt. 5–7). Finally, Jesus was sent to walk in and with people in a particular culture and time. Jesus did not provide esoteric teachings from a distant mountain or from deep in the desert; he walked with people, spoke their language, touched their sores, and gave them hope now and for the future. He held their children and was held, as a child, by his own mother.

So how is Jesus our role model for missionary work? There are two errors we must avoid in thinking about our mission in light of Jesus's mission. First, we must remember that Jesus was God: he claimed this identity, revealed it through his actions, and was recognized as such by the early church. We can easily develop a messiah complex, by thinking that we are just like Jesus. We must remember that we do not have the power to save people or situations; we can only point to Jesus as the savior, teacher, healer, and exorcist. Our ministry is derivative of the life and ministry of Jesus Christ. This may seem quite obvious, and yet many missionaries act like they are the savior of their particular mission field or their particular people group. Second, we must avoid seeing Jesus as so completely different (fully God, but not so human, really) that we end up reducing our missionary work to moral or ethical platitudes. Jesus healed, he cast out demons, and he taught with authority and power. He expected those whom he sent to do this—to an even greater extent (John 14:12)! Jesus is our model in ministry, but not as redeemer—for there is only one redeemer. He is our model and example, but he is also the wisdom and power of God. We are invited to participate in his ministry as on a missionary team. However, all the power and wisdom of this missionary team flows *from* Jesus *through* us.

Jesus's final instructions in John 20 (as well as in Matthew, Mark, and Luke—see below) were clearly for his followers. All of his disciples were to

37. "Just as (*kathōs*) the Father sent (*apestalken*) me, so also I (*kagō*) send (*pempō*) you."

follow him, and that meant to follow him out into the world. According to Dale Allison, one of the three major themes that we know of in the life of Jesus Christ is that he sent out individuals on his behalf, "extending his ministry through their own activities, including preaching."[38] Thus it follows that, "Christianity's missionary impulse was not born solely of post-Easter circumstances," for it had a pre-Easter expression, and "to join in Jesus' ministry was to repeat to some extent what he proclaimed."[39] Jesus fully expects his followers to receive not only him, but also his commission. We are sent, as the Father sent Jesus Christ, and in this way we are Christians: those who bear Christ and his message to the world.

If we are sent in the pattern of Jesus with a message to the world, then our message is both about Jesus and the Kingdom Jesus proclaimed. "If anything is clear in Jesus, it is that the announcement and demonstration of the Kingdom are at the very core of his message and life."[40] We have spoken about the good news and evangelism, but it is important to remember that the good news Jesus proclaimed was the good news of the Kingdom. "Jesus went throughout Galilee, teaching in their synagogues, proclaiming the good news of the kingdom, and healing every disease and sickness among the people" (Matt. 4:23). The good news of the Kingdom includes the restoring of right relationships prophesied in the Old Testament—a new social order marked by *shalom*—and this includes liberation from illnesses, diseases, and demons.[41] To be blind or lame was to be poor, so healing meant restoration to society, the ability to work and contribute to family and community. Children were marginalized—the Kingdom of Jesus Christ brought children to the center of God's realm (Matt. 18:1–10). Women were considered inferior to men—Jesus honored women and women became the first witnesses of the resurrection (John 20, Luke 24:1–12). Lepers were outcast, lonely, and without hope—Jesus healed them, touched them, and restored them to the community (Matt. 8:1–4, etc.). And, of course, if demons have been cast out, "then the kingdom of God has come upon you" (Matt. 12:28). The Kingdom of God is judgment on other lords and kings, it is liberation, and it is the subsequent restoration of God's righteous rule. It is announced and demonstrated, and it is entered through the doorway of repentance. Missionaries, sent as Jesus was sent, proclaim the Kingdom of God in their presence and praxis.

38. Allison, *Constructing Jesus*, 25. The other two are the memorable way Jesus's sayings are fashioned, and Jesus was an itinerant teacher who used much of the same material in different locations.

39. Ibid., 26.

40. Ron Sider, "What If We Defined the Gospel the Way That Jesus Did?" in Brian Woolnough and Wonsuk Ma, eds., *Holistic Mission: God's Plan for God's People* (Oxford: Regnum, 2010), 18.

41. Brief summary statements in the Gospels of Jesus's ministry make this clear: Mark 1:38–39; Matt. 4:23 and 9:35. See also the instructions given to his disciples: Matt. 10:7; Mark 3:14; and parallels.

Mission of Jesus: Four Windows of Scripture

There are many passages we might look at in the New Testament to zero in on the mission of Jesus, but I have chosen four that are especially helpful. The first passage is a window into the beginning of the mission of Jesus: his inaugural address found in Luke 4. The second passage we will look at is actually four passages of final instructions Jesus left that have guided the church through the ages and have been foundational for centuries of Christian mission. Our third passage is often called the beginning of the church:[42] the final instructions in Acts 1:8 and then the immediate fulfillment and understanding of the church in the world found in Acts 2. The last passage looks at the goal of mission: the heavenly vision found in Revelation 7.

1. Jesus's Inaugural Address, or the "Nazareth Manifesto": Luke 4:18–30

This has become a key passage in the past forty years or so, often for liberationist interpretations of Jesus, but the pericope is usually only read up to verse 20 or 21. It is important to read the whole pericope together, for the conclusion of the passage is in verses 28–31. Yet even the brief selection that Jesus reads from the Isaiah scroll is a sermon in itself and speaks clearly about liberation.

First, it starts out in a trinitarian fashion: the Spirit from the Lord is upon Jesus to enact the mission of God. Second, there is a major emphasis upon proclamation: the mission of Jesus involves verbal announcement of what God is doing. Third, the mission of Jesus involves special concern for the oppressed (imprisoned, blind, poor). In fact, the last line seems to point to the year of Jubilee (Lev. 25:8–55), in which land was returned to the poor who had had to sell land to pay their bills: "proclaim the year of the Lord's favor" (Luke 14:19). Fourth, there is a strong emphasis here on sending and empowering, beginning with the anointing and including the release of the prisoner. Finally, the special concern is for the most needy and helpless. If this is, in fact, Jesus's mission, it is focused on those who cannot help themselves. It is a saving work, a liberating work for those who have no other hope.

It seems likely that the Jewish listeners heard this announcement as announcing their imminent liberation from the heavy hand of Rome. "All spoke well of him" (v. 22) probably indicates that they liked what he said and assumed he was identifying himself as the liberator from Roman oppression. Jesus wanted none of this, so he immediately tells them two marginal stories from the Old Testament (these were not stories about major figures like David or Abraham) to redirect their thinking. With all of the blessings of God's chosen people recorded in the Old Testament, Jesus says: "Well, actually, it

42. This is, technically speaking, the beginning of the Jewish Christian church. The church for every nation and people is really birthed in Acts 10 with the direct inclusion of the Gentiles (Cornelius and his family).

is people like a widow from Zarethath in Sidon and an enemy general from Syria (Naaman) that I am talking about; these are the types of people I have come to redeem" (vv. 25–27, paraphrase). Here, Luke gives us a foretaste of the trajectory of Jesus's ministry. Most of Jesus's ministry was among and for the Jews, but we have forays and hints, such as this one, that his ministry will be for all nations. This was not appreciated by his Jewish listeners. So we also see, here, a foretaste of his rejection by the Jews—as he is taken out to a hilltop to be thrown off a cliff.

In both of the examples Jesus gives of God blessing non-Jews, we see the type of ministry that Jesus will have on earth: feeding the hungry (as illustrated by the widow from Sidon) and healing the sick (as illustrated in the story of Naaman). I believe that we have a double meaning here. First, Jesus is indicating to his hometown that these are the types of things he will do (and therefore these are markers of the Kingdom). Second, Jesus is saying that this message that he is bringing has universal application: all people will have access to redemption, even (or especially) your enemies. It is a wonderfully tight overview of Jesus's mission: preaching, liberating, healing, and feeding. Incidentally, twice the Greek word for "forgive" is used: *aphesis*. It is used in the above passage to express the release of the captive and the setting free of the oppressed. Forgiveness means to "be freed."

2. *Final Instructions: Matthew 28:17–20; Mark 16:15–16; Luke 24:45–50; John 20:21–23*

We turn now to Jesus's final discourses, as recorded by each of the Gospel writers. The last words a person speaks are very important—in fact, when it comes to a parent, a spouse, or a coach, last words are usually the *most* important. In each of the Gospels there is a form of final address with specific instructions given to Jesus's followers. The most familiar is that of Matthew, which occurs at the very end of his biography of Jesus.

> When they saw him, they worshiped him; but some doubted. Then Jesus came to them and said, "All authority in heaven and on earth has been given to me. Therefore go and make disciples of all nations, baptizing them in the name of the Father and of the Son and of the Holy Spirit, and teaching them to obey everything I have commanded you. And surely I am with you always, to the very end of the age." (Matt. 28:17–20)

But there are other final instructions given by other Gospel writers. We have already looked at John (20:21–23), but here are the other two from Luke and Mark.

> Then he opened their minds so they could understand the Scriptures. He told them, "This is what is written: The Messiah will suffer and rise from the dead

> on the third day, and repentance for the forgiveness of sins will be preached in his name to all nations, beginning at Jerusalem. You are witnesses of these things. I am going to send you what my Father has promised; but stay in the city until you have been clothed with power from on high." When he had led them out to the vicinity of Bethany, he lifted up his hands and blessed them. (Luke 24:45–50)

> He said to them, "Go into all the world and preach the gospel to all creation. Whoever believes and is baptized will be saved, but whoever does not believe will be condemned." (Mark 16:15–16)[43]

Acknowledging the major differences in the telling of these stories, it is even more remarkable that they express certain common themes and some common detail. There are five elements that are common in all these commission narratives. First, all of these accounts have Jesus sending out his followers: "As you go," "Go into all the world," "I am sending you." There is also a command to stay, but that command is given to tell them to wait for the Holy Spirit (Acts 1:4) before they go out and continue his mission. Second, all the Gospels have Jesus sending his followers out to "all nations" or to "all the world" (in John this aspect of sending is found earlier).[44] Third, in each commission story Jesus's followers, who are becoming apostles ("sent ones"), are to preach or teach: to continue the teaching of Jesus. There is specific content to Jesus's teaching, and in Matthew we read that Jesus says the apostles will be "teaching [new disciples] to obey everything I have commanded you" (Matt. 28:20). This is what Paul calls "the gospel": all that Jesus taught and did. In parallel with this command, Mark (16:15) says that Jesus commanded them to "preach the gospel." Fourth, Jesus's content is focused on a message of forgiveness and/or repentance. This is probably assumed in the Matthean commission, but in the others it is explicit: "Repentance and forgiveness of sins will be preached in his name to all nations" (Luke 24:47). From the earliest ministry of John the Baptist, preparing the way for Jesus, the concern has been for people to repent of the behaviors and the powers they were living under and turn to Jesus. The message has not changed from the beginning of the story until the end: people are to repent, obey what Jesus has commanded, and be baptized to be saved (Mark 16:16). Finally, in Jesus's final words to his followers, he points to the Holy Spirit as the power for this global ministry to every nation on earth. Put in the context of this present volume, chapter 8 (the Holy Spirit) must follow chapter 7 (Jesus Christ).

3. Founding of the Church: Acts 1:8 and Acts 2

A third scriptural window on the mission of Jesus is to the establishment of mission in the earliest Jesus community—with the coming of the Holy

43. This is from the longer ending of Mark.
44. See John 17:18, 21–23.

Spirit. It is instructive to see the continuity between the commissions mentioned in the Gospels and the community that forms in Acts. In 1:8 we read, "But you will receive power when the Holy Spirit comes on you; and you will be my witnesses in Jerusalem, and in all Judea and Samaria, and to the ends of the earth." The Gospels spoke both of the central role of the Holy Spirit in continuing the work of Jesus Christ in the world and the global nature of the commission (here given as the "ends of the earth"). In chapter 2 of Acts, we see that the Holy Spirit does indeed come in power: he is neither quiet nor demure in this first entrance. There are three "signs" that accompany the arrival of the Spirit: tongues as of fire were seen, a strong wind was heard, and local people miraculously speak in foreign languages. In a type of reversal of the Tower of Babel, people are now brought together or united through language. This happens because they are worshiping God, rather than trying to rise above God. It is a powerful symbol of the will of God and the work of the Holy Spirit to acknowledge and bless cultural diversity, diversity brought together through the worship of God in Christ.

Then, in continuity with Luke 4:18–30 and the commissioning passage, there is preaching: a message about Jesus Christ (the gospel) with a call to repent: "Everyone who calls on the name of the Lord will be saved. . . . Repent and be baptized, every one of you, in the name of Jesus Christ for the forgiveness of your sins. And you will receive the gift of the Holy Spirit" (Acts 2:21, 38). What followed, again, shows clear continuity with the ministry of Jesus and the commands of Jesus. They repented, were baptized, and continued to listen to the apostles' teachings about Jesus. A new community was formed reflecting Luke 4:18–30: the poor were provided for by the wealthy, and miracles and signs followed (seen later in Acts: healings and exorcisms). The church begins with the presence of the Holy Spirit, preaching, and the formation of a Kingdom of God community. The earliest missionaries, the apostles, were home missionaries—reaching pilgrims, people from many languages, and caring for the poor.

4. The Future Hope: Revelation 7:9–17

One of the best ways to uncover the meaning of mission and the nature of our calling in mission is to look at the goal. This goal is expressed in Revelation, in which we catch glimpses of what the eternal worship of the Lamb looks like. Revelation 7 is a condensed picture of heaven, along with a sideglance toward what has been conquered in order to reach this heavenly realm. I like to summarize the passage in a simple little phrase: "many languages, one Lamb, and no tears."

The first thing we notice is the repetition concerning cultural diversity: "a great multitude that no one could count, from every nation, tribe, people and language . . ." (Rev. 7:9). Four synonyms are used to express the reality of cultural diversity in heaven. Not just a few different people, but people from "every" ethnic group (*ethnos*). They will all be present, and that means that there has been intentional cross-cultural witness in this world. All languages would not be represented unless all languages would have God's Word expressed to them. Here is a strong argument for translation, learning foreign languages, and for moving to live among people from other groups, with different religions and cultures.

Second, there is only one Lamb. With all of the cultural diversity in heaven, all attention is focused on the Lamb (who is the Shepherd). The single worship of all nations (as well as all celestial creatures) is possible as everyone submits to the great Shepherd of the sheep. It is a paradox—a lamb being a shepherd—but it is apt symbolism for the two great names for Jesus in Revelation: sacrificial Lamb and reigning Lord. All creatures are focused upon the Lamb. If this is the case in heaven, then we should be moving this way ourselves now, and we should be leading the nations to this place of worship of Jesus Christ.

Finally, in the heavenly realm, as we see it in Revelation 7, there are no more tears. All of those issues that created tears in this world—hunger, thirst, exposure, illness, and of course, death—will be gone in heaven as God wipes away every tear (vv. 16–17). If this is the case in heaven, once again, it should also preoccupy our lives here on earth. Mission involves alleviating suffering in this life and pointing to eternal glory with Jesus Christ. They are really the same thing, since we only have this ministry through the power of his Holy Spirit, and we have learned this through the wisdom of Jesus, the Word made flesh.

Thus, in these four windows from Scripture we can see both the breadth of Christian mission as ushering in the Kingdom of God, and the focus and foundation of God's mission in Jesus Christ. From the announcement of his intended ministry in Luke to the final heavenly existence, there is a continuity of concerns for inclusion in Christ, and liberation from sin through Jesus Christ.

Postscript: *ReJesus* and Christian Mission

In the first evangelism class I ever taught, there were about thirty-five students from Southeast Asia, most of them from Singapore, Malaysia, and Indonesia. I did a little informal survey by asking everyone to stand up who had led (or helped to lead) at least one person to faith in Jesus Christ in the past year. The whole class stood up, and a surge of inadequacy flooded over me. I was sitting down at the time. I raised the stakes a little: "If you have led five or more people to faith in the past year, stay standing." Four or five people sat down and so, assuming I was trapped in some cultural misunderstanding (like asking how many Japanese want to receive Jesus Christ as their Savior, and having everyone dutifully raise their hand), I explained what I was asking. Everyone seemed to be perfectly clear about my query. "Ten people; if you have helped to lead fewer than ten people to Christ in the past year, please sit down." Most of the class now sat down. It was becoming obvious that my students were deeply involved in evangelism, since most were in some way involved in leading five to ten people to faith over the course of a year. Some were still standing, and so I continued to raise the stakes. When I got to fifty, only Mark was still standing. I remarked loudly under my breath, "Well, you must be some type of an evangelist or something."

"Yes, sir, I am. I am an evangelist."

He later told me his conversion story: On the night when he beat up a man with a lead pipe and threw him in a storm drain, assuming he was dead, Mark sat down to drink a bottle of whiskey and then kill himself. At the age of fifteen, he had killed a man—he saw little hope for his own future. Providentially, his illiterate mother had rescued a Gideon's New Testament from the trash and put it on a shelf. Mark picked it up and started reading a biography of a man he had only heard of. Jesus was considered an enemy of the Chinese Triad gangs in Singapore. As a last act, before killing himself, Mark glanced over the first pages of Luke, and he was captivated by the story of Jesus. When he got to the crucifixion, he was angry. He had come to respect, even love, this wandering teacher and miracle worker. Why was he being killed, and how could he forgive the people who were unjustly torturing Jesus to death? It was Jesus's forgiveness of his enemies that drew Mark in. Who was this man? By 6:00 a.m. Mark had finished reading and ran to the local church to wait for the pastor to show up to ask him about this Jesus. When they arrived in the pastor's study, a series of anxious questions were fired at the pastor: "Who was this Jesus? Where did he come from? Do you know what he did? He healed people and fed people who were hungry! But he was tortured and killed and he still forgave the people who were killing him. Who was Jesus? Do you know?"

"He was God," was the simple answer that was given, and it was the answer that changed Mark's life and turned him into a traveling evangelist, reaching out to other troubled youth in Southeast Asia. Jesus is captivating.

But Jesus is also a hot commodity. After a century and a half of a failed "search for the historical Jesus," and after a few decades of recovering the many Gnostic and nonorthodox Jesuses, a fresh batch of books are coming out about Jesus—in an effort to recover Jesus for the church. This is not an issue in Africa, most of Latin America, Asia, or the Pacific. It is a problem for the post-Enlightenment Western church. In the context of the hamstrung Jesuses of Marcus Borg, John Dominic Crossan, or John Shelby Spong, and the incomplete and mixed Jesus of Bart Ehrman, and the schizophrenic Jesus of Deepak Chopra (*Jesus: A Story of Enlightenment*), committed church authors are rediscovering Jesus for themselves. New books on Jesus are coming out with titles like Brian McLaren's *Everything Must Change: Jesus, Global Crises, and a Revolution of Hope* (2007); Rick James's *Jesus Without Religion: What Did He Say? What Did He Do? What's the Point?* (2007); and, one of the best-titled books on Jesus for the twenty-first century, Michael Frost and Alan Hirsch's *ReJesus: A Wild Messiah for a Missional Church* (2009). In all of these books, and scores of others, the concern is to recover Jesus for the church today. As Frost and Hirsch express it, there is a need to face squarely "the discontinuity between Jesus and the religion that bears his name."[45]

I am struck by the popularity of such books in the early decades of the twenty-first century, but I am even more in awe, like my student Mark above, at how remarkable and unusual and strangely attractive Jesus is on his own terms, as recorded by some of his friends. If we had no other secondary literature about Jesus, we might be led, like my student Mark, to say "Wow," then to worship, and finally to witness. It is a common progression, actually. Wow is the response of being in the presence of Jesus, the Lamb of God and Lord of galaxies. Wow is what led the ancients to the "gift of tears": "Pray with tears and all you ask will be heard. For the Lord rejoices greatly when you pray with tears."[46] The Puritans sought a moment of genuine conversion, which was a similar encounter with the Holy God in light of personal sin. It was called an "awakening," meaning that one was awakened to one's own sin and the need for God's grace. Wow leads to conversion and then to worship. The resurrected Jesus was a wow experience for his disciples. When they gathered on the mountain to receive their final instructions, "they worshiped him; but some doubted" (Matt. 28:17). Earlier, on the mount of transfiguration, it was the same; Peter did not know how to worship, but this seemed to be what he was searching for as he planned a building project. Many are still confused about worship and building programs today.

Worship involves rightly placing ourselves in God's presence and then receiving his benediction and commission. What I have tried to reveal in this chapter is that Jesus, the sent one of God, does call forth our amazement or awe (Wow!) and then, in the context of worship, we are led out in mission. In Revelation we see that worship itself is an act of humble conquest in mission; as Jesus is lifted up, he draws all people to himself (not necessarily to our church).

Jesus, the Missionary of God, is also the door of the sheepfold, holding all the flock together in safety. Human unity is found as we dwell in Christ. The more we stray from Jesus (who is the fulfillment of the Law and the Prophets), the further we stray from each other, the less power we have in mission, and the less clear is our witness or testimony (John 17). Church divisions and institutions are a witness to humanity's rebellion. The universal church must develop local structures, but to the degree that these forms are self-perpetuating and self-authenticating, and to the degree that they distinguish or divide rather than unite, to that degree they deny Christ. Each and every Christian, all churches, and even all of humanity will find its unity "in Christ."

45. Michael Frost and Alan Hirsch, *ReJesus* (Peabody, MA: Hendrickson, 2009), 5.
46. Evagrios the Solitary, "On Prayer," in *The Philokalia* 1:58.

Furthermore, all people, no matter how Christian their heritage, how secular or religious they are, are invited to find their unity and peace in Jesus Christ. "Universalism" is a Christian term when it is applied to Christ's universal lordship over all of humanity. No person is excluded. Each time a drug lord, pimp, prostitute, student, or bank executive comes to the foot of the cross, the world becomes a better place and the Kingdom is spread like yeast in a loaf, or like a mustard seed. Jesus is the universal Lord who calls all to find their liberation, healing, and life in his realm. We are enlisted in this cosmic transformation, one person and one nation at a time.

We have seen in this chapter that Jesus Christ, the fulfillment of Old Testament prophecies, is the suffering Son whose death brings redemption and transformation. We have also seen that Jesus is both the wisdom and the power of God. Jesus as the wisdom of God is above, beyond, deeper, and prior to all human wisdom—our natural rational thought process would not lead us to something as profound as the death of Jesus on the cross being a historic event that brings victory over death. It is beyond human wisdom because it takes into account all of time and eternity, whereas our thinking is bound to and bound by our experience in this world. It is deeper than our wisdom because it deals with concerns that are foundational and more profound than any concern we can know about: conquest of Satan, killing the second death (Rev. 20:6 and 21:8), and renewing all of creation. Finally, this is a wisdom that is prior to all human wisdom because Jesus, the wisdom of God, has always been, and will always be, in fellowship with the Father and the Spirit.

Jesus is also the power of God, but again this is a power that is of a different order from human or earthly power. Here is a power beyond our understanding: a victorious power in apparent defeat. The power of God is Jesus Christ crucified and proclaimed. As Paul said to the Corinthians,

> I did not come with eloquence or human wisdom as I proclaimed to you the testimony about God. For I resolved to know nothing while I was with you except Jesus Christ and him crucified. I came to you in weakness with great fear and trembling. My message and my preaching were not with wise and persuasive words, but with a demonstration of the Spirit's power, so that your faith might not rest on human wisdom, but on God's power. (1 Cor. 2:1–5)

This passage is not about Paul's incompetence, but about the gospel's power and wisdom. It is possible in Christian mission to empty the gospel of its power. How? We do this when we substitute human wisdom and eloquence for the clear proclamation of "Christ crucified" (1 Cor. 1:23). Paul says he proclaimed the gospel "not with wisdom and eloquence, lest the cross of Christ be emptied of its power" (1:17). The gospel has power, when it is freed from our control or manipulation, and when it is under the control of the Holy Spirit. The Holy Spirit searches the deep things of God and, as it were, translates this to us, opening the reservoir of God's wisdom and power for us, and then showering us with gifts that enable us to minister to others. When this happens, we are transformed by the work of the Holy Spirit to be made more into the image of Jesus Christ. Christ opens the door of salvation, and the Spirit leads us in and remakes our tarnished image of God, which is the image of Jesus Christ.

> Now the Lord is the Spirit, and where the Spirit of the Lord is, there is freedom. And we, who with unveiled faces contemplate the Lord's glory, are being transformed into his image with ever-increasing glory, which comes from the Lord, who is the Spirit. (2 Cor. 3:17–18)

8

The Holy Spirit in Mission

Presence, Participation, and Power

A Tamil Indian colleague of mine teaching at a seminary in Singapore did a PhD in Scotland on *Living in Two Worlds: Pastoral Responses to Possession in Singapore*.[1] Possession here is in the singular. It is not a matter of what you have, but of what has you: demons. Dr. Solomon, writing about a particular area of concern in his pastoral ministry, took three years to study pastoral responses to exorcism: interviewing pastors in Singapore and studying the phenomenon theologically and through modern psychology and medicine. Most of the Tamil families in Singapore are Hindu, and the incidents of possession are noteworthy. At times, possession becomes a social deterrent or economic handicap. Families would first seek a Hindu priest to remove the demon and then, when they got desperate, they would call Reverend Solomon. Solomon notes that Singapore is a very modern and secular state, but it is also a very religious state. In this sense, it may be a model for developing nations throughout the world. People are becoming more religious even as their daily lives are more rooted in "this world" through technology. Solomon provides a model for mission—thinking about the spiritual realm, specifically the realm of the demonic—while remaining a modern medical doctor, very much indebted to modern science and technology.

1. Robert Solomon, *Living in Two Worlds: Pastoral Responses to Possession in Singapore* (Frankfurt am Main: Peter Lang, 1994).

The spiritual realm is just as real as the mental realm and the physical realm. A person may make decisions based upon their physical well-being (or illness), but a person will also make decisions based upon their emotional and mental state, and a person will also make decisions based upon their spiritual state. The spiritual realm is where the Holy Spirit, the Spirit of Jesus Christ, dwells. This realm is not in opposition to the physical realm, but it interpenetrates the physical. In Christian mission we proclaim Christ and we demonstrate Christ to others, but we affirm that the application of our words and works is a matter of the Holy Spirit. We do not convert and we do not save; these are works of the Holy Spirit of God. Although there is much discussion about the Holy Spirit among Pentecostals and charismatics, doctrine of the Holy Spirit is very light or anemic in most Catholic and Protestant theology of mission. A lucid and enriched understanding of the Holy Spirit in mission is needed.

Christian Mission and the Triune God

Christian mission is often misunderstood or misguided because of an inadequate doctrine of the Holy Spirit.[2] Protestant theology especially has been timid when talking about the Holy Spirit in its ecclesiology and certainly in missiology (if theologians talk about the mission of the church at all). One wing of the Reformation, often called the "Radical Reformers," emphasized the immediate inspiration of the Holy Spirit. However, a number of these movements became radical and violent. George Williams[3] identifies some of the extreme groups as "Revolutionary Spiritualists" (e.g., Thomas Müntzer and the Zwickau prophets, called Schwärmer—zealots, or fanatics) and "Revolutionary Anabaptists" (e.g., Melchior Hoffman). Their zeal for reform and mission led them to disregard other authorities, which often led them to extreme positions and actions. The inspirational and miraculous work of the Holy Spirit was held suspect by most Catholics and Protestants after these excesses were put down, and as a result, a vigorous theology of the Holy Spirit in the church did not develop among Protestants until the twentieth century.[4] This history still prevents a more integrated doctrine of the Holy Spirit for missiology today.

2. David Bosch spends only three pages on the Holy Spirit in his massive volume (*Transforming Mission: Paradigm Shifts in Theology of Mission* [Maryknoll, NY: Orbis Books], 113–15), and Tim Tennent, in a more recent volume, *Invitation to World Missions: A Trinitarian Missiology for the Twenty-first Century* (Grand Rapids: Kregel, 2010), discusses the Holy Spirit only around the book of Acts (specific acts of the Holy Spirit) and mostly around a narrow set of concerns such as cessationism (the belief that the miraculous gifts ceased to exist after the early church period), Pentecostalism, and Donald McGavran's "Homogenous Unit Principle" (409–31).

3. George Williams, *The Radical Reformation* (Philadelphia: Westminster, 1962).

4. See Killian McDonnell, OSB, "A Trinitarian Theology of the Holy Spirit?" *Theological Studies* 46 (1985): 191–227.

What makes Christian mission Christian is not only the work and centrality of Jesus Christ, but the power or effectiveness of the work itself, which comes through the Holy Spirit. Christian mission is not a project or a function of the local church, although it is often misrepresented or denuded by these false assumptions. In fact, Christian mission is a dynamic process whereby the Holy Spirit is at work in the elect to bear witness to the salvific and liberating work of Jesus Christ for all nations. The active agent—the power and the personality, the righteousness and the relationship—in Christian mission is the Holy Spirit. The Holy Spirit works both with power and personality, for he is the power of the creator God and he is the Spirit of the living Christ. The Holy Spirit also works in righteousness, for he is the *Holy* Spirit bringing about holiness in this world, and he is the one who relates the Word of God to God's people in both the Old and New Testaments. His mission is too large for any of our programs, or even our theological formulations, to encompass. As Lesslie Newbigin has said, "Mission is concerned with nothing less than the completion of all that God has begun to do in the creation of the world and of man. Its concern is not sectional but total and universal."[5] The Holy Spirit in Christian mission is doing more than we can ever do, plan, or even imagine. Mission is a work of the Spirit of the living God, and we are invited, even elected or chosen, to participate in this cosmic work.

Twentieth-century Christianity has been marked by three major global movements: the ecumenical movement, the movement of the Christian center from the north Atlantic to the global south, and the modern movement of the Holy Spirit.[6] All of these are related; in fact, the first two are a result of the third. The Holy Spirit is the Spirit of Jesus Christ ("The Lord is the Spirit," as Paul says in 2 Cor. 3:17). It is the work of the Holy Spirit to bring greater Christian unity in witness and to reach the least and the lost. Thus the tremendous growth of Christianity among the impoverished and the oppressed points to the heart of Jesus Christ for the world. Jesus's heart is toward those who are in greatest need; it is a matter of divine justice and divine love. Christian mission always requires abandonment to the work of God—through his Holy Spirit—that will reflect the "Sacred Heart of Jesus." This is a Roman Catholic category of spirituality, but it should be embraced by all Christians: the Sacred Heart of Jesus expresses the great love and concern of Jesus who moves out in mission to the most needy.[7]

We have said that mission must be understood to be the work of God the

5. Lesslie Newbigin, *The Open Secret: Sketches for a Missionary Theology* (Grand Rapids: Eerdmans, 1978), 62.

6. See David Barrett's *World Christian Encyclopedia*, edited with Todd M. Johnson and George Kurian (Oxford: Oxford University Press, 2001); and Jason Mandryk's *Operation World*, 7th ed. (Colorado Springs: Biblica, 2010).

7. Illustrations of the Sacred Heart of Jesus often have a crown of thorns on the heart, a sword through the heart, or flames symbolizing the pain and suffering of Jesus for the world.

Father, through the work of the Son, and in the power of the Holy Spirit. What exactly do we mean by the Holy Spirit, and how do we understand the power of the Holy Spirit? A century ago this chapter would not have been written, because those who were beginning to emphasize the Holy Spirit (globally) were newer fringe players in the missionary movement: Pentecostals and indigenous church movements. In the past century, however, it has become clear that the Pentecostal, charismatic, and indigenous Christian movements have taken center stage in the historical movement of Christianity.[8] These Christian movements are windswept with the power and unpredictability of the Holy Spirit.

Bigstock.com/zatletic

Sacred Heart of Jesus reveals the suffering of Jesus for the world. Devotion to the Sacred Heart is devotion to what breaks Jesus's heart.

Holy Spirit and the Church

As I have proceeded in my study, it has come home to me again and again that when we study mission, we are really studying the nature and purpose of God's chosen people. The *co*-mission from God was given to the followers of Jesus as the seed of the church in Matthew 28, and as formation for the church in Acts. Therefore, when we look at the role and place of the Holy Spirit, we must keep before us that it is in, for, and through the church that the Holy Spirit works. The commission was Jesus-breathed and Spirit-infused (John 20:21–22). God's mission is not an individualistic mission, although God uses individuals. It is not a matter of self-actualization, although the individual self is sanctified by participating in mission. Mission, sanctification, and church must all be held together as we talk about the Holy Spirit, the power and presence of God in mission.

In 1952, Lesslie Newbigin delivered the Kerr lectures at Trinity College in Glasgow. As an ecumenical leader and missionary, he chose as his topic to

8. See, for example, Gary B. McGee, *Miracles, Missions and American Pentecostalism* (Maryknoll, NY: Orbis Books, 2010); Philip Jenkins, *The Next Christendom, The Coming of Global Christianity* (Oxford: Oxford University Press, 2002); Mark Noll, *The New Shape of World Christianity: How American Experience Reflects Global Faith* (Downers Grove, IL: IVP Academic, 2009); and Jehu J. Hanciles, *Beyond Christendom: Globalization, African Migration and the Transformation of the West* (Maryknoll, NY: Orbis Books, 2008).

contribute to answering the question, "By what is the church constituted?" After talking about the meaning of church, biblically considered, he examined the Protestant answer (the congregation of the faithful), the Roman Catholic answer (the church is the body of Christ), and the Pentecostal answer (the church is the community of the Holy Spirit). It is amazing that Newbigin, nine years before the first Pentecostal churches joined the WCC, was already talking about Pentecostalism on par with Roman Catholicism and separately from Protestantism. He understood that Pentecostalism is not just a breed of Protestantism, but a major expression of the church. Newbigin did not include in his lectures the fourth major family of Christianity: Orthodoxy. However, if he did, he would probably conclude that, for Orthodoxy, the church is constituted by its participation in, and representation of (in liturgy), the Great Tradition of the church.[9] Thus, there are four basic ways in which the church is understood to be constituted, and all four, I submit, are important to include in our understanding of the mission of the church. The church is rooted in the Great Tradition, representing the body of Christ, as a gathered community, in the power of the Holy Spirit.

What is more important in this chapter is that the emphasis on the Holy Spirit is an essential element in our understanding of church in its missionary life. Moreover, I want to take the next step and say that the "Pentecostal" nature of the universal church is the Holy Spirit who directs and empowers all of Christian mission. The Holy Spirit is the gift for the church in its mission. Understanding something of the power and purpose of the Holy Spirit will free churches, religious orders, and mission societies from divisions and disappointments that develop because of false assumptions of how God can and will (or should) act. The Holy Spirit, we must remember, is not tame—and therefore he is not completely predictable. However, the Holy Spirit is the Spirit of Jesus Christ, and therefore he does bring wisdom, truth, and power. The Holy Spirit points to Jesus Christ, and so he can be, and should be, studied and contemplated. Since there are some things that can be known about the Holy Spirit, we can be confident in excluding any type of mission that is inconsistent with the person of Jesus Christ. In this chapter, we want to begin by looking at the early church and the place of the Holy Spirit, realizing that our understanding must have some historical continuity with the church as it was first formed. This does not mean that we repeat exactly what happened, but it does mean that we understand that we are the same church and our essential DNA structure and genetic code will be found in these early years. Secondly, we will look at the Holy Spirit in the rest of the Bible to note the continuity there is with the work of the Holy Spirit throughout Scripture. Next, we will look at the Holy Spirit and contextualization. Since the Holy Spirit applies

9. This would be partially true. The central role of the Holy Spirit in worship and in the world is an important characteristic of Orthodoxy.

the work of Christ to individuals in context, we study contextual issues under the doctrine of the Holy Spirit in mission. Before concluding, we look at the Holy Spirit and other religions. How do we understand other religions and Christian witness to people of other faiths in light of the work of the Holy Spirit in people and cultures? These are important issues—in fact, I would argue these are central issues—for global Christian witness today.

It is remarkable that, even though scholars recognize the central role of the Holy Spirit in the book of Acts, when it comes to discussions of mission and the church, this important truth seems to be forgotten. David Bosch, who was a New Testament scholar, identified the Holy Spirit as central for the missionary paradigm in Luke. "The ministry of the earthly Jesus is already portrayed in terms of the initiative and guidance of the Spirit."[10] This is Bosch's first and strongest point regarding the Lukan paradigm—after this brief discussion, the Holy Spirit drops out of his volume.[11] Others have looked at the Holy Spirit through the book of Acts alone, but have pulled up short of viewing the Holy Spirit theologically and through all of Scripture.[12] In this section, we will look at the Holy Spirit in the early church (Acts, letters, and early noncanonical Christian material), and in the next section we will fill out this understanding of the Holy Spirit with other biblical material.

The Holy Spirit in Acts and the Ancient Church

The Holy Spirit is mentioned throughout Acts a total of fifty-nine times.[13] It is important to see how Luke describes the work of the Holy Spirit, because the book of Acts is the record of missionary encounters in the power of the Holy Spirit. Acts depicts the Holy Spirit *directing mission* ("the Holy Spirit said, 'Set apart for me Barnabas and Saul,'" Acts 13:2), and *empowering for mission*. At times the Holy Spirit is clearly the leading actor: sending Philip to Gaza by an angel, and then returning him miraculously to Azotus; keeping the apostles out of Asia and Bithynia (16:6–7); and then urging Paul not to go to Jerusalem (21:4). The most common way the Holy Spirit is active in mission

10. Bosch, *Transforming Mission*, 113.

11. There is a brief mention that the Holy Spirit is mysterious and is involved in revealing truth even to those who are from other religious communities. We will pick up on this second important issue later in this chapter.

12. See, for example, the very interesting discussion of Acts 2:1–47 by Howard Peskett and Vinoth Ramachandra in *The Message of Mission* (Downers Grove, IL: InterVarsity, 2003), 208–24. See also Tim Tennent's discussion of the Holy Spirit (again through Acts) in *Invitation to World Missions*, 409–31.

13. It is interesting that the Holy Spirit is mentioned fairly evenly through Acts until Paul is arrested and taken off to Rome. Chapters 22 to 28 only have one reference to the Holy Spirit, and that is at the end when he says that the Holy Spirit spoke through the prophet Isaiah (28:25).

in Acts and early Christian writings, however, is *through words*. The Holy Spirit inspires bold proclamation (4:8–31) and clear teaching about Jesus Christ (*The Shepherd of Hermas*, mandate 11:8–12). Another common way the Holy Spirit is seen to move in Acts and in the ancient church concerns foretelling. The Holy Spirit foresaw and told about Jesus through the prophets. The Holy Spirit spoke through Isaiah (Acts 28:25–28), and those who reject the teachings about Jesus in the Old Testament are seen as rejecting the Holy Spirit (Acts 7:51). Justin Martyr went as far as to call the Holy Spirit the "prophetic Spirit" because of the number of prophecies about Jesus Christ in the Old Testament (*Apology* 6, 32). Irenaeus concurs, explaining, for example, that the finger of God that wrote the Ten Commandments was the Holy Spirit (*Demonstration of the Apostolic Preaching*, 26). In Clement's first letter to Rome (chap. 16) he quotes Isaiah 53:2–12 and remarks, "the Holy Spirit has declared . . ." A number of individual odes in the *Odes of Solomon* talk about the Spirit of the Lord speaking truth (3:10) or "speaking through my members" (6:2 and 16:5). Thus, we must remember that verbal inspiration was seen as one of the most important works of the Holy Spirit in earliest Christianity.

Irenaeus points not only to the Old Testament prophets as speaking the words of the Holy Spirit, but to the New Testament Gospel writers as well. "The Holy Spirit says by Matthew: Now the birth of Christ was on this wise" (*Demonstration* III, xvii. 1). The early Christian writers carried this understanding of the Holy Spirit a step further. Not only are words inspired by the Holy Spirit (prophets and apostles), but the inspired words are then applied or interpreted to the believer who is prepared to receive them. In the case of Acts 10, an extended family of God-fearers in Cornelius's house heard the preaching of Peter applied to their lives, and spoke in tongues and praised God (two signs of the Holy Spirit).

In later centuries, monks and spiritual writers, quoting from 1 Corinthians 12:8, talk about "*spiritual knowledge*" being given by the Holy Spirit: "Such knowledge unites man to God through experience, but does not move him to express outwardly what he knows. . . . Spiritual knowledge comes through prayer."[14] The Holy Spirit works in the believer to inspire or connect the divine words with the intellect: "Only the Holy Spirit can purify the intellect, for unless a greater power comes and overthrows the despoiler, what he has taken captive will never be set free. . . . We must make ourselves a dwelling-place for the Holy Spirit. Then we shall have the lamp of spiritual knowledge burning always within us."[15] Thus, the Holy Spirit works with words, but with words and ideas that bring about conversion, understanding, and an ability to dwell with the very mind of Christ. For the ancients, as well as for the apostle Paul, this spiritual knowledge is of a different order, but not completely divorced

14. St. Diadochos of Photiki, "On Spiritual Knowledge," in *The Philokalia* 1:255.
15. Ibid., 260.

from the rational knowledge we learn by rote. "We have received not the spirit of the world, but the Spirit that is from God so that we may understand the gifts bestowed on us by God. And we speak of these things in words not taught by human wisdom but taught by the Spirit, interpreting spiritual things to those who are spiritual" (1 Cor. 2:12–13 NRSV). Preaching for conversion to Christ is preaching, but when it is of the Spirit, there is a new consciousness of divine things, and a new being that is created (Gal. 2:19–20; Col. 2:6–14). This is one of the dominant ways the Holy Spirit's work is described in the ancient church.

The Holy Spirit also *gives people visions* of heaven (which was predicted, Acts 2:17); Stephen, as he is being martyred, has a vision of Christ in his glory (7:55). When the Spirit-induced vision came, Stephen shifted from sermon into prayer. It is interesting that while giving his suffering witness to Jesus Christ, he saw Christ in glory. It became a moment of public testimony, sealed in blood, with the focus on Jesus in glory. Later martyr stories also include visions, prayers, and testimonies in the Holy Spirit at death (*Martyrdom of Polycarp* XII to XIV). The close association of public witness and worship[16] is integral to mission theology as well as to the nature of the church. We see in Acts other incidences where the Holy Spirit moves people to worship. In Acts 2, 10, and 19, people speak in tongues and praise God when the Holy Spirit comes upon them. Thus, there is a close connection in missionary outreach with the coming of the Holy Spirit to proclaim and to praise God. Worship is the natural (or better yet, the "spiritual") outcome of gospel proclamation. The Holy Spirit works through human speech, and at times the Holy Spirit overwhelms human speech. The Holy Spirit works through normal vision, and at times the Holy Spirit overwhelms normal human vision to give the ability to see heavenly things.

We also see that the Holy Spirit *brings power*: power for transformation, for working miracles and healing, for clear and strong preaching, and for obedience to the law. As we have seen, the Holy Spirit points to Jesus in preaching as well as in visions. Thus, the transformative power of the resurrection of Jesus Christ—which brought victory over sin and death—is the same power of the Holy Spirit. The Holy Spirit has power because the Holy Spirit is God. Gregory of Nazianzus[17] provides the classic theological defense of this position, but it is also assumed in earlier writings, beginning with Matthew 28:19; Luke 4:1; and John 14:15–21. When Jesus speaks, the Holy Spirit is the voice. When Jesus draws a person to faith, it is his Spirit who speaks to the broken soul. Thus, it is the same power of God that raised Jesus from the dead, the same power that created the universe, who now works in the lives of individuals to bring about the complete conversion of their souls. This is expressed in many

16. And also, but less frequently, suffering is part of that witness.
17. Gregory of Nazianzus, *Fifth Theological Oration* 10.

ways in the early church. Paul talks about the Holy Spirit giving a person love for others (Rom. 5:5) as well as bringing them peace and joy (Rom. 14:17).

And of course he is called the *Holy* Spirit, and so we would expect the *work of sanctification* to also be part of his work (Rom. 15:16). The *Odes of Solomon* express this poetically as the Holy Spirit pruning us, or "circumcising me," meaning "uncovering my inward being towards him" (Ode 11:2). The Holy Spirit, as it were, cuts away what is preventing us from being exposed fully to God and therefore transformed by his glory. This image captures much of what is contained in the Pauline corpus concerning the work of the Holy Spirit. For example, in 1 Thessalonians Paul expresses his thanksgiving for the Thessalonians' good and faithful work in ministry. He says that these virtues in ministry come from the work of the Holy Spirit, which came to them with preaching the gospel.

> Our gospel came to you not simply with words but also with power, with the Holy Spirit and deep conviction. You know how we lived among you for your sake. You became imitators of us and of the Lord, for you welcomed the message in the midst of severe suffering with the joy given by the Holy Spirit. (1 Thess. 1:5–6)

In fact, most of Paul's letters begin with a theological section focused on the work of God in Jesus Christ, often with the coming of the Holy Spirit to seal this salvation (Eph. 1:13), followed by a practical section on how to live in the Spirit. As all of the ancient Christians knew, the ethical or virtuous life is dependent upon the work of Christ and the coming of his Holy Spirit. The grace of God makes the virtuous life in Christ possible. Love comes into the Christian life by the Holy Spirit, and love is the greatest of all virtues (1 Cor. 13). "To heal a person is the greatest thing one can do and excels all other virtues, because among the virtues there is nothing higher or more perfect than love for one's neighbor."[18]

Finally, when we look at the understanding of the Holy Spirit as *God, actively applying the work of salvation and sanctification*, we should remember that these discussions were taking place in the midst of an ancient society filled with gods and spirits. Monotheism itself was a radical departure from ancient polytheistic pagan culture. This made it very difficult in Christian apologetics, proclaiming a single God when there were so many personal and socially acceptable gods available. But as the local Gentiles began to grasp the concept of a single God, the early Christians then complicated matters by insisting that this single God was in three persons. Immediately, a local listener would revert back to thinking about multiple gods. This is one of the reasons that clarity about the identity of the Holy Spirit with the creator

18. St. Peter of Damaskos, "Short discourse on the Acquisition of the Virtues and on Abstinence from the Passions," in *Philokalia* 3:163.

God took such a long time. In the difficult context of polytheism, the ancient church taught about a Holy Spirit who is one with God and does the work of God in the world and in individual lives. They spoke resolutely about this in their apologetic and theological literature (Justin Martyr, Irenaeus, Cyril of Alexandria, etc.). Even though there were those around them who were persecuting the church and misreading its beliefs, these ancient Christian writers talk about the Holy Spirit as the very Spirit of God—the prophetic Spirit of God speaking through the ancient prophets and now applying the work of salvation to believers. In retrospect it was a bold move. The early Christians witnessed to pagans who believed in many gods, but continued to talk about their one God in three persons.[19]

What does this mean for our thinking about Christian mission today? First, we must recognize and articulate clearly for church members that God's mission is, from first to last, the work of the Holy Spirit. To put it negatively, mission is not dependent upon money, programs, or education. Empowerment for mission is more about prayer, devotion, and silence than about fundraising and seminars.[20] Too much missionary work is done as if the Holy Spirit did not exist or as if he only exists in the church during worship.

Second, we must recognize that what may seem "reasonable" in mission may be wrong. Related to our point above, there is much in ministry that appears reasonable (according to human reason), but it is in fact contrary to the Word of God working through the Holy Spirit. It may seem reasonable that a closely related ethnic group would be the best evangelists in a particular situation, but in fact this may be far from the truth. Many people thought that white North Americans would be the best evangelists for indigenous peoples from North America and Central America. However, anecdotal evidence seems to indicate that Koreans and Chinese communicate better to indigenous peoples of Central and North America. Again, it may seem reasonable that more people, or more programs, will reach more people, but the exact opposite may happen. Our doctrine of the Holy Spirit requires that we wait, listen, and respond to the Spirit's promptings.

19. Gregory Nazianzus attacks pagan belief that Christians really believe in three or two gods (*Fifth Theological Oration* 8).

20. Again, we can learn a great deal from the early Greek-speaking Christians who understood the difference between human reasoning and God who is Reason (Logos). It is a distinction worth retaining or recovering today. They called human reason *dianoia*, and they described it as "the discursive, conceptualizing and logical human faculty" of humans. In addition, God has given us an intellect, called *nous*, which is "the highest faculty in humans through which one 'knows God' by direct apprehension or spiritual perception" (*Philokalia* 1:362, 364). It is through the intellect that we gain insight into God, as a gracious work of his Holy Spirit. The intellect is nurtured through prayer, silence, and spiritual reading of Scripture. Both are needed (we do, after all, need to know how to read a budget, or buy a cheap airplane ticket), but we seek a ministry of transformation that is from the Spirit of God speaking to and empowering the "intellect" or *nous*.

Third, we must recognize the priority of spiritual labors (fasting, prayer, etc.) as opening the way for the Holy Spirit to work in mission. Here we can bring together some of our earlier historical discussions in part 1. All of the early monastic missionary work (Benedictines, East Syrians going to China, Basil's Rule) have as their priority spiritual "exercises," to use the expression of Ignatius. Jesus's first command to the disciples in mission, in fact, was not to go and "do something"[21] but to stay and wait for the Holy Spirit to come. Waiting is not passive, but is an active participation in the Spirit through prayer, fasting, and intentional silence. I am not talking about quietism (or laziness) here but rather the wisdom of stillness.[22] Think of Jesus praying through the night and then being empowered to conquer death, or of Elijah in the wilderness listening to God. We need to remind our overworked and overprogrammed twenty-first-century selves that if we don't wait, and if we don't listen, we are very likely to develop our own mission apart from the work of God in our midst.

Finally, it is worth remembering that the primary work of the Holy Spirit in the earliest Christian writings is of inspiration for speech, both writing and speaking. The Holy Spirit is a communications specialist. He is concerned to get the word out, and specifically to get the word out for people to be changed. We should also include in the communications category visions and dreams, because these are also given to people to turn their eyes and minds toward Jesus Christ. I do not want to downplay the importance of healings or other miracles of the Holy Spirit, but I do want to face the facts head-on. Neither am I saying that mission can be *only* words. We are making our observations from Scripture and from ancient Christianity. The evidence is incontrovertible: God has so designed us that words are powerful and they are fundamental. Communication through symbolic discourse is, on some level, a divine activity we are invited into. It is part of being made in the very image of God that we can communicate with each other and with God. As further evidence of this priority, it is worth remembering that John starts his biography of Jesus with "In the beginning was the word" (John 1:1). Jesus cast out demons with words, and he healed with both words ("Rise, take your pallet and walk") and touch. After the words are spoken, the life in the Spirit begins.

Holy Spirit and Spirit of God in the Old Testament

I have already made my first point about the Holy Spirit in Scripture in my discussion of the New Testament and earliest Christianity. The earliest Christians

21. Of course some people have the opposite problem of not doing anything. I am reminded of the interesting book written by young brothers, Alex and Brett Harris, *Do Hard Things: A Teenage Rebellion against Low Expectations* (Colorado Springs: Multnomah Books, 2008).

22. "Be still and know that I am God, I will be exalted among the nations, I will be exalted in the earth" (Ps. 46:10; see also Exod. 14:14; Ps. 37:7).

were of one mind that the prophecies about Jesus—in fact the writers of the Old Testament in general—were inspired by the Holy Spirit. They were so clear about this that they could say, "the Holy Spirit says in Isaiah." What else do we learn about the Holy Spirit and mission in the Old Testament?

When we look at the Holy Spirit in the Old Testament, it is like looking at Jesus in the Old Testament. In light of the fulfillment of Old Testament teachings, we can see what otherwise might have been missed or misconstrued. However, in light of the trinitarian understanding of God that developed in the ancient church, we can see both continuity and discontinuity between the Spirit of God from the Old Testament and the Spirit of the apostolic church. First, we look at some of the discontinuity. In the Old Testament, we read that the Holy Spirit comes upon warriors, bringing victory in war, and even giving them the strength to tear animals apart (Judg. 3, 6, and 14). We also read that God sent his Spirit to give the Israelites the skills required for the tabernacle's art and architecture (Exod. 31:2–5), and that the Spirit of God, through David, gave Solomon plans for his temple (1 Chron. 28:10–21). We note these instances as examples of work that the Holy Spirit empowered during a time when God's Kingdom was to be represented to the world as a political nation with buildings, laws, and land. This required military victory and the building of a tabernacle (and later a temple) for the sake of public witness to God. Under the new covenant, the Kingdom of God is present in people's hearts and in the church. We should, therefore, not expect the Holy Spirit to work in exactly the same way today.[23]

What do we see in the Old Testament's portrayal of the Holy Spirit that is in continuity with the understanding of Christian mission? First, there are many spirits in the Old Testament, and we can see that the Spirit of God is depicted (like Yahweh) as the supreme Spirit over all spirits (Judg. 9:23; 1 Sam. 16:11–23). There are spirits that will turn people away from God, but it is the work of the Holy Spirit to point to, and to do, the work of God.

Second, as with the early church, the Holy Spirit gives people words to say. This is not just a private affair, a prophet sitting in his study writing Hebrew poetry; it is often depicted as a public witness. In 1 Samuel 10:5–9 God tells Saul that he will prophesy, and Saul goes down to Gibeah and does in fact prophesy with a company of prophets. Prophetic speech was different from everyday speech, and as such it was recognized by outsiders as speaking the words of God.

Third, the Holy Spirit often comes upon a person, causing the person to speak truth directly to another individual or to give a speech directing others

23. The one exception would be individual giftedness by the Holy Spirit, which I believe would include the work of culture making: art, music, drama, etc. See Andy Crouch's *Culture Making: Recovering Our Creative Calling* (Downers Grove, IL: InterVarsity, 2008) for a fuller discussion of this concept today.

toward God's will.[24] As New Testament writers and early church apologists affirmed, these prophets were speaking under the guidance of the Holy Spirit.

Fourth, the Holy Spirit in the Old Testament comes upon people to bring about justice and righteousness. This is more clearly seen in the Old Testament than in the New; however, I believe it is found in the content of the later sections of Paul's and Peter's letters. God's Holy Spirit brings about holiness (which includes justice) by working through the people of God.

> Here is my servant, whom I uphold, my chosen one in whom I delight; *I will put my Spirit on him and he will bring justice to the nations*. He will not shout or cry out, or raise his voice in the streets. A bruised reed he will not break, and a smoldering wick he will not snuff out. In faithfulness he will bring forth justice; he will not falter or be discouraged till he establishes justice on earth. In his teaching the islands will put their hope. (Isa. 42:1–4, emphasis mine)

This concept of the Spirit of the Lord coming to bring about justice is seen in many places in Old Testament narrative and poetry. We should clarify that bringing about justice (or righteousness)[25] means dealing with sin. The Holy Spirit speaks truth and that includes exposing sin wherever it is found, especially among God's people. "But as for me, I am filled with power, with the Spirit of the Lord, and with justice and might, to declare to Jacob his transgression, to Israel his sin" (Mic. 3:8). The Holy Spirit is more than just the One who convicts of sin and brings justice in a cruel and unjust world. The Spirit of the living God is the very breath of God who creates (Job 33; Ps. 104:30) and brings life. The Holy Spirit enlivens and revives, or generates and regenerates (Isa. 32:14–15; 44:3–4).

There are many other observations we might make about the Spirit of God in the Old Testament, but I'll conclude with this: the Spirit of God is often recognized in his works by outsiders. King Nebuchadnezzar says a number of times in Daniel 4 and 5 that Daniel (whom he called Belteshazzar) has the "spirit of the holy gods" in him. Another dream interpreter and Hebrew working in the court of pagan royalty was also identified as having the Spirit of God in him: "The plan seemed good to Pharaoh and to all his officials. So Pharaoh asked them, 'Can we find anyone like this man, one in whom is the spirit of God?' Then Pharaoh said to Joseph, 'Since God has made all this known to you, there is no one so discerning and wise as you'" (Gen. 41:37–39).

To conclude, we will look again at a familiar passage that holds many of these issues together. The Holy Spirit is the Spirit of God that came upon

24. There are many examples of this: 2 Chronicles 20:14–15; 1 Chronicles 12:18; Ezekiel 3:24–25, etc.

25. The two English words use the same Greek word (*dikaiosune*), and at times the same Hebrew word (*tsedeq*). Righteousness means to live according to the right rule, which is according to the character of God. Similarly, the just law is enshrined in the character of God.

Jesus Christ at baptism. All that was prophesied about the Messiah was fulfilled in Jesus.

> The Spirit of the Sovereign Lord is on me, because the Lord has anointed me to preach good news to the poor. He has sent me to bind up the brokenhearted, to proclaim freedom for the captives and release from darkness for the prisoners, to proclaim the year of the Lord's favor and the day of vengeance of our God, to comfort all who mourn. (Isa. 61:1–2)

Other messianic passages (such as Isa. 11, 42, 53, and 59) also remind us of the connection between the Spirit of God, the fulfillment of the Spirit's predictions in Jesus Christ, and the application of that redemption (putting the Spirit of God within them) that comes with the pouring out of the Holy Spirit. In summary, after looking at the place of the Holy Spirit in the earliest church and throughout Scripture, we can agree with D. T. Niles who said, "The Holy Spirit is the missionary of the Gospel. It is He who makes the Gospel explosive in men's lives and in human affairs."[26]

One Spirit, Many Cultures (Communication and Contextualization)

As pastor of an English-speaking, mostly Chinese, congregation of four hundred in Singapore, I was asked to lead in a house-cleansing ceremony. Our church was made up almost solely of first-generation Christians, and the average age of the congregation was about twenty-one. A young girl, who we will call Song Mee, asked me one day after worship, "Pastor, will you come to my house and remove the idols and have a house cleansing for my family? My parents have become Christian and they want the idols removed." Raised a Presbyterian in the United States, this had not been part of my (very thorough) seminary studies. I was prepared to preach a theologically responsible three-point sermon, to preside over a Presbyterian communion service, and to do premarital counseling using various personality-inventory and spiritual-gift questionnaires. Idol removal and house cleansing were not even elective courses in my seminary.

Being quick witted, if not wise, I asked what Chinese dialect the parents spoke, for I was pretty sure that they were not English speakers. "Hokkien" was the response, and I immediately knew I was off the hook. "You should ask Pastor Tan to do this, since he speaks Hokkien. Your parents need someone to pray with them in their own heart language." And so I attended the house cleansing and blessing ceremony and, when it was done and the prayers and hymns were completed, we returned to the back of the church, unloaded the idols, put them in what looked like an outdoor grill, and burned them up.

26. D. T. Niles, *Upon the Earth* (New York: McGraw-Hill, 1962), 67.

In the process, I learned a great deal about how to complete the redemption process in a Chinese culture. I had some problems and questions with what was going on (did they need to burn the idols?), but I was impressed with the clarity of the thinking of the church leaders and the pastoral care given to the family. As I look back on this today, I use the language of "conversion of cultures" for what was going on. It is not just the conversion of individuals, not just the conversion of groups of individuals (or families), but it is the full conversion of life—conversion of cultures—that God seeks to develop through his chosen people. The individuals *and the house* needed a "baptism" into a new life. The conversion process would not have been complete if the idols had remained.

A basic definition of culture might be "the sum-total of the learned patterns of thought and behavior of any given society." There are hundreds of definitions of culture that focus more on religion, on family life, or on "common sense"—but it is taught patterns of thought and action that define a culture. Classical definitions of culture in the nineteenth and early twentieth centuries assumed that there was one universal culture. This led to cultural imperialism, which was fed by social Darwinism: certain cultures were considered superior, and thus all cultures must eventually lead to something that looks like Western culture. The period following World War II witnessed an evolution from a dynamic or empirical understanding of culture to a postmodern understanding.[27] It is this more empirical or dynamic definition that we are assuming here. Cultures vary, but as human communities, they answer the basic questions of humanity: how to live, how to die, and how to understand the meaning of life.

With the decline of traditional Christian communities in the West, a new discussion of mission to the West has developed, exploring the possibility of conversion of the West and the West as a mission field.[28] This discussion has helped to further dislodge the notion of a particular culture (the West) as in any way a paradigm of a universal culture or as *the* Christian culture. In the early twenty-first century we have the opposite problem: postmodern theorists find all cultures self-authenticating and valid as communities of discourse. Each culture creates meaning from its own experience, using its own language, and therefore truth is bound to particular cultures and their language symbols. Postmoderns, like Lyotard and Foucault, focus on language

27. See Stephen B. Bevans, *Models of Contextual Theology* (Maryknoll, NY: Orbis Books, 1992), 5–10, for a discussion of these changes following the ideas of Bernard Lonergan in *Method in Theology* (New York: Herder & Herder, 1972).

28. Most of these discussions were catalyzed by J. E. Lesslie Newbigin when he returned to England from his ecumenical and missionary work in India and Switzerland. See "Can the West be Converted," *Princeton Seminary Bulletin* 6, no. 1 (1985): 25–37. He describes his return to England and the new missionary encounter with the West in his autobiography, *Unfinished Agenda: An Autobiography* (Geneva: WCC, 1985).

as culture-creator and as the power of culture.[29] For our purposes, we do not need to understand postmodernity as much as the concepts of culture and culture-formation that we encounter in daily living. Few people (if any at all) live as if truth (for them) fully resides in their own culture formed by their own language. We do and must live in a world that honors the unique patterns and beliefs of different cultures, but also honors and values the need to communicate across cultures. Cultures are not completely distinct and self-authenticating; they interpenetrate and commune. If they were absolutely unique, world peace, trade, and even cross-cultural communications would not be possible. Therefore, we will start from the premise that cultures have unique features that come from their own contextually specific locations, but that all cultures are open to other cultures. I believe in the possibility and the necessity of translation.

What does this have to do with mission and the work of the Holy Spirit in cultures?[30] I would first like to give an often-misunderstood example from the Old Testament and then take a look at how we should understand cultural diversity and the work of the Holy Spirit in cultures. I will conclude this section with a brief look at idols, violence, sex, and power.

It is very troubling to study the long chapters of the Old Testament in which the Israelites are commanded to kill and completely crush local cultures. Most of us are at least a little in sympathy with Marcion, who believed that this Old Testament God was a different god than the God of Jesus Christ. However, a Christian understanding of culture requires us to understand religions, culture, and God's people first in the Old Testament before we proceed to think about the Holy Spirit and cultures today. Beginning with Abraham, God called out a family to make into a "nation," God's own people. They were to be dedicated to God, and through this family (or nation) all the families of the earth were to be blessed.

> I will make you into a great nation and I will bless you; I will make your name great, and you will be a blessing. I will bless those who bless you, and whoever curses you I will curse; and all peoples on earth will be blessed through you. (Gen. 12:2–3)

29. See, for example: Myron B. Penner, *Christianity and the Postmodern Turn: Six Views* (Grand Rapids: Brazos, 2005); *The Logic of Incarnation, James K. A. Smith's Critique of Postmodern Religion*, ed. Neal DeRoo and Brian Lightbody (Eugene, OR: Pickwick, 2009); or James K. A. Smith, *Who's Afraid of Postmodernism?: Taking Derrida, Lyotard and Foucault to Church* (Grand Rapids: Baker Academic, 2006).

30. The language is complex regarding cultures. When the Bible talks about nations, tribes, peoples, tongues, or *ethnos* (*panta ta ethnē* in Matt. 28:19), it is talking about a people who are identified with a specific culture. Each nation traditionally had its own language and gods or idols that it honored. Abraham is, by God's design and God's grace, being chosen (election is the doctrine here) to be a blessing to other nations or cultures, by being fully devoted to YHWH. A particular culture will be reshaped by worshiping a "new" God.

What we have here is the shaping of a culture. Nation (or people) is shorthand for an ethnic group or a cultural entity. Today, we might say the Shan of Myanmar, the Kadazan-Dusun of Malaysia, or the Afar of Ethiopia. Any nation or people who were to come into contact with this new "people of God" were to be blessed. This culture was to be the missionary presence of God.

After Israel's sojourn in Egypt, they became a pilgrim people on a journey to claim their own land. On the way, they are given the rules for society—or what we might call cultural standards (the Ten Commandments)—but they quickly became "stiff-necked," rejecting God's leadership and standards. Culture has a dual core of religion (ultimate beliefs) and language (modes of thought and communication). Surely two centuries of living in Egypt had reshaped what started out as the family of Abraham. After twelve generations or so, Egyptian ways would have become the way Israel, too, lived and viewed the world. Then came the wilderness years. Forty years in the wilderness was like a period of cultural reshaping as the Israelites were fed and watered by God while his presence was marked through fire and smoke. A forty-year sojourn shaped them into a united culture after the mixed cultural life that developed after over two centuries in polytheistic Egypt.

The Ten Commandments were to become the backbone of Israelite culture. Other nations were already living in the "promised land," and these residential cultures had their own forms of worship and language. In order for his people to be a witnessing presence within these foreign cultures, God commanded that they must become a "holy nation," a nation set apart. They must not commingle with other cultural norms that were based on religious practices including the worship of idols. The most powerful way cultures are spread is through marriage and family life. In this ancient context, marriage would bring local idols, practices, and values into Israelite homes. Yahweh worship is first and foremost worship of the one God—only and absolutely. Everything else follows from the first two commandments: no other gods, no other worship. But, like a long-drawn-out tragedy, the history of Israel in the Old Testament is testimony to how God's people, again and again, rejected God's design for them and adopted local worship as they intermarried. Compromises developed into lost loyalty, which brought on God's judgment, exile, and restoration. When it came to receiving other religions, God was uncompromising. Being the people of God meant fundamentally that they were devoted to Yahweh only.

Now we turn to King Solomon, his great building program, and his unquenchable lust for power and women. God's command to build a temple was fulfilled in Solomon's amazing building program (1 Kings 5–8). The temple was built to be as magnificent as the God they worshiped (1 Kings 5 and 6). However, Solomon took nearly twice as long to build his own house and, in addition, he had oppressed many of his own people in order to build the two "homes." Solomon also accumulated many foreign women in his "household." In doing this, he took his eye off of God. Avarice, lust, oppression, and finally idolatry became cultural companions of the king—and thus of his people. It is not the case, however, that these other cultures were evil in and of themselves. God points out the problem that would (and did) bring judgment down on Solomon and his progeny: "But if you or your descendants turn away from me and do not observe the commands and decrees I have given you and go off to serve other gods and worship them . . ." (1 Kings 9:6). The issue was worship—the concern of the first two commandments, expressed so clearly as the core of the law recited in the *Shema*: "Hear O Israel: The LORD our God, the LORD is one. Love the LORD your God with all your heart and with all your soul and with all your strength" (Deut. 6:4–5).[31]

When we read of Solomon's downfall (or the judgment that will descend after he dies), we first find out that he loved women from six different ethnic groups, and then we learn which gods or idols they worshiped. Solomon began to worship Molech, Milcom, Chemosh, and Astarte.[32] The women turned his heart away from God, but my guess is (and the future judgment proves this) that it was Solomon's sin, not the sin of the women, that turned his heart away from God.

The point is, in the normative understanding of cultures, the core of a culture is found in its worship. Athenians worshiped Athena, and Celts worshiped Lug. A god defined and directed a people. Until the modern age of religious pluralism and tolerance of difference, there was no other option. When cultures collided, they either avoided conflict by turning around, or they prepared for a cultural battle that would end in the conquest of one over another. God's plan was for all cultures to be blessed—not annihilated. They would be blessed as they worshiped correctly the God who created them. King Solomon is an example of missed witness because of disobedience that brought a new, unholy center to Israelite culture. Each and every culture needs to be recentered.

Guidelines for Understanding Culture

We turn now to look at four guidelines to help us understand cultures and the witness of God through the Holy Spirit in diverse cultures.

1. God loves cultural diversity. We must start with the affirmation that cultural diversity is blessed by God in the Bible. God does not like all types of diversity but, as we noted previously, God seems to love diversity of culture, age, and gender.[33] We see, for example, in the heavenly vision in Revelation 7, that there are many languages and tribes and peoples worshiping the Lamb.

31. "Love the Lord your God" is used nine times in Deuteronomy.

32. According to the NRSV.

33. According to Genesis, the idea of complementary male and female human forms was God's idea. The concept is confirmed in marriage and reaffirmed in the Spirit's coming upon men and women in Acts in fulfillment of the prophesy of Joel 2:28.

This type of cultural diversity is a good thing, and so, in our missionary work, cultural diversity should be encouraged, not diminished. However, for many centuries, local cultures were not respected or honored, in large part because of the classicist (imperial) notion of culture mentioned above. There are far too many stories of missionaries coming to a village and bringing about a conversion *to* Western culture, rather than the conversion *of* the local culture. There is a world of difference. The first notion is based on the false concept that there is one Christian culture. The second is based upon the notion that God loves cultural diversity and that it is the missionary's responsibility to find ways of bringing Christ in as a local, as a long-lost relative, as a brother. The missionary participates in releasing God's Spirit to dwell in and reform each and every culture. John 1:14 is a foundational statement, a theological powder keg for mission in one verse.

> The Word became flesh and made his dwelling among us. We have seen his glory, the glory of the one and only Son, who came from the Father, full of grace and truth.

The simple phrase "made his dwelling among us" means "tabernacled among us," and it points back to the Israelites in the wilderness, carrying around the tentlike tabernacle so that God's glory could dwell among his people. And so, God's glory was walking among specific Jews who spoke a specific Aramaic dialect and ate specific Middle Eastern food at a particular time. This specific culture, food, and language was received and honored. And in that specific culture, and (by extrapolation from the Great Commission in Matt. 28) into each and every culture, the glory, grace, and truth of God are to be enthroned. As we read through the Acts of the Holy Spirit, we see the encounter of missionaries with cultures (see especially Acts 10–12). This naturally leads to our second point about culture and the Holy Spirit.

2. All cultures are marked by the image of God.[34] Thus, all cultures have within them the capacity to glorify God (to point to God) and to communicate with God. As collectives of individual humans who are created in God's image, cultures also bear that mark or capacity. If cultures are really collections of individuals made in God's image, then we can expect to see something of God's image in every culture. A brief thought experiment should help. Start by

34. It is awkward to take a whole section to talk about a concept that is not defined, but Christian understandings of the *imago Dei* are quite diverse. However, most all definitions center on characteristics that are found in God, that reflect God: rule, moral life (righteousness), communication, and capacity to love. See Eugene TeSelle's entry in the *Cambridge Dictionary of Christianity*, ed. Daniel Patte (Cambridge: Cambridge University Press, 2010). My favorite definition of "image of God" is found in John Bowden's *Christianity: The Complete Guide* (New York: Continuum, 2006) in the glossary: "The condition in which human beings were created according to Genesis 1:26. There is much discussion as to what this might be." Well said.

thinking of a specific culture. Quite often when we think of a specific culture we focus on what bothers us, or what (we think) is sinful in this culture. But now can you think of some ways that God's image is present in that culture, despite its sinfulness? Don Richardson talks about "redemptive analogies" as bridges of redemption in cultures.[35] It is true, many cultures have bridges of redemption, like ancient stories, myths, or values that point toward God. Some are much closer to the revelation we find in Christ than others. However, there are other ways we can find marks of the tarnished but still present image in cultures. Here is an example.

Most East Asian cultures are marked by a Confucian heritage. One of the core beliefs of Confucianism is the importance of harmonious relationships. The following are the five primary relationships that should be governed by *li*:[36]

Ruler and subject
Father and son
Husband and wife
Oldest son and younger brothers
Elders and juniors (friends)

Each of these relationships is to be nurtured by reciprocity or *shu*. For example, the ruler is to show benevolence to the ruled, and the subjects are to show loyalty to their rulers. The father is to show kindness to his son (children) and the son is to express filial piety (devotion of a son) to the father. There is much to be commended in this understanding of social order. Although at times the Confucian requirement to honor ancestors becomes a bondage of the living to the dead, this East Asian custom is an extension of the biblical mandate to "honor your mother and father." These aspects of East Asian culture portray something of the image of God, the moral life of God, for humanity. My point is a simple one: every culture still carries something of the image of God, even if, for a season, the culture at large has become very dark or some of the customs or habits have become idolatrous.

Although there have been some theologians who have argued that the image of God has been erased with the fall into sin, most Christians express the fall as a tarnishing of the image.[37] The ancient Christians wrote a great deal about the *imago Dei*, focusing upon the themes we are looking at here: its original glory, its corruption, and the hope of its restoration. They find the concept of the image of God helpful in explaining the work of Christ for the individual

35. Don Richardson, *Peace Child* (Glendale, CA: Regal Books, 1974), and *Eternity in their Hearts* (1981; Ventura, CA: Regal Books, 2005).

36. *Li* is an important Confucian concept that means "right," "custom," "ritual," "etiquette," or "morals."

37. Second Corinthians 3:18 hints at such an understanding of reflecting God to others.

and for cultures. Like a mirror that has tarnished, it can no longer reflect the image of God clearly. Jesus comes and restores that image—cleaning off the mirror. In his "Homily on our Lord's Birth from the Holy Virgin," Narsai (ca. 399–ca. 502), writing from Persia, describes the work of God in the incarnation in the following way:

> His corrupted image He willed to renew under the name of a birth, because He again moulds it in the crucible of the Spirit and renews it.[38]

He goes on to explain the importance of recovering the tarnished "image" through the coming of the true and pure image to human clay. This naturally leads to my third point regarding cultures—their fallen state or tarnished image.

3. All cultures, like the humans that form them, are fallen and therefore in need of redemption. All cultures, since the expulsion of Adam and Eve from the garden, have turned dark and cloudy, although the image of God is still evident to the eyes of faith. Thus, when we look for the image of God in all cultures, we need to also be aware of the basic tendencies of sin, what we might call the entropy of sin that pulls all cultures downward. Without the preserving and redeeming work of the Holy Spirit, all cultures tend toward one of three vices. First, cultures easily drift toward the self-worship of nationalism that sees the entire world as revolving around one's particular nation.[39] It is easy to point fingers when we mention this sin (German nationalism in the late nineteenth and early twentieth centuries; Japanese nationalism at the same time, etc.), but in each and every border skirmish, in each imposition of an empire's will upon others, and even in modern nationalisms that have led to regional wars, we see a good thing (unity) gone bad.

Closely related to the sin of nationalism is tribalism and its root cause, ethnocentrism. Once again, we can probably think of much that is of value in our particular culture, but what we are looking at here is how such cultural loyalty turns into an ultimate loyalty. We see this in tribal warfare, in which even Christians kill Christians and Muslims kill Muslims. In tribalism, ethnic identity trumps all other values: including nation, religion, and sometimes even one's own family.

Finally, a sector of one's culture or society may be elevated to the level of idolatry—a far more subtle evil, but equally destructive. Material goods may become an idol, and so a culture may be led to do whatever is necessary to accumulate or protect their goods. An ideology may become an idol, as happened in the Soviet Republic and in Mao Zedong's China. A communist ideology became a national idol and millions of people (made in God's image)

38. F. G. McLeod, trans., *Narsai's Metrical Homilies on the Nativity, Epiphany, Passion, Resurrection and Ascension*, Patrologia Orientalis 40.1 (Turnhout, Belgium: Brepols, 1979).

39. A modern nation-state (which I am talking of here) is made up of many cultures united by a common national identity and a core of commonly shared values.

died as a result. A slave ideology or a commercial ideology can also develop among a people. What is happening in all of these cases is that ultimate loyalty, which should always be reserved for God alone, is given to other things or other (inferior) ideas.

To carry this just one step further, it has been observed that idolatry always tends toward violence. Most idols begin as something good, which soon is asked to bear more than it was intended to bear. For example, communism has good basic concerns for communal justice and the welfare of all individuals. Yet the basic concept of justice soon turns toward required "sharing," which is ordered by rulers, and before long people are put in prison or reeducation camps for resisting the "natural process" of economies. Vinoth Ramachandra in *Gods That Fail* describes this same process with Adam Smith's "occult notion of an 'invisible hand' steering human self-interest to socially beneficent ends."[40] What started out as an optimistic description advocating a free-market economy has become something very dark. Ramachandra explains the development from theory to idolatry:

> There are reasons, then, for believing that Smith would be horrified by the modern alliance of big business interests with political parties . . . and the combination of private wealth and public squalor that has come to characterize American and European cities at the end of the 20th century. . . . While commentators may disagree among themselves as to how Smith is to be read, there is no doubt that many modern economists and governments have made of "market forces" a quasi-religious deity far more powerful than anything worshipped in pre-modern cultures. And in the name of that deity, they have thrown men and women out of work, added insult to injury by blaming the poor for their own poverty, justified the ruthless accumulation of wealth by a few, and squandered the earth's non-renewable resources.[41]

When ideas or things become idols, they become demanding; their relative value is turned into absolute loyalty. When idols are threatened, they become defensive and even violent because the life of an idol is dependent upon its worshiper. In addition, whatever we give our loyalty to shapes us, makes us into its (or his or her) image. Once we are shaped into the image of another, it becomes very disruptive when we try to tear ourselves away. Thus, we must not be surprised when violence erupts at the presentation of the gospel; idols that are threatened become violent. And almost anything—religion, a political system, a lifestyle, or even a relationship—can become an idol. The Holy Spirit speaking into idolatry may elicit a violent, definitive response. We should not be surprised by this, for Jesus was threatened by demons—idols with personality—and the demons felt threatened by his presence.

40. Vinoth Ramachandra, *Gods That Fail* (Downers Grove, IL: InterVarsity, 1996), 110.
41. Ibid., 111.

> What do you want with us, Jesus of Nazareth? Have you come to destroy us? I know who you are—the Holy One of God!" "Be quiet!" said Jesus sternly. "Come out of him!" The evil spirit shook the man violently and came out of him with a shriek. (Mark 1:24–26)

I believe when Paul talked about "authorities" and the "powers of this dark world" it is this spiritual battle of ultimate loyalty to which he is referring (Eph. 6:12).

4. The Holy Spirit works in cultures as he does in individuals. The Holy Spirit confronts cultural sin, empowers cultures for change, and draws cultures toward the Triune God, using individuals to affect this change in particular contexts. Again, as with individuals, we can see some cultural reform without Jesus Christ, but full redemption and living into the fullness that God intended will not happen without the proclamation and reception of Jesus Christ. Redemption of cultures is much more complex than with individuals, because it involves relationships across the culture and with other cultures. The redemption of a culture might mean that artwork will begin to reflect greater truth and will contain some image or message of hope. The full conversion of a culture will also mean greater wholeness in relationships: children respecting parents, parents taking responsibility for raising their children, and the elderly being cared for by the community. The full conversion of a culture will also mean the dedication of individuals and communities to stand against injustices and violence, to resist the dehumanizing practices and habits within the larger society, and to refuse to be defined by money or a job.

When the Holy Spirit enters a culture, as individuals are coming to faith in Jesus Christ, there are two movements we see and should promote: the movement of conversion and change, and the movement of contextualization. The first is a confrontation, the second an adaptation. Let's look first at the confrontation.

The Lun Bawang (called Muruts by the British) of North Borneo (today Sarawak) was a culture that was centered on the production and consumption of "burak," a local rice wine. I say centered, because they would put aside the first rice of the harvest to make the wine, and they would consume it at all celebrations (engagement, marriage, birth, harvest, planting, etc.). Personal hygiene, basic house maintenance, and cultivation were ignored because producing and consuming the liquor took priority. Alcoholism and infighting caused their numbers to decline from the late nineteenth to early twentieth centuries—from seventeen thousand to less than five thousand in 1905. The story is told in *Drunk Before Dawn*[42] that when the Lun Bawang began to convert in the 1940s, the culture changed dramatically. Wine production decreased (almost ended), life span increased, marriages stayed together, and the overall health and education level of the people rose. In this case, there was

42. Shirley Lees, *Drunk Before Dawn* (Kent: OMF International, 1979).

one cultural element that had become an idol—and when it was confronted, many other cultural norms were transformed.

The study of Christian expansion is the ongoing story of such transformations—whether it be Toyohika Kagawa and the social reforms that were introduced in Japan, the transformation of New England society under the Great Awakenings, or the change in laws and the treatment of people under Constantine's rule[43]—conversions of individuals are intrinsically related to the conversions of cultures. In the Great Welsh Revival (1904–5), the young preacher Evan Roberts, after having a lengthy vision or experience of heaven, prayed that God would "bend" him. He then preached a message about God bending people: bringing them to the point of repentance and into new life. The Welsh revival was about changed lives, changed families, and changed villages and towns. The brokenness of cultures reveals the need for redemption of cultures—for cultures to be bent. This bending is often seen in changes in law, art, habits, and institutions that point more to the Kingdom than they do to earthly idols.

How does the Holy Spirit work in such change, and how does this help us understand the role of Christian missionary work? I think it is helpful to return to John 1 and the image of Jesus walking among us. The Holy Spirit's presence in the very life of the believers is now the presence of Jesus Christ among people. When Jesus would walk among people, through towns and along the road, there were three basic responses he made to those around him. First, he provided teaching as to how they were to live. "It has been said . . . but I say to you . . ." (Matt. 5, multiple occasions). "Suppose one of you has one hundred sheep and loses one of them . . ." (Luke 15:4). Secondly, he confronted the sinfulness of the few. "You brood of vipers! How can you who are evil, say anything good?" (Matt. 12:34). He confronted sinful practices, ideas, and demons. The particular practices he confronted in society were often practices that promoted injustice and oppression. Thirdly, Jesus affirmed what was good and right, what reflected the Kingdom and its values. "Don't be afraid, from now on you will fish for people" (Luke 5:10). "I am willing, 'Be clean'" (Luke 5:13). Jesus walking among people is not unlike the role of the missionaries, who are to "always carry around in our body the death of Jesus, so that the life of Jesus may also be revealed in our body" (2 Cor. 4:10). As a vessel of the Holy Spirit (2 Cor. 4:7) the missionary walks among people to bring something of the glory of Christ into specific contexts. As the Holy Spirit then enters cultures, he lifts them up from their broken and damaged state, and as a culture is lifted up, it is cleaned off and set on a higher plane. It is a helpful image to think of the Holy Spirit as actually entering into a culture (where he belongs), lifting it up, and cleaning it off. This lifting and cleaning work is an ongoing process that is only finally complete at the eschaton. It

43. See Peter Leithart's *Defending Constantine: The Twilight of an Empire and the Dawn of Christendom* (Downers Grove, IL: InterVarsity, 2010).

is an ongoing process of God that continues after individual conversions. The goal, as is so evident from the teaching of Jesus, is the full conversion of individuals and relationships.

The second movement we can talk about, as the Holy Spirit moves into a culture, is that of contextualization. The Spirit of God does not take on one particular culture; he desires to take on each and every culture. When we mentioned above that the Holy Spirit enters into a culture, we are talking about how the Spirit "puts on" a local context. When talking about the history of mission in chapter 2, we noted that the Jesuits adapted the message to different cultures, through translated prayers and liturgies, through artwork, through methods of relating to royalty, and through acceptance of certain cultural ritual practices. We have also seen the original instructions of the SCPF: "Do not bring any pressure to bear on peoples, to change their manner, customs, and uses, unless they are evidently contrary to religion and sound morals." This is an interesting way to look at the missionary imperative to encourage contextualization of the gospel (or Kingdom adjustments): respect or honor basic customs and manners, but seek to reform immoral behavior and misleading worship (religion). We can see this distinction in Paul's letters, between what is required by faith (right belief and moral practice) and what is *adiaphora* (things indifferent, or outside of moral law). In each of his letters he establishes what faith entails and how we should then live into it—in a few places we see that some things just do not matter. In 1 Corinthians 8, for example, Paul mentions that food offered to idols is a sensitive subject. Some people still believe in idols, and they may think you are honoring them (or deriving some power from them) by eating their food. In deciding the matter of what to eat (or where to eat), Paul is concerned that he (and supposedly also "we") follow another principle that is more important than personal freedom: becoming "all things to all people" in order to win them (1 Cor. 9:19–22). Here Paul is talking about context and the gospel. We might imagine a missionary from England, who greatly enjoys steak and fish and chips, working in India, among Hindus. His freedom to eat meat would become a stumbling block to his witness. There are innumerable examples of appropriate dress for witness, appropriate ways of addressing others, and even appropriate reading material, which will either build bridges or walls. However, contextualization is much bigger than this.

Five Models of Contextualization

The best presentation of the issues of contextualization has been written by Stephen B. Bevans, SVD.[44] In this carefully nuanced volume, Bevans describes

44. Stephen B. Bevans, SVD, *Models of Contextual Theology* (Maryknoll, NY: Orbis Books, 2002).

the contextual imperative in mission (along with its attendant issues), and then he presents five models. I give them here, briefly, because the models themselves show the complexity of contextualization and why it is something that must be done in community, and with frequent reference to Scripture, Tradition, and the context itself.

The first model is the *translation model*. This model (used by the Jesuits) assumes that the gospel has a specific, unchanging message that can be translated into any other language (culture). The model assumes that we are not talking about a word-for-word translation, but something closer to a dynamic equivalence that will communicate the same meaning and have the same impact on the receiving culture that the message had in the original culture.

Second is the *anthropological model*. This type of contextualization is not in contrast to the first model as much as it holds a different emphasis. Here the question that is asked is, "How can local culture be continued or preserved?" The concern is to retain cultural continuity, recognizing that this means the "validity of the human as the place of divine revelation and as a source (*locus*) for theology that is equal to . . . scripture and tradition."[45] Revelation is meaningless (the word is carefully chosen) if it is not in the flesh, expressed in human form.

Third is the *praxis model*. Here the primary concern is to see the outworking of the gospel in appropriately expressed social change. This model comes out of the liberation theologies of the 1960s and 1970s—a time when much theology was done only with words. The power of transformation was hardly visible. The resultant concern for the poor and marginalized was really the recovery of some of the basic gospel concerns we spoke about in the last chapter. The gospel, in any particular context, will practically (praxis) express itself in revelatory Kingdom action for local people.

The fourth model is the *synthetic model*. It is synthetic in three ways. First, it brings together a synthesis of the three models mentioned above: holding the value of translation and retention of tradition, operating with concern for the retaining of cultural expressions, while moving out into appropriate action. Second, it is synthetic in that it brings together cultural elements from more than just the host culture, helping the faith to be articulated between cultures. It is, third, synthetic in the sense of being dialectical, as an "on-going dialogue between faith and culture or cultures."[46]

Finally, the last model is more theoretical and personal than the others, the *transcendental model*. This model begins with the world of the subject, the individual convert, rather than with the world of objects (the world out there). In this model, different questions are asked than are asked in the other

45. Ibid., 56.
46. Ibid., 90.

four models, for it is concerned about what is happening within the mind of the individual more than in the observable world.

> How genuine is the religious experience I am trying to interpret, how well does my language express this experience? How free of bias am I? Do I feel comfortable with a particular expression of my religious experience? . . . Do I really understand what I am trying to articulate?[47]

Although these models are helpful for a missionary entering into a new culture, it is also helpful to remember two warnings about contextualization. A foreign missionary may be very interested in contextualization, seeking to find ways of lifting local art forms or patterns of life as "Christian." The local newly converted Christian, however, may have a very different view of things. What is fascinating and interesting to the missionary (Chinese dragons as a major theme in Chinese art) may be, for the young Chinese convert, a reminder of the evil past. I have seen attempts by missionaries to build lecterns and communion tables with carved dragons—they were rejected by the local Chinese converts. I wrote a hymn for a new congregation in Singapore and had it put to (what I thought was) lovely Chinese music. The hymn was sung once by an all Chinese choir and then put away for good. As far as I know it was never sung again, because these English-speaking Chinese did not like the tune. Contextualization must come out of the lives and experience of a local community of faith. Outsiders can and should be in dialogue about what is appropriate, but God's Spirit is more than able to guide the local Christian community without outsiders imposing what may very well be the exact opposite of what they are trying to promote. Appropriate cultural expressions usually come out of the local community of believers.

The Holy Spirit in Disenculturation and Enculturation

Related to this concern is the concept of "disenculturation" or "decontextualization," which often occurs in the early stages of conversion.[48] When a person is converted to Christ, their life is reoriented, and by extension a culture or village will also be reoriented. Often symbols of the past life overlap. A village that used to practice head-hunting, for example, might identify other cultural symbols (knives, house architecture, dance, or instruments) with the former way of life and its violent practices. Thus, most new converts step far away

47. Ibid., 104–5.

48. This concept I first read about when Richard Lovelace's book *Dynamics of the Spiritual Life: An Evangelical Theology of Renewal* (Downers Grove, IL: InterVarsity, 1979) first came out. It has stuck with me, because it was my own experience upon conversion, and I have observed it time and again in the lives of converts in North America and in Asia.

from many cultural norms in the early period after conversion. For a culture, it may take months, years, or generations to reappropriate some of these cultural elements. Richard Lovelace calls this reappropriation "re-contextualization." It is necessary for people in a given cultural context to be allowed to make these decisions, but the meaning of these symbols is in their own mind and heart. Outsiders (the missionary) may ask questions or guide (by giving examples from other cultures) but not impose. This has been the error of many missionaries in the past who made connections regarding pagan practices and instruments that were not necessarily in the mind of the local people (e.g., the use of African drums). Thus, we can look at the advice given by the pope (Gregory) in far-off Rome to missionaries working among the pagan Brits as only part of the truth. On the surface his advice (see sidebar) seems very helpful, but it ignores the (likely) need for disenculturation that these converts would need in order to distance themselves from the spirits of their ancestors. The pull back to Egypt (the pre-Christian life) is very strong and requires a clear break from the past.

We might ask what it would mean for a young convert to return to the temples of their ancestors, now as a Christian. What would be in the convert's mind and heart as a worshiper? It may be that the convert would continue worshiping ancestors and spirits and demons even while attending the Mass. Or, it may be more like cleansing someone's home of idols and then rededicating the home to the Triune God. Conversion almost always involves rejection of the old in one way or another. How this will happen, what it will mean, and what type of recontextualization will be possible must be determined locally. It is an ongoing dialogical task.

Pope Gregory's Advice (about 601) to Abbot Mellitus on Using Pagan Temples

"[We] . . . have come to the conclusion that the temples of the idols among that people should on no account be destroyed. The idols are to be destroyed, but the temples themselves are to be aspersed with holy water, altars set up in them, and relics deposited there. For if these temples are well-built, they must be purified from worship of demons and dedicated to the service of the true God. In this way, we hope that the people, seeing that their temples are not destroyed, may abandon their error and, flocking more readily to their accustomed resorts, may come to know and adore the true God."[a] If only it were so easy.

a. From Bede, *Ecclesiastical History of the English People*, ed. Betram Colgrave and R. A. B. Mynors (Oxford: Oxford University Press, 1969), 1.30.

The Possibility of "Over-Contextualization"

The fascination with cultural contexts can also lead to the contextual tail wagging the gospel dog. It is possible to become so fascinated with a local culture (even a local culture of your own) that you over-contextualize the presence of the gospel to such an extent that the gospel itself is lost. Contextualization is like artwork and, like all artwork, it is often a matter of what is in the eye of the beholder. What is appropriate for a first-generation Christian may not be appropriate for a third-generation Christian and vice versa. We will look at this in greater detail in the next chapter, but some emergent and missional leaders in the West seem to work so hard to affirm the local culture (in dress, music, place to worship, etc.) that anything specifically Christian is almost incidental. How Christian exactly is a meeting in a bar, discussing religion over a few beers and calling it "worship"? How is this proclaiming the good news of redemption in Jesus Christ? Maybe it is, in fact, proclaiming the gospel loud and clear. On the other hand, it may be doing the exact opposite.

These are dynamic issues of communication, and so they are in need of periodic review and reevaluation in light of how others (outsiders) are responding. A church or missionary may find themselves becoming irrelevant even though they "fit" in a local cultural context so neatly. Such a smooth "wearing" of a local context may be tantamount to wearing camouflage; the fit is so good that the missionary or church is indistinguishable from the cultural background. Jesus and Jesus's people stand out some, because they rub against the grain of every culture. Globalization, with its constant influx of new ideas and forms, makes this process even more complex (and exciting). However, it is first and foremost a work of the Spirit—and this makes it possible to do the impossible.

In summary, we note that cultures are like an individual human person in that they are both created in the image of God and fallen. Every culture is capable of great words and works of grace, but each and every culture is also capable of demonic oppression, deceit, and destruction. Cultures are a web of significance expressed in thought patterns, habits, art and artifacts, food, and, most powerfully, language and religion. The introduction of the gospel in any culture is a work of the Holy Spirit, and it is a work the church is invited into. Cultures or nations are God's primary vehicle for the expression of his glory in this world. Thus, contextualization is a primary task of the church's missionary calling. How contextualization takes place is in part the responsibility of the missionary, but primarily it is the responsibility of the local converts. After conversion, as the gospel seeps into the various crevices and wrinkles of a culture, there will be contrasting responses of pulling away from cultural norms and lifting up and cleaning off destructive accretions. Often, since ultimate meaning and loyalties are being challenged, this work of the Holy Spirit brings conflict, and cultures experience violence. This is all reasonable and understandable when we think about buildings, food, art, and even language. When it becomes more difficult is when we focus on one of the two central elements of meaning in a culture: religion. How does the Holy Spirit enter into religion or bring about the conversion of religious expressions?

The Triune God and the Plethora of Religions

At a Christian gathering in 1993 in the United States, the following prayer to the goddess Sophia was given:

> We are women in your image. With the hot blood of our wombs we give form to new life. . . . With nectar between our thighs we invite a lover. We birth a child. With our warm body fluids we remind the world of its pleasures and sensations.[49]

After this prayer, women were invited to receive a red dot in the middle of their forehead, a sign of the sixth chakra, or seat of divine wisdom.[50] A middle-aged Indian woman, whose grandfather was a convert to Christianity from Hinduism, refused to have a dot placed on her forehead. She explained to the surprised Anglo-American Presbyterian, "When I was a young girl in Ludhianna, India, I came home from school one day with a red dot on my forehead and my mother sat me down and said, 'Honey, why do you have that red dot on your forehead?' I explained that some of my friends had them at school and they asked if I wanted one too. I thought it looked nice. My mother explained we should never have a red dot on our heads. Then she said, 'We are Christians. When you were young, we brought you to church, baptized you, and the priest took holy oil and marked the sign of the cross on your forehead in the name of the Father, Son, and Holy Spirit. You have been marked already by the cross of Jesus Christ.'" In this Indian Christian's mind, being marked by the Spirit of the living God meant something very deep and serious. She understood that one could be "marked" or set aside for other uses and for other service—but she was set aside to serve the Triune God alone. Each religion is its own "web of significance";[51] or, to put it as Paul Tillich does, "A mixture of religions destroys in each of them the concreteness which gives it its dynamic power."[52]

49. Stephen Goode, "Feminists' Crusade Sparks Holy War," BNet, CBS Interactive Business Network, accessed June 4, 2011, http://findarticles.com/p/articles/mi_m1571/is_n30_v10/ai_15640006/.

50. Used mostly in Hinduism, the meaning of the red dot, or *bindi*, is varied, but in all cases it carries religious meaning related to meditation, wisdom, and centering oneself (often meditating on a god or goddess or on the merits of the Buddha).

51. Clifford Geertz (referring to Max Weber) writes of cultures as being webs of significance that we spin ourselves. I am applying the same concept to religion, because religion is at the core of cultural meaning. Geertz expressed it this way: "Believing, with Max Weber, that man is an animal suspended in webs of significance he himself has spun, I take culture to be those webs, and the analysis of it to be therefore not an experimental science in search of law but an interpretative one in search of meaning. It is explication I am after, construing social expression on their surface enigmatical." From Geertz, "Thick Description: Toward an Interpretive Theory of Culture," in *The Interpretation of Cultures: Selected Essays* (New York: Basic Books, 1973), 5.

52. From his last of his four Bampton Lectures (delivered in the fall of 1961), titled, "Christianity Judging Itself in the Light of Its Encounter with the World Religions," published in *Christianity and the Encounter of World Religions* (Minneapolis: Fortress, 1994), 61.

There is no issue in today's missiology that is more contested and at the same time more important than the nature of the multitude of religions and the Christian belief in one God as revealed in Jesus Christ. This would not be much of an issue if Jesus had been more understanding, more tolerant, of his own religious friends. However, Jesus was pretty strong on false belief and false (or hypocritical) action, and the Old Testament is even stronger. We should begin this section by noting that Jesus's harshest words were to those closest to his own beliefs—the Jews—and he seemed the most tolerant, or open, to those furthest (it is good to remember Luke 4:23–30 at this point). By analogy, it would be good for us to be strongest in our critique of the church and more gracious to those who seem furthest from Jesus (but who may be very close!).

I spent a year trying to decide where to put the discussion on religions in a missiology book that is focused on a trinitarian approach to mission. It was in a moment of sudden insight that I realized that our struggle with "religions" is that we usually start with Jesus (which is not a bad idea) rather than the Holy Spirit (which I think is a better idea). Simply put, I have come to believe that God's Spirit is at work in all peoples and his Spirit seeks to recover the image of God in each person and in every culture. The same Holy Spirit who applies redemption to us, and gives us spiritual gifts, is also working in the lives of people of other loyalties. Therefore, when we talk about other religions, we are talking about ultimate loyalties that reflect both truth and error. This has been recognized throughout the twentieth century, especially in earlier gatherings of the International Missionary Council. Thus, we can and should affirm that Christian witness to someone of another faith involves a spiritual awareness of God's presence in others, even while the Holy Spirit is calling others to the cross. For example, Cornelius was not a Christian (he was a seeker, a God-fearer), but God's Holy Spirit spoke to him and led him to the man who would deliver the message of Jesus Christ to him (Acts 10).

Another reason for placing the discussion of religions in this chapter on the Holy Spirit is it reflects that reality, and all theology, in the end, must connect with real people and real situations. I have interviewed many people from Africa and Asia who were raised in other religions (mostly Muslims, Hindus, and Buddhists), and all have had some definite experience of the Holy Spirit *before* they were Christian. Some had reoccurring dreams calling them to Jesus, some had a demon cast out, and one had a vision of heaven in which the angels were playing Sri Lankan instruments. If people of other faiths have experiences of the Holy Spirit, and if all people are made in the image of God, and if the Holy Spirit is the One who works to restore that image in redemption, then missiology should place the study of other faiths under the topic of the Holy Spirit.

Christian mission, as we have noted, is the mission of God bringing forth his glory for the nations of the world. It is a work of the Triune God, whereby nations or cultures are honored and "lifted up." Religions are part of every culture, and therefore Christian mission speaks to the religious dimension of each culture. We must avoid two temptations when it comes to Christian mission and religions. On the one hand, it is too easy in the globalized free market economy of religions to see religions as items on a shelf that can be taken or ignored. According to this mind-set, religions are neutral variables in any culture, and therefore we can ignore religious belief and then get on with the real mission of doing justice and loving mercy. But religions are never neutral, and if we treat religions as a commodity, we are misunderstanding both the role of religion and the religious person. Secular Western governments have made this mistake in foreign policy decisions in Iran, Iraq, Pakistan, and Afghanistan. Christians should know better.

The second temptation is to make religion everything, and view the gospel as needing to attack each religion. Religions are not so easily reified (made into a thing) and are much more complex and relational than this view allows for. When we speak about religions, we need to speak about religious people: people who have particular faith commitments. Therefore, we do not want to pretend that religions are so small a thing (like the color of a shirt we might wear), nor so great a thing (like the only concern of Christian mission). Religious belief and practice is always expressed in languages and cultures; it can be all-consuming for a people or nation, or a nation can try to ignore it—but it is always present. Jesus Christ seeks to dwell in each culture, and therefore religious beliefs and practices will become important as the Holy Spirit works to bring forth faith and sanctification.

As we have seen in the above brief look at the Holy Spirit in the Bible, God's Spirit reaches out and calls people to himself. We have looked at the Spirit speaking through preachers, evangelists, prophets, and even to pagan kings (Pharaoh of Egypt and King Nebuchadnezzar) and religious non-Christians (Cornelius). In each of these cases, God's Spirit is drawing people closer to himself, to a greater understanding of who God is and what his will is for individuals. Revelation by the Holy Spirit is a call to repentance and obedience. As we now look at Christian mission and religions we reaffirm this theological truth: God is the One who, through his Holy Spirit, draws people to Jesus Christ. We are invited to participate in communicating his love and mercy for his greater glory.

Having said this, we remember that the gospel has often been carried to people of other faiths in both appropriate and inappropriate ways. Christian mission has a checkered past. It is important to remember the violence and inappropriate work of the Spanish using the *Requirimento* in the Americas; mission was mixed with conquest and monks were caught in the cross fire. It is also important, however, to remember the careful study of religions that marked the work of the Jesuits in Japan, Vietnam, China, and India, as well as the work of people like Ziegenbalg and Plutschau in India, Hudson Taylor in China, and many others. Recognizing the work of the Holy Spirit requires us to do careful study of other religions and cultures, so as to be a servant of the other. Those whom we love, and those whom God loves, deserve to become known by us. Mission is about communication, and communication involves relationship. The more intimate a relationship, such as communicating the deep love of God, the more knowledge and empathy is required. Thus, we take time to point out major themes in studying other religions, so as to be faithful communicators of the gospel.[53]

Points of Religious Contact

Christian mission to people of other faiths involves much more than any single concern (such as salvation or peacemaking). I think it is helpful to think about relating to people of other faiths with several different points of contact: areas that we need to discuss with our neighbor of another faith. Each of these areas becomes an opportunity for better understanding and is an opportunity for the Holy Spirit to bring about conversion or (for the missionary) sanctification.[54] Later we will talk at length about evangelism as part of Christian mission to people of other faiths, but here we look at the fundamental issue in a missional encounter: listening, understanding, and engaging.

Salvation/Salvations

First, although it is not the only issue, we do relate to our Buddhist or Muslim neighbor concerning salvation and the afterlife; but we have to be careful, because another religious person may have a very different view of salvation. Therefore, we need to ask what they seek to be saved from, how that might happen, and what an afterlife might look like. Most religions are based on the intuition that "the world is not right and I am not right." The Bible calls

53. This is not a book primarily on religions, on the history of religions, or on witnessing to people of other faiths. There is a huge and, like the universe itself, constantly expanding corpus of material on these topics. I mention a few here by way of introduction. The best new Roman Catholic approach to religions is the *Catholic Engagement with World Religions: A Comprehensive Study*, ed. Karl J. Becker and Ilaria Morali (Maryknoll, NY: Orbis Books, 2010). An excellent volume that includes a survey of major scholars from an evangelical perspective is that of Veli-Matti Kärkkäinen, *An Introduction to the Theology of Religions: Biblical, Historical and Contemporary Perspectives* (Downers Grove, IL: InterVarsity, 2003). A creative and fair approach to religions for Christian mission is done by Terry Muck and Frances S. Adeney, *Christianity Encountering World Religions: The Practice of Mission in the Twenty-first Century* (Grand Rapids: Baker Academic, 2009). Paul Knitter's *No Other Name: A Critical Survey of Christian Attitudes Toward the World Religions* (Maryknoll, NY: Orbis Books, 1985) is one of the most well-reasoned from a progressive prospective.

54. We can actually say that dialogue with the other will bring about conversion, if we are listening carefully—if we mean by this conversion to a deeper understanding of God. This is what I mean by sanctification.

this sin; the Buddha identified suffering (the first Noble Truth) as the main problem. The cause of this problem (suffering) for Buddhists is attachment, and so the call to salvation is a call to become completely unattached. Many people do not even understand what they are saved from, or what the goal of their religion is, so a dialogue may produce little light and more questions than answers. Seeking answers together, however, will open up the relationship to further understanding regarding salvation. How we view the afterlife will determine how we live in this life.[55]

Revelation

The second issue for dialogue is revelation. Some people of other faiths have no concept of the revelation of truth from God, or Allah, or Brahman—only a personal enlightenment. A Theravada Buddhist does not believe in God, so there is no "one" to reveal further truths. Others have even higher views of revelation in a sacred text than most Christians have (I am thinking of Islam here). Who reveals, and how truths are revealed, are both important questions to ask. To follow up, however, we would want to know if that revelation can be apprehended by all people or, like Gnosticism, is it a secret or private knowledge? What does the person say about, or know about, God? Is God even knowable or, like in many religions, is God known only as a distant creator who abandoned creation and now can only be known indirectly through ancestors? Are there many names for God, no name, or a single name? What are the primary and secondary characteristics of God? Is God loving? Is God frightening?

Ethics and the Moral Life

Third, we must relate to people of other faiths as we live in community and as we make moral and ethical decisions in community. All Christians live in pluralistic contexts. If a single Christian family is living in Saudi Arabia or Algeria, they are living in a multireligious context, and they will need to negotiate public morals and ethics. We make decisions for the welfare of society, as well as for the peace and justice of the public realm, *with* people of other faiths. How do our neighbors think about abortion, about war, about technology, about justice? This is often the strongest area for interreligious relationship, because Muslim and Christian mothers both want their young

55. Contra John Hick, who, speaking about the afterlife, said: "Whether it involves continued separate individuality we do not know and we ought not to care. Sufficient that, whatever its nature, our destiny will be determined by the goodness of God." He then quotes from John Robinson's book *But That I Can't Believe!*: "Death may be the end. So what? . . . Nothing turns on what happens after death." From John Hick, *God and the Universe of Faiths* (Oxford: One World Publications, 1993), 186. See chap. 10 for a larger discussion of salvation and religious pluralism.

children to avoid drugs, violence, and premarital sex. Buddhist and Christian men are concerned about job security and medical bills. As we discuss these moral and ethical issues, we get back to the cause of beliefs and values, and when this happens we are getting closer to the Kingdom of God. Where there will be tension is when we talk about the degree of tolerance and pluralism that we will support. Do we wish to build a pluralistic, just, and harmonious society together? What about the *dhimmi* (non-Muslim protected community) and the *ummah* (Muslim community)? How can Christians live peaceably and faithfully when restrictions are put on practices that flow out of beliefs? This is one of the major issues today for Christian mission in Islamic contexts: is it possible to build a just society together? There have been historic instances where Christians have lived in more-just Islamic realms, and there have been times when Christians lived in Muslim realms that have been deathly oppressive.

Evil

The topic of evil must come up at some point, and if it doesn't we need only read the front page of the morning paper. For some religious people, evil is not really so bad, it is simply not being quite good enough, sort of like not finishing your homework. For others, evil has personality and is constantly plotting to bring the downfall of people and nations. Along with this discussion will come the discussion of pain and suffering. Quite often interreligious discussions or relationships begin in pain: the death of a family member, a family tragedy, or a diagnosis of cancer. This is the time to listen carefully to how the person understands suffering, death, and the presence of evil. The first funeral I did was that of a young woman who committed suicide. She was the only Christian in a Buddhist family, and she killed herself over a broken heart. Not only was the family Buddhist, but they did not speak English, and I did not speak Mandarin. They had all types of questions—as did I. "Lord, why does my first funeral have to be a young woman, a suicide, and the only Christian in a Buddhist family?" Church members brought food to the family every night for two or three months. They stayed around the home, talking, praying, and listening. In the midst of all the discussions about evil and suffering, the family finally found comfort in Jesus Christ. The parents, siblings, and newborn nephew were all baptized the next year. This is not to say that all tragedies lead to God, but it does demonstrate that tragedies strip away our insulating comfort and expose us directly to the big problems in life. When this happens, people are often looking for a good shepherd.

Jesus

Jesus will eventually come up in a dialogue with people of other faiths. Most people are more interested in Jesus than they are in his followers, and that is a good thing. Christians who are struggling to be faithful to Jesus

Christ will often do things that cause cognitive dissonance: "You took your vacation at a refugee camp in Iraq?" "You teach illegal immigrants to speak English every Friday night?" As a history professor in Shanghai, China, once said to his students, who were studying the history of missions in China, "If you want to understand why these Christian missionaries came all the way to China and worked so hard to set up schools and hospitals, you have to study about Jesus. They are trying to follow Jesus." So, when the time comes, it is important to be able to explain about Jesus—not as a doctrine, but as a person. "Read the Gospel of Mark, and tell me what you think." Some religions have already pegged Jesus as a prophet (but the information about him in the Bible is not accurate), or as an avatar (a really good one, but one of many). They may disagree with your estimate of Jesus, but at some point in the dialogue you need to allow Jesus to speak.

Truth Claims

As a final issue, and as a type of catchall category, we relate to other religions on the basis of their truth claims. Truth claims include what we say as well as how we judge truth from error. "Why do you say that?" will be asked time and again as we seek to understand truth claims from others. Some truth claims will never be harmonized; for example, either humans are creatures (created by God), or humans are part of God (Brahma). There is a world of difference between these two claims, and the closest we can get to harmonizing them is probably to talk about the *imago Dei* that is in each person. Other truth claims, once they are voiced, will draw us close together because all truth is God's truth. Thus we can expect to find much that is true in the Buddhist, or Shintoist, or even the Daoist. This is why we are discussing religions under the Holy Spirit. The same Spirit who placed the moral concern of honoring parents in the Confucianist's mind caused me to write the Ten Commandments on a piece of cardboard for my children many years ago. And so we read together: "Honor your father and your mother so that your days may be long . . ."

Theologies of Religion

This is not the place to review the theology of religions, but it is necessary to be able to think about religions theologically, and I still think the paradigm developed by David Bosch in the 1970s is the most helpful and one that best explains all the evidence.[56] Before giving his Christian theology of religions,

56. *Theology of Religions* (Pretoria: University of South Africa, 1977). This volume was designed as a study guide for the Department of Missiology and Science of Religion at the University of South Africa.

Bosch outlined the following earlier paradigms that have been present in the twentieth century:

1. Relativism: All religions are paths to the one truth. This is represented by Ernst Troeltsch, William Hocking, Paul Tillich, and William Cantwell Smith.
2. "Not to destroy but to fulfill": This is represented by Georges Khodr, Kaj Baago, and J. N. Farquhar.
3. Revelation and religion in antithesis: This is represented by Karl Barth.
4. Abiding paradox: Christian faith and other religions. This is represented by Emil Brunner and Hendrik Kraemer.

Bosch then talks about the two lines of thought in the Bible that lead to opposite conclusions if they are not braided together. First is the universal line that points to God as Lord of all the nations and peoples. God's inclusion of other nations reveals his intent to include them in the future. The other line is exclusive, and this also is found throughout the Bible: "There is no other name under heaven given to mankind by which we must be saved" (Acts 4:12). After discussing biblical passages related to the exclusive and inclusive view of people of other religions, Bosch gives his "Tripolar Christian Theology of Religions."

Most people doing theology of religions are working with two poles (good or evil; or religious consciousness of a person and a real revelation from God), or they are working with one pole ("religion emerges from within man himself"). Following Peter Beyerhaus, Bosch outlines the three poles involved in a Christian theology of religions in the following manner:

1. A person's *religious awareness* of, and concern for, God
2. God's involvement with humanity, through *revelation*
3. The sphere of *demonic* influence

A Christian theology of religion must take into account these three variables. Thus, we can understand any religion as these three working together in the mind of the individual and in the collective spirit of the culture or nation.

We can use this tripolar framework to understand Christianity as a religion. There are times that Christians are aware of God's revelation, and they receive it and follow it. At other times, they receive God's revelation, but they are also listening to the evil one, turning grace into law and freedom into servitude. Christians, under a demonic influence, kill other Christians over the formulation of the Eucharist, and they have also tortured other Christians for false claims about being a witch. How do we make sense of the dark deeds that Christians have done without seeing something of the demonic at play? By the same token, we can make sense of other religions as also having an awareness of God's revelation, but as also listening at times to another voice that pulls them away from God. We have to be humble and cautious in thinking this way, for many people have caused great damage pointing the finger at a person or religion and calling it evil. That is not how this model is to be used. We use this model to make sense of the good that is in other religious people and the evil that we might find in the church, and vice versa. When Don Richardson discovered that the Dani of Papua had developed a central cultural value of treachery, he thought there was no way they could understand about Jesus: Judas was the real hero to the Dani. But, when he tried to end intertribal warfare, he learned about the culturally developed method of peace whereby the chief of one of the tribes gives his own child to the chief of the warring tribe. The child is raised, and lives his whole life, with the other tribe. As long as the child is alive, there is peace between the tribes. This "peace child" is just as important to the Dani as the value of treachery. In a sense, all religions have some treachery and some peace child. In interreligious dialogue, we hope to come to the point of being able to name the peace child—and then introduce him to the other.

The Holy Spirit and Religions: A Postscript

The great Indian evangelist and wandering monk Sadhu Sundar Singh wrote a book with a memorable title: *With and Without Christ: Being Incidents Taken from the Lives of Christians and of Non-Christians which Illustrate the Difference in Lives Lived with Christ and Without Christ.*[57] It is a fascinating little study on the difference Jesus makes in people's lives, whether they are called Christian or not. It is also interesting to find that those Christians who do not have Christ (we all have met them) are no different than the Hindu lying on a bed of nails to purify his thoughts and remove his sins. Following Jesus's lead, Sundar Singh explains that the poor and inadequate are more drawn to Jesus and follow Jesus more often than the rich and powerful.

> As the magnet draws steel, not gold or silver, so the cross of Christ, draws sinners who truly repent and turn in their need to Him, but not those who trust in their own goodness and are satisfied to live without him.[58]

As early as the 1920s, Sundar Singh was aware of many Indians and Nepalese who were following Christ, but who were not identified as Christians. Today, we talk about unbaptized believers, secret believers, and even Muslim followers of Isa. Religious titles are less the issue than being marked with the

57. Sadhu Sundar Singh, *With and Without Christ* (New York: Harper & Brothers, 1929).
58. Ibid., 75.

cross (as our Indian woman was as a child). Those who have the Spirit, whose image of God is being refashioned or polished, will reflect Christ to others in all that they are. If they do not, if they resist that work of the Spirit, they are in fact "Christians without Christ."

What we have looked at above is, I believe, an approach to understanding the Holy Spirit missiologically. The missionary encounter through the Holy Spirit is not easily described and certainly not easily controlled. What I have presented here is an approach to the Holy Spirit in mission that opens doors to ecumenical sharing in mission, while at the same time pointing to issues that speak to us all. How did we get to the place where we are today? Most missionaries of the nineteenth and early twentieth centuries who traveled to Asia or Africa did not expect their mission work would involve healing the sick, raising the dead, or casting out demons. They were cessationists: the miraculous gifts and work of the Holy Spirit had ended—they thought. However, even before the rise of Pentecostalism in the West, missionaries in Asia and Africa began to encounter apostolic-like ministry in the lives of their new converts. Young Korean converts did not have a Calvinist theology of cessationism, and so their ministry was built upon biblical and cultural expectations. "When Korean evangelists began to heal the sick through prayer and exorcism, the missionary response was mixed and ambivalent." The Koreans had the Bible and their cultural context, and so they prayed for healing and they cast out demons. Shamans had such power, so it was expected that any priest of the high God would have power to heal.[59]

Western missiology has tended to talk about the Holy Spirit either in abstract theological terms or as the absolute actor in mission. The first would include the conciliar Protestants, most Roman Catholics, and even evangelicals who, in the past half century, have had a rich discussion of trinitarian mission.[60] The second would include the Pentecostals, African and Asian indigenous churches, and (more recently) the charismatic churches. Mainstream missiology discusses the work of the Holy Spirit in general terms, as the work of God in salvation, humanization, or liberation.[61] Spirit churches speak specifically about the Holy Spirit both as enabling the work of God in conversion and sanctification, and as the One who gives gifts for empowering mission. Spiritual churches expect the mission history described in Acts to continue—and

59. Sean C. Kim, "Reenchanted: Divine Healing in Korean Protestantism," in *Global Pentecostal and Charismatic Healing*, ed. Candy Gunther Brown (Oxford: Oxford University Press, 2011), 268–69.

60. For a brief overview of this, see Stephen Bevans and Roger Schroeder, *Constants in Contexts: A Theology of Mission for Today* (Maryknoll, NY: Orbis Books, 2004), chap. 9, "Mission as Participation in the Mission of the Triune God (*Missio Dei*)," 286–304.

61. Major books on missiology, such as David Bosch (*Transforming Mission* [Maryknoll, NY: Orbis Books, 1991]), and the companion primary source reader edited by Norman Thomas (*Classic Texts in Mission and World Christianity* [Maryknoll, NY: Orbis Books, 1995]) do not even list the Holy Spirit in the index.

therefore major breakthroughs in mission are expected through dreams, healings, visions, or casting out demons (power encounters). The recovery of this larger place for the Holy Spirit in mission is a gift from the non-Western churches as much as from the global Pentecostal movement. Cultures that have not been "disenchanted" by Western secularization experience and expect God to work within the integrity of their own cultures. Most indigenous cultures are peopled with spirits, and the Holy Spirit enters as the Lord over the spirits. The Holy Spirit is the missionary, in the pattern of Jesus Christ, binding up the brokenhearted, but also casting out demons and healing the sick. The same Holy Spirit who spoke to Zechariah in the temple may speak to priests and shamans, and *marabou*.

In this magnificent calling, the missionary must not assume *how* the Spirit of God will work. The missionary should be ready to be surprised but should also be alert, attentive, and prepared. Preparation involves the study of cultures (including languages) and religions, but preparation also means time to pray, wait, listen, and be still. The encounter with the Holy Spirit, which at times involves the encounter with other spirits, is more than a human can endure. Our life is in Christ, and so our strength in mission is not our own. Empowerment in mission, more than from any other source, comes from humility—even from emptiness. The ancients had it right, spending so much time talking about the supreme need for humility—for many it is the supreme virtue (Phil. 2). I end this chapter talking about humility because I am a historian. I have seen the great pride, confidence, and racism that have marked so much Christian mission in the past. In all of these cases, Jesus Christ is misrepresented. The Holy Spirit, however, is welcomed in the house that is swept clean, and cleaning involves repentance and confession.

> As wax cannot take the imprint of a seal unless it is warmed or softened thoroughly, so a man cannot receive the seal of God's holiness unless he is tested by labors and weaknesses. That is why the Lord says to St. Paul: "My grace is sufficient for you: for My power comes to its fullness in your weakness."[62]

62. St. Diadochos of Photike, "On Spiritual Knowledge," 94. Quoted from *The Philokalia* 1:291.

PART 3

The Suffering and Glory of the Church

The Church in Mission Today

I have presented the following scenario many times while teaching missiology and, for the most part, every student knows exactly what I am talking about—and most of them begin to cheer for church A or church B before I finish the descriptions.

> In a medium-sized city in North America there are two churches, both of which are very committed to Christian mission. Church A is located on the rim of the city with an easy commute to the city center. This church is fairly wealthy, and they have a tradition of using much of their money to reach out to high school students who are not Christian, and to international students who attend the local college. In fact, a number of families have taken in foreign students, letting them live in their homes, providing food, and taking the students with them to worship services. A number of foreign students and high school students have become Christian over the years through this hospitality. The church also has sent out two couples who are working among unreached people groups in the Middle East and in East Asia. They have a long-standing tradition of having an annual mission conference, with mission speakers and a special mission program for the youth. Church A is very mission minded.

> Church B is also very mission minded. In the 1960s, when many urban churches were closing or moving to the suburbs, Church B stayed in the city and has continued to have a relevant and faithful witness to the urban poor. They sponsor their own soup kitchen, staffed with a full-time director and a host of volunteers. They have also organized suburban churches to donate furniture and clothing to families whom they are helping to get off the streets and into their own housing. Two nights of the week, the church is a hub of activity; one night for AA meetings and the other for NA meetings. As they work on next year's budget, Church B plans to set up a free medical clinic in what was formally the church's education building. The second floor of the building they hope to renovate for literacy and basic computer classes for people in the community.

If you have been following the argument of this book carefully, a number of issues are now clamoring for your attention. I have described two composite churches I have known, which are serving in the same city. They are less than five miles apart, but, in terms of mission involvement, they have almost no common ground. Another story will illustrate how dichotomous mission can become even within the same denomination and in the same city.

I was invited to be on a presbytery committee to help the presbytery decide how a surplus of mission money should be spent. The chair of the committee began with this loaded sentence (a year later he regretted saying it): "Well, I think we all know what mission is, so what are some options as to how we can spend this money?" I was the lone one who made life difficult for the committee. I simply said, "Actually, I don't think we know at all what mission is. I think it is likely we have very little agreement about mission. It might be good to start by talking about how we define it." A year later, we had completed our discussion and were finally prepared to talk about how to spend the money. About two-thirds of the people on the committee assumed mission was caring for the poor in your neighborhood. About one-third assumed mission was sending people out as missionaries, or supporting mission trips, or partnering with church leaders overseas. Not only were we divided in our understanding of what to do, we also had huge gaps in our understanding of the *missio Dei*. What a church believes about God and the mission of the Triune God will eventually alter the church's budget and their calendar. Programs, relationships, property, and worship should all be shaped by our understanding of the *missio Dei*.

As we move to the practice of mission, I am aware that most people reading this book are not preparing to be missionaries, so the discussion will be wide-ranging enough to include cross-cultural missionaries and also local church members. Therefore, the focus of this final section, part 3, is on the missional DNA of the church. Another way of looking at this is to say that we are moving from a trinitarian theology of mission to ecclesiology: the study of the nature and life of the church. We will be asking the following questions: "What does *a* church, as well as *the* church, look like when it is faithful to mission, living into the suffering and glory of God in the world today?" "What does it mean to live God's mission faithfully in the twenty-first century?" "If one is preparing to be an overseas missionary, what type of church is the missionary planting or supporting in a different cultural context?" "How does the church leader, at 'home' or on overseas mission, understand the nature of the church, the goal of its mission, and the nature of the task?" In short, "How does the church participate in the answer to the Lord's Prayer: 'Thy Kingdom come on earth as it is in heaven'?"

However, before we rush into answering these questions, we have a problem that must be faced head-on: after centuries of modern mission and after a century of theological discussions about the place of Christian mission in the church, missiology is still more of an annex to the church rather than its central purpose. Mission is still viewed as a function or an activity of local churches rather than as the purpose of the church. In contrast, our discussion about God the Father who sent his Son to redeem the nations makes it clear that mission is part of God's very life. And the Trinity and his mission are prior to the church. Or, as it has been often quoted: "The church does not have a mission—God's mission has a church."[1] This makes sense to most modern missiologists, but most Christians are not missiologists. Therefore, before moving forward, I want to make sure that we are clear about the nature of the church as called into existence by God for the purpose of fulfilling his mission. The problem is not an imaginary one; it has been recognized by many Christian scholars.

In 1959, at the height of WCC and IMC discussions about the missionary nature of the church, Stephen Neill, Anglican historian, bishop, and missionary, said "that ecclesiologies have all 'been constructed in light of a static concept of the Church as something given, something which already exists. . . . As far as I know, no one has yet set to work to think out the theology of the Church in terms of the one thing for which it exists,' i.e., mission."[2] What is amazing about this statement is that the ecumenical church had been talking about the missionary work of the church since 1910, and over fifty years later this statement was still fairly accurate. As a systematic theologian recently confided to me, "I am a systematic theologian, but I focus on the *missio Dei*. Therefore, I have had no seminaries interested in my teaching systematic theology. I am perceived as a missiologist, not as a theologian."

While Neill was making his observation, ecumenical theologians were in fact developing an ecclesiology that took seriously the nature of the church from its origins. Just two years later, in 1961, R. Pierce Beaver expressed what a minority of theologians were concluding about the church and its mission:

1. This has become a popular saying with many variations on the second phrase: it is mission; mission has a church; the church is mission.

2. Quoted from John G. Flett, *The Witness of God: The Trinity,* Missio Dei, *Karl Barth, and the Nature of Christian Community* (Grand Rapids: Eerdmans, 2010), 62.

> The apostolate or mission of the Church has its roots in the creative, the revelatory—illuminating the redemptive-revelatory work of God. . . . And as God sent His Son, so the Son has sent his body, the Church, empowered by the Holy Spirit, to preach the Gospel of reconciliation to the whole world. The Church exists primarily to witness to this good news, and every other function of the Church is subsidiary and contributory to this purpose.[3]

At the very same time (1961), Johannes Blauw in his critical survey of the biblical theology of mission, *The Missionary Nature of the Church*, reflected some of the same conclusions about the nature of the church:

> So far as theology is concerned, missions have often been regarded as a by-product. And when attempts have been made to treat them as a theological problem, the reaction from the theological and church side has not been satisfactory. At this point a great change has come about in the last few decades. The result of the theology of the Old and New Testament points more and more in the direction of the universal and missionary character of the Church; and systematic theology is keeping up its end.[4]

However hopeful Blauw was about the biblical theology movement as a bridge to mission and systematic theology, I think it is fair to say that his optimism overstepped reality. In fact, systematic theology does not today point to the missionary nature of the church, and ecclesiology continues to eschew the missiological nature of the church's calling and identity. What we have summarized in the past three chapters will not be found in most books on systematic theology or ecclesiology.

In our history section, we traced how missiologists and ecumenists developed a theology of the church that came out of the church's origins and that expressed its purpose in mission, but this theology has still not become the dominant way of understanding the church. The church is still largely defined as a "given" institution with its primary identifying marks (for Protestants) coming from the sixteenth- and seventeenth-century reformations. These marks are the pure preaching of the Word and lawful administration of the sacraments (and later was added the exercise of discipline in matters of doctrine and holiness of life). These identifying marks of the church came out of a context where there was little to no missionary activity in the church at all: Reformation Europe. In an effort to unite a dividing church during the Reformation period, the Diet at Augsburg was called for by the emperor and,

3. "The Apostolate of the Church," in Gerald Anderson, ed., *The Theology of the Christian Mission* (New York: McGraw-Hill, 1961), 258–68. This was said, even though in 1950 Hoekendijk had defined the church as "the function of the Apostolate, and instrument of God's redemptive action in this world" (see chap. 5).

4. Johannes Blauw, *The Missionary Nature of the Church: A Survey of Biblical Theology of Mission* (New York: McGraw-Hill, 1962), 10.

attended mostly by Germans, the Lutheran party was asked to make their confession. In the confession, the first two marks of the church are given in Article Seven. In 1540 Calvin signed a revised edition of the Confession, giving broad Protestant support for this definition of the church.[5] For Calvin,

> the object of his interest is Christianity as it then existed—the perspective of "mission to the ends of the earth" did not present itself to him. . . . Calvin was thus of the opinion that the "wonderful fullness of the gifts of the Spirit" was only imparted to the church in the earliest times to "adorn" the beginning of Christ's kingdom, to command respect for the gospel at its start and to announce that this was the time of divine visitation prophesied by Joel.[6]

Mission was not a part of the essence of the church and, to make matters worse, the power of mission (the Holy Spirit and his gifts) was also fenced out theologically. Most Protestants and Roman Catholics through the middle of the twentieth century would concur.

We must be clear that this minimalist definition of the church, given as the two primary marks of Word and sacrament, is an ad hoc definition: it comes out of a Christendom context in which everyone was understood to be some type of Christian, and the non-Christians were the "Turks at the gate."[7] The church, for Protestants, was defined as a given institution trying to maintain unity through worship (namely, preaching and sacraments). Roman Catholics actually defined the church in a similar manner, with much more emphasis given to order through the tradition of the church and ultimately residing in the Curia. Mission was present for Roman Catholics, but it was mostly an activity of religious orders. Therefore, the understanding of the church was also more institutional than missional, more static than dynamic. Most ecclesiologies up to the present time are built upon these foundations.[8] This explains the fix we are in regarding ecclesiology.

5. Calvin's theology had a great influence upon Anglican theology, Reformed churches throughout Europe, and even many Baptists. This helped to make what started out as a Lutheran definition of "church" become an ecumenical Protestant understanding. See also Alister E. McGrath, *Christian Theology: An Introduction*, 3rd ed. (Oxford: Blackwell, 2001), 482.

6. Lukas Vischer, *Pia Conspiratio: Calvin's Commitment to the Unity of the Church* (Louisville: PCUSA, Office of Theology, Worship and Education, 2007), 54.

7. The second purpose of the Augsburg Diet was to plan war against the invading Turks.

8. For example, Edward Schillebeeckx, in *Church: The Human Story of God* (New York: Crossroad, 1990), talks obliquely about mission in his section on the church in the power of the Holy Spirit and as the community of God (144–86), where he concludes with orthodoxy being proven by an orthopraxis that is seen in forms of liberation. A much more conservative and more systematic approach is that of Millard J. Erickson, who is concerned that too much "attention is given to the mission of the church than to its identity and limits or boundaries" (*Christian Theology*, 1028). Then after a long discussion of the need to have a philosophical understanding of "church," he presents a biblical study of terms for church (1030–41; not unlike Schillebeeckx, *Church*, 146–54), and then he talks about the functions of the church in chap. 50 (1051–68). In

There are hopeful signs, however, and they are found in many places. First, the global church is a missionary church, and these discussions about the definition of the church and its purpose will eventually resolve themselves as the practice of the church, and then will become expressed in ideas about the church. It is unlikely that a church living by the mission of God would define "church" as anything but the missionary body of Christ. Second, the documents of the Second Vatican Council, especially the "Dogmatic Constitution on the Church" (*Lumen Gentium*) are becoming the common way of speaking about the church. This influence is broadly ecumenical. Third, movements like the "Gospel in Our Context," the missional church movement, and the emerging church movement (among others) are all built upon an understanding that the church is missionary by its very nature. The arrival of the adjectival form of mission—missional—in 1998[9] is a sign both that mission has become part of the essence of the church and that it might actually be possible to talk about a church that is not missional: that is, if we have to specify a church as missional, it is possible to have one that is not. I prefer to see it as a positive development, giving us a vocabulary for how we understand our local church and lifting up the key element that has been missing. We should note that most of these movements have been influenced by ecumenical theology, the theology of Vatican II, and the missionary expression of the non-Western church.

Finally, there has been a greater interest in recent years in returning to the four marks of the church enshrined in the Nicene Creed, rather than the two marks of the Reformation. In the third paragraph of the Nicene Creed, under the Holy Spirit, we read the following: "We believe in one, holy, catholic, and apostolic church." The discussion revolves around the last of these adjectives, apostolic. Apostolic has been interpreted three different ways. It means that we confess the church that is founded upon the teachings and work of the apostles of Jesus Christ; there is a line of continuity from the teaching of Peter, John, Paul, and so on, to the teaching of the church today. It also means, to the Roman Catholic Church, that we follow the apostolic office as providing the unity and authority today as in the age of the apostles. Finally, it means that we believe in a church that is "sent" just as the apostles were sent. The apostles were both those who passed on the Great Tradition, providing authority and order for the early movement, and the ones who were sent by

---

this section he does not list "mission," but instead he lists four functions: evangelism, edification, worship, and social concern. Alister E. McGrath, in his *Christian Theology*, gives a history of the doctrine of the church, he then discusses basic themes of the church, and finally he talks about the Nicene marks of the church. In this final discussion, he mentions briefly the apostolic nature as including proclaiming the good news, but even in discussing Vatican II and *Lumen Gentium*, he does not mention missionary or mission as part of the nature of the church (chap. 15, 476–507). McGrath does not have mission in his glossary either.

9. See Darrell Likens Guder, "From Mission and Theology to Missional Theology," in *Princeton Seminary Bulletin* 24, no. 1 (2003): 36–54.

Jesus and who established a cross-cultural church on three continents. It has been suggested that we might recover this missional meaning of the church by reciting this line of the creed backwards: We believe in the apostolic church, which is catholic, holy, and one.[10] It is unlikely the creed will be revised, but it is illuminating and, I think, accurate,[11] to put apostolic prior to catholic, holy, and one.

Before talking specifically about the church in mission, or the church as the body of the *missio Dei*, I would like to look at some of the contemporary theology that has rekindled this understanding. Karl Barth has been one of the strongest voices in developing a consistent understanding of the church's missionary vocation.[12] English readers of Barth do not realize the depth and careful attention to "mission" that Barth showed—in part because of translation. Where the English reader might look for "mission," Barth used *Sendung* (mission), but he also used *zeugen* (to witness) and other forms of the same word (*Zeugen*, *Bezeugen*, *Zeuge*, *and Zeugnis*). At times, clearly referring to the *missio Dei*, he spoke of *Aufgabe* (the task) and *Auftrag* (commission). For Barth, as Flett explains,

> The "task" is not a secondary step besides some other more elemental Christian being or form of piety. The community "commission" expresses the whole of Christian existence; it is the community's concrete visible form. If the community fails to perform this commission, then she fails to exist as a Christian community.[13]

Barth understood the church to be gathered together as a missionary community. For Barth, apostolicity was the primary test of the church, for the Christian who is in this church of Jesus Christ "has no option but to sprint into the breach between Jesus Christ, whom it is given her to know, and those to whom is not yet given to know Him." He further explains that not only in going, but also in its holy existence, the church will be, "showing them by her existence that what she expects is really before them too."[14] Thus, the church *only* exists as it is a herald.

Another theologian who was heavily involved in ecumenical theological discussions, and who therefore understands the missionary nature of the church, is Jürgen Moltmann. In his volume *The Church in the Power of the Spirit*[15]

10. This was the challenge that was given by George Hunsberger to Darrell L. Guder as he was editing the important book *Missional Church: A Vision for the Sending of the Church in North America* (Grand Rapids: Eerdmans, 1998).

11. It is accurate both theologically and historically (the church was first sent before it had the later concerns about unity), because mission is the theological foundation for the church.

12. See John Flett's *The Witness of God: The Trinity,* Missio Dei, *Karl Barth, and the Nature of Christian Community* (Grand Rapids: Eerdmans, 2010).

13. Ibid., x.

14. Ibid., 263, quoting Barth, *Church Dogmatics* IV/3.2, 933.

15. Jürgen Moltmann, *The Church in the Power of the Spirit* (Minneapolis: Fortress, 1993). The volume was dedicated to the World Council of Churches.

The Church Exists Only as Herald: Karl Barth

John Flett summarizes how Barth understood the relationship between the church's existence and its proclamation to the world: "The apostolic community 'can never in any respect be an end in herself but, following the existence of the apostles, she exists only as she exercises the ministry of a herald.' And so the community 'does not exist *before* her commission and later acquire it. Nor does she exist *apart* from it, so there can be no question whether or not she might have to execute it. . . .' Her essential direction is 'outwards to mission, to the world, because she is not merely based upon the apostolate but is identical with it.'"[a]

a. Flett, *Witness of God*, 265, quoting Barth, *Church Dogmatics* IV/1, 724; IV/3.2, 779; and II/2, 430.

Moltmann recognizes that one of the major rediscoveries in theology has been the recognition of the missionary and ecumenical nature of the church.[16] As we have noted earlier, ecclesiology that came out of the Reformation was contextual, but this is no longer our context. The Protestant Reformers' context was Christendom Europe, dominated by a Roman Catholic Church they sought to reform. They were focused on remaking the church as a place for proper preaching and celebration of the sacraments, not (like Paul) the movement to reach the nations. Consequently, any remnant of missionary obligation was lost, overshadowed by theological repositioning. In short, the church was defined as an institution among Christians, not as a movement for non-Christians. Ecclesiology was an in-house discussion. Moltmann not only begins his volume discussing the missionary and ecumenical nature of the church, he also ends the volume talking about four marks of the church, with an extended discussion of its apostolic or missionary calling. In this final section, titled "The Apostolate in Suffering," Moltmann says both that the church in Christ is only catholic and holy "through the apostolic witness," and that "apostolicity is the church's special historical designation."[17] It bears repeating that Moltmann identifies the church's missional reality in suffering. "Participation in the apostolic mission of Christ therefore leads inescapably into *tribulation, contradiction and suffering*. The apostolate is carried out in the weakness and poverty of Christ, not through force or the strategies of force."[18]

Lesslie Newbigin would affirm this, and he extends the meaning of the apostolic witness in the following way:

16. Ibid., 7–15.

17. Ibid., 357.

18. Ibid., 361. There are many other theologians who are now working with these categories, but this sample should help. Before becoming pope, and in the aftermath of the Second Vatican Council, Benedict XVI described the church in similar language: the future Pope John Paul II, Cardinal Karol Wojtyla of Cracow, wrote in 1972 that in the shadow of Vatican II we must emphasize "that the Church is by its nature a Missionary body and the People of God is *in statu missionis*." From *Sources of Renewal* (New York: Harper & Row, 1980), 398.

> The local church is a signpost, a foretaste, and an instrument of the Kingdom of God.[19]

The church extends the ministry of Jesus Christ and, by the power of the Holy Spirit and in continuity with the apostles, is the instrument ushering in the Kingdom. I will keep this understanding of the church in the following chapters.

In different language, but with similar concerns, Jesuit Daniel Izuzquiza of Spain describes the church's presence and life in the following way:

> Regarding the identity of the church . . . it is necessary, first, to create and to strengthen a real community in which alternative relationships take place; it is necessary to nurture the social embodiment of Christian practices. It is important to provide a communal experience in which everyone is welcomed and no one is excluded. Finally it is indispensable to build up a community in which God's presence shines.[20]

Here we can see that the church, through its radical acceptance of others and its "alternative relationships" is a signpost pointing to the Kingdom and, for those who participate, it is a foretaste of the Kingdom. As the church becomes the social embodiment of Christian practices, it is functioning as an instrument of the Kingdom of God. There are many ways of expressing this threefold nature of the church, but signpost, foretaste, and instrument is both elucidating and memorable.

We have looked briefly at the disconnect between the church as described by systematic theologians and the church as understood by those who are involved in mission (the World Council of Churches, Second Vatican Council, etc.). This is one of the greatest tragedies of twentieth- and twenty-first-century theological education. The long shadow of Christendom has blocked the original and ongoing purpose of the church to be a witnessing and worshiping presence as the body of Christ on earth. Until the breech can be bridged, until the church can again be seen as primarily for others, there will be little change in Christian understanding of the church in the theological enterprise.

In the following chapters, we will build upon this understanding of the church and describe its meaning and work as a worshiping and sending community (chap. 9), as a community which bears witness to Christ (chap. 10), as a community of the city (chap. 11), and then as a global community in partnership (chap. 12).

19. Newbigin mentions this in a number of places. See "The Church: A Bunch of Escaped Convicts," in *Reform*, no. 6 (June 1990): 6.

20. Daniel Izuzquiza, *Rooted in Jesus Christ: Toward a Radical Ecclesiology* (Grand Rapids: Eerdmans, 2009), 40.

9

Church

The Community of Worship and Witness

The church, the body of Christ, has two basic purposes for its existence: worship and witness.[1] All other functions point to and should aid in fulfilling these two purposes. A church that is not worshiping or is not working at worshiping with greater humility and joy has lost the empowering purpose of its existence. Worship increases our power, for in worship we rightly place ourselves before God, and so we empty ourselves more and more in unbroken praise. Empowerment is not the purpose but the by-product of praise. We become who we are meant to be, and who we are meant to be is a glorious community of glorious individuals reflecting the image of God to the world.

As a healthy organism breathes in and breathes out, so the church goes out in mission and returns to receive needed oxygen in community worship. We can look at these two primary meanings and functions of the church as the temporal and the eternal: mission is temporary (until the eschaton), and worship is eternal. However, we can also look at mission as something that will simply be of a different order in the eschaton: then witness will be given as "declaring his glory among the nations," with the nations now fully represented (e.g., Ps. 96 and Rev. 7). As the church goes out in mission, the church

1. I will use the words "witness" and "mission" here interchangeably. Jesus's command that initiated the church used both words: Matthew 28:19, "Go" (*poreuthentes*); Acts 1:8, "you will be my witnesses" (*mou martyres*). The title "witness" encompasses all that the church is to be in its sentness, as it gives testimony to what God has done.

is the presence of Jesus Christ among the nations: loving, healing, including, proclaiming, and reconciling.

Of course it is always possible, and it is generally humanly likely, that these two elements will be out of kilter, or misplaced. It is all too easy to reduce everything to mission and to neglect purposeful and Christ-honoring worship. It is also quite likely that any local church will become preoccupied with its own community and worship, neglecting the "weightier matters" of witness and justice. God has designed the body of Christ to find health, and individual members of that body to find their meaning, in devotion to Christ and in discipleship of the nations. The weekly rhythm that God the creator placed in creation itself mandates rest and devotion to God, as well as work (as we serve as "underlords" for God). Witness without worship is a vain human invention. Worship without witness is deception, as if we are truly honoring God while we disobey his clearest and last command.

In the Orthodox Church, where worship is central to the meaning of the church's identity, there is also the understanding that worship is not an end in itself. Alexander Schmemann, in his *Introduction to Liturgical Theology*,[2] writes about the tendency for worship to become the sole purpose of the Christian community.

> No matter how paradoxical it may sound, what obscures the meaning of worship is that it has become for the faithful an object of love, indeed almost the sole content of Church life. . . . That is that worship has ceased to be understood as a function of the Church. On the contrary, the Church herself has come to be understood as a function of worship. . . . Having ceased to be the expression of the church, worship has also ceased to be the expression of the Church in relation to the world. It is no longer seen as the leaven which raises the loaf, as the love of God directed toward the world, as a witness to the Kingdom of God, as the good news of salvation as new life. On the contrary, worship is experienced as a departure out of the world for a little while, as a "vent" or a break in earthly existence, opened for the inlet of grace.

He goes on to say that the original success of Christianity was related to the fact that "Christianity was preached as a saving faith, and not as a saving cult." His distinction here is that Christianity, or more exactly the church, is centered on and comes into being in the *kerygma*, or the preaching of the Messiah to the nations. When this happens, the Christian church comes into being. The church "is not an end, but a means" to bring about the Kingdom. There are no sharp distinctions between worship and mission, or the cultic practice within the four walls of the church and the missional outreach beyond those walls.[3]

2. Alexander Schmemann, *Introduction to Liturgical Theology* (London: Faith Publishing, 1966), 83.

3. The quotation above was brought to my attention by Timothy J. Becker.

Romanian Orthodox theologian Ion Bria comes at the understanding of the church not through *kerygma* but through *leitourgia* (liturgy, or work of the people).[4] Here is another Orthodox approach that links this missional expression of the church with the heart of worship. In this case, Bria deepens and broadens the understanding of liturgy, explaining that it continues after the worship liturgy.

> Each of the faithful is called upon to continue a personal "liturgy" on the secret altar of his own heart, to realize a living proclamation of the good news "for the sake of the whole world." Without this continuation the liturgy remains incomplete. . . . The sacrifice of the Eucharist must be extended in personal sacrifices for the people in need. . . . The continuation of the liturgy in life means a continuous liberation from the powers of evil that are working inside us.[5]

Bria's discussion is more far-ranging and nuanced than we can cover here. He discusses the Trinity (in community) as the foundation for this missional outreach; he mentions the centrality of *Basileia* (Kingdom) in Orthodox worship and how such preaching of the Kingdom of God is a challenge to unjust structures; he reminds us that the table of the Lord is a sign of the gathering of the nations; finally, through many other images, he points to the center of worship as the center of the Christian life—the rule of God in all of life.[6] The work of the people as liturgy flows out into the work of the people in the world, and the glory of this work returns to worship in praise and thanksgiving.

I find it helpful to employ the image of yin and yang to visualize this understanding of the church. Yin and yang is an ancient Chinese concept that understands the universe as harmony finding expression in the balance and interplay of yin (dark, passive, downward, cold, contracting, feminine, and weak) and yang (bright, active, upward, hot, expanding, masculine, and strong). The shape gives a sense of constant movement and of interplay. The two are not the same, but they work in harmony, and at times it is difficult to see where one begins and the other ends. In Chinese thought these two energies cause everything to happen.

The two foundational purposes of the church—worship and witness—work together like yin and yang. When one collapses into the other, the church does not exist as it was intended; it becomes something different. When they work

4. Ion Bria, *The Liturgy after the Liturgy: Mission and Witness from an Orthodox Perspective* (Geneva: WCC, 1996).

5. Bria, *Liturgy*, 20, quoting from Ion Bria, ed., *Martyria-Mission: The Witness of Orthodox Churches Today* (Geneva: WCC, 1980), 67.

6. Bria notes that this Orthodox understanding has come out of WCC discussions since the 1970s. See *Liturgy*, 19–22.

The yin-yang symbol is one of the most ancient Asian symbols showing the harmony of nature in opposing forces or energies.

in perfect harmony, the witness brings people to faith and brings them to worship the Triune God, and the worship moves people to confession, repentance, and then out to witness.

Additionally, the church is a divine and human community centered on unbroken praise and witness. If the church is the body of Christ, it is both human and divine. The church, however, is made up of the first Adam, and so its humanity is broken and its image-bearing is marred.[7] The church praises the creator and redeemer God and witnesses to his work on behalf of all creation. It has been said that the church is the only institution whose sole existence is for its nonmembers. That is true on two levels: the church exists to honor and praise God alone; and the church exists to proclaim and show the saving work of God to all who live, to every tongue, and tribe, and nation. The church is the body of Christ, pointing to the Father, and living sacrificially for the sake of the world—a world that is still in rebellion.

What does it mean that the church has a divine reality and a divine purpose? This means that the Spirit and the power of the living God reside in the church, not because the church is a human institution with worldly power and influence, but because the church is, in part, divine. As hard as this is to believe, as we slog through our worship services and argue over budgets and buildings, Jesus Christ has chosen to reside in the church. This does not mean Jesus Christ resides in the Methodist, Presbyterian, or Mennonite church. Jesus Christ resides in the body of Christ—in the local assembly of disciples, which is the expression of the church through the ages and throughout all the earth. If we want to know what Jesus Christ is doing in the world through the church, we need to look at the global and historical church: the worldwide church through the ages. It is in this sense—the church carrying out the mission of proclamation and praise in the world—that Jesus's remark should be understood: "Very truly I tell you, whoever believes in me will do the works I have been doing, and they will do even greater things than these, because I am going to the Father" (John 14:12). The church is more than an institution and more powerful than most of us could ever imagine. The Orthodox are very clear on the divine aspects of the church and the church's existence in Christ.

We can also describe the divine nature of the church as the preferred residence of the Holy Spirit. Earlier, we spoke of the Holy Spirit revealing

7. This image of the tarnished *imago Dei* that acts like a mirror comes from 2 Cor. 3:18, "And we, who with unveiled faces all reflect the Lord's glory, are being transformed into his likeness with ever-increasing glory, which comes from the Lord, who is the Spirit."

truth and pointing to the image of God in cultures and peoples. However, the primary place where the Spirit resides, and calls people to reside, is the church—the Kingdom in formation, the foretaste of the Kingdom. We know this is true because the gifts of the Holy Spirit are given to the church for ministry—for service (Eph. 4:11–14; 1 Cor. 14). These gifts reveal the divine nature of the church in specific powers of ministry: they reveal the church as a divine community.

But the church is also a human community, and as a human community its expression of the image of God is fallen. We can expect the church to do great things—but at the same time we should not be surprised if the church is a great embarrassment. As a sinful human community, the church often falls into the temptation of self-absorption or self-worship. We can and should expect this to be an ongoing battle. It is expressed in a number of ways, but almost every way that the church's sinful side compromises its divine mission is a matter of being subverted by power or by improper contextualization. Here are some of the major ways that the church's sinfulness compromises its divine mission:

- racism and prejudice
- unwillingness to change
- idolatry
- unwillingness to face sin
- affluence or avarice
- injustice

Many of these compromises are cultural traits in the West today, which should be critiqued by the church, in light of the gospel—instead they often pollute the gospel through the church. Any church that is unwilling to change to reach its own youth (not to mention the youth in its neighborhood) has become captive to culture—to an older culture. Any church that will not confront its own affluence—wealth that stops their ears from hearing the cries of the poor—is expressing its fallen humanity. Such churches need to be remade into the image of God. The human aspect of the church must be transformed to be a new humanity in Christ. Although the church is both human and divine, its

Orthodox View of the Church

Father John McGuckin explains how Orthodoxy understands the nature of the church. The church is understood "as a mystery of the 'life in Christ'; a society of believers, certainly, but more fundamentally, the extended power of Christ's saving work as manifested and concretized in the world, and in the next age. The Church, rooted as it is in this age, yet moving already out of it to its transcendent destiny with the glorified Christ, is at heart an eschatological mystery that cannot entirely be at home in the present world order, and cannot fully be glimpsed within."[a]

a. John McGuckin, *The Orthodox Church: An Introduction to Its History, Doctrine and Spiritual Culture* (Hoboken, NJ: Wiley-Blackwell, 2010), 238.

human elements must be transformed in the same way an individual is transformed: by confronting sin, along with the bondage and guilt that it brings, every time it tries to find a home in the church.[8] A church that does not face the need for ongoing conversion or transformation is no longer a signpost of the Kingdom. Some might say that such an institution no longer functions as a church of Jesus Christ.

Thus, the church is bipartite twice over: in worship and witness, and in humanity and divinity. But, of course, every local church is more than these two functions with a dual nature. On a weekly basis, a church will have catechism classes; a pastor will visit the sick, marry the engaged, and bury the dead; lay leaders will teach children, balance budgets, and give offerings to the poor and the homeless; and they might write checks to support missionaries. All of these activities are functions that should be seen in the light of the double-dual nature of the church, lest the church be falsely centered around programs or activities. In the rest of this chapter we will look at what it means for the church to be a community built around witness and worship.

Community

Celebrating seventeen hundred years of existence, the Armenian Catholicos of Cilicia, Aram K'eshishean, wrote the following concerning the nature of the church as a community:

> The church is a community of faith. Under no circumstances should we lose this very concept of the church. Being a community of faith, the church is also a common mission. Our Lord Jesus Christ did not establish an institution that came to be called "church." He gave a particular mission to his disciples: Go forth into all the world and preach the Gospel to every creature (Mark 10:15). In fact the *raison d'être* of our church, its true richness and real value is neither in its structure nor in its hierarchy, neither in its theology nor in its spirituality. Its true richness lies in its missionary engagement, evangelistic witness and diakonal action. We should remind ourselves that mission does not come from the church; the church acquires its real nature, unique identity and

8. Another way the church is a fallen community of Christ is in its mixture of the elect and the nonelect into a single community. Many of those who do not honor Christ will join and participate in the church, and some will eventually come to faith. However, the local church is not the Kingdom of God, and so there will be tares among the wheat ("For we acknowledge and confess, that darnel, cockle, and chaff may be sown, grow, and in great abundance lie in the midst of the wheat: that is, the reprobate may be joined in the society of the elect, and may externally use with them the benefits of the word and sacraments; but such being but temporal professors in mouth, but not in heart, do fall back and continue not to the end," Scots Confession, chap. 25). This makes both mission and community life in the church very difficult at times.

> true vocation from mission. Hence a church becomes church when it fulfills its missionary calling.[9]

In this statement, K'eshishean reminds us that the local church community is a witness as well as a place of worship. This is where Newbigin's designation of the church as signpost, foretaste, and instrument is helpful. How the church lives in community points to what the Kingdom is like. When people see how Christians treat others and how they love one another, the world learns about the Kingdom of God. Here is where we can readily see that worship and witness meld into one another. When a local group of believers are called into community, they begin to relate to one another as redeemed individuals, no longer in the insecurity of their sin, but as people who recognize their need for redemption. There is a wholeness and a stability that comes with forgiveness. These new relationships are a signpost of the Kingdom of God.

The church as community is formed in extreme loyalty and in humble submission. When Jesus called people to follow him, he expected them to drop everything—even to the point of denying family members—and enroll in a new family focused on his leadership and care. It was a pilgrim community in which all members were devoted to the leader and therefore everyone's needs were met. Since it was a traveling community, it was not possible to cling to possessions. Personal possessions prevented close community relationships and the ability to move. And so we can learn something about the church as community in the band of followers Jesus first called together.

The same was true in the community formed by the Holy Spirit after Jesus ascended to heaven (Acts 2). Thus the community Jesus called together and the growing community called together by Jesus's Spirit have similar characteristics. Here we see in Acts how this earliest community of Jesus's followers gathered and lived.

> Peter replied, "Repent and be baptized, every one of you, in the name of Jesus Christ for the forgiveness of your sins. And you will receive the gift of the Holy Spirit. The promise is for you and your children and for all who are far off—for all whom the Lord our God will call." With many other words he warned them; and he pleaded with them, "Save yourselves from this corrupt generation." Those who accepted his message were baptized, and about three thousand were added to their number that day. They devoted themselves to the apostles' teaching and to fellowship, to the breaking of bread and to prayer. Everyone was filled with awe at the many wonders and signs performed by the apostles. All the believers were together and had everything in common. They sold property and possessions to give to anyone who had need. Every day they continued to meet together in the temple courts. They broke bread in their homes and ate together with glad and

9. Thanks to my pastor, Rev. Paul Roberts, for pointing this out to me. Aram K'eshishean, *The Armenian Church beyond the 1700th Anniversary* (Antilias, Lebanon: Armenian Catholicosate of Cilicia, 2001), 16.

> sincere hearts, praising God and enjoying the favor of all the people. And the Lord added to their number daily those who were being saved. (Acts 2:38–47)

Early believers are unified by the confession of Jesus Christ through repentance and the experience of forgiveness: this is the foundation of Christian community. This community does not just accept people and try to ignore sin. Christian community—the church—is a gathering of those who have repented and been forgiven; because of this, it is a community of humility. Christian community is not the cult of the accomplished but the church of the defeated.

Christian community is further united by baptism—the mark of death. Baptism holds multiple layers of symbolism, but the two most important symbolic images are the washing away of sins, and going down to die and then rising again. The old has not just been reformed or cleaned up a little, it has actually died; it has been buried, and a new life has begun.

Another element of this Christian community is that it is set apart from this "corrupt generation." As we will see later, this does not mean a complete separation from the world; it means that the community is to be counter-cultural. We read in Paul's letters, as well as in the epistles of Peter, that there were sinful behaviors that were constantly tugging the early Christian community back into old patterns of life. The community of the church was called to fight against these behaviors and remain different from the common culture. To function as a signpost of the Kingdom, the community life and lifestyle must be eschatological—pointing to the Kingdom of God.

This early Kingdom community was also a thoughtful community—listening to the apostles teach about Jesus Christ. Once a member was baptized, they "devoted themselves to the apostles' teaching" (Acts 2:42)—seemingly enrolling in a sort of community school that taught them how to grow into their new life. The community school involved teachings from those who walked with Jesus, and this teaching was done in the context of worship: "breaking of bread and prayer." Attentiveness to the teachings of the apostles is itself an act of worship. It was only natural that, in listening to the words of Jesus and about Jesus, the supreme work of Jesus on the cross would be honored in Eucharistic joy. In listening to the apostles, this early community couched learning in sacrament, and combined mental growth with spiritual devotion. We then see that this early community exhibited signs to the outsiders: "Everyone was filled with awe at the many wonders and signs performed by the apostles" (Acts 2:43). Later in Acts, we see what some of these "wonders and miraculous signs" were, but here it is enough to note that the community was both countercultural and empowered by the Holy Spirit. Witness occurred as an outpouring of the power of God to others. Worship and devotion to Christ spills out in powerful and observable manifestations.

Education about Jesus also led to a new way of thinking about personal identity and personal possessions. Their identity was in Jesus Christ and in attending to his will, not in the things (or even people) in which they previously found identity. Rather than thinking of items as "mine" they were thought of as being held in common (*koina* for common or community). This community's new identity in Christ was expressed in concrete ways—the community functioned as a healthy family: caring for and sharing with each other. Their communal identity led them to spend much time together in the temple (today the church building) and in homes (sharing meals). Remarkably, the dual gathering of Christian community (in large buildings and in homes) was evident in this very first community of believers in Jerusalem. It is no stretch of the exegetical mind to see that, from the beginning, communities centered in Christ had larger and smaller gatherings. The church, and maybe any local church, should see itself as breaking bread in homes and as gathering in a larger body. This earliest community resulted in a public witness seen in the good reputation they had among their neighbors, and this resulted in many more coming to faith and joining the community. Here is a way of summarizing characteristics of the earliest Christian communities:

1. Repentance and forgiveness
2. Centered in Jesus Christ
3. Resisting cultural sins
4. Baptism
5. Teachings about Jesus Christ in the context of worship
6. Corporate worship: Eucharistic celebration and prayer
7. Shared goods
8. Time together: ate meals in homes
9. Respected in their communities
10. More people coming to faith (evangelism)

If I was writing a book about the church, I might want to go into greater detail about this community. That is not my purpose here, but it is still necessary to note the close relationship between the community's core values and its witness. For example, teaching and worship easily move into sharing goods and eventually adding more people to the fellowship. Any local church is a dynamic, worshiping community living in common, with a common confession. The results flow out into the world both as a *model* for greater society, and as a *call* to confession: the foundation for community. What follows are five ways the church is both a model for greater society and a call to confession and repentance.

First, the church community, as a community of repentance and confession, breaks down barriers. We read in Ephesians 2:11–22 that the wall between Jews and Greeks has been torn down and the two are now one in Jesus Christ.

What we often forget is that this new unity between different ethnic peoples starts in Ephesians 2:1–8. We were all dead in our sins, and we were made alive by Christ through grace. Therefore, unity of different peoples begins with grace and the forgiveness of sins. What follows is a community of great diversity: "In Christ Jesus, you are all children of God through faith, for all of you who were baptized into Christ have clothed yourselves with Christ. There is neither Jew nor Gentile, neither slave nor free, nor is there male and female, for you are all one in Christ Jesus. If you belong to Christ, then you are Abraham's seed, and heirs according to the promise" (Gal. 3:26–29). The universal church, as well as each local church, is to live into this identity. In some cultures, where there are many languages in one diocese or town, it may be very hard to live into this type of unity. However, the concept and concern should always be before the local church. All prejudices and racism must be identified and then confessed. This is why the community must be built upon confession of sin and confession of Christ.

A quick story will illustrate this point. I was the pastor of a church in Singapore that was nearly all educated, English-speaking Chinese people. The language of worship and education was English, although many of the church members spoke Hokkien or Mandarin at home. Most of the members were first-generation Christians, having been raised in Buddhist, Confucianist, Daoist, or "free-thinker" homes. When looking for land for a church home, after years of not having our own worship space, this congregation was given the opportunity to buy a property in "Little India." There were two Hindu temples within a fifteen-minute walk of the property, and most of the people in the neighborhood were Indian, Sri Lankan, or Bangladeshi; many of them were migrant laborers. When talking about the property, one very wealthy church member was shocked that we would even consider buying a property in Little India. "Pastor, did you ever think of what it would be like for my young daughter to walk to the bus stop in *that* neighborhood at night? We are a Chinese church." Fortunately, the leadership of the church had greater theological and pastoral integrity than this one person—so they bought the property. The wealthy man took his family elsewhere, and eventually the church began a separate service for Sri Lankan, mostly Sinhalese, migrant workers. Over 130 were baptized in the first three years of their ministry. A local church must tear down walls that divide cultures, even while it affirms cultural integrity.

The only way forward in a world that is so divided and "tribal" is to freely confess prejudices and step into the new world of unity in Christ. Walls are torn down in a Christian community, and this is a sign to the surrounding society. Walls of race, language, economic status, and age (children learning from the elderly, and the elderly caring for youth) all must be dismantled in a Christian community. It is an ongoing concern for every church, one that is never fully completed, for the propensity to wall-building is a strong human urge driven by fear. One of the greatest opportunities and concerns for many churches in the world today is the migration of people. Chinese are moving from rural areas to the big cities, Filipinos are moving in from the southern Philippines to Sabah, Mexicans and Guatemalans are moving into Texas, Colorado, California, and many other states. Other people are moving into formerly single-ethnicity neighborhoods in global cities ("Germantown" is no longer purely German; it is now part African and part Asian). Church as a community of broken walls means greater diversity and an increase in intentional outreach as local churches live into this calling.

Second, the church reflects the Kingdom to others as it is a teaching-worshiping community: teaching both in the context of worship and of the missionary calling of the church (Matt. 28:19–20). Following Jesus's final command to teach disciples of all nations "to obey everything" that Jesus has commanded is part of the transformation process of the local Christian community. This is not teaching as in classroom teaching so much as it is Christian discipleship or devotion to Christ. The community learns as they share the Word and the sacraments together. Related to this concern for teaching, the community must reflect the transformation that has started in each person's baptism. Not all Christian communities reflect Jesus Christ in their relationships and their work. Large portions of Paul's letters are concerned with matters of growing in holiness—the church living like they are reflecting Christ.[10] Jesus's little community of followers were called disciples (learners). We see something of how learning is to take place in the church by following Jesus, with the disciples, through the Gospels. As a worshiping and missional community, any and every church is to be a place where children are learning stories and memorizing the words of Scripture and, at the other end of the age spectrum, the elderly continue to learn even as they teach others.

Third, as a community of worship and witness, every local church must work toward greater and greater levels of holiness. Founded upon the grace of God, which calls us to confession and repentance, the community is ever welcoming, but also ever transforming. No sin is so great that it excludes a person from God's love. His grace brings about the complete transformation of the individual and the community.

> Therefore, I urge you, brothers and sisters, in view of God's mercy, to offer your bodies as a living sacrifice, holy and pleasing to God—this is your true and proper worship. Do not conform to the pattern of this world, but be transformed by the

10. First Corinthians, for example, is mostly about instructions regarding how to live as a community (don't take others to court, don't allow teachers to divide you, live chaste lives and remove those who refuse to do so, don't cause a weaker brother or sister to stumble, etc.). Galatians involves a rebuke for continuing to be divided over ethnic identity, and a rebuke to those who live "according to the flesh" (5:16–21). Ephesians has a long list of sins that are to be kept out of the church (4:17–5:20). The community is to be holy.

> renewing of your mind. Then you will be able to test and approve what God's will is—his good, pleasing and perfect will. (Rom. 12:1–2)

Transformation of the individual toward holiness begins in the mind—with the thought life. All of the ancients knew this, and so they focused on the mind and the intellect as they walked the path toward greater holiness. This is not a matter of works; it is a matter of taking God at his word that sin has been conquered and so we can now move toward holiness. Growth in virtues, rejection of sin and its temptations, should be the environment of the Christian community. The very air that the community breathes should give holiness to the body and soul. Those who associate with this community should find support in helping to end addictions, to controlling anger, lust, or revenge. The local church is not made up of perfect people, but we should expect the community to be on the way to holiness: growing in its capacity to name sin, to repent, and to strengthen the resolve to live humbly for others.

Throughout the ages, many Christians have come up with schemes to describe the ladder to holiness, or to higher levels of love, or steps to the higher Christian life. We find these patterns in the Roman Catholic Church, in Puritan and Pietist traditions, as well as in the Orthodox and the Pentecostal church. St. Peter of Damaskos,[11] a medieval monk, describes the way to holiness this way:

> First, we must recognize that the starting point of all spiritual development is the natural knowledge given us by God, whether this comes through the Scriptures, by human agency, or by means of the angel that is given in divine baptism. . . . If the baptized person keeps these commandments, the grace of the Holy Spirit is preserved in him. Then, alongside of this knowledge, there is our capacity to choose. This is the beginning of our salvation; by our free choice we abandon our own wishes and thoughts and do what God wishes and thinks.[12]

Holiness, or growth in virtues, is a work that is enabled by grace. "Continue to work out your salvation with fear and trembling, for it is God who works in you to will and to act in order to fulfill his good purpose" (Phil. 2:12–13). A church that is growing in holiness is attractive to people who are trapped in sin and see no hope of change. This will be seen, practically, in relationships—for love is only seen in relation to another, and sanctification is really a matter of growing in love. Thus, a church that is growing in holiness will find ways of loving and caring for the needy, the deaf, the blind, and those with other personal challenges. Children will be listened to, cared for, and find a place

11. St. Peter is the largest contributor to volume 2 of *The Philokalia*. He summarizes the work of others, after reading Scripture and the scrolls of many other monks and theologians. His dates are uncertain, but are not later than the eleventh century, since he does not mention Symeon the New Theologian.

12. St. Peter of Damaskos, "The Treasury of Divine Knowledge," in *Philokalia* 2:76.

of safety and growth. People with addictions—whether to drugs, alcohol, or sexual behaviors—will find a place where they are helped and supported along the road to healing and holiness. As the earliest Christians grew in holiness, they changed their attitude toward possessions, and surely this was noticed by outsiders. A church that, in all humility, seeks to be released from all the forms and shapes that sin takes in their lives is being remade in the image of God, and this is attractive to outsiders (Acts 2:47).

Fourth, the community must develop smaller communities in which genuine, caring, and loving relationships, marked by forgiveness and trust, can flourish. This expression of Christian love seldom develops unless there are small groups of committed relationships. We have noted that Jesus used this model with his small wandering group of disciples, and the earliest church also had meetings in homes. The historian Herbert Butterfield (1900–1979) was one of the few modern and respected historians of Christianity who openly discussed and struggled with questions of faith and historical meaning. In an essay published the year of his death he discussed, as a historian, the meaning and importance of small groups in history. The title of his essay is, "The Role of the Individual in History."[13] In this essay, he says that the cell group (small cells that make up a larger community) seems to be "the appointed way by which a mere handful of people may open up a new chapter in the history of civilization." Butterfield observed that the "cell community" is the strongest organizational unit in world history for the following reasons:

- It is a remorseless self-multiplier.
- It is exceptionally difficult to destroy.
- It can preserve its intensity of local life while vast organizations quickly wither when they are weakened at the center.
- It can defy the power of governments.
- It is the appropriate lever for prying open any status quo.

Many have thought that the modern cell structure in local churches, developed after World War II, was a unique and modern invention. As Butterfield

13. This is found in a volume edited by C. T. McIntire called *Writings on Christianity and History* (Oxford: Oxford University Press, 1979), 24. It is interesting to note that the Marxist, G. V. Plekhanov, published an article of the exact same title in 1898 in *Nauchnoye Obozrenie* (Scientific Review) under the pen name of A. Kirsanov. Plekhanov was one of the pioneer Marxists in Russia, who was exiled to Switzerland, later returned, and was opposed to Lenin's interpretation of the revolution. Of interest, he ended his 1898 essay with these words, "And it is not only for beginners, not only for great men that a broad field of activity is open. It is open for all those who have eyes to see, ears to hear and hearts to love their neighbors. The concept *great* is a relative concept. In the ethical sense every man is great who, to use the Biblical phrase, 'lays down his life for his friend.'" Early Marxists who were developing communist theory were greatly indebted to the teachings of Jesus.

has pointed out, however, it has a long history and is not necessarily a uniquely Christian invention. It seems to be imbedded in the very DNA of humanity to seek and cling to small groups as part of larger communities. In the church, there should be intentional and concerted efforts to keep cell groups vital. In times of disruption and division, the cell group adapts and continues to survive. History is filled with examples of cell groups becoming the life-stream for Christianity during times of oppression, as well as in times of extreme avariciousness. Even in prisons, ironically, a cell group ministry can be the foundation for a Christian community.

Finally, the community holds together around the common confession and foundational virtue of humility. My point here is that the community itself is not an absolute value: the Triune God is the center and the supreme value of the church. When the saving faith of Jesus Christ, and his lordship in all areas of life, is compromised, there is no longer a Christian community. A community may itself become an idol, an ultimate value or concern, and when this happens the soul of the church has departed. A community may exist for a long time after it has given up the glory of Christ, but we must recognize that it is then no longer "[carrying] around in our body the death of Jesus so that the life of Jesus might also be revealed in our body" (2 Cor. 4:10). Churches can move off center in many ways: they may soften their theology, they may drop the need for confession, they may call just that which is unjust, or they may promote sin as a virtue. When this happens, it is important that the community reaffirm its center, find ways of confessing its sin, and then seek to return. When this renewal does not come, another sin enters as a last resort to save the remnant: division.

Separation or division in a Christian community can be an act of obedience, as when Paul tells the Corinthians they must expel the unrepentant sinner (1 Cor. 5). The healthy community cannot allow the immoral brother or sister, or the heretical teacher, to lead the community away from Christ. There are also times, however, when the community itself praises sinful behavior or wrong teaching. What should be done then? Jesus's concern, expressed in his high priestly prayer, was for Christian witness. Our unity is the visible sign or the fruit of our confession, repentance, and worship of the Triune God:

> My prayer is not for them alone. I pray also for those who will believe in me through their message, that all of them may be one, Father, just as you are in me and I am in you. May they also be in us so that the world may believe that you have sent me. I have given them the glory that you gave me, that they may be one as we are one—I in them and you in me—so that they may be brought to complete unity. Then the world will know that you sent me and have loved them even as you have loved me. (John 17:20–23)

As we have said, unity is not an ultimate value, however, it *is* vital if the church is going to have a credible witness to the nations. What we see in this passage is that unity is found in Christ. There are times when a church no longer honors Christ in its worship, life, or witness. When we have determined, with careful discernment, that this has happened, we have to decide where the glory of Jesus Christ is now to be found. Great Christian leaders have disagreed about this in times of trial. Here are a few situations in which the social context forced the church to make decisions regarding their worship and witness.

- Korean Christians under Japanese imperial rule being required to worship at a Shinto Shrine in the early and mid-twentieth century
- German Christians who were to honor the German culture (*Volk*) over other cultures (including Jews) in the mid-twentieth century
- Persian Christians who were to honor the Zoroastrian Shrines in third- and fourth-century Persia

Any community that ceases to become a signpost or foretaste of the Kingdom becomes a community at the crossroads. Either decisions will have to be made as to how to return to its proper role as witness to the broader community, or painful and damaging separation will be necessary. It may be necessary for a person or group to leave a local community, for the community is always human and divine—not completely divine. In addition to the community at Corinth, we should also remember 2 Peter 2, for false teachers really exist and, like a spreading cancer, they can kill the body. There are no easy answers in these contexts: at times Christians seem overly anxious to leave, and at other times they are lulled into theological and spiritual lethargy, not realizing that they no longer reflect the glory of God in their community. The local Christian community is always on the road, but it is on a road to greater holiness and greater love, seeking the welfare of those with whom the people come in contact. As the local community worships, it becomes a witness, taking on the very will of the Triune God whose love goes out to all of creation. We turn now to worship as one of the two essential elements of the church.

Worship

Earlier, I mentioned Alexander Schmemann's warning that worship is not to become "an object of love," or "the sole content of church life." Christian worship is one of the two great purposes of the church. In 1987 I flew from New York City to Bangkok, Thailand, and then arrived in Rangoon (now Yangon), Burma (now Myanmar). My visit was an act of service to deliver vitamins, money, and clothing to a friend's wife. When my suitcase was inspected, I was pretty sure they would send me back to Bangkok. However, the inspectors seemed not to care what they found, they were just interested in doing their duty and, as far as I could tell, that meant stirring up everyone's suitcase. Two days later, I was with my new friends (mostly ethnic Chin and Karen pastors and professors) worshiping along with six hundred or so ethnic Chins, far away from their homeland near the border of India. As the Chin people have converted to Christianity, their academic level has risen, their economic status has risen, and now many have come to the capital to work and to study. I understood little of the two-and-a-half-hour worship service, but parts of it were translated through my new friend. Two things stood out. First was the beautiful music that was led by the youth mission team that had come all the way down from the Chin Hills to describe their ministry of evangelization. "Every Chin a Baptist (I translated this to 'Christian') by 2000," was their prayer and vision. Worship was filled with glorious singing and a wonderful vision of the Chin being fully dedicated to Jesus Christ. The second thing that remains vivid to this day was the moment my host whispered, "You need to go forward and bring greetings."

"What does it mean to 'bring greetings?'" I queried. I was told (with no crack of a smile) that it meant they wanted to hear a sermon, but I should pause every once in a while and say, "And I bring greetings from . . ." and then fill in with the names of relatives or churches. It was not legal for foreigners to teach or preach in Burma. I stood in front of that crowd of six hundred people, all focused on me, and I felt completely exposed in my inadequacy and lack of preparation. "What in the world do I have to say to them?" Roaming dogs, chickens, and other animals seemed to become still—I was alone—lost in a prayer for meaning. "What does it mean that I am here?" I imagined that I might soon be sending letters to my family from a Burmese prison. I uttered a prayer, and suddenly the grace of God gave me some clarity. I had nothing to offer them, and we had nothing in common except for our faith in Jesus Christ. I stepped forward and began, "When I was sixteen years old, a friend invited me to a Bible study in her living room on a Sunday afternoon . . . and I bring greetings from my parents who live in Arkansas." I ended my "greetings" by telling them how I finally learned about Jesus and decided to entrust my life to him, to seek to serve him all my days. I had brought about fifteen greetings from numerous cities, but more importantly I had, almost accidentally, centered the worship where it belonged: at the foot of the cross.

Christian worship, like Jesus taking Peter, James, and John to the Mount of Transfiguration, involves coming away from a type of ecstatic experience of holiness and then returning to brokenness (Matt. 17). As Edith Humphrey expresses so well, worship involves *ecstasy*:

> "Standing outside" oneself; it thus refers to the abandonment of self as one goes out to the other. . . . It is that ecstatic movement which, it seems, enables the mysterious *intimacy* shared between the Divine Persons. Or, perhaps it is the other way around—does the shared intimacy allow for the ecstatic freedom?

> Intimacy and ecstasy, at any rate, are mutual states, each nourishing or attending the other.[14]

Christian worship is not just a sociological or psychological event, it is a deeply and fully human and divine event that is centered on the Trinity and on the incarnation. In worship, we are invited into the very presence of the Triune God to honor and proclaim redemption through the Son. "In fact, the two things go together: we proclaim Jesus as Savior in public, and then we celebrate the Trinity within the household of the church."[15] All true worship flows out of gratitude or thanksgiving, and this is why so many of the great spiritual theologians through the ages have prayer and worship with tears. Tears for one's own sin, for the sins of the world, and for the church were a common theme in early Syriac literature, and even St. Augustine talks about the gift of tears.[16] Worship flows out of thanksgiving for what God has done for us in light of our own sinfulness. Tears of repentance move us to thanksgiving and then praise.

There is a natural flow to Christian worship that can be remembered through body movement. We enter as a community and lift praises to God as we stand with outstretched arms. Ancient Christians would face to the east and, as the sun was rising, they would stand in the form of a cross praising God in prayer and song for the resurrection of Christ from the dead. Standing and singing praises is an appropriate and ancient way to enter into worship.

> Shout for joy to the LORD, all the earth.
> Worship the LORD with gladness;
> come before him with joyful songs.
> Know that the LORD is God.
> It is he who made us, and we are his;
> we are his people, the sheep of his pasture.
>
> Enter his gates with thanksgiving
> and his courts with praise;
> give thanks to him and praise his name.
> For the LORD is good and his love endures forever;
> his faithfulness continues through all generations. (Ps. 100:1–5)

Thus, we begin worship standing in praise and thanksgiving. Then, once we come into God's holy presence, we are reminded of who we are in his holiness and we bow down on our knees. For the ancients, the taproot of spirituality is to

14. Edith Humphrey, *Ecstasy and Intimacy: When the Holy Spirit Meets the Human Spirit* (Grand Rapids: Eerdmans, 2006), 3.

15. Ibid., 9.

16. St. Augustine, "Prayer for the Gift of Tears," trans. M. F. Toale; see Lectionary Central, http://www.lectionarycentral.com/trinity10/Augustine2.html.

Embodied Worship, Movement, and Mission

Christian worship can be summarized as a movement from standing, to kneeling, to sitting, to going. Thus, the Christian life is embodied in worship and mission. We enter worship with praise (standing) and then are moved to confession (kneeling); we listen to the Word proclaimed (sitting) and then we move out in mission (going). It is a basic movement of life in Christ: the movement of the people of God.

recognize the "fear of the Lord." "For when God is thanked, He gives us still further blessings, while we, by receiving his gifts, love Him all the more and through this love attain that divine wisdom whose beginning is the fear of God (Prov. 1:7)."[17] Moved by this fear to humility, and even to tears, we go to our knees and confess our sins. Confession follows praise, and so kneeling follows standing. After confession, both as a community and as individuals, we sit. Sitting, we attend to the Word, to the teaching of the apostles in imitation of the earliest Christians. We hear the Word of the Lord spoken, and then we participate in the Word enacted as mystery or sacrament. Word and sacrament, hearing and participating, go together. I realize that not all churches celebrate the Eucharist with every worship service and, as John Calvin recognized, it is not always possible. However, it is theologically appropriate and, in terms of *kerygma*, it completes the proclamation of the Word. Most ancient and traditional Eucharistic services rehearse or reenact the salvation story, pointing to the sacrifice of Jesus Christ. Traditional Eucharistic prayers (*anaphora*, or a prayer of offering as part of Eucharist) remind the community to look to God,[18] to remember the work of Jesus Christ, to call upon the Holy Spirit (*epiclesis*), to lift up the church and the world while at the altar (or Lord's Table), and then to watch as the body is broken, the blood is poured out, and then to come forward as a community to share in the death that conquers life.[19]

If we ignore the importance of this great Eucharistic tradition, we weaken the connection between worship and witness. Lesslie Newbigin tells the story of sharing the Eucharistic meal in a rural village in Tamil Nadu (South India) with many curious onlookers listening and looking in. After he finished quizzing new converts on the meaning of their faith (catechetical instruction), there was a time of worship including baptism and sharing of the Eucharist. He observed that it was very likely that when the missionary (himself) returned

17. St. Peter of Damaskos, "Spurious Knowledge," in *Philokalia* 2:199.

18. The *Sursum Corda* is found in most all of the ancient rites: Priest: "The grace of Our Lord Jesus Christ, the Love of God the Father, and the communion of the Holy Spirit be with you all." People: "And with your spirit." Priest: "Lift up your hearts." People: "We lift them up to the Lord." Priest: "Let us give thanks to the Lord." People: "It is proper and right."

19. The World Council of Churches' document "Baptism, Eucharist and Ministry" provides ecumenical understandings of the Eucharist and worship, and the Lima Liturgy gives an example of a liturgy that helps to unite Christians in some of the deep traditions from the past.

the next month, many of those looking in would be sitting inside seeking instruction themselves. Then, soon, many who were participating in the Eucharist, sharing in the death of Jesus, would become ambassadors of Christ (2 Cor. 5:18–21). This is the normal pattern of worship—through Word and sacrament focusing on Jesus as Savior and calling others to enter into the life of Jesus Christ.

Other Eucharistic prayers, such as the Anglican "Prayer of Humble Access," express the same theology of humility, calling upon God for mercy and grace:

> We do not presume to come to this thy Table, O merciful Lord, trusting in our own righteousness, but in thy manifold and great mercies. We are not worthy so much as to gather up the crumbs under thy Table. But thou art the same Lord, whose property is always to have mercy: Grant us therefore, gracious Lord, so to eat the flesh of thy dear Son Jesus Christ, and to drink his blood, that our sinful bodies may be made clean by his body, and our souls washed through his most precious blood, and that we may evermore dwell in him, and he in us. *Amen.* (Book of Common Prayer, 1662 edition)

Thus, after standing in praise, we go down to our knees in humble confession, sit to receive the Word spoken and enfleshed, and, finally, we respond by going. The final movement in worship is not to sit or even stand but to walk—filled with praise, thanksgiving, and Christian unity, and overflowing with words that bear witness and a life that provokes questions. I mentioned earlier that if Jesus is lifted up—an act of worship—he draws all people to himself. It is a matter of witness to lift him up.

Keeping worship from becoming an end in itself, however, may involve some very practical measures. Visual representations of mission or of the world are helpful in worship. Some churches have flags of nations, or they light a mission candle, or they may have a mission prayer book in the pews. Each worship service, during the Eucharistic prayers for the world, a mission or missionary can be lifted up in prayer from the mission prayer book. The key is to have the church leadership find appropriate ways to keep the world and its needs before the worshiping community. I once attended a church that had a massive wood carving of the world (possibly fifteen meters long) along one of the side walls that had carved in bold letters the reminder: "All of the World is on God's Heart." Every worship service was symbolically taking place before the nations as the congregation listened to the Word and lifted up the nations in Eucharistic prayer. Worship can also reinvigorate witness by issuing reminders of the global church through music, liturgies, guest preachers, and testimonies. The key is to make sure that the local congregation is a "house of prayer for the nations," and not a local cult gathering (Isa. 56:7; Mark 11:17). Worship is not therapy, nor is it an end in itself. Worship draws us into the presence and will of God.

Mission and the Local Church

The local church is an outpost of the Kingdom. It is a sanctuary, but it is much more. It is a school of Christ, but it is also a place of equipping missionaries for the surrounding culture. Worship overflows into mission, even as mission results in worship. About six years ago, while I was standing in church singing the opening song, a man from the neighborhood came down the aisle on crutches and stood next to me. The lyrics for the music were in the bulletin and also on the screen in front of the sanctuary. Earl, the visitor, didn't look at either. He looked at the cross, and then he looked at the people. Later, I found out that he was illiterate. I took him to the fellowship hall after worship and heard his story: Earl had been an alcoholic for nearly thirty-two of his fifty years; he got into a halfway house; then, that very morning, Earl woke up and God told him, "Earl, you need to go to worship." He told me that he just walked outside, lifted up his eyes, and, seeing our church, he just walked in. I suppose I became his first Christian friend. I asked him if he was a Christian, and he responded with great excitement, "That's it, that's what I want, I want to be a Christian." I struggled with how to help in the discipleship of a man who was illiterate. I had an old cassette tape recorder, so I checked out from our library audio tapes that had the Gospels read in a modern translation. Every other day, Earl and I exchanged tapes until, finally, Earl got through the Gospels, and then he got out of the halfway house. I tell you this story because sometimes people do just walk in and say, "I want to become a Christian." For these people, we need to be present, alert, and open. It would be wrong to suggest that an "attractional" model is entirely bad. Jesus attracted a good number of people through his ministry, although many did not stay faithful. People do walk into churches seeking God, but most of those who come to faith are found by a church, or church members, going out in mission. The local church should have a missionary posture; it must see itself as a missionary presence in each place, in each parish. This is how the earliest Christians understood their place in society.

Local Church as Missionary Presence in the Ancient Church

The *Letter of Diognetus* is a fascinating letter for understanding the early church within broader society, even though it is a text without a context.[20] Dating from somewhere after the middle of the second century, the letter gives a description of Christian life in a pluralistic world and then defends Christian belief and life as good and healthy. At this time, Christians were threatened with persecution, and so this letter (possibly a composite letter) functioned as a defense of the faith. There are important issues raised in this ancient letter

20. From Paul Foster, "The Epistle of Diognetus," *The Expository Times*, January 1, 2007, 162–68.

for our understanding of the church as missional presence in the twenty-first century. The author first places his letter in context, explaining some of the questions Diognetus had for him about how Christians live. "You want to know . . . how they worship [God], while at the same time they disregard the world and look down on death and . . . the source of the loving affection that they have for each other" (chap. 1). We see here that many in the early church had a "disregard" of the world, meaning a detachment from worldly concerns (2 Cor. 5:16; Rom. 12:1–2; Phil. 3:7–9).[21] Christians are preoccupied with the things of God, and the things of God include "loving affection" for each other. In fact, this preoccupation with showing care and concern for others marked early Christians as almost a "new race." It is a way of life that finds personal fulfillment in God and in participating in God's love for others.

The letter then goes on to explain that Christians do not follow the "stupidity" of idolatry ("You Gentiles adore these things, and in the end you become like them," 2:6) and the "superstition of Judaism." Judaism is seen as superstitious because the sacrificial system, food taboos, and "mutilation of the flesh" are seen as attempts to control God (chaps. 3 and 4). Chapters 5 and 6 reveal a great deal about how the early Christians lived in the world, and how it is that they had such a missional impact. First, Christians were not separated from the surrounding culture but were embedded in their own culture: speaking the same language, wearing the same clothes, and eating the same food as those around them. "They do not follow an eccentric manner of life" (5:2) is the way this is expressed. Christians live in and take on the local context, whether it is as local believers or as missionaries sent to take on a newer culture. This is the incarnational principle we have spoken of. In contrast, some other religious peoples did (and do) set themselves apart. Later, Christians do this as well (in some monastic lifestyles), but in this early document, Christians are clearly embedded in the surrounding culture and also show "loving affection" to others. Next, we read that even though Christians are embedded in their culture, they hold onto that culture lightly. Christians are not fully identified by or attached to the cultures in which they live. "They live in their own countries, but only as aliens. They have a share in everything as citizens, and endure everything as foreigners" (5:5).

How can Christians live within their own culture, but as foreigners? How are Christians embedded in local contexts and yet also detached from them? In a word, Christians live the life of Christ in the world. Christians do not follow the local culture in its moral and ethical decisions, for they live according to a much higher order of existence. For example, Christians do not abort or expose unwanted children (5:6). Christians remain faithful in marriage (5:7). "It is true they are 'in the flesh,' but they do not live 'according to the flesh'" (5:8). As

21. Detachment was a strong and important concept of Christian discipleship in early Christianity. See St. Isaiah the Solitary, "On Guarding the Intellect," in *Philokalia* 1:27.

Tertullian Describes Christian Character as Witness

In *Apology*, Tertullian remarks on how Christian behavior is different from pagan culture; this difference becomes a witness to the surrounding society. "But look at the Christians! There you have quite another story; not a man of them is ashamed of [accusations], not a man regrets. . . . If he is denounced [as a Christian] he glories in it; if he is accused, he does not defend himself; when he is questioned, he confesses without any pressure; when he is condemned, he renders thanks." (1.12–13)

a summary statement, we read that, "[Christians] go far beyond what the laws require" (5:10). Christians go beyond what the laws or customs require because of love: Christians have greater love for all people, including the weak and indefensible. As a local congregation, we should show greater love for those outside our congregation than those outside show even for their own people. Others may not love or care for their own unborn, handicapped, or elderly, but Christian love fills in the gaps of love and justice.

In addition, we see clearly that these early Christians lived simply—but it was not a burden for them. "They are poor, and yet they make many rich" (5:13). Even though they were dressing, eating, and speaking like local people in their cultural contexts, early Christians were "completely destitute," "dishonored," "defamed," "reviled," and even "punished as evildoers" (5:13–17). Like a soul in a body, dispersed throughout the body and giving it life, so are Christians in the world (chap. 6). It is a fascinating conclusion to this section of the letter that Christians, hated and rejected, living very simply and even in poverty, are yet precious to the surrounding society ("the body"). Other apologists of the early centuries, such as Tertullian (see sidebar), concur.

Tertullian's observation is an interesting window into the character of early Christians when they were accused and then taken to trial to receive punishment, or possibly to become martyrs. We see this in many martyrdom stories: the accused Christians are not angry and violent; like their Savior, they are gentle and humble. The ancient Christians, probably in light of their persecution, followed the humble Christ in their own trials. Gentleness became one of the central virtues of Christians in the world. "There is scarcely any other virtue which the demons fear as much as gentleness," says Evagrios the Solitary, then listing the many saints in Scripture who were marked by gentleness.[22]

This is just a brief look into the way Christians lived in a pluralistic society during the ancient Christian period. Although in some ways the Christians "fit in" quite well, in other ways they did not. Some of their moral and ethical commitments of love and justice broke or bent the larger culture, which

22. "On Discrimination," in *Philokalia* 1:46. Some recent scholars have reminded us that martyrdom in the early church was a complex matter of cultural predispositions concerning death and exaggerated claims about the numbers and types of martyrdom. See Candida Moss, *Ancient Christian Martyrdom: Diverse Practices, Theologies, and Traditions* (New Haven: Yale University Press, 2012).

resulted in the persecution of Christians. Many Christians—nearly crushed by cultural resistance—eventually denied the faith. What we see here is a reminder of the position the church should take today—finding ways to fit into a local cultural context but remaining clear about what cannot be denied, what must not be lost in the adaptation to the culture.

Two Redemptive Structures

Another issue that came up during the early period of Christianity, and that we looked at in chapter 1, is the matter of the local church being superseded by monastic structures for mission. Most cross-cultural and much local missionary work has been done not from a local church base but from monasteries or special mission structures. Ralph Winter recognized that, historically, Christianity has had two missionary structures.[23] The local church, carrying out mission in a local context, he called a *modality*. A modality is the basic grouping in any society—the synagogue in the time of Jesus, and the local church or *ekklesia* in the apostolic age. People from all ages are included in this group and no "second" level of commitment is required. In addition to the modality, there is also the *sodality*—a structure designed to carry out a specific task. A sodality may be all men, all women, all youth, or only adults. The sodality has a more specific calling, such as medical missions or, as in some Roman Catholic orders, special charism for education or to provide care for the dying. The sodality has a Jewish parallel in the Jewish evangelistic bands at the time of Jesus (Matt. 23:15). The sodality is more flexible, more focused, and it may be self-supporting or supported by local churches (like Paul's missionary actions).

Local churches today should not limit their missionary expression to support of their local organizational structure (sodality). I believe Ralph Winter has clearly shown, through history and through Scripture, that *both* structures are part of God's redemptive plan. As awkward as it may be at times, especially when apportioning time or money, God's mission has always been carried out by individuals—through both local churches (modalities) and missionary organizations (sodalities).

What this means for each local church is twofold. First, the fact that early Christians borrowed from contemporary patterns and structures frees us up to find contemporary patterns for mission and adapt them. This may include the

23. "The Two Structures of God's Redemptive Mission," originally delivered as an address in August 1973 at the founding of the "Asia Missions Association" in Seoul, Korea. Later this was published and is most easily found in print form in *Perspectives on the World Christian Movement* (Pasadena, CA: William Carey Library, 2009), 244–53. Darrell Guder elaborates further, "It appears that the work of God's Spirit in carrying out the mission of God is not to be restricted to one institution form. Whenever the church tries to do that there is reaction, both in the form of renewal and in the form of division. In terms of institution structure, the Spirit does list where it will." *The Continuing Conversion of the Church* (Grand Rapids: Eerdmans, 2000), 184. See all of chap. 8, "The Conversion of the Institutional Church," 181–204.

use of technology and media for mission, but it may also involve complex webs of partnership (which we will look at in chap. 12). Second, each local church needs careful reflection on their missionary outreach within their context, considering how partnering with or establishing sodalities for specific ministries may enhance the work of the *missio Dei* in their locale. Reaching youth in schools, neighborhoods, or universities usually involves a special missionary outreach or sodality structure. Many churches will (and should) partner in such a work. Similarly, outreach to immigrants, to prisoners, or to the homeless will also involve cooperation and special missional structures. The *missio Dei* in any local community is as varied as the life and ministry of Jesus Christ, now empowered by his Spirit. It involves a variety of appropriate structures, both modalities (planting new churches) and sodalities (missionary structures).

Contemporary Issues in Local Mission

I would now like to look at six contemporary questions for the local church as it lives into God's missional presence. The first question is a way of seeing the local community: "How can we understand our local missional context?" What we are talking about here is social analysis of our locale. A church that is in a small town in a rural area has much less difficulty doing a social analysis of their "mission field" because there is greater homogeneity within the community. What is it that the attentive local church should be looking for as it analyzes its own mission field?

1. Ethnic patterns: what groups live here and in which areas do they live?
2. Age patterns
3. Economic status of various groups
4. Communication and transportation lines
5. Educational level
6. Major institutions in the area
7. Economic patterns (manufacturing, service industries, etc.)
8. Religious beliefs and membership

In addition to doing a factual, objective analysis from census data and other data available, there should also be a subjective analysis of the community. The church's leadership team should walk the neighborhood, stopping in stores, schools, restaurants, and other establishments. They should take time to talk to people along the road, on the bus, or in the park. In this way, a leadership team will develop a missional awareness of their neighborhood. Most church contexts are very complex and it takes time to take the pulse, to know the hopes and fears of local people. A church must begin their missional journey with listening and attentiveness.

The second and third questions narrow in on some of the information we learn from this careful social analysis, both the objective and the subjective aspects. The second question we need to ask is, "Who are the immigrant groups in our social context, where are they from, and what does their social profile look like?" In most places in the world, people are moving beyond their ethnic boundaries.[24] Some are "moving up" because of better jobs and greater economic opportunities, while others are "moving out" to escape famine or violence. Some are students, some are professionals, and some are illiterate. Our missional presence must be directed according to the people God has brought into our midst. In major cities of the world, an important group of migrant people are students. Education is generally seen as the key to the better opportunities that the entire world is seeking. International students are generally eager to meet local people and to know that they are accepted. They are interested in learning about local customs, holidays, and family patterns. Local churches should find ways of equipping their parishioners to become oases of hospitality for international students. Many of the world's dictators and doctors studied in Christian environments where local Christians could have met their basic needs and pointed them to their ultimate need for a savior. Unfortunately, there are many international students who could affirm the experience of Mahatma Gandhi who said he liked Jesus, but, after his experience with Christians in England and South Africa, he found it best to imitate the Sermon on the Mount and reject Jesus as Savior and Lord.[25]

Other immigrants come to different countries as a matter of survival. These are among the neediest people in our communities. They may be migrant workers in the Middle East and East Asia, or they may be political refugees in Europe and North America, but they will not survive without help. Governments help with relocation programs, but churches need to be the first and strongest friends of immigrant populations. These dependent populations searching for a home provide an opportunity for local churches to show something of the *hesed*[26] love of God. "Where is God?" they may be asking as they struggle to learn a new language and transportation system and adjust to a new climate. God should be seen in the incarnation of his body, the local church, which welcomes the foreigner.

24. See, for example, Russell King's *People on the Move: An Atlas of Migration* (Los Angeles: University of California Press, 2010). For a focus on African migration, see Jehu Hanciles, *Beyond Christendom: Globalization, African Migration and the Transformation of the West* (Maryknoll, NY: Orbis Books, 2008).

25. Margaret Chatterjee, *Gandhi's Religious Thought* (Notre Dame, IN: University of Notre Dame Press, 1983); S. K. George, *Gandhi's Challenge to Christianity* (Ahmedabad: Navajivan, 1947).

26. *Hesed* (*Chesed*) is the Hebrew word for the loving-kindness of God. There is no one word that can be used to translate *hesed* because it includes faithfulness, kindness, love, grace, and compassion.

Third, when looking at the results of the social analysis, we want to ask, "Where are the poorest and neediest in our midst?" There are many ways in which we can and should be involved in local missionary work, but one aspect of mission that we *must* identify and then engage in is ministry among the neediest. Poverty and injustice should be like magnet north, turning the compass of our missional involvement in their direction. Unfortunately, often the daily patterns of our lives make the poor and the oppressed invisible to us. We may depend on finding them, however, in prisons, in group homes, in drug rehabilitation centers, or under bridges at night. In some cities, they may be found in brothels, in dark alleys, or in factories that function as sweatshops. Jesus said, "The poor you will always have with you," and yet we often forget that this little phrase, in the context of an act of worship (Matt. 26:6–12), means that today, now, we are to use our money for the poor.

The early Christians were known for taking care of the poor—especially widows and orphans who were especially defenseless within the surrounding culture. Basil the Great is known to have established, in Cappadocia, what was considered a "city of hospitality." His work has been an inspiration for Christians through the ages, and it might be helpful to be reminded and inspired once again:

> Here disease was regarded in a religious light, disaster thought to be a blessing in disguise, and sympathy put to the test. Food, shelter and medical care were provided without charge. Because of its scale, Basil's astonishing "city," in which the unwelcome were made welcome, was regarded as one of the wonders of the world.[27]

Basil was a great influence upon the leaders of the Catholic Worker movement, through its leaders Peter Maurin and Dorothy Day. If we look carefully, we will find many other great saints—from the earliest church, through the Middle Ages, and up to the present—who knew that the *missio Dei* must run through the places of greatest darkness and pain, the places that seem completely hopeless. It is in such places, and with such people, that the light of the gospel is most needed and most clearly seen. Every local church should ask, "Who are the neediest?" and then set out to meet their needs.

Fourth, we should ask, "Are there events and institutions that we need to establish in order to meet needs and serve our community?" The local church should be the one place in every community in which people are asking what their community needs. It may be that a medical clinic is needed, or a free dental clinic. I visited a church in Upper Egypt that saw that the most desperate need in that area was for a multireligious institution to be established to end female circumcision. The local church, led by laypeople, gathered together

27. Jim Forest, *All Is Grace: A Biography of Dorothy Day* (Maryknoll, NY: Orbis Books, 2011), 121.

women, community leaders, and leaders from the two local mosques, and in a couple of years they reeducated families, teachers, and parents and brought an end to the practice. This particular work of this local church made the national newspapers.

Paying attention to the local community may reveal that the community needs healthy gathering places or wholesome gathering events. In some cities, it means reclaiming the streets: bringing families and young people back to playgrounds and side streets. Many churches are providing street fairs and sports leagues to bring communities together in moral and safe contexts. Other churches are using their buildings seven days a week to offer free tutoring for children, language classes for immigrants, computer literacy for the unemployed, and AA classes for people with ongoing addiction problems. A local church can be a catalyst for community building as part of the cultural mandate, or what we called earlier the "full conversion of cultures."

A fifth big question that we need to answer in light of taking leadership in community activities is the following: "To what degree can the local church cooperate with people of other faiths in local mission and social ministry?" This is not an easy question to answer. In many Western countries Christians are strongly encouraged to cooperate in all mission with all people. In certain contexts, this is appropriate—nothing is compromised and much good is done (as illustrated above by the church in Egypt). However, there are times when cooperation becomes compromising, as not all social issues are commonly evaluated as to their social good. Should Christians cooperate in a local medical clinic when young girls are given free birth control or abortions, or when end-of-life issues are handled in a pragmatic or mechanistic fashion? Concern to intervene with drug addiction should be something we can work on across religious lines, but are we really saving someone from addiction when our hands are tied from meeting the deepest need of the individual? Anyone working with drug addicts will tell you that it is important to change behavior patterns: not just behaviors that need to stop but also behaviors that need to begin. Jesus talks about this in Matthew 12:

> When an evil spirit comes out of a person, it goes through arid places seeking rest and does not find it. Then it says, "I will return to the house I left." When it arrives, it finds the house unoccupied, swept clean and put in order. Then it goes and takes with it seven other spirits more wicked than itself, and they go in and live there. And the final condition of that person is worse than the first. (Matt. 12:43–45)

In many areas of community outreach, cooperation is essential: local churches need to work cooperatively with other religions to provide basic health care, to maintain open dialogue between religious leaders, and to feed the poor. But if our ability to talk about the center of our faith is hindered, we need to rethink our cooperation. However, there are times when there is no other choice (this was the case in Nepal until the constitutional reforms of 1989, and was the witness of many of the White Fathers in North Africa).[28] At such times we serve faithfully in silence.

Apostolicity of the Laity

In an important development in Roman Catholic theology, Pope Paul VI issued the decree *Apostolicam Actuositatem* ("Apostolate of the Laity"), which outlined the important role that the laity play in the mission of the church. Recent decades have seen this theology of mission reinforced, not only in the Catholic Church, but in global Christianity. "In the Church there is a diversity of ministry but a oneness of mission. Christ conferred on the Apostles and their successors the duty of teaching, sanctifying, and ruling in His name and power. But the laity likewise share in the priestly, prophetic, and royal office of Christ and therefore have their own share in the mission of the whole people of God in the Church and in the world" (par. 2).

The sixth question that needs to be asked, and one of the biggest questions of the past fifty years, is, "What is the role of the laity in mission, and how can the clergy enhance and promote lay missional involvement?" Many people in the West have come to believe that mission is the responsibility of the clergy. Beginning with the Second Vatican Council, however, there was a countermovement that recognized the ministry of the *laos* ("people," from which we get the term "laypeople" or "laity"). Numerous documents coming out of the council focused on the role of the laity, a major change from earlier councils and writings. The Dogmatic Constitution on the Church speaks clearly about the role of the laity in mission, but no document speaks so clearly as the *Apostolicam Actuositatem* ("Decree on the Apostolate of the Laity").

The laity is specially gifted in a variety of ways for carrying out the mission of God, to the end that the "Kingdom come on earth as it is in heaven." The role of priestly or clerical members is to aid in converting, equipping, and sending out the laity.

> They [the laity] exercise the apostolate in fact by their activity directed to the evangelization and sanctification of men and to the penetrating and perfecting of the temporal order through the spirit of the Gospel. In this way, their temporal activity openly bears witness to Christ and promotes the salvation of men. Since the laity, in accordance with their state of life, live in the midst of the world and its concerns, they are called by God to exercise their apostolate in the world like leaven, with the ardor of the spirit of Christ. (par. 2b)

28. Aylward Shorter, *The Cross and the Flag in Africa: The White Fathers during the Colonial Scramble (1892–1914)* (Maryknoll, NY: Orbis Books, 2006).

We often forget that most of the evangelization in the world, most of the translation of the Bible, most of the work for justice, and most of the care for the poor has been done by laypeople. Great movements of students for the evangelization of the world have been fired up by students, not by pastors. It is imperative that each local church find ways of releasing and empowering the laity to do the work of the mission of God. This is not the place to trace the clericalism of the church, but I do want to note that the church has often struggled with what might be called "clerical creep." A church can become slowly more dependent upon full-time, professional Christians—leaving the masses of the faithful behind in the process.[29]

The importance of laity in the *missio Dei* became clear to me when our little church was asked to start a new church at the Presbyterian High School in Singapore. I was the only ordained pastor in a church that already had a core of about four hundred, and a smaller worship group of about forty or forty-five. How could I ever manage to lead a third service on Sundays? The elders' answer to this question was simply to call for thirty or forty laypeople to leave the main church and start the new church—and so they did. I watched in amazement, offering very little, except prayer, encouragement, and the performance of occasional baptisms and Lord's Supper celebrations. Similarly, in many parts of Africa and Asia where the church is growing rapidly, there are not enough ordained clergy to preach and lead congregations. Laypeople are not only leading these churches but also evangelizing villages and cities. Thus, laypeople are not only involved in mission; they are the initiators of mission. "Mission does not proceed from the pope, nor from a missionary order, society, or synod, but from a community gathered around the word and the sacraments and sent into the world."[30] Even as greater numbers of laity are involved in mission, there is a countervailing movement of hierarchical expectation in mission. Thus, it is necessary to find ways in *each* church to empower and direct laity in mission in *each* place, as well as around the world.

Pete Scazzero is the pastor of a church of about twelve hundred members in Queens, New York, that has over sixty different nationalities represented, including people from Puerto Rico, Guatemala, Honduras, Nicaragua, Mexico, Singapore, China, Nigeria, Algeria, and India. Living in the midst of one of the most diverse mission fields in the world, Pete did an extended study on the role of the laity and the meaning of mission. Part of his response was the "Full-Time Ministry I.D." This is a business card that everyone in the church carries as a reminder of their own identity and responsibility in God's mission. The card says:

29. For a discussion of this "clerical creep," see William R. Burrows, *New Ministries: The Global Context* (Maryknoll, NY: Orbis Books, 1980), 75–114. See also Yves Congar's *Lay People in the Church* (Westminster, MD: Newman, 1957).

30. David Bosch, *Transforming Mission: Paradigm Shifts in the Theology of Mission* (Maryknoll, NY: Orbis Books, 1991), 472.

Full-Time Ministry I.D.
This certifies that I am a full-time minister (i.e., servant) of Jesus Christ.
I am called to:

1. allow Christ to transform me
2. create and shape
3. build community, and
4. push back the powers of evil,

. . . at work, church, family, neighborhood and wherever I go.[31]

After a series of sermons on the meaning of being a missional presence in all areas of life, Pete began to encourage members to give testimonies of their lives in the marketplace as "full-time ministers." A crossing guard gave a testimony of how God had called him to make the intersection in front of a primary school a safe place for children. If a child forgot their lunch, he lent them money to buy one; and if a child forgot their homework, he called a parent. He created a loving and peaceful environment for children. A hairdresser spoke about how God had called her to help women feel good about themselves and to listen and pray for her clients. A few had so appreciated her "ministry" that they came to her church to discover the faith that they had seen and enjoyed in her presence. Here is a model for a local church in which everyone can understand themselves as uniquely gifted and called by God to their neighborhood.

It is far too easy to see mission as a professional occupation rather than as a high and holy vocation to which God has called all of his children. Each and every person called to Christ is sent by Christ. Some are sent around the world, others are sent across the street. However, all are sent as ambassadors and reconciling agents with a life to share, as well as a message to speak. For each and every one in the church, worship spills out into witness and witness leads to worshiping the Triune God. The local church is the place where worship takes place and where people (*laos*) are called to bear witness.

In this chapter, we have spoken of witness mostly in terms of what we do. In the next chapter, we want to look more closely at what it means to be a witnessing or evangelizing community. The good news is for sharing, but too many have experienced the good news as something that was communicated to them by pounding, shouting, or threatening. Others have never even heard of the good news, and so they wonder how good it could be if no one has bothered to share it with them.

31. This card has a copyright by New Life Fellowship, Queens, New York. Used by permission.

10

Witnessing Community

Evangelism and Christian Mission

In the six years we had been friends with Akram, we had taken him to the Singapore Zoo with our family, we had had meals together, and we had even visited him for a public holiday in his home. He had let us into the struggles of life as a Malay Muslim in a Chinese-dominated country, and he had confided in us his own struggles with his family and with his job. We had become good friends. Most of all, speaking as a father, he had been like an uncle to our four children. We shared everything a family would share, except the most important area of our life, which we shared only in a small way—Akram had given us a copy of the Qur'an to read, and I had given him a small, pocket (easy to hide) New Testament. We had read each other's holy book and had some brief discussions. I had also taken him to a large, well-done evangelistic rally that focused on Christian care for the poor and needy. After the rally, we went out to a restaurant and had a conversation about Christianity and about Jesus. So we had shared a bit about our religious beliefs and life—but we did not share a common understanding. But, as I look back sixteen years later, I can still say that Akram had become one of our best friends—one of our only Muslim friends.

One Christmas Eve, we had Akram over for dinner and the kids were excited, because he said he had some presents for them. We were pleased and then, when the kids opened the presents, we were embarrassed—he bought nicer gifts than we had ever bought our kids. Our Muslim friend was spoiling our Christian kids. We had a great time together, and the kids were wired from the combination of ice cream, presents, and having Akram over. Finally we got them all down to bed, said their prayers, and then we sat down to have a cup of tea with Akram while looking over the beautiful skyline of Orchard Road in Singapore. After a moment of silence, with Christmas carols playing softly in the background, Akram shot up and said, "You're not trying to convert me, are you?"[1]

Clarity about Witness

There is much confusion and a great deal of criticism concerning evangelism today. Christians encounter resistance from many quarters of society (especially in the West), and this resistance has paralyzed many Christians from even thinking about evangelism. Evangelistic paralysis has led to doubts about its purpose. When evangelism is talked about, and engaged in, technologies and technique seem to have taken over the priority of relationship and attentiveness. Public criticism and confusion over the message and method of evangelism combine to make it a major missiological concern. Our purpose here is to regain some clarity about what it means to bear witness to Jesus Christ, for evangelism is, at heart, introducing Jesus Christ to others and inviting them to become partakers in his Kingdom.

One sunny afternoon a student from China came into my office and announced that I was his adviser. I checked with the admissions office and, sure enough, I had a last-minute student in my class. Since I had been to Beijing a number of times, we had much to talk about. Trying to be sensitive to the church situation in China, I asked if he were part of the three-self or the unregistered church movement. He politely said, "Oh, sir, I am not a Christian." This was rather odd, since I teach at a Christian seminary that prepares people for Christian ministry. After a quick prayer for a way forward I then asked if he would like to meet other Chinese in the city, and of course he responded with a healthy, "Yes sir!"

"Hello, Pastor Chan, I have a student here from China who has just arrived from Beijing and he would like to meet other Chinese people in the city. . . . Sunday morning? That would be great. . . . OK, I will have him wait outside his dorm at 9:30 on Sunday." The student was pleased to meet so many Chinese-speaking people (mostly graduate students and recent graduates) and I was happy to introduce him to a Christian community of his own culture. Over the months, the good folks at the Chinese Christian Church picked up Chong Kau every Sunday morning and, after worship, they took him to a church member's house for lunch. Every Wednesday evening they picked him up for dinner and then for Wednesday evening Bible class. I spoke to Chong

1. The story is finished at the end of this chapter.

Kau about Jesus Christ, the human condition, and our need for a savior. However, he always got hung up on the concept of sin. In his own words, "My friends and family have always told me I am a good boy. I always obey my father, showing filial piety, and I do my school work. I don't think I am a sinner." Six months later, Chong Kau came into my office and announced, "I have become a Christian."

"You have? Tell me how that happened." He said that every week at worship he was assigned the task of running the overhead projector (these were the days before digital projectors). In this way, he was singing and looking at the lyrics of all of the worship songs for six months. He said that, as they sang the beautiful songs about God's greatness and his goodness and mercy, he became overwhelmed. He could not imagine anyone so good. "I could never be that forgiving and loving, and so I began to realize my separation from God. I wanted to know this God who loved us so much that he sent his Son to die for us." Two months later, he announced that his girlfriend—who was studying at Harvard—had also become a Christian. Again, I asked him how it happened. "Oh, very expensive, sir," was the honest reply. In the days before cheap long-distance phone calls, he was paying huge telephone bills to talk to his girlfriend—a PhD student in religions—as she would ask many serious questions about Christianity. After months of nightly quiz sessions, she gave her life to Jesus Christ. My wife and I attended the worship service in which they were both baptized. Chong Kau was filled with questions, which were finally answered by a church community, by his study of Scripture, and by a number of Christians who were willing to listen and take time to explain about Jesus again and again.

Evangelism involves both reasoning and relationship, both the mind and the heart. How a person comes to faith is always mysterious, and yet after it happens, we can tell a meaningful and coherent story. When I first met Chong Kau, a materialist philosopher and communist, I had no idea how he might come to faith, but in retrospect the narrative is something we can understand; in light of Scripture, it all makes sense.

No other sector of the Christian faith is as sensitive and controversial, and yet as glorious and vivifying as evangelism. Those who have been with people as their lives have been redeemed by Christ look upon those relationships and those times as the most memorable in their Christian lives. Missionaries, knowing the great joy that others receive when hearing about conversions, are often tempted to exaggerate claims and embellish stories. This, however, does not take away from the truth that Jesus spoke when talking about lost things:

> I tell you . . . there will be more rejoicing in heaven over one sinner who repents than over ninety-nine righteous persons who do not need to repent. . . . I tell you, there is rejoicing in the presence of the angels of God over one sinner who repents. (Luke 15:7, 10)

On the other hand, those who have been badgered by insensitive evangelists—evangelists who rely on human technique rather than trust the Spirit of God—have little time for the concept of evangelism at all. They might even use contentious language when talking about the concept: evangelism is "spiritual colonialism" or "religious imperialism." Those who evangelize are "narrow-minded fundamentalists" who have "no tolerance of other religions" and "no sensitivity to the beauty and value of other religions." As we mentioned in the last chapter, this divide can lead to an unfortunate dichotomy in our churches, a dichotomy that denies the fullness of Christ and the power of his Spirit in the church. It is no exaggeration to say that a healthy commitment to Christian witness, pointing to Christ and calling others to faith in Christ, is vital not only for mission but for the entire twenty-first-century church. Growth, which includes numbers, is evidence of life.

Another part of our problem with evangelism today is that we still suffer the effects of modernity, which creates a false dichotomy between the spiritual and the physical, the religious and the secular, and which polarizes truth from values. Consequently, most well-educated people in the world today assume a choice has to be made between spiritual and physical explanations and concerns. Educated people often assume that scientific and sociological explanations lead us to truth, but personal choices are merely "values" and have no claim to be true. For these individuals, peace and justice will only be brought about by the best political thinkers rationally arriving at the most logical and just solutions. At the other extreme, some might find the only answer to spiraling violence and injustice is to help bring about the conversion of gang leaders or of oppressive politicians. However, the Kingdom of God is

"Good News": What Does "Evangelism" Mean?

Technically speaking, "evangelism" is the practice or study of telling the good news. In Roman Catholic thought, we more frequently hear the term "evangelization," which is a broader term, including most of what Protestants call "mission" and most of what this whole book is about. Here we focus on presenting the good news to others and helping to usher them into the Kingdom. David Bosch remarked that evangelism is not a separate part of mission, but it is the heart of mission: "Evangelism is the core, heart, or center of mission. We do not believe that the central dimension of evangelism, as calling people to faith and new life, can ever be relinquished. I have called evangelism the heart of mission. With evangelism cut out, mission dies: it ceases to be mission."[a]

a. David Bosch, "Evangelism: Theological Currents and Cross-Currents Today," *International Bulletin of Missionary Research* 11, no. 3 (July 1, 1987): 98–103.

much more beautiful and much more complete than this false choice between science or values. By ourselves, we can never convert a person, we can never eradicate poverty, and we can never conquer corruption in government. But we are graciously invited to participate in the holistic and mysterious work that God's Holy Spirit is already doing. Our responsibility is to bring Christ into all of these situations by the way we live and the way we speak, as a life pointing to something higher, deeper, and greater than we ever imagined (Col. 4:2–6). And then we, in the pattern of Jesus Christ, offer others the same invitation we received.

I dedicate this chapter to deepening the understanding of Christian witness centered in the evangelistic message and appeal. Witness is a broader category that includes evangelism, but also includes other actions or relationships that testify to God. As we enter the twenty-first century, there is a common assumption among many Christians that evangelism is a communal act and it has a communal goal. This is true, for the church—as the body of Christ with all of the gifts given to it—is given this calling corporately. Much is made of the need for witness to start from a growing Kingdom community (*koinōnia*) and for Christian witness to also end in a growing Christian community.[2] Especially in contemporary cultures that are marked by loneliness, brokenness, and alienation, this emphasis upon community is not only helpful, it is necessary. However, we should also remember that there are times when evangelism simply cannot spring from a community. At times it is a lonely,[3] or at least an *alone*, experience—we have to be careful with generalizations.

In this brief chapter, we will look at major themes in evangelistic witness in the twenty-first century. This will include a discussion of the content of the message, the relationship between evangelism and social justice, Jesus as a pattern for evangelism, the meaning of conversion, the necessity of humility in evangelism, fine-tuning our witness, the issue of salvation (heaven and hell), and the question of converting Muslims. There is something to offend pretty much everyone in this chapter, but I also hope to provide some encouragement and guidance. I will conclude the chapter with the end of my story about Akram and what this might say about evangelism and people of other faiths.

2. Evangelism through community, often described as an organic or attractional model, is important, but limited. In the nineteenth century, Horace Bushnell promoted such a model (especially for children of the church) in his important book *Christian Nurture* (1847). I mention it here simply to remind the reader that there may be something to learn today from such a popular model of an earlier period. Bushnell, however, is writing from a Christendom perspective where it was assumed most everyone in society had some sort of Christian belief. A helpful survey that gives paradigms of theology of mission is found in Francis Adeney, *Graceful Evangelism: Christian Witness in a Complex World* (Grand Rapids: Baker Academic, 2010), 59–98.

3. For example, Philip and the Ethiopian (probably a Nubian) eunuch in Acts 8 is an example of lonely evangelism.

Something to Believe In, Someone to Believe

Evangelism calls people to believe something that is not commonly thought: to think differently about the world and about themselves and then to live into that belief. Evangelism is a call to belief, and by extension it is a call to values, community, and actions. However, it would be easy to miss this message of belief in many of the evangelism programs and books that have been written in the past twenty or thirty years because of their primary emphasis upon behavior, community, and values.[4] Although seldom expressed so directly, the focus of most recent work is upon the need, in a postmodern world, for evangelism to be focused upon community building and fighting against injustice. But *participation in* divorced from *loyalty to* is a misrepresentation of the Kingdom proclaimed by Jesus and the gospel proclaimed by Paul. Jesus called people to faith, and faith is a synonym for belief, trust, or loyalty. It is a subtle shift in evangelism to move from saying, "The community is important to witness" to saying, "The community is the evangelist." The *Holy Spirit* is the evangelist, and the Holy Spirit calls people to absolute loyalty, not to a church, fellowship, or community, but to God in Jesus Christ. Truth claims enfleshed in a community are important (Jesus proclaimed a Kingdom, not simply individual salvation), but we do not put our trust in a community, for all communities, like all people, are broken and open to even greater fallenness. This is a subtle, but important, distinction.

Evangelism is about beliefs and truth claims. It is news. Evangelism calls people to abandon false claims about the world and about themselves and to embrace good truth (or news) about God and about themselves. Stepping into this new truth results in transformation, which comes about by the Holy Spirit of God who inhabits all truth. In the end, the convert will live differently because they have encountered the way, the truth, and the life.

A parable from counseling may help. A woman went to a counselor and, after two hours, she had revealed a personal biography filled with the pain of rejection, verbal abuse, and mild physical abuse. The woman—I will call her Mary—could not make decisions because she had been so devastated by years of abuse and rejection. She had no personal resources left, because she

4. I am thinking here of the great impact that some "emergent" literature, as well as some of the broader interpretations of "missional" church, have had on the theology of evangelism. Many of these works are germinated as a reaction to fundamentalist notions of church in the past, or to more complacent cultural forms of Christianity. As a result, evangelism is critiqued as abrasive and confrontational, and so the new forms of outreach often come across as social engineering more than communicating a clear message. Agreeing to prescribed social behaviors (social justice issues, or meeting in a particular "third place") is substituted for communicating content. It is the lack of a clear message, not the concern for relationship and justice, that is my concern here. There are many examples, but Brian McLaren in *Everything Must Change: Jesus, Global Crises and a Revolution of Hope* (Nashville: Thomas Nelson, 2007) sets the tone in his first two highly autobiographical chapters (1–30).

had come to believe the lie told her by her own family: "You are not of any value; you are no good; the world would be better off without you." She was utterly lonely. "Counselor A" decided it would be best to help Mary do the right thing, and so made up a list of things for Mary to do. She was to go out and get a job, make new friends, and watch happy movies with her family. Of course, Mary's life was so damaged from years of humiliation that she could not simply make new friends. Mary felt even worse when she tried to do this. She could not suddenly change and enjoy the company of others. Mary concluded that she must actually be the worthless person she had been told she was. "Counselor B" came into this situation and said something quite different. Counselor B identified with Mary, having been rejected and almost killed early in life. Later in life, Counselor B had experienced other forms of rejection, as all of the counselor's friends had abandoned the counselor when things became difficult. Then Counselor B said something transformative to Mary: "You are believing a lie about yourself and about this world. Let me tell you how beautiful you are and how much you are really loved—and even how much people are counting on you. On top of all of this, God loves you more than you can imagine." This did not bring immediate healing, but Counselor B was beginning to deal with the root of the problem, a problem that begins with our thoughts about ourselves and about the universe. At the foundation of all our actions or inactions are thoughts—how we think about ourselves, our world, and God.

I am not a counselor, but I know enough about people to know that it is never enough to tell a paranoid person, "Don't be paranoid," or to tell a humiliated and lonely young woman, "Be strong and have fun with others." Healing requires a much deeper work, built on truth. A person must *think* differently, not just *do* certain things. Forgiveness, the root of healing, wholeness, and holiness, begins in the mind and relationship together. Thoughts bear fruit in actions, and so God came as the Word made flesh, teaching about the Kingdom of God. It is a mystery that some people, when they hear the truth about themselves, are liberated from the lies of the past, while other people just do not have ears to hear how much they are loved by God. Jesus had the same problem, or maybe we should say the same experience.

> This is why I speak to them in parables: "Though seeing, they do not see; though hearing, they do not hear or understand. In them is fulfilled the prophecy of Isaiah: 'You will be ever hearing but never understanding; you will be ever seeing but never perceiving.'" (Matt. 13:13)

Not all will believe the truth about God's forgiveness, but all need to hear it. Evangelism is not a demand for certain behaviors. Evangelism is an offer, a gift, an opportunity. Paul's letters outline the progression from belief in God's grace to action; from faith to virtues. Faith means absolute trust in a particular belief and, in this case, the belief is an incarnate person. Thus, we do not preach virtues or spiritual gifts to the unspiritual. For those outside of the household of faith, God offers himself as healing and redeeming truth. "Faith comes from hearing the message, and the message is heard through the word about Christ" (Rom. 10:17). After his long discussion on faith in the early chapters of Romans,[5] Paul turns to his listeners and says he expects transformation, or a new life, to be lived in light of this new knowledge.

> Therefore, I urge you, brothers and sisters, in view of God's mercy, to offer your bodies as a living sacrifice, holy and pleasing to God—this is your true and proper worship. Do not conform to the pattern of this world, but be transformed by the renewing of your mind. (Rom. 12:1–2)

Therefore, I want to be clear that evangelism involves communication of a message and encouragement to trust that message. It is much more than that, but it is never less than that.

> It is not so often acknowledged that evangelism means calling people to believe something which is radically different from what is normally accepted as public truth, and that it calls for a conversion not only of the heart and will but of the mind.[6]

But Christianity is not just about signing off on a catechism or memorizing and repeating certain facts. Facts—historical facts—are the foundation, but they are not the building of faith. Faith, or trust, needs an object, and as Christians the object of faith is a person, not a principle or a precept. Conversion is not like signing a contract—unless we are talking about a marriage contract. Conversion is more like falling in love—there is a complete turning of the head. When we fall in love, it is with a specific person who has our trust. *This* falling in love is just much bigger and more dynamic.[7]

Evangelism is about Jesus Christ. It is hard to imagine a person starting anywhere else, or focusing on any other idea, doctrine, or person than Jesus Christ when trying to communicate the Christian faith. We might start with the analogy of a bridge, but the bridge is always to Jesus Christ—not to the

5. By "faith," Paul means trust in specific knowledge. Some rejected that knowledge and lived in enmity with God (Rom. 1:28–32). Having faith means living into specific truths from God that bring liberation to the individual and reconciliation in community.

6. Lesslie Newbigin, *Truth to Tell: The Gospel as Public Truth* (Grand Rapids: Eerdmans, 1991), 2.

7. Falling in love with God, and even the analogy of marriage, is a consistent image for God's relationship with his people. See for example, Hosea; Eph. 5:21–33; Isa. 54:5; 62:5; and the Song of Songs. In the Old Testament the image of God's people being faithful or not faithful is the same language of marriage (as is seen in Hosea). The loving relationship is sealed with a marriage covenant.

The Person of Jesus

When people or people groups in the non-Western world come to faith, they are generally enamored with Jesus, his words, life, love, and grace. In recent years, it has become clear that emerging Christian communities in the West are also identifying with Jesus more than with a theology, denomination, or set of precepts. The following is from an expansive study done on emerging communities in North America and the UK.

"There is a strong and indissoluble link between the teaching of Jesus and the good news he embodied and proclaimed. His message both announced and inaugurated the reign of God on earth. . . . It is this kingdom hope that inspires emerging church leaders as they seek to realize that promise within their communities, striving for them to become servants and signs of that kingdom. . . . In concrete terms, emerging church leaders look to Jesus as the one who initiated the work of the kingdom in Israel, and their hope is to point to the kingdom through their communal practices in postmodern culture today."[a]

a. Eddie Gibbs and Ryan K. Bolger, *Emerging Churches: Creating Christian Community in Postmodern Cultures* (Grand Rapids: Baker Academic, 2005), 47.

church, not to Christianity, not to my denomination, and certainly not to my particular eschatology. Almost every recent book about evangelism makes it clear that the message is the Messiah: that our words are to focus on the Word.[8] Many issues will be brought up in evangelistic settings, but these issues should arise in the context of Jesus, as the invited guest who soon turns out to be the host. When a contemporary issue is broached we want to ask together, "What would Jesus say in such a situation?" or "Does Jesus's life or do Jesus's words provide any guidance here?"[9] And, after questions have been aired, we ask in return, "What do you think about Jesus?"

Thus Christianity is about truth in personal relationship. Most religions of the world are concerned about suffering and death, and the answers that religions give are generally in the form of prescriptive behaviors. Jesus, however, came teaching and opening the door to relationship with himself and therefore with the Father. Jesus is an attractive person. Almost any evangelist will tell you that evangelism as a process is more like introducing a person

8. See, for example, Richard Peace, *Holy Conversation: Talking about God in Everyday Life* (Downers Grove, IL: InterVarsity, 2006), 39–58; Ronald J. Sider, *Doing Evangelism in Jesus' Way: How Christians Demonstrate the Good News* (Nappanee, IN: Evangel, 2003); Elaine A. Heath, *The Mystic Way of Evangelism: A Contemplative Vision for Christian Outreach* (Grand Rapids: Baker Academic, 2008). In Heath's book, the *kenotic* (self-emptying) model of Jesus is central to her whole argument.

9. Rick Richardson has an example of this in *Evangelism Outside the Box: New Ways to Help People Experience the Good News* (Downers Grove, IL: InterVarsity, 2000), 48.

to their best friend than it is like teaching a class. At the age of sixteen, I attended my first real Bible study, and the evangelist wisely chose to study the life of Jesus. I didn't know all of the theology—in fact, I am sure I got much of the theology wrong during my first years as a Christian—but I was clear that I wanted Jesus: first as my friend and defender, and later as my life. When the leader asked if I wanted to give my life to Jesus Christ, it seemed quite a simple decision: "Of course! Who wouldn't want to give their life to such a wonderful person?" In chapter 7 we heard about the young man who had been in a Chinese triad society and who, before killing himself, read the life of Jesus and then could not go through with it. Jesus is bigger than life. Christianity is an invitation to be in relationship with Someone bigger than life, in fact with Life itself.

Evangelism and Justice: No Longer Partners

For the past century or so, it was common to talk about two distinct but essential elements of Christian mission: evangelism and justice. Such an approach is misleading. Since evangelism is about Jesus, and Jesus was an integrated whole human being, it makes no sense to give a dichotomous reading of Jesus's love for humanity. Jesus's love covers our deepest personal needs and the greatest social injustices. In fact, as we all know, they are of the same fabric. Another way we can see this holistic view of Jesus's love is to remember that the word for justified (*dikaioō*)[10] is the same word for "righteous." One Greek word describes both our legal status and our moral status. So, in evangelism, we start with a single quality of God in Jesus Christ—love—rather than starting with a dichotomy of word and works, or evangelism and justice, or preaching and social justice.[11]

We should be a little suspicious if a person talks about "both sides" of the life of Jesus. In the past it was common to use such language, to talk about the mission of God as two dance partners (evangelism and social justice) or as two sides of the same coin. But these analogies are not just inadequate, they are misleading. Jesus was a whole person, filled to overflowing with the kenotic, self-emptying love of God. Jesus's love is far deeper, wider, and more expansive than we can imagine. His love is as personal as his forgiveness of those who killed him, and it is as large as his suffering love for the sins of the world.

Christians who are informed about their faith, who can explain why they do what they do, are giving an *evangelistic message* when they give up their

10. This means we are now justified before God who is the righteous judge. To be justified is to be righteous.

11. The "Lausanne Covenant" (1974) assumes this dichotomy in section 5 under "Christian Social Responsibility": "Although reconciliation with other people is not reconciliation with God, nor is social action evangelism, nor is political liberation salvation, nevertheless we affirm that evangelism and socio-political involvement are both part of our Christian duty."

holiday to feed the poor or to serve in rehab homes for the elderly. They are pointing to Jesus Christ, and they can make the connection between evangelical faith and evangelical life. At the same time, Christians are making a *social statement* when they lead prisoners or illegal aliens to faith in Jesus Christ. The violent criminal who meets the Lord of the universe in forgiving and cleansing love will cost the city less money and will bring greater justice to local communities. Ron Sider tells the story of a Mennonite pastor in Philadelphia who had been an "angry black militant who hated white people. He once told me that if he had met me back then, he might have killed me. I'm glad he met Jesus first!" says Sider.[12] Evangelistic witness is the good news demonstrated and described. We are not all evangelists, but all Christians are required to be able to explain their faith when others ask about their life. It is interesting that when Peter talks about this type of preparedness, he puts it in the context of Jesus's life, words, and suffering, which we are to emulate.

> But even if you should suffer for what is right, you are blessed. "Do not fear their threats; do not be frightened." But in your hearts revere Christ as Lord. Always be prepared to give an answer to everyone who asks you to give the reason for the hope that you have. But do this with gentleness and respect, keeping a clear conscience, so that those who speak maliciously against your good behavior in Christ may be ashamed of their slander. It is better, if it is God's will, to suffer for doing good than for doing evil. (1 Pet. 3:14–17)

Christians live counter to all cultures, because they have hope. Hope shines like a bright star in a dark world of hopelessness, injustice, loneliness, and oppression. Hope is seen in the lives of individuals who dedicate their free time to offering literacy classes for the illiterate, even though they can only reach a few. Hope is seen in a small church continuing to gather in a home in North Africa when there have only been five or six true conversions in four years. Hope is seen in the lone lawyer taking on a large corporation because truth and justice are at stake. Hope is seen in the decision of the wealthy banker moving into an economically depressed area of the city without any plan but to pray and see how God might use him. All Christians are to live into such hope and to be ready to explain where that hope comes from. This unity of witness was expressed clearly in the "Cape Town Commitment" in 2010.

> If the gospel is not deeply rooted in the context, challenging and transforming underlying worldviews and systems of injustice, then, when the evil day comes, Christian allegiance is discarded like an unwanted cloak and people revert to unregenerate loyalties and actions. Evangelizing without discipling, or revival

12. Sider, *Doing Evangelism*, 75.

> without radical obedience to the commands of Christ, are not just deficient; they are dangerous.[13]

Some people are gifted evangelists and they will be more consciously involved in proclaiming the good news to people during the week. These are the people who have no problem talking to a person on the train, striking up a conversation with the checkout person in the supermarket, and bringing new friends with them to church. We should pray that their numbers increase, but we should also pray that they will evangelize in the pattern of Jesus—who not only preached good news but also brought good news in the way he cared for the needy and oppressed. Evangelists should have eyes to see the wounds of the world and offer the healing touch of grace. We turn now to Jesus and how he brought the good news of the Kingdom.

Witness in the Pattern of Jesus Christ[14]

Whenever I think of witness in the pattern of Jesus Christ, I think of my freshman year in college and my roommate Jerry. I was from the North—a young Christian filled with hope and a message. Jerry was from a small town in the Bible Belt and he was filled with desire—desire to run away from all the culture-Christianity[15] in his past. I played soccer and went to Bible studies, and Jerry spent time looking for a good fraternity. "Roomie, they have all this free beer! Kegs out on the lawn—why don't you come with me this Friday night?" Jerry pledged a fraternity, and I struggled with finding Christian fellowship, playing soccer, and finding time to study. About five months into our year as "the odd couple," Jerry suddenly woke up one night and shouted, "Roomie, I had a vivid dream and I need your help!" Half awake, and filled with ungodly thoughts about how to find a different roommate, I turned on the light. He

13. Cape Town Commitment, II.B.2 (28) This is found under the heading "Christ's Peace in Ethnic Conflict."

14. One of the earliest and still standard books on evangelism in the pattern of Jesus is Robert Coleman's *The Master Plan of Evangelism*, first published in 1963 (New York: Fleming H. Revell). He now has a follow-up book entitled *The Heart of the Gospel: The Theology behind the Master Plan of Evangelism* (Grand Rapids: Baker Books, 2011).

15. Culture-Christianity is Christianity that is so dominated by a particular culture, nation, or ideology that it requires all others to accept the culture to become Christian. A particular culture directs the development of the theology and thus excludes other cultures. Many of the attentive Christians in Germany during the time of the rise of the National Socialists Workers' Party (Nazi) recognized the problem of German folk Christianity (one form of culture-Christianity), and so many of the writings of people like Dietrich Bonhoeffer and Karl Barth opposed the uncritical alignment of the German Christians with the Nazi Party. The "Barmen Declaration" is one of the best examples of resistance to this form of culture-Christianity. Culture-Christianity always resists the fulfillment of the Great Commission, because Christ's commission requires all nations and cultures to be included at the foot of the cross.

told me his dream: "I was walking in the hot sun with not a cloud in the sky. I was thirsty and tired and then I looked up on a hill and there was a big shade tree that looked so inviting—and Jesus was standing under the tree." "Who?" I said. "Jesus—he was standing under the tree, looking cool and smiling at me. Then he said to me—he spoke right at me in my dream—'Jerry, come up here with me.' It scared the heebie jeebies out of me." With an uncharacteristic degree of clarity in the middle of the night I simply said, "Jerry, Jesus is calling you to follow him. Will you do it?" And so he did. We prayed in the middle of the night and, as far as I know, Jerry continues to be a follower of Jesus today.

I think of this as evangelism in the model of Jesus because in this case Jesus really did call my roommate to come to him. Additionally, Jesus offered to fill Jerry's deepest need, not necessarily give him what he wanted. Jerry badly wanted to please people, to be part of a group. Jesus gave him what he really needed: comfort and refreshment. Also, in Jerry's dream Jesus gave a call—he asked for a step of faith. Many stories of Jesus in the Bible show Jesus as giving a sometimes gentle and sometimes strong call to commitment (e.g., Matt. 19:21: "If you want to be perfect, go, sell your possessions and give to the poor, and you will have treasure in heaven. Then come, follow me"). Finally, throughout this middle-of-the-night conversion, Jesus made no demands; he simply offered grace.

> Come to me, all you who are weary and burdened, and I will give you rest. Take my yoke upon you and learn from me, for I am gentle and humble in heart, and you will find rest for your souls. For my yoke is easy and my burden is light. (Matt. 11:28–30)

Jesus is our model, both in terms of his approach and in terms of the basic content of his message, and yet, unlike Jesus, we do not point to *ourselves*, nor do we call people to follow *us*. Some pastors and missionaries seem to be confused in this matter. Our message is given in the third-person singular; Jesus's message was given in the first-person singular.

Variety of Approaches

Reading through the Gospels, noting Jesus's major encounters with people, there is no single pattern that emerges. Evangelism is as varied as the people Jesus encountered, and so we too must resist any dominant pattern or approach. Jesus's interactions with people reveal the following:

- Jesus spoke his message directly to some people, but with most he gently led the conversation as a discussion.
- For some people he performed deeds of mercy, and to others he communicated his message with words alone.

- To some people he issued a direct call or challenge, but with others he did not.
- With many he told stories and parables, inviting people to think deeply about the Kingdom of heaven.
- To some people he brought peace and calm, but to others he brought division.
- Many of his teaching moments were during times of trial, injury, illness, and death (funerals).
- In many of his encounters he used questions and only a few statements.
- His witness was out of weakness—not from a position of strength or power.
- His witness was lived out as he healed, fed, and touched people, and exorcised demons.
- His witness involved some hard, demanding teachings and a call to repentance.
- His witness was often an offer of grace or relief through a relationship with him.

These observations reveal some of the varied ways in which Jesus proclaimed the good news of the Kingdom. In all of this there is a consistent call to change loyalties, from self (money, family, religion) to Jesus and God's Kingdom. This is an important distinction: while his methods were diverse, they were in service to a unified call—toward unqualified loyalty to Jesus and his Kingdom.

Responses to Jesus

There were also a variety of responses to Jesus. We might expect that all encounters with Jesus the evangelist would end with a conversion, but this is not the case. Many resisted, some walked away, and others plotted to kill him. It is somewhat reassuring that Jesus, God in the flesh, did not have unqualified success in evangelism. His offer honors the integrity of the individual will, a will created by Jesus himself. How did people respond to Jesus's evangelism?

- Some people responded to Jesus by dropping everything and following him immediately.
- Some people walked away from his challenge.
- Some people followed for the big show (healings, exorcisms, and food), but turned away when the call became more difficult or more demanding.
- Some people not only responded but became immediate evangelists—bringing others to Jesus.

- Some people wanted to follow Jesus secretly, fearing what others might say.
- Some of the people who seemed to be closest to him denied him.
- Some people followed him, then denied him, but later died for him.

If we look carefully, we can see in Jesus's varied approaches and these diverse responses the two threads of grace and judgment: grace for the needy and judgment on the self-satisfied. Jesus said to the self-righteous teachers of the law, "It is not the healthy who need a doctor, but the sick. I have not come to call the righteous, but sinners" (Mark 2:17). Evangelizing in the pattern of Jesus will mean that we are clear about Jesus's message, but are also humble enough to realize our inability to speak as clearly as Jesus did to the needs and to the pride of others. As with Jesus, evangelism for us is a creative communication of mercy through prayer.

Evangelism in the pattern of Jesus is especially appropriate during times of transition. Funerals proclaim the resurrection and remind people of their own mortality. Weddings mark covenant commitments and point to the covenant love of God for his people. Baptisms are a reminder of the possibility of dying to sin and being raised up to newness of life. Life's transitions are places where the good news is at home. Jesus's evangelism took place mostly on the highways and byways of life, not in a religious setting (the temple). Jesus was the evangelist of God, eating meals with his friends and acquaintances, walking through fields, spending time with fishermen, and even asking for a cup of water at a well.

Conversion Is Once and for All and It Happens Again and Again

Evangelism is not mere announcing. I am reminded of one of the early black-and-white films about the life of Jesus that depicted Jesus walking quickly through grain fields shouting out to the people in the fields, "Repent, the Kingdom of God is at hand." No time to wait for a response, Jesus seemed to be trying to maximize how many people he could make contact with each day. Evangelism is not like this, and neither was Jesus's ministry. Evangelism is an intimate form of communication that seeks a response. Jesus did not say, "Go make converts"; he did say, "Go make disciples." Conversion is not the goal, but it is the passageway to becoming a disciple. What this means is that evangelism must not be limited to rallies, movies, tracts, or billboards. All or any of these may be helpful, but if there is no intent to invite a response or to make a call to commitment, then Jesus has been misrepresented. This is where Reformed theologians must be careful not to hide behind the doctrine of predestination: "I am doing my duty by announcing the reign of God; it is up to God to do the rest." This type of evangelistic quietism is just an excuse for disobedience.

Evangelism is faithful and imaginative communication that implores others to step into the Kingdom, to join the family, and to accept their adoption as sons and daughters. There may be a fine line between badgering people and inviting a response, but there is definitely a rather large fat line between inviting a response and not inviting a response.

I have taught evangelism courses for eighteen years, and I start each class with a testimony from someone who has come to faith from a non-Christian background. I do this because it helps me learn about God's creativity, and it helps the class see again and again the joy that a person experiences when they come to faith. Some have come from Hindu, Buddhist, or Muslim backgrounds, but most were raised completely outside of any religion or were only tangentially involved in Christian activities when they were young. As the person is giving their five- or ten-minute testimony, I generally write key words on the board. What these testimonies have illustrated, over the years, is that the approach of Jesus and the responses to Jesus mentioned above are born out in twentieth- and twenty-first-century evangelism. Here are some of the themes that repeat themselves in the personal testimonies of salvation I have recorded over the past eighteen years.

Ten Characteristics of Contemporary Evangelism and Conversion

1. There is always an initial contact with a Christian who is alert and willing to talk about faith in Jesus Christ (not just about "church"). Jesus was the subject.
2. Soon, after an initial contact, many other Christian relationships develop. The person is not related to just one Christian, but to a network of people.
3. A community (a small group, church, or fellowship) will invite the person to attend meetings, worship, prayer, or a Bible study.
4. At times the contact and evangelist have a lot in common (a type of elective affinity),[16] but more often the contact and evangelist have very little in common, and may not even be the same age or have any interests in common.
5. Somewhere along this journey, the future convert begins reading the Bible, usually (but not always) with some guidance from Christians.
6. From contact with Christians and from the reading of the Scriptures come questions, both theoretical and personal. Some of the questions are never answered.
7. Quite often a crisis event or crossroad in life is an important element in the conversion story. A death, an illness, a family divorce, or some

16. First used by Max Weber in his book *The Protestant Ethic and the Spirit of Capitalism* (1905) where he described a resonance between the ethics of Protestantism and the basic needs and principles of capitalism.

other event begins the search for some, but for others a major event concludes the search and helps to lead the person to faith.

8. It is hard to put a time period on the process from first contact to baptism, but most often it seems to take from six months to three years. Some people hear and respond the first time, others live with faithful Christian witness all around them for a decade or more.
9. Most people can remember significant points of understanding or special "breakthroughs" during this pilgrimage. Sometimes these breakthroughs were at a meeting, sometimes when they were alone, and sometimes as part of a conversation.
10. Change in life and lifestyle always happens as the denouement of the testimony. Jesus Christ is not just an add-on. When he enters a person's life, there is a whole new foundation for decisions and a new pattern for life. All testimonies end with descriptions of how their lives changed.

Pluralistic contexts, such as Western societies, offer a unique opportunity to speak into public spaces, but with every evangelistic benefit there seems to be a countervailing difficulty. Many pluralisms resist universal stories, but the gospel is nothing if not a universal story. In non-Western worlds, different patterns develop depending upon the context. In each local context, Christians should take time to look at typical patterns—to be aware of how Christ becomes attractive, understood, and then received. Don Everts and Doug Schaupp have noted that, for all contexts, it is of primary importance for the evangelist to live faithfully, and therefore attractively. When we live in ways that are faithful to the gospel of Christ, it is *unusual* and therefore attractive. Christian involvement and participation in society is deep and

Postmodern Skeptics Coming to Faith

A recent publication identifies a pattern for how contemporary people in the United States have been coming to faith. In *I Once was Lost: What Postmodern Skeptics Taught Us about Their Path to Jesus*,[a] Don Everts and Doug Schaupp identify a pattern from their interviews with people who have come to faith (mostly college students) in the past few decades. These individuals generally move from not trusting anyone religious, to developing enough trust to be a friend, and then toward curiosity. After some time, they develop some openness to new ideas, then move to a point of actually seeking, and finally make a commitment in conversion. One of Everts and Schaupp's main points is that the process in a post-Christian world begins with building trust and developing some genuine curiosity.

a. Don Everts and Doug Schaupp, *I Once Was Lost: What Postmodern Skeptics Taught Us about Their Path to Jesus* (Downers Grove, IL: InterVarsity, 2008).

wide, but it is also unique. The Christian whose life is "normal" blends into the surrounding culture, and therefore is just as captive to the culture as everyone else. In contrast, Jesus's life raised questions because of his radical acceptance of the marginalized; so should ours. Conversion is from one thing to something else. Therefore, the life that is being lived on earth, but in the Kingdom realm, is itself a call to change/conversion—or at least the possibility of conversion.

One final note needs to be made about conversion, and that is that conversion is both a one-time event (or, to put it differently, the conclusion of a process) and something that happens again and again. On the one hand, we can take the one-time event as the original call to discipleship. Jesus expressed this call by asking some to drop their nets, others to go sell all they had, and others to be born again. All of these are one-time conversions or "turning around points" in a person's life. When I prayed the sinner's prayer at the age of sixteen, I knew that I had turned a corner and that there was no turning back. The first verse I memorized was Luke 9:62, "No one who puts a hand to the plow and looks back is fit for service in the kingdom of God." I put my hand to the plow at one specific time and for all of time.

But, after that initial conversion, there are many other "turnings" in the Christian life. These later conversions are not the full turn to a new life in Christ—they are a turning back *again* to Christ, and each turn involves discovering something new. In fact, we go through many conversions as we first come to faith and then as we grow as disciples of Christ. Many people and many churches go through a number of conversions.[17] This is partially because very few people know the whole story when they come to faith in Christ. In fact, most people come to faith for a specific reason that is only a small part of who Jesus is. Some confess their sins and join the church because they are enjoying fellowship and community like they had never known it before. Some, like Chong Kau, come to faith because they learn about the beauty and love of God. Others come to faith because they have been healed and they know that in Christ they can have wholeness. None of these beginnings will stay in that limited, small house of faith. As they learn more and step further into obedience, God's house becomes bigger; it is not just a little place for me and my family, it is a whole Kingdom that involves all the nations and speaks to all the longings and cries of the world. Each time we go back to Jesus, there is a deeper conversion of belief and life. And if we do not return again and again to see the greater glory of God in Christ, then our kindergarten faith will not be able to speak to the university issues we confront in our lives. Conversion is a once-and-for-all event that prepares a person and a community for an ongoing life of conversions to Christ.

17. I think of the wonderful title of the book *The Continuing Conversion of the Church* by Darrell Guder (Grand Rapids: Eerdmans, 2000).

Witness in Humility and Suffering

There is a cost to conversion and a cost to leading a person through the process of conversion. The individual coming to faith must count the cost (Luke 14:27–28), evaluating if they can really "carry the cross" that is required of a disciple. No evangelistic message is complete if it simply promises health and happiness. In fact, the promise that Jesus gives is that we will be redeemed by him, received by him, and then likely rejected because of him. The concept of following in the suffering path of Jesus is found throughout the Gospels, but Paul summarizes is most directly: "For it has been granted to you on behalf of Christ not only to believe in him, but also to suffer for him" (Phil. 1:29). All this is true for followers of Jesus. As disciples obey Christ in evangelistic witness, there is a further call to humility, self-denial, and suffering. Why is this the case? Because when we live into our witness, we are saying with our lives that time with other people—other people who are resistant to the gospel or even angry at God—is important. This will mean that at times we are lonely, not getting the affirmation and support that we think we need from our Christian community. An evangelist is exposed, living on the frontiers of faith, in a place where common values are not shared and where even the language may be difficult. Evangelists working in Islamic contexts may know the cost most dramatically, often living in daily fear of being exiled or imprisoned. Some evangelists live on a more dangerous edge than others, but all evangelists live on an edge. The edge between faith and unbelief is a place of great danger, but also a place of great opportunity and joy.[18]

Part of my ongoing conversion was to learn of the Messiah's identity with the poor and with prisoners. It began when my wife and I read some Advent readings that included Isaiah 61:1. I sat there on my couch and thought, "Jesus was identified with the needy and with prisoners, and I don't even know any really needy people. I don't even know where the prison is." So I was converted to Jesus's view of my community. I found the local prison and asked if I could visit some prisoners. After three or four weeks of training, I was assigned to two prisoners to visit twice a week. The learning curve was pretty steep for me, and yet I had no question that I was at least heading in the right direction. As part of my ongoing discussions and studies with my two new friends, I found out that one of them needed to pay off some debts before the courts would consider early release. He asked me if I could lend him money to pay a particular bill: $250. I was a little bit leery, but I reasoned that, since he was in prison, he wasn't going anywhere soon. Well, as you may have guessed, I was taken advantage of—when I was paid back the check bounced, I had to

18. It is tempting to add here the popular belief that the Japanese and Chinese characters that together mean "crisis" are made up of "danger" and "opportunity." However, this is not true, as sinologist Victor H. Mair of the University of Pennsylvania has proven: http://www.pinyin.info/chinese/crisis.html.

pay extra bank fees, and my prison friend was soon released—with a copy of the New Testament and $250 of my money.

Missionaries sell their belongings to travel across borders and across the world to tell people about the Kingdom of God. Many sacrifice careers, family relations, or their lives so that others may hear of Jesus. To carry out witness in their university, some Christians move out of their "Christian ghettos" to live among international students or to live in a fraternity house. Some retired folks give up an easy retirement to open their home to their neighbors or to new immigrants, leading them to faith in Christ. Evangelism requires the death of something—security, comfort, relationships—so that new life can be planted. The seed of faith must be planted in broken, aerated, and irrigated soil. The work of sowing seed is just that: work.

I knew an especially gifted evangelist, an eighteen-year-old university student. I will call her Tanya. Tanya was excited to go to the big university both to learn (many students still say this!) and to meet non-Christians and invite them into the Kingdom. One of her first accomplishments in her new dorm was to be the first person to get a citation for putting up signs in "unacceptable" places. After removing the signs and placing them in appropriate places, she waited for Wednesday night. The signs simply read: "Prayer meeting for fourth floor every Wednesday night at 11:00 in room 404." Six or eight people came, but one stood out. A Japanese girl from a Buddhist and Shintoist family came and sat on the bed watching and listening as the other girls prayed on their knees. It was rather uncomfortable, to say the least, for the girls to have someone staring at them as they prayed. But, she came the second week, and the third, and for the whole fall semester. Early in the spring semester, the Japanese girl asked Tanya, "Can you teach me to pray?" This led to a discussion about trusting your life to Jesus and then not only praying to him, but actually having him pray for you. It took time, and it was not comfortable, but this Japanese girl did come to faith. She then transferred to continue her studies in Japan because, as she said, "So many of my Japanese friends do not know about Jesus." Tanya also sacrificed some of her (far more enjoyable) time with Christian friends to spend time with the women's rugby team. She soon found out that this particular team was made up of "hard living" women who drank a lot; many of them were sexually active with each other. It was an uncomfortable community for this young Christian girl, but she gave up the time she wanted to spend with others to spend time with those who needed to hear the gospel.

Evangelism will require a change in priorities, a change in location, a change in calendar—it will mean taking up the cross of Christ. The normal Christian life is a life of witness, and a life of witness counts the cost and enters into the struggles of the Kingdom. Witness, as Jesus reminds us, will not always be welcome, and it will not always be comfortable. Jesus's words, "Unless a kernel of wheat falls to the ground and dies, it remains only a single seed. But if it dies, it produces many seeds" (John 12:24), refers not only to the convert but also to the evangelist.

Fine-Tuning Our Witness

Whether we are moving across the ocean to tell the good news of the Kingdom or walking across the street, there are some characteristics of Christian evangelism that should be part of each person or each Christian community. I call this fine-tuning our witness, since these are finer points than what has been mentioned above. For some people, these aspects of evangelism will be new, opening new doors for witness, but for others they will simply be gentle reminders. The first essential aspect of evangelism is Scripture. From the earliest Christian communities, Christians have been united in their understanding that the Scriptures point to Jesus and are about Jesus. This has a very practical application in evangelism. If we are going to give witness to Jesus Christ, we need to know Scripture and have portions memorized. It is not enough to be able to find a reference or look for a Scripture that is similar to the issue that has been raised. We need to look into the eyes of our new friend, perhaps a friend who is under a lot of pressure at work, and say to them, "Jesus has said, 'Come to me, all you who are weary and burdened, and I will give you rest. Take my yoke upon you and learn from me, for I am gentle and humble in heart, and you will find rest for your souls. For my yoke is easy and my burden is light'" (Matt. 11:28–30).

We don't throw Scriptures at people in hopes that some of them will stick; we should instead have Scripture, especially the Gospels, so woven into our lives that we can't help but speak with the words of Scripture. To the person who feels that their life is too dark and sinful for God to accept them, we should be able to respond naturally that God knows that. He knows that "all have sinned and fall short of the glory of God" (Rom. 3:23), and Jesus did "not come to call the righteous, but sinners to repentance" (Luke 5:32). It cannot be emphasized enough that evangelism must flow out of the living stream of Scripture, both memorized and enfleshed in our lives.

Secondly, testimonies are also important for evangelism. This has always been the case in the church, from the very beginning. The witness of Polycarp that was recorded as "The Martyrdom of Polycarp"[19] has been an encouragement to Christians and a witness to nonbelievers. The testimonies of Saul, who became Paul, and of Simon, who became Peter, are paths of conversion for others to read and follow. When a person gives a testimony of what God has done in their life, or in their family, it becomes undeniable evidence of

19. Found in Cyril C. Richardson, ed., *Early Christian Fathers* (New York: Collier Books, 1970), 149–58. Also found at http://www.earlychristianwritings.com/text/martyrdompolycarp-lightfoot.html and at http://www.ccel.org/ccel/schaff/anf01.iv.iv.html.

the truth about which they are speaking. Each testimony points to what God has done for an individual. Testimonies do not have to be "success stories," but they do have to be genuine.

Our daughter, while teaching English in China, was invited to a church member's house for tea one afternoon. Unsure of where the house was located, she asked a local high school student to show her the way. After winding their way through streets and walled properties, they finally came to the gate of the woman's house and rang the bell. When the lady came to the house she greeted Caroline and then, looking at the boy, said, "And who are you?" He identified himself as Caroline's guide and, without missing a beat, the woman said, "Are you a Christian?" He said no and immediately she said, "Good, then please come in for tea," whereupon she spent a good part of an hour ignoring Caroline and giving the young man her testimony. Her testimony was mostly about how, after being baptized, her husband turned against her and moved out. She was left to raise the two children by herself. The Christian life was not all a bed of roses (in fact there were many thorns), but it was the truth of God's faithfulness to her even through difficult times that was the heart of her testimony. What a testimony does is point to the work of God in our lives. It is not *our* testimony; it is *God's* testimony, pointing to the work of God in, to, and through us.

Thirdly, evangelism requires that we think creatively about how to meet people on their terms, in their context. This is where Max Weber's concept of elective affinity is helpful. There are certain patterns and interests we have in common that bring groups of people together. Often by identifying our interests and then looking to see where outsiders who share those interests are, we have an immediate bridge of trust and communication. Upon returning back to the States and starting to teach evangelism, I noticed that, not only was I no longer involved in evangelism, but I didn't even have any places of contact with non-Christians, except through my children. Since I coached soccer and basketball, I decided to work with my boys on evangelism. For six years, I met with high school boys, having breakfast at 6:30 in the morning (that's right, high school boys can get up at 6:00 a.m.), telling jokes, talking about sports, and studying the Gospel of Mark. We all liked jokes, they were all involved in sports teams, and I was interested in them learning to follow Jesus. Others have found ways to get involved in chess clubs, quilting groups, bowling teams, photography classes, the volunteer fire department, or even tattoo parlors as a way to meet people and begin relationships. Without a connection to others, especially through common interests, it is nearly impossible to share the good news. This is something that usually requires intentional decisions and a change in lifestyle.

Fourthly, it is important to remember that even the most secure and confident individual is broken and lost. If we stay around long enough and listen carefully enough, we find out that all people are in need. I have taught a course on "evangelism in context" in which I have students watch commercials for an hour, three different times. They are to record what they learn about: what is sold, why it is being sold (why we need this product), and what this says about the advertiser's view of the public. It is a very interesting exercise, which essentially reveals that all advertising is pitched to our insecurities. We must have a lot of insecurities, because there is a lot of money being spent in advertising. Advertisers point out that we smell, we have bad breath, we are wearing the wrong clothes, we are driving a slow and ugly car, our hair is bad (or the wrong color), and we are too fat. Playing on these insecurities, they come in to "save" us by providing the product we need. People are lost and needy—all of us, including myself. "We all, like sheep, have gone astray" (Isa. 53:6). We are all lost sheep—and so is our neighbor. The evangelist enters as a guide to point the way to refreshment and acceptance. One of the most famous definitions of an evangelist is that given by Sri Lankan evangelist and ecumenist D. T. Niles: "One beggar showing another where to find the bread." We are all needy, no matter how satisfied and secure we may look on the outside.

An evangelist helps a person to become vulnerable and transparent; this process involves helping a person become open to their own needs, and therefore the evangelist must be discerning and gentle. When Jesus begins to enter a person's life, he enters all of the recesses of the past, all of the hurts and sins of the present, and all of the fears and idolatry we have about "our" future. Evangelism has to do with ideas and beliefs, but these ideas are intensely personal, even as they are universally applicable. Jesus's encounter with the woman at the well is a case in point (John 4:4–42). When they meet, she holds him at bay—keeping conversation away from the personal—by talking about Jews and Samaritans, then Jacob and the well, and finally about water. Jesus, however, will not be kept at a distance—he moves right in and says, "Go call your husband and come back." In saying this, he goes to the heart of her brokenness and her loneliness. When Jesus brings redemption, he brings redemption to all areas of a life. The entrance to the Kingdom is on our knees in confession of sin and then repentance. Confession requires exposure, so the evangelist must be gentle and firm with the call of Christ.

Finally, it is essential to remember that all of this is beyond us. It is impossible to be a perfect evangelist. If Jesus, who I think was the perfect evangelist, was rejected at times, how are we going to know if our rejection is truly a rejection of God or if the person is rejecting our poor approach and skills? Evangelism is a matter of discernment and prayer, relationship with the Triune God, and linking that relationship with our neighbor. In building bridges from the heart of God to the heart of our neighbor we will be living in prayer, interceding on behalf of others. This is the priestly and most important work of evangelism. Individuals and churches are invited into this sacred space on behalf of our neighbors, and on behalf of unreached people across the globe. Evangelism is a prayerful ministry.

Evangelism and Salvation

There are certain theological flash points that are sure to rouse interest, even among the most moribund of Christian communities. Salvation—who's in and who's out—is one of those flash points today. Recently, I was at a memorial service for a relative. The event was more New Age than Christian. There were luminescent balloons, brightly colored clothes, poignant stories, and funny songs—but no mention of God, Jesus, salvation, or heaven at this celebration of the life of a former elder in a Presbyterian church. No clergy were invited, although I (a Presbyterian clergy member) sat quietly in the sixth row, incognito. After the service I sat around with other relatives, in theological shock at what I had just experienced, when slowly an uncle began to ask me about my work and then about what I thought about other religions and about salvation. For the next hour, four of us had a fairly typical discussion about "good Buddhists," about our common humanity, and one person even talked about everyone going to their *own* heaven (Jewish heaven, Muslim heaven, Hindu heaven, etc.). It was a spirited discussion that generated neither heat nor light—but it did generate some interest. Death and the afterlife concern every person and every nation; we all share life as something that is fatal.

Evangelism has to do with good news that relates to this life and the next. It is not just a matter of enlisting people in God's Peace Corps program, or a way to make bad people better and unjust situations more just. Evangelism concerns this world, but it also relates to ultimate questions and the fate of humanity. Our dilemma is that we want to affirm all people (which is a good and true impulse, since all people are marked with the *imago Dei*) while at the same time affirming what we know about God and salvation from Scripture (which speaks of heaven and hell). Hans Küng has neatly listed some options that have evolved regarding the truth in other religions, and of course this would include the truth regarding salvation.[20]

1. The atheists' position: No religion is true *or* all religions are equally untrue.
2. The absolutists' position: Only one religion is uniquely true. One form of this is the earlier Roman Catholic theology of *extra ecclesia, nulla salus* (no salvation outside of the church).
3. The relativists' position: Each religion is true *or* all religions are equally true.
4. The inclusivists' position: One religion is true for all *or* all religions have some part of the truth of the one religion.

20. "Towards an Ecumenical Theology of Religions: Some Theses for Clarification," in Hans Küng and Jürgen Moltmann, eds., *Christianity Among World Religions* (Edinburgh: T&T Clark, 1986), 119–25.

For our purposes, it is helpful to see this variety of opinions and then to acknowledge that Christians of different stripes hold these various positions today. However, this paradigm is misleading, because it is based upon an abstract concept of "truth" and it focuses on a modern concept of "religion," rather than on the person of Jesus Christ. If we are going to think Christianly about salvation and evangelism, we need to do it on Christian terms, and that means following the trinitarian approach outlined in chapters 6, 7, and 8. How do we proceed?

First, before we get caught in a number of conversations and issues for which we have no answers, it is best to start with what we *cannot* know—for what we *cannot* know should not prevent us from faithfulness in what we *do* know. This would lead us to agnosticism ("We really cannot be sure about salvation at all"), for we would be paralyzed from making any kind of personal commitment if we needed to know everything before we acted. An example from everyday life may help. Even though we may not completely understand the workings of an airplane, we know enough to step on, sit down, and buckle up. We "believe" in airplanes and we live as if they can fly, even though we (or at least I) have many questions about how they actually defy gravity. Although we do not have a complete knowledge of aeronautical engineering, we are not agnostic about United Airlines or Cathay Pacific—we are still willing and able to go up in the plane.

The following are some questions and issues that we cannot know the answer to in this life. Therefore, it is best to set these issues aside for later times of private intellectual speculation and move on to what we do know.

1. We cannot know the actual state, condition, or place of hell.
2. We cannot know the exact state, condition, or place of heaven.
3. We cannot know exactly who will be found in either place (although we may have some pretty good ideas).
4. To further expand on number 3, we cannot know the fate of those who came before the death, resurrection, and ascension of Jesus Christ, nor can we be sure of the fate of those who have never heard of Jesus Christ.[21]

However, not knowing the actual state, condition, or place of hell does not mean that hell is not real or that it is not something to be avoided.[22] Suffering

21. The work of Jesus Christ includes his ascension and therefore we cannot really talk about the work of redemption or salvation being completed until Jesus has ascended to the right hand of the Father (the seat of authority).

22. There is a doctrine of the "restoration of all things" (*apokatastasis*) that was first systematically taught by Origen in the third century (*First Principles* 3.6.6). In brief, this doctrine has often been interpreted as meaning that all people (angels and even Satan himself) will be saved and restored, through purgation. This has been a minority position in the church through the ages; even among the proponents and those who discussed it as a possibility (Origen, Gregory of

and judgment for disobedience in the Old Testament,[23] as well as threats of hell and punishment in the New Testament, are not incidental or peripheral arguments of Jesus (Matt. 5:22, 29; 10:28; 23:15, 33; Mark 9:42–48; and Luke 12:5). An understanding of the punishment or exile[24] of those who are "unfaithful" is a precondition for understanding Jesus's teachings, as well as the teachings of Peter and of Revelation. Second Peter chapter 2 does not make sense if it is read as an idle warning, like a mother saying, "If you touch my cake I am going to cut off your hand." Peter's warnings are consistent with the grace offered in Jesus Christ and the judgment on sin. Judgment is always the backdrop to grace. Judgment is always a real possibility for the "ungodly" ("unrighteous").

> If he rescued Lot, a righteous man, who was distressed by the depraved conduct of the lawless (for that righteous man, living among them day after day, was tormented in his righteous soul by the lawless deeds he saw and heard)—if this is so, then the Lord knows how to rescue godly men from trials. (2 Pet. 2:7–9)

Neither does lack of knowledge prevent most people from belief in heaven. The Kingdom of heaven is one of Jesus's major concerns, but what we can understand of heaven (concerning rooms, food, and relationships) is mostly metaphorical and allegorical language. We cannot know everything about heaven. So it is for all four of the statements above. We cannot know all about these four issues, but we *can* know something—enough to be faithful.

Secondly, salvation is much more beautiful and integrated a concept than merely an escape from hell into heaven. Salvation is a much larger concept than what happens after death. I have preferred to use the word "redemption," which shows continuity with the Old Testament (sacrifices and prophecies) and is more holistic in its depiction of the saving work that God has done in Jesus Christ. However, the words "save" and "salvation" are important to use because this is also the language of Scripture: Jesus's very name reveals that "God is

---

Nyssa and Gregory of Nazianzus, Ambrosiaster, Evagrios of Pontus), there is no strong univocal theology. See Frederick Norris's brief discussion under "Apokatastasis," in John McGuckin's *Westminster Handbook on Origen* (Louisville: Westminster John Knox, 2004), and Edward Moore's historical discussion of the concept in relation to Stoic philosophy and Gnosticism: http://www.romancatholicism.org/origen-apokatastasis.htm.

23. First Chronicles 10 says that Saul was killed (and a violent death it was, including having his head removed) "for his unfaithfulness; he was unfaithful to the Lord in that he did not keep the command of the Lord; moreover, he had consulted a medium, seeking guidance and did not seek guidance from the Lord" (vv. 13–14). All of Judah was sent into exile to Babylon "because of their unfaithfulness" (9:1; cf. Neh. 9:16–31). This is not a description of hell, but it does describe punishment for being unfaithful. Similarly, the exodus is a "type" of salvation of which Jesus's death and resurrection (conquering sin) is the "arch-type."

24. The Old Testament images of exile (from God's presence) as a punishment and exodus (liberation from Egypt) as salvation are very important for our understanding of a Christian view of salvation and punishment.

the savior." Salvation[25] involves our redeemed life lived now, in Christ, as well as our life of suffering faithfulness for others, and our eternal life in Christ. Salvation "wholeness" comes through confession of sin and repentance, but it has physical, emotional, social, and spiritual implications (Ps. 32). Salvation divides us from some people and unites us to others (including family members: Matt. 12:48–50). Salvation has comprehensiveness to it that we seldom recognize. It relates to all of a person, all relationships, and all of creation. A person or culture cannot be redeemed quietly, on the side, with no one noticing.

Thirdly, we must remember that salvation is in and through Jesus Christ. I have spoken of this in the theological section, but we should remember here as well that evangelism among people of no faith, or of a strong faith, or of a weak and amorphous faith, is still the good news about Jesus Christ. Whether we are particularists about salvation (only those who trust in Jesus will be saved) or universalists about salvation (everyone is saved through Jesus), we still speak with the voice of Acts 4:12, "Salvation is found in no one else, for there is no other name under heaven given to mankind by which we must be saved." There is a clarity about this ("no other name," "under heaven," "must be saved") that will not let us go elsewhere.

Fourthly, we can and should be clear about what salvation is from. "To save" is a transitive verb. One must be saved from something and to something. Jesus saves (following the Old Testament language we have referred to) from exile and slavery. Whether people realize it, acknowledge it, or avoid it, sin is the ever-present enemy of every human being, dragging us down to sickness, death, and separation from God. We are saved from our sins and the results of sin: "Your faith has healed you" (Matt. 9:22; Mark 10:52). We are also saved from the unseen powers: "Jesus rebuked the demon, and it came out of the boy, and he was healed at that moment" (Matt. 17:18). Remembering that exorcism was a major and uncontested ministry of Jesus, we can see that salvation is from demons, as well as from sin and its results (illness and death).[26]

25. A very good overview of the questions regarding salvation is given in the article on "Salvation" (by Daniel Patte) in *The Cambridge Dictionary of Christianity*, ed. Daniel Patte (Cambridge: Cambridge University Press, 2010). For contemporary discussions on salvation, see: Ivor J. Davidson and Murray A. Rae, *God of Salvation: Soteriology in Theological Perspective* (Burlington, VT: Ashgate, 2011). For an interesting study of salvation in dialogue with Confucianism, see Paulos Zhanzhu Huang's *Confronting Confucian Understandings of the Christian Doctrine of Salvation: A Systematic Theological Analysis of the Basic Problems in the Confucian-Christian Dialogue* (Leiden: Brill, 2009). For a good introductory study of salvation, religions, and universalism in the Bible, see Terry Muck and Frances S. Adeney, *Christianity Encountering World Religions: The Practice of Mission in the Twenty-first Century* (Grand Rapids: Baker Academic, 2009). These volumes, with their bibliographies, will introduce one into the major issues and debates concerning salvation.

26. Not all illnesses are directly caused by sin, so we want to be careful not to assume that salvation brings complete health. Paul had a particular illness that he prayed for, but it stayed with him. Paul was saved, nonetheless (2 Cor. 12:7–10).

Fifthly, we know that resurrection is understood in continuity with the Old Testament paradigm as understood by Paul. When Rabbi Paul defended himself before the governor, he said, as if it were common knowledge, that *all* people will be resurrected—but not all people will be resurrected to the same place. "I believe everything that is in accordance with the Law and that is written in the Prophets, and I have the same hope in God as these men themselves have, that there will be a resurrection of both the righteous and the wicked" (Acts 24:14–15). Thus, resurrection as the doorway to eternal life is understood as a key concept in both salvation and judgment. Resurrection was so important in Paul's preaching that he even said that he was to be tried in Jerusalem concerning his teaching about the resurrection of the dead (Acts 24:21). The resurrection is for all: resurrection into eternal life (and thus avoiding the "second death"[27]) is for the righteous, or those who are made righteous. "The righteous will live by faith" means they will be resurrected to new life after death (Rom. 1:17).

Sixthly, we know that the evangelist is God's normal method for bringing salvation to others. Reconciliation with God, a communion of two individuals, is brought about through personal relationships with others. There are times when a person comes to faith without another person present, but this is rare, and even then there is soon another person in the story. Some may come to faith through dreams, or reading a book, or reading the Bible by themselves, but these are all extraordinary methods. Isaiah 52 was recognized as a fulfilled prophecy in Jesus and the apostles after him (Rom. 10:15):

> "Therefore in that day they will know
> that it is I who foretold it.
> Yes, it is I."
> How beautiful on the mountains
> are the feet of those who bring good news,
> who proclaim peace,
> who bring good tidings,
> who proclaim salvation. (Isa. 52:6–7)

Salvation is brought through human relationships, through language, pointing to the Word made flesh who brings eternal life.

Finally, we can know for sure that salvation, as part of the call of God, is not an end in itself, but is for a purpose: to declare God's glory and to live fully in and for Jesus Christ. The wonder and joy of salvation is not only for personal fulfillment or happiness (it often brings unmerited suffering); it is the privilege of participating in God's ongoing mission in the world. Emil Brunner, in his classic work *The Word in the World*,[28] describes the meaning of this unique salvation in the following manner:

27. Revelation 20:14.
28. Emil Brunner, *The Word in the World* (New York: Charles Scribner's Sons, 1931), 108.

> The Word of God which was given in Jesus Christ is a unique historical fact, and everything Christian is dependent upon it; hence everyone who receives this Word, and by it salvation, receives along with it the duty of passing this Word on; just as a man who might have discovered a remedy for cancer which saved himself, would be in duty bound to make this remedy accessible to all.

And here we see the connection between evangelism ("make this remedy accessible to all"), salvation ("remedy for cancer"), and the church that we spoke of in the last chapter. We continue Brunner's quotation, found on the same page:

> Mission work does not arise from any arrogance in the Christian Church; mission is its cause and its life. The Church exists by mission, just as a fire exists by burning. Where there is no mission, there is no Church; and where there is neither Church nor mission, there is no faith.

There is much we cannot know or understand about the Kingdom of heaven, about salvation, and about the obligation for mission and evangelism. However, what we do know, in no uncertain terms, is that our responsibility to make the announcement of the good news, or to give the witness to what God has done, is integral to our identity in Christ, to our task as Christians, and to our own salvation.

> For when I preach the gospel, I cannot boast, since I am compelled to preach. Woe to me if I do not preach the gospel! If I preach voluntarily, I have a reward; if not voluntarily, I am simply discharging the trust committed to me. (1 Cor. 9:16–17)

Every Christian is an ambassador for Christ "as though God were making his appeal through us" (2 Cor. 5:20). It may be a matter of our own salvation, if we do not proclaim Christ to those who have not heard. So the Christian should be occupied with his or her own obedience rather than trying to answer unanswerable questions. God is just and loving, and he can be trusted with those other difficult questions.

Am I Trying to Convert Muslims?

At the beginning of this chapter I began a story about our Christmas Eve with Akram. When he shot his question at me, I did not have time to look up a good answer, nor did I have time to call a good missionary, nor to seek out a Muslim convert for advice. I looked to my wife, thought about Peter denying Christ, and then said to Akram, "Am I trying to convert you? Let me tell you this, Akram: we are good friends. You have been, from the beginning, a great friend—not only to us, but to all of our kids. Our friendship is a sure thing and something for which we are very grateful to Allah.[29] However, there is nothing greater, more beautiful, or important to me and my family than Jesus Christ. As your friend and as a friend of Jesus Christ, I cannot imagine holding back from you that which is most important to us. There is nothing greater that I could ever wish for you, or pray for, than that you would come to know Jesus and follow him. And so, yes, I would like you to know the same love that we have received from Allah in Jesus. However, if you do not choose to follow Jesus, we will still be your friends. We greatly appreciate your friendship, Akram."

Are there friendships, are there acquaintances, for which we should not have an evangelistic concern? Let's ask it another way: are there people who should not know about Jesus? I don't think anyone should be denied the opportunity to know the love of God in Jesus Christ. We have no idea how God may bless in this life and the next, when our neighbor hears about Jesus Christ. What is an appropriate approach or method for evangelism, and when is it an appropriate time to speak—these are important questions, but they are based on the prior commitment that we cannot deny Christ if we are in Christ. Good news is for sharing, and good news is for all people.

29. Allah is not the Muslim name for God, nor a Muslim god. Allah is Arabic for God, the way Deus is Latin for God. Allah is also the name for God in Bahasa Malay, the language of Akram.

11

Urban Community

Mission and the City

> It was the best of times, it was the worst of times, it was the age of wisdom, it was the age of foolishness, it was the epoch of belief, it was the epoch of incredulity, it was the season of Light, it was the season of Darkness, it was the spring of hope, it was the winter of despair, we had everything before us, we had nothing before us, we were all going direct to heaven, we were all going direct the other way—in short, the period was so far like the present period, that some of its noisiest authorities insisted on its being received, for good or for evil, in the superlative degree of comparison only.
>
> Charles Dickens, *A Tale of Two Cities*

Cities are studies in contrast, and they always have been.[1] Every city is both Jerusalem and Babylon; it can be a place of refuge, but it is also the place of refugees, displaced families, and persecuted minorities. Cities contain temples, cathedrals, and basilicas—demonstrating the great creativity of humanity as it brings glory to God. But cities also contain

1. "On the one hand the city stands for all that is evil—a city that is full of devils, foul and corrupting; and on the other hand, the city stands for all that is noble, full of the glory of God, and shining with a clear and brilliant light. . . . Every city has been a Babylon and every city has been a New Jerusalem." From Josiah Strong, *The Challenge of the City* (New York: Young People's Missionary Movement, 1907), v.

slave forts, slums, drug houses, and casinos. There are no simple ways to talk about the city—both its value and its evils—for complexity and diversity are part of its very nature. God's mission in the city seeks to lift up the work of the Spirit, while confronting the evils that crush the defenseless. Cities are often experienced as a battlefield of cultures, in which vices proliferate and yet people pray for peace. As the prophet Jeremiah wrote to exiles in one city from another:

> Thus says the Lord of hosts, the God of Israel, to all the exiles whom I have sent into exile from Jerusalem to Babylon: build houses and live in them; plant gardens and eat what they produce. Take wives and have sons and daughters; take wives for your sons, and give your daughters in marriage, that they may bear sons and daughters; multiply there, and do not decrease. But seek the welfare of the city where I have sent you into exile and pray to the Lord on its behalf, for in its welfare you will find your welfare. (Jer. 29:4–7 NRSV)

In a fascinating book on the city written in 1911, Charles Hatch Sears writes from an optimistic social gospel perspective, and yet he depicts ministry in the city as warfare. He says,

> To show that this progress is an earnest of a brighter future, that while the force now attaching to the city problems unaided can never win the victory, the initial success fully justifies a renewed and more vigorous attack.[2]

This warfare image is used to express the enormity of the struggle and the sense that "forces" are allied against the church. "The reserve forces of every denomination must be directed to the city attack."[3] Although warfare imagery may, in some ways, be apt, I prefer to use the terminology of redemption rather than war, for our cities already hold far too much violence. Redemption is, as we have seen, the heart of the *missio Dei*.

Why a Chapter on the City in a Book on Mission?

In the not too distant past, most churches had two types of mission structures: foreign missions and national missions. Often there was very little connection between the two, but in the early period of missionary work in North America, "national" mission began to blend into foreign mission work (in which missionaries had to learn an indigenous language to reach their "neighbors") as missions began to indigenous Americans. In the late nineteenth century, cities became special places of mission, as the needs and concerns in large urban

2. Sears was the general secretary of the New York City Baptist City Mission Society. Charles Hatch Sears, *The Redemption of the City* (Philadelphia: Griffith & Rowland, 1911), vi.
3. Ibid., 237.

centers began to mirror needs and concerns of foreign missions. Settlement houses were established to care for immigrants. Food pantries and kitchens were set up to feed the poor, and groups like the YMCA and the Salvation Army ministered to the urban poor through Christian witness and compassion. Thus, foreign mission again became a local or national mission.

At the same time that missionaries in India were establishing hospitals, clinics, schools, and feeding programs during times of famine, cities in the West had many of these same needs. And, in addition, Western cities had extremes of poverty and wealth and great migrations of people from European nations. Urban centers became the new mission frontier of national missions. Some immigrants to Western cities were very strong Christians but with very great social need. Other new arrivals were poor migrants, looking for a job, with little active religious life. Poverty flowered into slums, with their attendant disease, hunger, and homelessness. Most of these social needs were met either by churches, or not at all.

Globally, missionaries have always anchored their ministries in cities: Seoul, Rio de Janeiro, Calcutta, Hong Kong, Edessa, Alexandria, and Constantinople have all been mission centers. What makes "the city" the subject of a chapter in a book on mission is the enormity of the field of ministry in large urban centers and the growing multicultural nature of our cities. As mentioned earlier, a church in Queens, New York, has sixty-three nationalities among its members. Queens itself has many more nationalities than this. Thus, the very size, complexity, and growth of cities in the last century make urban centers a primary place of mission.

In 1900, of the ten largest cities in the world, only one was in Asia (Tokyo), and only London had more than five million people (6.5 million).[4] Fifty years later, after two world wars and two major genocides (Armenian and Jewish), there were six cities of over five million people and three cities in the top ten were in Asia (Tokyo, Shanghai, and Calcutta). This illustrates very rapid growth, but it is nothing compared to what happened between 1950 and 2010. In sixty years, planet earth has gone from one to twenty-three cities containing more than ten million people—and thirteen of those cities are in Asia. This massive increase has come about both through natural population growth and through migration. People have been moving from the countryside to the city and from poor nations to more wealthy nations, looking for jobs and food. It is a common sight in many developing nations to see men waiting near street corners for a truck to (hopefully) pick them up as a day laborer. If they get a day's work, they may be able to feed their family for another day or two. Many of the largest cities in the world have populations larger than many nations. Tokyo (32 million) and Seoul (20.5 million) are both larger than over 160 na-

4. Statistics come from Tertius Chandler, *Four Thousand Years of Urban Growth: An Historical Census* (Lewiston, NY: St. David's University Press, 1987).

tions of the world.[5] The forty largest cities all contain over five million people and are therefore larger than most mission fields of the nineteenth century.

In 1800, only 3 percent of the world's people lived in urban areas; by 1900 the percentage had only grown to 14 percent. Over the next fifty years the number grew to 30 percent, and today it is over 50 percent.[6] Thus, most of the people who are in need of Christian mission and ministry live in urban areas. The growth of the cities, their global influence, and the growing problems these cities are experiencing make them the primary place of missionary outreach. Such rapid growth has meant that cities cannot build infrastructures quickly enough to handle new urban dwellers—so vast numbers live in slums. There are now over one billion people who are living in slums worldwide, a staggering picture of a great human tragedy at our doorsteps.[7] Unfortunately, according to the United Nations Human Settlements Programme, that number may double to two billion by 2020.[8] Thus it is not only the size of twenty-first-century cities that should turn the missional mind toward them, it is also the enormous number of very poor people living on the edge of life and death. Cities have always held both the very rich and the very poor, but today's cities hold slums the size of the largest cities of the nineteenth century. Jesus's special concern for the poor and marginalized is a call for us to enter the world's cities, and especially their slums. The rediscovery of the poor (now understood as God's preferential option for the poor) in 1968 at the Roman Catholic Latin American Bishop's Conference (CELAM), has influenced more than just Catholic perceptions of mission. The slums of cities prevent hundreds of millions of people from hearing or experiencing anything of the love of God. In the words of the first CELAM meeting in Medellín, Columbia, in 1968, "Poverty marginalizes large groups. Poverty as a collective act is an injustice that claims to heaven."[9] Because of this and other statements coming out of Latin America (including some from the Lausanne Congress in 1974),[10] the global church has been more aware of the need not only to develop a theology of poverty, but to look first to the places of greatest suffering. Thus, greater priority in mission has been given to the slums, to sex trafficking, and to disaster relief. In large urban areas, poverty often marginalizes large groups quite efficiently.

5. For current statistics on the largest agglomerations (cities over one million), see the following website: http://www.citypopulation.de/world/Agglomerations.html. Almost all current population statistics today are found on websites rather than in reference books.

6. United Nations, *World Urbanization Prospects: The 2007 Revision*.

7. Quoted from Scott Bessenecker, ed., *Quest for Hope in the Slum Community: A Global Reader* (Waynesboro, GA: Authentic, 2005), 3.

8. Now called Un-habitat: http://www.unbrussels.org/agencies/habitat.html. The UN identified 828 million slum dwellers in 2010.

9. CELAM, 1968, 51. Quoted from Jorge Mario Flores Osorio, "Praxis and Liberation in the Context of Liberation Theory," in Maritza Montero and Christopher C. Sonn, eds., *Psychology of Liberation* (New York: Springer Science and Business Media, 2009), 25.

10. Lausanne Covenant section 5 is on "Christian Social Responsibility." Its language is similar to earlier Roman Catholic language: liberation, reconciliation, and justice for the poor.

Another reason to focus a whole chapter on the city is the great suffering that has occurred in cities in the past half century. When we list a few major cities, it doesn't take long to remember some of the great human tragedies that have occurred: Kosovo, Nanjing (Nanking), Dresden, Hiroshima, Mogadishu (*Maqadīshū*), Kigali (Rwanda), Port au Prince. This is not to say that great human suffering does not occur in the wilderness, for it does. However, what makes cities great and important is the very thing that magnifies human suffering: population.

Because of the ethnic diversity in most cities of the world, cities are places that link people across language and geography. People who travel to cities also continue to communicate with family and friends in their place of origin: migrants are bicultural. Cities are also places where reconciliation is both possible and a necessity. Cities are a unique missiological situation, and so I want to look first at how cities should be understood biblically and theologically; then we will look at the nature of cities sociologically and historically; and finally I will suggest some ways in which cities should be approached missiologically.

The City, Biblically and Theologically Considered

The concept of city, as a place of spiritual life and conflict, is a major theme in the Bible. The city symbolizes the grace of God as well as human hubris and evil. The first city spoken of in the Bible is the city of Enoch, built by Cain, who murdered his brother. One might think this means that biblical imagery portrays the city as the work of fallen and violent humanity; however, Cain had assumed he would be a restless wanderer after God's punishment and that anyone who saw him would kill him. It was God's mercy that put a "mark" on Cain to protect him, and he was able to build a city and dwell with others in peace. The city, from the beginning, was a place of refuge and community.

As noted in the opening paragraphs of this chapter, the meaning or story of cities is really a "tale of two cities." Cities, theologically speaking, represent God's mercy and presence, but they also represent all that is opposed to God's rule. In this section, I want to look at these two images and explore what this means for mission work. First, we will look at the city as designed by God, the master designer, and set apart as sacred space. Then we will look at the reality of cities as places that accumulate power and oppression. Finally, we will look at eschatology—the hope of a sacred urban future prepared for us by God.

City as Sacred

The city is not the result of the fall of humanity; it is part of God's design.[11] Embedded in the first chapters of Genesis are the goodness of creation;

11. I am greatly indebted to Meredith Kline and his self-published *Kingdom Prologue*, 2 vols. (South Hamilton, MA, 1981–83), for the following discussion. In addition, I am using my

humanity's commission to name, order, and multiply; and the responsibility of humanity to bear the image of God in a social setting. God's command to multiply, fill the earth, and subdue it will eventually point to the city as a place of commerce, order, and worship.

> The cultural mandate given to Adam and Eve in the garden to fill, rule, and subdue the earth (Gen. 1:28) was nothing more than a mandate to build the city. Human culture to follow them was to take city form.[12]

When Cain built a city he was not continuing in sin but responding to the cultural mandate of ordering and naming: he named the city after his son, Enoch. The city is to be a place of fulfilling the cultural mandate given to humanity in creation. Thus, the city is a place of worship—in which Yahweh is present and honored. The city is a place of safety and refuge. We read in Numbers 35 that certain cities were specifically set up as places of refuge to protect individuals from revenge. Thus, cities should be seen as safe places. Walls are built around cities for protection, and this explains why, when Jerusalem was rebuilt, one of the major aspects of the return from exile was the rebuilding of the wall (Jeremiah). Cities are also, as seen in Scripture, to be places of truth telling and proper judgment. The city gate is the place of justice where cases are heard and, symbolically, error and deceit are kept out (e.g., Deut. 17:5; Josh. 20:4). The poor, the lame, and the blind receive alms at the city gate—reflecting both mercy and justice. Job 29 illustrates the full meaning of proper judgment at the city gate. We know from the law, as expounded in Deuteronomy, that the poor of the land (both Israelites and local) were to be cared for (Deut. 15:11). When Job looks back with longing on the life he used to lead, he uses the way in which he rendered judgment and mercy at the city gate as part of his defense. He recalls how young and old persons alike viewed him with respect and spoke highly of him because of his righteous and just actions toward the poor, fatherless, blind, lame, needy, and strangers (Job 29:7–25). The city is to be a place where such justice and refuge is prevalent. Justice, biblically considered, has a strong thread of moral virtue woven into it. The just are humble, and the unjust or wicked are proud. The city is to be a place of the righteous humble who care for the needy and speak truthfully (Isa. 26:1–6).

Jerusalem was the paradigmatic city, representing the justice, truth, and mercy of God in all of its dealings. "Jerusalem will be called the Faithful City"

---

class notes from his biblical exegesis class (1981) and the work of Harvie M. Conn, "Genesis as Urban Prologue," in Roger Greenway, ed., *Discipling the City: A Comprehensive Approach to Urban Mission* (Grand Rapids: Baker, 1992). Kline's book is now published as *Kingdom Prologue: Genesis Foundations for a Covenantal Worldview* (Eugene, OR: Wipf & Stock, 2006).

12. Conn, "Genesis as Urban Prologue," 15. Kline describes the city as "Interim World Structure" guided by "divine ordinance."

(Zech. 8:3) and is the place where Yahweh uniquely resides—in the temple. Yahweh, however, did not reside only in Jerusalem, because he is the God who sits over all of creation and therefore over every city. Therefore, when God's people were in exile in foreign cities, they were commanded to pray and work for the good of their adopted cities (Jer. 29:5–7). Unlike the local deities of the world, almost all of which were confined to specific cities, Yahweh was not bound to Jerusalem—as magnificent as the city and the temple were. In Jeremiah 29:5–7 the Israelites are commanded to carry out, within foreign cities, the same cultural mandate found in Genesis 2. They are to raise families, seek peace and prosperity, and pray for the city in which they reside. God's people, even if they are a minority, must work for the betterment of the city in which they live. Additionally, when the enemy comes into a city, we have some indication that they are to be cared for and given mercy—even when they deserve punishment. In 2 Kings 6 we read that when the Arameans came to kill the prophet Elisha, they were struck with blindness and led by Elisha into the Hebrew city of Samaria. Rather than allowing the king of Israel to kill his enemies, Elisha commanded the Israelites to instead prepare a feast for them and allow them to return to their home camp (2 Kings 6:22–23).

Mercy, wisdom, and righteousness are to be defining qualities of the city. We read in Proverbs that "wisdom calls out in the city," expecting people in the city to respond to the call (Prov. 1:20–28; 8:3; etc.). When the inhabitants do not respond to wisdom's call, they reap judgment and punishment. People in the city are to be righteous in all of their dealings, and when they are, the city prospers and there is great joy (Prov. 11:10). There is a God-ordained order or ecology to the city whereby righteousness and care for the poor and needy bring prosperity, which has to do with both family life and financial security (Zech. 8:3–13).

City as Evil

The city, as ordained by God, was to be a place of justice, a place of proper worship, and a place of care that would establish God's Kingdom on earth. And yet we do not see cities as we have described them above. Cities, like individuals, are fallen—and since there are so many fallen people within a given city, we see both greater accumulations of evil and an abundance of opportunities for grace. When the city is bent by human pride, and when the righteous are mocked, the city suffers economic ills and people and families collapse.

Jacques Ellul held an extreme view of the city: he said all cities are Babylon, and therefore what was said of Babylon is true of every city.

> Babylon, the great city, or Babylon the Great. The biggest in the world. No one can rival her, not even Rome. Not because of her historical greatness, but because of what she represents mythically. All the cities of the world are brought together in her, she is the synthesis of them all (Dan. 3 and 4; Rev. 14 and 18). . . .

> There is everything for sale, the bodies and souls of men. She is the very home of civilization and when the great city vanishes, there is no more civilization, a world disappears. . . . Babylon, Venice, Paris, New York—they are all the same city, only one Babel always reappearing, a city from the beginning mortally wounded: "and they left off building the city."[13]

Ellul's position is pessimistic in the extreme. All cities are fallen, and so we see greater and lesser degrees of evil prospering at the expense of the powerless. Biblically, there are some cities that are seen by God as so reprehensible that they must be utterly destroyed (Josh. 6; 8). Some of the most difficult passages of Scripture are descriptions of the destruction of cities as God's people claim the promised land.

Related to the conquest of the promised land, we must remember that what defines the core of the fallen city is its worship. This is seen from the very beginning, in the plain of Shinar, when arrogance reigned and the people sought to build a tower reaching to God. The sin of Babel was the worship of human pride (Gen. 11). Throughout Scripture, we see again and again that worship is the center of the city, which means that the evil of a city is false worship. We become what we worship, and so the sins of Sodom and the judgment of Sodom come about because of false worship (Gen. 19:1–29). People cry out to God because of the injustice and immorality of the city. God hears their cries.[14]

We see the central importance placed on worship in many places in the Old Testament. One of the most telling is when the ark of the covenant was captured by the Philistines and brought into the temple of Dagon in the city of Ashdod. In the morning, the Philistines found that Dagon had fallen face down before the ark—in fact his head and hands had fallen off (1 Sam. 5). Worship defines a city, and when the presence of Yahweh comes into a city, all others must submit. A city's false worship precedes judgment and destruction, even (or especially) when the city is built by God's people. Omri built the northern capital of Samaria, but it was Ahab and his Phoenician queen, Jezebel, who built the temple to Ba'al in the center of the city (1 Kings 16:31–33). Injustice followed false worship as seen, for example, in the murder of Naboth for his vineyard (1 Kings 21). Pride and avarice reigned under Ahab's rule, and the city suffered as a result. Cities that no longer seek God and his will are likened to a prostitute, seeking false lovers and living false lives: "See how the faithful city has become a prostitute! She once was full of justice; righteousness used

13. Jacques Ellul, *The Meaning of the City*, trans. by Dennis Pardee (Grand Rapids: Eerdmans, 1970), 20–21.

14. There has been much discussion about the meaning of Sodom's sin, but the use of the verb "to know" likely means to have sexual relations (Gen. 19:5), for just a few verses later we see the parallel, when Lot offers his two daughters to the Sodomites (v. 8). This was also the unbroken understanding of the sin of Sodom in the Jewish tradition (see Jude 1:7). Unbridled sexual lust was not their only sin, but it was one of the most obvious and memorable.

to dwell in her—but now murderers!" (Isa. 1:21).[15] When cities turn against God and his prophets, even the Messiah weeps (Luke 19:41). And yet, although the Savior himself weeps over the city, hope is on the horizon—coming from "outside the city gate" (Heb. 13:12).

City as Hope

Reflecting the basic salvific pattern of creation, fall, and redemption, we see the city as sacred, evil, and hopeful. The city of hope is the promised future in which the great saints of the past placed their hope. Abraham and the long list of Old Testament saints had faith in God and in God's future, even though they died without seeing it for themselves.

> They [were] looking for a country of their own. If they had been thinking of the country they had left, they would have had opportunity to return. Instead, they were longing for a better country—a heavenly one. Therefore God is not ashamed to be called their God, for he has prepared a city for them. (Heb. 11:14–16)

Later in Hebrews, we read that we in the present, not only the saints of the past, are looking for "the city that is to come" (Heb. 13:14). The future or goal of God, and the future into which we are invited in mission, is described as a city. Earlier, we looked at four windows of mission from the New Testament, the last one being the heavenly vision found in Revelation 7. That vision is elaborated further in Revelation 21 and 22. When God gives us a glimpse of the future he has prepared for us, we need to be willing to lean into that future in our mission today.

However, before looking at the characteristics of the heavenly city, Revelation reveals the destruction of the evil city—a necessary prerequisite. The evil city, Babylon, has, as it were, infected all the cities of the earth.

> For all the nations have drunk the maddening wine of her adulteries. The kings of the earth committed adultery with her, and the merchants of the earth grew rich from her excessive luxuries. (Rev. 18:3)

Babylon is brought down and all the saints, apostles, and prophets rejoice at her fall. She is judged for her treatment of God's spokespersons: "In her was found the blood of the prophets and of God's holy people" (18:24). Consequently, all the saints sing "Hallelujah."

The heavenly city that is to come is not like Babylon—an effort of the human spirit that serves the human spirit—for this New Jerusalem is given as

15. Much of the prophetic literature against the Hebrews concerns their injustices, unnecessary bloodshed, and neglect of the weak and defenseless. See, for example, Habakkuk 2.

Ephrem the Syrian on Paradise

Ephrem, in "The Harp of the Spirit" (306–73), wrote a series of "Hymns of Paradise" that reflect on the theological meaning of paradise from the first chapters of Genesis. He understands paradise as the place (the garden) in Genesis 1 and 2, but also as our presence with God now, in this life, and finally as our life in the heavenly garden—pictured in Revelation 21 and 22. Ephrem breathes new meaning into the symbolism of the heavenly city in Revelation in his discussion of paradise (7.21–22). "Nothing there in Paradise is useless: both grass and roots bring benefit and profit; whoever tastes them is rejuvenated, whoever breathes in their scent grows fair; in the bosom of its blossoms and flowers is hidden a veritable treasure, a gift for those who pluck it; the fruits of Paradise bear rich wealth for those who gather them. None toil there, for none go hungry there, none endure shame there, for none do wrong there."[a]

a. Translated by Sebastian Brock, *Hymns on Paradise by St. Ephrem* (Crestwood, NY: St. Vladimir's Seminary Press, 1990), 126.

a gift of God and is centered on worship of God. In one sense, the heavenly city is the church, "prepared as a bride, beautifully dressed for her husband" (Rev. 21:2; cf. Eph. 5:25–32). The heavenly city outlines the destiny and mission of the church: there is no crying or pain, and there is no more death and therefore no more mourning (Rev. 21:4). The city of God, as with all cities, is centered on worship—only now, in the heavenly city, there is no temple and no tabernacle; God himself is present. God's presence is what prevents tears and mourning and even thirst and hunger. The justice that was to mark the city from the beginning is now a reality. Economic justice prevails, and all people are fed and protected because those who would prevent justice have been removed from the city of God.

> The cowardly, the unbelieving, the vile, the murderers, the sexually immoral, those who practice magic arts, the idolaters and all liars—they will be consigned to the fiery lake of burning sulfur. This is the second death. (21:8)

Like all cities, this city also provides protection: a wall protects the citizens from plagues, violence, and from those who would oppress the heavenly citizens. It is a safe city. It is a city that is illuminated by the glory-presence of God where all of the nations meet in harmony (21:23–26). As a recapitulation of Genesis 2, we read that the river of life flows through the heavenly city, and the tree of life is there—providing fruitful harvests. The curse from Genesis 3 is taken away (22:3). In a word, the heavenly city is a world of love.[16]

16. From a sermon by Jonathan Edwards.

Reflecting on these characteristics of the city of hope, the heavenly city, we can begin to see how it directs the mission of the church in the largest, most complex cities in the world. Thus we have looked at the city as part of God's design from the beginning, its broken and evil expression in the present world, and the hope it gives us for the future. But what is a city and how does it function in the world?

What Is a City, and What Does It Mean?

Three Foundational Functions of Every City

A city, biblically and sociologically considered, has three functions: to be a place of sacred space, a place of commercial activity, and a place of safety and social order. Its first function, and its primary organizational concern in ancient times, was to be a place of worship. Any and every city from ancient times was built to honor a god or goddess: Athens for Athena, Lyons for Lug, Constantinople for the Triune God, and Ashdod for Dagon.[17] According to Joel Kotkin, for the earliest cities in Mesopotamia it was the "priestly class that emerged as the primary organizers of the new urban order. . . . Priests set the calendars that determined times for work, worship, and for feasting for the entire population."[18] Temples were the first marketplaces, not only in Mesopotamia, but also in Asia and Africa. Cities have always had this sacred function, and if we look at the evolution of cities, worship was the primary collective force in urban development.

Secondly, cities function as commercial centers, as places where goods can be traded and labor bought or hired. Cities are providers. People who first came to cities because of the sacred space, came again to trade grain for tools or tools for grain. Commercial activity is also the furnace for creativity and artistic expression; consequently we see that cities produce and attract culture makers: artisans, sculptors, poets, philosophers, and musicians.

Thirdly, cities provide a place of safety. Walled areas were designed on hills to keep out marauding migrants and wild animals. In a city, a sick person could be cared for and the weak would have community and protection. As Kotkin notes, when cities no longer provide safety and security they become dysfunctional and people move out or the city begins to decline (as in the late Roman Empire).[19] Although today we often think of cities as dangerous habitations,

17. One great reminder of this in Asia is to look for the wats, stupas, mosques, or temples in cities (or to remember the sacred cities of Angkor, Varanasi, Yangon-Shwedagon), and in the West to look for the cathedrals. When the British colonized, they built Anglican cathedrals, and later Roman Catholic, Anglican, and Reformed churches.

18. Joel Kotkin, *The City: A Global History*, 4th ed. (New York: Modern Library, 2005), 4.

19. Kotkin remarks of the decline of Rome, for example, "Now the Empire, no longer capable of acquiring new territories, was on the defensive, struggling mightily, and at great expense, to

as late as the nineteenth century and into the early twentieth century, cities were understood as safe places for refugees, migrants, and immigrants. On the Statue of Liberty in New York Harbor is the poem "The New Colossus" written by Emma Lazarus. It says, in part:

> "Keep, ancient lands, your storied pomp!" cries she
> With silent lips. "Give me your tired, your poor,
> Your huddled masses yearning to breathe free,
> The wretched refuse of your teeming shore.
> Send these, the homeless, tempest-tost to me,
> I lift my lamp beside the golden door."[20]

All three of these themes—sacred space, commercial hub, security or social order—are essential to the healthy working of any city. When one or more are unhealthy, a city becomes unhealthy and begins to decline. Pathological commercial enterprises like monopolies, the Mafia, or the Chinese Triad hurt all citizens of a city. When crime goes unchecked, or worship and the cultural values that are derived from worship no longer hold, a city begins its decline. Many of the world's megacities today "increasingly seem to lack a shared sense of sacred space, civic identity, or moral order. . . . Even affluent cities without moral cohesion or a sense of civic identity are doomed to decadence and decline."[21]

Three Basic Functions in the Twenty-First Century

These three themes or functions that make up every city drive other characteristics that are important for our understanding of mission in and to the city. Because cities attract people (to worship, to trade, and for safety) there is always a greater diversity of people in the city than will be found in villages or in the countryside. The diversity of languages, food, and cultural practice requires cities to have a greater tolerance for difference. Cities often offer a place and a community for people who were not welcome in their home country or village. This diversity makes possible greater artistic achievement and engenders academic development. New ideas, philosophies,

---

protect its vast network of cities. With the breakdown of security and easy communication, long distance trade declined. Over the ensuing centuries the currency, the denarius, was consistently debased" (*The City*, 35).

20. The poem's title refers to the Colossus of Rhodes, which was a thirty-meter-high statue erected at the harbor of Rhodes to commemorate the city-state's victory over Cyprus. Both statues have a religious significance: the Colossus is a statue of the Titan Helios (god of the sun; in Latin, *Sol Invictus*), and the Statue of Liberty represents "Libertas," the Roman goddess of freedom. Again, gates or entrances to cities are very important. Babylon means "Gate of the Gods" (*Babi-ilani*).

21. Kotkin, *The City*, xvii.

and inventions often come out of urban environments. People produce plays, music, buildings, and they communicate through media with other cities and with their place of origin. Cities have a major cultural influence upon countries and empires. It is important, for the sake of the mission of God to every nation of the world, to understand the critical role that urban culture makers have.

When the three functions of a city turn in upon themselves, however, they often create and reinforce injustice and oppression rather than providing the protection and harmony in which creativity flourishes. A few examples will illustrate this point. Cities are supposed to protect children and families, and yet it is estimated that there are about 160 million children on the streets of cities today. This would make street children the seventh or eighth largest country in the world by population—a country the size of Nigeria (the largest country in Africa).[22] In the late twentieth century, slums (the mother of street children) have expanded dramatically in the developing countries of the world.

Rapid urbanization in the past half century means that urban infrastructures (water, sewage, education, roads) have not kept up with the teeming masses moving into the cities. The result is underemployment and slums. Although some countries (India and China) have decreased the number of slum dwellers within their borders in the twenty-first century (by 227 million), in most areas of the world slums are growing—which means that more and more people are exposed to diseases caused by unhealthy living conditions.[23] Overall, the number of slum dwellers has increased by fifty-five million since the turn of the century, and the number is still growing. Two-thirds of the world's slum dwellers live in Africa, and in some countries in sub-Saharan Africa over half of the population live in slum conditions. For these people, most of the functions of the city are not working for them: they are not safe, they do not have access to commercial activity—and yet many are still deeply devout Christians.

Cities should function as safe places, but with the size and complexity of cities today, cities have instead become safe havens for criminals. Gangs and criminal societies function as local authorities in many cities (or in parts of cities), and these illegal authorities prey upon the defenseless. Illegal economic activity is oppressive to the poor, because there is no just ordering of the

22. Jeff Anderson, "The Street Children Scene," in Bessenecker, *Quest for Hope*, 222. Anderson notes that there are four types of street children: (1) those who have no home, whose parents died or abandoned them; (2) those who may go home to sleep at night, but home is so terrible they prefer to live in the streets; (3) those children who live at home and sell cigarettes or tissue on the streets to help the family; and (4) those children who live on the streets and may go to school, but whose home situation is so terrible they seldom go home.

23. John Vidal, "227 Million Escape World's Slums, UN Report Finds," *The Guardian* (online edition), March 22, 2010, http://www.guardian.co.uk/world/2010/mar/22/slums-un-report.

exchange of goods and services. Illegal economic activity usually builds its dark kingdoms on lower human appetites; the world's economy is laden with illegal trade in arms, sex trafficking, pornography, and illegal drugs. Many governments seek to recoup lost income by supporting immoral services such as gambling: mammon is god.[24]

There is much that can be said about the broken functions of the city, but one final comment is in order. In the shadow of the slums is generally found some of the greatest accumulation of individual wealth. It would be wrong to say that the immoral accumulation of wealth is greater than ever, or is as great as ever, for the variables are too great and the examples from history are so vast and remarkable. How can we compare the salaries of big bankers and the CEOs of multinational corporations today with the Mongol emperors, the czars of Russia, or the rulers of Songhay and other kingdoms in Africa?[25] This has been the history of humanity, the vice of avarice emerges where there are opportunities to accumulate wealth—even if it's on the backs of the poor. In the past, one of the most lucrative forms of immoral accumulation of wealth was slavery, but today practices like drug dealing, sex trafficking, and others mentioned above dominate. Other immoral activities, although marginally legal, are banking and business practices that make possible the accumulation of wealth in the presence of oppressive poverty. What this means is that part of the answer to redemption for the city is usually found within the city. The resources, in terms of human capital and financial opportunity, are present to meet the needs of the poorest of the poor. What is missing is the connection; a moral and spiritual bridge is needed to connect the greatest needs of the world with the human actors who have the ability to be God's agents of reconciliation and redemption.

24. The great modern icon of government-sponsored immoral activity ("If you can't beat them, join them") is the Marina Bay Sands in Singapore. The contrast with nineteenth-century symbolic buildings (churches and temples and mosques) could not be greater.

25. From the fascinating *Ta'rikh al Fattash: The Timbuktu Chronicles, 1493–1599*, ed. Christopher Wise, trans. Christopher Wise and Hala Abu Taleb (Trenton, NJ: Africa World Press, 2011), we read the following concerning the Kayamaga princes: "It is said that he (the prince) kept one thousand horses tied up inside his palace. . . . Each horse had his own brass vessel into which he urinated. Each drop of urine passed neatly into this vessel, whether it was day or night. No manure could be seen under any of these horses. Each of them had three persons in attendance who were seated nearby: the first one saw to it that the animal was fed, the second, that he had plenty to drink, while the third attended to his urine and carried out his manure" (82). The remarkable wealth from West African Muslim cities was not a new thing. In the fourteenth century the wealth was just being discovered by poor and backward Europeans: "The early 14th century Muslim King Mansa Musa (1307–37) of Mali was wealthy enough that on his pilgrimage to Mecca he is reported to have sent 500 slaves ahead of him to prepare the way. His overflowing gifts of gold (approximately 50,000 oz.) as he passed through Egypt had the effect of reducing the value of gold overall in North Africa." Quoted from Dale Irvin and Scott Sunquist, *History of the World Christian Movement*, vol. 2 (Maryknoll, NY: Orbis Books, 2012), chap. 2, "African Christianity in the Sixteenth Century."

Some of History's Lessons Regarding the City

History provides us with both inspiration and warning concerning God's mission to the world's cities today. We want to look back at a few of these now, as a way of moving forward. I will focus on both structure and spirituality of urban mission as we take a quick look at some historical urban missional vignettes.

Earliest Christianity Was Mostly Urban

Earliest Christianity moved from city to city, along trade routes, emerging as a largely urban religion.[26] We know this from tracing Paul's missionary journeys, but we also know this from the earliest apostolic writings: Clement wrote to the Romans, Ignatius wrote to seven urban churches on the way to his martyrdom in Rome, Polycarp wrote to Christians in Philippi.[27] These early letters deal with typical urban themes of church order, heresies,[28] care for the poor, and the Christian life lived in contrast to popular urban life.

One great example of saintly ministry in the city (and there are many others) is St. Ephrem the Syrian. Ephrem was a deacon in Nisibis, and then, after Rome surrendered Nisibis to the Persians, he was a teacher and deacon in Edessa. In Edessa, many heretical schools of thought were vying for dominance, and Orthodox Nicene Christianity was viewed as simply a smaller sect. Ephrem fought for orthodox teachings by writing hymns to be sung to popular Syrian music. Then he organized choirs to sing his orthodox theology. Because the tunes were familiar, Edessans themselves began to sing orthodox theology. Another major urban problem that Ephrem faced was disease. In 372 and 373 the plague came to Edessa, killing many people and leaving others homeless and without food. Ephrem organized food drives during the famine, he set up houses in the city to care for the sick and dying (some of the earliest hospitals), and eventually he himself died of the plague in 373. Under his leadership, Edessa became a "Blessed City" on the borderlands between the Roman and Persian empires, revered as the first kingdom to accept Christianity.[29]

26. Wayne Meeks's study *The First Urban Christians* (New Haven: Yale University Press, 1983) combines biblical and extrabiblical material to do a thorough sociological study of the earliest Christians. More recently, a sociologist, Rodney Stark, in *Cities of God: The Real Story of How Christianity Became an Urban Movement and Conquered Rome* (San Francisco: HarperSanFrancisco, 2006), provides more statistics as part of his larger argument to show how Christianity moved from being planted in cities to being critical to urban development. His discussion includes the cities as places of heresy and heretical schools.

27. By 300 CE, 50 percent of urban areas in the Roman Empire were reached by the gospel, but 90 percent of rural areas were unreached. Apostolic ministry moved from city to city.

28. "Larger cities were more likely than smaller cities to have heretical schools. . . . Nearly 2/3rds of the larger cities did shelter heretical schools as compared with only 13% of the smaller cities" (Stark, *Cities of God*, 162). See all of chap. 6 on Gnosticism and heresies (ibid., 141–81).

29. J. B. Segal, *Edessa: The Blessed City* (Piscataway, NJ: Gorgias, 2001). It was considered a blessed city because of the Christian presence in the early centuries before the rise of Islam.

We can't go through all of the great saints who developed ministries to address specific urban situations, but it is worth noting that for most of them *there was no division between concern about heresy and concern for justice and mercy*. Ephrem is known for his great hymns and his pioneering work in leading a city to care for the neediest among them. What is taught will determine how one lives, and how one lives can influence how a city develops.

Monastic and Urban Synergy

Coming out of the persecutions of the early centuries and the sudden acceptance by the Roman Empire, many Christian leaders took to the deserts in order to remain faithful to Christ. Other saints, however, survived persecution by leaving the cities and, while in the wilderness regions, developed a spirituality hearty enough for the city. Basil of Caesarea was one of these and, as such, he demonstrates the synergy between monastic life and urban mission.

Basil was from a strong Christian family, a family that produced many Christian leaders, including his grandfather, who was martyred for the faith. Educated in Athens, Basil returned home "a practiced rhetorician. He was puffed up beyond measure with the pride of oratory and looked down on the local dignitaries, excelling in his own estimation of all the men of leading and position."[30] After a search for spiritual life among the ascetics in Syria, Egypt, Palestine, and even in Persia, Basil returned to provide leadership as priest and then as Bishop of Caesarea. His life was marked by a dual desire to return to desert monasteries and to "care for the flock." The care that was needed included clearheaded teaching about the Trinity (in opposition to the Arians) and care for the poor and the sick. He and his good friend Gregory of Nazianzus preached and wrote theology as a way of giving leadership to local Christians. He organized communities of monks (coenobitic, from *koine*, or "in common"), and in his *Longer Rule* he defended the need for monks to live together among people, in cities. Quiet and solitude, he said, was needed to draw near to God—but community was needed to care for one another.

During famine and drought Basil organized the church to feed the poor. He even gave to others out of his own wealth. It was reported that he gave his family inheritance to care for the poor in his own diocese. Basil established what may have been the first "soup kitchen," actually preparing food for the poor rather than merely distributing grain. Basil is also famous for his letters,

30. At least this is his brother's estimation. Gregory of Nyssa praises their sister, in *Life of Macrina*, describing her impact on other family members. "Macrina took him in hand, and with such speed did she draw him also toward the mark of philosophy [theology] that he forsook the glories of this world and despised fame gained by speaking, and deserted it for this busy life where one toils with one's hands." Taken from the abridged version in John W. Coakley and Andrea Sterk, eds., *Readings in World Christian History* (Maryknoll, NY: Orbis Books, 2008), 1:149.

encouraging people to resist many of the temptations of the city (avarice, immorality) and to give to the poor. He took a personal interest in helping former prostitutes and criminals reform through Christian virtues. Along with other bishops of the period, we see in his sermons that Basil preached directly against government officials who were oppressing the poor or who were not dispensing justice. Finally, Basil built a major building outside of the center of Caesarea called the Basiliad. It was a place for the poor, sick, and needy, and included a poorhouse and a hospital, with attending hospice care. In short, it was in urban areas that Christians developed hospitals, soup kitchens, and poorhouses. But these social services were developed by theologians who, with the same breath they used to pray for the sick, preached to the spiritually misguided. Social reform, spiritual reform, and theological reform developed as a triune call to Christian obedience.

Sodalities for Cities

Franciscan spirituality and later patterns of "Modern Devotion" (fourteenth- and fifteenth-century Europe) were also started as, or developed into, a special spiritual life for the urban areas of Europe and then for the non-Western world. One of the urban ministries for the poor that developed and later became a global ministry was founded by the Florentine Pietro Borsi in 1240.[31] Borsi was a layman who, as a porter, was disgusted by the language and behavior of other porters. He boldly called for their moral and religious reform, and, as they began to reform, they raised money to care for the sick and dying in the city of Florence. Upon Borsi's death, the group of porters took the name Brothers of Mercy, or *Misericordia*. Of particular note is the fact that moral reform in the city was developed into ministries of mercy for the dying. Throughout the Spanish and Portuguese empires (for the influence of the Brothers of Mercy spread from Italy to Iberia) lay brothers (and later the religious order) provided organized nursing care (some of the first), established hospices, and purchased cemeteries for the poor.

Nineteenth-Century Moral Reform in the City

In the modern period, almost all social reform was started or inspired by Christian initiative to alleviate suffering and provide greater opportunities for those who were neediest in the growing cities during the Industrial Revolution. For example, the concept of "settlement houses" was first pioneered by an Anglican couple, Reverend Samuel and Henrietta Barnett, in the most impoverished East London parish (St. Jude's) in 1877. Concerned about the crowded conditions and lack of opportunities for the poor in London, they first initiated evening classes, concerts, and other cultural opportunities, in

31. Susan and Joanna Horner, *Walks in Florence* (London: Strahan 1873), 1:93.

Nineteenth-Century Moral Reform and the City

The nineteenth century was the century of moral reform in Western civilization, in large part because of the rapid growth of urban centers and the lack of infrastructure to support immigrants. Enlightenment discoveries did not provide Enlightenment constraints or virtues. In the West, thousands of societies and movements, most of them coming out of Catholic or evangelical reform, began to meet specific needs. One such society, the New York Female Reform Society (NYFRS), was established to prevent prostitution, to lead women out of prostitution, and then to provide education and help for future employment. The first meeting of the NYFRS in 1835 connected the Great Commission with urban social ills like prostitution, alcoholism, and homelessness. "It was the last command of our Savior to preach the gospel to every creature; and while our missionaries have been laboring to do this from house to house, and through the streets and lanes of the city, several females, professing a wish to forsake their sins, have been thrown into their hands and provided for in the society's house." Urban blight was a missionary concern.

large part with the cooperation of the young urban scholar Arnold Toynbee.[32] This mother house of settlement houses developed into a university extension program: bringing wealthy and bright scholars to live in East London to provide education and to struggle alongside local residents for better conditions in the community. Toynbee himself helped to establish libraries for the poor, and his close work with the poor (and relentless pace of activity) probably led to his early death at the age of thirty. Settlement houses spread across the Atlantic to New York and then to Chicago, where the famous "Hull House" was established in 1889. The Hull House was founded by Ellen Gates Starr (1859–1940) to care for immigrants in the city. After visiting London, she returned and started kindergartens and adult education and literacy classes, and soon became an activist fighting for child labor laws.

The nineteenth century is known for many social reform movements, mostly, but not exclusively, initiated by Roman Catholics and evangelicals: newer religious orders among Catholics, the rise of the YMCA, temperance movements, women's rights movements, workers' rights movements, and the Salvation Army, as well as spiritual movements like the businessmen's prayer meetings that started in the wake of the economic collapse of 1857.

These movements focused money, attention, and organization on caring for the neediest. Jeremiah Lanphier began a prayer meeting for laymen in New York City in 1857, which ignited a prayer revival and an evangelistic

32. This Toynbee (1852–88) was the uncle of the more famous universal historian Arnold Joseph Toynbee (1889–1975).

movement, and became the taproot of many lay organizations for the urban poor. Within six months, noon prayer meetings of thousands of businessmen and other city dwellers were taking place in New York, Pittsburgh, Boston, Chicago, and other metropolitan centers. It has been estimated that over a million Americans were converted through this unusual urban businessmen's revival. Not only were many businessmen converted, but this marks the advent of businessmen as leaders within evangelicalism, and the advocacy and support of the business approach to mission and Christian institutions. Many of the connections that developed from the businessmen's prayer meetings developed into cooperations for building YMCAs and settlement houses.[33]

Twentieth Century: Social Gospel and the City

Many great urban reformers are still widely known and studied today. People like Washington Gladden and Walter Rauschenbusch raised the consciousness of Christians in the early twentieth century to the social nature of Christianity—the central teaching of Jesus on the Kingdom of God—and then focused this theology on the needs of modern Western cities. Called the social gospel, the greater emphasis Gladden and Rauschenbusch placed upon urban problems was important for many later ecumenical Christian leaders. This American approach to urban social issues was picked up globally. One of the most influential Asian Christians of the twentieth century was Kagawa Toyohiko (1886–1960). While attending the new Presbyterian seminary in Kobe, Japan, Kagawa tried to carry out Jesus's concern for the poor by moving into the slum district of Shinkawa to care for the poorest of the poor. Seeing firsthand the interrelationships of urban ills (poor education, injustice, poverty, inadequate housing, etc.), he founded a labor movement in that same slum district. After studies at Princeton Theological Seminary, he nurtured his conviction that Christianity must convert the soul to active love. Kagawa lived his life in such a way that it pointed others in that same direction.

For Kagawa, the religion Jesus taught is a religion of life. People who are fully alive, people who are living strongly, can understand it; those who deny life, who do not want to live, cannot get its meaning. The God of Jesus is a God of action. People who stay at home, read their Bibles, pray and meditate, and do nothing for the poor who beg for help before their very doors—such people will find the God of Jesus unintelligible. Only through the active movement of love will these people intuitively come to know the God of action.[34] Kagawa made no distinction between saving from sin and saving from the oppression and suffering of this world. He would not tolerate oppressive conditions and

33. Taken from Dale Irvin and Scott Sunquist, *History of the World Christian Movement* (Maryknoll, NY: Orbis Books, 2012), vol. 2, chap. 21.

34. From chap. 1 of Kagawa's *The Religion of Jesus*, trans. Helen F. Topping (Philadelphia: John C. Winston, 1931).

unnecessary suffering. He helped to organize farm cooperatives and labor unions, and he fought for women's suffrage with the same zeal that he preached Jesus. It is hard to imagine how this social activist had time to write, but in addition to his outspoken criticism of Japanese aggression and the oppression of labor, he wrote 150 books, many of which are still in print in English translations today. Kagawa took the teachings of Jesus into a predominately Buddhist and Shintoist culture—at the height of Japanese imperialism—and brought about much of the social transformation of Japanese society that would not fully develop until after World War II.

Many of the examples of urban missionary activity were people of great means who gave up their position and their possessions for the urban poor or oppressed. It is a common theme, and it should remind us that ministry to the wealthy is both for the sake of the wealthy themselves and for the sake of the poor who are waiting to become their partners in urban transformation.

Race and Reconciliation

In the United States, one of the largest urban issues has been racism and the need for reconciliation. Christian leaders like Martin Luther King Jr. (1929–68) taught Christians of all colors to resist policies, laws, and practices that dehumanized and divided. His participation in the Montgomery, Alabama, bus boycott[35] helped to unite Christians in resistance to unjust public policies. He stated that the purpose of the Montgomery bus boycott was "reconciliation[,] . . . redemption, the creation of the beloved community." The results of this boycott included the formation of the Southern Christian Leadership Conference (1957) whose main goals included desegregation and voter registration for African Americans. "The beloved community," a type of Kingdom community, was always King's goal. Later, King helped organize other peaceful marches of resistance, including the famous 1963 March on Washington. At that march, King used his well-honed rhetoric ("I have a dream!") to give the entire nation a united vision of a more blessed community than most had ever experienced.

The civil rights movement, of which King was one of the most important leaders, led to improved policies, laws, and the possibility of greater justice and reconciliation in many cities. King was assassinated while taking up the cause of black sanitation workers in Memphis, Tennessee. From the time of Christ's crucifixion "outside the city gate" up to the present, the city has been a priority in God's work of redemption. Whether it was the preaching, singing, and social work of Ephrem in Edessa, or King in Memphis, the city has been a place to declare and display God's justice and God's righteousness. Today this call takes on an even greater importance.

35. Public places, including buses, were often segregated, giving better seating and services to whites over nonwhites.

"I Have a Dream": Martin Luther King Jr.

King's famous speech was a Christian vision, communicated to a pluralistic and racially mixed polis, delivered in the capital city—the heart of the nation:

"We cannot be satisfied as long as a Negro in Mississippi cannot vote and a Negro in New York believes he has nothing for which to vote. No, no, we are not satisfied, and we will not be satisfied until justice rolls down like waters and righteousness like a mighty stream.

"I am not unmindful that some of you have come here out of great trials and tribulations. Some of you have come fresh from narrow jail cells. Some of you have come from areas where your quest for freedom left you battered by the storms of persecution and staggered by the winds of police brutality. You have been the veterans of creative suffering. Continue to work with the faith that unearned suffering is redemptive."[a]

a. Quoted from http://www.usconstitution.net/dream.html.

Mission in the City

We turn now to look at basic themes and guidelines for global urban missional initiatives.

One City

I lived in a small city that has been in constant decline for the past half a century. Pittsburgh was at one time one of the largest cities in the United States (eighth in 1910), but now it ranks fifty-ninth, with about three hundred thousand citizens, and it is shrinking. The once-thriving steel mills have closed, and so many people have left the "rust belt" of the Northeast looking for manufacturing jobs elsewhere. Pittsburgh does not have the population base to support the basic services of fire, police, public transportation, schools, and other social services. Downsizing is a much-too-common euphemism for more lost jobs, more hopelessness, and more homelessness. As with so many cities in North America, government agencies tried to revitalize the city without thinking about people. Buildings—nice, new, shiny buildings—were built—displacing local people struggling to survive on limited incomes. They were displaced into crowed areas with poor services and poor public transportation. Poor housing, poor schools, insufficient funds for infrastructure, and a lack of jobs all combine to bring about a perfect storm of economic decay and rising crime. Gangs and drug trafficking thrive in such contexts. I walked a lot in Pittsburgh and would frequently pass homeless folks, large homes divided into apartments by slum lords, and then a few huge mansions owned by professionals. Each year in Pittsburgh, about a person a week is murdered—mostly drug-related shootings. Many of the neighborhoods in my former city look hopeless.

In the United States as a whole, family structures—the foundation for the cultural mandate of the city that we looked at earlier—are breaking down. About 41 percent of all births in the United States are out of wedlock.[36] There is a correlation between family breakdown, poverty, and education in the United States—in fact, in every society. Young boys in the East End of Pittsburgh, where I lived, have little hope, with poor schools, poor transportation, poor housing, street violence, and few fathers to stand with them. Gangs prey upon young men by the time they are twelve. One local pastor wanted to look up the young men he had worked with twenty-one years ago, a youth fellowship of twenty boys, and discovered that six are now dead (before the age of thirty-five) and four are in prison. And these were not kids off the streets to begin with; these were the boys who grew up in the church and were involved in youth group and weekly worship. Gangs and the promise of drug money suck the hope and the life out of young men and their families. Cities—my city, all cities—are mission fields today.

> And so Jesus also suffered outside the city gate to make the people holy through his own blood. Let us, then, go to him outside the camp, bearing the disgrace he bore. For here we do not have an enduring city, but we are looking for the city that is to come. (Heb. 13:12–14)

Urban Webs of Needs and Hopes

Most large cities have overwhelming needs. If a single church, or even a denomination, were to try to take on a city's needs alone, depression and hopelessness would soon paralyze further action. What makes these needs so overwhelming is their intertwining nature: poor housing and unclean water lead to poor health, and poor health is compounded by the lack of medical care for the poor. Homelessness is both a cause and a result of broken families, and broken families have greater financial problems, and thus education and health suffer. Unjust urban zoning, or rezoning, often forces the poor from their homes or even from temporary shacks. When this happens, the economically marginalized often lose their jobs, or families are broken up as the father migrates, searching for work to feed his family. The city is a complex network of many levels: transportation, communication, education, public services, and urban symbols.[37] On the other hand, a city is simple: it is merely a larger

36. From the US Census statistics. In 2000 the figure was 62 percent of African American children were born out of wedlock. For Asian Americans it was 17 percent; whites, 29 percent; Hispanics, 53 percent; and Native Americans, 53 percent. The national average was 41 percent.

37. I am thinking here of the identity that urban dwellers attach to their cities of habitation. In the West people identify with schools, sports teams, history, or reputation. Some cities

and more complex family of relationships, finding ways to meet needs and express justice and mercy.

Outline for Urban Missional Engagement

In this final section, I want to identify eight *urban mission issues* that need to be considered in urban mission, no matter what continent the city is in. This list of issues is not exhaustive, but it is a way of seeing the city with Kingdom eyes and a way of understanding how issues interact in the city. This is also a way to begin to pray and plan to penetrate the city as a gracious and merciful presence.

1. *Navigating the web of urban needs*: Most books on urban ministry point out the interrelationships among urban needs that, on the surface, seem completely unrelated. I point out here eight interrelated needs that must be considered in looking at a city as a mission field.

A. Housing: In most urban areas, the problem of squatting on government land and the unhealthy living conditions that come with poorly constructed or maintained housing is always a problem. Most local churches involved in ministry to the poor will soon find themselves involved in housing issues. Churches can provide temporary housing when appropriate, but the larger issues of access to land, housing, loans, and basic public services (water, power, etc.) must be discussed early on.

B. Health care: Many of the causes of urban diseases and high infant mortality rates are simple matters with complex solutions. Political intrigue often raises its ugly head when people seek to solve basic health care issues for the poor in slum areas; many governments would rather not admit they have a problem. But the statistics are overwhelming as to the need for basic health care in the world's slums.

C. Food: Malnutrition is not only a problem in drought-stricken areas of Africa or Asia. Malnutrition is found in most major cities of the world, in both developing and developed cities. Often the problem is transportation, but more often it is economics: the poor do not have the money to buy good food in the city. When they were in the country, they could often pick food or raise food to eat. Migration to the city, however, requires money to buy food, and money only comes from jobs.

D. Jobs: Unemployment is a major problem in most urban areas, as hundreds of millions of people have moved to cities looking for work and a better future. Cities have not been able to respond quickly enough in developing manufacturing or service sectors. Many times it is not the ability to respond but the will of the leaders that prevents job creation. Doors have to be opened to make job creation a possibility. In some cities it is laws that have to be passed (or

---

identify with their religious history, commercial importance, or the status of being a leading city in the region or the nation.

Eight Urban Mission Issues

Those working in urban missions must do the following:

- Navigate the web of interrelated urban needs: housing, health care, food, jobs, education, church planting, racial and tribal reconciliation, and justice.
- Understand the need to reach the extremes of urban society.
- View reconciliation as a priority.
- Understand the church as the first and last hope for the city.
- Seek harmony between large churches and small Christian fellowships.
- Recognize the need to uncover immoral and unethical activities.
- Understand the purpose of buildings.
- Recognize the importance of evangelizing migrants and transients.

revoked); in other cities capital investment is needed. However, even if jobs are available, many of the poor do not have the education or training to fill these jobs. Often, if newer immigrants are well educated, they take the new jobs for which local people are not qualified, leaving a large unemployed sector.

E. Education: When street children are asked what their hope is for the future, what they would rather be doing instead of living on the streets, they say they would rather be in school.[38] Most illegal immigrants and many legal immigrants see education as the key for a better life—for them and for their children. Without basic literacy (something early settlement houses provided) and some specific training in skills, there is little hope for the poor. Christianity has been the religion, among all the religions of the world, that has always emphasized education.

F. Church planting: When churches are planted in different areas of a city, children, widows, and the needy have access to a community of support. Churches in the cities, even the poorest of local communities, offer hope to the hopeless; the church functions as an extended family. When there is no church, there may or may not be a social service agency or NGO that will step in. It is the responsibility of the church, however, to be the healing and merciful presence of Christ in every area of the city. If we care about the poor in the city, we will plant "beloved communities," so that the city might become more of a "blessed city" in each urban community.

G. Racial and tribal reconciliation: Healthy church communities will point toward the Kingdom of God in their reconciliation of diversity. Cities, of all places, must be the place where churches embody what it means to resist racial purity or tribal division. The vision of Revelation 7 and Jesus's sermon in Luke 4 must always be before the church leaders. In the words of Ephesians,

38. See Anderson, "Street Children," 225.

churches in cities must remember, "Now in Christ Jesus you who once were far away have been brought near by the blood of Christ." Christ must be the peace of local churches, showing to the city and to the world that the dividing wall of hostility has been broken down (Eph. 2:13–15). This will not happen except through culturally diverse leadership committed to reconciliation as a central pillar in its expression of orthodoxy. One of my favorite watchwords for a local urban church says, "We are a Christ-centered and intentionally cross-cultural family." Reconciliation must always be intentional, or it will not happen at all.

H. Justice: A church that has established reconciliation among its members, even a tentative and sensitive reconciliation, will have the platform from which to proclaim and seek justice for the poor. Urban economic and political systems are rife with unjust traditions that need to be challenged in the name of the God of justice. However, no one wants to hear another unjust hypocrite call for justice.

> From the least to the greatest,
>   all are greedy for gain;
> prophets and priests alike,
>   all practice deceit.
> They dress the wound of my people
>   as though it were not serious.
> "Peace, peace," they say,
>   when there is no peace. (Jer. 8:10–11)

Justice is not something we yell about from a safe place—it is our job to live justice for the poor and then call others, mainly the church, to walk together in this justice. Justice requires truth telling, although, in our media-driven age, truth is often difficult to identify or to appreciate. It is a missional responsibility to work for the peace and justice of the city and to raise up truth tellers.

2. *The church must reach the extremes of urban society*: The answer to grinding poverty, slums, street children, and sex trafficking in our cities must involve the most wealthy and powerful, along with the neediest. Urban areas develop great extremes of poverty and wealth, and all need to be reached. We should be reminded of the conversions of some of the wealthy bishops in the early church who gave all their money to the poor, and allow this example to be a call to the redistribution of wealth.[39] There is much to criticize in the leadership of Emperor Constantine, yet his conversion freed the church to minister to the poor. St. Basil's father was martyred for being a Christian,

39. From the three basic principles of urban ministry of John Perkins and his Christian Community Development Association: redistribution (more just distribution), relocation, and reconciliation. See *Let Justice Roll Down* (Ventura, CA: Regal, 1976) and *With Justice for All: A Strategy for Community Development* (Ventura, CA: Regal, 2007).

but Basil, living after the conversion of Constantine, was able to establish soup kitchens and hospitals for the needy. Urban mission must realize that the preferential option for the poor does not mean complete neglect of the rich or the influential. We are called to minister to both extremes.

3. *The priority of reconciliation:* We have spoken of this above, but we list it here again as a reminder that the local church must be a reconciled community in the city. The truthfulness of its message and integrity of its call are at stake here. Reconciliation (or the lack thereof) is something that is immediately obvious, and therefore it becomes a signpost for the surrounding community and for all new members.

4. *Recognizing the church as the first and last hope for the city*: Traveling through slums in Mumbai, through West Philadelphia, or through the sprawling shanty towns of Jakarta, it is evident that the local church is often the first and last hope for people. This has been the legacy of black churches in the United States. When the only economic activity left is a few pawnshops and liquor stores, the black church remains. This is one of the reasons the poorest churches need ongoing support, and why new, small churches need to be planted in urban areas. A local church becomes an outpost as well as a clinic.

> Each local church is located in a particular neighborhood. Its first mission responsibility must therefore be to the people who live there. The congregation is strategically placed to reach the area around it.[40]

Any mission strategy that ignores this apparently "weak" witness is not looking with spiritual eyes. These earthen vessels contain the glory of God in each place.

5. *Harmony between large churches and small gatherings in neighborhoods*: Related to number 4 above, there is always a need for large churches: cathedrals that are reminders of the global Christian family and that have the leverage to address complex situations. Ministry from the bottom, or from the neediest to the neediest, is a priority in urban ministry. This is reflected in the small churches planted in each neighborhood. However, large churches can become places in which to establish medical clinics and literacy programs and to host ESL and AA[41] meetings. It is hard for a small church to meet larger needs, but, with large and small working together, a community can be transformed.[42]

6. *Uncovering immoral activities that corrode lives*: From earliest times, the city has been a place in which immoral leadership can find protection. Great evil is done to the city, and to individual lives and families, through

40. John R. W. Stott, *The Living Church: Convictions of a Lifelong Pastor* (Downers Grove, IL: InterVarsity, 2011), 50.

41. English as a Second Language and Alcoholics Anonymous.

42. I am grateful for the work of Mark Gornik, Tim Keller (*Church Planter Manual*, 2002), and Pete Scazzero, all working in New York City, which has shown the role of larger churches in working with local communities to meet urban needs.

the easy availability of drugs, alcohol, pornography, abortion, prostitution, and gambling. The economics of these activities are staggering, and the way these vices have embedded themselves in local economic, technological, and social structures is even more troubling. For example, in recent years the term "gendercide" has been coined to explain the systematic removal of female fetuses.[43] Many cultures value male children over female children and modern technology (ultrasound) makes it possible to selectively abort baby girls. In some sections of China and India, 130 to 140 boys are born for every 100 girls. This is going to result in millions of frustrated men who will never be able to get married, but will be looking for sexual partners. Easy abortion for gender reasons will thereby increase the cost of a prostitute and increase activity in sex trafficking. Speaking against abortion has become both a gender-equality issue and a slavery issue.[44]

These vices have enormous economic power. The pornography industry brings in over fifty billion dollars annually (globally) and is very progressive in its use of technology. The profits from human trafficking (for both forced labor and prostitution) are estimated to be only a little less: about forty-five billion dollars.[45] Gambling has become socially acceptable, and even labeled a political virtue when used to help increase local government income. The dark side of gambling is always the economically depressed person or family who places their hopes and dreams in a lottery ticket (every week or every day) as a way to solve their financial problems; the poor get poorer. In effect, governments are providing social services for the poor, but they are paying for those government programs with money earned on the backs of the poor. Immoral activities redirect capital away from the greater social good, and in the end the city, its citizens, and its future are wagered on brief pleasures, while a few people become very wealthy.

Finally, when the church takes on immoral activity, it should expect to suffer for its witness. Mission to, or witness against, drug traffickers, for example, is very dangerous. Pastors and priests in Mexico who sponsor alcohol and drug rehabilitation programs have been killed or kidnapped for their support of such programs. Church leaders who resist the abuse of women by teaching them to read—which lessens the chances of them being taken into forced labor—also expose themselves to persecution.

43. See http://www.gendercide.org/what_is_gendercide.html.

44. See the fascinating paper by Elizabeth M. Wheaton, Edward J. Schauer, and Thomas V. Galli entitled, "Economics of Human Trafficking," produced by the "Not For Sale Academy" in San Francisco, http://nfsacademy.org/wp-content/uploads/2011/02/Wheaton-Economics-of-Human-Trafficking.pdf.

45. The numbers for immoral and illegal activities are very hard to validate, but they do show the enormity of the economic power these vices have globally. See the International Labour Office's working paper by Patrick Belser entitled, "Forced Labour and Human Trafficking: Estimating the Profits" (Geneva: ILO, 2005), http://digitalcommons.ilr.cornell.edu/cgi/viewcontent.cgi?article=1016&context=forcedlabor. Belser admits that his statistics are likely all underestimated.

7. *Understanding the purpose of buildings*: Earlier, we explored how cities in the past have been built according to three major needs: worship, commercial activity, and social order or safety. While I do not think that mission to the city absolutely requires big buildings, there is still a need for buildings in urban mission. These buildings may be multifunctional, providing soup kitchens, clothing stores, medical care, and literacy programs, along with a place to worship. Buildings are not sufficient for urban mission, but they are necessary, even if it is only the smallest edifice. In Seoul, and now in Beijing, Singapore, and Bangkok, church buildings are a reminder to the city of a Christian presence and of the opportunity to be part of the church. There are times when a building is simply not possible, as when governments will not allow buildings for Christian worship. However, when it is possible, the Christian building becomes a meeting place. It is wrong to say that buildings do not matter at all for Christian witness in the city, but it is also wrong to depend on buildings to build the mission.

Sometimes a building is important because it is "planted" in the midst of a squatter settlement or a refugee camp. While visiting Yangon in 1993, I was taken about twenty kilometers out of town to see where thousands of citizens had been "relocated" so a Japanese construction firm could build a new hotel in the urban center of the city. These people were simply taken from their apartments, put on buses, and shipped out of town. The next day, most of them could not get to work, for there was no bus service to the city. In a short period of time, they went from being urban workers to rural squatters with no tools for farming, no clean water, and no transportation. A church building needed to be built there to provide hope, basic services, and a place of refuge.

8. *Evangelizing "people on the way"*: Cities are great borderlands in which communities overlap and people frequently pass through on their way to another job, or another opportunity (education being one of the most important).[46] Therefore, mission to the city should identify "people on the way," who happen to be our neighbors for a season—or for a generation. One of the most important groups of migrants in the West is international students. They usually come for one to six years, bringing with them great hopes, deep needs, and often unrealized potential for the Kingdom. Many international students are Christians who are seeking to serve while they are in the West. After I spoke at a church in Alexandria, Egypt, a father came up to me and said something that I am sure many Christian parents have wanted to say: "My son is a strong Christian who will be in your city for three or four years. He will be looking for a church, not just for fellowship, but as a place where he can minister. He has a great desire to reach out to the poor and to

46. There are an estimated three hundred thousand international students studying in the UK (from the UK Council for International Student Affairs) and about six hundred and seventy thousand in the USA (Chronicle of Higher Education). See http://www.ukcisa.org.uk/about/statistics_visas.php and http://chronicle.com/article/Number-of-Foreign-Students-/49142/.

be involved in evangelism." Later, I met his son, and he did get involved in a local multicultural church.

Other people on the way, either looking for jobs or working as immigrants on short-term contracts, are in great need of support. Away from family, many young women and men need to be shown the love of God in Jesus Christ, and many churches are doing admirable work reaching out toward and then building up those who are passing through.

> He defends the cause of the fatherless and the widow, and loves the foreigner residing among you, giving them food and clothing. And you are to love those who are foreigners, for you yourselves were foreigners in Egypt. (Deut. 10:18–19)

I have heard of amazing ministries to Filipino amahs in Malaysia and Singapore, to Sinhalese health care workers in Singapore, to Chinese construction workers in the Middle East, and to Filipino migrant workers (mostly illegal) in Sabah. Some of these return to their countries as Christians and become educated church planters. In our cities, the foreign mission field is often brought to our doorstep, if only we have eyes to see and hearts that break at the loneliness and hopelessness that our new neighbors sometimes experience.

In the end, all missional work in the city must be done in partnership: churches from the region working together, churches and nongovernment (and government) agencies working together. The city calls for ecumenical unity, and this involves not only the full conversion of cultures (the city), but also the full conversion of the church. It is hard for Christians to extend grace by cooperating in city ministry, and yet it is crucial. Such cooperation brings greater grace to the city, but it also becomes a sign that Jesus Christ is, in fact, in the city—loving each city block in and through local churches. It gives hope to the poor and the outcast, and it becomes a sign to the oppressor and unjust ruler. For the city is, in the end, a hopeful sign and a promise from God.

> No longer will there be any curse. The throne of God and of the Lamb will be in the city, and his servants will serve him. (Rev. 22:3)

12

Global Community

Partnership in Mission

Of all the major themes in mission that I could focus on in an introductory book, I have chosen the church (chap. 9), evangelism (chap. 10), the city (chap. 11), partnership (chap. 12), and spirituality (chap. 13).[1] I believe these issues, plus one issue I have interwoven in various chapters—religions—are the major concerns for mission in the twenty-first century. Partnership may be the hardest to defend, historically or theologically, and yet most people involved in mission oversight or missionary leadership recognize the importance of this issue. Every place of mission is a place of partnership in the twenty-first century.

I focus on partnership in mission first because of technology. The availability, immediacy, and economy of communications and transportation that have

1. By means of comparison, David Bosch ends his masterful volume *Transforming Mission: Paradigm Shifts in the Theology of Mission* (Maryknoll, NY: Orbis Books, 1991) with thirteen "elements of an emerging ecumenical missionary paradigm." Writing in the late 1980s and early 1990s, Bosch was aware that he was writing in a "period of transition, on the borderline between a paradigm that no longer satisfies and one that is, to a large extent, still amorphous and opaque" (366). His elements were: (1) mission as the church-with-others, (2) mission as *missio Dei*, (3) mission as mediating salvation, (4) mission as the quest for justice, (5) mission as evangelization, (6) mission as contextualization, (7) mission as liberation, (8) mission as inculturation, (9) mission as common witness, (10) mission as ministry by the whole people of God, (11) mission as interfaith witness, (12) mission as theology, and (13) mission as action in hope. As valuable as these final discussions are in *Transforming Mission*, they do not point the way forward as much as they describe the resources that were available at the time to shape a missiology.

developed in recent decades have linked unlikely Christians together as never before in mission history. Individual churches can communicate directly with synods, presbyteries, or parishes around the world with little or no oversight or previous knowledge. Individuals or small groups can travel easily, and often decide on their own to "help" a church in another country. Much of this help is impulsive and counterproductive—missiologically speaking—because it ignores partnership as a means of and mode for mission.

Secondly, there is also an ecclesial reason to discuss partnership in missiological terms: the breakdown of major confessions and denominations and the rise of independency and local autonomy. Before decolonialization there were a few main players in global missions: major denominations, religious orders, and mission societies. National church councils and the WCC were the primary meeting places for global cooperation in mission. This is no longer true. In the past few decades, the major Western players and major church councils have greatly decreased in influence and size. They have been replaced by thousands of local societies, indigenous churches, NGOs, and non-Western churches and missions. The expansion of Christianity in the past half century has also meant the diversification of structures and organizations. Christian mission is much harder to grasp, but it is much more active from and to all the corners of the world. Moving from hierarchical Western missions to a global network of mission requires greater partnership in each place.

Thirdly, partnership has come to the fore because of the sudden reorientation of global Christianity that has occurred in recent history.[2] In almost any country to which a missionary might be sent, there are now local Christian gatherings or even a mature Christian church. In earlier years, missionaries sent from the West often went to regions where there was no Christian witness at all (and perhaps even no roads or maps). At that time, there were no Christians—of any Christian family—with whom to partner. Now, if a person is going to a formerly "unreached" region, she or he will usually find a number of Christian groups present, even if they only have a fragile existence.

Partnership has become a central issue because of technology, the diversification of Christianity, and the global spread of Christian communities. The global context we now live in illustrates the need for partnership, and theology reveals both the necessity and manner of partnership in mission.

"Partnership" is a frequently used word, but its actual meaning is quite difficult to pin down. In the following pages, I want to define the concept as

2. Much has been written about this remarkable shift in Christianity that occurred in the twentieth century. Andrew Walls says it was the most significant century for Christianity outside of the first century. See "Christianity across Twenty Centuries," in Todd M. Johnson and Kenneth R. Ross, *Atlas of Global Christianity* (Edinburgh: Edinburgh University Press, 2009), 48. See also the articles by Todd Johnson and Sun Young Chung, "Christianity's Centre of Gravity, AD 33–2100" (ibid., 50–53); and Daniel Jeyaraj, "The Re-emergence of Global Christianity, 1910–2010" (ibid., 54–55).

clearly as possible—in part by showing how this concept is rooted in the nature of the Trinity. Then I will look briefly at the history and meaning of the concept today and the basic types of partnership that should be considered. Finally, I introduce ten issues in world mission today that require careful partnership in mission. But first, three stories will illustrate this concern. These three stories are examples from Asia and from the former Soviet Republic; they are composite stories, in order to protect the ministries involved, but they are fairly representative of actual mission situations.

Three Partnership Stories

In country X in Southeast Asia, Christian mission has begun to open up in recent decades—with the surprising result that people are coming to faith at a previously unheard-of rate. In previous centuries, the work in this area had been predominantly Roman Catholic, but now the largest work is Protestant, and it is more diverse than ever before. I visited orphanages, homes for battered women, training centers, and Bible schools run by five different Protestant groups. Roman Catholic work has also returned to this country and is carried on by both lay and religious orders. I counted at least ten denominations at work when I visited, but I have heard that there are actually over one hundred denominations. Different ecumenical or fellowship groups have been started in order to bring about some cooperation, but there is little genuine fellowship and partnership. In addition to over one hundred denominations at work in this small country, there are missionaries from at least twenty foreign countries helping with development work and church planting. I visited five different Bible schools in the country, but I understand that there are many more. Despite the noble efforts of a few great leaders, most of the work in country X is led by individuals with strong personalities or by mission societies that have primary accountability to their organizations or home countries. In the few areas where there is true cooperation, outstanding work is being done.

Country Y is a predominately Muslim nation with a strong, but small, Christian minority. As with most countries in the world, there is a large influx of foreign workers and other migrants looking for jobs and homes. Slums of undocumented foreigners grow on the outskirts of the cities, and children of these foreign workers walk the streets looking for handouts. These children are caught between cultures, countries, and economies; most of them were born in country Y, but they do not have birth certificates, and, therefore, as stateless children, they have no rights, cannot attend school, and cannot receive medical help. A retired missionary from the West noticed the thousands of stateless children idle on the streets, often getting involved in illegal activities in order to earn some money for the family. She began a small "school" of sorts, inviting all kinds of people to pitch in. No one gets paid anything for teaching at the school, and all of the supplies are donated: chairs, markers, tables, paper, clothes, and most of the food for daily snacks. I have met Anglicans, Catholics, Presbyterians, Lutherans, and Baptists helping out at the school. The people who are serving there come from at least seven countries. Some local churches are more committed than others, but most people don't ask who is "sponsoring" the school. I believe this is because of the personality of the retired missionary, who gently includes all who will help—and all who help find themselves equally important to the task.

Country Z is of the former Soviet Republic.[3] After the fall of the Iron Curtain, thousands of Christian groups from all over the world began to look for ways to be involved in mission in Russia and its former satellite nations. Much of the mission work was insensitive and poorly thought out. Some of the mission work was done with no awareness of the existence of the Orthodox Church and therefore no concept that Orthodox churches might be partners with them in God's greater mission. There was much proselytizing and building of personal kingdoms. One pastor in country Z developed a partnership with Americans from a well-meaning and wealthy church. It was like a dream come true, after so many years of oppression and poverty, to have such abundant support from a rich American church. If the Christians in Z needed warmer clothes, the Americans sent clothes. If they needed medicine, the Americans sent medicine. If they needed a bigger or better church (according to American perception), then they sent money and builders and built a bigger church. After three years, the pastor in Z woke up and said to himself, "What effect is all of this 'missionary work' having on my congregation? Local clothes stores are not doing well because so many free clothes are available from the United States. My church members are not willing to sacrifice for others because they have developed the understanding that the Americans will provide. As the American mission grows, our church atrophies." They had become a welfare church.

History of a Concept: The When, Where, and Why of Partnership

Although the modern concept of partnership in mission began with the discussions at the Jerusalem meeting of the IMC in 1928, actual partnerships began much earlier. Of course, the earliest partnerships were Western missionaries from various countries and denominations (or religious orders) cooperating together in an overseas country. But one of the earliest and most interesting partnerships involves an indigenous Christian in the Caribbean who was pioneering work among slaves when European missionaries came to help. Moravian missionaries arriving in St. Thomas met Rebecca Protten, who had been evangelized by her Dutch owner, taught to read the Bible (and the Dutch

3. From Peter Greer and Phil Smith, *The Poor Will Be Glad: Joining the Revolution to Lift the World out of Poverty* (Grand Rapids: Zondervan, 2009), 49–62.

Partnership Concerns, circa 1928

At the International Missionary Council meeting in Jerusalem in 1928, a statement came out that recognized the need for greater partnership in global mission. It was recognized that churches in Asia could teach Christians in the West a lot about mission. "Lastly, we urge that every possible step be taken to make real the fellowship of the Gospel. The churches of the West send missions and missions-of-help to the churches of Africa and Asia. We believe that the time is come when all would gain if the younger churches were invited to send missions-of-help to the churches of Europe and America that they may minister of their treasure to the spiritual life of those to whom they come."[a]

a. This is from the IMC statement on "The Christian Message" that came out of the Jerusalem meeting. *The Jerusalem Meeting of the International Missionary Council*, vol. 1, *The Christian Life and Message in Relation to Non-Christian Systems of Thought and Life* (London: IMC, 1928), 410.

Book of Martyrs), and then bought her own freedom. She became a traveling evangelist and an irritant to slave owners on the island. When the German Pietists arrived as missionaries to the Caribbean (1732), Rebecca became their most trusted translator and evangelist. She was taken to Germany for further training, whereupon she was ordained in 1746; the first woman of color ever ordained. This is a unique early partnership of a local indigenous missionary with Western missionaries.

Another type of partnership that developed in the Protestant world is illustrated by the Danish-Halle mission to India, in which a Danish king sent out a mission of German missionaries who received much financial and prayer support from England. It became a model for much early Protestant missionary work—to be multidenominational and multinational. As we have seen, the idea of partnership gave way to the strong tides of denominationalism in the nineteenth century. From that point on, partnership involved denominations carrying out their own missionary work, but also talking together about how to cooperate as denominations. Conferences were held that encouraged certain types of partnership, beginning with the 1860 Liverpool Conference that focused on both national (UK) and international missionary work. Partnership continued to be promoted through such conferences and through specific comity arrangements in which regions would be divided between various missions. These conferences pointed to greater cooperation and unity in mission, but their influence and vision were limited to cooperation, as opposed to integral partnership.

A major step forward occurred after World War II at the 1947 Whitby, Ontario, IMC meeting where the phrase "Partnership in Obedience" became etched in IMC and WCC history. It was recognized at this meeting that Western churches were greatly weakened, and that churches in many other regions of the world were no longer "younger churches."[4] The distinction between older and younger, or mother and daughter, churches was no longer helpful. These differences were erased by the concept of partnership in obedience, which expressed the radical notion that Christian churches around the world share in the mission of God together and so should also share the resources, suffering, and glory of God's mission. There is no such thing as second-class or inferior churches—no matter what they may look like or however old they may be. Christian witness should always be done in common solidarity.

The meaning of this concept was explained by Stephen Neill, who helped to draft the Whitby statement.[5] Neill had attended four meetings that focused on the new concept of mutuality and partnership in mission, from July 1947 (Whitby) to September 1948 (Amsterdam, First Assembly of the WCC). In between these two meetings was the eighth Lambeth Conference of Anglican bishops and the inauguration of the important Church of South India (September 1947). In *Christian Partnership*, Neill's final lecture was on the church union that formed the Church of South India. He calls it "A Dangerous Experiment." The organic union that took place in South India was, for many ecumenical thinkers of the time, the supreme goal of all partnership and cooperation in mission: different churches uniting to become one new church. However, since that time—a time symbolized by the founding of the United Nations and the WCC—the organic union model has not predominated. With the proliferation of churches and missions has come a messiness in ecumenism and partnership that was completely unanticipated. But just like the WCC, which requires respect and open dialogue among different communions, so partnership requires respect and open dialogue in participation in God's mission. Reconciliation in the world must be built upon reconciliation of the church, but what will this look like, and what goals and standards should we set?

What Is Partnership?

Partnership, theologically speaking, is grounded in four basic theological and biblical concepts: the Trinity, Jesus's high priestly prayer, the church as the

4. Andrew Walls is uncompromising in his evaluation of what happened to Christianity in Western Europe in the twentieth century (not just after two world wars). "Between the beginning of the twentieth century and the present day, western Europe has moved from Christian heartland to Christian wasteland, and there has been a degree of withering in the West as a whole." Johnson and Ross, "Christianity across Twenty Centuries," 48.

5. *Christian Partnership* (London: SCM, 1952). The James Long Lectures of the CMS, which were later printed up as this volume, were delivered in 1950. For a different perspective, see Max A. C. Warren, *Partnership: The Study of an Idea* (London: SCM, 1956).

body of Christ, and the apostolic missions in the New Testament. We will briefly look at each of these before discussing some guidelines for partnerships.

Trinity and Partnership

Max Warren (1904–77), one of the most celebrated leaders of the Church Missionary Society, wrote a standard explanation of the concept of partnership.[6] Along with others ecumenists, he roots the idea in the doctrine of the Trinity. God is in community, and as the three persons of the Godhead express love in self-giving attentiveness to the other and to all of God's creation, so we also learn to participate in community. Love is the primary designation of God, and love at all times indicates attention to the other and self-emptying for the other. God's oneness, however, is the foundational word about God. In terms of missional partnership, this should remind us that we are equal partners. We all stand before God as created beings invited into partnership with God. As humans, we all are distinct persons with distinct personalities and gifts, but we are all "one" in essence: we are all created in the image of God. Partnership looks like the Trinity: one nature in all persons, each person distinct.[7] The mystery of the Trinity—in its unity and diversity, its single nature and three persons—is to be expressed in the mystery of the church in mission. What is the mystery of the church in mission? It is the fact that God dwells within humanity, bringing about unity of witness. The mystery is that the church is the body of Christ in unified mission, bringing liberation to all nations (Eph. 3:4–11; Col. 1:24–29). This leads to the second theological foundation for partnership: Jesus's prayer in the garden before his betrayal.

"That All of Them May Be One . . ."

The second theological foundation for partnership is found in the very important prayer recorded for us in John 17, often called Jesus's high priestly prayer. The whole prayer shows Jesus's concern for the continuation of the mission given to him by the Father. It is a missionary prayer that has become the prayer of the ecumenical movement. Without looking at the whole prayer, it should be noted that it is put in the context of Jesus's suffering (he is aware of his coming end, v. 11), the attendant glory that will come through this suffering (vv. 1, 4, 5), and the continuation of his mission in truth, holiness, and unity. Although John 17:13–25 is the foundation for Christian unity and ecumenical witness, it is also a guideline for all Christian mission. All Christian mission must express God's Word which is truth (v. 17), through suffering and

6. Warren, *Partnership*, 38.

7. Enoch Wan, "The Trinity: A Model for Partnership in Christian Missions," *Global Missiology* 3, no. 7 (April 2010). See the full article at http://ojs.globalmissiology.org/index.php/english/article/viewFile/138/397.

rejection (vv. 14–15); it must express the unity of the Godhead (vv. 21–26); and its purpose is that the world would know that Jesus was sent by the Father to bring glory to God (v. 23). Thus, all mission must seek the unity found in the Godhead, which is a unity of purpose, of coordinated action, and of truth. Partnership is too weak a word for the high calling in mission that is envisioned here. Jesus is in the Father, the Father is in the Son, believers are in the Son and the Father, and the Son is in believers (vv. 21–26).

> Furthermore . . . the community's unity is based on God's unity and makes it visible. Unity is given to the church, created together with her essence. It cannot be achieved by human hand, but it must be maintained in fidelity to the origin; it is not a goal to be achieved, but a gift given to the church. If she renounced her unity, she would defile her essence and would be unfaithful to her vocation.[8]

Missionaries in every context would do well to study this remarkable prayer together, and recognize that partnership in unity is given to us as a gift from God. This unity requires Christians of all backgrounds and communions to work, act, and live as a single body in each community.

The Body of Christ

The third theological foundation for partnership is the wonderful image of the church as a body. Paul plays with this image in a number of places, indicating that he carried the same concern as Jesus regarding the importance and the difficulty of Christian witness being united.[9] Jesus experienced division among his own disciples, and Paul experienced division among the churches he served. In both cases, this division misrepresented God before the world. The church is a single body with diverse ethnic groups. In Ephesians 3, Paul explains that now the Gentiles and Israel are members of the same body in Christ (v. 6). We should, therefore, expect mission to involve cooperation among different ethnic groups. The body of Christ is also diverse in spiritual gifts, talents, and abilities. This is a good thing for mission: everyone is not doing the same thing with the same abilities (1 Cor. 12). Such understanding of the diverse parts of the body should and must lead to partnership. The body must be coordinated to allow the foot to run or kick with freedom, while the arm takes the lesser role of helping to counterbalance the body. When the fingers type or hold a book, other parts of the body rest.

The body image is an apt and dynamic picture of partnership: we need to be listening, attentive to others in their ministry, always ready to step in to

8. Francis Anekwe Oborji, *Concepts in Mission: The Evolution of Contemporary Missiology* (Maryknoll, NY: Orbis Books, 2006), 157.

9. Paul uses this as a dominant image of the church: Romans 7:4; 1 Corinthians 10:16; 12:12–31; Ephesians 3:6; 4:12–32; 5:25–33; and Colossians 3:15.

support when appropriate. When a group or an individual launches out into missionary work with no regard for others who live in that region or who have also been sent to that region, it is like an amputation has taken place. No missionary work done that is "cut off" from the body will endure, except by the surprising grace of God. There is always a cost when missionary work develops out of personal agenda rather than from true body life. The earliest mission letters that we find in the New Testament are a testimony of how the early church struggled to carry out mission in partnership.

Partnership in the Apostles' Mission Work

The apostles understood something of partnership even before Jesus prayed his high priestly prayer. They had been sent out as ambassadors of Christ earlier, in a group of twelve and a group of seventy-two (Matt. 10; Luke 10). In each case, they were sent out in pairs—partnership was required. The apostles seem to have copied this pattern. For example, Paul is often held up as a great pioneer missionary, but he worked closely with many others: Luke, Silas, Timothy, Sosthenes, Mark, Barnabas, Epaphroditus, Euodia, Syntyche, Clement, Epaphras, Onesimus, Demas, Nympha, Archippus, Titus, Tychicus, Priscilla, and Aquila. All of these are listed in his letters, and he also mentions other groups or churches that are partners in the ministry with him.

In Philippians and Romans, we get a glimpse into this earliest partnership model. Paul begins his correspondence to the Philippian church by reminding them of his prayers and their partnership: "In all my prayers for all of you, I always pray with joy because of your partnership in the gospel from the first day until now" (1:4–5). The idea of partnership in the gospel carries out Jesus's concern in his prayer, that we might be one. It is also an expression of the body imagery, whereby unity and cooperation are found in working together to proclaim and live out the gospel. In both Philippians and Thessalonians, Paul expresses partnership as more than a compromise or business arrangement; it is a deep and abiding love for each other. "Since I have you in my heart . . . all of you share in God's grace with me. God can testify how I long for all of you with the affection of Christ Jesus" (Phil. 1:7).

Later in the first chapter of Philippians, Paul struggles with the desire to be immediately with Christ (since his imprisonment seems to point to death) or to be saved to labor with and for the Philippians. For him, laboring on behalf of others (in imitation of Christ) is more important than immediately being in the presence of Christ (vv. 21–26). The secret to this type of partnership is found in chapter 2: humility. Jesus is the model, and emptying oneself is the image Paul uses.[10] Later, in chapter 3, he completes the connection between partnership and suffering, even dying for others: "I want to know Christ—yes,

10. *Kenosis* is the Greek word for "to make empty or void." It is an extreme word used here for completely emptying oneself for the sake of loving others.

to know the power of his resurrection and participation in his sufferings, becoming like him in his death" (3:10). Partnership requires this type of attitude that ultimately recognizes our partnership together as our partnership in suffering with Christ.

In Romans, we read that Paul understands his ministry as a partnership, even when writing to people he has not yet met. We should also note that he regards the Romans as part of his "mission field," and yet he also comes to learn from them.

> God, whom I serve with my whole heart in preaching the gospel of his Son, is my witness how constantly I remember you in my prayers at all times; and I pray that now at last by God's will the way may be opened for me to come to you. I long to see you so that I may impart to you some spiritual gift to make you strong—that is, that you and I may be mutually encouraged by each other's faith. I do not want you to be unaware, brothers and sisters, that I planned many times to come to you (but have been prevented from doing so until now) in order that I might have a harvest among you. (Rom. 1:9–13)

Mutuality in mission means that partnership is not just about working shoulder to shoulder—it is about mutually learning from the other and supporting each other. It is remarkable that Paul, the great apostle and author of about one third of the New Testament, talks about mutuality even among those who are just coming to faith. The conclusion is inescapable: There is no person who is not in need of mutual support and partnership in mission. There is no situation in which one person has nothing to offer the partnership.

Some Guidelines for Partnership in Mission

Partnership is more than a static concept of unity, tolerance, or helping one another. Mission partnership, based on the above biblical and theological concepts, is dynamic unity in mission, on the road or in the trenches. Partnership is dynamically involved in the world and centered in unity with Christ. Therefore, partnership in mission is less like a unified business and more like a soccer team moving toward a goal—facing constant resistance and continuously moving and reconfiguring. Because there is movement within partnership, it is important to establish guidelines as opposed to rules, and, as with all relationships, it is important to forgive and reevaluate consistently. To use a marriage analogy, rarely should partnerships end in a divorce, and yet there are times when violence or abuse requires separation. Times like this do not indicate that God is not faithful or that he has withheld his unity from us; rather, sometimes the disobedience of part of the body is so great that it damages the witness of the whole body. Such separations are never good, and must

Eight Guidelines for Partnership

- Ask: "Who are the local partners already at work?"
- Maintain worship in Christian unity.
- Make sure unity is both personal and corporate.
- Identify and name the type of partnership.
- Be clear about each partner's own gifts and limitations.
- Encourage both local initiatives and outside perspectives.
- Encourage the broadening of the understanding of partnership.
- When possible, seek long-term partnerships.

always be a last resort; however, a "unity at all costs" perspective may end up costing Christian witness.

Based upon historic lessons and a theology of the Trinity and the body of Christ, I offer the following guidelines for discussion and as a means of solidarity in mission.[11]

1. When considering mission to a new region, a new people group, or in response to new areas of injustice, it is necessary to first ask, "*Who are the local partners* who are already at work in this situation, and how can we best relate to them?" This is not to say that mission must only take place under the direction of local Christians, but local Christians should have a primary hearing. Often local church unity is encouraged when outside groups come in to be involved missionally. As the mission society (or church) initiates, they should bring other Christians together and listen to their concerns and suggestions. We should never expect complete agreement, but we should never ignore a united voice from indigenous Christians. Too much damage has been done to Christian witness by foreign Christians (usually with more money than the local Christians) who moved forward without any concern for local Christian communities.

2. It is important to live a partnership that expresses *Christian unity in worship*. Can we worship together on occasion, or can we find ways to pray

11. There have been many guidelines regarding mission partnership over the past decades. See Sherron Kay George, *Called as Partners in Christ's Service: The Practice of God's Mission* (Louisville: Geneva, 2004). In this volume, see especially Appendix C, "'Presbyterians Do Mission in Partnership' Policy Statement," 120–24. See also the following statements conveniently found in Philip Wickeri's *Partnership, Solidarity, and Friendship: Transforming Structures in Mission* (Louisville: Worldwide Ministries Division, 2003), 21–28: (1) Christian Conference of Asia and Council for World Mission 1999 statement on approaches to partnership that are *rejected*; (2) "Guidelines for Sharing" from the WCC World Consultation on Koinonia, El Escorial, 1987; and (3) "Basic Principles: A Synthesis Taken from the United Church of Christ in the Philippines Document 'Partnership in Mission'" (1992).

The Anglican Communion has ten principles for partnership: (1) local initiative, (2) mutuality, (3) responsible stewardship, (4) interdependence, (5) cross-fertilization, (6)integrity, (7) transparency, (8) solidarity, (9) meeting together, and (10) acting ecumenically. From the Anglican Communion website http://www.anglicancommunion.org/ministry/mission/resources/guidelines/partnership10.cfm.

together? It is very important that partnership be rooted in the deepest spiritual levels and not become a business transaction. We keep this rootedness when we find ways of worshiping the Triune God together, and praying with and for each other. Historically, it has been on the missionary frontiers that Eucharistic fellowship has been the least divided. Missional existence must continue to push back divisions in and through worship. Despite the many obstacles developed over centuries of divisions and separate contextual development, partnership in mission means that we pray and move toward greater and deeper worship in Jesus Christ.

3. Partnership must always be *both personal and corporate*: there must be both individual partnerships at the local level and more official relationships with institutions. In our zeal to be in full communion with local Christians and other missions, it must not be forgotten that we may very well lose our union with our own church and/or mission. Individuals need to relate together and know each other's gifts and needs, but institutions need to agree to walk together also. Partnership involves both individuals and institutions walking and living together in mission.

4. Discuss and then identify the *type of partnership* that is then agreed upon. Some partnerships are temporary, as when churches come into a region where there has been a natural disaster. Churches often partner in mission to rebuild homes after a hurricane or tsunami. Outsiders may be involved in helping to feed and rebuild for a few weeks or for a few years. In these situations, the partnership is temporary and goal specific. Other temporary partnerships might include helping to build a Bible school program using foreign faculty until local faculty can be trained. Or a mission might help, for a season, to reach an unreached people group and, once a church is established, it may be time for that mission to move on. Some partnerships involve twinning (two churches, conferences, synods, or presbyteries) working in partnership, while others will involve multiple groups of different types. Whatever the number of organizations involved, it is important to discuss openly, from the beginning, each group's purpose, goals, and expectations before deciding how to work and worship together.

5. Each group must be clear about *their own gifts and limitations*.[12] One of the major difficulties in partnership, and often where the greatest damage is done, is the use of money: a gift for one partner and a limitation for the other. In almost every partnership, one group has more money than the other. Early discussions must take place openly and honestly as to how to prevent paternalism, dependency, or a welfare mentality regarding money.[13] This is also something that must be reevaluated periodically. Giftedness also may

12. The image here is of the Lord's Table (not a conference table), worshiping around the broken body of Christ, while being the body of Christ for the world.

13. See Jonathan Bonk, *Missions and Money: Affluence as a Western Missionary Problem*, rev. ed. (Maryknoll, NY: Orbis Books, 2007).

include evangelism, care for the poor, knowledge, training, and prayer. These and other gifts should be part of the discussion, each partner asking, "What can we contribute to this partnership?"

6. Encourage both *local initiative and outside perspective.* Outsiders bring the gift of perspective, bringing various cultures and contexts into comparison with the local context. Local people, however, know their own context better than the outsider ever will; the local person also has to live with the decisions and the work of the outside missionary. The missionary will need to know and understand local laws, customs, and relationships to other religions and the local government authorities. Missionaries must listen carefully from the start. Partnerships always begin with the missionary at the school of local church and local culture.

7. Always encourage *broadening the understanding of partnership* to include other Christian groups. When local Protestants and Catholics are in conflict, the outside partner can and should raise some questions about forgiveness and greater reconciliation for the future. This does not mean ignoring the past; it means recognizing the past, talking about the past, working to forgive the past, and then building greater trust for the future. The sins of the past should not bind the hope of unity in mission for the future. Any partnership can soon become a new type of division, but ever-growing circles of cooperation in mission can be the antidote.

8. When possible, seek *long-term partnerships.* It takes a long time to build strong cross-cultural relationships in mission. Language learning is just one of the important cultural concerns that needs to be overcome; there is also the problem of cultural values and assumptions. Long-term relationships say to the local church, and to the surrounding culture, that fidelity is important. A covenant-initiating God, who prefers the analogy of husband and wife to describe his relationship to the church, will be revealed more fully in long-term commitments. What this will usually mean is that there will be a person, persons, or family(-ies) that will move in order to be present with the local partners. One of the greatest weaknesses of contemporary missional partnership is that they are based upon long-distance travel, without the attending close and ongoing relationships that residence provides. Some people from the mission or church need to make the long-term commitment to be bridge persons for the partnership, giving up their own lives for the sake of partnership in mission. It goes without saying that the persons who are sent should be fully supported and approved by both the receiving and sending churches.

Partnership Contexts: How Does Partnership Enhance Christian Mission?

Not only does Christian theology point to cooperation and partnership in mission, but the size and complexity of global concerns to which the church should speak *requires* this partnership. No one individual, church, or even national church can solve the major issues of violence and human trafficking, nor can they alone reach the mass of unreached people in the world. The *missio Dei* requires that we work together as the body of Christ, not building personal kingdoms, but looking forward in our ministry to the city built by God (Heb. 11:10).

Today, the concept of partnership has been deepened by various popular ecclesiologies in the West. Building Christian community is often seen as a matter of orthodoxy. The church is community, and as that community is caring for its own, its caring fellowship reaches out to others as a type of missional presence. Both the missional church movement and emerging movements see the local community as more than a collection of baptized Christians—it is a family whose love flows out to others.[14] I think it is helpful to see that such an emphasis on community is flowing in the same direction as the emphasis upon partnership in mission. With this commitment to partnership affirmed, then, what are some of the major issues that local churches and individual missions should focus on in global mission today? In other words, how can we see missional partnership working to liberate and redeem within our fallen world?

1. *Partnership makes common witness to societies and governments possible.* Every government, no matter how just or unjust, no matter how strong or weak, has a love-hate relationship with the church. Christians, growing in their own discipleship, will seek for ways to care for the poor, the lost, and the oppressed. As Christian communities become stronger, they begin to be a blessing to society: feeding the hungry, caring for the homeless, teaching morals and ethics. The history of hospitals, drug rehab centers, schools, and relief work is very much a Christian history. However, all governments also resist the church, for the church requires absolute covenant loyalty. Christians, in baptism, are marked with a loyalty to a power higher than the state. Governments need their citizens to serve the state and its leaders; Christians seek to serve Christ and his mission, and often the two come into conflict. You cannot serve God and mammon, nor can you serve Jesus and nationalism.

In the past, many governments were Christian in orientation, if not in essence, and so Christians found that many of their values and desires were supported by the state. This was true for a period of time, mostly in the West and the Middle East. Now, there are very few governments in the world that are outwardly sympathetic to Christianity, not to mention being supportive of the church. This means that Christians, in most political contexts, need to

14. Brian McLaren ends his analysis with a community of action (*Everything Must Change: Jesus, Global Crises and a Revolution of Hope* [Nashville: Thomas Nelson, 2007], 291), and Michael Frost and Alan Hirsch end their *ReJesus* (Peabody, MA: Hendrickson, 2009) with a community (chap. 7, 165–89). Base Christian Communities also focus on the critical importance of the community for witness. See Jeanne Hinton's *Walking in the Same Direction: A New Way of Being Church* (Geneva: WCC, 1995).

work together to live out their Christian lives in faithful and consistent ways. Most of the assumptions about governments and religion that prevailed in the post–World War II era no longer hold. It was assumed that communist governments would persecute Christians and that Christian witness and worship would be considered acts of civil disobedience in communist states; this is partially true today, and yet some of the most rapidly growing churches are in communist countries. It was assumed that the world's Western democracies would provide freedom for worship and witness; yet today Christianity is being marginalized in the West, in subtle (and sometimes not-so-subtle) ways. In most countries of the world, Christians have to work together to provide a united witness, and to find ways of being a blessing to their own countries. Foreign missionaries must listen carefully to local Christians and follow their lead. In areas of ecology, missionaries working closely with local Christians often see what local people don't see: strip mining, deforestation, soil erosion, and air and water pollution. Racism and types of oppression are also more visible when cross-cultural missionaries are working closely in partnership with local church leaders. Hidden peoples—those who are all around us, but for some social or cultural reason, are invisible to us—are seen more easily when missionaries and local Christians work in partnership. In Islamic contexts, partnership is critical in giving hope to oppressed Christian groups, and, from the other angle, helping the missionary to understand the parameters for Christian witness. In brief, local political possibilities and sensitivities require close partnerships among missionaries, and among missionaries and local Christian communities.

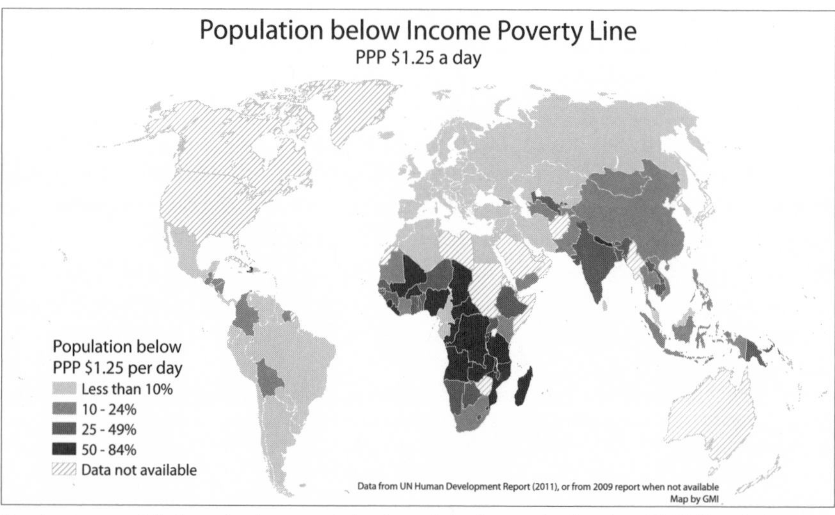

Here is a map on global poverty where poverty has been defined as earning less than $1.25 US a day.

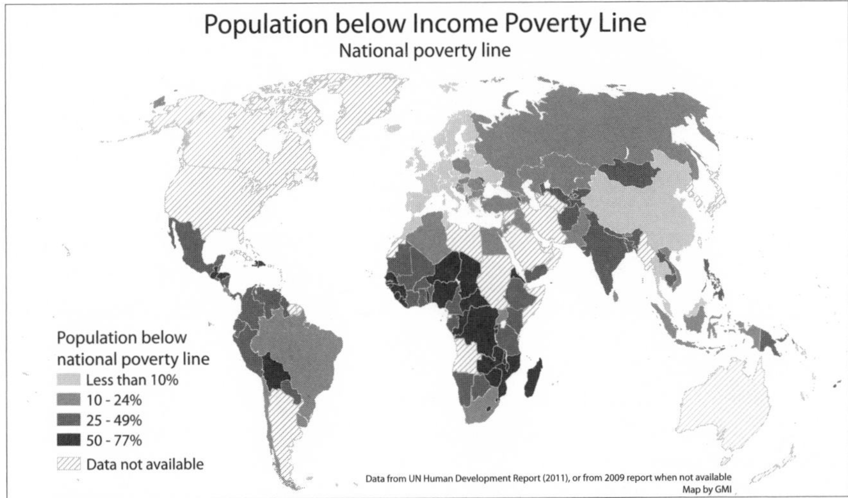

Here are the global rates of poverty, using each country's definition. The darker the shading, the higher the rate of poverty.

2. *Partnership is essential for literacy and education.* Literacy is directly related to poverty, as the maps here indicate. An even closer relationship is demonstrated when we isolate illiteracy among women. In places where women are denied access to literacy and education, poverty and the index of human suffering increases. Two-thirds of the world's illiterate are women, and where women are illiterate, the rates of infant deaths are higher and women's health is greatly compromised. There is also a relationship between religion, literacy,

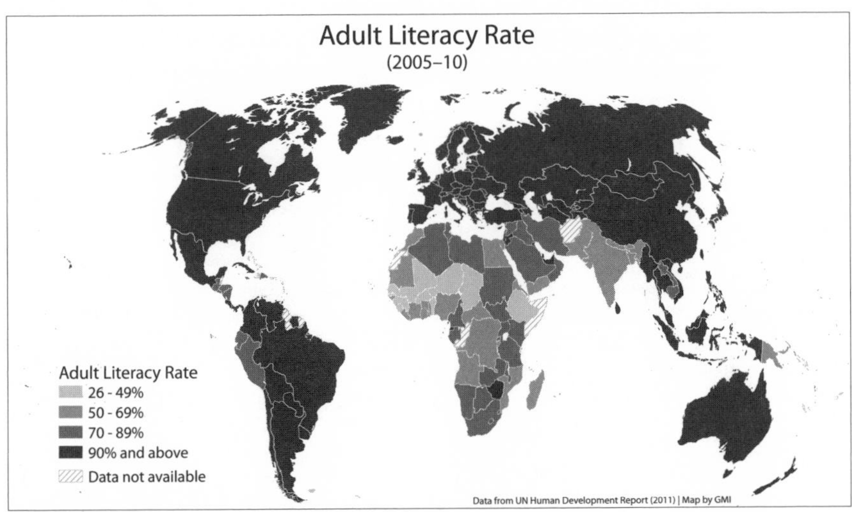

Literacy rates in the world. The darker shades reflect higher rates of literacy.

and health. Although only about forty-three of the 192 countries of the United Nations have a great disparity between the literacy of men and of women, seven of the top nine with the greatest disparity are Muslim countries.[15] Communist and Christian nations do not have such a great disparity; in fact, they have the highest literacy rates in the world.[16] Without going into greater detail, it should be noted that the reason partnership is necessary in the difficult area of illiteracy is because some of these cultural issues require complex wisdom and diverse actors to bring about change. I am familiar with, and have already mentioned, a local Protestant church that, in partnership with Orthodox Christians, helped to bring about the end of female circumcision in an Egyptian city. It required sensitive work with Muslims and literacy work with all women. The project could not have moved forward if the women of that city were unable to read materials and then talk about those materials together. Over half of the women in Egypt cannot read, so literacy is foundational for other justice issues.

Education at all levels is a global need, but it must be education that is appropriate and effective. It may be counterproductive to bring an efficient Western educational program for pastors or missionaries into Turkey, or Pakistan, or Mozambique. Let me rephrase that: it *will* be counterproductive to bring in Western programs to train leaders in these areas. It is not just the arrogance of Westerners that causes the problem (for many Asians and Africans much prefer Western education)—it is the fact that all education is a matter of communication and all communication is culturally signified. Thus, especially at the leadership level, education must be a matter of partnership: bringing in the best technology and pedagogy, and then allowing the local context to shape and rework the material and the method. Often this will require trust and hard decisions regarding who is the appropriate educator and whose ideas are to be dropped. Education is one of the keys to global justice and evangelism, and it requires carefully negotiated partnerships in order to be effective.[17]

3. *Partnerships are required in the midst of suffering and tragedy.* Churches in secure settings should partner with persecuted Christian churches in order to provide them with a voice and a watchful eye. In mission we cannot rely on the local news to inform us about tragedies and places of human suffering.

15. In these countries, women's literacy rate is less than 50 percent of men's: Mali, 49 percent; Benin, 49 percent; Yemen, 47 percent; Mozambique, 46 percent; Ethiopia, 46 percent; Guinea, 42 percent; Niger, 35 percent; Chad, 31 percent; and Afghanistan, 28 percent. Ethiopia is about 34 percent Muslim and Mozambique is about 18 percent Muslim.

16. See the United Nations statistics on illiteracy: http://unstats.un.org/unsd/demographic/products/socind/illiteracy.htm.

17. One quick example will help to illustrate the problem. In training pastors, is it appropriate to have all of the education take place in classrooms with a lecturer in the front of the room and the students all dutifully taking notes? This Western university model has limitations, and yet it is so often imitated in areas where learning is much more a matter of community and practice.

Most often we get much better information from local Christians and from resident missionaries. A few years back, we had a Karen student from Myanmar studying with us. The American seminary students became good friends with him, but after lunch one Thursday the relationship took on a whole different meaning. The student showed a brief, locally produced video showing the way the military treated the Karen people in Myanmar. The levels of human suffering and ongoing insecurity portrayed in the video were completely unknown to the American students. African American students, who have their own struggles in American culture, began to see other types of oppression and ethnocentrism twelve time zones away. Students began to look for ways to help, and later a group of students went on a type of mission trip to visit the student when he returned home. Partnerships that work to alleviate suffering in the world involve developing genuine friendships.

Human suffering comes in many forms, and involves many interconnected issues and relationships. The complexity of issues involved in a famine in Somalia, or a tsunami and earthquake in Sumatra, require local Christians in close communication with foreign Christians who view that region as a place of missional involvement. Seldom does the foreigner understand how to "fix things." Because of local customs, laws, and habits, partnership is necessary to get the right aid to the right people, in the right place, at the right time.

Partnerships that address tragedy and disaster should also not end quickly. They require long-term commitment, because it is more effective to work toward long-term solutions rather than just patch up the leaks in social systems. Many regions have periodic suffering due to climate, religious beliefs, government policies, corruption, and education. Rivers flood almost annually in Bangladesh, a country built on silt with over eight hundred different rivers. How can a local church or a single mission step in to alleviate human suffering in a context so vast with a problem so massive? Long-term partnerships with local Christian leaders and with mission agencies and churches can begin to help people move forward.

One of the issues that has surfaced in the past decades, regarding responding to local tragedies, is the need to use local resources as much as possible. International agencies and missions are needed and appreciated, but bringing in foreign supplies when local supplies are available, or bringing in foreign labor when local labor is available, undermines local economy. It should be considered a justice issue when powerful foreign countries (not only Western) refuse to buy locally to serve locally. Foreign relief workers should buy as much of the food and as many of the supplies as they can from local markets. Thus, in the midst of tragedy, local markets can be stimulated by foreign involvement.

4. *Partners are necessary for evangelistic outreach*. Most people who commit to Christ will do so through the witness of someone within their own culture; this is what Ralph Winter, at the Lausanne International Congress

on World Evangelization, called E-1 evangelism.[18] And yet the vision of John in Revelation 7:9–12 will not be fulfilled without cross-cultural evangelistic outreach. Winter called evangelism among those of a similar culture E-2 evangelism, whereas evangelism among those of a completely different culture and language he called E-3 evangelism. When Koreans work among ethnic Koreans in China, for example, that would be called E-2 evangelism. When Chinese people from China are partnering with the Koreans, they are also involved in E-2 evangelism. But a Filipino evangelist entering the team would be involved in E-3 evangelism. All are needed, and at times the most distant person culturally may open minds to the gospel more easily than the person who is the neighbor.

All people groups will not be reached unless there are cross-cultural missionaries willing to move into local cultures, learn the language, and act and speak in ways that point to Jesus Christ. Local Christians must be in partnership with them, helping these missionaries to adapt to local cultures, to adopt appropriate practices, and to acquire the necessary trust. With the great migrations of people in the world today, partnership in outreach is even more critical. Turks in Germany can be reached by teams involving Turkish Christians working with Americans, Lebanese, and Germans. Muslim Africans in Detroit or New York can be reached by intercultural teams that include African Christians. Three- or four-way partnership and support is a delicate matter to negotiate, but also a great opportunity for representing the Kingdom even while proclaiming the Kingdom to unreached people.

5. *Partner with other local churches to sponsor a people group.* Closely related to partnership for global evangelism is the need for partnerships to reach unreached people groups. Coming out of that same talk that Ralph Winter gave in 1974 was the notion that God intends to reach groups of people (ethnic groups), not individual people. Mission strategy, therefore, should plan to reach unreached people groups, rather than every individual person, with the gospel. This turn in theology and strategy has had a big impact upon evangelical mission thinking (and later on ecumenical mission thinking). In most areas of the world, partnerships can be developed to reach specific minority peoples. However, there are times and places when there really are no local partners, or when possible partners are not able to be of help. Some local partners, for example, have no interest in reaching a particular local ethnic minority, because that people group is their cultural enemy or oppressor. When this is the case, it will be necessary for missionaries to take wise and careful initiative despite local Christian prejudice. This must be done with great sensitivity and care. When an outsider (the cross-cultural missionary) see what locals cannot because of local prejudices, the missionary is bringing

18. "The Highest Priority: Cross-Cultural Evangelism," in J. D. Douglas, ed., *Let the Earth Hear His Voice* (Minneapolis: World Wide Publications, 1975), 213–41.

the gift of vision, helping them see the mission field in their own midst. This is a problem throughout the world: ethnic blind spots or missionary prejudice. We all learn to live with our own blind spots and our own prejudices, but missionary partnership helps to challenge them. Again, the categories of E-1, E-2, and E-3 evangelism are critical here. In addition, a fourth category—E-0 evangelism—helps to explain what is going on in local contexts. E-0 evangelism involves bringing about the conversion of local Christians, what Darrell Guder wisely called "the continuing conversion of the church."[19] When foreign missionaries help local Christians see the mission fields in their midst, they are aiding in E-0 evangelism, the conversion of local Christian communities.

6. *Partners are able to share resources*. Tremendous inequities have always existed in the world, but we are more aware of them today because of the communication revolution. In the time of Jesus, there was no middle class: there was an extremely wealthy class of royal families and masses of peasants eking out a living from the soil or the sea. Christian partnership is founded on a basic concept of Christian community, or the sharing of gifts and talents: *koinōnia* means to share or hold things in common. Holding all things in common is an ideal that should not be quickly tossed aside. This means that each and every partnership must be able to speak candidly about what they can bring—even as a sacrifice—to bless the mission of God. However, no gift is a static gift—a type of detached investment, as it were. Every gift that is given (hands to work, money to pay for medical care, food, teachers, etc.) comes as a relationship. A teacher is also a friend, companion, and praying coworker. A gift of money for a building comes with the prayers and advice (not directives) of the home church or mission. Sharing resources means sharing our lives. This may seem like a simple concept, easily learned in kindergarten—but it is seldom so.

In the early twenty-first century, a presbytery in the United States sent a delegation of pastors and elders to discuss their formal partnership arrangement with the Presbyterian Church of Sudan. When they had their major meeting, the elders from the United States sat on the dirt floor in a Sudanese meeting house to discuss the meaning of their partnership. The questions that were before them were, "What do we have to offer each other?" and, "What does partnership mean for us, whose lives are so different and who live so very far away from each other?" After an awkward silence of over a minute, one of the well-meaning American elders blurted out, "We see that many of your people are hungry and food is in short supply. We could send you food." Immediately the head Sudanese elder spoke out—stopping the Americans from pulling out their checkbooks. "No. Do not send food. You can never feed all of our people. That is our responsibility to work out. We need teachers. Many people are coming to Christ, but we are so poorly

19. Darrell Guder, *The Continuing Conversion of the Church* (Grand Rapids: Eerdmans, 2000).

educated about the gospel. We need you to teach us so we can be faithful to Christ in Sudan." Although money or food may seem like the obvious gifts to bring, the local community may have different priorities or different methods of meeting local needs.

Money, of course, is one of the biggest potential conflicts in partnerships. Korean, Japanese, or British missionaries working in places like Malawi or Haiti experience a huge financial culture shock. If the missionary from the West or from East Asia were to live according to their home lifestyle in Haiti, they would be cutting themselves off from the local people. In 1996, Jonathan J. Bonk published the most thorough presentation of issues related to money and mission, titled *Missions and Money: Affluence as a Western Missionary Problem.*[20] It is his contention that the huge disparities between rich and poor in mission require the rich to divest themselves of the burden of wealth and find ways to live not only *with* but *as* a local believer. In a later article,[21] he describes his own experience in Ethiopia of living on his missionary allowance of $1,200 a month (1975) while the local literacy teachers, whom he was supervising, were making $8 a month with no benefits. Bonk's book and article "show how both the effectiveness and the integrity of decent, well-meaning missionaries and mission organizations can be compromised when theory and practice are at demonstrable odds with those of the Lord they proclaim."[22] Sharing of resources for missionaries from wealthy countries must begin with a soul-searching assessment of their own personal identity: how important to me is life insurance, running water, air conditioning, or a personal car? If money unnecessarily alienates the missionary from local people, any other sharing of resources will be meaningless.

One final note regarding the sharing of resources: spiritual gifts of healing, exorcism, teaching, knowledge, as well as skills such as plumbing, water purification, and computer technology must be included in the discussion of what various partners have to offer. Money must not get in the way of the equal valuing of gifts and skills.

7. *Partnerships working against poverty*. Statistics are enigmatic; they can quickly become incarnate in many different forms, supporting many different social agendas. Recent scholarship has indicated that the global poverty rate is declining, and yet those living in particular contexts of drought and war can tell you with no hesitation that poverty and starvation are as bad as ever. The actual numbers have not gone down. In certain regions poverty never seems to abate; the issues are so complex that missionaries seem to have nothing to

20. Jonathan J. Bonk, *Missions and Money: Affluence as a Western Missionary Problem*, rev. ed. (Maryknoll, NY: Orbis Books, 2007).

21. Jonathan J. Bonk, "Missions and Money, Affluence as a Western Missionary Problem . . . Revisited," *International Bulletin of Missionary Research* 31, no. 4 (Oct. 2007): 171–76.

22. Ibid., 172. This article focuses on the role wealthy missionaries should assume based on the biblical concept of the "righteous rich."

Poverty Is Relational

Bryant L. Myers, who worked for thirty-three years with World Vision International, provides a holistic understanding of poverty that includes cultural, social, political, religious, and economic systems. Overall, he reminds us, poverty is relational. "Poverty is a result of relationships that do not work, that are not just, that are not for life, that are not harmonious or enjoyable. Poverty is the absence of shalom in all its meanings. It is interesting to note that this view is consistent with the Hebraic worldview, in which relationships are the highest good, while alienation is the lowest. All five poverty frameworks provide explanations that rest on the idea of relationships that are fragmented, dysfunctional, or oppressive."[a]

a. Myers, *Walking with the Poor*, 143.

offer but prayers and resignation. The prayers are good; the resignation is not. The poverty rate is down among certain populations in India, Latin America, and East Asia, but in some places the situation is as hopeless as ever.[23] In these regions, and when working against the greatest suffering in the world, Christians should not only partner but be absolutely united in finding answers to the causes of poverty. Then Christian institutions should work to partner with the agencies, governments, and local people who are part of the larger solution. Quite often, the ecumenical church (especially in its international expression) is able to open doors to solutions that no one else can open.

There is no silver bullet for global poverty—in each location Christian missionary work must engage the various causes as a whole. Thus, partners must ask questions about bank loans, literacy, public access to clean water, and the causes of diseases as part of their Christian witness. Even when other economic reforms are not in place on a national level, Christian partnerships can still help to develop local businesses and educational enterprises through micro-finance.[24] The best evangelistic work in poverty situations may come through concrete steps taken, in partnership with mission agencies, to alleviate

23. See Jeffrey D. Sachs, *The End of Poverty: Economic Possibilities for Our Time* (New York: Penguin, 2005). Sachs was Special Advisor for the United Nations Secretary-General Kofi Annan on the Millennium Development Goals. One does not have to agree with all of Sachs's economic theory to benefit from his intriguing analysis of why some countries advance so rapidly out of the poverty pit, and others seem never to shake off crippling poverty. His analysis of poverty in Africa (focusing on disease more than corruption and the colonial past) and his discussion of India's market reforms are helpful. A more complete discussion of poverty (causes, experiences, and theology) is found in Bryant L. Myers's excellent volume *Walking with the Poor: Principles and Practices of Transformational Development*, rev. ed. (Maryknoll, NY: Orbis Books, 2011).

24. See, e.g., Peter Greer and Phil Smith, *The Poor Will Be Glad* (Grand Rapids: Zondervan, 2009).

poverty and disease.[25] Most of the solutions to poverty involve local initiative and creative thinking but require outside support and guidance. Partnership is of the essence in the struggle against cycles of poverty and cycles of dependence. The best investments that outsiders can make will always have to do with empowering local communities through literacy, education, business loans, community organization, and skills training. Investments need to be built upon and need to nurture deeper relationships, as broken relationships are the root of poverty.

8. *Partnerships help to resist dehumanization and injustice.* Early Christian preoccupation with vices and virtues may seem quaint and distant from twenty-first-century mission work, and yet vices still corrode the work of the Kingdom in every instance. John Cassian was one of the first to come up with Christian vice and virtue lists (he lists eight of each).[26] It is interesting that the three he speaks about the most drive the three major international vices that become oppressive in the injustices they perpetuate: unchastity (sex trafficking and pornography), avarice (greed and corruption), and anger (violence). International partnerships are necessary to deal with dehumanizing behaviors such as buying (or capturing) young girls for the sex trade, arms trafficking, gambling, and pornography. It is the international and complex nature of these immoral businesses that requires partnerships.

Avarice, the greed for wealth (even if justly gained), is at the root of many of the most dehumanizing practices in the world. Malaysia has quickly become the largest producer of palm oil, the cost of which has been the loss of much farmland and tens of thousands of acres of virgin forest. Many of these forested regions were the homes of smaller ethnic groups who now are unable to grow their own food; they have to look for jobs on the palm plantations. Corruption, greed, lack of local representation, and ignorance have all conspired to block Malaysian minorities out of the economic growth their country is enjoying. A similar story could be told, with only a few changes, for many of the developing and underdeveloped nations of the world. Partnership in mission requires missionaries to take time to listen to the local stories of injustice and find ways to act together to bring about the redemption of these cultures. The massive killing in southern Sudan, before its independence in 2011, was in large part due to arms trading making guns easily available to different ethnic groups in the south. There are very few "innocent" outside nations. Arms have been sold to Sudan from the former USSR, the United States, Iran, China, and other countries.[27] Reconciliation and peace talks were needed between ethnic

25. The two are closely related. "Is disease a cause of poverty, a result of poverty, or both? The commission concluded that causation runs strongly in both directions. Poor health causes poverty and poverty contributes to poor health." Sachs, *End of Poverty*, 204.

26. For easy access, see "On the Eight Vices," in *Philokalia* 1:73–93.

27. Mike Lewis, "Skirting the Law: Sudan's Post CPA Arms Flow" (Geneva: Graduate Institute of International and Development Studies, 2009).

groups in the south due to the increased violence encouraged by the escalating availability of arms. It takes wise partnerships to be peacemakers in such a volatile situation where governments stand to profit from local violence.

9. *Partnerships are necessary in the witness to people of other living faiths.* One of the most promising areas of Christian partnership is in Christian witness to people of other living faiths. On the one hand, Christians living as a minority community are vulnerable and exposed to a majority faith that has the allegiance of the regional or national government. On the other hand, Christians are usually drawn closer together in ecumenical trust and common witness when living as a minority faith. Unity is always important for the church's witness, but it is absolutely essential when the church is exposed as a minority community.

Partnership in mission is important, as Christians from outside nations identify with local Christians living in minority under a majority faith. This identification makes it clear to the local officials that Christian participation locally affects a global community. Christian witness is not a local or private anomaly but a public and global testimony. When international partnerships unite in witness through relief efforts, this becomes a testimony to the local culture: the wall of partition is broken down. Many religions, in Asia especially, are monocultural on a local level. To be Tamil is to be Hindu, to be Thai is to be Buddhist. Christian multicultural partnerships reveal something of the character of the Kingdom, as Christians grow in trust and mutual sharing.

One important argument for continuing to encourage strong mission work from the West is to demonstrate the falseness of the assumption that all Western Christians are oppressive imperialists. As Western (or wealthy) Christians work in partnership, often under the leadership of local Christians, the world sees something different, something winsome that is a reflection of the Kingdom of heaven. When Christians give up their homes and jobs to teach English, or to help with literacy or water purification, they are both providing a window into the Kingdom, and they are acting as preemptive peacemakers. There is much violence against Christians in the world, and stepping out in mission to some of the neediest areas (which are often some of the most violent areas) can be a way of participating in God's Kingdom of peace. In partnership, local Christians will determine the ways Western missionaries should be involved, the types of work that is appropriate for them, and the places they should live.

Epilogue: A National Church Leader Reflects on Partnership[28]

Partnership is a spiritual matter, not merely an organizational ploy or a pragmatic necessity. The following statement from an interview with a national

28. See http://berkleycenter.georgetown.edu/interviews/a-discussion-with-reverend-heng-cheng-evangelical-fellowship-of-cambodia.

church leader in Asia expresses some of the difficulties and the promise of partnership in a missional context.

> Our challenge was how different churches could work together and how we could mobilize them. There were so many different strands. I came from a very conservative Christian tradition (Pentecostal) but was also very open. For two years I went to meet with each pastor individually, to encourage the pastors to work together. It was not easy, and there were many conflicts. But people would not talk about them when they met face to face. [Our] culture is that when there is a problem, you say there is no problem. You keep the problem in your heart. A fellowship cannot be made by force; it has to be made from the heart. By meeting people one by one I tried to reach their hearts.
>
> We agreed that there were four basic things we could do together. The first was to come together, as the body of Christ. Christ has many parts that were different; his body had arms, legs. But the body is one body. And there is one Bible. So there can be differences—the denominations are not uniform—but we can come together. We began by eating together. That is nondenominational. The [mainline Protestants] and [Pentecostals] thus began to meet and eat together. The second stage was to pray together. Everyone has to pray; if you do not pray, it is not church. The third was to recognize that we would all die, so that was another way we came together. And marriage and family was another common point. So as the fellowship, we began by sharing meals together, eating together. We began to go to funerals of members of other denominations. So slowly we began to come together.
>
> [Regarding development work] Between 1996 and 2000 it was not easy to do development work. So I went to talk to [one NGO], as it was receiving funds from the government and from [overseas] churches. I went to talk to other NGOs. They needed partners. They said, "We have the money." It was easy to raise funds at that time. We were starting from the darkness, and people wanted to help. But the [local] churches were not easy. The church organizations lost a lot of money. They tried to do quick development in a community, but they did not understand the hearts and minds of the [local] people. People had suffered so much. They had seen so much violence. It was as if their hearts were in prison; they were still living in fear. . . . They were hungry for God. And they needed everything. But the organizations did not understand that [the local people] had to develop themselves. They wanted to develop for them. But that does not change anything. When the project is finished, everything is gone. There is no sustainability. And some people were working for salaries, for promotions in organizations. In the churches, people were working with the heart, for no salary. And after the organizations leave, the church is left.
>
> So I argued that we needed partnerships, and that we needed to support together a holistic approach. The approach could not be about bread alone or about the Word alone. It had to train leadership. But I did not agree to give the funds to the church or to the community. Where we could help was in pointing to what are the needs.
>
> [Regarding foreign missionaries] Some come for very short visits and some stay longer. Many come to us for advice. We work with some of them. There

> are some tensions and problems. Some talk to the government and work with them, and some do not. [We] represent 80 percent of church members in [the country], and we try to have a common voice. Because of this, we provide a powerful voice to talk with the government.
>
> Many of the short-term missionaries come from Western Europe and America. They are the largest group [here]. There are more and more from Korea and the Philippines. There are some special problems there, especially with the Koreans, who tend to want to work alone and who want to be the boss, in control. Some Filipino churches try to copy the Koreans. There is a problem with authority, and they are reluctant to put the [local] churches in front. Now there are more than four hundred Korean missionaries here and more than two hundred Filipinos.

Here we can see candidly expressed the hopes, vision, and frustrations of partnership with other Christians in mission. Locally, it involves sharing in the lives of Christians from other fellowships and churches. Eating together, talking, praying together, attending weddings and funerals are all important dimensions of partnership in mission. With the great influx of missionaries, the concern is to make sure that these outsiders take time to listen and learn from the local Christian. All missionaries coming into a foreign country should remember this church leader who is frustrated with the outsiders who "are reluctant to put the [local] churches in front." At the same time, this insightful church leader recognizes and tells us of the central importance of partnership in mission. Partnership begins with listening.

13

Spirituality and Mission

Suffering and Glory

We have been working with the thesis that God's mission is enacted through temporary suffering and humiliation for God's eternal glory. All of history and all of the nations are included in this grand design of God's redemption. However, the key to the redemption of the world is in the liberation of individuals, within specific cultures, called into communities of the King. Individuals matter. All of creation is in view.

Our journey through the history of God's mission, the theology of God's mission, and the expression of that mission has revealed the fragile nature of God's redemptive plan, as well as the glorious work that has been done through his church, the body of Christ. The fragile nature of God's mission has been seen in individuals faithfully proclaiming and serving despite cultural opposition and, at times, the resistance of other Christians. What could be more remarkable than that the broken and violent church coming out of two world wars converted and became a suffering servant once again? We have lived through that age. The strong and proud church of Western imperialism has become once again an earthen vessel. And now that broken church is being led in the mission of God by the growing non-Western church. The mission of God is a movement that carries the strength and steadfast love of God in a fragile and imperfect vessel known as the church.

In these last pages, I want to lift up some of the major lessons we have learned through this journey, lessons that are illustrations of scriptural guidance, and then we will look at why spirituality must be the final (and the first) word in missiology.

Recap: A Few Lessons from History

One of the most important lessons I hope you have gleaned from this text is the periodic occurrence of new movements, new orders, new people, and new centers. I will call this the *wineskin factor* (Matt. 9:17; Mark 2:22; Luke 5:37–39). The mission of God is not confined to any wineskin. In fact, when any particular wineskin becomes old and hard, a new one comes along to hold and then spread the good wine of the gospel. It is a great struggle, and something that most church leaders will deny, but every Christian institution is a human invention—a response to God—in service to the mission of God. When it ceases to be such, when it ceases to serve the two basic purposes of the church (worship and mission), it becomes obsolete. Some wineskins are revived, as when old leather is oiled and becomes flexible and expandable once again. We have seen how new structures, especially religious orders (Franciscans, Dominicans, Jesuits) rose under the leadership of people who recognized the need for mission. In each case, it was a missional purpose that called these orders into existence. Later movements, some considered heretical and others embraced by the church, arose to reach out to the common people (Waldensians, Sisters and Brothers of the Common Life, and early Protestant missions). Seldom do old structures completely die off, for there is always the possibility of resurrection. Yet history seems to point to the need for grace and magnanimity when it comes to new movements and new structures. The spirit of the movement and its sense of purpose are what should be held in view. New movements become divisive (1) when they refuse to embrace the Great Tradition, (2) when they refuse to work with others, or (3) when others block them out of fellowship. Church unity is a matter of fellowship and fidelity to truth—not a matter of structures.

Another important theme that has emerged again and again is that of avarice, or the struggle against Babylon. We have seen groups that began in poverty and simplicity but, within generations, were given land and buildings and soon became preoccupied with wealth. Some churches started out as churches of martyrs, but once they gained public acceptance they became defenders of the wealthy. Concern for the poor and zeal for reaching the unreached has often faded behind preoccupation with accumulation. Uneven economic growth, magnified greatly since the Industrial Revolution, has caused confusion in missionary work. Is it the clear presentation of the gospel that is bringing people to church, or is it the offer of food, good education, and other side benefits? Western missionaries have struggled with economic inequities when working in underdeveloped nations.

Another important lesson we have learned is that the mission of God is more diverse than we can ever imagine. We can study the variety of approaches and institutional structures for the rest of our lives and still not know all of the great variety of ways God's mission has been carried forward. We have seen emperors and kings send out missionaries, and we have seen businesspeople serve as missionaries. We have seen Africans brought to Europe to become educated to return as missionaries, and we have seen released slaves go out on their own to serve as missionaries to slaves. We have seen multi- and non-denominational missions, but we have also seen missions as denominational church-planting agencies. We have seen mission stations set up, almost as small self-contained communities or kingdoms, but we have also seen wandering individuals proclaiming repentance like John the Baptist. In this great diversity, we should remember not to hold too tightly to a single approach or even a few approaches. We must return again and again to our basic theology of mission and evaluate new structures and ideas in light of a broadly envisioned ecumenical and evangelical theology. Such a theology as we have described here is focused on the Trinity, but is as diverse as all human cultures.

Another recurring lesson is the importance of the laity in God's mission. Most people in the world will come to faith because of a neighbor or relative, not because of a priest or bishop. Most people in the world who will be cared for, who will be taught to read, or who will be saved from crippling poverty, will be thanking a Christian layperson. The church has always been the people of God whose priesthood is through Jesus Christ, the high priest. In the twentieth century, the importance of laity in mission has been reaffirmed in both Protestant and Catholic theology. Edinburgh 1910 stated, and later conferences affirmed, that evangelism "is incumbent on every member of the Church. . . . The missionary task demands from every Christian, and from every congregation, a change in the existing scale of missionary zeal and service."[1] One of the great movements that has opened up the laity to mission has been the Spiritual movement of the nineteenth and twentieth centuries. Spiritual renewals are democratic in nature, in the pattern of Acts 2 and as prophesied in Joel 2. Thus, all people receive power to engage in God's mission. The outpouring is not for individual edification (although that does happen); it is an endowment of power for mission.

Another lesson, often neglected, is the importance of youth in God's global mission. Many of the early movements of religious orders were founded by young men and women, not by seasoned church leaders. St. Dominic was in his early twenties when he began to lead others by giving away all he had to the poor. St. Francis was in his twenties when he gave away all he had and began his life of evangelical poverty for the poor. The earliest Protestant missions from the United States were inspired by college students. Ignatius of Loyola and his early followers were all university students. John Sung, the great Chinese itinerant evangelist, began his ministry before finishing seminary. Sadhu Sundar Singh was in his teens when he had a vision of Christ and began his ministry. All of these individuals sparked major movements that transformed

1. World Missionary Conference, Edinburgh, 1910, *The History and Records of the Conference* (New York: Fleming H. Revell, 1910), 9:109.

the face of global mission—and they were all in their teens or twenties. "Your sons and daughters will prophesy, your young men will see visions" (Acts 2:17).

Although there are many other lessons we could derive from the history and theology sections of this text, the one that has shaped this volume is the relationship between suffering and glory. God's mission, as we have seen, is more often than not the story of suffering witnesses or sacrificing saints. And yet, the larger story is one of glory: suffering is the path; glory with great joy is the end. Governments of all kinds know that there is a derivative type of glory—a reflection of God's glory in this world as a result of missionary work. Secular Chinese scholars know that the earliest Chinese words for modern physics, math, music, and chemistry were developed by missionaries. The East German government turned the German Pietist buildings in Halle into a communist museum as an example of "from each according to their ability, to each according to their need."[2] When the poor are fed and when criminals become a blessing, we are beginning to see a glimpse of God's glorious Kingdom on earth, as it is in heaven. It is an open secret.

Mission as Christian Spirituality

Christian mission is too often detached from its source of power and inspiration—the Holy Spirit. A future missionary or pastor in the city cannot become qualified to lead in frontiers of justice and faith simply by sitting in a classroom, taking notes, and then passing tests. And yet we expect this to happen all the time. A missionary is qualified not by knowledge but by wisdom—spiritual wisdom. The thrust of this volume is that mission is the work of God (*missio Dei*) in which we are invited to participate by humble submission to Jesus Christ, the light for the nations (*lumen Gentium*). Thus mission is participation with the Holy Spirit. As another writer has said:

> Simply put, I believe we need to recover a sense of immediacy and action in our spiritual practices. Perhaps what we need is a path for discipleship that is more like a karate studio than a college lecture hall. . . . [We need a] practical approach to spiritual formation that is serious about Scripture, action-focused, communal, experiential and connected to real world challenges and opportunities.[3]

In 1978, David Bosch gave a series of lectures to the Mennonite Missionary Study Fellowship on the topic of spirituality: "A Spirituality of the Road."[4] His

2. This story was told by Professor Richard Lovelace in teaching about the social transformation that took place under the German Pietists in the eighteenth century. It was still considered exemplary in the twentieth century.

3. Mark Scandrette, *Practicing the Way of Jesus: Life Together in the Kingdom of Love* (Downers Grove, IL: InterVarsity, 2011), 14.

4. Later published as *A Spirituality of the Road* (Scottsdale, PA: Herald, 1979).

lectures, built around Paul's Second Letter to the Corinthians, pointed away from self-serving understandings of spirituality and away from the isolated monastic model. The spirituality of mission follows the way of the cross. But what does spiritual formation with a trajectory of missional engagement look like? Few people involved in spiritual formation and spiritual direction will read this, and yet I believe that what follows should guide all spiritual movement toward holiness.[5] The divisions between spiritual formation and missional formation, or between silence and action, are false dichotomies. Here I offer seven elements of spiritual formation for mission. These are not uniquely missiological elements, but I describe each with an eye to our participation in the *missio Dei*. Spirituality is for the world.[6]

Silence

We start our discussion of the spirituality of mission where Jesus started, and where the church started—in prayer and silence. Jesus's first command in mission is not to go, but to wait: "Do not leave Jerusalem, but wait for the gift my Father promised, which you have heard me speak about" (Acts 1:4). The secret to the spiritual life, and therefore to the missional existence, is to wait for the Holy Spirit. The spiritual life is life in the Spirit, and the Holy Spirit is the very Spirit of Jesus Christ. The Holy Spirit will lead the Christian in the ways of Jesus Christ, who loved the nations, spoke truth, and led by example in the way of suffering obedience. The ancient church knew, and the greatest spiritual leaders of the ages have all experienced, the empowerment that comes from silence, and the contrasting frustration and mess that follows constant activity. One of the most influential movements in Eastern Orthodoxy was the Hesychasm (silence or stillness) of the thirteenth and fourteenth centuries. It was not a new movement, for it was rooted in early spirituality that called ascetics to solitude and attentiveness.

> So it is right always to wait, with a faith energized by love, for the illumination which will enable us to speak. For nothing is so destitute as a mind philosophizing about God when it is without Him.[7]

We might add that nothing is so destitute as a missionary proclaiming the Kingdom without having first listened to the King.

5. This is not a common word for a Reformed theologian to use; however, the Orthodox, Wesleyan, and most of the Pentecostal tradition speak this language. It is good biblical language for all Christians (Matt. 5:48).

6. The central role of spirituality was understood by Bosch and the members of his department of missiology at the UNISA. See J. N. J. Kritzinger and W. Saayman, *David J. Bosch: Prophetic Integrity, Cruciform Praxis* (Dorpspruit, South Africa: Cluster, 2011), 1–9.

7. St. Diadochos of Photiki, "On Spiritual Knowledge," in *Philokalia* 1:254.

But silence is not just an Orthodox practice; evangelicals often talk about their "quiet time," or taking a "retreat of silence." The spirituality of silence is as old as the Psalms. "Be still, and know that I am God; I will be exalted among the nations, I will be exalted in the earth" (Ps. 46:10). Stillness or silence before God leads to knowledge of God and to the praise of God among the nations. John Sung, traveling evangelist in East Asia, was once on a ship with a very talkative woman from an apostolic (Pentecostal) church. She talked until 12:30 in the morning and Sung noted in his diary:

> This alerted me to the fact that much talk leads to failure. I was regretful that I had often engaged in meaningless small talk that benefited no one. . . . From now on, I would learn to keep silence before God.[8]

In the early days of the ecumenical movement, there was a clear message given about the need for silence and reflection in mission. In a statement from the 1928 Jerusalem meeting, we read the following:

> But in these hurried and feverish days there is also more need than ever for the deepening of our spiritual life through periodical detachment from the world and its need in lonely communion with God. We desire also to call for a greater volume of intercessory prayer.[9]

Silence and solitude, stillness and attentiveness, make it possible to receive the gifts God offers us, which enable our participation in his mission. Power in mission comes more from stillness and patience than from academic study and planning. But stillness is not the same as emptiness—stillness is openness to God's Spirit and God's Word.

Scripture

Visiting a mission training center in Korea, I once happened upon forty or so new missionaries who were preparing to be sent all around the world (quite literally) in just a few weeks. Their preparation involved some linguistics training, but mostly they were being equipped by reading the Bible; all forty were reading through the whole Bible. It takes a little more than a week, and they do it in community—stopping at the end of each day to allow time for the slower readers to catch up. This submersion in Scripture should be part of all missionary training, so that they will be devoted to the tradition that is rooted in the gospel message. In 2 Thessalonians 2:13–17, we read the admonition

8. Shangjie Song, *The Diaries of John Sung: An Autobiography*, trans. Stephen L. Sheng (Brighton, MI: Luke H. Sheng and Stephen L. Sheng, 1995), 164.

9. *The Jerusalem Meeting of the International Missionary Council*, vol. 1, *The Christian Life and Message in Relation to Non-Christian Systems of Thought and Life* (London: IMC, 1928), 410.

that we are to be devoted to the truth (the gospel) as it has been taught by the apostles either by word of mouth or in letters. Such knowledge will make it possible to act and speak with the same spiritual depth. The missionary must reflect gospel life, and this cannot happen unless gospel knowledge is firmly at home in the missionary heart. In the ancient church, spiritual theology was written as if one were opening up passages of Scripture. Scriptures are quoted throughout ancient Christian writings, reflecting a knowledge of Scripture—all of Scripture—that we seldom see or experience today.

Spiritual formation for mission should involve learning all of Scripture, and it should include memorizing portions of it. Psalm 119, the longest Psalm, makes it clear how important God's words (law, precepts, statutes, etc.) are for life and holiness. "I have hidden your word in my heart that I might not sin against you" (v. 11) is a good place to start. A spirituality for mission will necessarily involve reading other books and articles, but all other writings must be in service of the knowledge of Scripture. The only way God's Word can be a light, or even a "fire shut up in my bones" (Jer. 20:9), is if the Word of God is first in our heads. God will bring to remembrance what we have learned from his Word; it will be available for the Spirit's inspiration, if we have it in our heart.

Community

In the previous chapter we discussed partnership—part of which is living into the simple truth that the body of Christ, not lone-star Christians, is the witness to the gospel. This communal witness—reflecting the triune presence of God—requires work, repentance, and self-denial in this world. The communal nature of Christianity is in stark contrast to many other religions in which devotion is a strictly private matter. For Buddhism, salvation or nirvana is a solitary pursuit. Moksha, in Hinduism, is also an entirely personal matter. The Christian life cannot be lived alone, although at times faithful missionaries are very lonely. Love requires relationship, and God is love. God himself is in community and calls us to a Kingdom community, not to personal or individual release. What this means for missional formation is that the spiritual life must be nurtured in submission to others. There is no place for the lone-star missionary or spiritual guru in God's mission.

We have seen how the understanding of mission has moved from church planting (church centered) to participating in the mission of God (God centered). And yet the church is still the basic structure of mission. The local church is a missional presence in each time and place. It is a community that points to the Kingdom community. This was reaffirmed at the 1938 Madras meeting of the IMC:

> It is the Church and the Church alone which can carry the responsibility of transmitting the Gospel from one generation to another, of preserving its purity,

> and of proclaiming it to all creatures. . . . The place where this task is centered is the local church or congregation.[10]

Although periods of silence and solitude are important, spiritual formation must happen in and with a larger community of believers. Christianity, and therefore Christian mission, is communal, cooperative, and mutually submissive.

Repentance

The great Reformation debates of the sixteenth century began with arguments about penance: what does it really mean to repent? Luther wrote ninety-five statements about what it means to repent and how the individual and the church are involved in that penance. The first thesis says, "Our Lord and Master Jesus Christ, when He said *Poenitentiam agite*,[11] willed that the whole life of believers should be repentance." The two most frequently spoken prayers in the world are the Lord's Prayer and the Jesus Prayer. Both have strong elements of seeking mercy through *metanoia*, or repentance:

> Forgive us our debts as we forgive our debtors.
>
> Lord Jesus Christ, Son of God, have mercy on me, a sinner.

All great spiritual directors know that the prideful heart has no place in the Kingdom of God. The person who would try to hide vice from God and others is in direct opposition to the basic posture of repentance before God. Only on our knees or prostrate before God can we receive what God has for us and, through us, for others.

All of the great spiritual leaders of the church have known this basic truth: humility and penance guide us into the presence of God. It is for this reason that the ancients (and later the mystics, Pietists, and Puritans)[12] encouraged meditation upon our own death. This is not a morbid exercise—it is a healthy view of self.[13]

10. International Missionary Council, *The Madras Series: 1938 Findings* (New York: IMC, 1939), 24, 26.

11. "Repent" or "Do penance." From the Latin Vulgate, this is the same command that John the Baptist gives in preparing the way for Jesus's arrival (Matt. 3:2).

12. Johann Arndt, the great founder of German Pietism, in his book *True Christianity* writes in book 1, chap. 22 (titled "A True Christian Can Be Known in No Way Better than by Love and the Daily Renewal of His Life. He Is the Branch of a Tree"): "Think on the short span of this life, how much you have avoided the practice of Christian virtues. . . . As a man desires to die, so ought he to live. You do not wish to die as an ungodly man; therefore you ought not to live as on ungodly man. If you wish to die as a Christian you must live as a Christian. . . . A servant must always be prepared to appear before his master if his master calls him." From Peter Erb, trans., *Johann Arndt: True Christianity* (New York: Paulist Press, 1979), 119.

13. There are numerous examples of the need to meditate on our own death. St. Philotheos of Sinai, in his "Forty Texts on Watchfulness," gives three "gates" to the way of spiritual attentiveness

> Finally, recalling Judas' death by hanging, let us beware of acquiring again any of the things which we have already renounced. In all this we should remember how uncertain is the hour of our death, so that our Lord does not come unexpectedly and, finding our conscience soiled with avarice, say to us what God says to the rich man in the Gospel: "You fool, this night your soul will be required of you."[14]

Awareness of our own death prevents materialism, what is called the vice of avarice. In other texts, we learn that being aware of our own mortality helps to keep us alert and watchful in prayer.[15] Such humility and penance make it possible to serve others, while pride or *self*-esteem negates our spiritual endeavors for others. Repenting, we receive our real esteem or value, which is from God alone. A person who is repentant and humble is able to endure hardships and stay focused on service to others despite loneliness or suffering. The Roman Catholic martyr in Algeria Charles de Foucauld was strong enough to be a lone witness to Christ in the desert, among Muslims; the secret to his strength is found, in part, in his identity with Christ's suffering and death.

> We cannot possibly love him without imitating him. Since he suffered and died in agony, we cannot love him and yet want to be crowned with roses while he was crowned with thorns. . . . To prepare oneself constantly for martyrdom, and accept it without a shadow of reluctance, like the divine Lamb, in Jesus, through Jesus, for Jesus. I must try and live as if I were to die a martyr today.[16]

Reflecting on our own death and on Christ's passion removes any lingering pride and reminds us of our own mortality, frailty, and need for forgiveness.

Repentance, as Martin Luther noted, is something that is to mark the whole life of the believer. Repentance—identified by Bosch as the "courage to be weak"—opens the doorway to spiritual power for mission. Only in honest weakness is the power of God released in missional existence.[17]

Action

All Christian spirituality should be seen as a gentle dance of the personal and communal, of silence and action, and of study and reflection. Our sanctification through spiritual disciplines is for the sake of others. Jesus came to serve and we, as his disciples, "put on Christ"; we serve at his bidding and under his power. As we serve, we are being formed into the likeness of

("the noetic Jerusalem"): (1) Silence of your tongue, (2) self-control in food and drink, and (3) mindfulness of death, for this purifies intellect and body (*Philokalia* 2:17).

14. John Cassian, "On the Eight Vices," in *Philokalia* 1:82.

15. Mark the Ascetic, "On Those Who Think that They Are Made Righteous by Works: Two Hundred and Twenty-Six Texts," in *Philokalia* 1:128.

16. Robert Ellsberg, ed., *Charles de Foucauld* (Maryknoll, NY: Orbis Books, 1999), 25.

17. Bosch, *Spirituality of the Road*, 75.

Christ, the Suffering Servant. The temptation is to make the goal of spiritual formation personal excellence, inner peace, or outward joy. If we do this, spirituality easily devolves into personal therapy, and spiritual directors can easily be tempted to function as counselors or psychologists. No, the purpose of spiritual formation is not personal edification but social transformation and evangelical engagement. Spiritual directors should be more like physical therapists than psychologists; the physical therapist pushes, stretches, and demands hard work so the leg will be able to carry the body in the future.

Formation is for others, not for the self alone. The self must be transformed *so that* it will be able to hear and respond to God's call to serve others. Salvation is not just for the self, and neither is sanctification. When Ezra was preparing to lead in the rebuilding of the temple and the return to worship of Yahweh, it was said of him that he "had set his heart to study the law of the LORD and to do it, and to teach the statutes and ordinances in Israel" (Ezra 7:10). His personal study was to flow out into obedience and then lead others to know and to follow the law. As we step out in obedience, trusting God's very Spirit to go before us, we become formed into the likeness of Jesus, the Missionary of God. When we do not step out in obedience, we draw back from our own formation in the Spirit. Spirituality that does not point toward outreach and service is not Christian spirituality; it may have elements of Christian spirituality, but it is anemic and incomplete. The Spirit of the living God enters the heart to apply forgiveness and empower for ministry—always both.

Attentiveness

One of the greatest gifts a missionary can have is that of attentiveness and discernment. To be attentive is to be watchful and alert toward others and toward God's Spirit. It is possible to be silent, to read Scripture, to be active in mission, and yet not be attuned to the needs and cries of the needy around you. It is possible, and it is also far too common. Our spiritual formation for mission must train us to be attentive to the cries of the needy—to the voice of God in the loneliness of death and suffering. This means that spiritual formation must help us, in community, to pay attention.

In 2011, John Stott (1921–2011) passed away. He was a great spiritual and missional leader for generations of students and for the evangelical wing of Protestantism. What few people know is how attentive he was to Scripture and to the needs of the world. Furthermore, he was aware that his personal decision making needed to be in line with the understanding he developed through attentiveness. Although he came from a wealthy home, Stott chose, in retirement, to live in a two-room flat built over the garage of the parsonage where he had been rector. He chose not to buy books, but to use the London libraries, as a matter of thrift. He lived simply and used all of the profits from his books to support pastors and theologians in poorer countries. He chose not to get married, and not to accept the call to be a bishop, so he could focus on his writing and speaking ministry. Attentive to Scripture and attentive to the needs of others, Stott's life reminds us of the need for the missionary to be attentive, focused, and faithful.

Love

Love is the goal as well as the means of the Christian life. It is only by stepping into the extravagant love of God that we are able to express that love for others. All the great saints of the past understood that love was the center of God's being and the goal of all human life and relationship. Julian of Norwich, one of the greatest English mystics and the first woman to write in English, titled her book about the visions of God that were given to her *Revelations of Divine Love*.[18] To look at God is to look at love. Love has a face; it is a concrete rather than an abstract noun. Love is not just a quality or characteristic, it is also a verb: "The noblest and most precious thing one can speak of is love. . . . True divine love, which you must nourish within yourself, can be recognized by the love you bear your neighbor."[19]

One of the many significant sermons of Jonathan Edwards is entitled, "Heaven Is a World of Love."[20] It may be possible to be so heavenly minded that a person is of no earthly good; on the other hand, heavenly mindedness may also provide resolve and direction for this earthly existence.

> Here I remark that the God of love himself dwells in heaven. Heaven is the palace or presence-chamber of the high and holy One, whose name is love, and who is both the cause and source of all holy love.[21]

God, in whose image we are made and are being remade, is holy love. Spiritual formation remakes us into people whose love overflows sacrificially.

Throughout the history of the church, the supreme quality of missional spirituality has been the same as it is for all Christians—love for others expressed in humility. At the 1928 Jerusalem IMC conference, the final report stated,

> Our approach to our task must be made in humility and penitence and love: in humility, because it is not our own message which we bring, but God's, and if in our delivery of it self-assertion finds any place we shall spoil that message

18. Julian of Norwich, *Revelations of Divine Love*, trans. M. L. del Mastro (Liguori, MO: Triumph Books, 1994).

19. Johannes Tauler, "Sermon 76," in *Johannes Tauler: Sermons*, trans. Maria Shrady (New York: Paulist Press, 1985), 169.

20. "Heaven Is a World of Love (Charity and Its Fruits, Sermon Fifteen, 1738)," in *The Sermons of Jonathan Edwards: A Reader*, ed. Wilson H. Kimnach, Kenneth P. Minkema, and Douglas A. Sweeney (New Haven: Yale University Press, 1999), 242–72.

21. Ibid., 244.

> and hinder its acceptance; in penitence, because our fathers and we ourselves have been so blind to many of the implications of our faith; in love because our message is the Gospel of the Love of God, and only by love in our own hearts for those to whom we speak can we make known its power or its true nature.[22]

The taproot of all virtues or gifts is love. Not unlike many of the great saints in the past, the focus here is on a consistent life in love that will spill out into missional presence. Without love, the missionary is a clanging symbol or a noisy gong (1 Cor. 13:1).

Icons of Spirituality: Missionaries of the Past

With this understanding of spiritual formation and mission, we can look back at missionaries of the past and see how this formation was part of their lives.[23] The Christian practice of icons (images of saints) and the practice of saints' days have been used by God to guide and correct Christians of the present by reflection on the characteristics of saints of the past. When we look at an icon of John the Baptist, we may reflect on his call to repentance. In a similar way, Christians have used missionary biographies to reflect on the work and wisdom of missionaries in the past. It may be instructive to do the same today, with the awareness of the spiritual qualities and disciplines that undergird missionary life.

For example, we can learn something of the temptations to grandeur that missionaries face when reporting on their work. Amy Carmichael, Church of England missionary to India, downplayed successes in reporting her missionary work:

> It is more important that you should know about the reverses than about the successes of the war. We shall have all eternity to celebrate the victories, but we have only the few hours before sunset in which to win them. . . . So we have tried to tell you the truth—the uninteresting, unromantic truth.[24]

22. "The Christian Message: Go and Make Disciples of All Nations," in *The Jerusalem Meeting of the International Missionary Council*, vol. 1, *The Christian Life and Message in Relation to Non-Christian Systems of Thought and Life* (London: IMC, 1928), 407.

23. Or how it was not part of their lives. All missionaries are human and, like studying the Bible, we can find the Spirit of God working in their lives, but we can also see where they have denied their Savior through their actions.

24. Amy Carmichael, *Things as They Are: Missionary Work in Southern India* (New York: Fleming H. Revell, 1900), 158. Quoted from Ruth Tucker's *From Jerusalem to Irian Jaya* (Grand Rapids: Zondervan, 1983). Amy is reported to have received a letter from a young woman considering missionary work who asked what missionary work was like. Amy's response was, "Missionary life is simply a chance to die." See Elizabeth Eliot's biography of Amy Carmichael, *A Chance to Die: The Life and Legacy of Amy Carmichael* (Old Tappan, NJ: Fleming H. Revell, 1987).

Other missionaries write about their suffering, the deaths of their colleagues, the conversions of villages, and even their despair. And so, missionary biographies can function as icons—pointing us to God's faithfulness for the nations. Here is also a way to break down the divisions in the global church, as we learn to honor the spiritual life and sacrifice of missionaries from traditions and communions that are not our own. An African independent church leader can become a guide for a Malaysian Anglican, and a Jesuit working in China can become a model for a Methodist in Minneapolis.

Mission as Sacrifice

In 1987, David Bosch interviewed for a position at Princeton Theological Seminary. I was serving on the search committee and, after he gave a lecture to a packed crowd that included some difficult questions,[25] we went back to his apartment and prayed. The tall and burdened missiologist prayed for South Africa and that he would hear the voice of his sisters and brothers in South Africa as to what he should do. I prayed that they would tell him to come to the United States, but I sensed my prayer was in vain—for the tall, stately missiologist and Bible translator on his knees before the throne of God was an image of humility and obedience that was beyond me. I found out later that his church needed him in the struggle against apartheid, and so he turned down a position in the United States, but he did return to Princeton to write a little book on his sabbatical: *Transforming Mission*. The image of the great scholar on his knees, praying that he would know the will of his people, and then being willing to submit to their will for him, will always be with me.

A second image is equally etched in my mind. Bosch spoke to a student fellowship group about how missionaries have been portrayed in the past and how missionaries have viewed themselves in the past. Bosch said that in the nineteenth century missionaries were viewed as pioneers; to be a missionary meant you were a pioneer and a hero for the world. Later, under colonial structures, missionaries lived on mission compounds and were often imaged as models; local people would watch how the missionary lived and worshiped and they would imitate this Christian model. Today, Bosch said (prophetically), missionaries need to step back and see that, like Christ, the missionary must be understood as sacrifice—not as pioneer or model—but sacrifice. In the pattern of Jesus Christ, the missionary must lay down their life for their friends. As in many other things, David Bosch was correct.[26] The missionary

25. "Why do you stay in the church that is oppressing the black South Africans through the racist policy of apartheid?" His answer was classic Bosch, "There is not a day that I do not wonder if I have made the right decision. However, if I leave the Afrikaner Church, they will no longer have to listen to me, and read every word I say."

26. See David Bosch's *Spirituality of the Road*.

is called to die. It is a profound and deep mystery that God has woven into the fabric of redemption.

This understanding of missionary spirituality was expressed clearly in the prayer of one of the first missionaries of the Pontifical Institute for Foreign Missions (PIME). Father John Mazzuconi was martyred in 1855, after only three years of missionary work in the region of New Guinea. His missionary prayer has been prayed by PIME missioners for over 160 years; it is a humble prayer that is full of love for others, concern for all people to hear the gospel, and his willingness to sacrifice himself.

> Most Holy Trinity, Father, Son and Holy Spirit, I a poor sinner, with sincere gratitude and love for your infinite goodness, which I had the opportunity to know through your precious grace, and moved in my innermost being by the unutterable misfortune of so many of my brothers who in distant lands have until now been beyond reach of the beautiful light of the Gospel, have decided at the cost of any sacrifice, even should I lose my life, to give myself totally for the salvation of those souls that also cost the Redeemer's blood.
>
> Blessed the day when I will be allowed to suffer greatly for such a holy and humane cause, but more blessed still the day when I should be found worthy to shed my blood for it and to meet death with all its torments.
>
> My God, you inspire me with these proposals so much greater than my weak forces, sustain me with that almighty spirit that first filled your holy Apostles.
>
> Most Immaculate Mary, our advocate and most loving mother, obtain for us the grace to bring to the ends of the earth the adored name of your divine Son and your sweet name, Mary. Guardian Angels of the nations, Holy Apostles Peter and Paul, St Francis Xavier, pray for us.
>
> Amen.

Missionary existence is life in Christ, and life in Christ is a call to be faithful unto death. Much is communicated about the gospel of salvation through a weak, poor, and suffering servant. Less is communicated about the gospel through a comfortable and wealthy short-term visitor. The call to missionary service is the call to come and die. Renowned missionaries such as Charles de-Foucauld, David Brainard, William Wade Harris, John Mazzuconi, and Mother Teresa have known this. But so too did the tens of thousands of forgotten and nameless missionaries from every continent. They can be our teachers. They were attentive to the call of discipleship, knowing that it was of no value to gain the world—so why try? They were not ashamed of the Son of Man, and they did not try to save their lives (Mark 8:31–38).

Missionaries should always be aware that the entire world is watching them. As never before, today missionaries are held suspect, having been identified with colonial, imperial, and business interests for centuries. In speaking about the missionary vocation, specifically religious orders, the Second Vatican

Council said the following about the religious (or more generally about the missionary) vocation:

> Indeed from the very beginning of the Church men and women have set about following Christ with greater freedom and imitating Him more closely through the practice of the evangelical counsels, each in his own way leading a life dedicated to God. . . . Since the Church has accepted their surrender of self they should realize they are also dedicated to its service. This service of God ought to inspire and foster in them the exercise of the virtues, especially humility, obedience, fortitude and chastity. In such a way they share in Christ's emptying of Himself (cf. Phil. 2:7) and His life in the Spirit (cf. Rom. 8:1–13).
>
> Faithful to their profession then, and leaving all things for the sake of Christ (cf. Mark 10:28), religious are to follow Him (cf. Matt. 19:21) as the one thing necessary (cf. Luke 10:42) listening to His words (cf. Luke 10:39) and solicitous for the things that are His (cf. 1 Cor. 7:32).
>
> It is necessary therefore that the members of every community, seeking God solely and before everything else, should join contemplation, by which they fix their minds and hearts on Him, with apostolic love, by which they strive to be associated with the work of redemption and to spread the kingdom of God.[27]

The missionary must not be diverted from "seeking God solely," even as she or he pursues justice, peace, and mercy.

The Glory of God

The final word in mission is glory—not suffering. The final word is God's glory that will be revealed through the church in this age and in the age to come. The great saints in the past, through their obedience and sacrifice, have pointed to and helped to reveal God's glorious presence and his self-authenticating and overflowing love. When a household turns "from darkness to light, and from the power of Satan to God, so that they may receive forgiveness of sins and a place among those who are sanctified by faith in [Jesus]" (Acts 26:18), more of God's glorious Kingdom is being revealed. When a village turns from materialistic pursuits or from the worship of idols to the worship of God in Christ, more of God's glory is being revealed. As different races and nations come together to resist child pornography or illiteracy, light is beginning to break through. Individuals thrive in the light of God's glory, and nations need the glory of God if peace and justice are to break forth on the earth.

Some may think it dangerous to reflect too much on glory, or on the future that God promises his people. Is it escapist to dream and meditate on the glory of God in the new creation? I think it can be very healthy, because in doing so we are thinking about what is sure and true. This world, with its

27. From "Decree on the Adaptation and Renewal of Religious Life," *Perfectae Caritatis* 5.

wealth, oppression, lies, and deception is not what will last—and so if we do not lift our eyes, we are being shaped by what is transient, rather than what is eternal. Paul says very clearly:

> Since, then, you have been raised with Christ, set your hearts on things above, where Christ is, seated at the right hand of God. Set your minds on things above, not on earthly things. For you died, and your life is now hidden with Christ in God. When Christ, who is your life, appears, then you also will appear with him in glory. (Col. 3:1–4)

It is easy for missionaries—caught in political, cultural, and spiritual battles, and struggling with finances and illness—to lose hope. God's glory, however, is sure, and this should be our guide and our anchor within the storms of global mission. We should be shaped in our thinking and our living by a vision of Christ reigning in glory. And so I conclude with a trusted ancient Christian writer, Ephrem the Syrian, who is recognized as a saint in both Eastern and Western churches. Ephrem describes the contrast between the struggle in this world and the reality and beauty of the paradise of God's future glory:

> In the world there is struggle,
> in Eden, a crown of glory;
> at our resurrection
> both earth and heaven will God renew,
> liberating all creatures
> granting them paschal joy, along with us. . . .
> The Lord of all
> is the treasure store of all things:
> upon each according to his capacity
> He bestows a glimpse
> of the beauty of His hiddenness,
> of the splendor of His majesty.
> He is the radiance who, in his love,
> makes everyone shine
> —the small, with flashes of light from Him,
> the perfect, with rays more intense,
> but only His Child is sufficient
> for the might of His glory.[28]

28. Hymn 9 from Sebastian Brock, trans., *St. Ephrem the Syrian: Hymns on Paradise* (Crestwood, NY: St. Vladimir's Seminary Press, 1990), 138, 145.

Appendix

Twentieth-Century Ecumenical Councils

Year	IMC/CWME[a]	L&W/C&S[b]	WCC[c]	F&O[d]	RCC	Evangelical
1910	Edinburgh					
WWI						
1921	IMC					
1925		Stockholm				
1927				Lausanne		
1928	Jerusalem					
1937		Oxford		Edinburgh		
1938	Tambaram-Madras		[Utrecht]			
WWII						
1947	Whitby					
1948			Amsterdam			
1952	Willingen			Lund		
1954			Evanston			
1957–58	Ghana					
1961			New Delhi			
1962–65					Vatican II	
1963	Mexico City			Montreal		
1966		Geneva				Wheaton and Berlin

a. International Missionary Council, later called the Council on World Mission and Evangelism of the World Council of Churches.
b. Life and Work, later called Church and Society of the World Council of Churches.
c. World Council of Churches.
d. Faith and Order of the WCC.

Year	IMC/CWME[a]	L&W/C&S[b]	WCC[c]	F&O[d]	RCC	Evangelical
1968			Uppsala		Medellin-CELAM[e]	
1972–73	Bangkok					
1974					4th Synod 1st FABC Taipei[f]	Lausanne[g]
1975			Nairobi			
1978				Bangalore		Willowbank, Bermuda
1979		Boston			Puebla-CELAM	
1980	Melbourne					Pattaya (L&WEF)
1982				Lima	FEBC	
1983			Vancouver			
1986					Manila-FEBC	
1989	San Antonio	(Seoul, JPIC)		Budapest		Manila (LCWE)
1990						
1991			Canberra			
1992 1993				Santiago de Compostela	Santo Domingo-CELAM	
1995					Manila-FEBC	(GCOWE)[h] Seoul
1996	Salvador da Bahía, Brazil			Moshi, Tanzania		
1997						(GCOWE) Pretoria, S. Africa
1998			Harare, Zimbabwe			
2000					Saphram, Thailand-FEBC	
2004				Kuala Lumpur		(LCWE) Pattaya
2005	Athens					
2006			Porto Alegre, Brazil			
2007					Aparecida, Brazil	
2009		Geneva		Crete, Greece	Manila (FABC)	
2010	Edinburgh					Capetown (LCWE)
2012					Ho Chi Min City-FABC	
2013			Seoul, South Korea			

e. CELAM: Latin American Episcopal Conference (RCC).

f. FABC: Federation of Asian Bishops' Conference.

g. Begins a new evangelical movement for mission: The Lausanne Covenant for World Evangelization (LCWE).

h. GOCWE: Global Consultation on World Evangelization.

Bibliography

History of Mission and Ecumenics

Beaver, R. Pierce. *Ecumenical Beginnings in Protestant World Missions: A History of Comity*. New York: Nelson, 1962.

———. *From Missions to Mission*. New York: Association Press, 1964.

———. "The Legacy of Rufus Anderson." *Occasional Bulletin of Missionary Research* (July 1977): 94.

Bliss, Edwin Munsell. *Encyclopedia of Missions: Descriptive, Historical, Biographical, Statistical*. New York: Funk & Wagnalls, 1891.

Bosch, David. "Evangelism: Theological Currents and Cross Currents Today." *International Bulletin of Missionary Research* 11, no. 3 (July 1, 1987): 98–103.

Bowden, Henry Warner. *American Indians and Christian Missions: Studies in Cultural Conflict*. Chicago: University of Chicago Press, 1981.

Brockey, Liam Matthew. *Journey to the East: The Jesuit Mission to China, 1579–1724*. Cambridge, MA: Harvard University Press, 2008.

Carmichael, Amy. *Things as They Are: Missionary Work in Southern India*. New York: Fleming H. Revell, 1900.

Clark, Allen D. *History of the Korean Church*. Seoul: Christian Literature Society of Korea, 1961.

Colgrave, Bertram, and R. A. B. Mynors. *Ecclesiastical History of the English People of Bede*. Oxford: Oxford University Press, 1969.

Davies, Ronald E. *Jonathan Edwards and His Influence on the Development of the Mission Movement from Britain*. Cambridge, UK: Currents in World Christian Project, 1996.

Del Mastro, M. L. *Revelations of Divine Love: Julian of Norwich*. Liguori, MO: Triumph Books, 1994.

Dennis, James. *Christian Mission and Social Progress: A Sociological Study of Foreign Missions*. Vol. 1. New York: Fleming H. Revell, 1897.

Diamond, Jared. *Guns, Germs, and Steel: The Fates of Human Societies*. New York: Norton, 2005.

Edwards, Jonathan. *Ethical Writings: The Works of Jonathan Edwards*. Vol. 8. New Haven: Yale University Press, 1989.

Eliot, Elizabeth. *A Chance to Die: The Life and Legacy of Amy Carmichael*. Old Tappan, NJ: Fleming H. Revell, 1987.

Ellsberg, Robert, ed. *Charles de Foucauld*. Maryknoll, NY: Orbis Books, 1999.

Emilsen, William W. *Gandhi's Bible*. Delhi: ISPCK, 2001.

Equiano, Olaudah. *The Interesting Narrative of the Life of Olaudah Equiano*. 2nd ed. New York: Bedford St. Martins, 2006.

Erb, Peter, trans. *True Christianity: Johann Arndt*. New York: Paulist Press, 1979.

Flick, Alexander Clarence. *The Rise of the Medieval Church*. New York: Putnam & Sons, 1979.

Forest, Jim. *All Is Grace: A Biography of Dorothy Day*. Maryknoll, NY: Orbis Books, 2011.

Fox, Frampton F. *Edinburgh 1910 Revisited Gives Us Friends: An Indian Perspective on 100 Years of Mission*. Bangalore, India: CMS, 2010.

Friedman, Thomas L. *The World Is Flat: A Brief History of the 21st Century*. New York: Farrar, Straus & Giroux, 2005.

George, S. K. *Gandhi's Challenge to Christianity*. Ahmedabad: Navajivan Publishing House, 1947.

González, Justo. *The Story of Christianity*. 2 vols. San Francisco: Harper & Row, 1984/1985.

Green, Michael. *Evangelism in the Early Church*. London: Hodder & Stoughton, 1970.

Guder, Darrell L. *The Continuing Conversion of the Church*. Grand Rapids: Eerdmans, 2000.

Hanciles, Jehu. *Beyond Christendom: Globalization, African Migration and the Transformation of the West*. Maryknoll, NY: Orbis Books, 2008.

Hastings, Adrian. *A World History of Christianity*. Grand Rapids: Eerdmans, 1999.

Hogg, William Richey. *Ecumenical Foundations: A History of the International Missionary Council and Its Nineteenth-Century Background*. New York: Harper & Brothers, 1952.

Howard, David M. *Student Power in World Missions*. Downers Grove, IL: InterVarsity, 1979.

Hutchinson, Mark, Donald Lewis, and Richard Pierard, eds. *A Guide to Global Evangelicalism*. Downers Grove, IL; InterVarsity, 2012.

Irvin, Dale T., and Scott W. Sunquist. *History of the World Christian Movement*. 2 vols. Maryknoll, NY: Orbis Books, 2001/2012.

Jenkins, Philip. *The Next Christendom: The Coming of Global Christianity*. Oxford: Oxford University Press, 2002.

Johnson, Todd, and Kenneth R. Ross. *Atlas of Global Christianity 1910–2010*. Edinburgh: Edinburgh University Press, 2009.

Jongeneel, Jan A. B., Scott W. Sunquist, and Peter Tze Ming Ng, eds. *Christian Mission and Education in Modern China, Japan and Korea: Historical Studies*. Hamburg: Peter Lang, 2008.

———. *Philosophy, Science and Theology of Mission in the 19th and 20th Centuries*. 2 vols. Frankfurt am Main: Peter Lang, 1995/1997.

K'eshishean, Aram. *The Armenian Church Beyond the 1700th Anniversary*. Antilias, Lebanon: Armenian Catholicosate of Cilicia, 2001.

Kalu, Ogbu. *African Christianity: An African Story*. Pretoria: University of Pretoria, 2005.

Kolodiejchuk, Brian, M.C., ed. and commentary. *Mother Teresa, Come Be My Light: The Private Writings of the "Saint of Calcutta."* New York: Doubleday, 2007.

Korieh, Chima J., ed. *Olaudah Equiano and the Igbo World History, Society and Atlantic Diasporo Connections*. Trenton, NJ: Africa World Press, 2009.

Koschorke, Klaus, Frieder Ludwig, Mariano Delgado, and Roland Spliesgart. *A History of Christianity in Asia, Africa, Latin America, 1450–1990*. Grand Rapids: Eerdmans, 2007.

Krabill, James R., Walter Sawatsky, and Charles E. Van Engen. *Evangelical, Ecumenical and Anabaptist Missiologies in Conversation: Essays in Honor of Wilbert R. Shenk*. Maryknoll, NY: Orbis Books, 2006.

Kraemer, Hendrik. *World Cultures and World Religions: The Coming Dialogue*. London: Lutterworth, 1960.

Latourette, Kenneth Scott. *A History of Christian Missions in China*. New York: Macmillan, 1929.

———. *A History of the Expansion of Christianity*. 7 vols. New York: Harper & Brothers, 1937–45.

Leithart, Peter J. *Defending Constantine: The Twilight of an Empire and the Dawn of Christendom*. Downers Grove, IL: InterVarsity, 2010.

Lewis, Mike. "Skirting the Law: Sudan's Post CPA Arms Flow." Geneva: Graduate Institute of International and Development Studies, 2009.

Longfield, Bradley J. *The Presbyterian Controversy, 1922–1936: Fundamentalists, Modernists and Moderates*. New York: Oxford University Press, 1991.

MacMaster, Richard K. *A Gentle Wind of God: The Influence of the East Africa Revival*. Scottdale, PA: Herald, 2006.

Manikam, Rajah Bhushanam, ed. *Christianity and the Asian Revolution*. New York: Friendship Press, 1954.

Matthews, Shailer. *The Social Gospel*. Boston: Pilgrim Press, 1910.

McGavaran, Donald Anderson. *The Bridges of God: A Study in the Strategy of Missions*. London: World Dominion Press, 1955.

McIntire, C. T., ed. *Writings on Christianity and History*. Oxford: Oxford University Press, 1979.

Metzger, John. *The Hand and the Road*. Louisville: Westminster John Knox, 2010.

Miller, Jon. *Missionary Zeal and Institutional Control: Organizational Contradictions in the Base Mission on the Gold Coast, 1828–1917*. Grand Rapids: Eerdmans, 2003.

Moffett, Samuel Hugh. *A History of Christianity in Asia*. 2 vols. Maryknoll, NY: Orbis Books, 1998/2005.

Moran, J. F. *The Japanese and the Jesuits: Alesandro Valignano in 16th Century Japan*. New York: Routledge, 1993.

Moreau, Scott, Gary R. Corwin, and Gary B. McGee. *Introducing World Missions: A Biblical, Historical and Practical Survey*. Grand Rapids: Baker Academic, 2004.

Morton, Daniel O. *Memoir of Rev. Levi Parsons: Lute Missionary to Palestine*. New York: Arno, 1977.

Neill, Stephen. *A History of Christianity in India*. Cambridge: Cambridge University Press, 1985.

———. *A History of Christian Missions*. Middlesex, UK: Penguin, 1986.

Noll, Mark A. *The New Shape of World Christianity: How American Experience Reflects Global Faith*. Downers Grove, IL: InterVarsity, 2009.

Pagan, Luis Rivera. *A Violent Evangelism: The Political and Religious Conquest of the Americas*. Louisville: Westminster John Knox, 1992.

Patte, Daniel. *Cambridge Dictionary of Christianity*. New York: Cambridge University Press, 2010.

Pegg, Mark Gregory. *A Most Holy War: The Albigensian Crusade and the Battle for Christendom*. New York: Oxford University Press, 2008.

Raboteau, Albert J. *Canaan Land: A Religious History*. New York: Oxford University Press, 2001.

Robert, Dana. *American Women in Mission: A Social History of Their Thought and Practice*. Macon, GA: Mercer University Press, 1996.

———, ed. *Converting Colonialism: Visions and Realties in Mission History, 1706–1914*. Grand Rapids: Eerdmans, 2008.

Ross, Andrew C. *A Vision Betrayed: The Jesuits in Japan and China, 1542–1742*. Maryknoll, NY: Orbis Books, 1994.

Sachs, Jeffrey D. *The End of Poverty: Economic Possibilities for Our Time*. New York: Penguin Books, 2005.

Sanneh, Lamin. *Abolitionists Abroad: American Blacks and the Making of the Modern West Africa*. Cambridge: Harvard University Press, 1999.

Schnabel, Eckhard J. *Early Christian Mission*. 2 vols. Downers Grove, IL: InterVarsity, 2004.

Seward, Desmond. *The Monks of War*. New York: Penguin Books, 1972.

Shaw, Ryan. "A Haystack that Changed the World." *Evangelical Missions Quarterly* 42, no. 4 (October 2006): 480–85.

Shorter, Aylward. *The Cross and the Flag in Africa: The White Fathers During the Colonial Scramble, 1892–1914*. Maryknoll, NY: Orbis Books, 2006.

Shrady, Maria, trans. *Johannes Tauler: Sermons*. New York: Paulist Press, 1985.

Smith, George. *The Life of William Carey, DD: Shoemaker and Missionary, Professor of Sanskrit, Bengali and Marathi in the College of Fort William, Calcutta*. London: John Murray, 1887.

Sng, Bobby E. K. *In His Good Time: A History of Christianity in Singapore, 1819–2002*. Singapore: Bible Society of Singapore / Graduates' Christian Fellowship, 2003.

Stark, Rodney. *The Rise of Christianity: How the Obscure, Marginal Jesus Movement Became the Dominant Religious Force in the Western World in a Few Centuries*. Princeton, NJ: Princeton University Press, 1996.

Stark, Rodney, and Roger Fink. "Catholic Religious Vocations: Decline and Revival." *Review of Religions Research* 42, no. 2 (2000): 135–45.

Sunquist, Scott. *Time, Cross and Glory: Understanding Christian History*. Downers Grove, IL: InterVarsity, forthcoming.

Sunquist, Scott, and Caroline N. Becker. *A History of Presbyterian Missions, 1944–2007*. Louisville: Geneva, 2008.

Thomas, Norman E. *Classic Texts in Mission and World Christianity*. Maryknoll, NY: Orbis Books, 1995.

———. *Missions and Unity: Lessons from History, 1792–2010*. Eugene, OR: Cascade Books, 2010.

Tierney, Brian. *Great Issues in Western Civilization*. Vol. 1. New York: Random House, 1972.

Tucker, Ruth. *From Jerusalem to Irian Jaya: A Biographical History of Christian Missions*. Grand Rapids: Zondervan, 1983.

Verstraelen, Frans J., Arnulf Camps, Libertus A. Hoedemaker, and Marc R. Spindler. *Missiology: An Ecumenical Introduction: Texts and Contexts of Global Christianity*. Grand Rapids: Eerdmans, 1995.

Vischer, Lukas. *Pia Conspiratio: Calvin's Commitment to the Unity of the Church*. Louisville: PCUSA, Office of Theology, Worship and Education, 2007.

Von Germeten, Nicole, ed. *Sandoval Treatise on Slavery*. Indianapolis: Hackett, 2008.

Wahbe, Thaurat. "The Practices of Mission in Egypt: A Historical Study of the Integration Between the American Mission and the Evangelical Church of Egypt, 1854–1970." PhD diss., London School of Theology, 2008.

Walls, Andrew F. *The Cross-Cultural Process in Christian History*. Maryknoll, NY: Orbis Books, 2002.

———. *The Missionary Movement in Christian History: Studies in the Transmission of Faith*. Maryknoll, NY: Orbis Books, 1996.

Warneck, Gustav. *Outline of a History of Protestant Missions from the Reformation to the Present Time*. Translated by George Robson. New York: Fleming H. Revell, 1906.

Williams, George. *The Radical Reformation*. Philadelphia: Westminster, 1962.

Winter, Ralph D. *The Twenty-Five Unbelievable Years, 1945–1969*. Pasadena: William Carey Library, 1970.

Wise, Christopher, ed. *The Timbuktu Chronicles, 1493–1599: Ta'rikh al Fattash*. Trenton, NJ: Africa World Press, 2011.

Mission: Bible and Theology

Adeney, Francis. *Graceful Evangelism: Christian Witness in a Complex World*. Grand Rapids: Baker Academic, 2010.

Allen, Roland. *Missionary Methods: St. Paul's or Ours?* London: Robert Scott, 1912.

———. *Pentecost and the World: The Revelation of the Holy Spirit in the "Acts of Apostles."* London: Oxford University Press, 1917.

———. *The Spontaneous Expansion of the Church, and the Causes Which Hinder It*. Grand Rapids: Eerdmans, 1962.

Allison, Dale. *Constructing Jesus: Memory, Imagination, and History*. Grand Rapids: Baker Academic, 2010.

Anderson, Gerald. "American Protestants in Pursuit of Mission: 1886–1986." In *Missiology: An Ecumenical Introduction*, edited by F. J. Verstraelen, A. Camps, L. A. Hoedemaker, and M. R. Spindler. Grand Rapids: Eerdmans, 1995.

———, ed. *The Theology of the Christian Mission*. New York: McGraw-Hill, 1961.

Anderson, Gerald H., and Thomas F. Stransky, CSP. *Mission Trends No. 1: Crucial Issues in Mission Today*. New York: Paulist Press, 1974.

Anderson, Ray S. *An Emergent Theology for Emerging Churches*. Downers Grove, IL: InterVarsity, 2006.

Anderson, Rufus. *Foreign Missions: Their Relations and Claims*. New York: Charles Scribner, 1869.

Ariarajah, S. Wesley. *The Bible and People of Other Faiths*. Geneva: WCC, 1985.

Arias, Mortimer. *Announcing the Reign of God: Evangelization and the Subversive Memory of Jesus*. Philadelphia: Fortress, 1984.

Barrett, David B., George T. Kurian, and Todd M. Johnson. *World Christian Encyclopedia: A Comparative Survey of Churches and Religions in the Modern World*. New York: Oxford University Press, 2001.

Bassham, Rodger C. *Mission Theology, 1948–1975: Years of Worldwide Creative Tension—Ecumenical, Evangelical, and Roman Catholic*. Pasadena: William Carey Library, 1979.

Bavinck, John Herman. *An Introduction to the Science of Missions*. Translated by David H. Freeman. Philadelphia: P&R, 1960.

Bevans, Stephen. *Models of Contextual Theology*. Rev. ed. Maryknoll, NY: Orbis Books, 2002.

Bevans, Stephen, and Roger Schroeder. *Constants in Context: A Theology of Mission for Today*. Maryknoll, NY: Orbis Books, 2004.

Becker, Karl J., and Ilaria Morali. *Catholic Engagement with World Religions: A Comprehensive Study*. Maryknoll, NY: Orbis Books, 2010.

Blauw, Johannes. *The Missionary Nature of the Church: A Survey of Biblical Theology of Mission*. New York: McGraw-Hill, 1962.

Bonk, Jonathan, ed. *Between Past and Future: Evangelical Mission Entering the 21st Century*. Evangelical Missions Society, 10. Pasadena: William Carey Library, 2003.

———. *Missions and Money: Affluence as a Western Missionary Problem*. Maryknoll, NY: Orbis Books, 1996.

———. "Missions and Money: Affluence as a Western Missionary Problem . . . Revisited." *International Bulletin of Missionary Research* 31, no. 4 (October 2007): 171–76.

Bosch, David J. *A Spirituality of the Road*. Scottdale, PA: Herald, 1979.

———. "The Theology of Mission." *Verbum SVD* 15 (1973): 79–91.

———. *Theology of Religions: Missiology and Science of Religion*. Pretoria: University of South Africa, 1977.

———. *Transforming Mission: Paradigm Shifts in Theology of Mission*. Maryknoll, NY: Orbis Books, 1991.

———. *Witness to the World: The Christian Mission in Theological Perspective*. Atlanta: John Knox, 1980.

Bowden, John, ed. *Christianity: The Complete Guide*. New York: Continuum, 2006.

Boyd, Robin. *The Witness of the Student Christian Movement: "Church Ahead of the Church."* Geneva: WCC, 2007.

Bria, Ion. *The Liturgy after the Liturgy: Mission and Witness from an Orthodox Perspective*. Geneva: WCC, 1996.

———. *Martyria Mission: The Witness of Orthodox Churches Today*. Geneva: WCC, 1980.

Brunner, Emil. *The Word and the World*. Lexington: American Theological Library Association, 1965.

Bühlman, Walbert. *The Church of the Future: A Model for the Year 2001*. Maryknoll, NY: Orbis Books, 1986.

———. *The Coming of the Third Church*. Maryknoll, NY: Orbis Books, 1976.

Burrows, William. *New Ministries: The Global Context*. Maryknoll, NY: Orbis Books, 1980.

———. "A Seventh Paradigm? Catholics and Radical Inculturation." In *Mission in Bold Humility: David Bosch's Work Considered*, edited by William Saayman and Klippies Kritzinger. Maryknoll, NY: Orbis Books, 1996.

Chan, Edmund. *Built to Last: Towards a Disciplemaking Church*. Singapore: Covenant Evangelical Free Church, 2001.

Chatterjee, Margaret. *Gandhi's Religious Thought*. Notre Dame, IN: University of Notre Dame, 1983.

Coleman, Robert. *The Heart of the Gospel: The Theology Behind the Master Plan of Evangelism*. Grand Rapids: Baker Books, 2011.

———. *The Master Plan of Evangelism*. New York: Fleming H. Revell, 1963.

Cone, James. *Black Theology and Black Power*. New York: Seabury, 1969.

Congar, Yves. *Lay People in the Church*. Westminster, MD: Newman, 1957.

Costas, Orlando. *Christ Outside the Gate: Mission Beyond Christendom*. Maryknoll, NY: Orbis Books, 1982.

———. *The Church and Its Mission: A Shattering Critique from the Third World*. Wheaton: Tyndale House, 1974.

———. *The Integrity of Mission: The Inner Life and Outreach of the Church*. San Francisco: Harper & Row, 1979.

———. *Liberating News: A Theology of Contextual Evangelization*. Grand Rapids: Eerdmans, 1989.

Court, John M. *New Testament Writers and the Old Testament: An Introduction*. London: SPCK, 2002.

Cragg, Kenneth. *The Call of the Minaret*. New York: Oxford University Press, 1956.

Crossan, John Dominic. *The Historical Jesus: The Life of a Mediterranean Jewish Peasant*. San Francisco: HarperSanFrancisco, 2000.

———. *Who Killed Jesus? Exposing the Roots of Anti-Semitism in the Gospel Story of the Death of Jesus*. San Francisco: HarperSanFrancisco, 1996.

Crouch, Andy. *Culture Making: Recovering Our Creative Calling*. Downers Grove, IL: InterVarsity, 2008.

D'Costa, Gavin, ed. *Christian Uniqueness Reconsidered: The Myth of a Pluralistic Theology of Religions*. Maryknoll, NY: Orbis Books, 1990.

Davidson, Ivor, and Murray A. Rae. *God of Salvation: Soteriology in Theological Perspective*. Burlington, VT: Ashgate, 2011.

Dawson, Gerrit. *Jesus Ascended: The Meaning of Christ's Continuing Incarnation*. Phillipsburg, NJ: P&R, 2004.

de Lubac, Henri. *Catholicism: Christ and the Common Destiny of Man*. London: Burns & Oates, 1950.

———. *The Church: Paradox and Mystery*. Shannon, Ireland: Ecclesia Press, 1969.

———. *The Splendour of the Church*. San Francisco: Ignatius, 1986.

Devanandan, Paul D. *The Gospel and Renascent Hinduism*. London: SCM, 1959.

Douglas, J. D., ed. *Let the Earth Hear His Voice*. Minneapolis: World Wide Publications, 1975.

Driver, John. *Images of the Church in Mission*. Scottdale, PA: Herald, 1997.

Dulles, Avery. *Models of the Church*. Garden City, NY: Doubleday, 1974.

Dupuis, Jacques. *Christianity and the Religions: From Confrontation to Dialogue*. Maryknoll, NY: Orbis Books, 2002.

Escobar, Samuel. *The New Global Mission: The Gospel from Everywhere to Everyone*. Downers Grove, IL: InterVarsity, 2003.

Everts, Don, and Doug Schaupp. *I Once Was Lost: What Postmodern Skeptics Taught Us About Their Path to Jesus*. Downers Grove, IL: InterVarsity, 2008.

Farhadian, Charles E., ed. *Christian Worship Worldwide: Expanding Horizons, Deepening Practices*. Grand Rapids: Eerdmans, 2007.

Farquhar, John N. *The Crown of Hinduism*. London: James Nisbet and Co., 1954.

Flett, John G. *The Witness of God: The Trinity,* Missio Dei*, Karl Barth, and the Nature of Christian Community*. Grand Rapids: Eerdmans, 2010.

Foster, Stuart J. "The Missiology of the Old Testament." *International Bulletin of Missionary Research* (October 2010): 205–8.

Frost, Michael, and Alan Hirsch. *ReJesus: A Wild Messiah for a Missional Church*. Peabody, MA: Hendrickson, 2009.

———. *The Shape of Things to Come: Innovation and Mission for the 21st Century Church*. Peabody, MA: Hendrickson, 2003.

Fullenbach, John. *Church: Community for the Kingdom*. Maryknoll, NY: Orbis Books, 2002.

Gallagher, Robert L., and Paul Hertig, eds. *Mission in Acts: Ancient Narratives in Contemporary Context*. Maryknoll, NY: Orbis Books, 2004.

Geertz, Clifford. *The Interpretation of Cultures: Selected Essays*. New York: Basic Books, 1971.

George, Sherron Kay. *Called as Partners in Christ's Service: The Practice of God's Mission*. Louisville: Worldwide Ministries Division, PCUSA, 2004.

Gibbs, Eddie, and Ryan K. Bolger. *Emerging Churches: Creating Christian Community in Postmodern Cultures*. Grand Rapids: Baker Academic, 2005.

Glassar, Arthur. *Announcing the Kingdom: The Story of God's Mission in the Bible*. Grand Rapids: Baker Academic, 2003.

Gnanakan, Ken. *Kingdom Concerns: A Theology of Mission Today*. Leicester, UK: Inter-Varsity, 1989.

Goppelt, Leonard. *Typos: The Typological Interpretation of the Old Testament in the New*. Translated by Donald M. Madvig. Grand Rapids: Eerdmans, 1982.

Greenway, Roger. *Go and Make Disciples: An Introduction to Christian Missions*. Philipsburg, NJ: P&R, 1999.

Greer, Peter, and Phil Smith. *The Poor Will Be Glad*. Grand Rapids: Zondervan, 2009.

Guder, Darrell. "From Mission and Theology to Missional Theology." *Princeton Seminary Bulletin* 24, no. 1 (2003): 36–54.

———. *The Incarnation and the Church's Witness*. Eugene, OR: Wipf & Stock, 2005.

———. *Missional Church: A Vision for the Sending of the Church in North America*. Grand Rapids: Eerdmans, 1998.

Gutiérrez, Gustavo. *A Theology of Liberation: History, Politics and Salvation*. Maryknoll, NY: Orbis Books, 1973.

Harrington, Wilfrid J. *Revelation*. Sacra Pagina 16. Collegeville, MN: Liturgical Press, 1993.

Hauerwas, Stanley, and William H. Willimon. *Resident Aliens*. Nashville: Abingdon, 1989.

Heath, Elaine A. *Mystic Way of Evangelism: A Contemplative Vision for Christian Outreach*. Grand Rapids: Baker Academic, 2008.

Hick, John. *God and the Universe of Faiths*. New York: McMillian, 1973.

Hinton, Jeanne. *Walking in the Same Direction: A New Way of Being Church*. Geneva: WCC, 1995.

Hocking, William Ernest. *The Coming World Civilization*. New York: Harper & Brothers, 1956.

———. *Rethinking Missions: A Layman's Inquiry after One Hundred Years*. New York: Harper & Brothers, 1932.

Hoekendiijk, Johannes. "The Church in Missionary Thinking." *International Review of Missions* 41 (1952): 324–36.

Hoffman, Ronan. "The Changing Nature of Mission." *Washington Service* 19, no. 1 (Special Issue, 1968).

Hogg, A. G. *The Christian Message to the Hindu*. London: SCM, 1947.

Hogg, William Richey. "Some Background Considerations for *Ad Gentes*." *International Review of Missions* 56, no. 223 (July 1957): 281–90.

Huang, Paulos Zhanzhu. *Confronting Confucian Understandings of the Christian Doctrine of Salvation: A Systematic Theological Analysis of the Basic Problems in the Confucian Christian Dialogue*. Leiden: Brill, 2009.

Humphrey, Edith. *Ecstasy and Intimacy: When the Holy Spirit Meets the Human Spirit*. Grand Rapids: Eerdmans, 2006.

Hunsberger, George R. *Bearing the Witness of the Spirit: Lesslie Newbigin's Theology of Cultural Plurality*. Grand Rapids: Eerdmans, 1998.

Hunsberger, George R., and Craig Van Gelder. *The Church between Gospel and Culture: The Emerging Mission in North America*. Grand Rapids: Eerdmans, 1996.

Izuzquiza, Daniel. *Rooted in Jesus Christ: Toward a Radical Ecclesiology*. Grand Rapids: Eerdmans, 2009.

James, Rick. *Jesus without Religion: What Did He Say? What Did He Do? What's the Point?* Downers Grove, IL: InterVarsity, 2007.

Johnson, Todd M., and Kenneth R. Ross, eds. *Atlas of Global Christianity*. Edinburgh: Edinburgh University Press, 2010.

Jones, E. Stanley. *Christ at the Round Table*. New York: Abingdon, 1928.

———. *Christ of the Indian Road*. New York: Abingdon, 1925.

Kähler, Martin. *Schriften zur Christologie and Mission*. Munich: Chr. Kaiser Verlag, 1908.

———. *The So-Called Historical Jesus and the Historic Biblical Christ*. Translated and edited by Carl E. Braaten. German original, 1896. Philadelphia: Fortress, 1964.

Kärkkäinen, Veli-Matti. "How to Speak of the Spirit among Religions: Trinitarian Prolegomena for a Pneumatological Theology of Religions." In *The Work of the Spirit: Pneumatology and Pentecostalism*, edited by Michael Welker. Grand Rapids: Eerdmans, 2006.

———. *An Introduction to the Theology of Religions: Biblical, Historical and Contemporary Perspectives*. Downers Grove, IL: InterVarsity, 2003.

———. *The Trinity: Global Perspectives*. Louisville: Westminster John Knox, 2007.

Kim, Kirsteen. *The Holy Spirit in the World: A Global Conversation*. Maryknoll, NY: Orbis Books, 2007.

Kimball, Dan. *The Emerging Church: Vintage Christianity for all Generations*. Grand Rapids: Zondervan, 2003.

King, Russell. *People on the Move: An Atlas of Migration*. Los Angeles: University of California Press, 2010.

Kirk, J. Andrew. *What is Mission? Theological Explorations*. Minneapolis: Fortress, 2000.

———. *A New World Coming: A Fresh Look at the Gospel for Today*. Basingstoke, UK: Marshalls, 1983.

———. *The Mission of Theology and Theology as Mission*. Valley Forge, PA: Trinity Press, 1997.

———. *Losing the Chains: Religion as Opium and Liberation*. London: Hodder & Stoughton, 1992.

———. *The Meaning of Freedom: A Study of Secular, Muslim and Christian Views*. Carlisle, UK: Paternoster, 1998.

———. *Handling Problems of Peace and War*. Basingstoke, UK: Marshall Pickering, 1988.

———. *God's Word for a Complex World: Discovering How the Bible Speaks Today*. Basingstoke, UK: Marshall Pickering, 1987.

———. *Mission under Scrutiny: Confronting Contemporary Challenges*. Minneapolis: Fortress, 2006.

Knitter, Paul F. *No Other Name? A Critical Survey of Christian Attitudes Toward the World Religions*. Maryknoll, NY: Orbis Books, 1985.

Köstenberger, Andreas J. *The Missions of Jesus and the Disciples According to the Fourth Gospel with Implications for the Fourth Gospel's Purpose and the Mission of the Contemporary Church*. Grand Rapids: Eerdmans, 1998.

Köstenberger, Andreas J., and Peter T. O'Brien. *Salvation to the Ends of the Earth: A Biblical Theology of Mission*. Downers Grove, IL: InterVarsity, 2001.

Kraemer, Hendrik. *The Christian Message in a Non-Christian World*. New York: Published for the IMC by Harper & Brothers, 1938.

Kritzinger, J. N. J., and W. Saayman. *David J. Bosch: Prophetic Integrity, Cruciform Praxis*. Dorpspruit, South Africa: Cluster Publications, 2011.

Küng, Hans, and Jürgen Moltmann, eds. *Christianity among World Religions*. Edinburgh: T&T Clark, 1986.

Larkin, William J., and Joel F. Williams. *Mission in the New Testament: An Evangelical Approach*. Maryknoll, NY: Orbis Books, 1998.

Lingenfelter, Sherwood. *Transforming Culture: A Challenge for Christian Mission*. 2nd ed. Grand Rapids: Baker Academic, 1998.

Lonergran, Bernard. *Method in Theology*. London: Darton, Longman & Todd, 1972.

Lovelace, Richard. *Dynamics of the Spiritual Life: An Evangelical Theology of Renewal*. Downers Grove, IL: InterVarsity, 1979.

Maidstone, Graham, ed. *Mission-Shaped Church: Church Planting and Fresh Expressions of Church in a Changing Context*. London: Church Publishing House, 2004.

Mandryk, Jason. *Operation World*. 7th ed. Colorado Springs, CO: Biblica, 2010.

McDonnell, Killian. "A Trinitarian Theology of the Holy Spirit." *Theological Studies* 46 (1985): 191–227.

McGee, Gary B. *Miracles, Missions and American Pentecostalism*. Maryknoll, NY: Orbis Books, 2010.

McGrath, Alister E. *Christian Theology: An Introduction*. 3rd ed. Oxford: Blackwell, 2001.

McKee, Robert. *Story: Substance, Structure, and Style and the Principle of Screenwriting*. New York: HarperCollins, 1997.

McLaren, Brian D. *Everything Must Change: Jesus, Global Crises, and a Revolution of Hope*. Nashville: Thomas Nelson, 2007.

Miller, Donald. *A Million Miles in a Thousand Years*. Nashville: Thomas Nelson, 2009.

Moltmann, Jürgen. *The Church in the Power of the Spirit: A Contribution to Messianic Ecclesiology*. London: SCM, 1977.

———. *The Crucified God: The Cross of Christ as the Foundation and Criticism of Christian Theology*. New York: Harper & Row, 1974.

———. *Theology of Hope: On the Ground and the Implications of a Christian Eschatology*. London: SCM, 1967.

Mounce, Robert. *The Book of Revelation*. Rev. ed. Grand Rapids: Eerdmans, 1977.

Moyise, Steve. *Evoking Scripture: Seeking the Old Testament in the New*. New York: T&T Clark, 2008.

Muck, Terry, and Frances S. Adeney. *Christianity Encountering World Religions: The Practice of Mission in the Twenty-first Century*. Grand Rapids: Baker Academic, 2009.

Müller, Karl. *Mission Theology: An Introduction*. Nettetal: Steyer Verlag Wort und Werk, 1987.

Myers, Bryant L. *Walking with the Poor: Principles and Practices of Transformational Development*. Rev. ed. Maryknoll, NY: Orbis Books, 2011.

Myklebust, Olav Guttorm. *The Study of Missions in Theological Education*. 2 vols. Oslo: Egede Instituttet, 1955–57.

Neill, Stephen. *Christian Partnership*. London: SCM, 1952.

Nevius, John L. "Methods of Missionary Work." In *The Chinese Recorder*. 1886; repr., New York: Foreign Mission Library, 1895.

Newbigin, J. E. Lesslie. "Can the West be Converted?" *Princeton Seminary Bulletin* 6, no. 1 (1985): 25–37.

———. "The Church: A Bunch of Escaped Convicts." *Reform* 6 (June 1990).

———. *A Faith for this One World?* New York: Harper, 1961.

———. *The Finality of Christ*. Richmond: John Knox, 1969.

———. *Foolishness to the Greeks: The Gospel and Western Culture*. Grand Rapids: Eerdmans, 1986.

———. *The Gospel in a Pluralist Society*. Grand Rapids: Eerdmans, 1989.

———. *The Household of God: Lectures on the Nature of the Church*. New York: Friendship Press, 1954.

———. *The Open Secret: Sketches for a Missionary Theology*. Grand Rapids: Eerdmans, 1978.

———. *The Other Side of 1984: Questions for the Churches*. Geneva: WCC, 1983.

———. *Proper Confidence: Faith, Doubt and Certainty in Christian Discipleship*. Grand Rapids: Eerdmans, 1995.

———. *Signs Amid the Rubble: The Purposes of God in Human History*. Edited by Geoffrey Wainwright. Grand Rapids: Eerdmans, 2003.

———. *Tell the Truth: The Gospel as Public Truth*. Grand Rapids: Eerdmans, 1991.

———. *Unfinished Agenda: An Autobiography*. Geneva: WCC, 1985.

Niles, D. T. *Buddhism and the Claims of Christ*. Richmond: John Knox, 1967.

———. *The Preacher's Task and the Stone of Stumbling*. New York: Harper & Brothers, 1958.

———. *Upon the Earth: The Mission of God and the Missionary Enterprise of the Churches*. New York: McGraw-Hill, 1962.

Oborji, Francis Anekwe. *Concepts of Mission: The Evolution of Contemporary Missiology*. Maryknoll, NY: Orbis Books, 2006.

Onwubiko, Oliver A. *Missionary Ecclesiology: An Introduction*. Nsukka, Nigeria: Fulladu Publishing Co., 1999.

Padilla, C. René. *Mission Between the Times: Essays on the Kingdom*. Grand Rapids: Eerdmans, 1985.

Panikkar, Ramundo. *The Unknown Christ of Hinduism*. London: Darton, Longman & Todd, 1964.

Peace, Richard. *Holy Conversion: Talking About God in Everyday Life*. Downers Grove, IL: InterVarsity, 2006.

Percy, Walker. *The Moviegoer*. New York: Knopf, 1961.

———. *The Second Coming*. New York: Macmillan/Picador, 1999.

Peskett, Howard, and Vinoth Ramachandra. *The Message of Mission*. Downers Grove, IL: InterVarsity, 2003.

Piper, John. *Let the Nations Be Glad: The Supremacy of God in Mission*. 2nd ed. Grand Rapids: Baker Academic, 2003.

Pocock, Michael, Gailynn Van Rheenen, and Douglass McConnell. *The Changing Face of World Missions: Emerging Contemporary Issues and Trends*. Grand Rapids: Baker Academic, 2005.

Porter, Stanley E., ed. *Hearing the Old Testament in the New Testament*. Grand Rapids: Eerdmans, 2006.

Protestant/Orthodox/Roman Catholic Consultation on Dialogue with Men of Other Faiths. "Christians in Dialogue with Men of Other Faiths." *International Review of Missions* 56, no. 233 (1967): 338–43.

Ramachandra, Vinoth. *Faiths in Conflict? Christian Integrity in a Multicultural World*. Downers Grove, IL: InterVarsity, 1999.

———. *Gods That Fail: Modern Idolatry and Christian Mission*. Downers Grove, IL: InterVarsity, 1996.

———. *The Recovery of Mission: Beyond the Pluralist Paradigm*. Grand Rapids: Eerdmans, 1996.

Richardson, Rick. *Evangelism Outside the Box: New Ways to Help People Experience the Good News*. Downers Grove, IL: InterVarsity, 2000.

Robert, Dana. "The Origin of the Student Volunteer Watchword: The Evangelization of the World in our Generation." *International Bulletin of Missionary Research* 10, no. 4 (October 1986): 146–50.

Robinson, John. *But That I Can't Believe!* London: Collins, 1967.

Roxburgh, Alan J. *The Missionary Congregation: Leadership and Liminality*. Philadelphia: Trinity Press, 1997.

Rynearson, Edward K. *Retelling Violent Death*. Oxford: Oxford University Press, 2001.

Saayman, William, and Klippies Kritzenger, eds. *Mission in Bold Humility: David Bosch's Work Considered*. Maryknoll, NY: Orbis Books, 1996.

Samartha, S. J., ed. *Faith in the Midst of Faiths: Reflections on Dialogue in Community*. Geneva: WCC, 1977.

Samuel, Vinay, and Chris Sugden, eds. *Mission as Transformation: A Theology of the Whole Gospel*. Oxford: Paternoster/Regnum, 1999.

Scandrette, Mark. *Practicing the Way of Jesus: Life Together in the Kingdom of Love*. Downers Grove, IL: InterVarsity, 2011.

Schillebeeckx, Edward. *Church: The Human Story of God*. New York: Crossroad, 1990.

Schmemann, Alexander. *Introduction to Liturgical Theology*. Portland, ME: American Orthodox Press, 1966.

Schmidlin, Joseph. *Catholic Mission Theory*. Translated by Matthias Braun. Techny, IL: Mission Press, S.V.D., 1931.

Schreiter, Robert. *Reconciliation: Mission and Ministry in a Changing Social Order*. Maryknoll, NY: Orbis Books, 1992.

Schwarz, Christian A. *Natural Church Development: A Guide to Eight Essential Qualities of Healthy Churches*. St. Charles, IL: ChurchSmart Resources, 1996.

Scudieri, Robert J. *The Apostolic Church: One, Holy, Catholic and Missionary*. Chino, CA: R.C. Law, 1996.

Sider, Ronald J. *Doing Evangelism in Jesus's Way: How Christians Demonstrate the Good News*. Nappanee, IN: Evangel Publishing House, 2003.

———. "What If We Defined the Gospel the Way That Jesus Did?" In *Holistic Mission: God's Plan for God's People*, edited by Brian Woolnough and Wonsuk Ma. Oxford: Regnum Books, 2010.

Singh, Sadhu Sundar. *With and Without Christ: Being Incidents Taken from the Lives of Christians and Non-Christians which Illustrate the Difference in Lives with Christ and Without Christ*. New York: Harper & Brothers, 1929.

Skreslet, Stanley H. *Comprehending Mission: The Questions, Methods, Themes, Problems, and Prospects of Missiology*. Maryknoll, NY: Orbis Books, 2012.

———. *Picturing Christian Witness: New Testament Images of Disciples in Mission*. Grand Rapids: Eerdmans, 2006.

Snow, Donald B. *English Teaching as Christian Mission: An Applied Theology*. Scottdale, PA: Herald, 2001.

Solomon, Robert. *Living in Two Worlds: Pastoral Responses to Possession in Singapore*. Frankfurt am Main: Peter Lang, 1994.

Song, Shangjie. *The Diaries of John Sung: An Autobiography*. Translated by Stephen L. Sheng. Brighton, MI: Luke H. Sheng and Stephen L. Sheng, 1995.

Speer, Robert E. *The Finality of Jesus Christ*. New York: Fleming H. Revell, 1933.

Stanley, Brian, ed. *The World Missionary Conference, Edinburgh, 1910*. Grand Rapids: Eerdmans, 2009.

Stott, John R. W. *The Authentic Jesus: The Certainty of Jesus in a Skeptical World*. Downers Grove, IL: InterVarsity, 1985.

———. *Christian Mission in the Modern World*. Downers Grove, IL: InterVarsity, 1975.

———. *The Living Church: Convictions of a Lifelong Pastor*. Downers Grove, IL: InterVarsity, 2011.

———. *Our Guilty Silence*. Grand Rapids: Eerdmans, 1967.

Strachan, R. Kenneth. "Call to Witness." *International Missionary Review* 53, no. 210 (1964): 191–200.

Stransky, Thomas. "The Observers at Vatican Two: A Unique Experience at Dialogue." *Centro Pro Unione* 63 (Spring 2003): 8.

Strauss, David Friedrich. *The Life of Jesus Critically Examined*. Translated by George Eliot. Edited by Peter C. Hodgson. Philadelphia: Fortress, 1972.

Sunquist, Scott. "A Wide Embrace: The Heart of Christ for Mission Today." Lecture given at OMSC, January 12, 2007.

Tennent, Timothy C. *Christianity at the Religious Roundtable: Evangelicalism in Conversation with Hinduism, Buddhism and Islam*. Grand Rapids: Baker Academic, 2002.

———. *Invitation to World Missions*. Grand Rapids: Kregel, 2010.

Thangaraj, M. Thomas. *The Common Task: A Theology of Christian Mission*. Nashville: Abingdon, 1999.

Thomas, M. M. "The Absoluteness of Jesus Christ and Christ-Centered Syncretism." *Ecumenical Review* 37 (1985): 287–397.

———. *The Acknowledged Christ of the Indian Renaissance*. Madras: CLS, 1970.

———. *Man and the Universe of Faiths*. Madras: CLS, 1975.

———. "The Meaning of Salvation Today." *International Review of Mission* (1973).

———. "Salvation and Humanization." *International Review of Mission* (1971).

Tillich, Paul. *Christianity and the Encounter of the World Religions*. New York: Columbia University Press, 1963.

Travis, John. "The C1 to C6 Spectrum: A Practical Tool for Defining Six Types of Christ-Centered Communities Found in the Muslim Context." *Evangelical Missions Quarterly* 34, no. 4 (October 1998): 407–8.

Van Engen, Charles, Dean S. Gilliland, and Paul Pierson, eds. *The Good News of the Kingdom: Mission Theology for the Third Millennium*. Maryknoll, NY: Orbis Books, 1993.

Van Gelder, Craig, ed. *Confident Witness: Changing World, Rediscovering the Gospel in North America*. Grand Rapids: Eerdmans, 1991.

———. *Ministry of the Missional Church: A Community Led by the Spirit*. Grand Rapids: Baker Books, 2007.

Van Rheenen, Gailyn. *Missions: Biblical Foundations and Contemporary Strategies*. Grand Rapids: Zondervan, 1996.

Vatican II Documents. All references to the documents of the Second Vatican Council are taken from the Vatican's website, where they can be read in any of the official languages. See http://www.vatican.va/archive/hist_councils/ii_vatican_council/.

Verkuyl, Johannes. *Contemporary Missiology: An Introduction*. Grand Rapids: Eerdmans, 1978.

Visser 't Hooft, W. A. *The Ecumenical Movement and the Racial Problem*. Paris: UNESCO, 1954.

———. *The Genesis and Formation of the World Council of Churches*. Geneva: WCC, 1982.

———. *No Other Name: The Choice between Syncretism and Christian Universalism*. Philadelphia: Westminster, 1963.

Wacker, Grant. "Pearl S. Buck and the Waning of the Missionary Impulse." *Church History* 72, no. 4D (2003): 852–74.

Wan, Enoch. "The Trinity: A Model for Partnership in Christian Missions." *Global Missiology* 3, no. 7 (April 2010).

Warren, Max A. C. *Partnership: The Study of an Idea*. London: SCM, 1956.

Weber, Max. *The Protestant Ethic and the Spirit of Capitalism*. London: Unwin Paperbacks, 1985.

West, Charles C., and David M. Paton, eds. *The Missionary Church in East and West*. London: SCM, 1959.

Wickeri, Philip. *Partnership, Solidarity and Friendship: Transforming Structures in Mission*. Louisville: Worldwide Ministries Division, 2003.

Witherington, Ben. *Revelation: The New Cambridge Bible Commentary*. Cambridge: Cambridge University Press, 2003.

Wright, Christopher J. H. *The Mission of God: Unlocking the Bible's Grand Narrative*. Downers Grove, IL: InterVarsity, 2006.

Yong, Amos. *Beyond the Impasse: Toward a Pneumatological Theology of Religions*. Grand Rapids: Baker Academic, 2003.

Zahniser, A. H. Mathias. *The Mission and Death of Jesus in Islam and Christianity*. Maryknoll, NY: Orbis Books, 2008.

Zwemer, Samuel M. *Thinking Missions with Christ: Some Basic Aspects of World-Evangelism: Our Message, Our Motive, and Our Goal*. Grand Rapids: Zondervan, 1934.

Urban

Bakke, Ray, with Jim Hart. *A Theology as Big as the City*. Downers Grove, IL: InterVarsity, 1997.

———. *The Urban Christian: Effective Ministry in Today's Urban World*. Downers Grove, IL: InterVarsity, 1987.

Bessenecker, Scott, ed. *Quest for Hope in the Slum Community: A Global Urban Reader*. Waynesboro, GA: Authentic Media, 2005.

Chandler, Tertius. *Four Thousand Years of Urban Growth: An Historical Census*. St. Davids, PA: University Press, 1987.

Conn, Harvie, and Manuel Ortiz. *Urban Ministry: The Kingdom, The City, and the People of God*. Downers Grove, IL: InterVarsity, 2010.

Ellul, Jacques. *The Meaning of the City*. Translated by Dennis Pardee. Grand Rapids: Eerdmans, 1970.

Fuder, John. *A Heart for the Community: New Models for Urban and Suburban Ministry*. Chicago: Moody, 2009.

Gornik, Mark R. *To Live in Peace: Biblical Faith and the Changing Inner City*. Grand Rapids: Eerdmans, 2002.

Greenway, Roger, ed. *Discipling the City: A Comprehensive Approach to Urban Mission*. 2nd ed. Grand Rapids: Baker, 1992.

Grigg, Viv. *Companion to the Poor: Christ in the Urban Slums*. Monrovia, CA: MARC Publications, 1990.

———. *Cry of the Urban Poor: Reaching the Slums of Today's Mega-Cities*. Waynesboro, GA: Authentic Media, 2004.

———. *The Spirit of Christ and the Postmodern City*. Wellington, New Zealand: First Edition Publishers, 2009.

Keller, Timothy. *Church Planter Manual*. New York: Redeemer Presbyterian Church, 2002.

Kimbrough, S. T., Jr. *Urban Mission: Two Viewpoints*. New York: General Board of Global Ministries of the United Methodist Church, 2001.

Kline, Meredith G. *Kingdom Prologue: Genesis Foundations for a Covenantal Worldview*. Eugene, OR: Wipf & Stock, 2006.

Kotkin, Joel. *The City: A Global History*. 4th ed. New York: Modern Library, 2005.

Meeks, Wayne. *The First Urban Christians*. New Haven, CT: Yale University Press, 1983.

Montero, Maritza, and Christopher Sonn, eds. *Psychology of Liberation*. New York: Springer Science and Business Media, 2009.

Perkins, John. *Let Justice Roll Down*. Ventura, CA: Regal, 1976.

———. *With Justice for All: A Strategy for Community Development*. Ventura, CA: Regal, 2007.

Peters, Ron. *Urban Ministry: An Introduction*. Nashville: Abingdon, 2007.

Sears, Charles Hatch. *The Redemption of the City*. Philadelphia: Griffith & Rowland, 1911.

Segal, J. B. *Edessa: The Blessed City*. Piscataway, NJ: Gorgias, 2001.

Stark, Rodney. *Cities of God: The Real Story of How Christianity Became an Urban Movement and Conquered Rome*. San Francisco: HarperSanFrancisco, 2006.

Strong, Josiah. *The Challenge of the City*. New York: Young Peoples' Missionary Movement, 1907.

Toyohiko, Kagawa. *The Religion of Jesus*. Translated by Helen F. Topping. Philadelphia: John C. Winston, 1931.

United Nations. *World Urbanization Prospects: The 2007 Revision*. New York: United Nations, 2007.

Van Engen, Charles, and Jude Tiersma, eds. *God So Loves the City: Seeking a Theology for Urban Misison*. Monrovia, CA: MARC, 1994.

Villafañe, Eldin. *Seek the Peace of the City: Reflections on Urban Ministry*. Grand Rapids: Eerdmans, 1995.

Ancient Christian Writings

Apostolic Fathers (Early Christian Collection). Loeb Classics Series. Translated by Bart D. Ehrman. Cambridge, MA: Harvard University Press, 2003.

Berthold, George C. *Maximus the Confessor: Selected Writings*. New York: Paulist Press, 1985.

Cassian, St. John. *The Conferences*. Translated by Boniface Ramsey. Mahwah, NJ: Paulist Press, 1997.

Coakley, John W., and Andrea Sterk, eds. *Readings in World Christian History*. Vol. 1, *Earliest Christianity to 1453*. Maryknoll, NY: Orbis Books, 2004.

Deane, Sydney Norton, trans. *St. Anselm, Cur Deus Homo*. Chicago: Open Court, 1903.

Drijvers, H. J. W., trans. *Book of the Laws of Countries by Bardaisan of Edessa*. Assen: Van Gorcum, 1965.

Ephrem the Syrian. *Hymns on Paradise*. Introduction and translation by Sebastian Brock. Crestwood, NY: St. Vladimir's Seminary Press. 1990.

Evans, G. R., trans. *Bernard of Clairvaux: Selected Works*. New York: Paulist Press, 1987.

Foster, Paul. "The Epistle of Diognetus." *Expository Times*, January 1, 2007.

Jones, Christopher, ed. *Apollonius of Tyana by Philostratus*. Loeb Classics. Cambridge, MA: Harvard University Press, 2006.

Keble, John, trans. *Five Books of St. Irenaeus, Bishop of Lyons, Against Heresies*. Oxford: J. Parker, 1872.

Keselopoulos, Anastes. *Man and the Environment: A Study of St. Symeon the New Theologian*. Translated by Elizabeth Theokritoff. Crestwood, NY: St. Vladimir's Seminary Press, 2001.

Maloney, George, SJ. *Symeon the New Theologian: The Discourses*. New York: Paulist Press, 1980.

McGuckin, John. *The Orthodox Church: An Introduction to Its History, Doctrine and Spiritual Culture*. Hoboken, NJ: Wiley-Blackwell, 2010.

———. *Westminster Handbook on Origen*. Louisville: Westminster John Knox, 2004.

McLeod, F. C., trans. *Narsai's Metrical Homilies on the Nativity, Epiphany, Passion, Resurrection and Ascension*. Patrologia Orientalis 40.1. Turnhout: Brepols, 1979.

Nikodimos of the Holy Mountain and Makarios of Corinth. *The Philokalia*. 4 vols. Translated and edited by G. E. H. Palmer, Philip Serrard, and Kallistos Ware. London: Faber & Faber, 1979–99.

Pegis, Anton C., FRSC, ed. and trans. *Thomas Aquinas: Summa Contra Gentiles*. Notre Dame, IN: University of Notre Dame Press, 1955/1975.

Richardson, Cyril C. *Early Christian Fathers*. New York: Collier Books, 1970.

Schaff, Philip, ed. "Gregory Nazianzus, Theological Orations." In *Nicene and Post-Nicene Fathers of the Christian Church*. 2nd series, vol. 7. Edinburgh: T&T Clark, 1898.

Slivas, Anna M., trans. and ed. *The Asketikon of St. Basil the Great*. New York: Oxford University Press, 2005.

St. John Climakos. *The Ladder of Divine Ascent*. Translated by Colm Luibheid and Norman Russell. New York: Paulist Press, 1982.

Timothy I (Patriarch). *Apology of Patriarch Timothy of Baghdad before the Caliph Mahdi*. Translated and edited by A. Mingana. In *Woodbrooke Studies*. Vol 2. Cambridge: Heffer, 1928.

Wallace-Handrall, J. M., trans. *Bede's Ecclesiastical History of the English People*. New York: Oxford University Press, 1988.

Primary Sources on Mission and Ecumenics

Abbott, Walter M., ed. *The Documents of Vatican II*. Translated by Joseph Gallagher. New York: Guild, 1966.

Barth, Karl. *Church Dogmatics*. Edinburgh: T&T Clark, 1961.

Briggs, John, Mercy Amba Oduyoye, and Georges Tsetsis, eds., *A History of the Ecumenical Movement*. Vol. 3, *1968–2000*. Geneva: WCC, 2004.

The Evanston Report: The Second Assembly of the World Council of Churches 1954. London: SCM, 1955.

Fey, Harold Edward, ed. *The Ecumenical Advance: A History of the Ecumenical Movement*. Vol. 2, *1948–1968*. Philadelphia: Westminster, 1970.

Gairdner, W. H. T. *Echoes from Edinburgh, 1910*. New York: Fleming H. Revell, 1910.

International Missionary Council, ed. *The Jerusalem Meeting of the International Missionary Council, March 24–April 8, 1928*. 8 vols. New York: International Missionary Council, 1928.

———. *The Madras Series: 1938 Findings*. 7 vols. New York: International Missionary Council, 1939.

———. *The Witness of a Revolutionary Church: Statements Issued by the Committee of the International Missionary Council, Whitby, Ontario, Canada, July 5–24, 1947*. New York: International Missionary Council, 1947.

Lausanne Movement. "Cape Town Commitment." http://www.lausanne.org/ctcommitment.

Newbigin, J. E. Lesslie. *One Body, One Gospel, One World: The Christian Mission Today*. London: IMC, 1958.

Oldham, J. H. *Christianity and the Race Problem*. London: SCM, 1924.

Orchard, Ronald K., ed. *The Ghana Assembly of the International Missionary Council 28 December to 8 January, 1958: Selected Papers with an Essay on the Role of the IMC*. London: Edinburgh House, 1958.

Rouse, Ruth, and Stephen Charles Neill, eds. *A History of the Ecumenical Movement*. Vol. 1, *1517–1948*. Philadelphia: Westminster, 1954.

Song, Choan-Seng. *Growing Together in Unity: Texts from the Faith & Order Commission on Conciliar Fellowships*. Geneva: Faith & Order, 1978.

Stott, John. *Making Christ Known: Historic Mission Documents from the Lausanne Movement, 1974–1989*. Grand Rapids: Eerdmans, 1996.

Student Volunteer Movement for Foreign Missions. *Students and the Present Missionary Crisis*. New York: SVMFM, 1910.

World Council of Churches, ed. *Bangkok Assembly, 1973: Minutes and Reports of the Assembly*. New York: WCC, 1973.

———. *The Church for Others and the Church for the World: A Quest for Structures for Missionary Congregations*. Geneva: WCC, 1967.

———. *Jesus Christ Frees and Unites: Section Dossiers for the Fifth Assembly of the World Council of Churches*. Geneva: WCC, 1975.

———. *Man's Disorder and God's Design*. The Amsterdam Assembly Series New York: Harper Brothers, 1949.

———. *New Delhi to Uppsala: 1961–1968; Report of the Central Committee to the Fourth Assembly of the World Council of Churches*. Geneva: WCC, 1968.

———. *Uppsala Speaks: Section Reports of the Fourth Assembly World Council of Churches, Uppsala 1968*. Edited by Norman Goodall. Uppsala: World Council of Churches, 1968.

World Council of Churches, and David M. Paton, eds. *Breaking Barriers: Nairobi, 1975*. London: SPCK, 1976.

World Missionary Conference, Edinburgh, 1910. *The History and Records of the Conference: Together with Addresses Delivered at the Evening Meetings*. New York: Fleming H. Revell, 1910.

Scripture Index

Isaiah

Jeremiah

Ezekiel

Daniel

Hosea

Joel

Micah

Habakkuk

Zechariah

New Testament

Matthew

Mark

Luke

John

Acts

Romans

1 Corinthians

2 Corinthians

Galatians

Ephesians

Philippians

Colossians

1 Thessalonians

2 Thessalonians

2 Timothy

Hebrews

James

1 Peter

2 Peter

1 John

Jude

Revelation

Subject Index